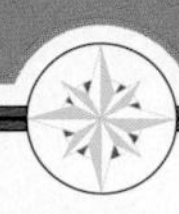

EYEWITNESS TRAVEL

DENMARK

MONIKA WITKOWSKA
JOANNA HALD

LONDON, NEW YORK,
MELBOURNE, MUNICH AND DELHI
www.dk.com

Produced by Wydawnictwo Wiedza i Życie, Warsaw

SENIOR GRAPHIC DESIGNER Paweł Pasternak
EDITORS Maria Betlejewska, Joanna Egert-Romanowska
AUTHORS Joanna Hald, Marek Pernal, Jakub Sito, Barbara Sudnik-Wójcikowska, Monika Witkowska

CARTOGRAPHERS Magdalena Polak, Olaf Rodowald, Jarosław Talacha
PHOTOGRAPHERS Dorota and Mariusz Jarymowiczowie
ILLUSTRATORS Michał Burkiewicz, Paweł Marcza
GRAPHIC DESIGN Paweł Pasternak
DTP Elżbieta Dudzińska

For Dorling Kindersley
TRANSLATOR Magda Hannay
EDITOR Matthew Tanner
SENIOR DTP DESIGNER Jason Little
PRODUCTION CONTROLLER Rita Sinha

Reproduced by Colourscan, Singapore

Printed and bound in China by Toppan Printing Co. (Shenzhen), Ltd

First American Edition, 2005
10 11 12 13 10 9 8 7 6 5 4 3 2 1

Published in the United States by DK Publishing, 375 Hudson Street, New York, New York 10014

Reprinted with revisions 2008, 2010

Published in Great Britain by Dorling Kindersley Limited.

A catalog record for this book is available from the Library of Congress.

ISSN 1542-1554
ISBN: 978-0-75666-144-1

FLOORS ARE REFERRED TO THROUGHOUT IN ACCORDANCE WITH EUROPEAN USAGE; IE THE "FIRST FLOOR" IS THE FLOOR ABOVE GROUND LEVEL.

Front cover main image: Frederiksborg Slot, Northwestern Zealand

The information in this DK Eyewitness Travel Guide is checked regularly.

Every effort has been made to ensure that this book is as up-to-date as possible at the time of going to press. Some details, however, such as telephone numbers, opening hours, prices, gallery hanging arrangements and travel information are liable to change. The publishers cannot accept responsibility for any consequences arising from the use of this book, nor for any material on third party websites, and cannot guarantee that any website address in this book will be a suitable source of travel information. We value the views and suggestions of our readers very highly. Please write to: Publisher, DK Eyewitness Travel Guides Dorling Kindersley, 80 Strand, London WC2R 0RL, Great Britain.

◁ **Colourful 18th-century houses and yachts on Nyhavn, Copenhagen**

CONTENTS

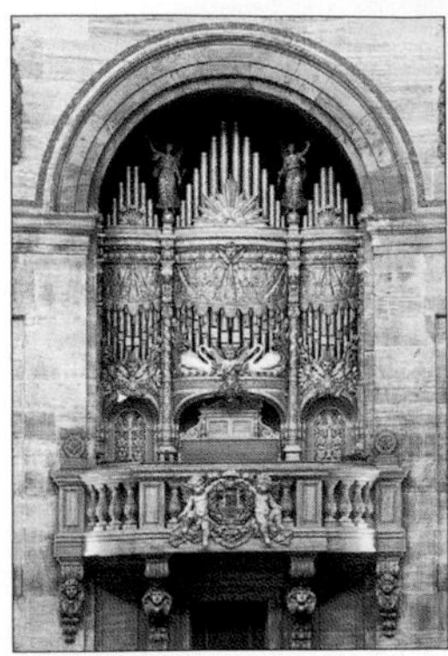

Church organ, Copenhagen

INTRODUCING DENMARK

Amalienborg and Marmorki... Copenhagen, seen from th...

Trumpeters' monument standing near Copenhagen's Rådhus

The Lille Tårn (Little Tower), Frederiksø

Christiansborg, Copenhagen

HOW TO USE THIS GUIDE

This guide will help you get the most out of a visit to Denmark. The first section, *Introducing Denmark*, provides information about the country's geographic location, its history and culture. The sections devoted to the capital and other large cities, as well as to individual regions, describe the major sights and visitor attractions. Information on accommodation and restaurants can be found in the *Travellers' Needs* section. The *Survival Guide* provides practical tips on everything a visitor may need to know, from money and language to getting around and seeking medical care.

COPENHAGEN

This section has been divided into three parts, each devoted to a separate part of the city. Sights outside the capital's centre are described in the *Further Afield* section. All sights are numbered and plotted on the area map. Detailed information for each sight is given in numerical order.

Pages referring to Copenhagen are marked in red.

A locator map shows where visitors are in relation to other areas of the city.

1 Area Map

For easy reference the sights are numbered and plotted on the area map, as well as on the main map of Copenhagen (see pp108–11).

Sights at a Glance lists the sights in an area by category: churches, museums and art galleries; streets and squares; parks and gardens.

A suggested route for sightseeing is indicated by a dotted red line.

2 Street-by-Street Map

Provides a bird's-eye view of the town centre described in the section.

Star Sights indicate parts of buildings, historic sights, exhibits and monuments that no visitor should miss.

3 Detailed Information

All the major sights of Copenhagen are described individually. Practical information includes addresses, telephone numbe the most convenient buses trains, and opening hour

1 Introduction
This section deals with the landscape, history and character of each region, revealing how it has changed over time, and describing its current attractions.

DENMARK REGION BY REGION

In this guide Denmark is divided into seven regions, each of which has a separate section devoted to it. The most interesting cities, towns, villages and sights worth visiting are marked on each regional map.

2 Regional Map
The regional map shows the main road network and the overall topography of the region. All sights are numbered, and there is also information on public transport and getting around.

Boxes highlight interesting aspects or people associated with a sight.

Each region of Denmark can be found by using the colour code. The colours are explained on the inside front cover.

3 Detailed Information
Towns, villages and major tourist attractions are listed in numerical order, corresponding with the area map. Each entry contains information on important sights.

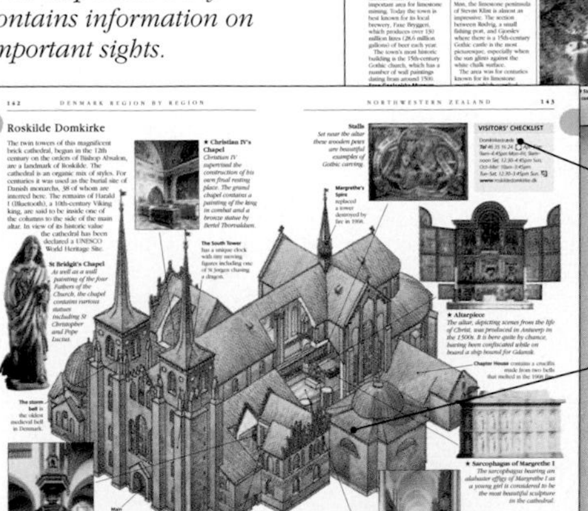

The Visitors' Checklist provides practical information to help plan your visit.

4 Major Sights
At least two pages are devoted to each major sight. Historic buildings are dissected to reveal their interiors. Major towns and town centres have street maps with the principal sights marked on them.

INTRODUCING DENMARK

DISCOVERING DENMARK

An island kingdom, linked to Germany by a land border and to Sweden by a magnificent bridge, Denmark has a substantial coastline: a mix of sandy beaches, fjords and pretty fishing villages. Inland lie colourful towns, forests, castles, lakes and Viking remains. Jutland is the country's mainland and Zealand its largest island. Funen is known as "the Garden of Denmark" and Bornholm "Scandinavia in miniature". The vibrant capital, Copenhagen, shares the relaxed friendliness that pervades the entire country.

Visitors at Legoland®

The colourful illuminations of Tivoli by night

COPENHAGEN

- **Architectural surprises both old and new**
- **Fabulous shops and bars**
- **The magic of Tivoli**

City of castles and canals, palaces, parks and gorgeous gardens, Denmark's capital offers many architectural surprises. Amid a skyline of copper roofs, domes and redbrick towers, the strange spires of **Børsen** *(see p85)* and **Vor Frelsers Kirke** *(see p88)* intrigue, while the modern "**Black Diamond**" *(see p88)*, the stunning **Operaen** *(see p89)* and **Tycho Brahe Planetarium** *(see p92)* dare to be different.

For art lovers, the **Statens Museum for Kunst** *(see pp62–3)* and **Ny Carlsberg Glyptotek** *(see pp78–9)* are a must, while style queens will be spoilt by the shops, restaurants and nightlife that the city is renowned for.

Joyous **Tivoli** *(see pp76–7)* delights visitors of all ages and any trip should include a visit to the **Little Mermaid** *(see p54)* – "small and close to the sea" – said to be the perfect symbol of Denmark.

NORTHWESTERN ZEALAND

- **Hamlet's castle, Kronborg**
- **On the Viking trail**
- **Karen Blixen's home**

This region is packed with historic sights, including the great castles of **Kronborg Slot** (Elsinore in Shakespeare's Hamlet, *see pp126–7*), **Frederiksborg Slot** *(see pp132–3)* and **Fredensborg Slot** *(see p129)*. Follow in the wake of the Vikings at **Trelleborg** *(see p147)* and **Roskilde** *(see pp140–41)*, where the cathedral *(see pp142–3)* is a World Heritage Site. Culture vultures enjoy writer **Karen Blixen**'s evocative home *(see p121)* and modern art at the striking **Louisiana Museum** *(see pp122–3)*.

Outdoors, choose between sandy beaches, beautiful lakes *(see pp130–31)*, forests, or the world's oldest fun park at **Bakken** *(see p120)*.

SOUTHERN ZEALAND AND THE ISLANDS

- **Pristine beaches**
- **The spectacular white cliffs of Møn Klint**
- **Family-friendly resorts**

This relaxed, family-friendly region has miles of coastline, pristine beaches, lakes and a scattering of islands. Worth a visit are the cliffs at **Møns Klint** *(see p168)* and **Stevns Klint** *(see p170)*, the moated **Vallø Slot** *(see p171)* and medieval **Køge** *(see p171)*.

Children love the giant roller coaster at **BonBon-Land** *(see p157)*, **Knuthenborg Safari Park** *(see pp160–61)*, and the family activity resorts such as **Lalandia** *(see p162)* and **Marielyst** *(see p167)*.

Chalk cliffs of Møns Klint, rising up out of the Baltic

FUNEN

- **Odense, birthplace of Hans Christian Andersen**
- **Preserved towns and sights**
- **Sealife encounters**

The writer Hans Christian Andersen was born in **Odense** *(see pp178–9)*, but there is a fairytale old-world

Regal Egeskov Slot, surrounded by water

feel to the whole island: market towns have cobbled streets and half-timbered houses; manor houses, palaces and castles dot the rolling landscape. Romantic **Egeskov Slot** *(see p177)* is particularly well preserved.

For getting close to the local sea life there is Fjord&Bælt in **Kerteminde** *(see p176)*.

SOUTHERN AND CENTRAL JUTLAND

- **Family fun at LEGOLAND®**
- **Peaks and lakes of Silkeborg**
- **Lively Århus**

Denmark's peninsula is packed with attractions, including the very popular **LEGOLAND®** *(see pp192–3)*. Historic towns and excellent museums compete for your attention while walkers and cyclists flock to the **Silkeborg Lake District** *(see p187)*. **Rømø** *(see p196)* has one of the widest beaches in Europe.

Also worth a visit are runic stones in **Jelling** *(see p191)*, medieval **Ribe** *(see p191)* and, when night falls, the friendly bars of **Århus** *(see pp188–9)*, Denmark's second city.

NORTHERN JUTLAND

- **Peaceful Limfjorden**
- **Remote and artistic Skagen**
- **Aalborg's medieval quarter**

The peaceful **Limfjorden** *(see pp210–11)* cuts its watery way across this region of forest and farmland, famed for its picturesque towns, windswept dunes and diverse birdlife.

Artists have found much inspiration from the extra-ordinary light here, many settling in the fishing village of **Skagen** *(see p205)*.

Historic sights include manor houses, a "living history" open-air museum, **Hjerl Hedes Frilandsmuseum** *(see p207)* and the bustling medieval quarter of **Aalborg** *(see pp208–9)*. Try the potent *akvavit* (Danish schnapps), produced in the town.

Picturesque Gudhjem, seaside centre for arts and crafts

BORNHOLM

- **Mediterranean climate**
- **Fortified round churches**
- **Art and crafts**

This tranquil "sunshine island", where vineyards and Mediterranean flowers thrive, boasts steep cliffs, rift valleys, moors, bogs and memorable beaches. Bornholm is also known for its white **round churches** *(see p221)* and the atmospheric ruins of **Hammershus Slot** *(see p220)*. Artists and craftsmakers flock here, and there are workshops and galleries all over the island – the pretty, well-preserved towns of **Svaneke** *(see p223)* and **Gudhjem** *(see pp208–9)* are good places to start looking.

GREENLAND AND THE FAROE ISLANDS

- **Life outdoors from whale-watching to dog-sledding**
- **Unspoilt island life on the Faroe Islands**

Greenland, a huge ice-covered island lying within the Arctic Circle, offers adventure: from whale spotting trips out of **Nuuk** *(see p232)*, dog-sledding across frozen fjords from **Uummannaq** *(see p233)*, to cruising among icebergs in Disko Bay and summer hikes in the "**Valley of Flowers**" *(see p233)* – even hunting and fishing with the Inuit. In this unforgettable landscape, visitors encounter brightly coloured towns and ice in all its forms and pristine beauty.

Close-knit communities snuggle by fjords on the **Faroe Islands** *(see pp234–7)* where craggy mountains meet the sea and millions of seabirds nest on soaring cliffs. The air is clean and clear, the ever-changing light plays on a steep, sheep-grazed landscape, and the views are magnificent.

Coast of Mykines, one of the Faroe Islands

Putting Denmark on the Map

Denmark is situated between the North Sea to the west and the Baltic Sea to the southeast. Most of Denmark consists of Jutland, a peninsula that covers 29,766 sq km (11,493 sq miles). The rest of the country consists of some 400 islands, of which the largest are Bornholm, Funen and Zealand. Far to the north, Greenland and the Faroe Islands are self-governing overseas regions of Denmark.

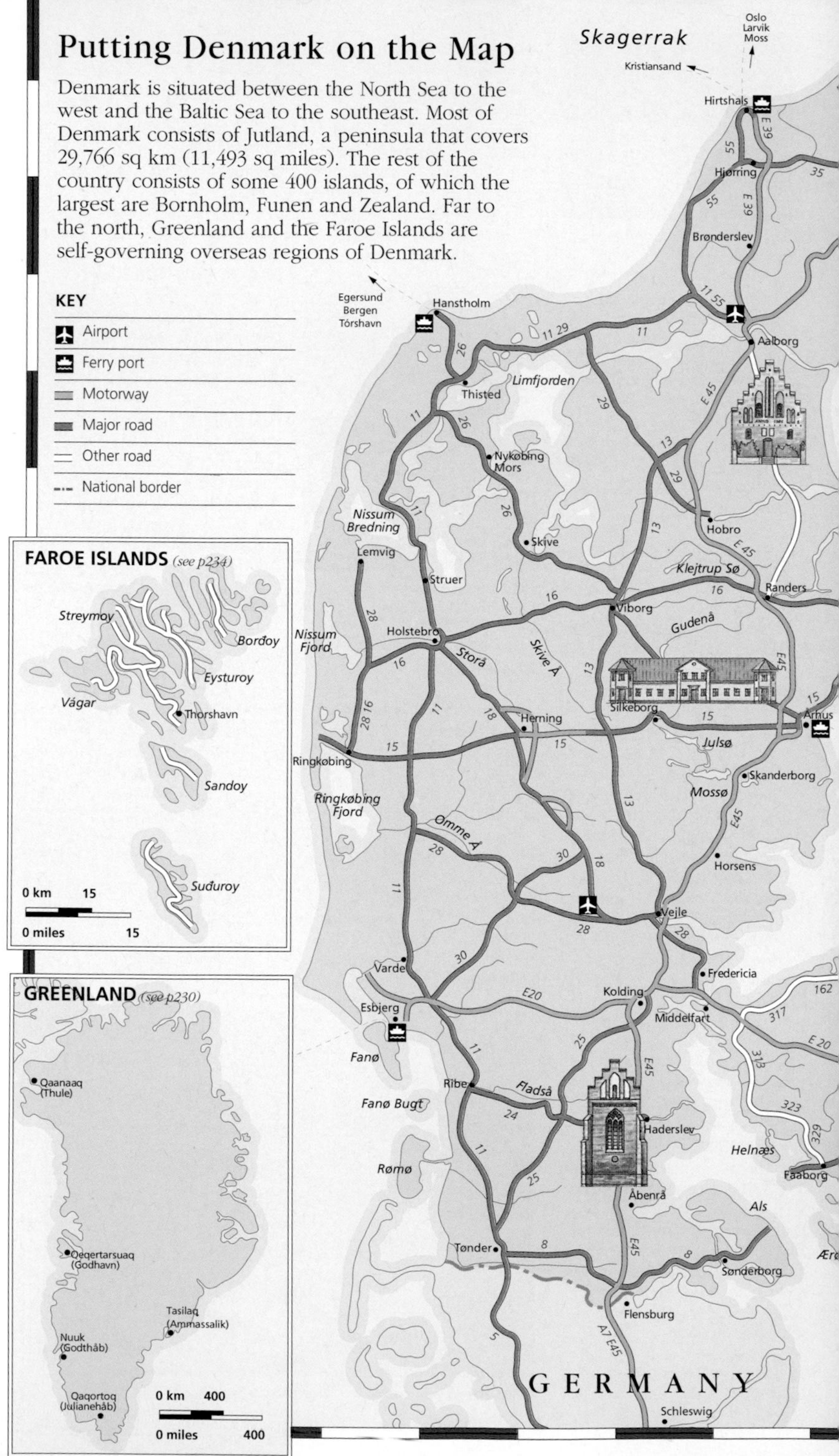

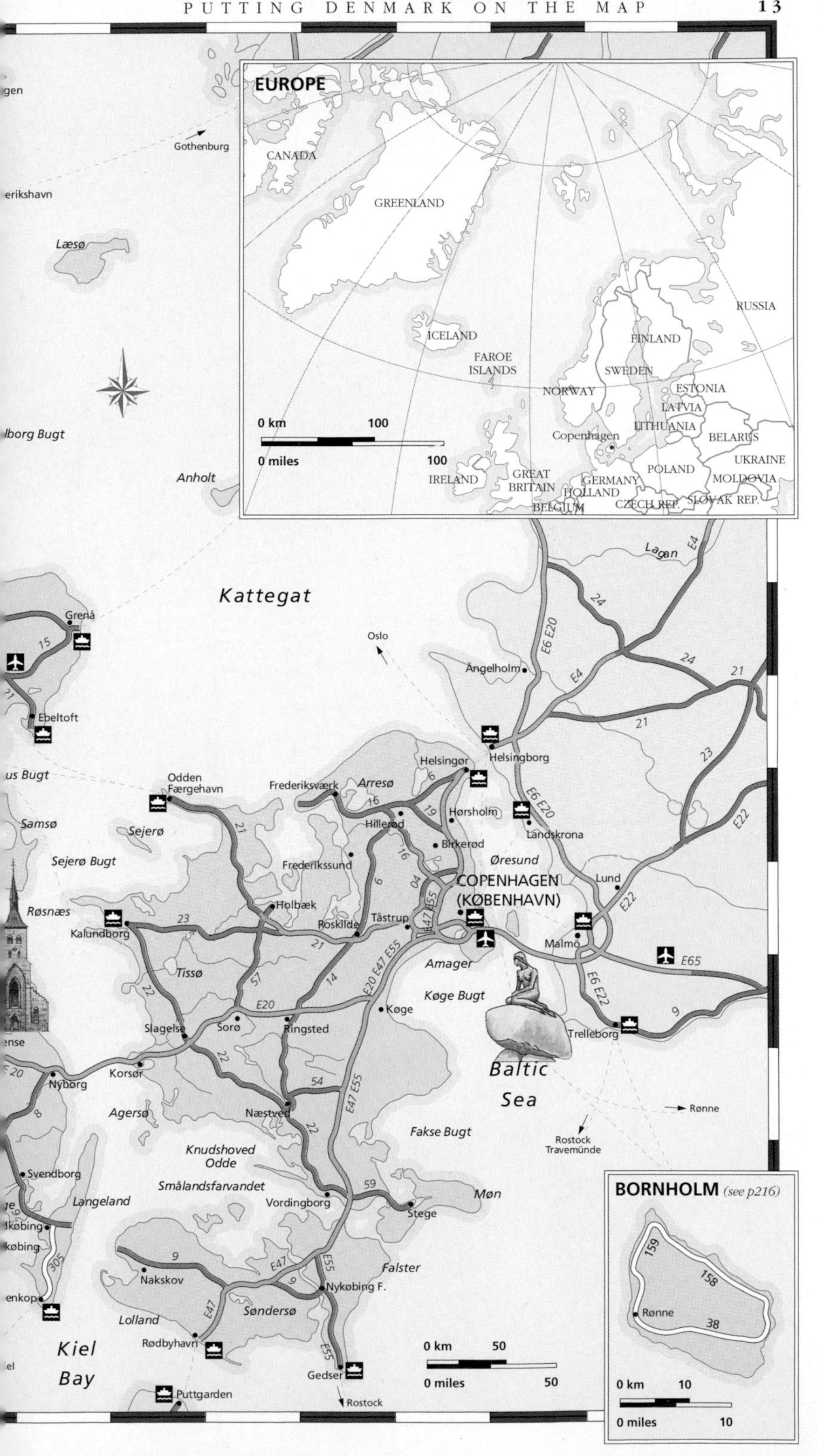
EUROPE
CANADA
GREENLAND
ICELAND
FAROE ISLANDS
NORWAY
SWEDEN
FINLAND
RUSSIA
ESTONIA
LATVIA
LITHUANIA
BELARUS
UKRAINE
MOLDOVIA
POLAND
GERMANY
HOLLAND
BELGIUM
CZECH REP.
SLOVAK REP.
GREAT BRITAIN
IRELAND
Copenhagen
0 km 100
0 miles 100
Gothenburg
Læsø
Anholt
Kattegat
Grenå
Ebeltoft
Oslo
Ängelholm
Helsingborg
Helsingør
Lagan
Odden Færgehavn
Frederiksværk
Arresø
Hillerød
Hørsholm
Birkerød
Landskrona
Samsø
Sejerø
Sejerø Bugt
Frederikssund
Øresund
COPENHAGEN (KØBENHAVN)
Lund
Røsnæs
Holbæk
Kalundborg
Roskilde
Tåstrup
Malmö
Tissø
Amager
Køge Bugt
Køge
Slagelse
Sorø
Ringsted
Trelleborg
Korsør
Nyborg
Baltic Sea
Agersø
Næstved
Rønne
Fakse Bugt
Knudshoved Odde
Rostock Travemünde
Svendborg
Smålandsfarvandet
Langeland
Vordingborg
Stege
Møn
Nakskov
Falster
Nykøbing F.
Søndersø
Lolland
Rødbyhavn
Kiel Bay
Gedser
Puttgarden
Rostock
0 km 50
0 miles 50
BORNHOLM (see p216)
Rønne
0 km 10
0 miles 10

UDSTILLINGER

A PORTRAIT OF DENMARK

Denmark is most famous for its association with the Vikings and the writer Hans Christian Andersen. It has, of course, far more to offer visitors, including miles of sandy coastline, beautiful countryside and historic buildings. Copenhagen, the country's capital, has a rich cultural life and world-class museums.

Denmark, the southernmost and most continental of the Scandinavian countries, occupies over 480 islands, of which about 100 are inhabited. It acts as a bridge between mainland Europe and Scandinavia and is linked with the European continent by a narrow stretch of land, in the southern part of the Jutland peninsula, at the border with Germany.

Although not part of the Scandinavian peninsula, the Danes are linked with their northern neighbours by ties of common history and culture. There are also linguistic similarities and Danes can easily converse with people from Sweden or Norway.

Porcelain doll in traditional costume

The country has strong links with two autonomous regions: the Faroe Islands and Greenland, both of which are represented in the Danish parliament. Denmark exercises control over their banking, foreign policy and defence.

Denmark is a low-lying country with wide stretches of cornfields, moors and forests, including Rebild Bakker – Denmark's only national park. In addition, it has vast sand dunes, fjords and long stretches of beach. The country's immaculate towns and villages, with colourful houses adorned with flowers, include many examples of half-timbered design.

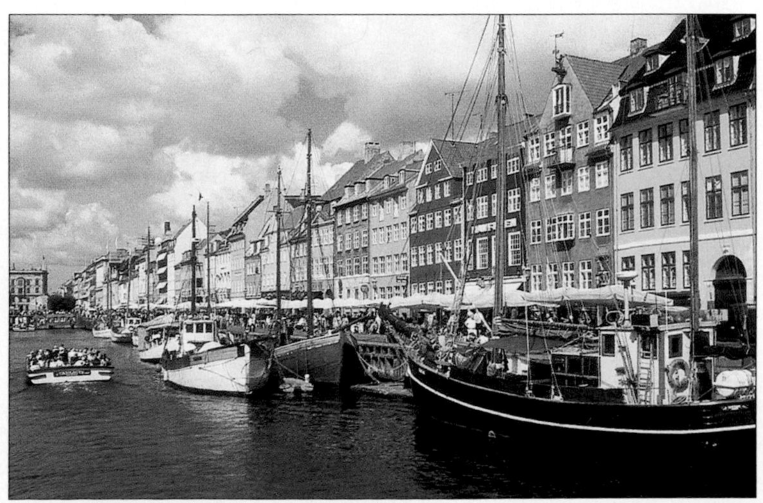

Picturesque houses along the bank of Nyhavn, Copenhagen

◁ **The "Black Diamond" extension to Det Kongelige Bibliotek (The Royal Library), Copenhagen**

Changing of the guards at Amalienborg Slot, Copenhagen

Majestic castles, palaces and historic churches pepper the Danish landscape. There are also many Viking ruins, as well as older remains including ancient dolmens dating from the Stone Age.

Denmark is acknowledged to be a peaceful and liberal country, with a well-organized transport system and a comprehensive system of social welfare. It has enviably low levels of crime and corruption. In rural areas it is not unusual to see stalls by the roadside on which local farmers have left their produce on sale unattended.

Statue of the Little Mermaid – a symbol of Copenhagen

Charming half-timbered house in Rønne, on the island of Bornholm

TRADITIONS AND POLITICS

The national flag – the Danneborg – is the world's oldest and the Danes demonstrate their patriotism by unfurling it during state and family celebrations. According to legend, the flag takes its origin from a banner, bearing a white cross on a red background, which was dropped from heaven to rally the Danish knights during a battle fought in present-day Estonia in the early 13th century.

The Danes are proud of their heritage and in summer many families visit Viking villages in order to sample the lives of their distant ancestors. Most Danes regard the fact that their monarchy is the oldest in the world with pride. The present queen, Margrethe II, has been on the throne since 1972 and is the first female monarch in Denmark since the 14th century. In addition to performing all ceremonial functions, this popular queen is credited with transforming the monarchy into a modern institution.

In political matters, the monarchy's influence is limited by the Danish constitution. The direction of national policy is determined in the Folketinget, the chamber in Christiansborg Slot, Copenhagen, where the country's 179 members of parliament sit. About a dozen parties are represented in parliament. Elections take place every four years and over 90 per cent of those eligible to vote turn out at election time. Most important national issues are decided by popular vote, however. Decisions made in referenda have included the Danes' approval of a constitutional amendment allowing a woman to inherit the throne in 1953 and, in 2000, the rejection of the euro.

View of Gammelestrup, Jutland, surrounded on all sides by water

SOCIETY AND EVERYDAY LIFE

Denmark is largely inhabited by ethnic Danes who are ancestors of the Teutonic tribes that once populated all of Scandinavia.

Harald I (Bluetooth), Denmark's second king, was baptised as a Catholic in 960 and Denmark remained a Catholic country until well into the 16th century. During the 16th century the ideas of the German Protestant reformer Martin Luther won widespread support and Lutheranism became the official religion of Denmark with the accession of Christian III in 1534. Today, about 90 per cent of the population are Protestant, and although the churches remain fairly empty, many Danes subscribe to a tax that supports the Church.

Although Denmark is largely an ethnically homogenous country, relaxed immigration policies introduced in the 1960s helped to establish small communities of foreign nationals from outside Europe. Copenhagen is home to significant numbers of Turks and Palestinians as well as new arrivals from Iraq and Afghanistan.

When it comes to bringing up children, many parents continue with their careers after taking parental leave. The progressive welfare system enables most women to return to work, at least part time.

Harbour and sailing boat jetty, Maribo (Lolland)

Denmark's famous liberalism is perhaps best illustrated by "Christiania", a hippy commune that sprang up in 1971. Allowed to remain as a social experiment, it is inhabited by about 900 people seeking an alternative lifestyle.

Father and son feeding pigeons in one of Copenhagen's open squares

The Danes are similarly relaxed when it comes to issues such as marriage. The country's divorce rate is one of the highest in Europe and nearly 20 per cent of couples co-habit without ever getting married. Abortion has been available "on demand" since the 1960s.

ECONOMY AND ECOLOGY

The Danish economy is fairly robust and the country has the EU's highest per-capita Gross National Product and a high standard of living.

Denmark was for centuries a land of farmers and fishermen. Today only 5 per cent of the country's population are employed in agriculture. Fishing, however, is still an important sector of the economy. The country is a major exporter of fish and is also known for its dairy and pork products. Other exports include beer, furniture and home electronics.

The Danes attach great importance to environmental issues. The country has an extensive network of alternative energy sources and the state-subsidized power-generating windmills are a common feature of the landscape. These supply over 15 per cent of the country's energy needs. Major investments are also made in the use of solar power and the island of Ærø, south of Funen, has one of Europe's largest solar power stations. All new building projects are scrutinized to minimize the impact on the environment. Danes take great care of their coastline, many resorts have been awarded the blue flag, denoting clean beaches. Recycling domestic waste is normal practice in Denmark, as is the use of environmentally friendly packaging (80 per cent of the country's paper production comes from recycled sources).

Seaside scenery in Allinge, Bornholm

CULTURE, ART AND DESIGN

Oven-smoked fish, a popular delicacy

Denmark's cultural events range from major music festivals to local parades and concerts. Even smallish towns consider it a point of honour to organize festivals and concerts, putting on anything from classical music to pop and rock. One of the largest events is the July rock festival in Roskilde, which attracts over 70,000 visitors. Copenhagen's July jazz festival, held every year since 1978, is one of the top events of its kind in Europe and has attracted top performers including Dizzy Gillespie, Miles Davis and Oscar Peterson.

Sculpture from Holmegård

Denmark has a wide variety of wonderful museums, including the Ny Carlsberg Glyptotek *(see pp78–9)* and the Nationalmuseet *(see pp84–5)*, both in Copenhagen, as well as the Arken and Louisiana museums, which are within easy reach of the capital. The Nationalmuseet devotes much of its space to exhibits relating to Danish culture and history, but it also has world-class collections of Greek, Roman and Egyptian artifacts. Among the Glyptotek's collection are examples of 19th-century European painting, representatives of Denmark's "Golden Age" *(see pp42–3)* and works by major international artists such as Pablo Picasso and Francis Bacon.

Many smaller museums and galleries are spread throughout the country. Some of these are devoted to the life and work of famous Danish individuals such as the composer Carl Nielsen and sculptor Bertel Thorvaldsen. Then there are more unusual museums, such as Roskilde's Viking Ship Museum *(see p141)*.

Among the country's best-known architects and designers are Ole Kirk Christiansen, inventor of LEGO®; Jørn Utzon, creator of the Sydney Opera House; and Arne Jacobsen, a pioneer of Danish modernism famous for his furniture and minimalist tableware. Prominent examples of Danish applied art include jewellery by Georg Jensen and sleek audio and visual equipment by Bang & Olufsen.

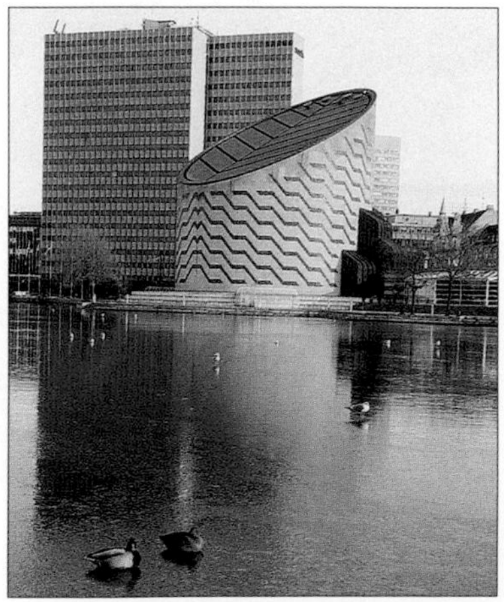

Ultra-modern Tycho Brahe Planetarium, Copenhagen

Danish Landscape and Flora

More than three quarters of Denmark is less than 100 m (330 ft) above sea level. Most of its landforms are of glacial origin, which adds variety to the lowland scenery. Forests, whose wholesale destruction was halted in the 19th century, occupy only a small percentage of the landscape and include commercial forests planted with spruce and fir, and natural forests dominated by beech and oak. Pastures and meadows are also distinctive features of the landscape and most of these are given over to crop cultivation and the rearing of livestock. A large portion of Denmark's highly diversified coastline consists of dunes, marshland and tidal flats.

DANISH FAUNA

Many mammals, including elks and bears, have disappeared in Denmark. What forests remain provide a habitat for deer, marten, wild boar and hare. Excellent nesting grounds are a haven for many birds including geese, storks, swans and sandpipers. The largest wild animal to be found in Denmark is the red deer, while polar bears can still be found in Greenland.

ZEALAND
The island covers an area of 7,000 sq km (2,702 sq miles), and has a diverse landscape. In its northern section, on the outskirts of Copenhagen, there are fragments of natural forests – all that remains of a vast former wilderness. Elsewhere, the island has lakes, beaches and pasture land.

Seaside Centaury (Centaurium littorale) *is a species associated with salt flats, but can also sometimes be found growing on seaside sands.*

White Helleborine (Cephalanthera damasonium) *is an orchid with creamy-white flowers, and is often found in forests.*

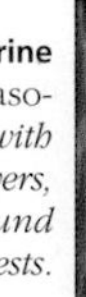

Helleborine (Epipactis) *is found in several different varieties in Denmark. This orchid can be recognized by its labium, which is divided into two parts.*

BORNHOLM
This island, largely composed of volcanic rock, has a mild climate. Its rugged granite cliffs, with stone rubble at their base, rise to over 80 m (262 ft) in height. At its northeastern end the well-preserved deciduous forests grow to the edge of the cliffs. The southern coast has long stretches of white sand beaches.

Bird's Eye Primrose (Primula farinosa) *is a rare peat bog species, which in Denmark is found only in isolated clusters.*

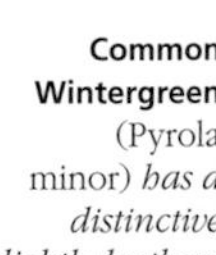

Common Wintergreen (Pyrola minor) *has a distinctive rosette of slightly leathery leaves; it grows in forests and deciduous woodlands, on acid soil.*

Wild Strawberry (Fragaria vesca) *grows on woodland glades and banks. Its small red berries are sweet and fragrant.*

Five species of seal *can be found on the coast of Greenland. The largest of these is the hooded seal, the male of which can weigh up to 400 kg (884 lbs). The Inuit still rely on seals for clothing and food.*

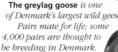

The greylag goose *is one of Denmark's largest wild geese. Pairs mate for life; some 4,000 pairs are thought to be breeding in Denmark.*

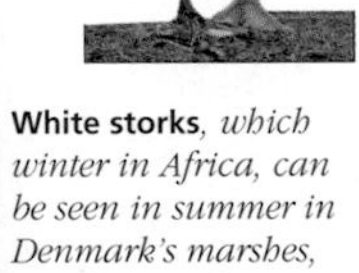

The mute swan *is Denmark's national bird and can be found in many parks and ponds throughout the country.*

White storks, *which winter in Africa, can be seen in summer in Denmark's marshes, meadows and pastures.*

FUNEN

The island that separates Jutland from Zealand is famous for its scenery and is known as the "garden of Denmark" because it produces much of the country's fruit and vegetables. The terrain in the north of the island eventually levels out into marshland, while in the south it is more hilly.

JUTLAND

Lakes, which occupy about one per cent of Denmark's total area, are clustered mainly in the central part of Jutland. Yding Skovoj, Denmark's highest peak, can also be found here and is 173 m (568 ft) above sea level. Himmelbjerdget is 147 m (482 ft) above sea level and is a famous viewpoint.

Mountain Arnica (Arnica montana), *contrary to its name, is also found growing on lowlands, meadows, pastures and by roads. It is a valuable medicinal plant.*

Sea Rocket (Cakile maritima) *is a delicate plant associated solely with Funen's sandy coast.*

Sea Holly (Eryngium maritimum) *is a typical plant of the seaside dunes and comes in white and grey varieties.*

Field Fleawort (Senecio integrifolius) *is a rare species, found in meadows, grasslands, pastures and woodlands.*

Gentian (Gentianella) *is in danger of extinction and is legally protected in Denmark and many other European countries.*

Cinquefoil (Potentilla) *belongs to the rose family. There are several varieties growing in Denmark with yellow flowers.*

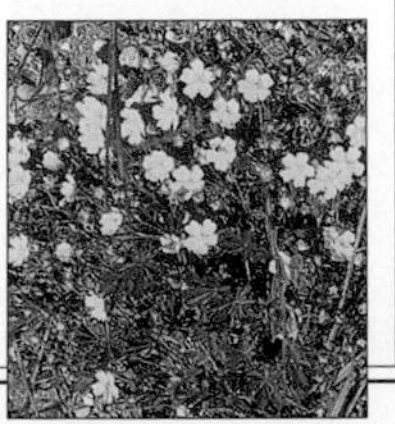

Danish Architecture

Denmark's architecture includes many of the styles found elsewhere in Europe. The country's vernacular architecture includes 17th-century fortress churches and half-timbered houses. The influence of Baroque and Dutch Renaissance dominated the style of palaces built in the 17th and 18th centuries. Denmark's native character re-established itself with Neo-Classicism at the end of the 19th century and this trend has continued with contemporary landmark designs.

Dutch Renaissance Frederiksborg Slot, built mainly in the 17th century

ROMANESQUE ARCHITECTURE

The first Danish churches were built of wood, but they were quickly replaced by Norman structures that were usually constructed of granite. The 10th to 12th centuries marked the arrival of brick and stone Romanesque architecture, exemplified by the churches in Viborg and Ribe. Village churches, such as the one in Hover, Jutland, were usually built as single-aisle structures, with an apse or presbytery. The historic round churches found on Bornholm represent a very distinctive style. These medieval fortress-like buildings were built in the 12th century and were used not only for religious purposes but as places of refuge. Three-storeys high, the top two storeys were used for storage rooms and also provided shelter for the local population in times of danger.

Portal finial in the form of a pediment, with ornamental carvings

The portal tympanum has been decorated with a granite relief depicting the Deposition from the Cross, reminiscent of the reliefs found in the churches of northern Spain.

Ribe Domkirke *is a prime example of a Romanesque cathedral. Built on the site of a wooden structure, this stone building was begun in 1150. One of its most notable features is the "Cat's Head" door on the south side.*

Sankt Bendts Kirke, *Ringsted, was built during the reign of Valdemar I (1152–82) as a tomb for his father, Canute III. Later, more royals were buried here including Valdemar I. Its rich architecture encompasses an imposing edifice with a front tower, a presbytery enclosed with an apse and a mighty transept.*

Round churches were used as shelters during enemy raids.

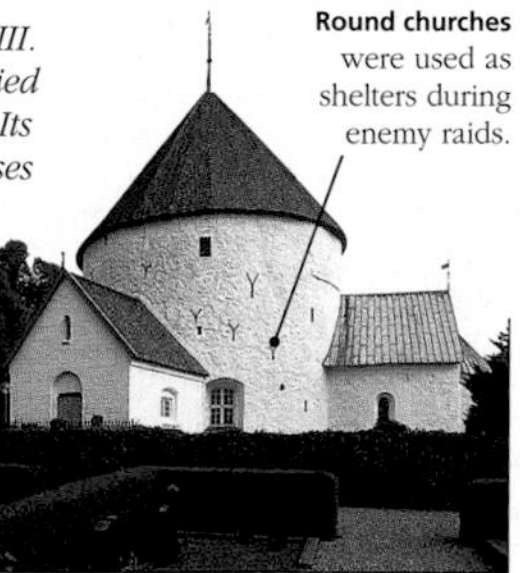

Nylars' round church on Bornholm, built around 1150

GOTHIC ARCHITECTURE

One of the earliest Gothic buildings in Denmark is Roskilde's Domkirke (Cathedral), founded by Bishop Absalon in 1170. The most prominent example of the mature Gothic is the cathedral church in Odense. The introduction of red brick is an important element of the Danish Gothic style. Other typical features of Gothic architecture are its severe forms, ornate decorations and a façade that features stepped peaks. Many Gothic buildings have whitewashed or polychromatic interiors.

Sankt Knuds Domkirke *in Odense is a magnificent example of pure Gothic church brickwork. Most of the cathedral is 13th-century but the finely detailed gilded altar dates from the early 16th century and is the work of Claus Berg, a master craftsman from Lübeck.*

RENAISSANCE ARCHITECTURE

Danish Renaissance architecture grew out of the church's practice of importing architects for major projects in the late 16th century. Dutch architects and craftsmen were employed by Frederik II, and later by Christian IV in the 17th century, to build grand palaces such as Frederiksborg Slot in Hillerød and Kronberg Slot in Helsingør.

Triton figure from the Neptune fountain at Frederiksborg, by Adrian de Vries (c.1615)

Gables with richly-carved ornaments

Jens Bangs Stenhus, Aalborg, *is, along with the Børsen (Stock Exchange), Copenhagen, and the quaint streets and crooked houses of Christianshavn, a fine example of town architecture from this period.*

Kronborg Slot, a stately castle built in 1585 by Frederik II, and later rebuilt by Christian IV

BAROQUE ARCHITECTURE

From the mid-17th to mid-18th centuries Baroque in Denmark left its mark mainly on residential architecture. The best examples are Copenhagen's palaces – Charlottenborg and Christiansborg – along with the grand residence in Ledreborg. The main force behind Baroque in Denmark was the architect Nicolai Eigtved. His greatest achievement was the Frederikstad district in Copenhagen, which was built in a French style and intended as a royal quarter.

Audience Room in Frederiksborg Slot with moulded decorations

Fredensborg Slot *is a sumptuous early-18th-century castle and was built by Frederik IV to a design by Johann Cornelius Krieger in an Italian Baroque style.*

Altar from Vor Frelsers Kirke (Our Saviour's Church), Copenhagen

20TH-CENTURY ARCHITECTURE

In the early part of the 20th century Danish architecture began to reflect a desire for better design in housing and everyday objects, resulting in Modernism and, subsequently, Functionalism. A major result of this trend was the creation of the Design Council at the Association of Architects, in 1907. Characteristics of modern Danish architectural practice are an honest use of materials, clean lines and an abundance of natural light.

The "Black Diamond", *an extension of Det Kongelige Bibliotek (The Royal Library), Copenhagen, represents a Neo-Modernist trend that is gaining favour in Denmark.*

Water emphasises the visual link with a ship

Arken's Museet for Moderne Kunst *(Museum of Modern Art) was designed by the then 25-year-old architect Søren Robert Lund, in metal and white concrete, and is a splendid example of Danish Deconstructivism.*

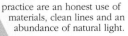

Danish Design

Logo for Danish food chain

LEGO® bricks, chairs by Arne Jacobsen, audio-visual equipment by Bang & Olufsen, jewellery by Georg Jensen: all are recognized throughout the world as examples of a Danish aesthetic. Design has a high profile in Denmark and constitutes an important source of revenue for the country, as well as being a major element of the national identity, supported by many institutions. Two good places to learn more about the traditions and history of Danish design are the Kunstindustrimuseet (Museum of Art and Design) and the Danish Design Centre, both of which are in Copenhagen.

Danish glass *is admired throughout the world. The Holmegård factory was founded in the first half of the 19th century and initially employed workers brought over from Norway.*

Bang & Olufsen *high-fidelity products have been manufactured since 1925. The beauty of these products resides in the discreet use of the latest technology, which is coupled with audiophile performance.*

Large windows blur the boundary between a room's interior and the outside.

Furniture designer Kaare Klint *was fascinated by the possibility of combining ergonomics with traditional furniture design. His designs draw on many sources including pieces from 18th-century England.*

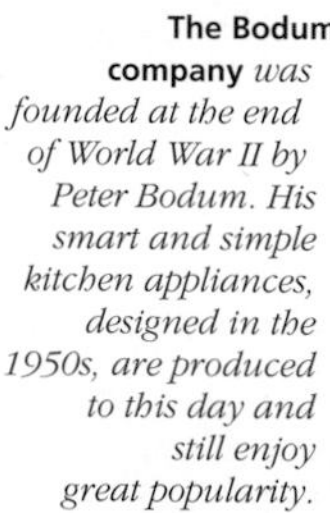

The Bodum company *was founded at the end of World War II by Peter Bodum. His smart and simple kitchen appliances, designed in the 1950s, are produced to this day and still enjoy great popularity.*

LEGO® *is the name of the toy company founded in 1932 by Ole Kirk Christiansen. Christiansen started by producing wooden toys and, in 1958, introduced the now familiar plastic building bricks. The well-known brand name is a contraction of the Danish phrase* leg godt *("play well").*

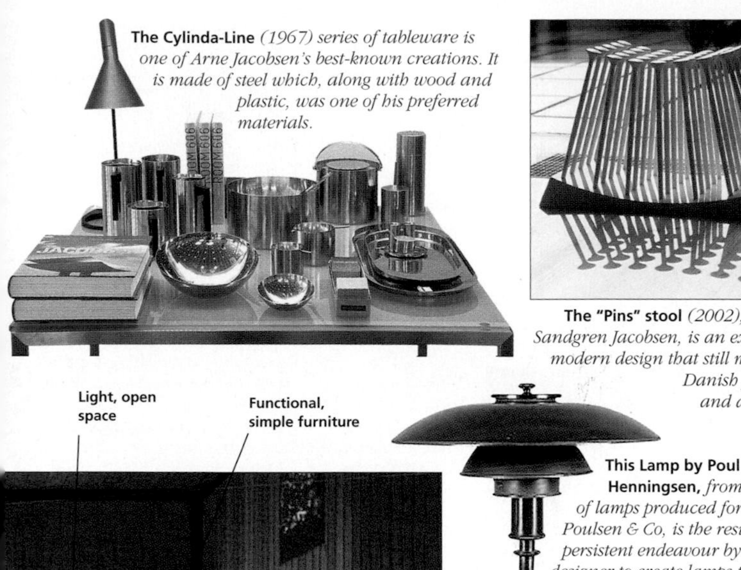

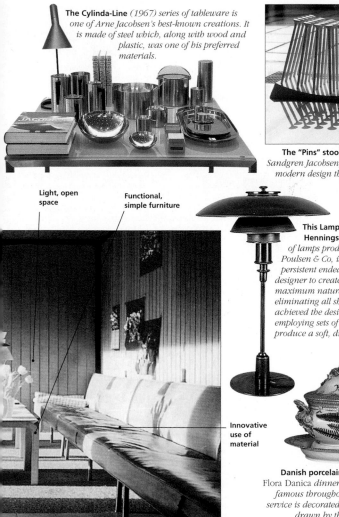

The Cylinda-Line *(1967) series of tableware is one of Arne Jacobsen's best-known creations. It is made of steel which, along with wood and plastic, was one of his preferred materials.*

The "Pins" stool *(2002), by Hans Sandgren Jacobsen, is an example of modern design that still maintains Danish precision and aesthetics.*

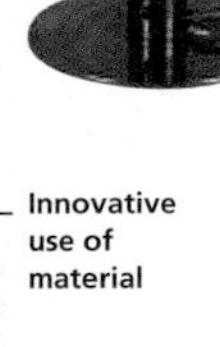

This Lamp by Poul Henningsen, *from a series of lamps produced for Louis Poulsen & Co, is the result of a persistent endeavour by the designer to create lamps that give maximum natural light, while eliminating all shadows. He achieved the desired result by employing sets of shaped shades to produce a soft, dispersed light.*

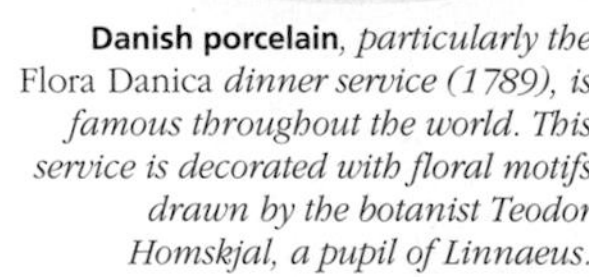

Danish porcelain, *particularly the* Flora Danica *dinner service (1789), is famous throughout the world. This service is decorated with floral motifs drawn by the botanist Teodor Homskjal, a pupil of Linnaeus.*

DESIGN FOR LIVING

Following World War II, Danish architects began to take an interest in the architectural styles of a number of other countries, drawing on many influences to produce open-plan house designs. This trend is, perhaps, best exemplified by houses that architects have built for themselves, such as the home of Jørn Utzon in Hellebæk, erected in 1952.

ARNE JACOBSEN

Born in 1902, Arne Jacobsen is the unquestionable "star" of Danish design. In his youth, Jacobsen was fascinated by the work of the Swiss-born architect Le Corbusier, especially his focus on functionality. As a designer Jacobsen created many well-known pieces including the Ant (1951). This plywood chair could be stacked and was the forerunner of chairs found in schools and cafés all over the world today. The majority of Jacobsen's chair designs, including the Egg and the Swan, are still being produced. He died in 1971.

Danish Art

Both painting and sculpture have an important place in the history of Danish art. Sculpture flourished particularly during the Late Gothic and Mannerist periods, but above all, thanks to the genius of sculptor Bertel Thorvaldsen, during the so-called "Golden Age" in the early 19th century, which saw a flowering of Danish expression. Painting also flourished during this period and the formal portraiture of earlier painters such as Jens Juel began to be replaced with lively depictions of everyday life by artists such as Christoffer Wilhelm Eckersberg and his student Christen Købke.

***View from the Loft of the Grain Store at the Bakery in the Citadel* (1831), Christen Købke**

***Wounded Philoctetes* (1774–75), Nicolai Abildgaard (Statens Museum for Kunst)**

OLD MASTERS

There are many well-preserved medieval works of art in Denmark, including Romanesque paintings and, in the churches of Zealand, the cycles of frescoes dating mainly from the 12th century.

The subsequent centuries were dominated by formal portraiture. Among the most outstanding, and the largest in size, are the oil paintings on display in Rosenborg Slot in Copenhagen, produced after 1615 by Dutch artists including Reinchold Timm and Rembrandt. The artists working for Christian IV, in Kronborg, included the Dutch painter Gerrit van Honthorst, who painted for the court of Denmark between 1635 and 1641. During the reign of Frederik IV the influences of French painting became more pronounced. During the Rococo period a French influence was also present and can be seen in the works of Scandinavians such as Johan Salomon Wahl and Carl Gustaf Pilo. The turning point in the development of Danish painting came with the founding of the Royal Academy of Fine Arts in 1754. Its alumni included many prominent painters from the period such as Jens Juel and Nicolai Abildgaard, who studied in Rome, from 1772 to 1776.

THE "GOLDEN AGE"

The period between 1800 and 1850 saw a great surge in creativity. One of the prime movers of the "Golden Age" *(see pp42–3)* was Christoffer Wilhelm Eckersberg, who drew much of his inspiration from the native Danish landscape, as well as from scenes of everyday life. He had studied in Paris where he was taught by Jacques Louis David to see nature for what it was. Eckersberg returned to Denmark, fired with the belief that truth is beauty. He brought back the precision of Neo-Classicism and made it a dominant trait in Danish painting. Portraiture during the "Golden Age" was also of a very high standard. Among the other outstanding artists of the period are Christian Albrecht Jensen and Christen Købke.

MODERN ART

After 1880 Realism and Naturalism ruled supreme in Danish painting. Their most famous exponents was the Skagen School, which placed an emphasis on natural light and its effects. Among the leading members of this school were Peder S. Krøyer and Anna and Michael Ancher. Around 1900, Danish painting came to be dominated by Symbolism. The situation changed just before World War I, when new trends, such as the

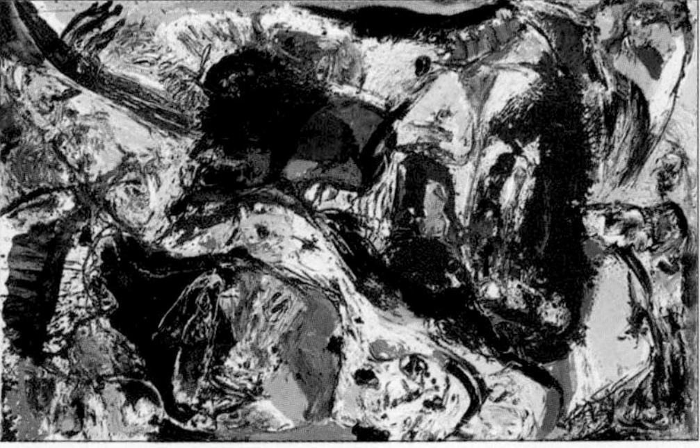

***Dead Drunk Danes* (1960), Asger Jorn**

experiments with form by the Expressionists and Cubists, began to challenge existing traditions in art. The ranks of Danish Cubists included Jais Nielsen and Vilhelm Lundstrom. One of the most important phenomena of the 1950s was CoBrA (Copenhagen–Brussels–Amsterdam), a movement that tried to give free expression to the unconscious. One of the movement's founders was the Danish artist Asger Jorn, whose vivid abstract paintings have received international acclaim.

High altar of Roskilde Domkirke, 16th century

SACRED ART

Before turning to Protestantism Danish churches were richly decorated. In the 16th century, after the Reformation, many frescoes were painted over, as they were considered to be examples of Catholic flamboyance. Surviving to this day are a few gilded altars dating from the Romanesque period (12th–13th centuries); two of them are still found in their original locations, in Sahl and Stadil churches. Some outstanding altarpieces were created in the Late Gothic period (late 15th and early 16th centuries) by woodcarvers from Lübeck, notably Claus Berg. Berg's work, which includes the main altar in the cathedral in Odense, is particularly striking. Filled with emotional charge and high in drama, his carving maintains a realism of detail that is typical of work found in southern Germany.

The Renaissance high altar in Roskilde Domkirke was made in Antwerp in 1560. It was originally intended for Gdansk, until it was requisitioned by Danish customs authorities.

The 17th century saw a culmination of the Reformation. At that time large sums of money were spent on building churches and chapels, notably Holmens Kirke in Copenhagen, for which Frederik III ordered a sumptuously decorated altarpiece sculpted from raw oak wood.

SEPULCHRAL SCULPTURE

With the passing of the medieval era, funereal or sepulchral sculpture began to enjoy success in Denmark. Characteristic of this period are the works of the sculptor and architect Cornelius Floris of Antwerp, who designed the tomb of Christian III (d.1559) in Roskilde Domkirke (Cathedral), west of Copenhagen. It is made of multi-coloured marble and extraordinarily richly ornamented, with an open plan colonnade that contains two statues of the monarch. This is one of Europe's largest royal tombs from this period.

Self-portrait, by Bertel Thorvaldsen

Renaissance tombs and epitaphs of the aristocracy, found in great numbers throughout Denmark, were more modest, and usually limited to a single slab of stone bearing the image of the deceased in a prostrate position, with an inscription. A new type of tombstone appeared in the 17th century. Its main creator

Tomb of Christian III in Roskilde Domkirke, by Cornelius Floris

was Thomas Quellinus of Antwerp. His marble tombs realistically depicted the deceased, and were accompanied by personified images of his virtues.

MODERN SCULPTURE

Prior to the 19th century sculpture was treated in Denmark solely as a means of portraying the monarchy. This art form began to be taken more seriously with the establishment of the Royal Academy, however, and among its early exponents were Johanes Wiedeweilt (d.1802) and Nicolai Dajon (d.1823). Sculpture was only elevated to a high form of art, however, by Bertel Thorvaldsen (d.1844), who created an austere variety of Classicism based on his in-depth studies of classical antiquity while in Rome. After working in southern Europe for many years, Thorvaldsen returned home to a hero's welcome in 1838. He bequeathed many of his finest works to the city of Copenhagen on condition that a museum was established in which to house them (Thorvaldsens Museum, *see p85*).

DENMARK THROUGH THE YEAR

Denmark is roughly on the same latitude as Moscow and southern Alaska but has a fairly mild climate. The coldest months are January and February, and most events and festivals are scheduled for spring and summer. The Danes like to enjoy themselves, and during the summer holiday season the whole country comes alive, with almost every town having its own festival. Denmark is not a large country yet it hosts many world-class events, including one of the oldest rock-music festivals, in Roskilde, which is attended by many major international acts. The world-famous Copenhagen jazz festival also attracts top performers. As elsewhere in Europe, religious festivals such as Christmas are widely observed and provide an opportunity for people to spend time with their families.

A clown dressed for Copenhagen's carnival

Royal family at the official celebrations of the Queen's birthday

SPRING

Spring arrives slowly in Denmark, but its advent is welcomed with great celebration around the country. The biggest of the festivals is Copenhagen's Whitsun Carnival, when the streets fill with Danes dressed in colourful costumes to mark the end of the long winter.

MARCH

Aalborg Opera Festival *(1st half of Mar)*, Aalborg. In early March opera lovers congregate to hear some of the world's best performers.

APRIL

Birthday of Queen Margrethe II *(16 Apr)*, Copenhagen. The Danish queen is very popular, and on this day large crowds of loyal Danes congregate outside Amalienborg Slot to sing "Happy Birthday", which is accompanied by the ceremonial changing of the Livgarden (royal guards).
Store Bededag *(4th Friday after Easter)*. Common Prayer Day or Great Prayer Day is a movable Easter feast. Following the introduction of Protestantism to Denmark in the 16th century, the church calendar was revised and several feasts were combined into one – the Store Bededag. On this day many Danes eat wheat buns – *varme hveder*.
CPH:PIX *(late Apr)*, Copenhagen. This is the biggest international film festival in Denmark. Film entries include Scandinavian producers, as well as many world-famous directors.

MAY

Arbejdernes Kampdag *(1 May)*. Rallies are held to mark Labour Day.
Pinsedag. Whitsunday.
Viking Market *(1st weekend in May)*, Ribe. Held at the Viking Museum, this annual event recreates a Viking marketplace complete with displays of Viking crafts.
Aalborg Carnival *(2nd half of May)*, Aalborg. Four days of spring celebrations including a firework display and a parade.
Ølfestival *(20–22 May)*, Copenhagen. Arranged by the Danish Beer Society, this lively beer festival includes stalls, music and, of course, lots of beer to sample.
Copenhagen Marathon *(late May)*, Copenhagen. This race attracts amateur and elite runners from many European countries.
Whitsun Carnival *(Whitsun weekend)*, Copenhagen. This three-day event includes a parade, dancing and special activities for children.

Viking Market, Ribe

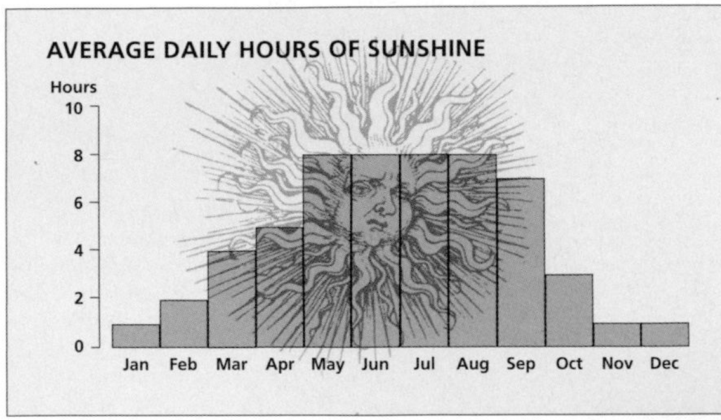

Hours of Sunshine
Most sunny days occur in late spring and early summer but visitors can also expect some fine weather through until September. November, December and January are generally the cloudiest months.

SUMMER

Summer festivities begin with Midsummer Eve (23 June) when bonfires are lit on many beaches. Numerous attractions are scheduled for the summer holidays – from local one-day events to major festivals.

Roskilde Festival – one of Denmark's most popular events

JUNE

International Kite Festival *(mid-Jun)*, Fanø.
River Boat Jazz Festival *(end Jun)*, Silkeborg. Jazz bands perform all around Silkeborg, some on boats.
International Sand Sculpture Festival *(spring to autumn)*, various towns. Competition to build the best sand sculptures.
Sankt Hans Eve *(23 Jun)*. Midsummer Night is celebrated around camp fires.

JULY

Ringridning *(Jul)*, several towns in Sønderjylland. At this colourful festival, horse riders use a lance or spear to target a series of metal rings suspended in mid-air.
Roskilde Festival *(begin Jul)*, Roskilde. For more than three decades this rock festival has been attracting some of the biggest names in music. Past performers include Bob Dylan, Bob Marley and David Bowie.

Jazz Festival, Copenhagen

Copenhagen Jazz Festival *(early Jul)*, Copenhagen. For two weeks jazz, blues and fusion blast out of almost every public space in the city.
Århus International Jazz Festival *(mid-Jul)*, Århus. A second opportunity in this month to hear some top-class jazz.
Hans Christian Andersen Plays *(end Jun–early Aug)*, Odense. Andersen's tales are staged in the Hans Christian Andersens Hus garden.

AUGUST

Cultural Harvest. Festivals celebrated in castles and stately homes, including exhibitions and theatre.
International Clown Festival *(mid-Aug)*, Klampenborg. A 10-day meeting of clowns and other performers from around the world.
Hamlet Summer *(early to mid-Aug)*, Helsingør. Performances of Shakespeare's *Hamlet* and other works are staged in Kronborg Slot.
International Film Festival *(mid-Aug)*, Odense.
Schubertiade *(mid-Aug)*, Roskilde. Top musicians perform a selection of the works of Franz Schubert.
European Medieval Festival *(end of Aug)*, Horsens. For two days the town is transformed into a 15th-century city.

Re-creating the Middle Ages at Horsens's European Medieval Festival

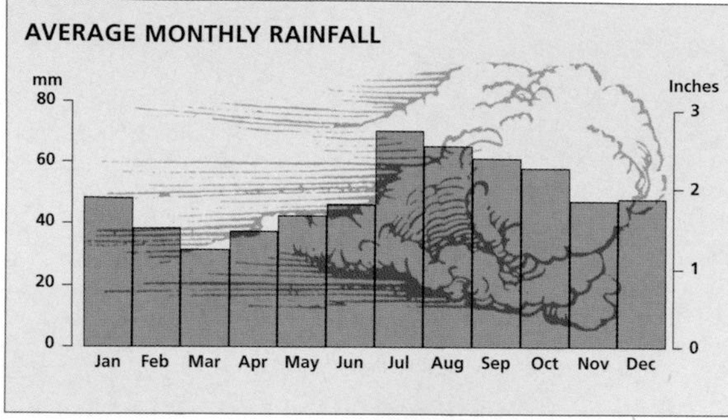

Rainfall

July is one of the warmest, but also one of the wettest, months. The best time to visit is in late spring, when it is warm and there is very little rain.

AUTUMN

Early autumn provides the final opportunity to stage outdoor performances of jazz and theatre. The beginning of October marks a transition between the carefree holiday season and the beginning of the new school year with months of hard work and study ahead. Theatres stage their first-night performances, and cold autumn evenings bring music-lovers into the clubs.

Israels Plads flower market, Copenhagen, in early autumn

SEPTEMBER

Golden Days *(2 weeks in Sep)*, Copenhagen. This bi-annual event celebrates Copenhagen's rich cultural heritage and city life.
Limfjorden Race *(early or mid-Sep)*, Løgstør. Scandinavia's biggest annual sailing event.
Tourde Gudenå *(mid-Sep)*, Skanderborg. Kayak and canoe contest attracting many participants and spectators.
Copenhagen International Film Festival *(end Sep)*, Copenhagen.

Father Christmas Parade during Christmas celebrations in Tønder

OCTOBER

Cultural Night *(2nd Fri in Oct)*, Copenhagen. A night when it is possible to visit many exhibitions, museums, castles, theatres and churches, including some buildings that are usually closed to visitors.
Tivoli Halloween *(3rd week Oct)*, Copenhagen. Witches, lanterns and pumpkins.
Antiques Fair *(end Oct or early Nov)*, Copenhagen. Antiques and rare coins fair.
Copenhagen Gay and Lesbian Film Festival *(end Oct)*, Copenhagen. International gay and lesbian film festival.

NOVEMBER

Tivoli Christmas *(Nov–Dec)*, Copenhagen. Numerous events for the young and young at heart in Tivoli as Christmas draws closer. Among the attractions are a Christmas market, ice-skating on a frozen artificial lake and the chance of spotting a Christmas pixie.
Copenhagen Irish Festival *(1st half of Nov)*, Copenhagen. Four days of celebrations and plenty of Irish music.
Tønder – The Christmas Town *(mid-Nov)*, Tønder. A colourful parade featuring a multitude of Father Christmases, accompanied by marching bands, passes along the main street of the town.
Feast of St Morten *(10 Nov)*. St Morten's Evening is often marked by roasting a goose.
CPH:DOX *(mid-Nov)*, Copenhagen. This is the largest documentary-film festival in northern Europe.

Street vendor roasting almonds on a Copenhagen pavement

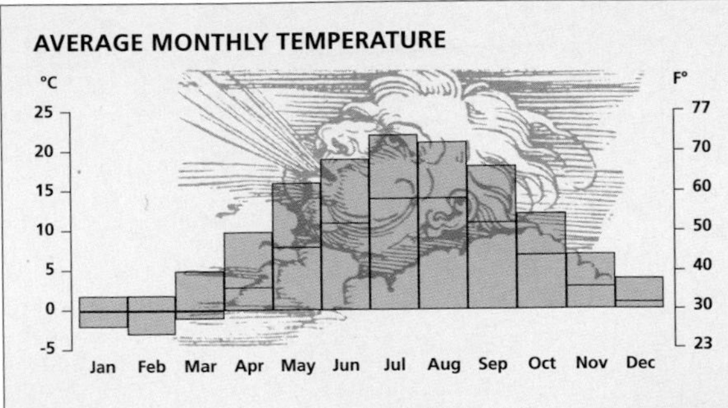

Temperature
This chart shows the average maximum and minimum temperatures for each month. Summer temperatures reach about 20° C (68° F), although temperatures can top 25° C (77° F). Winters can be cold with the temperature often dropping below zero, though severe frosts are rare.

WINTER

Winter is the quietest time of the year. Little happens and the weather is not conducive to outdoor entertainment. The Christmas period abounds in concerts, however. These are often staged in churches and feature choral ensembles singing psalms and carols. Denmark's streets are beautifully decorated and illuminated at this time and Christmas fairs are held throughout the country, with plenty to eat and drink, and the occasional parade.

DECEMBER

Jul *(24–26 Dec)*. The Danes celebrate Christmas in family circles. As in most of Europe, children play a central role. Danes tend to celebrate on Christmas Eve, decoratinag the tree the night before Christmas and often hanging it with real candles. The traditional Christmas dinner is also eaten on the 24th and usually consists of roast duck with red cabbage and potatoes. Rice pudding is eaten for dessert; whoever finds the hidden almond gets a prize.

Symphony orchestra performing for Aalborg's New Year concert

JANUARY

Nytårsdag *(1 Jan)*. New Year's Day witnesses a boisterous welcome to the New Year in Denmark. Many towns stage firework displays, while classical concerts are performed in most major cities.
Winter Jazz Festival *(late Jan or early Feb)*, Copenhagen. Jazz festival, held since 1979.

FEBRUARY

Copenhagen International Fashion Fair *(early Feb)*, Copenhagen. Top Scandinavian and European fashion designers present their latest collections.
Fastelavn *(last Sun before Lent)*. Shrovetide is a time for fun and games. The Danish tradition of "knocking a cat out of the barrel" is still practised by children in fancy-dress. Originally the barrel, hanging from a string, contained a real cat, which was held to be a symbol of evil. Today, the barrel contains sweets, toys and fruit, which eventually fall to the ground.

New Year fireworks in Tivoli, Copenhagen

PUBLIC HOLIDAYS

New Year *Nytår* (1 Jan)
Maundy Thursday
Good Friday
Easter Day *Påske*
Labour Day *Arbejdernes Kampdag* (1 May)
Common Prayer Day *Store Bededag* (Apr/May)
Ascension Day *Kristihimmelfartsdag*
Whitsunday, Whitmonday *Pinse*
Constitution Day (5 Jun)
Christmas Day (25 Dec)
Boxing Day (26 Dec)

THE HISTORY OF DENMARK

Denmark's history has long been associated with the sea. Viking raids on England and elsewhere between the 9th and 11th centuries marked the beginnings of Danish influence and by the late Middle Ages Denmark had a tight grip on trade in the Baltic. The country later lost its position as a world power, but continues to play an important role in the international arena.

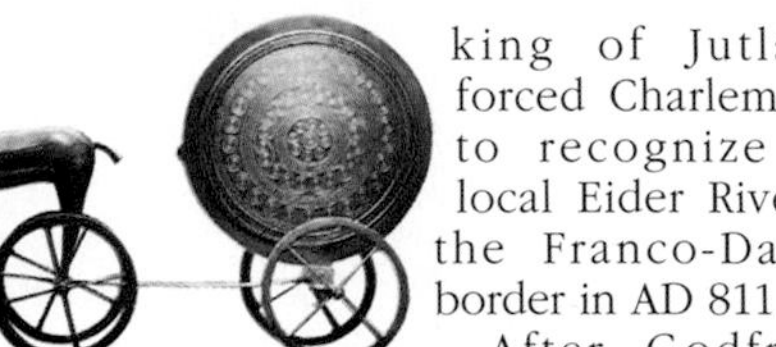

Bronze-Age cult object displayed at the Nationalmuseet

The earliest evidence of human existence to be found in Denmark dates from about 12,000 BC. Between 3900 and 1700 BC the first agricultural settlements began to emerge. Denmark's Bronze Age dates from around 1800 BC and jewellery and cult objects have been unearthed from this period. By about 500 BC iron had largely replaced bronze.

UNIFICATION

During the late Iron Age (5th and 6th centuries AD) a Nordic tribe known as Danes began to take control of the Jutland peninsula, forming a social order based around tribal structures.

As a result of the threat from the south presented by the Frankish empire under Charlemagne, these clans began to co-operate as a defensive measure. The Danish strategic position was strengthened in about AD 737 by the building of the Danevirke, a rampart that cut across the Jutland peninsula. This wall, and the forces of Godfred, king of Jutland, forced Charlemagne to recognize the local Eider River as the Franco-Danish border in AD 811.

After Godfred's death, rivalry between different clans again brought chaos. The first ruler to restore unity was Gorm the Old, the son of a Norwegian chieftain who had conquered the Jutland peninsula in the late 9th century. Gorm's son, Harald I (Bluetooth) took the throne in AD 950 and extended his power base across the rest of Denmark. Harald I's conquest enabled the widespread adoption of Christianity, which not only unified the country but also appeased Denmark's Frankish neighbours.

Increased security gave new impetus to a series of Viking *(see pp34–5)* raids on the British Isles and Ireland. These raids made it possible for Danish kings to win control of England and, for a period, an Anglo-Danish kingdom was formed under Canute I (The Great), who ruled as monarch of Denmark, England and Norway until his death in 1035.

TIMELINE

12,000 BC Earliest evidence of man in Denmark

Cover of a stone urn from the Bronze Age

9th century Danish Viking raids on British Isles and France

811 Army of Charlemagne stopped by Danevirke wall

1018–1035 Reign of Canute I. Unification of Denmark, England and Norway

12,000 BC | 4000 BC | AD 500 | 750 | 1000 | 1100

3900–1700 BC Earliest agricultural settlements

5th–6th century Danes occupy the Jutland peninsula

737 Building of the Danevirke rampart

Clay pot, 1700–500 BC

1013 Sweyn I conquers England

c.985 Harald I (Bluetooth) unites Jutland, the islands and southern Sweden

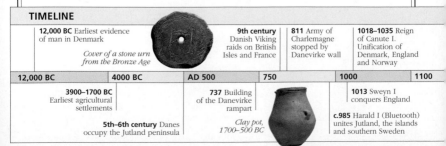

◁ Danish flag descending from heaven during Valdemar II's campaign in present-day Estonia in 1219

The Vikings

The term Viking is generally used to refer to the Scandinavian peoples who journeyed overseas in wooden ships, between AD 800 and 1100, to raid and trade throughout the North and Irish seas and along the rivers of eastern and western Europe. Early Viking raiders targeted monasteries for their wealth and the ferocity of these lightning raids spread terror throughout Christian Europe, giving rise to the image of Vikings as plunderers and rapists. In fact these pagan people were expert sailors and ventured as far as North America where they traded in such items as tusks and pelts.

Ornament
This silver ornament, found in Lindholm Høje in 1952, represents a typical piece of Viking jewellery.

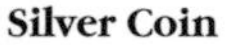

Silver Coin
The Vikings established trade routes to the East and the West. From the 9th century, silver coins, such as this one from the market place of Hedeby, were used as currency.

Strong ropes holding the mast

Sails were made from sheep's wool or flax and were often worth more than the rest of the boat.

Viking Chieftain
In the 19th century a view of Vikings began to take hold, which saw them as barbarians. This portrait by Carl Haag is typical of the common image. Actually they were skilled craftsmen, traders, and hunters.

The bow and stern of a Viking ship had the same shape, enabling it to make a rapid change in direction.

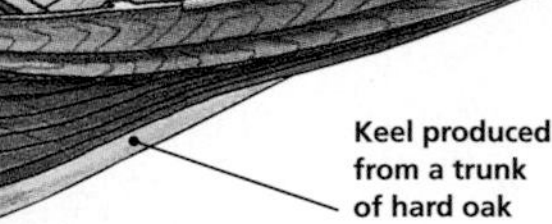

Keel produced from a trunk of hard oak

Figurehead
The stems of ships were decorated with figureheads, in the form of a snake or a dragonhead. The loss of a figurehead was believed to be a bad omen.

VIKING SHIP
Viking warships were usually about 28 m (92 ft) in length. The longest one ever found measured nearly 70 m (230 ft). Along with a 60-strong crew of oarsmen, they could carry as many as 400 people.

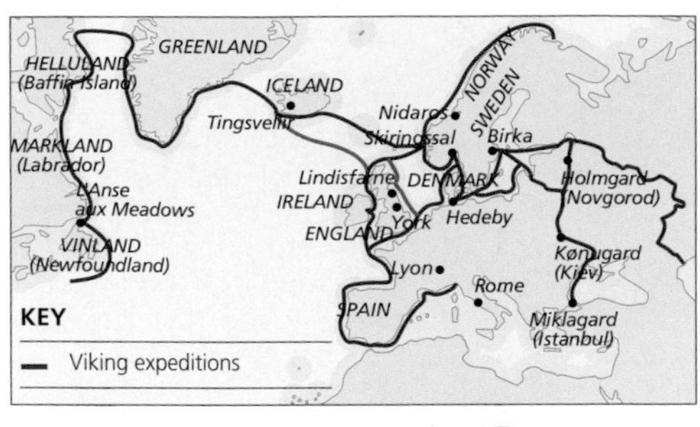

Woman Statuette
The independent and self-reliant Viking women ran their homes and farms for many months when their men went out to sea.

The ship's planking was made of overlapping planks of oak and joined together with nails. Any gaps between the planks were sealed with tarred wool or fur.

Viking sailing ships had a very shallow draught and could sail in waters less than 1 m (3.3 ft) deep.

Viking Raids
Early raids were carried out only during spring and summer. From about 845, Vikings began wintering at the mouths of foreign rivers, making raids possible throughout the year.

VIKING ARCHITECTURE

Few Viking buildings, which were built of earth, wood and stone, have survived. The best preserved are the round fortresses erected during the reign of Harald I (Bluetooth), in the late 10th century, at strategic points around Fyrkat (eastern Jutland), Aggersborg (northern Jutland), Trelleborg (Zealand) and Nonnebakken (Funen). These fortified settlements were surrounded by circular embankments 120 m (394 ft) in diameter, 12 m (39.4 ft) wide and rising to a height of 4 m (13 ft).

The Frykat fortress included 16 huge buildings containing domestic quarters, and was probably inhabited by between 800 and 1,000 people. Close to where the fortress stood, there is now a replica Viking farmstead including houses and outbuildings.

This replica longhouse, *near Fyrkat, was built using authentic tools and materials, with knowledge gained from archaeological research.*

Viking house doors, *such as this one in Frederikssund, was heavily built as a defence against intruders as well as the forces of nature.*

Valdemar I removing a pagan statute on the coast of Rugia

THE MIDDLE AGES

King Canute's son Hardicanute died in 1042 and the Anglo-Danish kingdom disintegrated as the successors of Denmark's eighth monarch, Sweyn II (1047–74), began fighting each other for the throne. As royal supremacy weakened, the power of wealthy landowners and church leaders grew and this early medieval period of Denmark's history is scarred by internal strife and corruption.

This period of unrest came to an end with the succession of Valdemar I (The Great) in 1157. He reunited the country and enacted Denmark's first written laws (the Jutland Code). With help of the powerful Bishop Absalon, he made a series of successful raids against the Wends in eastern Germany. By the time of Valdemar II's succession, Denmark had won control of Meklenburg, Holstein, Lübeck and Estonia, making it one of the greatest powers in northern Europe.

Denmark's pre-eminence ended in 1227 when the country was defeated by its German vassals at the Battle of Bornhøved. As a result, Denmark was forced to give up much of its recently acquired territory and, following the death of Valdemar II in 1241, the Danish monarchy lost much of its power. As a result, successive monarchs were forced into enacting a number of laws which for the time were quite progressive. These changes included the end of imprisonment without just cause (1282) and the establishment of the first supreme court in 1360.

THE KALMAR UNION

One of the greatest achievements of King Valdemar IV (1340–75) was to arrange the marriage of his daughter Margrethe to Norway's King Haakon. Margrethe succeeded in forming the Kalmar Union, an alliance uniting Denmark, Norway and Sweden under a common sovereign. The main aim of the union was to counter the dominance of the Hanseatic League, which under the influence of Germany dominated trade in the region.

Queen Margrethe, regent of Denmark and the initiator of the Kalmar Union

TIMELINE

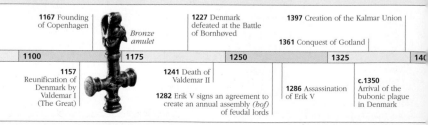

- **1157** Reunification of Denmark by Valdemar I (The Great)
- **1167** Founding of Copenhagen
- **1227** Denmark defeated at the Battle of Bornhøved
- **1241** Death of Valdemar II
- **1282** Erik V signs an agreement to create an annual assembly *(hof)* of feudal lords
- **1286** Assassination of Erik V
- **c.1350** Arrival of the bubonic plague in Denmark
- **1361** Conquest of Gotland
- **1397** Creation of the Kalmar Union

Bronze amulet

1100 | 1175 | 1250 | 1325 | 1400

Gustav Vasa persuading Lübeck authorities to join in the attack on Christian II

While each country remained free to follow their own policies, they were obliged to fight any wars together and elect a common monarch. In 1397, Margrethe's grand-nephew Erik of Pomerania was crowned king of Denmark, Norway and Sweden.

Initially, a long line of military successes, the introduction of customs duties in the Øresund (Sound) and a growing demand for Danish produce strengthened the country's position. Soon, however, Denmark's domination in the Baltic was challenged by the growing power of Sweden, which sought a greater influence in its own internal affairs. In 1520 the Danish king, Christian II, ruthlessly suppressed an insurrection by what is known as the Stockholm Bloodbath. Three years later, however, Sweden elected its own king, Gustav Vasa, effectively putting an end to the union.

Wooden altar by Abel Schrøder, 1661, in Holmens Kirke, Copenhagen

WARS WITH SWEDEN

Denmark's and Sweden's aims to gain control of Øresund lead to a long series of wars between the two countries during the 16th and 17th centuries. In addition to these battles, the major European conflict, the Thirty Years War, took place (1616–48). Denmark was involved from 1625 to 1629 and suffered a disastrous defeat, while Sweden, joining in 1630, gained power and wealth through the conflict. Renewed warring between the two countries ended in 1658 with Denmark losing all of its territories on the Swedish mainland. Two more wars occurred, 1675–79 and 1709–20.

TOWARDS ABSOLUTE MONARCHY

The strength of the monarchy had been increased by the introduction of Lutheranism in 1536, which placed the wealth of the Catholic church in the hands of the Crown. The king, however, was still elected by the nobility. Although political power was divided between the Crown and Council, the nobles often had the last say, especially in financial matters. After the defeats of 1658, state coffers were empty and King Fredrik III needed to assert himself and take control. This led to the instatement of absolute monarchy *(see pp38–9)*.

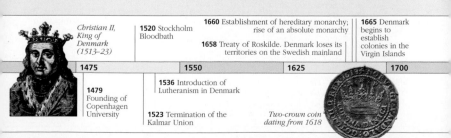

Christian IV, King of Denmark, welcomed in Berlin by the Brandenburg Elector, 1595

Christian II, King of Denmark (1513–23)

1479 Founding of Copenhagen University

1520 Stockholm Bloodbath

1523 Termination of the Kalmar Union

1536 Introduction of Lutheranism in Denmark

1658 Treaty of Roskilde. Denmark loses its territories on the Swedish mainland

1660 Establishment of hereditary monarchy; rise of an absolute monarchy

1665 Denmark begins to establish colonies in the Virgin Islands

1475 | 1550 | 1625 | 1700

Two-crown coin dating from 1618

The Era of Absolute Monarchy

Frederik III introduced hereditary monarchy in 1660 in an effort to curtail the power of the nobles of the Council *(see p37)*. In 1665, he took the matter further and passed the Royal Act, which declared the sovereign to be beyond the law and inferior only to God. Five years later Christian V became the first monarch to be crowned under the new system. The people seemed to prefer an almighty king to the old nobility, and kings continued to rule as absolute monarchs until 1848.

Frederik III
Crowned King of Denmark and Norway in 1648, Frederik III ruled until his death in Copenhagen castle in 1670. To this day, his grave can be found in Roskilde cathedral.

Academy of Knights
Denmark's elite schools were established by Frederik III. These academies became popular in the 17th century.

Frederiksborg Chapel
The Slotskirken (Palace Chapel) is where Danish kings were crowned from 1670 to 1840.

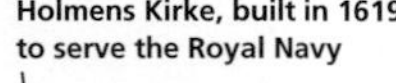
Holmens Kirke, built in 1619 to serve the Royal Navy

Holmens Canal
The Holmens Drawbridge enabled ships to enter the canal.

THE INTRODUCTION OF ABSOLUTISM IN DENMARK
The decision by Frederik III to introduce absolute monarchy in Denmark in 1665 was met with general approval. The ceremonial meeting between the king and the parliament has been immortalized in minute detail in many paintings including examples found in Rosenborg and Frederiksborg.

Copenhagen (c.1700)
Following the introduction of absolute monarchy the Danish capital's defences were strengthened.

Corfitz Ulfeldt
Corfitz Ulfeldt, son-in-law of Christian IV, was a typical example of the powerful nobility. After a disagreement with Frederik III, he switched sides and negotiated the Roskilde Treaty on Sweden's behalf in 1658.

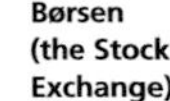
Colourful burgher homes were built in the form of narrow-fronted terraced houses.
Børsen (the Stock Exchange)
Numerous inhabitants of the capital attended the celebrations marking the introduction of absolute monarchy.
Boats moored along the canal
The king's troops

Frederik VII
In 1848 Frederik VII renounced absolute power and, with a new constitution, turned Denmark into a democratic country, with guaranteed freedom of speech.

ARCHITECTURE

The period of absolute monarchy brought with it many magnificent buildings. The most opulent examples of the residential architecture of this period include Charlottenborg in Kongens Nytorv, Copenhagen, which was completed in 1683 as a palace for the royal family *(see p69)*. Other outstanding buildings from this period are Ledreborg, a stately home designed by the architect Lauritz de Thurah *(see p139)*, Copenhagen's Børsen (Stock Exchange) and Amalienborg Slot *(see pp56–7)*, which was designed by Nicolai Eigtved, the architect also responsible for Copenhagen's Frederiksstad district.

Vor Frelsers Kirke *was built in 1696 by Lambert van Haven in Dutch Renaissance style. The spire was added by Lauritz de Thurah in 1752* (see p88).

Christian VII's Palace *at Amalienborg has typically opulent Rococo interiors, designed by Nicolai Eigtved and the sculptor Le Clerk.*

Painting by C.A. Lorentzen of the British attack on the Danish fleet, 1801

THE AGE OF REFORM

A peace treaty with Sweden signed in 1720 marked the beginning of the longest war-free period in Denmark's history. The absence of external threats encouraged economic growth and this in turn brought about a period of social change, which became more urgent as the French Revolution gathered pace. Under Frederik VI (1808–39) feudal obligations such as compulsory labour were abolished and large tracts of land were broken up and redistributed to peasants. At the same time landowners were given a role in government and compulsory education was introduced for all children under the age of 14.

THE NAPOLEONIC WARS

The outbreak of the Napoleonic Wars in 1796 eventually brought this period of peace and reform to a halt. Denmark, which derived major benefits from trade, tried to remain neutral in the face of the conflict in Europe but, in 1801, Britain accused Denmark of breaking the British trade embargo and attacked and destroyed the Danish fleet in Øresund. In 1807 the British, fearing the strengthening of a Franco-Danish alliance, struck again and bombarded Copenhagen for four days, inflicting heavy damage. By the end of the attack much of the city was ablaze and the naval yard was destroyed. The British then sailed away with what remained of the Danish fleet, which included 170 gunboats. In the aftermath of this assault, Denmark joined the continental alliance against Britain and Britain in turn blockaded Danish waters.

The war ended with the signing of the Kiel Peace Treaty in 1814 under the terms of which Denmark lost some 322,000 sq km (124,292 sq miles) of territory, including Norway. The new boundaries left Denmark

Peasants give thanks to Christian VII for abolishing serfdom, painting by C.W. Eckersberg

TIMELINE

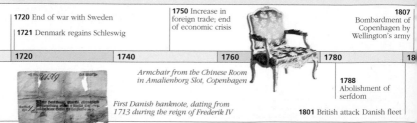

1720 End of war with Sweden

1721 Denmark regains Schleswig

1750 Increase in foreign trade; end of economic crisis

1807 Bombardment of Copenhagen by Wellington's army

1720 | 1740 | 1760 | 1780 | 18

Armchair from the Chinese Room in Amalienborg Slot, Copenhagen

1788 Abolishment of serfdom

First Danish banknote, dating from 1713 during the reign of Frederik IV

1801 British attack Danish fleet

Painting by C.W. Eckersberg depicting bombardment of Copenhagen in 1807

with a mere 58,000 sq km (22,388 sq miles), which included the Duchy of Schleswig, with its Danish-German population, and the Holstein and Lauenburg dukedoms.

The Napoleonic Wars had a catastrophic effect on Denmark. The British blockade led to famine and starvation while territorial losses and wartime destruction resulted in a bankrupt state treasury. Culturally, however, this was the beginning of Denmark's Golden Age *(see pp42–3)*.

Denmark's national emblem, 1774–1820

SCHLESWIG CONFLICT

Events in Europe, including the 1830 July Revolution in France, contributed to the weakening of absolute monarchy. With increasing force, demands were made for the creation of a representative government. Eventually, in 1848, pressure from liberal circles resulted in the enactment of a new constitution, putting an end to absolute monarchy.

The new constitution included the incorporation of the duchies of Schleswig and Holstein as permanent regions of Denmark. With the support of Prussia, the armies of Schleswig and Holstein rose up against the Danish authority. War ensued and ended in 1851 with the defeat of the duchies, but failed to solve the conflict. Trouble erupted again with even greater force, in 1863, when the Danish parliament agreed a new joint constitution for the Kingdom of Denmark and the Duchy of Schleswig. A year later, on the pretext of defending the German populations within the duchies, Prussia and Austria declared war on Denmark. Within months Denmark was defeated and the contested duchies were lost to Prussia and Austria.

The shock of defeat led Denmark to declare its neutrality and concentrate its efforts on rebuilding the economy. Danish agriculture entered a period of rapid growth, assisted by a high demand for grain in Britain, and the railway system was extended to cover much of the country. By the end of the 19th century Denmark had a well-developed economic base that included mature shipbuilding and brewing industries.

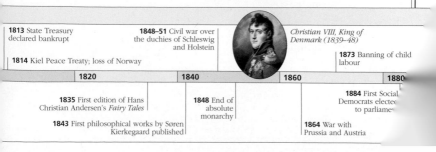

Return of Danish soldiers to Copenhagen in 1864, painting by Otto Bache

1813 State Treasury declared bankrupt

1814 Kiel Peace Treaty; loss of Norway

1835 First edition of Hans Christian Andersen's *Fairy Tales*

1843 First philosophical works by Søren Kierkegaard published

1848–51 Civil war over the duchies of Schleswig and Holstein

1848 End of absolute monarchy

Christian VIII, King of Denmark (1839–48)

1864 War with Prussia and Austria

1873 Banning of child labour

1884 First Social Democrats electe to parliame

1820 | 1840 | 1860 | 1880

Denmark's Golden Age

The period of political and economic turmoil that occurred during the Napoleonic wars, and the years immediately following them, witnessed an unprecedented flourishing of culture. The leading figures of Denmark's "Golden Age", which lasted throughout the first half of the 19th century, achieved recognition far beyond the borders of Denmark. Among the most prominent are the sculptor Bertel Thorvaldsen, the painter Christoffer Wilhelm Eckersberg and the romantic poet Adam Oehlenschläger. More famous than these, however, are the writer Hans Christian Andersen and the philosopher Søren Kierkegaard.

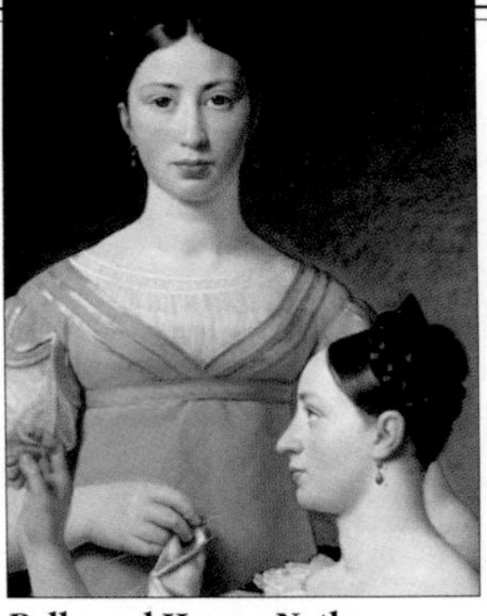

Bella and Hanna Nathansson
This portrait was painted by the "father of Danish painting" Christoffer Wilhelm Eckersberg.

Interior of a House
The drawing room of a Copenhagen merchant, portrayed in this painting by Wilhelm Marstrand, represents a typical interior of a middle-class home during the 1830s.

ertel Thorvaldsen
his sculpture (1817) of a shepherd is one of many Neo-Classical ues by Bertel Thorvaldsen.

Parade
Festivals, parades and fairs coloured the lives of Copenhagen's citizens.

H.C. Andersen Telling his Stories *An illustration from one of the earliest editions of Hans Christian Andersen's tales, which are some of the most famous works of children's literature.*

ARTISTS OF THE GOLDEN AGE

This painting, entitled *A Group of Danish Artists Visiting Rome* was painted in 1837 by Constantin Hansen. Like many painters of this period, Hansen learnt his craft abroad and returned to Denmark with a fresh perspective.

H.C. Andersen *Born in humble circumstances in 1805, the popular writer later socialized with the bourgeoisie and at court.*

Andersen's Inkpot *As well as writing nearly 200 fairy tales, Andersen also wrote novels, librettos and other works.*

Søren Kierkegaard *One of the forerunners of Existentialism, Kierkegaard (1813–55) described human life in terms of ethics, aesthetics and religion.*

THE GOLDEN AGE IN COPENHAGEN

Following the ravages that befell Copenhagen at the turn of the 18th and 19th centuries, including the 1807 British bombardment *(see p40)*, the city was rebuilt in a new form. Classicism became the dominant architectural style. Christian Frederik Hansen and other Danish architects often drew their inspiration from antiquity. Office buildings, as well as the new bourgeois residences, were adorned with columns, porticoes and tympanums. The most interesting buildings include Thorvaldsens Museum, the Domhuset (Court House) in Nytorv, and the Harsdorff Hus in Kongens Nytorv.

Thorvaldsens Museum *was built in 1848 and approved personally by the sculptor who had bequeathed his work to the city. This building is decorated with friezes by Jørgen Sonne* (see p85).

Vor Frue Kirke *was designed by Christian Frederik Hansen, who got his inspiration from Classical buildings. It had an imposing faåade, but no tower until Frederik VI declared that a tower was essential* (see p72).

Stockholm, Copenhagen and Oslo portrayed in a satirical magazine, in 1906

WORLD WAR I

Before World War I Denmark had maintained good relations with both Britain and Germany and with the outbreak of war the Danish government declared its neutrality. This brought considerable benefits to the country's economy, although a third of Denmark's merchant fleet was sunk during the conflict. Also, the war drew attention to the commercial and strategic importance of Denmark's colonies in the West Indies, and the USA bought the Virgin Islands from Denmark in 1917.

Germany's defeat in 1918 revived the old Schleswig-Holstein problem. Under the Treaty of Versailles, the area was divided into two zones and, after a referendum in 1920, the northern part of the former duchy was returned to Denmark. The southern zone remained with Germany.

WORLD WAR II

In September 1939, during Hitler's invasion of Poland, Denmark again confirmed its neutral status. This failed to stop the Third Reich from invading Denmark on 9 April 1940, and after a brief period of resistance by the royal guards at Amalienborg Slot Germany began a "peaceful occupation". Hoping to minimize casualties, the government in Copenhagen decided on a policy of limited co-operation. Opposition among ordinary Danes to this occupation was widespread, however, and in 1943 an increasingly strong resistance movement brought an end to the policy of collaboration. Following a wave of strikes and anti-German demonstrations, the government resigned and was replaced by a German administration.

The Nazis disarmed the Danish army and fleet and began to round up Danish Jews. Fortunately, most were spirited away at night in fishing boats by the Danish Resistance to neutral Sweden.

The final 18 months of the war saw the Danish Freedom Council, an underground movement that organized the Resistance, become

US State Secretary hands the Danish minister a cheque in payment for the Virgin Islands

TIMELINE

1914–18 World War I. Denmark remains neutral

Frederik VIII with his wife, Louise

1940 Denmark occupied by the Third Reich

1944 Iceland becomes a republic

1900 | 1915 | 1930 | 1945

1901 Adoption of democratic parliamentary government

1917 Sale of the Virgin Islands to the United States

1920 Schleswig-Holstein referendum

1933 Implementation of first social reform programmes

1949 Denmark becomes a co-founder of NATO

Christian X (1912–47)

1960 Denmark joins EFTA

Germans on the streets of Copenhagen during World War II

increasingly active. The Danish Resistance, which by 1945 had some 50,000 operatives ready to assist the Allies, did all it could to hamper the German war effort, including blowing up railway lines and sabotaging German-run factories. With the German surrender in 1945, a new government composed of Resistance leaders and pre-war politicians was formed in Denmark.

Margrethe II, Queen of Denmark

POSTWAR DENMARK

Thanks to the activities of the Resistance, Denmark was recognized as a member of the Allied Forces and joined the United Nations in 1945. In 1949 it joined the ranks of NATO. This move marked a departure from a policy of neutrality, which the country had followed since 1864. Denmark's participation in the Marshall Plan enabled the country to thoroughly modernize its industry and agriculture and laid the foundations for postwar prosperity. A new constitution, enacted in 1953, introduced a single-chamber parliament and changed the rules governing female succession to the throne. These new rules were applied in 1972 when Queen Margrethe II ascended the throne following the death of her father, Frederik IX.

Denmark did not participate in the talks which in 1957 resulted in the formation of the European Union, but in 1973, after a referendum, it became the first Scandinavian country to join the EU. Denmark's EU membership has remained a controversial subject with many Danes, however, and 87 per cent of the country voted against the adoption of the euro.

Throughout the 1960s and 1970s a series of reforms, including a generous system of social welfare and a virtual lack of censorship, bolstered the country's reputation as a liberal country. In the 1970s and 1980s Denmark entered a conservative phase with calls for curbs on immigration and tax cuts. However, it is still acknowledged as a tolerant society, with a high standard of living, a strong sense of social conscience and many positive policies towards protecting the environment. In 2009, Anders Fogh Rasmussen, the country's former prime minister, was appointed secretary general of NATO.

Anders Fogh Rasmussen, secretary general of NATO

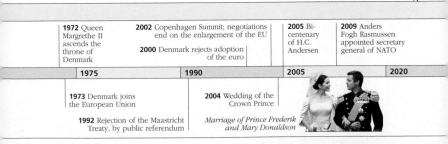

1972 Queen Margrethe II ascends the throne of Denmark

2002 Copenhagen Summit; negotiations end on the enlargement of the EU

2000 Denmark rejects adoption of the euro

2005 Bi-centenary of H.C. Andersen

2009 Anders Fogh Rasmussen appointed secretary general of NATO

1975 | 1990 | 2005 | 2020

1973 Denmark joins the European Union

1992 Rejection of the Maastricht Treaty, by public referendum

2004 Wedding of the Crown Prince

Marriage of Prince Frederik and Mary Donaldson

COPENHAGEN AREA BY AREA

Copenhagen at a Glance

Copenhagen's main attractions include its three royal palaces (Rosenborg, Amalienborg and Christiansborg), as well as numerous museums, churches and monuments, including the much-loved Little Mermaid. There is no shortage of parks. The most famous of these is Tivoli in the heart of the city. The city centre is compact and can easily be explored on foot. Enjoyable alternatives to walking are touring the city on a bicycle or riding one of the waterbuses that run along some of the most interesting canals.

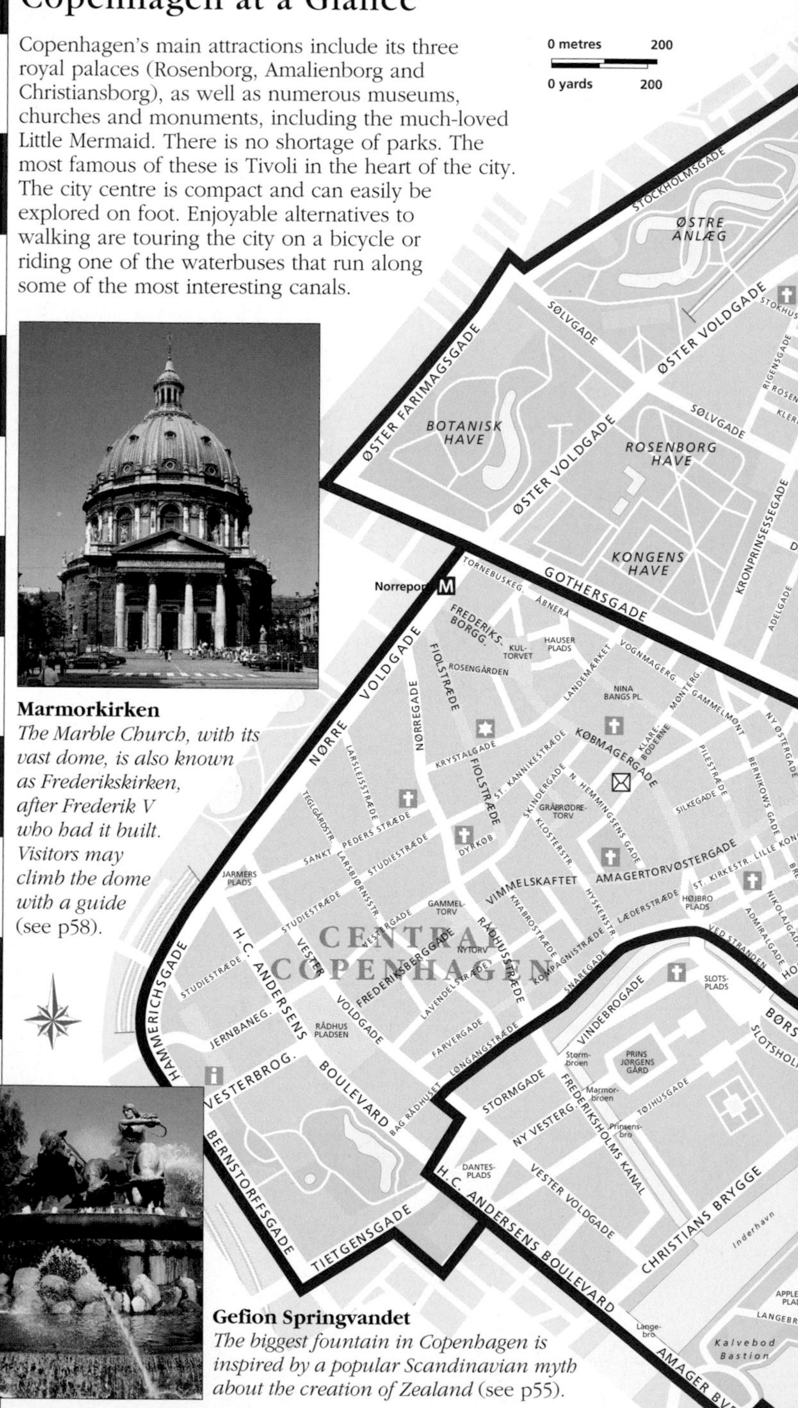

Marmorkirken
The Marble Church, with its vast dome, is also known as Frederikskirken, after Frederik V who had it built. Visitors may climb the dome with a guide (see p58).

Gefion Springvandet
The biggest fountain in Copenhagen is inspired by a popular Scandinavian myth about the creation of Zealand (see p55).

◁ **Royal guards sporting red uniforms and busbies and carrying drums**

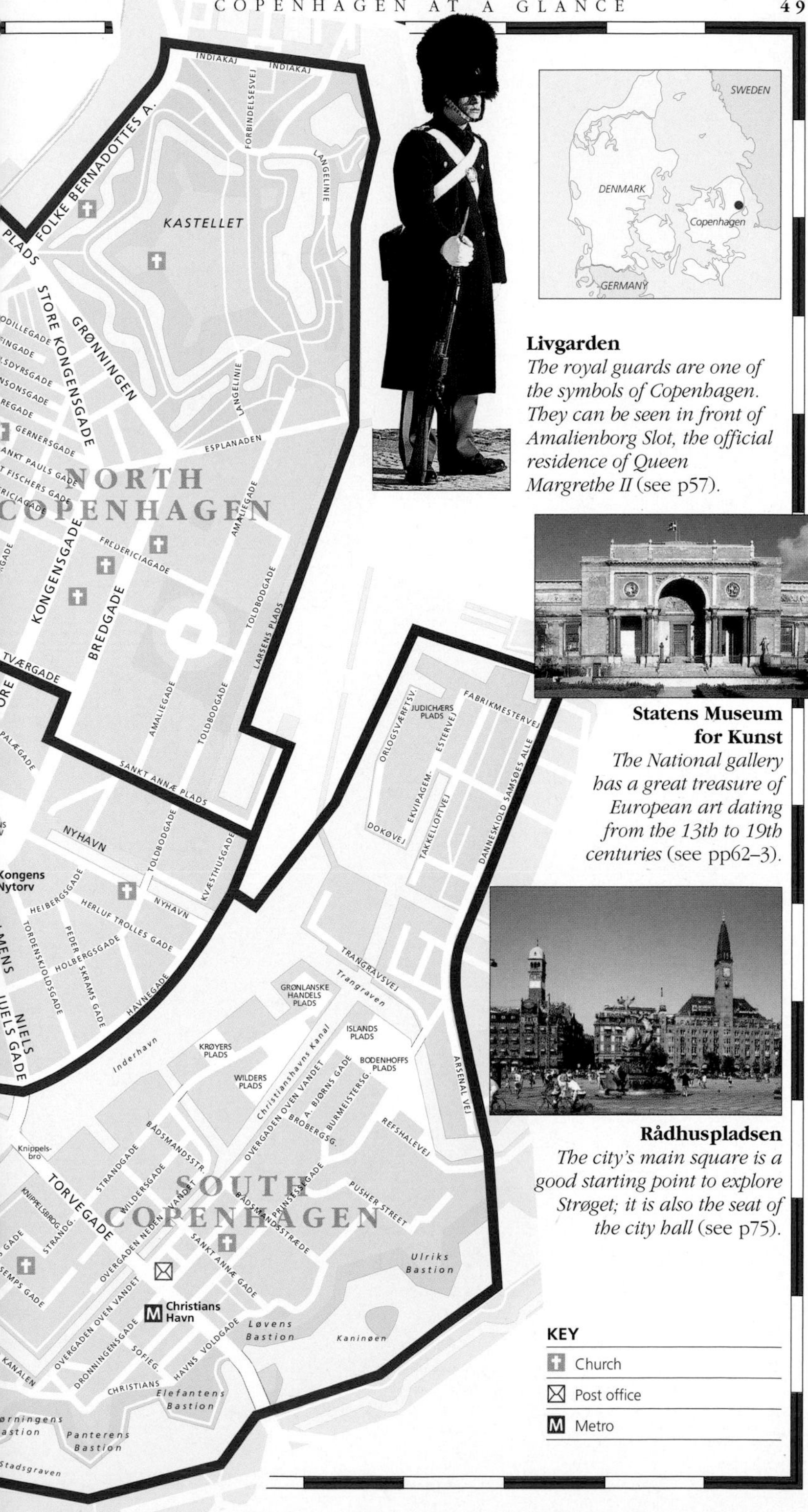

Livgarden
The royal guards are one of the symbols of Copenhagen. They can be seen in front of Amalienborg Slot, the official residence of Queen Margrethe II (see p57).

Statens Museum for Kunst
The National gallery has a great treasure of European art dating from the 13th to 19th centuries (see pp62–3).

Rådhuspladsen
The city's main square is a good starting point to explore Strøget; it is also the seat of the city hall (see p75).

KEY

- Church
- Post office
- Metro

NORTH COPENHAGEN

The north of the city is particularly attractive and includes the famous statue of the Little Mermaid *(Den Lille Havfrue)* and two royal palaces: Amalienborg Slot and Rosenborg Slot. The area also contains several interesting museums of a highly diverse nature – ranging from the Statens Museum for Kunst (Danish National Gallery), through to the Geologisk Museum (Geological Museum) and the Frihedsmuseet (Danish Resistance Museum). Standing close to one another are sacred buildings belonging to three different religions: the Protestant Marmorkirken, the Roman Catholic Sankt Ansgars Kirke and the Russian orthodox Alexander Newsky Kirke. North Copenhagen has masses of greenery. The gardens and waterfalls of Botanisk Have (Botanical Gardens) are well worth exploring, as is the King's Garden (Kongens Have), which surrounds Rosenborg Slot.

Emblem from a frieze decorating Marmorkirken

SIGHTS AT A GLANCE

Churches
Marmorkirken 8
Sankt Albans Kirke 3

Historic Buildings and Monuments
Amalienborg Slot pp56–7 7
Gefion Springvandet 4
Kastellet 2
The Little Mermaid 1
Rosenborg Slot pp60–61 12

Museums and Galleries
Davids Samling 9
Frihedsmuseet 5
Geologisk Museum 14
Hirschsprungske Samling 15
Kunstindustrimuseet 6
Livgardens Historiske Samling 11
Statens Museum for Kunst pp62–3 16

Places of Interest
Botanisk Have 13
Kongens Have 10

GETTING AROUND

This part of Copenhagen can be reached by taking the S-tog to Østerport or Nørreport or the metro to Kongens Nytorv and walking from there. Amalienborg is served by buses 1A and 15; Rosenborg by 6A and 173E.

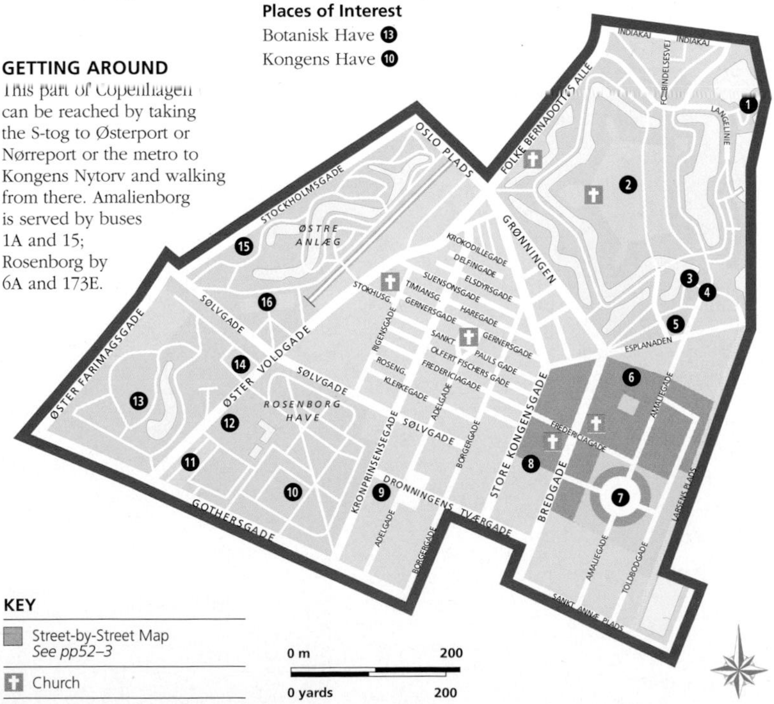

KEY

Street-by-Street Map *See pp52–3*

Church

0 m 200

0 yards 200

◁ **Marble Hall with 17th-century stuccowork, Rosenborg Slot**

Street-by-Street: Around Amalienborg Slot

The main reason to come to this part of Copenhagen is to visit Amalienborg Slot, the official residence of Queen Margrethe II, which is guarded by soldiers in traditional uniforms. The best time to visit is at noon, when the daily ceremony for the changing of the guard takes place. Frederik V made Amalienborg Slot the focal point of a new, smart district, which he built to mark the 300th anniversary of the Oldenburg dynasty, celebrated in 1748. In honour of the king the district was named Frederiksstaden.

Medicinsk-Historisk Museum, a medical museum, is housed in the former Danish Academy of Surgery and has on display some gruesome human remains as well as an old operating theatre.

Alexander Newsky Kirke is a Russian Orthodox church and was completed in 1883. It was a gift from Tsar Alexander III to mark his marriage to a Danish princess.

★ Marmorkirken

Also known as Frederikskirken, this church is just west of Amalienborg. Its huge dome rests on 12 pillars and is one of the biggest of its kind in Europe, measuring 31 m (102 ft) across ❽

KEY

- - - - Suggested route

STAR SIGHTS

★ Amalienborg Slot

★ Kunstindustrimuseet

★ Marmorkirken

★ Amalienborg Slot

Consisting of four almost identical buildings, the palace has been the main residence of the Danish royal family since 1794 ❼

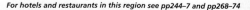

For hotels and restaurants in this region see pp244–7 and pp268–74

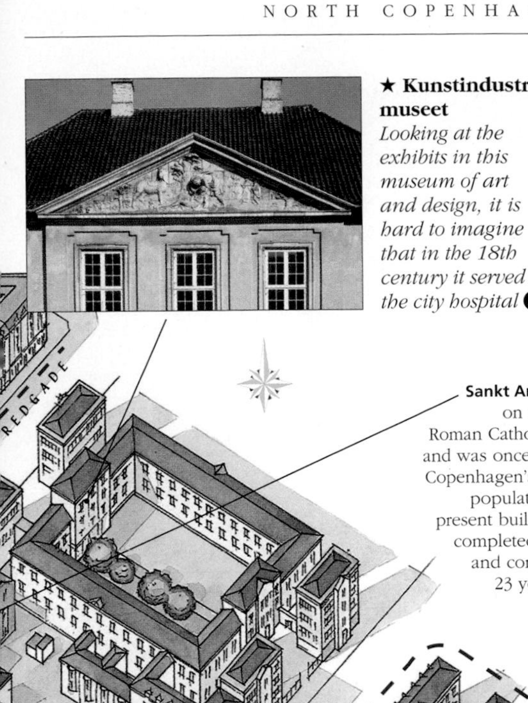

★ Kunstindustrimuseet
Looking at the exhibits in this museum of art and design, it is hard to imagine that in the 18th century it served as the city hospital ❻

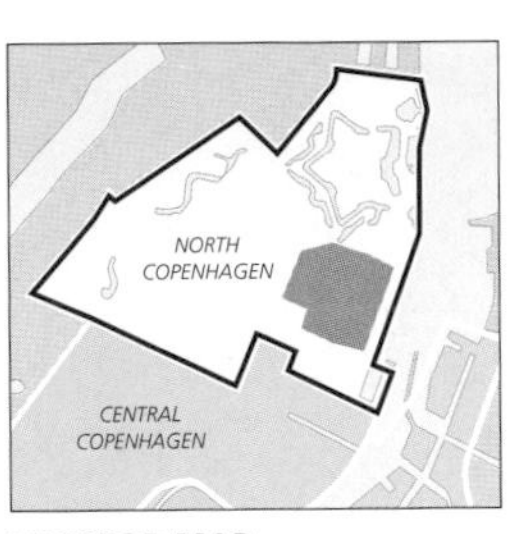

LOCATOR MAP
See Street Finder Map 2

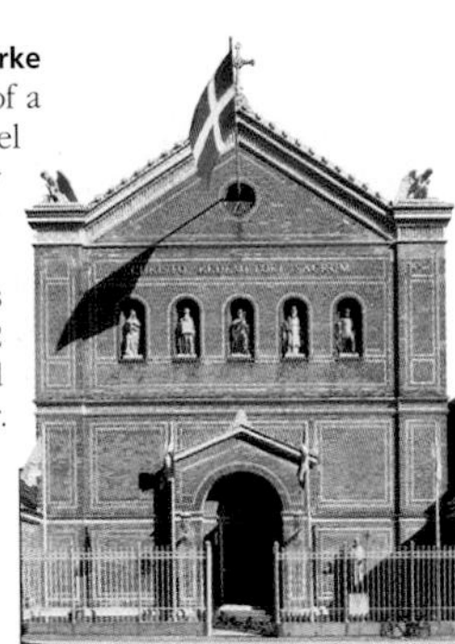

Sankt Ansgars Kirke on the site of a Roman Catholic chapel and was once used by Copenhagen's foreign population. The present building was completed in 1842 and consecrated 23 years later.

AMALIEGADE

EDERICIAGADE

TOLDBODGADE

TOLDBODGADE

Afstøbningssamling, or Royal Cast Collection, has over 2,000 sculpture casts, including a copy of the *Venus de Milo* and copies of statues from the Acropolis.

Amaliehaven is a modern park, donated to the city by the A.P. Møller shipping company in 1983. The gardens are next to Nyhavn and are a popular place for a walk.

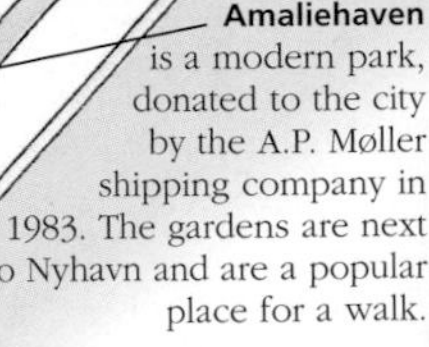

The Little Mermaid ❶

Langelinie. **Map** 2 F3. 🚌 *1A, 15, 19, 26.*

The tiny figure of the Little Mermaid *(Den Lille Havfrue)*, sitting on a rock and gazing wistfully at the passing ships, is Denmark's best-known monument. The sculpture, commissioned by Carl Jacobsen, head of the Carlsberg brewery, was inspired by the ballet version of *The Little Mermaid*, which in turn was based on Hans Christian Andersen's tale about a mermaid who falls in love with a prince.

The sculptor, Edvard Eriksen (1876–1959), wanted to use as his model Ellen Price, a prima ballerina who had played the part of the mermaid. However, when the dancer learned where the statue was to be located she refused to continue posing and allowed only her face to be used. As a result, the body was modelled on that of the sculptor's wife.

The final bronze cast was placed at the end of the harbour promenade in 1913. Since then, the sculpture has fallen victim to vandals and pranksters on a number of occasions. In 1961 she had her hair painted red. In 1964 her head was cut off; some time later she lost both arms and in 1998 she lost her head once again. Now, moved a little further towards the sea, she enjoys more peace.

The Little Mermaid, Copenhagen's most famous landmark

One of the buildings inside the Kastellet

Kastellet ❷

Map 2 E3. ***Tel*** *33 47 95 11 (for tours of the grounds).* Ⓢ *Østerport.* 🚌 *1A, 15, 19, 26.* ◯ *fortress grounds only.*

A fortress was first built on this site in 1626 but a Swedish attack in 1658 revealed its numerous weak points and on the orders of Frederik III the defences were rebuilt. The works were completed in 1663. The final structure, known as the Kastellet (Citadel), consisted of a fort in the shape of a five-pointed star surrounded by high embankments and a deep moat. In the 19th century the fortress was partially demolished and rebuilt once more. During World War II it was taken over by the occupying German forces who used it as their headquarters. It is now used by the Danish military, although the grounds and ramparts are open to visitors.

In the 19th century Kastellet served as a prison. The prisoner's cells were built against the church so that the convicts, unseen by the public, could participate in the mass by peering through small viewing holes cut into the walls.

Sankt Albans Kirke ❸

Churchillparken. **Map** 2 E3. ***Tel*** *39 62 77 36.* 🚌 *1A, 15, 19.*

This church was built in 1887 to serve the city's Anglican community and is named after Saint Alban, a 4th-century Roman soldier who converted to Christianity and suffered a martyr's death.

Churchillparken, just south of Kastellet

THE STORY OF THE LITTLE MERMAID

The heroine of Andersen's tale is a young mermaid who lives beneath the waves with her five sisters. The little mermaid rescues a prince from a sinking ship and falls in love with him. Desperate to be with the prince, she is seduced by a wicked sea witch into giving up her beautiful voice in return for legs so that she can go ashore. The price is high, and the witch warns the mermaid that should the prince marry another she will die. For a long time the prince adores his new, mute lover but in the end he is forced into marrying a princess from another kingdom. Before the wedding is to take place on board a ship, the mermaid's sisters swim to it and offer her a magic knife. All she need do is stab the prince and she will be free to return to the water. The mermaid cannot bring herself to murder the prince and, as dawn breaks, she dies.

Andersen surrounded by fairytale characters

Situated not far from the Gefion fountain, along Langelinie promenade in Churchillparken, the elegant Gothic church was a gift from Edward, Prince of Wales, who at the time was vying for the hand of Princess Alexandra, the daughter of Christian IX. They married in 1863, and the prince ascended to the throne as Edward VII in 1901. The church's interior has attractive stained-glass windows and a miniature copy of Bertel Thorvaldsen's sculpture – *St John the Baptist Praying in the Desert*. Religious services are still held here in English and the congregation often includes visitors to the city.

Gefion Springvandet ❹

Map 2 F4. 🚌 *1A, 15, 19.*

Built in 1908, the Gefion fountain is an impressive work by Anders Bungaard and one of Copenhagen's largest monuments. Its main feature is a statue of the goddess Gefion – a mythical Scandinavian figure. According to legend, the king of Sweden promised to give the goddess as much land as she could plough in one night. Gefion, who took him at his word, turned her four sons into oxen and harnessed them to a plough. By the time the cock crowed she had managed to plough a sizeable chunk of Sweden. She then picked it up and threw it into the sea, and so formed the island of Zealand. The hole left behind became Lake Vänern (whose shape closely resembles that of Zealand).

Danish armoured car in front of the Frihedsmuseet

Frihedsmuseet ❺

Churchillparken. **Map** 2 E4. ***Tel*** *33 13 44 11.* Ⓢ *Østerport.* 🚌 *1A, 15, 19.* ◯ *May–Sep: 10am–5pm Tue–Sun; Oct–Apr: 10am–3pm Tue–Sun.* **www**.frihedsmuseet.dk

The armoured car standing in front of the Danish Resistance Museum was built by members of the Danish underground movement and is one of the star attractions of this fascinating museum, which tells the story of Denmark's role during World War II.

Many of the secrets of sabotage are revealed and exhibits include a makeshift printing press, home-made weapons and police reports. Another section is devoted to the evacuation of Denmark's Jewish population, who were spirited away to Sweden by the Resistance. Photographs of resistance workers killed in action are especially moving, as are letters to family and friends written by those sentenced to be executed by firing squad.

The thorny issue of Denmark's collusion with Germany during World War II is also covered, and uniforms from the Danish Freikorps – volunteers who signed up to fight with the German army – are on display. It is estimated that almost 4,000 Danes died fighting for Germany.

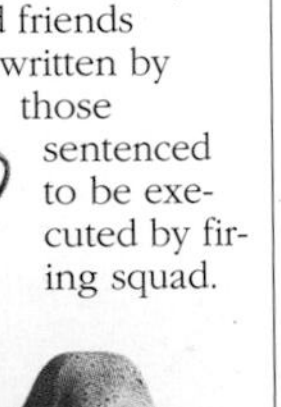

The goddess Gefion and her oxen, from the Gefion Springvandet

Kunstindustri-museet ❻

Bredgade 68. **Map** 2 E4. ***Tel*** *33 18 56 56.* Ⓢ *Østerport.* Ⓜ *Kongens Nytorv.* 🚌 *1A, 15.* ◯ *11am–5pm Tue–Sun.* **www**.kunstindustrimuseet.dk

Designed by the Danish architect Nicolai Eigtved and erected in the mid-18th century, the buildings that now house the Museum of Art and Design were originally the city hospital; it was here that the philosopher Søren Kierkegaard died in 1855. The hospital was closed in 1919 and today contains one of the largest collections of royal porcelain in Denmark including pieces from the famous *Flora Danica* service *(see p93)*, as well as furniture, Japanese ceramics, silverware and textiles. Exhibits on display range from medieval items to examples of contemporary design.

Nearby, on the same side of the street, is **Sankt Ansgars Kirke**, a Roman Catholic church that has a small exhibition devoted to the history of Danish Catholicism.

Amalienborg Slot ❼

The Amalienborg Palace complex consists of four buildings around an octagonal square. They were meant as residences for four wealthy families, but when Christiansborg Slot burned down in 1794, Christian VII bought one of the four palaces and turned it into a residence for the royal family. Designed by Nicolai Eigtved, Christian VII's Palace is renowned for its Great Hall, which has splendid Rococo woodcarvings and stucco decoration. Since 1885, the palace has been used mostly for royal guests and ceremonial purposes.

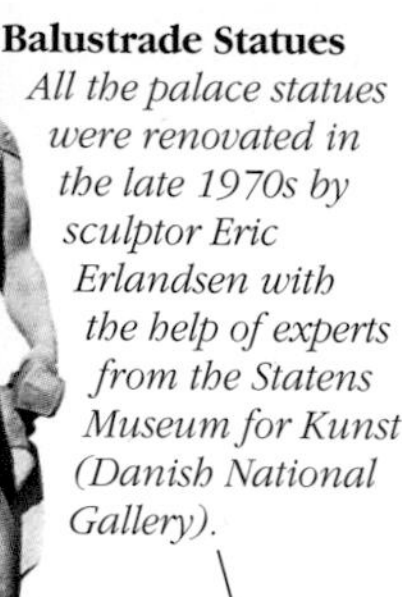

Balustrade Statues
All the palace statues were renovated in the late 1970s by sculptor Eric Erlandsen with the help of experts from the Statens Museum for Kunst (Danish National Gallery).

Gallery
The palace gallery has a beautiful ceiling and is the work of Fossatti. The French architect Nicolas-Henri Jardin designed the furniture.

Velvet Chamber
The tiled stove in this room comes from a factory in Lübeck. The silk velvet wall hangings were presents from Ludwig XV to an important high court official named Count Moltke.

★ Entrance Hall
The entrance hall has been renovated to appear as it would have done when the palace was first built. Its decorations have been recreated according to period designs. The statue of Andromeda is a cast of the original marble sculpture.

★ Knights' Chamber
This elegant room is an example of the artistry of Nicolai Eigtved and is the most beautiful Rococo chamber in Denmark.

VISITORS' CHECKLIST

Amalienborg Slot, Christian VII's Palace, Amalienborg Slotsplads. ***Tel*** *33 92 64 51. M Kongens Nytorv. S Nørreport. 1A, 15, 19, 26, 29, 650S, 901, 902. Jul–Sep: Sat & Sun. compulsory: 11:30am (Danish); 1pm & 2:30pm (English).* **www**.ses.dk/amalienborg

The royal guards, sporting bearskin hats, stand watch, day and night, in front of the palace.

Clock
This grandfather clock is one of many objects on display in the palace that were once used by the Danish royal family.

Changing of the Guard
Every day at noon, the Livgarden (royal guards) walk from Amalienborg Palace to Rosenborg Castle for the Changing of the Guard.

ROYAL RESIDENCE

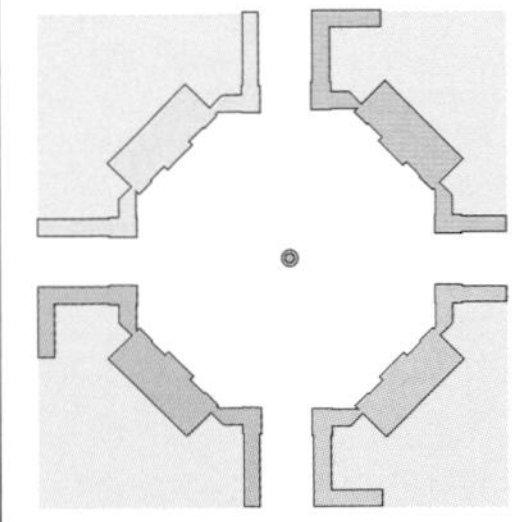

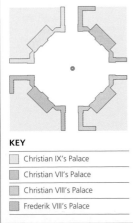

KEY

- Christian IX's Palace
- Christian VII's Palace
- Christian VIII's Palace
- Frederik VIII's Palace

The name Amalienborg actually refers to an earlier palace, built in 1669 by Frederik III for his young bride Sophie Amalie. The present complex consists of four palaces grouped around a square, collectively known as Amalienborg Slot, which is in the heart of Frederiksstaden. The equestrian statue of Frederick V in the middle of the complex is the work of French sculptor Jacques Saly who spent 30 years working on it. The statue reputedly cost as much as the entire complex.

STAR FEATURES

- ★ Entrance Hall
- ★ Knights' Chamber

Marmorkirken 8

Frederiksgade 4. **Map** 2 D4. ***Tel*** *33 15 01 44.* *1A, 15, 19, 26.*
Church *10am–5pm Mon–Thu & Sat, noon–5pm Fri & Sun.*
Dome *Sep–mid-Jun: 1pm, 3pm Sat & Sun; mid-Jun–Aug: 1pm, 3pm daily.* **www**.marmorkirken.dk

The vast dome of the Baroque Frederikskirken, also known as Marmokirken or the Marble Church, leads many visitors to suspect that its architect, Nikolai Eigtved, based his design on St Peter's Basilica in Rome. The church was named for Frederik V who wanted to celebrate the fact that his family had ruled Denmark for 300 years by building a new district in Copenhagen – Frederikssta-den – with the church as its focal point. When work began, in 1749, it was assumed that the church would be constructed of marble imported from Norway (hence its alternative name). However, it quickly became apparent that the cost of such a venture would exceed the financial resources of the treasury and in 1770 work was abandoned.

A century later the building was completed using local Danish marble. The most obvious feature of the church is its dome – one of the largest in Europe. Visitors can climb the 260 steps to enjoy wonderful city views from the top of the bell tower. Inside the church are frescoes by Danish artists. On the outside, the building has statues of Danish saints.

Davids Samling 9

Kronprinsessegade 30–32. **Map** 2 D5. ***Tel*** *33 73 49 49.* Ⓢ Ⓜ *Nørreport.* *1A, 15, 19, 26, 42, 43, 350S.* *1–5pm Tue–Sun (from 10am Wed & Thu).* **www**.davidmus.dk

The museum's founder, Christian Ludvig David (1878–1960), was a lawyer who donated his collection to the state in 1945. The main museum building is 19th century and, like others on this street, has a characteristic L-shaped floor plan. David's family had lived there since 1810, although he did not personally take possession of it until 1917. In 1968 the state donated the adjacent house, helping to accommodate the museum's growing collection.

17th-century bronze vessel from India, Davids Samling

The museum is best known for its extensive collection of Islamic art, which includes items from Spain, Persia, India and elsewhere. Among the many treasures, some of which date as far back as the 6th century, are ceramics, silks, jewellery and ancient daggers inlaid with jewels. The museum also houses a small collection of European art, as well as examples of 18th-century English, French and German furniture. There is also a collection of Danish silver dating from the 17th and 18th centuries.

Circular grand nave of Marmorkirken, decorated with wall paintings

Kongens Have 10

Map 1 C5. *6am–dusk.*

The King's Garden was established by Christian IV in 1606 and is Copenhagen's oldest park, retaining most of its original layout. In the 17th century the gardens supplied the royal court with fresh fruit, vegetables and roses to adorn the royal apartments.

Today, the shady gardens, criss-crossed by paths and with numerous benches, are one of the favourite places for Copenhagen's citizens to walk and relax. Here, visitors can also find one of the capital's most famous monuments. Unveiled in 1877, it is a statue of Hans Christian Andersen enchanting a group of children with some of his fairy tales.

Leafy Kongens Have surrounding Rosenborg Slot

Livgardens Historiske Samling 11

Gothersgade 100. **Map** 1 B5. ***Tel*** *45 99 40 00.* Ⓢ Ⓜ *Nørreport.* *5A, 6A, 14, 42, 43, 150S, 173E, 184, 185, 350S.* *11am–3pm Sun; May–Sep: also 11am–3pm Tue.* **www**.forsvaret.dk/lg

The Livgarden or royal guards, dressed in colourful uniforms and sporting furry busbies, are one of the symbols of Copenhagen. Many people come to watch them during the daily ceremony for the changing of the guard in front of Amalienborg Slot, but even their daily marches between Rosenborg and Amalienborg palaces are a popular sight.

For hotels and restaurants in this region see pp244–7 and pp268–74

Vast palm house, built in 1874, in Copenhagen's Botanisk Have

The museum is housed in a cluster of 200-year-old barracks and contains background information on the guards' history. Examples of their uniforms are on display along with weapons, paintings, documents, and musical instruments played by the guardsmen.

Rosenborg Slot ⓬

See pp60–61.

Botanisk Have ⓭

Gothersgade 128. **Map** 1 B4. ***Tel*** *35 32 22 22.* *5A, 6A, 14, 40, 42, 43, 150S, 173E, 184, 185, 350S.* Ⓢ M *Nørreport.* *May–Sep: 8:30am–6pm daily; Oct–Apr: 8:30am–4pm Tue–Sun.* **www**.botanik.snm.ku.dk

The 20,000 species of plants gathered in the Botanical Gardens include native Danish plants, as well as some highly exotic ones collected from around the world. The garden was established in 1872, on the grounds of old town fortifications. Bulwarks have been turned into rockeries, and the moat that once surrounded the fortified walls is now a lake filled with water and marsh plants.

The gardens themselves have much to offer. There is a small forest, waterfalls and greenhouses, one of which contains over 1,000 varieties of cactus. Elsewhere, it is possible to see coffee and pineapples growing. A special attraction is the roof-top walk in the steamy palmhouse.

Geologisk Museum ⓮

Øster Voldgade 5–7. **Map** 1 B4. ***Tel*** *35 32 23 45.* Ⓢ M *Nørreport.* *6A, 26, 150S, 173E, 184, 185.* *1–4pm Tue–Sun.* **www**.geologi.snm.ku.dk

Standing close to the eastern end of Botanisk Have, the Geological Museum opened in 1893 and occupies an Italian Renaissance-style building. Its carved stone decorations include rosettes, columns and arches.

The earliest museum exhibits are the meteorites on display in the courtyard. The biggest of these was found in Greenland in 1963 and, at 20 tonnes (17.86 tons), is the sixth largest in the world. On the ground and first floors are glass cabinets filled with minerals and fossils including the imprint of a jellyfish made over 150 million years ago. Elsewhere, there is an exhibition devoted to volcanoes, displays relating to the history of man and collections of dinosaur bones.

A separate section is devoted to oil and gas exploration and the geology of Denmark. Colourful stones and rock crystals are on sale in the museum shop.

Hirschsprungske Samling ⓯

Stockholmsgade 20. **Map** 1 C3. ***Tel*** *35 42 03 36.* Ⓢ *Østerport.* *6A, 14, 26, 40, 42, 43, 150S, 184, 185.* *11am–4pm Wed–Mon.* **www**.hirschsprung.dynamicweb.dk

This gallery, one of Copenhagen's best, owes its existence to the art patronage of Heinrich Hirschsprung (1836–1908), a Danish tobacco baron who supported many Danish artists. The Hirschsprung collection has been on public display since 1911 and is housed in a Neo-Classical building on the outskirts of Østre Anlæg park.

The collection includes works by prominent Danish artists from the 19th and 20th centuries such as Eckersberg, Købke, Bendz, Hansen, Anna and Michael Ancher, Johannes Larsen and Peder S. Krøyer. Among the works on display is a portrait of Hirschsprung himself, smoking a cigar, which was painted by Krøyer.

One of the exhibition rooms displaying the Hirschsprungske collection

Rosenborg Slot ⓬

This royal palace is one of Copenhagen's most visited attractions and contains thousands of royal objects including paintings, trinkets, furniture and a small armoury. Most impressive of all is the underground treasury containing the crown jewels and other royal regalia. The exquisite Dutch-Renaissance brick palace was erected in 1606, on the orders of Christian IV, to serve as a summer residence. It was used by successive monarchs until the early 18th century when Frederik IV built a more spacious palace at Fredensborg. In the early 19th century Rosenborg was opened to the public as a museum.

Marble Hall
The hall's Baroque décor was commissioned by Frederik III. The Italian decorator Francesco Bruno gave the ceilings new stuccowork and clad the walls with imitation marble.

★ Long Hall
17th-century tapestries decorate the walls of the hall, which also contains a collection of 18th-century silver furniture including three silver lions that once guarded the king's throne.

The spire-topped towers were converted from bays

Tower Stairway
Equestrian paintings, portraits, and a series of 17th-century floral water colours by Maria Merian are hung on the walls.

"The Rose"
The ceiling paintings and gilded wall linings found here were brought from Frederiksborg in the 19th century. The 18th-century chandelier was made in England.

STAR FEATURES

- ★ Long Hall
- ★ Treasury

For hotels and restaurants in this region see pp244–7 and pp268–74

★ Treasury
The underground treasury rooms house the royal jewels, including the Crown of Christian IV which weighs 2.89 kg (6.4 lbs).

VISITORS' CHECKLIST

Øster Voldgade 4A.
Map 1 C4. ***Tel*** *33 15 32 86.*
Nørreport. *6A, 26, 150S, 173E, 184, 185.*
Jan–May & Sep–Oct: 11am–4pm; Jun–Aug: 10am–5pm; Nov–Dec: 11am–4pm Tue–Sun.
1 Jan, 21–26 & 31 Dec.
www.rosenborgslot.dk

The Main Tower was originally shorter and was raised in the 1620s.

Mirror Cabinet
The mirrored room on the first floor dates from 1714 and was the fancy of Frederik IV, who had a connecting bedroom placed next door. It is the only room of its kind in Europe.

The third floor was completed in 1624 and was designed to provide space for the magnificent, long banqueting hall.

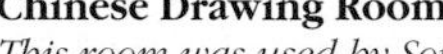

Chinese Drawing Room
This room was used by Sophie Hedevig, sister of Frederik IV. Some of its most distinctive items are the Chinese-style chairs, a guitar encrusted with ivory and tortoiseshell and bearing the princess's monogram, a 17th-century Japanese porcelain jug and an ebony table.

Royal Chamber of Frederik IV
The table standing at the centre of the room was given to Frederik IV in 1709 by the Grand Duke of Tuscany. The magnificent rock crystal chandelier was probably made in Vienna.

Statens Museum for Kunst ⑯

The Danish National Gallery houses a fascinating collection of European art. Among the Danish painters represented here are artists from the "Golden Age", such as Christoffer Wilhelm Eckersberg, and Skagen artists Anna and Michael Ancher. There are also works by Old Masters like Bruegel, Rubens and Rembrandt, as well as masterpieces by 20th-century giants such as Picasso, and contemporary installation art. Children have their own gallery and an inspiring workshop. In 2010 the works will undergo a major rehanging.

2nd floor

The New Wing, a striking Modernist structure by Anna Maria Indrio, opened in 1998 and is linked to the old building by a glass-roofed atrium.

Boys Bathing in Skagen, Summer Evening (1899)
The painting by Peder S. Krøyer is typical of the Skagen School in that it depicts an everyday scene from Danish life and perfectly captures the country's crisp light.

Girl with a Fruit Basket (c.1827)
The picture is one of many works in the museum by Constantin Hansen; one of the most famous Danish painters from Denmark's "Golden Age".

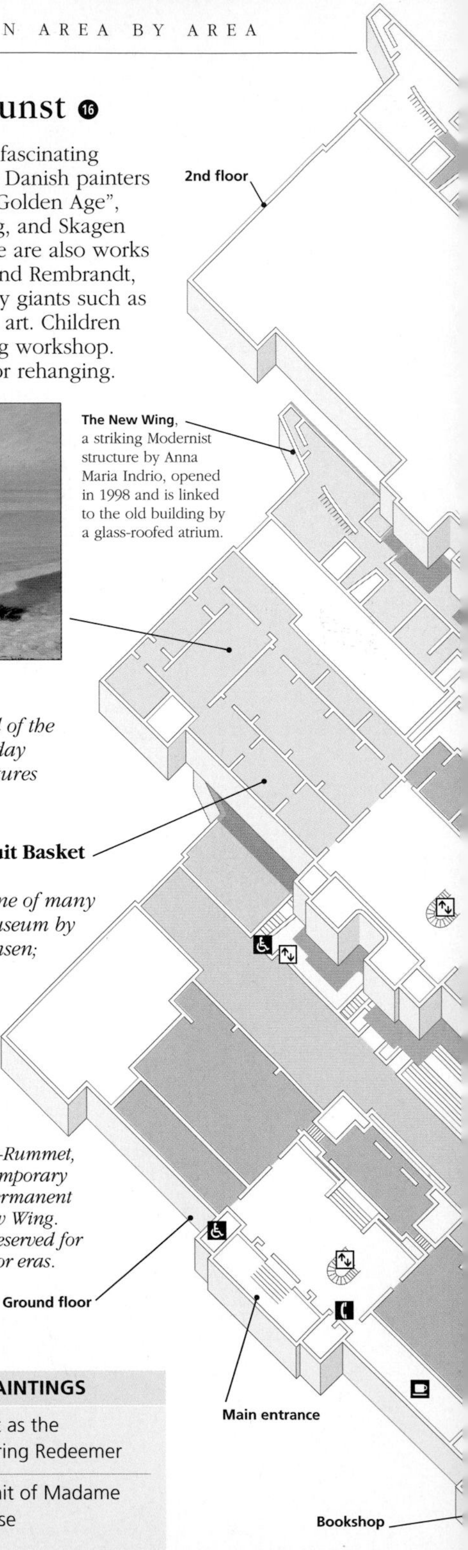

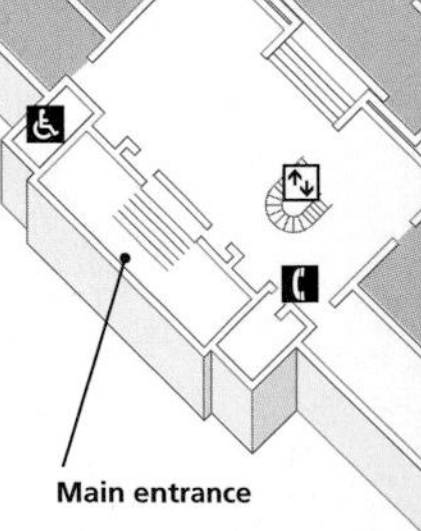

GALLERY GUIDE

Contemporary art exhibitions are held in X-Rummet, while Sculpture Street is the venue for contemporary Danish and international sculpture. The permanent collection is on the first floor and in the New Wing. The museum also has a number of spaces reserved for temporary exhibitions on particular artists or eras.

KEY

- 20th-century art
- X-Rummet
- Children's Art Museum
- Sculpture Street
- Non-Danish art, 1300–1800
- Temporary exhibitions
- Danish art, 1750–1900

STAR PAINTINGS

★ Christ as the Suffering Redeemer

★ Portrait of Madame Matisse

The Last Supper (1909)
Emil Nolde, a well-known representative of German Expressionism, has often pursued religious themes in his art.

VISITORS' CHECKLIST

Sølvegade 48–50. **Map** 1 C4. ***Tel*** *33 74 84 94.* Ⓢ *Østerport.* Ⓜ *Nørreport.* *6A, 26, 43, 150S, 173E, 184, 185, 350S.* *10am–5pm Tue–Sun (to 8pm Wed).* *(free to collections & some exhibitions).* **www**.smk.dk

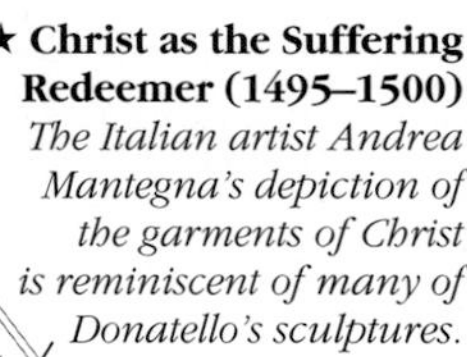

★ Christ as the Suffering Redeemer (1495–1500)
The Italian artist Andrea Mantegna's depiction of the garments of Christ is reminiscent of many of Donatello's sculptures.

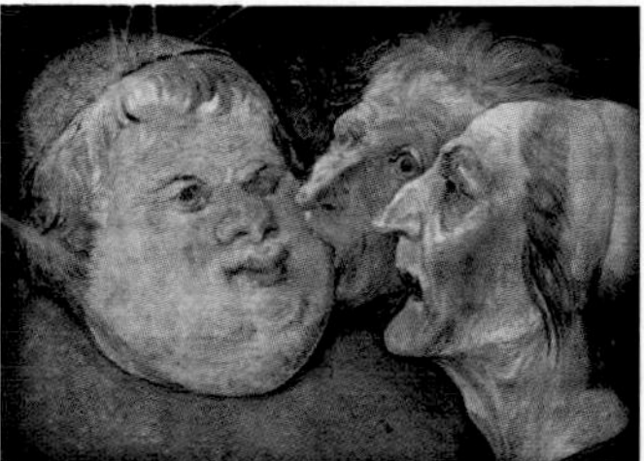

The Strife of Lent Against Carnival (1540–69)
This detail from a painting by Bruegel is typical of his earthy moralizing.

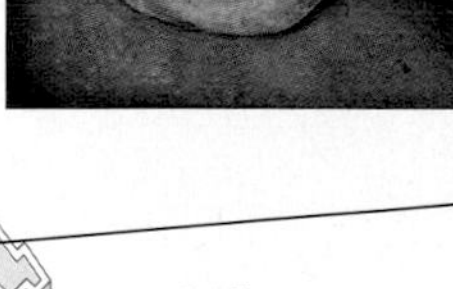

1st floor

Seated Woman (1934)
This sculpture by Henri Laurens shows the artist's move from sharp Cubist forms to more organic shapes.

★ Portrait of Madame Matisse (1905)
This portrait by Henri Matisse combines some of the most typical elements of Fauvism including simple lines and sharply contrasting colours.

CENTRAL COPENHAGEN

The Strøget, a chain of five pedestrianized streets, links the city's two main squares, Kongens Nytorv and Rådhuspladsen. Shops and restaurants line the promenade, which bustles with activity well into the night. Equally busy is Nyhavn, the city's canal district, where the streets are lined with café terraces and restored 18th-century houses. Central Copenhagen's many museums include the Ny Carlsberg Glyptotek, housing one of the world's best collections of painting and sculpture, and the Guinness World Records Museum. On a fine day it is well worth visiting the famous Tivoli amusement park and gardens. The Latin Quarter, located around the old university, has some pleasant traffic-free streets, such as Fiolstræde, which is lined with second-hand bookshops. A climb up the spiral walkway of the 17th-century Rundetårn (Round Tower) is rewarded by magnificent views over the city.

Façade detail, Latin Quarter

SIGHTS AT A GLANCE

Churches
Helligåndskirken 9
Sankt Petri Kirke 15
Vor Frue Kirke 16

Museums and Galleries
Guinness World Records Museum 6
Københavns Ravmuseum 2
Musikhistorisk Museum and Carl Claudius Samling 12
Nikolaj, Copenhagen Contemporary Art Centre 7
Ny Carlsberg Glyptotek pp78–9 22
Ripley's Believe It Or Not! 18

Streets and Squares
Gråbrødretorv 13
Højbro Plads 8
Kongens Nytorv 3
Nyhavn 1
Nytorv 17
Rådhuspladsen 20

Historic Buildings
Charlottenborg Slot 4
Det Kongelige Teater 5
Rådhus pp74–5 19
Rundetårn 11
Universitet 14

Gardens
Tivoli pp76–7 21

Theatres
Skuespilhuset 10

GETTING AROUND

Kongens Nytorv is served by metro and buses 1A, 15, 19, 26, 350S. The main transport terminal is Rådhuspladsen, served by buses 2A, 5A, 6A, 10, 12, 14, 26, 29, 33, 67, 68, 69, 173E, 250S.

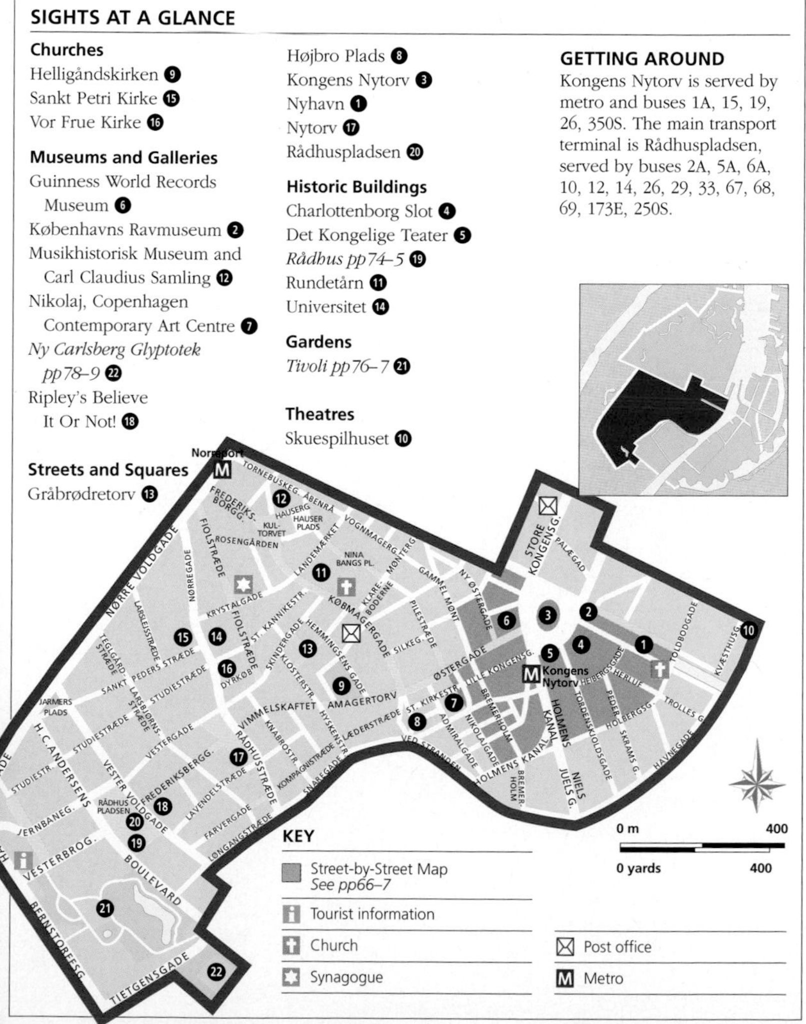

◁ **The picturesque Moorish façade of Restaurant Nimb in Tivoli**

Street-by-Street: Around Kongens Nytorv

During the late 17th century, Kongens Nytorv (King's New Square) was laid out to link the medieval parts of the city with its newer districts. Today, it is Copenhagen's biggest square and makes an excellent starting point for exploring the city. To the southeast it joins the picturesque Nyhavn district where historic ships belonging to the Nationalmuseet's collection can be admired from a canalside café. It also marks the beginning of Strøget, which has plenty of restaurants and bars as well as specialist shops and boutiques to tempt visitors.

Hotel d'Angleterre is one of the oldest and most exclusive hotels in Scandinavia *(see p68)* and has entertained many celebrities visiting Denmark.

Guinness World Records Museum

The museum collection includes numerous curios, including a figure of the world's tallest man (2.72m/8 ft 11 inches) ❻

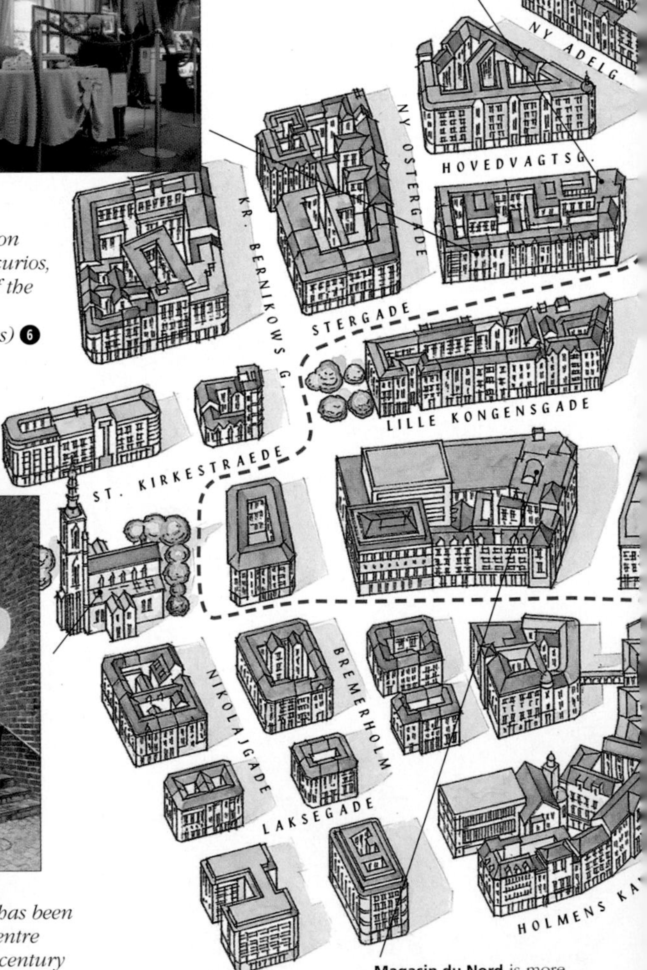

0 m 30

0 yards 30

Nikolaj

This former church has been used as a cultural centre since the early 20th century and was the venue for "happenings" in the 1960s. It is currently an exhibition gallery and concert hall ❼

Magasin du Nord is more than 100 years old and is one of the biggest and most exclusive department stores in Scandinavia.

KEY

- - - - Suggested route

For hotels and restaurants in this region see pp244–7 and pp268–74

★ Kongens Nytorv
Built in 1680 by Christian V, whose huge equestrian statue is at its centre, Kongens Nytorv is one of Copenhagen's most elegant squares and contains some of the city's finest buildings ❸

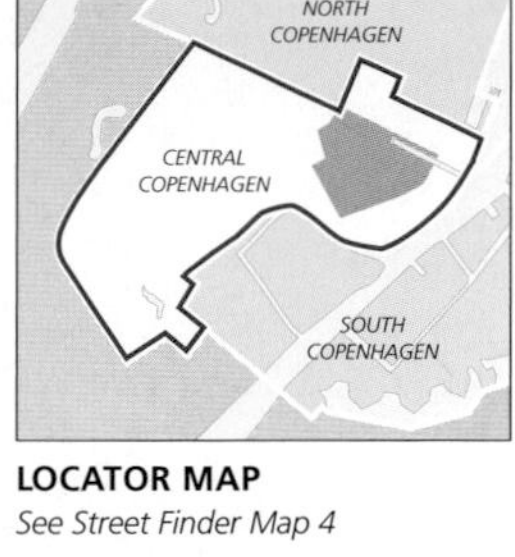

LOCATOR MAP
See Street Finder Map 4

Charlottenborg Slot
This is the oldest building in Kongens Nytorv, and is used by Det Kongelige Kunstakademi (The Royal Academy of Fine Arts) ❹

An anchor from a 19th-century sailing vessel has been transformed into a monument to the victims of World War II.

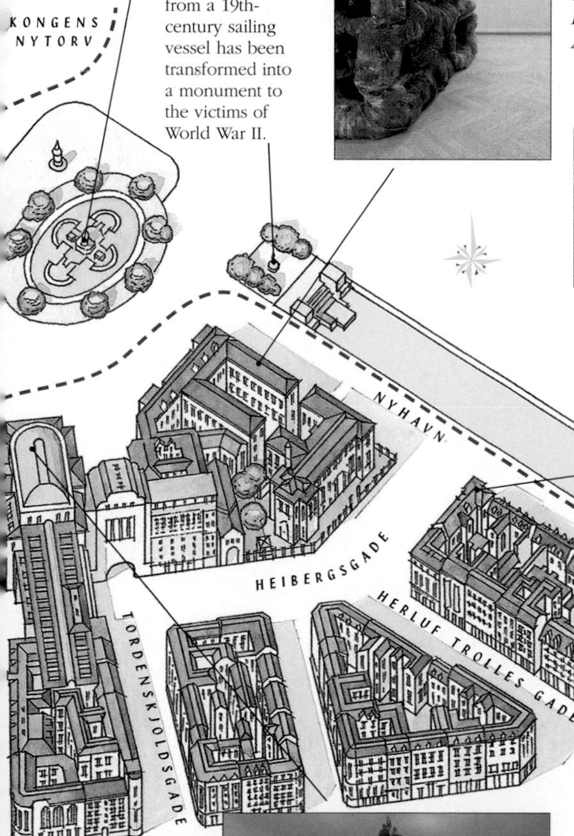

KONGENS NYTORV

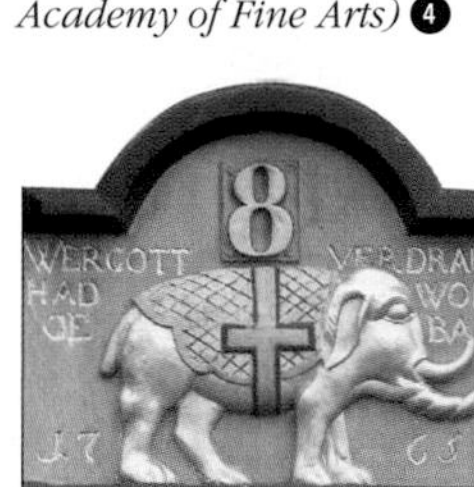

★ Nyhavn
The northern side of the canal is lined with colourful houses, many of which were once brothels frequented by sailors after months at sea ❶

NYHAVN

HEIBERGSGADE

HERLUF TROLLES GADE

TORDENSKJOLDSGADE

Pleasure boat rides along the 17th-century canal are one of the main visitor attractions. It has became a tradition that each year old sailing ships arriving in Copenhagen moor alongside Nyhavn.

★ Det Kongelige Teater
This 19th-century building houses a prominent theatre, staging both drama and ballet ❺

STAR SIGHTS

★ Det Kongelige Teater

★ Kongens Nytorv

★ Nyhavn

Nyhavn, lined with bars, restaurants and cafés

Nyhavn ❶

Map 4 E1.

Lined on both sides with colourful houses, this 300-m (328-yard) long canal, known as the New Harbour, was dug by soldiers between 1671 and 1673 and was intended to enable ships loaded with merchandise to sail into the centre of Copenhagen. Today, stylish yachts and old wooden boats are moored at many of the quays and, amid them, a 19th-century lightship, which is now used as a restaurant.

When Hans Christian Andersen lived here the area north of the canal was a notorious red-light district with a seedy reputation thanks to the cheap bars, rough-and-ready hotels, tattoo parlours and numerous brothels. Since then Nyhavn has smartened up a great deal (though a few tattoo parlours still remain) and is now one of the city's best-known districts. The boozy joints packed with sailors are long gone and have been replaced with bars, cafés and restaurants targeting a more prosperous clientele. The place is especially popular on warm summer evenings and many of the restaurants and bars can get extremely busy. The huge anchor found at the Kongens Nytorv end of the canal once belonged to *Fyen*, a 19th-century frigate, and has been used to commemorate Danish sailors who lost their lives during World War II.

Københavns Ravmuseet ❷

Kongens Nytorv 2. **Map** 4 D1. ***Tel*** *33 11 67 00.* M *Kongens Nytorv.* *1A, 15, 19, 26, 350S.* *May–Sep: 10am–6:30pm daily; Oct–Apr: 10am–5:30pm daily.* **www**.houseofamber.com

The private Amber Museum at the Kongens Nytorv end of Nyhaven is devoted to "Nordic Gold". On display are numerous specimens of this 30–50-million-year-old petrified tree resin, some of which contain fossilized insects such as flies, mosquitoes and termites. The exhibition boasts the biggest piece of amber found in the Baltic Sea, which was fished out of the water off the coast of Sweden in 1969. It weighs an impressive 8.886 kg (19.64 lbs) – most amber pieces rarely exceed 10 g (0.35 ounces). Another of the exhibits, displayed in a glass cabinet, is an amber sailing ship made in Gdansk. The exhibition occupies the upper floors of the historic building, which dates from the late 17th century. The ground floor is taken up with a shop where a range of amber products can be purchased including jewellery and knick-knacks.

An exhibit from the Amber Museum

Kongens Nytorv ❸

Map 4 D1.

King's New Square was created over 300 years ago. This is one of Copenhagen's central points and the site of Det Kongelige Teater (The Royal Theatre) and Charlottenborg Slot. As well as marking the end of Nyhavn, it is also a good starting point for exploring Strøget, Copenhagen's famous walkway, which is lined with shops and restaurants.

At the centre of this oval square is an equestrian statue of Christian V, on whose orders the square was built.

HOTEL D'ANGLETERRE'S ROMANTIC ORIGINS

In the mid-18th century Jean Marchal, a young hairdresser and make-up artist travelling with a troupe of actors, arrived in Copenhagen. Jean decided to settle in town and took the job of valet to Count Conrad Danneskiold Laurvig. At a reception, to which he accompanied the count, he met Maria Coppy, daughter of the court chef. They married in 1755 and, exploiting the culinary talents of Maria, opened a restaurant with a handful of bedrooms for passing travellers. Unfortunately neither lived long enough to fully enjoy the fruits of their enterprise. Their small hotel has survived and thrived, having undergone a great many changes including the addition of around 100 or so rooms. It now receives some of the world's most distinguished figures.

Hotel d'Angleterre

Equestrian statue of Christian V in Kongens Nytorv

The original sculpture was made in 1688 by a French artist. Unfortunately, with time, the heavy lead monument, which depicts Christian V as a sombre Roman general, began to sink, distorting the proportions of the figure. In 1946 the monument was recast in bronze.

Each June graduates gather in the square to dance around the statue as part of a traditional matriculation ceremony. In winter the square becomes an ice rink (skates are available for hire).

Kongens Nytorv was once filled with elm trees, planted in the 19th century. Sadly, these fell prey to disease in 1998 and the square has since been replanted.

Charlottenborg Slot ❹

Nyhavn 2. **Map** 4 D1. ***Tel*** *33 13 40 22.* M *Kongens Nytorv.* *1A, 15, 19, 26, 350S.* *noon–5pm Tue–Sun.* **www**.charlottenborg-art.dk

This Baroque palace was built between 1672 and 1683 for Queen Charlotte Amalie (wife of Christian V), and was named after her. In the mid-18th century King Frederik V handed over the palace to the newly-created Royal Academy of Fine Arts, and it is now filled with faculty and students. The building is also sometimes used as a venue for temporary art exhibitions, at which times its doors are opened to the public.

Det Kongelige Teater ❺

Tordenskjoldsgade 7. **Map** 4 D1. ***Tel*** *33 69 69 33.* ***Fax*** *33 69 69 19.* **www**.kgl-teater.dk

Anyone visiting the area around Kongens Nytorv is usually struck by the sight of the Royal Theatre, a vast Neo-Renaissance building that has been the main venue in Denmark since it was founded in 1748. The present building, which occupies the original site, dates from 1872. For many years, this theatre set itself apart by putting on ballet, opera and theatre in the same space. The complex includes two theatres – Gamle (old) Scene and Nye (new) Scene. Since the opening of Operaen, the striking opera house, across the harbour from Amalienborg Slot in January 2005 *(see p89)*, Det Kongelige Teater only hosts ballet and theatre.

One of Charlottenborg's portals

The statues at the front of the theatre celebrate two distinguished Danes who made contributions to the development of theatre and the arts. One is the playwright Ludvig Holberg, often hailed as the father of Danish theatre, the other is the poet Adam Oehlenschlager.

Guinness World Records Museum ❻

Østergade 16. **Map** 4 D1. ***Tel*** *33 32 31 31.* M *Kongens Nytorv.* *1A, 15, 19, 26, 350A.* *Jan–mid-Jun: 10am–6pm daily (to 8pm Fri & Sat); mid-Jun–Aug: 10am–10pm daily; Sep–Dec: 10am–6pm daily (to 8pm Fri & Sat).* *1 Jan, 24–25 Dec, 31 Dec.* **www**.guinness.dk

Visitors to the Guinness World Records Museum are welcomed at the entrance by a replica of the world's tallest man. Inside is a collection of the biggest, smallest, fastest, heaviest, longest and shortest, as well as a number of rooms in which visitors can try to beat a world record or experience how it feels to drive a car at 500 km/h (311 mph). A film showing how people from all over the world have trained for their record-breaking attempts can also be seen.

Entrance to the Guinness World Records Museum

Café situated in the former Sankt Nikolaj Kirke

Nikolaj, Copenhagen Contemporary Art Centre ❼

Nikolaj Plads 10. **Map** 3 C1. ***Tel*** *33 18 17 80.* Ⓢ *Nørreport.* Ⓜ *Kongens Nytorv.* *1A, 15, 19, 26, 350S.* *noon–5pm Tue–Sun (to 9pm Thu).* *(free on Wed).* **www**.kunsthallennikolaj.dk

This unique exhibition space, housed in a renovated 16th-century church, focuses on Danish and international modern art.

The first art exhibitions were held here in 1957 but the art centre really came to prominence in the 1960s when it was used by Fluxus, an important international group of avant-garde artists, that staged a number of innovative "Fluxus-performances" here. Some unique works remain from this period including a "juke box" by Fluxus organiser Knud Petersen, which has since been developed to contain more than 22 hours of experimental music, sound poetry, and the latest in audio art. The "Crying Space" by Eric Andersen is filled with tear-inducing objects and suggestions on the wall. Eleven hollow stones are there to collect visitors' tears.

As well as these permanent exhibits, Nikolaj puts on a number of temporary shows including an annual art exhibition for children.

Højbro Plads ❽

Map 3 C1.

This cobbled square is one of the most enchanting places in Copenhagen. Although at first glance it looks like a single large unit, it is in fact divided into Højbro Plads and Amagertorv.

Højbro Plads contains a vast monument to Bishop Absalon, who from his horse points out towards Christiansborg Slot on the other side of the canal. In Amagertorv, the former city market, is a 19th-century fountain with three birds about to take flight. It is named Storkespringvandet (The Stork Fountain) though the birds are actually herons.

The northern section of Amargertorv has an interesting twin-gabled house, built in 1616, in the style of the Dutch Renaissance. It is one of the city's oldest buildings and houses the Royal Copenhagen Porcelain Shop. Adjacent to it is the showroom of Georg Jensen, which specializes in upmarket silverware. A small museum is devoted to the work of Jensen and contains some of his early pieces.

STRØGET

The word "Strøget" ("pedestrian street") cannot be found on any of the plates bearing street names; nevertheless, all those who know the city are familiar with it. Copenhagen's main walkway runs east to west. It is made up of five interconnected streets: Østergade, Amagertorv, Vimmelskaftet, Nygade and Frederiksberggade. Pedestrianized in 1962, it has since become one of the town's favourite strolling grounds. Shops range from exclusive boutiques and second-hand clothes outlets to cafés and restaurants offering food from all parts of the world. There are also some pretty churches and squares and a handful of museums. Every day (when the Queen is in residence), at about 11:45am, the Livgarden or royal guards march along Østergade, heading for Amalienborg Slot for the changing of the guards.

Tourist train running along Strøget

Portal of Helligåndskirken – one of Copenhagen's oldest churches

Helligåndskirken ❾

Niels Hemmingsensgade 5. **Map** 3 C1. ***Tel*** *33 15 41 44.* *noon–4pm Mon–Fri; also 7pm–1am Fri.* **www**.helligaandskirken.dk

Dating originally from the early 15th century when it was an Augustinian monastery, the "Church of the Holy Spirit was built on an even an earlier religious site, founded in 1238. The church, which is one of the oldest in Copenhagen, acquired its towers in the late 16th century and its sandstone portal, originally intended for the Børsen (Stock Exchange), early in the 17th century. The building was ravaged by one of the city's great fires in 1728, and has been largely rebuilt, although some original 14th-century walls in the right-hand wing can still be seen. Now surrounded by a park, the church still holds religious services. It is also used for art shows and exhibitions, which provide an occasion to admire its magnificent vaults.

In the churchyard is a memorial to Danish victims of the Nazi concentration camps.

Skuespilhuset ⑩

Sankt Annæ Plads 36. **Map** 2 D5. ***Tel*** *33 69 69 82.*
www.skuespilhus.dk

Throughout the 1900s, a number of venues across the city were used to house the Royal Danish Theatre's Drama Department – with varying degrees of success. Although the need for a suitable playhouse was recognized as early as the 1880s, it was not until 2001 that the government unveiled plans to build a dedicated theatre.

The Royal Danish Playhouse was inaugurated in 2007. The strikingly modern building offers a range of performance spaces, including two main auditoria – the Main Stage and the Portscenen, seating 650 and 200 respectively – and the Studio Stage, which has seats for 100 people. There are also several open-air spaces, such as the waterfront foyer and the footbridge terrace, which are used for children's activities and other events.
In addition to its seasonal repertoire of plays, the theatre hosts ballets, public lectures, concerts and Q&As with playwrights, directors and actors.

Designed by Danish architects Boje Lundgaard and Lene Tranberg, the theatre cuts an impressive figure on the Copenhagen waterfront. The design incorporates a variety of materials: the dark cladding on the external walls was created with ceramic tiles; the outside of the stage tower is covered with copper; and the footbridge linking the foyer to Nyhavn and the harbourfront promenade is made out of oak.

Royal Danish Playhouse

Rundetårn's cobbled spiral ramp winding to its top

Rundetårn ⑪

Købmagergade 52A. **Map** 3 C1. ***Tel*** *33 73 03 73. 21 May–20 Sep: 10am–8pm daily; 21 Sep–20 May: 10am–5pm daily.*
www.rundetaarn.dk

The round tower, 35 m (115 ft) tall and 15 m (49 ft) in diameter, provides an excellent vantage point from which to view Copenhagen. Access to the top is via a cobbled spiral ramp, 209 m (686 ft) long, which winds seven and a half times around to the top. Over the years the Rundetårn has been damaged by several fires and part of the observatory was rebuilt in the 18th century.

Rundetårn was erected on the orders of Christian IV, and was originally intended as an observatory for the nearby university. It is still used by the university, making it the oldest working observatory of its kind in Europe.

In 1642, during the tower's opening ceremony, Christian IV is said to have ridden his horse up the spiralling pathway to the very top. Later on, in 1716, the Tsar of Russia, Peter the Great, allegedly repeated this stunt during a visit to Copenhagen and was followed by his wife Tsarina Catherine II, who, as legend would have it, climbed to the top in a coach drawn by six horses. The modern-day equivalent of such antics is an annual bicycle race; the winner is the person who cycles to the top and back again in the fastest time, without dismounting or falling off.

Musikhistorisk Museum og Carl Claudius Samling ⑫

Åbenrå 30. **Map** 3 C1. ***Tel*** *33 11 27 26. Oct–Apr: 1–3:30pm Tue, Wed, Sat & Sun; May–Sep: 1–3:30pm Tue–Sun. Guided tours by appointment.* **www**.natmus.dk

Copenhagen's Museum of Musical Instruments occupies three 18th-century buildings situated in the Latin Quarter. The ground floor is used for temporary exhibitions, while the upper floors house a permanent exhibition. The collection has been pieced together over the last hundred years and is divided into two sections – the Middle Ages to the 1900s and the 20th century. A huge variety of instruments from Europe, Asia and Africa is on display, including folk instruments and such rarities as one of Danish composer Carl Nielsen's pianos and a zither that once belonged to Frederik IX. The museum is also used as a venue for numerous music events including recitals of chamber music and jazz concerts.

Traditional 19th-century Swedish violin

Outdoor restaurant tables in Gråbrødretorv

Gråbrødretorv ⓭

Map 3 C1. *6A.*

This charming, cobblestone square is filled with music from buskers in summer when the restaurant tables spill out into the street. It is an excellent place in which to stop for a lunch. The square dates back to 1238, and its name refers to the so-called Grey Brothers, Franciscan monks who built the city's first monastery here. A great fire in 1728 destroyed the surrounding buildings; the present buildings date mainly from the early 18th century.

Universitet ⓮

Vor Frue Plads. **Map** 3 B1. Ⓢ Ⓜ *Nørreport.* *5A, 6A, 14, 42, 43, 150S, 173E, 184, 185, 350S.*
www.ku.dk/english

The cobbled Vor Frue Plads and its surrounding university buildings are the heart of the so-called Latin Quarter (Latin was once spoken here). Despite the fact that the university was founded by Christian I in 1479, the buildings that now stand in Vor Frue Plads date from the 19th century. They house only a handful of faculties including law; the remaining departments and staff have moved to the main campus, on the island of Amager, east of Copenhagen.

The vast, Neo-Classical university building stands opposite Vor Frue Kirke. It has an impressive entrance hall decorated with frescoes depicting scenes from Greek mythology, which are the work of Constantin Hansen. Adjacent to the university building is the 19th-century university library. On the library's main staircase is a glass cabinet containing fragments from a cannon ball that was fired during the British bombardment in 1807. The ball struck the library and ironically hit a book entitled *The Defender of Peace*. A number of second-hand bookshops are located along Fiolstræde, which runs up to the Universitet.

Sankt Petri Kirke ⓯

Sankt Peders Stæde 2. **Map** 3 B1. ***Tel*** *33 93 38 76.* Ⓢ Ⓜ *Nørreport.* *5A, 6A, 14, 42, 43, 173E, 150S, 350S.* *Mar–Nov: 11am–3pm Tue–Fri, noon–3pm Sat.* *11am Sat.*
www.sankt-petri.dk

Saint Peter's church has been the main church for Copenhagen's German community since 1586. It dates from 1450 but suffered serious damage in the course of a series of fires and the British bombardment of 1807. However, many of the bricks used in the building work are from the original structure. Particularly noteworthy is the "burial" chapel containing numerous tombs and epitaphs, mainly from the 19th century. There are also some interesting tablets commemorating the dead which can be seen on the church's outside wall.

Vor Frue Kirke ⓰

Nørregade 8. **Map** 3 B1. ***Tel*** *33 37 65 40.* Ⓢ Ⓜ *Nørreport.* *5A, 6A, 14, 42, 43, 150S, 173E, 184, 185, 350S.* *8am–5pm daily.*
www.koebenhavnsdomkirke.dk

Copenhagen's cathedral, Vor Frue Kirke (Church of Our Lady), has a somewhat sombre look and is the third consecutive church to be built on this site. The first, a small 12th-century Gothic church, was consumed by fire in 1728, while the next one was destroyed by British bombs in 1807 (the tower presented an excellent target for the artillery). The present structure dates from 1820 and was designed by Christian Frederik Hansen. Its interior is a veritable art gallery, full of sculptures by the prominent Danish sculptor Bertel Thorvaldsen *(see p85)*. Standing on both sides are marble statues of the 12 apostles; the central section of the altar has a kneeling angel and a vast figure of Christ – one of the artist's most famous masterpieces. Thorvaldsen is

Statue of Christ from the high altar in Vor Frue Kirke

The imposing Neo-Classical façade of the Universitet

Interior of Vor Frue Kirke, with statues by Bertel Thordvaldsen

is also the creator of the relief depicting St John the Baptist, seen at the entrance to the cathedral. During Sunday mass it is sometimes possible to see Queen Margrethe II among the congregation. In the past she used to occupy a special royal box. But attitudes have changed and today, not wishing to distance herself from her subjects, the Danish monarch is to be found sitting in the pews.

Nytorv ⓱

Map 3 B1.

Although Nytorv looks like one big square, it is in fact made up of two separate areas – Gammeltorv (Old Square) and Nytorv (New Square) which are separated by the Nygade section of the Strøget walkway. To the northwest of Strøget, Gammeltorv was a busy market place in the 14th century and therefore has the longest trading tradition in Copenhgen. Today, it is dominated by a small fruit and vegetable market along with stalls selling jewellery and all kinds of handicrafts.

Standing at the centre of the square is Caritas Springvandet (The Charity Fountain), which dates from 1609. This Renaissance treasure is the work of Statius Otto, and depicts a pregnant woman carrying one child in her arms and leading another by the hand – a symbol of charity and mercy. Water flows from the woman's breasts and also from the urinating boy at her feet (the holes were blocked with lead for reasons of decency in the 19th century). The fountain was commissioned by Christian IV to draw the public's attention to his charitable virtues. At one time it supplied the city's inhabitants with water brought along wooden pipes from a lake 5 km (3 miles) north of Copenhagen.

Nytorv was established in 1606 and for a long time was used by the authorities as a place of execution. The squares were joined together and given their present form soon after the city hall was destroyed by fire in 1795. The outline of the city hall can still be seen in Nytorv's pavement.

The striking Neo-Classical Domhuset, or Court House, with its six large columns, on the south side of Nytorv was completed in 1815 to a design by Christian Frederik Hansen, the Danish architect who worked on rebuilding the town after a fire in 1795. The materials used in the rebuilding work included those taken from the ruined Christiansborg Slot, and the resulting building is redolent of an ancient temple. The building was first used as the city hall, becoming the fifth seat of the town's authorities. In the early 20th century the city hall was moved to the Rådhus. The inscription seen on the front of the Domhuset refers to more recent function as a court house and quotes the opening words of the Jutland Code of 1241: "With law the land shall be built".

Ripley's Believe It Or Not! ⓲

Rådhuspladsen 57. **Map** 3 B2. ***Tel*** *33 32 31 31.* *2A, 5A, 6A, 10, 12, 14, 26, 29, 33, 67, 68, 69, 173E, 250S.* *Jan–mid-Jun & Sep–Dec: 10am–6pm Sun–Thu, 10am–8pm Fri–Sat; mid-Jun–Aug: 10am–10pm daily.* *1 Jan, 24, 25 & 31 Dec.* **www**.ripleys.dk

This museum is part of an American chain that is based on an idea of Robert L. Ripley, a radio presenter, comic book writer and adventurer, who dreamt up a freakshow in the early 20th century to stun and amaze his American audience.

The museum may well prove popular with children. Many strange exhibits are on display, some of which were collected by Ripley himself. Here, visitors can marvel at a man who eats bicycles or a doll covered in 7,000 buttons, wince at a collection of medieval torture instruments and shrunken voodoo heads, and be astounded by various freaks of nature including a fish covered in fur and a two-headed cow.

Nytorv, a colourful and bustling square

Rådhus ⓳

The red-brick Rådhus (City Hall), which opened in 1905, was designed by the Danish architect Martin Nyrop (1849–1921), who was inspired by Italian buildings but also employed some elements of Danish medieval architecture. Its large main hall, sometimes used for exhibitions and official events, is decorated with statues of Nyrop as well as three other prominent Danes – Bertel Thorvaldsen, H.C. Andersen and Niels Bohr. Though it is an official building, the Rådhus is open to visitors. It is well worth climbing the 298 stairs to the top of the 105-m (344-ft) tower to reach the city's highest viewpoint.

Ceilings
The Rådhus rooms and chambers are full of details and architectural flourishes such as intricate brickwork, mosaics and decorated ceilings.

Copenhagen's Emblem
This has changed little since the 13th century. It consists of three castle towers, symbolically drawn waves of the Øresund and images of the sun and moon.

★ Main Hall
This vast, rectangular hall on the first floor is flanked by cloisters and topped with a glazed roof. It has Italianate wall decorations and a number of sculptures.

Absalon's Statue
Standing above the main entrance is a gilded statue of Bishop Absalon, the 12th-century founder of Copenhagen.

★ World Clock
Jens Olsen spent 27 years building this clock. Its extraordinary mechanism was set in motion in 1955. One of its many functions is to provide a calendar for the next 570,000 years.

Clock Tower
The peals from the tower's bells are heard throughout the streets of Copenhagen and are also transmitted by radio across the whole of Denmark.

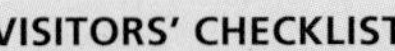

VISITORS' CHECKLIST

Rådhuspladsen. **Map** 3 B2. ***Tel*** *33 66 25 82.* Ⓢ *Central Station.* *2A, 5A, 6A, 10, 12, 14, 26, 29, 33, 67, 68, 69, 173E, 250S.* *10am–4pm.* *(in English) 3pm Mon–Fri, 10am Sat.* **Tower** *11am & 2pm Mon–Fri, noon Sat.* **World Clock** *8:30am–4:30pm Mon–Fri, 10am–1pm Sat.* **www.**kk.dk

Staircase
The stately rooms on the top floors are reached by graceful stairs with marble balustrades.

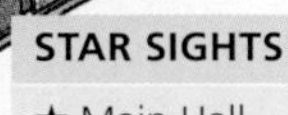

STAR SIGHTS

★ Main Hall

★ World Clock

Rådhuspladsen ⓴

Map 3 A2 & B2. Ⓢ *Central Station.* *2A, 5A, 6A, 10, 12, 14, 26, 29, 33, 67, 68, 69, 173E, 250S.*

This open space is the second biggest square in the Danish capital (after Kongens Nytorv). City Hall Square was established in the second half of the 19th century, following the dismantling of the western gate that stood on this site, and the levelling of the defensive embankments. Soon afterwards it was decided to build the present city hall, providing further impetus to the development of the surrounding area. The square has been pedestrianized since 1994 and is popular with shoppers and sightseers. It is also a gathering point on New Year's Eve.

A number of monuments in Rådhuspladsen are worthy of note. Standing immediately by the entrance to the city hall is the Dragon's Leap Fountain, erected in 1923. A little to one side, by Rådhus's tower, is a tall column, unveiled in 1914, featuring two bronze figures of Vikings blowing bronze horns. Close by, in Hans Christian Andersens Boulevard, is a sitting figure of Andersen, facing Tivoli gardens. Another curiosity is an unusual barometer hanging on a building that is covered with advertisements, located at the corner of Vesterbrogade and H.C. Andersens Boulevard. It includes a figure of a girl, who in fine weather rides a bicycle. When it rains she opens her umbrella. A nearby thermometer gives a reading of the daily temperature.

The Rådhus with its red brick elevations

Tivoli ㉑

When Tivoli first opened in 1843 it had only two attractions: a carousel with horses and a roller coaster. Today Tivoli is an altogether grander affair. Part amusement park, part cultural venue, part wonderland, it is one of the most famous places in Denmark and much loved by the Danes themselves, who regard it as one of their national treasures. Situated in the heart of the city, this large garden is planted with almost one thousand trees and blooms with 400,000 flowers during the summer. At night, when it is lit by myriad coloured bulbs, it is a truly breathtaking sight.

The Ferry Inn
Scenically located next to the jetty, this is one of 30 restaurants in Tivoli.

Frigate
The huge ship, known as St George's Frigate III, *is a floating restaurant, and is moored on Tivoli's picturesque lake – the remains of a former moat.*

Pantomime Theatre
Pantomime in Denmark dates back to the early 19th century. The Chinese-style pavilion hosts regular performances and is the oldest building in Tivoli gardens.

Main Entrance
The main gate, in Vesterbrogade, was built in 1896.

STAR SIGHTS

★ Pagoda

★ Restaurant Nimb

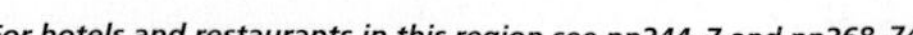

For hotels and restaurants in this region see pp244–7 and pp268–74

★ Pagoda

The tower, built in the style of a Chinese pagoda, houses a restaurant that has been here since its construction in 1900; it specializes in Chinese cuisine.

VISITORS' CHECKLIST

Vesterbrogade 3. **Map** 3 A2. ***Tel*** *33 15 10 01. Ⓢ Central. 1A, 2A, 5A, 6A, 10, 15, 26, 30, 40, 47, 65E, 250S. 11am–10pm Sun–Thu, 11am–11pm Fri & Sat. Summer season: mid-Apr–mid-Sep; Halloween season: mid-Oct; Christmas season: mid-Nov–end Dec.* **www**.tivoli.dk

Concert Hall

Tivoli's pastel-coloured concert hall was built in 1956 and updated in 2005. Concerts range from rock to symphonies, and in the basement is Europe's longest seawater aquarium.

Amusements

Rides and other amusements are scattered throughout the park. One of the most popular is the wooden roller coaster.

TIVOLI BOYS GUARD

A group of boys dressed in smart uniforms and marching to the beat of drums is a frequent sight when strolling along the park's avenues on weekends. According to promoters of the gardens, "the Queen has her own guards and the Tivoli has its own". Made up of about 100 boys, aged between 8 and 16, the Tivoli Boys Guard is smartly dressed in red jackets and busbies and covers some 300 km (186 miles) a year. The marching band was founded in 1844 and is one of Tivoli's four orchestras, the other three being the Symphony Orchestra, the Tivoli Big Band and the Tivoli Promenade Orchestra.

Boys Guard marching through Tivoli

★ Restaurant Nimb

This palatial Moorish-style restaurant is the ideal place to recharge your batteries after a day in Tivoli.

Ny Carlsberg Glyptotek ㉒

This world-class art museum boasts over 10,000 treasures including Ancient Egyptian art, Greek and Roman sculptures and a huge collection of Etruscan artifacts. It also exhibits a wealth of Danish paintings and sculptures from the era known as the Golden Age *(see pp42–3)* and exquisite works by French Impressionist masters such as Degas and Renoir. It has grown from the fine collection of sculptures *(glyptotek)* donated by Carl Jacobsen, founder of the New Carlsberg Brewery, and the museum now consists of three architecturally different buildings, the first one built in 1897 and the latest added in 1996.

★ Ancient Egyptian Art
The outstanding collection of Egyptian art ranges from delicate vases to monumental statues, such as this granite figure of Ramses II from the 2nd millennium BC.

Danish Sculpture
Sculptures representing the great artistic flourishing of Denmark's Golden Age include works such as Jens Adolph Jerichau's Penelope *(1840s), as well as many pieces by HW Bissen.*

★ The Kiss
This famous pair of lovers is one of 35 works by Auguste Rodin, which constitutes the largest collection of the artist's works anywhere outside France.

Alabaster Relief
This 9th-century BC relief depicting the Assyrian King Assurnasirpal II is part of the multifaceted collection representing the Middle East.

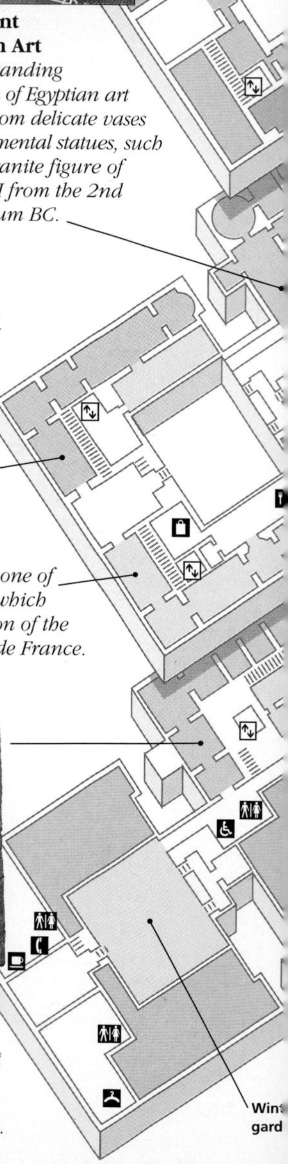

STAR EXHIBITS

- ★ Ancient Egyptian Art
- ★ Head of Satyr
- ★ The Kiss

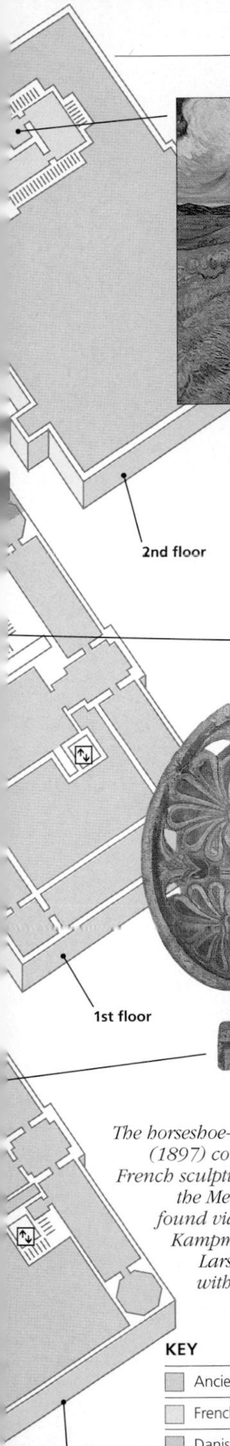

Landscape from Saint-Rémy
Along with this picture painted by Vincent van Gogh during his stay in a psychiatric hospital in 1889, the museum has numerous works by many of the Impressionists and Post-Impressionists, including Gauguin, Toulouse-Lautrec, Monet and Degas.

2nd floor

VISITORS' CHECKLIST

Dantes Plads 7. **Map** 3 B3. ***Tel*** *33 41 81 41.* *11am–5pm Tue–Sun.* *1 Jan, 5 Jun, 24 & 25 Dec.* *(free Sun and to under-18s).* *2A, 33, 69, 173E, 250S.* **www**.glyptoteket.dk

The Little Dancer
The statue of a 14-year-old dancer dates from 1880 and is one of the most famous sculptures to be produced by Edgar Degas.

★ Head of Satyr
This beautiful painted terracotta Head of Satyr *is part of the Etruscan collection, which includes vases, bronze sculptures and stone sarcophagi dating from the 8th to the 2nd century BC.*

1st floor

GALLERY GUIDE

The horseshoe-shaped Dahlerup Building (1897) contains mainly Danish and French sculpture. Ancient artefacts from the Mediterranean and Egypt are found via the Winter Garden in the Kampmann Building (1906). The Larsen Building (1996), rising within one of the courtyards of the Kampmann Building, houses French painting.

KEY

- Ancient Mediterranean
- French painting and sculpture
- Danish painting and sculpture
- Egyptian, Greek and Roman sculpture
- Temporary exhibitions
- Non-exhibition space

Ground floor

WINTER GARDEN

This green oasis of palm trees, planted under a glass dome, was included in the original design as a way of attracting visitors who might not normally be interested in art. It has always provided a pleasant place in which to stroll during a visit. Many visitors are drawn to the *Water Mother* sculpture by Kai Nielsen. Unveiled in 1920, it depicts a naked woman reclining in a small pool, surrounded by a group of babies. The Winter Garden is also used as a concert venue.

1698
efter egen Nytte
blot til Ørenslyst
Hjertet at
lade op min
Mal det alene,
at jeg maa Salmens
og Menighedens
enfoldigt tjene.

SOUTH COPENHAGEN

Criss-crossed by canals and waterways, this part of Copenhagen contains two areas that are about as different from each other as it is possible to be. The islet of Slotsholmen is dominated by Christianborg Slot, standing on the site of a fort built by Bishop Absalon in the 12th century, when there was nothing here but a tiny fishing village. The area flourished and in 1443 København, or "merchant's port", was made the Danish capital. Many historical sights are situated here.

Across the water is Christianshavn where the "free state of Christiania", an alternative community, has been in existence since the 1970s. Both Christianshavn and nearby Holmen have undergone a period of redevelopment, and the area has become one of Copenhagen's more fashionable districts. The city's striking opera house has taken centre stage with its location on Dokøen, an islet that was once used as a naval base.

Waterbus tours provide an enjoyable way of getting to know the area. Alternatively, a bicycle can be useful for exploring the many nooks and crannies of Christianshavn.

Dragon's tails on Børsen's spire

SIGHTS AT A GLANCE

Churches

Vor Frelsers Kirke 9

Museums

Nationalmuseet pp84–5 1

Orlogsmuseet 10

Thorvaldsens Museum 2

Tøjhusmuseet 6

Historic Buildings

Børsen 5

Christiansborg Slot pp86–7 4

Det Kongelige Bibliotek 7

Folketinget 3

Places of Interest

Christiania 11

Christianshavn 8

Operaen 12

GETTING AROUND

Christiansborg and Børsen can be reached by metro (getting off at Kongens Nytorv), and also by buses 1A, 2A, 15, 26 and 29. Christianshavn also has metro links with the rest of the city. Buses 2A, 19, 47, 66 and 350S stop close to Christiania. Waterbuses depart from Nyhavn.

KEY

- Street-by-Street Map *See pp82–3*
- Church
- Metro
- Post office

◁ **Three-storey organ, with a bust of Christian V, in the 17th-century Vor Frelsers Kirke**

Street-by-Street: Around Christiansborg Slot

Christiansborg Slot, with its adjoining palace buildings including the palace church, former royal coach house and royal stables, as well as Tøjhusmuseet, Det Kongelige Bibliotek and Børsen, are all situated on the islet of Slotsholmen. The palace derives its name from a castle that was built on this site in 1167 by Bishop Absalon. Opposite the palace, on the other side to the canal, is the Nationalmuseet, which has many exhibits relating to the history of Copenhagen and the rest of Denmark.

Thordvaldsens Museum
The collection confirms the genius of the Danish sculptor, whose tomb can be found in the museum courtyard ❷

★ Nationalmuseet
This museum was founded in 1807, though its origins date back to 1650 when Frederik II established his own private collection ❶

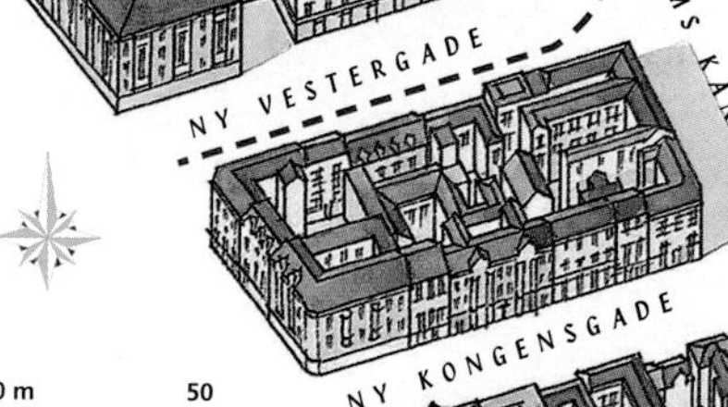

VINDEBROGADE

FR. HOLMS KANAL

NY VESTERGADE

TØJHUSGADE

BRYGHUSGADE

CHRISTIA BRYGGE

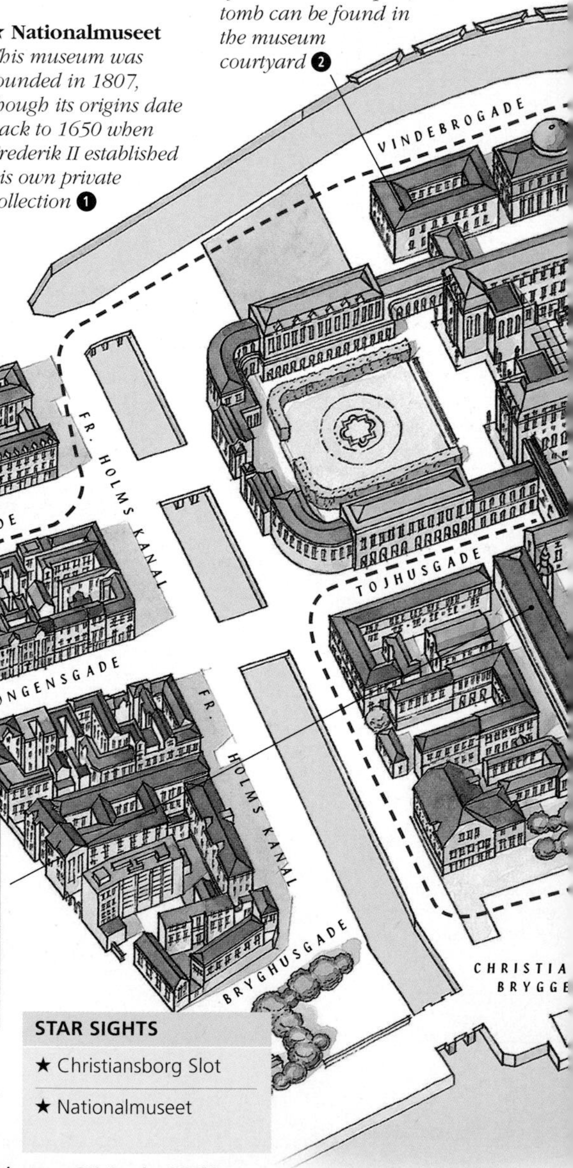

Tøjhusmuseet
Visitors interested in militaria will enjoy the huge array of arms and armour in this museum ❻

STAR SIGHTS

★ Christiansborg Slot

★ Nationalmuseet

For hotels and restaurants in this region see pp244–7 and pp268–74

★ Christiansborg Slot
Although this has not been the home of the royal family for more than 200 years, the palace rooms are still used for grand occasions, such as state banquets attended by Queen Margrethe II ❹

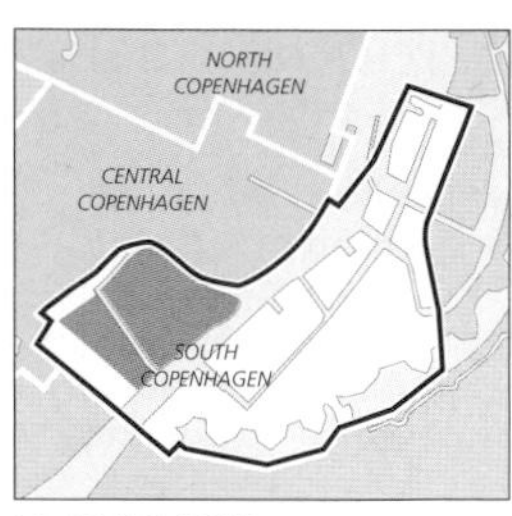

LOCATOR MAP
See Street Finder Maps 3 & 4

KEY

- - - - Suggested route

Folketinget
The Danish parliament building is open to visitors during the summer, when its members are on vacation ❸

BØRSGADE
SLOTSHOLMSGADE
BØRSGADE
CHRISTIANS BRYGGE

Børsen
The former Stock Exchange, with its spire sculpted in the form of entwined dragon tails, represents an outstanding example of 17th-century public architecture ❺

Det Kongelige Bibliotek
The library's "Black Diamond" extension, utilizing black glass and granite imported from Zimbabwe, is one of the capital's most innovative buildings ❼

Nationalmuseet ❶

Exhibits in this prestigious museum include many items relating to Denmark's history as well as artifacts from all over the world. It is worth allocating several hours for a visit. Among the vast array on display are Inuit costumes and tools, rune stones, priceless Egyptian jewellery and medieval church interiors. There is a good children's section, where kids will enjoy trying on armour or "camping out" in a Bedouin tent. All exhibits are labelled in English.

Antiquities
Greek pottery, Etruscan jewellery and Egyptian mummies are on display in the Egyptian and Classical section.

★ Inuit Culture
Included in the ethnographic section are rooms devoted to the Inuit containing many costumes, including a suit made of bird feathers, as well as traditional kayaks and harpoons.

3rd floor

Ethnography
Items from around the world include exhibits from Africa, India and Japan. One room is devoted to world music.

1st floor

Children's Museum

Helmet
This Bronze Age helmet, in the museum's pre-history department, dates from the 9th century BC and was found at Viksø on Zealand.

Main entrance

KEY

- Pre-history (1300 BC–AD 1050)
- Middle Ages & Renaissance (1050–1660)
- Tales of Denmark (1660–2000)
- Ethnography
- History of the Museum
- Royal Collection of Coins
- Ethnographic Treasures
- Near East & Antiquities

For hotels and restaurants in this region see pp244–7 and pp268–74

VISITORS' CHECKLIST

Ny Vestergade 10. **Map** 3 B2. ***Tel*** *33 13 44 11.* *1A, 2A, 6A, 12, 15, 26, 29, 33, 650S.* *10am–5pm Tue–Sun.* **www**.natmus.dk

GALLERY GUIDE

The collection is spread over four floors with pre-history on the ground floor. The medieval department shares the first floor with Ethnography, which continues on the second floor with a exhibits relating to the Inuit. A section designed to appeal to children aged between four and 12 is on the ground floor.

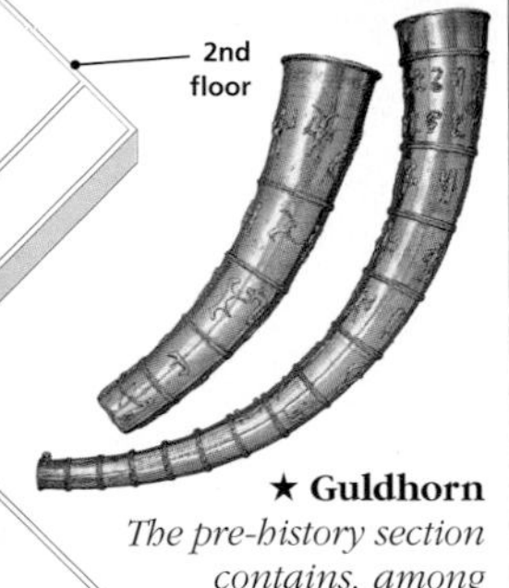

★ Guldhorn
The pre-history section contains, among other exhibits, fragments of golden horns forged around 400 BC.

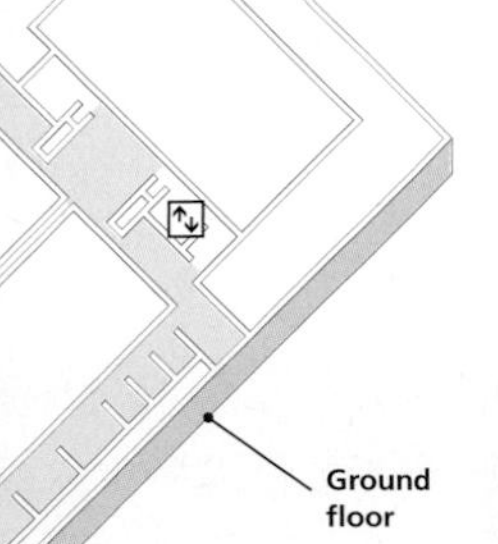

STAR EXHIBITS

★ Guldhorn

★ Inuit Culture

Thorvaldsens Museum ❷

Bertel Thorvaldsen Plads 2. **Map** 3 C2. ***Tel*** *33 32 15 32.* *Central.* *Nørreport, Kongens Nytorv.* *1A, 2A, 15, 26, 29.* *10am–5pm Tue–Sun.* **www**.thorvaldsensmuseum.dk

Located behind the palace church (Christiansborg Slotskirke), Thorvaldsens Museum was the first art museum in Denmark and opened in 1848. The Danish sculptor Bertel Thorvaldsen (1770–1844) lived and worked in Rome for more than 40 years, but towards the end of his life he bequeathed all his works and his collection of paintings to his native Copenhagen. The collection is placed in Christianborg's old Coach House. The building is worth a visit in its own right, with a frieze on the outside by Jørgen Sonne and mosaic floors within.

Despite the fact that he worked on some of his pieces for 25 years, Thorvaldsen's output is staggering and includes sculptures based on classical mythology, busts of well-known contemporaries such as the English poet, Lord Byron, monumental studies of Christ and a number of self-portraits. The museum also displays Thorvaldsen's drawings and sketches and includes items from his private collection of paintings and Egyptian and Roman artifacts.

Vaulted ceiling and decorative floor in Thorvaldsens Museum

Folketinget ❸

Christiansborg. **Map** 3 C2. *Jun–Sep: daily.*

The Folketinget is the Danish parliamentary chamber. Seating for the 179 members is arranged in a semi-circle with "left wing" MPs positioned on the left and "right wing" MPs on the right. The civil servants' offices occupy the largest section of the palace. Separate offices are used by Queen Margrethe II, whose duties include chairing weekly meetings of the State Council and presiding over the annual state opening of parliament in early October.

Christiansborg Slot ❹

See pp86–7.

Børsen 5

Slotsholmsgade. **Map** 4 D2. *to visitors.*

Copenhagen's former Stock Exchange was built between 1590 and 1640 on the orders of Christian IV, to a design by Lorentz and Hans van Steenwinckel. Today, the building houses the city's Chamber of Commerce and is not open to the public, but its stunning Renaissance façade, copper roofs, numerous gables and unusual spire have made it one of Copenhagen's best-known sights. Its sleek 54-m (177-ft) spire, carved to resemble the entwined tails of four dragons, is a city landmark. Topping the spire are three crowns representing Denmark, Sweden and Norway. Trade in goods continued at Børsen until 1857, when it was purchased by a private association of wholesalers who pledged to maintain the historic building.

Dragon tails forming Børsen's tower

Christiansborg Slot ❹

This palace stands on the site of five former buildings. A 12th-century fortress built by Bishop Absalon was torn down in 1369 and replaced by the Copenhagen Castle. Christian VI replaced this building with the first Christiansborg Palace, one of the grandest palaces in Europe. This burned down in 1794, forcing the royal family to move to Amalienborg. A second Christiansborg Palace, completed in 1828, was also damaged by fire in 1884. Work on the present palace was completed in 1928.

★ Throne Room
As in every royal palace, the Throne Room is one of the grandest rooms in Christiansborg. However, Queen Margrethe II is famous for her "common touch" and has apparently never sat on this magnificent royal seat.

Velvet Room
Completed in 1924, this room is noteworthy for its grand marble portals, reliefs and luxurious velvet wall linings.

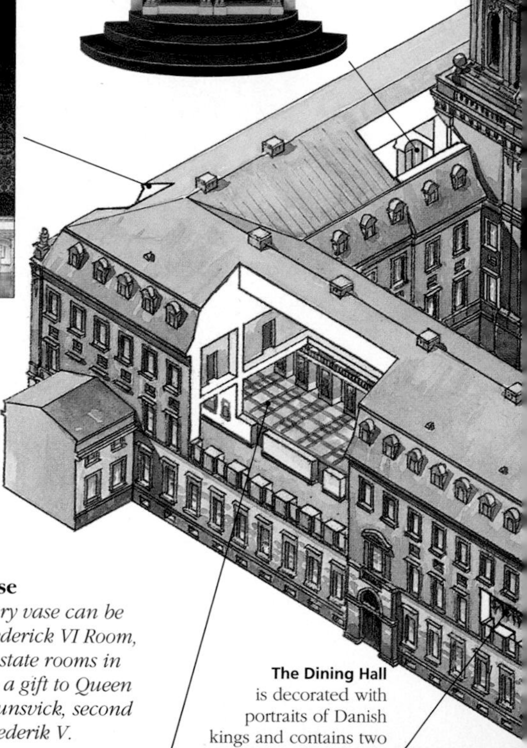

Decorative Vase
This 18th-century vase can be found in the Frederick VI Room, one of the many state rooms in the palace. It was a gift to Queen Juliane Marie of Brunsvick, second wife of monarch Frederik V.

The Dining Hall is decorated with portraits of Danish kings and contains two crystal chandeliers.

★ Great Hall
The 17 tapestries on display here were commissioned for the 50th birthday of Queen Margrethe II. They were made by Bjørn Nørgaard and depict key events from Denmark's history.

STAR FEATURES

- ★ Castle Ruins
- ★ Great Hall
- ★ Throne Room

For hotels and restaurants in this region see pp244–7 and pp268–74

Tower Hall
Copenhagen's tallest tower is 106 m (348 ft) high and topped with a 5-m (16-ft) crown. The tower's interior has a series of tapestries created by Joakim Skovgaard depicting scenes from Danish folk tales.

VISITORS' CHECKLIST

Christiansborg Slotsplads.
Map 3 C2. ***Tel*** *33 92 64 92.*
1A, 2A, 15, 26, 29.
Reception Rooms *Oct–Apr: 10am–4pm Tue–Sun; May–Sep: 10am–4pm daily. 11am (Danish), 3pm (English).*
Ruins *Oct–Apr: 10am–4pm Tue–Sun; May–Sep: 10am–4pm daily.* **www**.ses.dk/en

★ Castle Ruins
Under the palace are the ruins of the previous castles, including parts of Bishop Absalon's castle and the Copenhagen Castle.

Library
A small portion of the vast royal collection is housed here. The remaining volumes are kept at Amalienborg Slot (see pp56–7).

Alexander Hall
Bertel Thorvaldsen's frieze depicting Alexander the Great entering Babylon is displayed in this hall.

Tøjhusmuseet ❻

Tøjhusgade 3. **Map** 3 C2. ***Tel*** *33 11 60 37.* *1A, 2A, 15, 26, 29.* *noon–4pm Tue–Sun.* *(free on Wed).* **www**.thm.dk

The Royal Danish Arsenal was built between 1598 and 1604 and was one of the earliest of Christian IV's building projects. When completed, the 163-m (535-ft) long complex was one of the largest buildings in Europe and was capable of equipping an entire army. In 1611 the building was extended to include a harbour pool, which was situated next door in what are today the Library Gardens. The building now serves as a museum. Its collection covers the history of artillery from the invention of gunpowder up to the present day (exhibits include artillery guns as well as firearms). Suits of armour and military uniforms are also on display.

Cannon from the Tøjhusmuseet collection

Det Kongelige Bibliotek ❼

Christians Brygge, entrance from Søren Kierkegaards Plads. **Map** 4 D2. ***Tel*** *33 47 47 47.* *66.* *901, 902.* *10am–9pm Mon–Sat.* **www**.kb.dk

The Royal Library is an excellent example of how to merge two very different architectural forms. The

Gate leading to the old section of Det Kongelige Bibliotek

original library building is 19th century. The Neo-Classical building's courtyard has been transformed into a garden and contains a statue of the Danish philosopher and theologian Søren Kierkegaard. Next to the old building is the ultra-modern new library, linked by a special passage to its historic predecessor. Nicknamed the "Black Diamond" because of its angular black glass-and-granite exterior, the extension houses library and exhibition areas, the National Photography Museum, a concert hall and a restaurant and café. It is worth stepping inside, if only to see the vast ceiling mural by Per Kirkeby.

Christianshavn ❽

Map 4 D & 4 E.

This district, which is sometimes referred to as "Little Amsterdam" because of its many canals, can be explored on foot, by bicycle or by hopping aboard a waterbus. Built in the first half of the 17th century by Christian IV, Christianshavn was originally intended both as a fortified city and a naval base. The area was the site of the first boatyards established in Copenhagen, as well as the warehouses belonging to major shipping lines. It is also where most sailors and boatyard workers lived. Until recently, Christianshavn was known only as the site of the "free state of Christiania" and was considered to be unattractive, poor and neglected. Lately, however, Christianshavn, together with nearby Holmen, has blossomed thanks to a sustained programme of urban redevelopment. Run-down warehouses have been transformed into trendy restaurants, cafés, company offices and smart apartments, which are favoured by artists and young professionals.

Vor Frelsers Kirke ❾

Sankt Annæ Gade 29. **Map** 4 E2. ***Tel*** *32 54 68 83.* **M** *Christianshavn.* *2A, 19, 47, 66, 350S.* *daily.* **Tower** *11am–4pm daily.* **www**.vorfrelserskirke.dk

Our Saviour's Church is most famous for its extraordinary spire, completed in 1752, and accessible via a spiral staircase that runs around the exterior. Be warned – it takes considerable stamina

Yachting marina and houses built out over the water, in Christianshavn

to climb all 400 steps, not to mention a good head for heights. The spire is Copenhagen's second-highest panoramic viewpoint and once you have caught your breath at the top you will be rewarded with a fabulous view of the city from 90 m (295 ft) up.

The spire's creator was the architect Lauritz de Thurah, who struck upon the idea of a spiral staircase while visiting the church of Sant'Ivo alla Sapienza in Rome. Legend has it that Thurah was so obsessed by his work that when it was alleged that his encircling staircase wound up the wrong way he committed suicide by leaping from the top of the tower. The truth is more prosaic, however, as the architect died in his own bed, poor and destitute, seven years after completing the tower. The tale was nevertheless made into a movie by the Danish director Nils Vest in 1997.

Spiral stairs of Vor Frelsers Kirke's tower

The church itself is also worth visiting. It was built in 1696, to a design by Lambert von Haven. Inside, a Baroque altar by the Swede Nicodemus Tessin is adorned with cherubs. The huge three-storey organ dates from 1698. It has over 4,000 pipes and is supported by two giant elephants.

Orlogsmuseet ⑩

Overgaden oven Vandet 58. **Map** 4 E2. ***Tel*** *33 11 60 37.* *Christianshavn.* *2A, 19, 47, 66, 350S.* *noon–4pm Tue–Sun.* **www**.orlogsmuseet.dk

The Royal Danish Naval Museum's building dates from 1780 and was once a sailors' hospital. Among its exhibits are navigation instruments, ships' lights, figureheads that were once fixed to the bows of windjammers, and uniforms. A collection of over 300 model ships includes one that dates back to 1687.

Entrance to Christiania – a district promising an alternative lifestyle

Christiania ⑪

Map 4 D3 & E3. *Christianhavn.* *2A, 19, 47, 66, 350S.* **www**.christiania.org

The "free state of Christiania" has been in existence since 13 November 1971, when a group of squatters took over some deserted military barracks to the east of Christianshavn and established a commune. The local authorities initially tried to force the squatters to leave, but as the community's numbers swelled, the government decided to treat Christiania as a "social experiment". Today the community has about 900 residents.

The community has its own schools, infrastructure and system of government, which are financed in part by the proceeds of its cafés and restaurants and the sale of locally made handicrafts. Christiania was initially linked with hippy drug culture, and cannabis was openly sold and smoked here until the trade was outlawed in 2004.

Operaen ⑫

Ekvipagemestervej 10. **Map** 2 F5. ***Tel*** *33 69 69 69.* *66.* *901, 902.* *foyer: 3 hours before a performance.* *9:30am & 4:30pm Mon–Fri.* **www**.operaen.dk

The stunning Copenhagen Opera House opened in January 2005 on the island of Holmen in Copenhagen Harbour. For over a century the Danish Royal Opera shared a space with the Danish ballet and theatre companies at Det Kongelige Teater. The auditorium was designed by the prominent Danish architect Henning Larsen, whose works include the Ny Carlsberg Glyptotek extension and the Danish Design Centre. The modern building is clad in German limestone and covers 35,000 sq m (376,000 sq ft). It includes an 1,800-seat auditorium as well as a second, smaller stage.

Striking façade of Copenhagen's opera house

FURTHER AFIELD

There is plenty to see outside the city centre. Some attractions, such as the Tycho Brahe Planetarium, are within walking distance. Others, like the Carlsberg Brewery, Zoological Garden, or Assistens Kirkegård can be reached by bus. Sights even further afield are served by a network of modern suburban trains.

A visit to one or more of these places provides an alternative to the bustle of inner-city Copenhagen.

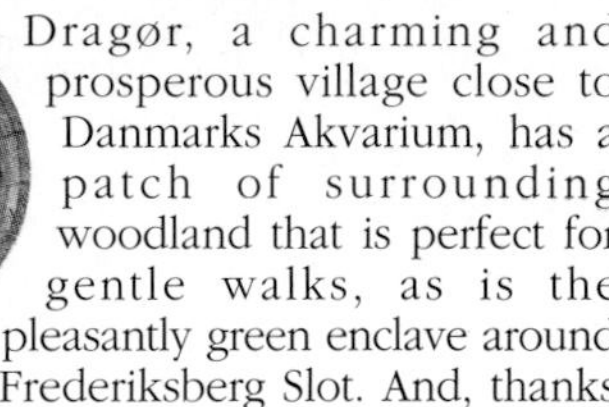

Tuborg brewery sign

Dragør, a charming and prosperous village close to Danmarks Akvarium, has a patch of surrounding woodland that is perfect for gentle walks, as is the pleasantly green enclave around Frederiksberg Slot. And, thanks to the bridge and tunnel that spans the Øresund (Sound), the long sandy beach and fine parks of Malmö in Sweden are only half an hour away. The bridge is a marvel of modern engineering and can be admired from Dragør's small harbour.

SIGHTS AT A GLANCE

Historic Buildings
Frederiksberg Slot 4

Places of Interest
Amager 12
Carlsberg Brewery 2
Danmarks Akvarium 9
Dragør 13
Experimentarium 8
Royal Copenhagen 5
Tycho Brahe Planetarium 1
Øresund Bridge 11

Parks and Gardens
Charlottenlund 10
Zoologisk Have 3

Museums
Arken Museum For Modern Kunst 14

Churches
Grundtvigs Kirke 7

Cemeteries
Assistens Kirkegård 6

KEY
City centre
Greater Copenhagen
Railway station
Airport
Motorway
Major road
Other road

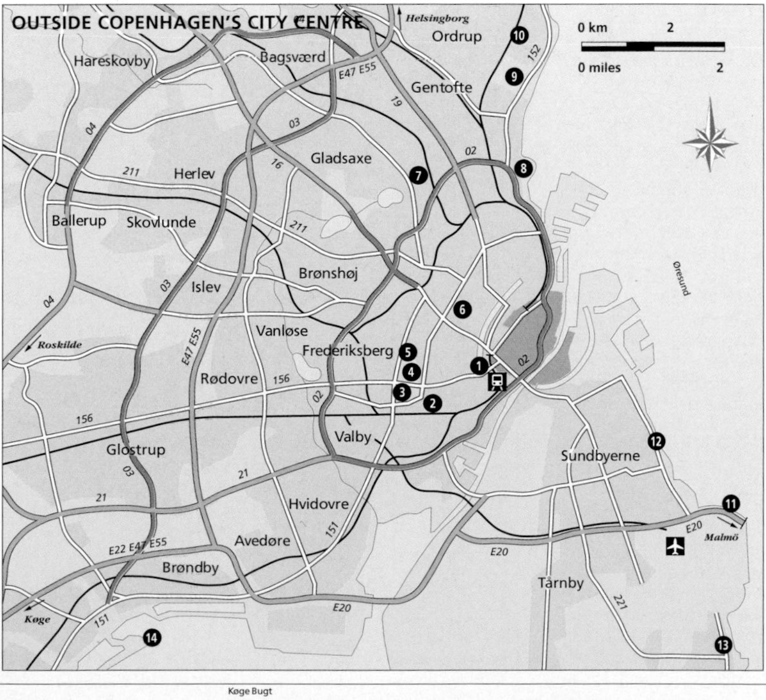

OUTSIDE COPENHAGEN'S CITY CENTRE

0 km 2
0 miles 2

◁ **Decorative lamps on Dronning Louises Bro (Queen Louise Bridge) east of the city centre**

Tycho Brahe Planetarium in the shape of a bevelled cylinder

Tycho Brahe Planetarium ❶

Gl. Kongevej 10. ***Tel*** *33 12 12 24.* Ⓢ *Vesterport.* 🚌 *12, 14, 15, 29, 831.* 🕘 *10:30am–9pm daily (from 1pm Mon); holidays: 9:30am–9pm.* **www**.tycho.dk

Copenhagen's planetarium is the largest of its kind in western Europe and is named after Tycho Brahe (1546–1601), the renowned Danish astronomer. Brahe is credited with the discovery of a new star in the constellation of Cassiopeia, in 1572, and with making important advances in our knowledge of planetary motion. One of the reasons his work is so impressive is that he made these advances before the invention of the telescope.

The planetarium opened in 1989 in a cylindrical building designed by Knud Munk. Built from sand-coloured brick, it appears at its most attractive when viewed from across the small lake, which was created in the late 18th century by damming the local river. The street in which the planetarium is located is the Old Royal Route (Gammel Kongevej), which was once travelled by royal processions heading for Frederiksberg Slot.

The planetarium houses a small astronomical collection, including antique telescopes. Films are screened in the planetarium's huge IMAX cinema, including one on the wonders of space travel.

Carlsberg Brewery ❷

Carlsberg Visitors Center & Jacobsen Brewhouse. Gamle Carlsberg Vej 11. ***Tel*** *33 27 12 82.* 🕘 *May–Aug: 10am–5pm Tue–Sun (to 7:30pm Thu); Sep–Apr: 10am–4pm Tue–Sun.* ● *national holidays.* *Jacobsen Brewhouse.* **www**.visitcarlsberg.dk, **www**.jacobsenbryg.dk

Carlsberg was founded in 1847 by Jacob Christian, whose father had worked at the king's brewery in Copenhagen. Jacob Christian chose this site on Valby Hill (now Frederiksberg Hill) because of the quality of the water nearby, and named his company Carlsberg (Carl's Hill) after his son. By the late 19th century the business had an international reputation. In 1882 Carl founded his own brewery, Ny Carlsberg (New Carlsberg), while his father's brewery was named Gamle Carlsberg (Old Carlsberg). Twenty four years later, in 1906, the two combined.

East entrance gate to the Carlsberg Brewery

This site no longer produces lager but has an information centre where visitors can learn about the manufacturing process and sample the beer.

In 2005, the Jacobsen Brewhouse opened in part of the old brewery. It is designed for the development of speciality beers and visitors can experience a live demonstration of brewing skills in the Visitors Centre, not to mention tasting the produce in a bar overlooking the shining copper kettles.

Along the same street are some examples of industrial architecture, including the intriguing Elephant Gate. Built in 1901, the gate consists of four 5-m (16-ft) high elephants made of granite shipped from Bornholm.

Giraffes in the city zoo, near Frederiksberg Have

Zoologisk Have ❸

Roskildevej 32. ***Tel*** *72 20 02 00.* Ⓢ *Valby.* Ⓜ *Frederiksberg.* 🚌 *4A, 6A, 18, 26, 832.* 🕘 *Jan, Feb, Nov & Dec: 9am–4pm daily; Mar: 9am–4pm daily (to 5pm Sat & Sun); Apr, May & Sep: 9am–5pm daily (to 6pm Sat & Sun); 1–26 Jun & 17–31 Aug: 9am–6pm daily; 27 Jun–16 Aug: 9am–9pm daily; Oct: 9am–5pm daily.* **www**.zoo.dk

Copenhagen's zoological garden was established close to Frederiksberg Slot in 1859, making it one of Europe's oldest zoos. Although not large by international standards, the zoo

Frederiksberg Slot, headquarters of the Danish Military Academy

has a good record of breeding in captivity. A wide selection of animals are kept here including giraffes, polar bears, elephants and lions. A tropical section houses butterflies and birds as well as some crocodiles. An additional attraction is the 42-m (138-ft) high wooden observation tower, built in 1905, which affords views as far as the coast of Sweden.

Frederiksberg Slot ❹

Roskildevej 28. ***Tel*** *36 13 26 00.* *Frederiksberg.* *4A, 6A, 18, 26, 832.* **Palace** *to visitors.* **Garden** *7am–sunset daily.*

Built between 1700 and 1735 this palace was the summer residence of Frederik IV who used it to entertain visitors including, in 1716, the Tsar of Russia, Peter the Great. The king is said to have enjoyed sailing along the park canals, while Copenhagen's inhabitants lined the banks and cheered.

The palace was designed in the Italian style by the architect Ernst Brandenburger following the king's visit to Italy. During the reign of Christian IV the building was enlarged with two additional wings, giving it its present horseshoe shape.

Since 1869 Frederiksberg Slot has been used by the Danish Military Academy. Having its origins in the Cadets' Corp established by Frederik IV in 1713, the school's emblem still bears the king's monogram. The school is not open to the public, though visitors are free to explore the grounds. The palace gardens, known as Frederiksberg Have, were laid out in a French style in the early 18th century. Later on they were transformed into a romantic rambling English park, criss-crossed with a network of canals and tree-lined paths, and dotted with statues and park benches.

Frederiksberg Slot stands on top of a hill and, for the people of Copenhagen, marks a notional boundary of the city. In the 18th century, when it was built, the palace stood outside the city limits and, even today, many locals refer to this area of Copenhagen east of the hill as the "village".

Royal Copenhagen Factory Outlet ❺

Søndre Fasanvej 9. ***Tel*** *38 34 10 04.* *Frederiksberg.* *4A, 14, 15.* *9am–4pm Mon–Fri,* *10am–5:30pm Mon–Fri, 10am–2pm Sat.* *public holidays, 1 Jan, 1 May, 5 Jun, 24 Dec.* **www**.royalcopenhagen.com

The Royal Copenhagen Porcelain Manufactory was founded by Christian VII in 1775 in order to supply the royal court with exquisite tableware worthy of a monarch. One of the first designs was a pattern known as Blue Fluted, which has since become a trademark of the company. To decorate a single plate in this distinctive blue-and-white pattern takes nearly 1,200 individual brush strokes. *Flora Danica*, however, is the more well known design, based on an ornate 1,800-piece dinner service that was created in the 18th century.

Production now takes place elsewhere, and the factory is used as a factory outlet. Royal Copenhagen is famous throughout the world and its products are especially popular with collectors in the USA and Japan. A wide variety of items is on sale in the centre's shop, including the Blue Fluted Mega line, Royal Copenhagen's current best-selling range, designed in occasion of the company's 225th anniversary.

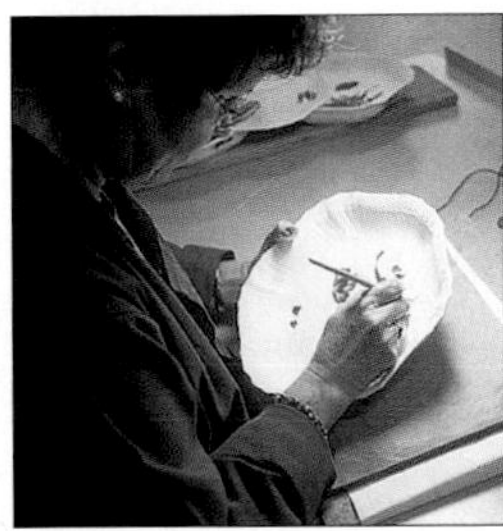
Decorating a plate at Royal Copenhagen

FLORA DANICA

This dinner service, decorated with floral designs copied from the *Flora Danica* encyclopedia of plants, was ordered in 1790 by Christian VII. The set was intended as a present for Catherine II of Russia. However, during the 12 years when the first *Flora Danica* was in production the Tsarina died, and the king decided to keep the set for himself. It was used for the first time in 1803 during a reception to celebrate the king's 37th birthday. Over 1,500 of the original 1,802 pieces have survived and are now in the possession of Queen Margrethe II. Copies of individual items are made to order and the methods of production hardly differ from those employed over 200 years ago. The pieces are hand-painted by artists who train for over 10 years to master the exquisite flower paintings. This kind of quality is expensive – a plate costs about 5,000 Dkr.

An example of *Flora Danica* tableware

Assistens Kirkegård, both a park and a cemetery

Assistens Kirkegård ❻

Kapelvej 2. ***Tel*** *35 39 93 04.*
Ⓢ Ⓜ *Nørreport.* 🚌 *5A, 66, 350S.*
◯ *Jan–Feb, Nov–Dec: 8am–4pm daily; Mar–Apr, Sep–Oct: 8am–6pm daily; May–Aug: 8am–8pm daily.*
www.kbh-kirkegaarde.kk.dk

In 1760 Copenhagen's graveyards were too small to accommodate victims of a plague that was assailing the city at this time. The plague first struck in 1711 and claimed 23,000 lives in all, reducing the city's population by a third. Assistens Kirkegård was established to supplement the existing provisions for burials.

Initially the cemetery was used only for burying the poor but, from the late 18th century, burial plots at Assistens came into fashion. The list of famous people who are buried here include Søren Kierkegaard, Niels Bohr and Hans Christian Andersen, as well as the artists Christoffer Wilhelm Eckersberg and Christian Købke.

The cemetery is also a pleasant park, and popular with many locals. Visitors are as likely to see buskers, joggers, cyclists and sunbathers as people tending the graves.

Grundtvigs Kirke ❼

På Bjerget 5B. ***Tel*** *35 81 54 42.*
Ⓢ *Emdrup.* 🚌 *6A, 42, 43, 66, 69.*
◯ *9am–4pm Mon–Sat (to 6pm Thu), noon–4pm Sun (to 1pm in winter).*
www.grundtvigskirke.dk

This unusual yellow brick church, remarkable not only for its size but also its highly original shape, was designed in 1913 by P.V. Jensen Klint. Standing almost 49 m (161 ft) high, it ranks as one of Denmark's largest churches and is designed in a Danish Modernist style. It was built between 1921 and 1940 on Bisperbjerg, the highest hill in Copenhagen, and paid for through public donations to honour the memory of Nicolai Frederik Severin Grundtvig (1783–1872) – a prominent clergyman, theologist and philosopher. In addition to his social work, this versatile man found time to write books and treatises, and composed some 1,500 hymns, many of which are sung to this day in Danish churches. For more than 10 years Grundtvig was a member of the Danish Parliament, and in 1861 he became an honorary bishop of the Danish Church.

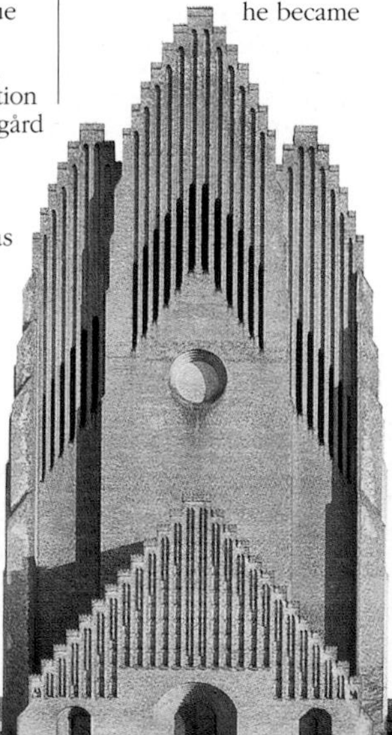

Front elevation of Grundtvigs Kirke, inspired by small village churches

The charismatic clergyman became famous in his country as the founder of the Danish Folkehøjskole (People's High School), a system that enabled those from the lower ranks of society to gain access to education. The shape of the church building symbolizes this sphere of his activities, being reminiscent of a typical Danish village church. On the other hand, the top of the tower is designed to resemble a church organ and alludes to the many religious hymns written by Grundtvig.

Hands-on fun for kids at Experimentarium

Experimentarium ❽

Tuborg Havnevej 7. ***Tel*** *39 27 33 33.*
Ⓢ *Hellerup or Svanemøllen.*
🚌 *1A, 14, 21, 166, 169, 179.*
◯ *9:30am–5pm Mon–Fri (to 9pm Tue), 11am–5pm Sat, Sun & hols.*
● *1 Jan, 23–25 Dec, 31 Dec.*
www.experimentarium.dk

The main idea behind this innovative science centre, in the Hellerup district of Copenhagen, is to bring science to life through hands-on exploration. Almost all the exhibits are interactive; there are about 300 experiments that can be independently performed by anyone.

The display area is huge and, not surprisingly, the place is hugely popular with children who run about trying out all the exhibits. Adults, too, will find much of interest, whether it be testing the latest in virtual technology, programming robots or experiencing an

For hotels and restaurants in this region see pp244–7 and pp268–74

Some of the many aquatic creatures to be found at Danmarks Akvarium

earthquake of 5.5 degrees on the Richter scale.

At every point, children are confronted with exhibits and puzzles to fire their curiosity, and tested with such imponderable questions as "Are there green rabbits?" and "Can you lift yourself?". Kids can try their hand at guiding a cargo vessel into harbour, test their emotions, check their hearing from the lowest to the highest frequencies, and learn how ice-dancers' hands affect the speed of their pirouettes. Environmental issues are high on the agenda and topics include how winds develop, what kind of climate can be expected in 100 years' time by simulating various concentrations of carbon dioxide emissions into the atmosphere, and methods of water conservation.

The Kids' Pavillion is a separate section where younger visitors between 3 and 6 years old can experiment with magnetism, build a house using a crane, hear what their voice sounds like backwards and decide whether the sounds of bird song or rain should fill a colourful section known as the "Poppy Wood".

All the exhibits are labelled in Danish and English, and there are numerous lectures and special exhibitions staged throughout the year.

Dried seahorse, Danmarks Akvarium

Danmarks Akvarium 9

Kavalergården 1, Charlottenlund. ***Tel*** *39 62 32 83.* *14, 166.* *Nov–Jan: 10am–4pm daily; Feb–May, Sep & Oct: 10am–5pm daily (to 8pm Wed); Jun–Aug: 10am–6pm daily (to 8pm Wed).* *1 Jan, 24, 25 & 31 Dec.* **www**.akvarium.dk

Copenhagen's aquarium is located in the grounds of Charlottenlund Slot and was founded in 1939. Although not as large as the Nordsøen Oceanarium in Hirtshals *(see p204)*, it is one of the oldest establishments of its kind in Scandinavia and still plays a major role in conservation, research and education.

It contains more than 90 glass tanks, the largest holding 85,000 litres (18,700 gallons) of water. The tanks are populated by over 300 species of fish from all over the world including sharks and sharp-teethed piranha. Among the other aquatic wildlife are a giant octopus, crocodiles and an electric eel (capable of producing up to 2,000 volts), as well as turtles, sponges, lobsters and many hundreds of brightly coloured tropical fish.

One of the most recent and unexpected arrivals is a young caretta turtle (an endangered species from the Caribbean) that was found washed up on one of Denmark's beaches on a December morning in 1999.

Charlottenlund 10

14, 166. *Charlottenlund St.* **Palace** *to visitors.* **Gardens**

A royal residence has stood on this site since 1690 but the present palace was built between 1731 and 1733 on the orders of Princess Charlotte Amalie. The princess, who remained single all her life, liked the place so much that it was soon named after her.

The building was remodelled in the 19th century, when its Baroque character gave way to a Renaissance style. A number of other Danish royals have enjoyed staying here including Frederik VIII and his wife, Princess Louise, who remained here until her death in 1926. The couple are commemorated by an obelisk at the rear of the building.

The palace is now used by the Danish Institute for Fisheries, but it is still possible to stroll in its surrounding gardens. The appearance of the park, with its pruned conifers and pleasant avenues, dates from the 1990s, though marked pathways and ponds remain from the 17th century. The vegetable garden dates from 1826 and once grew herbs and produce for the palace kitchen. There are a number of ancient trees in the grounds, notably two larches that stand at the rear of the palace and are considered to be the oldest of their kind in Denmark.

Charlottenlund Slot, surrounded by parkland

Øresund Bridge ⓫

Cost of one-way ticket: motorcycle – 150 Dkr; car up to 6 m (20 ft) – 275 Dkr, car with trailer – 550 Dkr; bus over 9 m (29.5 ft) long – 1,145 Dkr; no bicycles allowed; toll and passport control points are located on the Swedish side.
www.oeresundsbron.dk

In 2000, when Queen Margrethe II and King Carl XVI of Sweden jointly snipped the ribbon at the opening ceremony of the Øresund Bridge, it was the first time that the Scandinavian peninsula had been connected to mainland Europe since the Ice Age. Now, thanks to the bridge, the delights of Malmö, the largest city in southern Sweden, are only 35 minutes away from Copenhagen.

The bridge is the second longest fixed-link bridge in the world. The entire crossing is 16 km (10 miles) long and consists of (from the Danish side): a 430-m (1,411-ft) long artificial peninsula, a tunnel measuring over 3.5 km (2.2 miles) and running 10 m (33 ft) below the water, a 4-km (2-mile) long artificial island and a 7,845-m (25,738-ft) long cable-stayed bridge. From either side of the sound, the sight of the structure, with its huge 204-m (670-ft) high pylons, is truly impressive.

The bridge is a marvel of modern engineering. It has a two-level structure; the top is for motor traffic, the bottom for rail. At its highest point the bridge is suspended 57 m (187 ft) above the water. At the tunnel entrance, on both sides, are light filters designed to allow drivers to adjust to the dimmer conditions. About one thousand sensors are installed along the route as part of a fire alarm system, while over 220 CCTV cameras operate round the clock.

The idea of linking Danish Zealand with Swedish Skåne (Skania) first emerged some 130 years ago, but it was only in the 1930s that realistic projects concerning a bridge began to take shape. The agreement between the two countries to build the link was signed in 1991, and two years later work commenced. The bridge has proved to be popular and over 20,000 rail passengers and 10,000 cars make the crossing every day.

The Øresund region's economy has been boosted by the crossing, and it is becoming one of northern Europe's largest commercial centres. The bridge also forms part of an annual marathon run, the first of which took place in June 2000, before the official opening.

Wind turbines rising from the seabed east of Amager

Amager ⓬

3 km (2 miles) southeast of Copenhagen city centre.

For a great number of visitors arriving by plane, the island of Amager is the starting point of their exploration of Denmark. Lying a short way southeast of Copenhagen's city centre, Amager is the site of Copenhagen's international airport. It is also a place much appreciated by young people seeking inexpensive overnight accommodation – the island has the largest youth hostel in the city, offering 520 beds.

The north end of Amager is virtually in the centre of Copenhagen and from there it is possible to get to the area around Christiansborg. The south end is entirely different in character with farms and small fishing harbours including the picturesque village of Dragør. Amager's beaches, known as the Amager Strand, are on the east side of the island and are the nearest area of coast to the centre of Copenhagen.

Øresund Bridge linking Denmark and Sweden

For hotels and restaurants in this region see pp244–7 and pp268–74

The shoreline is mostly pebbly although there is the occasional patch of sand. The Strand is popular during summer as the shallow water and grassy areas for picnics and games make it ideal for families with children. Another attraction of Amager Strand is the Helgoland swimming pool complex. Since 1929 this has been the headquarters of an association known as "Cold Shock" whose members favour winter sea bathing.

Amager is a good point from which to admire the Øresund Bridge and the huge wind turbines that are situated 2 km (1 mile) east of the island's northern tip.

Dragør ⓭

12 km (7 miles) southeast of Copenhagen. **Museum** Havnepladsen 2. ***Tel*** *32 53 93 07.* *Jun–Sep: noon–4pm Wed, Thu, Sat & Sun.* **www**.museumamager.dk

This picturesque town to the southeast of Amager was until recently known only as the place to catch a ferry for Limhamn, on the Swedish side of the Øresund (Sound). The opening of a bridge brought about the closing of this route, and Dragør has since become a destination for those wishing to escape the hustle of central Copenhagen.

An exhibit from Dragør's museum

As far back as the Middle Ages, Dragør was a major centre for the Baltic herring trade. Later on, its inhabitants profited by piloting the boats that sailed across the Øresund. Many houses in Dragør still have distinctive observation towers, known as "Kikkenborg". The biggest of these stands by Lodshuset, a building that houses the local pilot service headquarters, which was established in 1684. Surprisingly, for a long time Dragør had no proper harbour and the boats were simply dragged ashore. The word "dragør" means a sandy or pebbly strip of land up which the boats were hauled. It was not until 1520 that Dutch settlers, inhabiting nearby Store Magleby, built a proper harbour. Once built, it developed fast and by the 19th century it was the third-largest port in Denmark (after Copenhagen and Helsingør), receiving large sailing ships. Today these maritime traditions are kept alive by a pleasant marina overlooking nearby Sweden and the stunning bridge.

Cutters moored in Dragør's harbour

The town is a pleasant place for a stroll with cobbled streets and pretty 18th-century yellow walled houses decorated with flowers. The local museum, housed in the old town hall building and a 17th-century harbour warehouse, has a collection of items devoted to Dragør's rich maritime past.

Arken Museum For Moderne Kunst ⓮

20 km (12 miles) south of Copenhagen city centre. Ishøj, Skovvej 100. ***Tel*** *43 54 02 22.* *Ⓢ to Ishøj and from there 128.* *10am–5pm Tue–Sun (to 9pm Wed).* **www**.arken.dk

Located a stone's throw from the beach, Arken Museum For Moderne Kunst (Arken Museum of Modern Art) is housed in a building designed by Søren Robert Lund and is intended to resemble a marooned ship.

The exhibition area occupies 9,200 sq m (99,000 sq ft), constituting one third of the available space. The museum's permanent collection is comprised mostly of Danish and Nordic art created after 1945 with an emphasis on installations, sculpture and graphic art. Many of the works on display are by Danish artists such as Asger Jørn and Per Kirkeby. Much of the collection consists of major installations, such as Palestinian-born Mona Hatoum's *Sous tension* (a huge wooden table surrounded by electrified kitchen utensils) and Olafur Eliasson's *Quadrible light ventilator mobile* (a mobile comprised of a light and four electric fans).

The building has proved to be as controversial as much of the work inside. Designed by Lund when he was 25 years old and studying at the Det Kongelige Kunstakademi (The Royal Academy of Fine Arts), it has an interior which follows few conventional rules. Its similarity to a ship is apparent not only from the external shape, but also when looking at details that include fake "rivets" and stairs resembling a companionway.

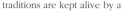

Bold outline of Arken Museum For Moderne Kunst

SHOPPING IN COPENHAGEN

Copenhagen has long been the commercial centre not only of Denmark, but also of an entire region that includes Zealand and, on the Swedish side, Skåne (Skania). Shopping here is a pleasurable experience, with many of the most interesting stores concentrated in just a few areas, often in buildings as interesting as their merchandise. Strøget and nearby pedestrian streets offer everything from designer labels and everyday fashion, to porcelain, crystal and antiques. Copenhagen is synonymous with the best in interior style and the decorative arts, while young Danish talent has turned the city into a fashion capital, too. An array of hip boutiques and quirky shops have helped to revitalise some previously run-down areas of the city and they deserve to be explored. Along the way, dozens of picturesque squares and cafés offer welcome respite for tired feet.

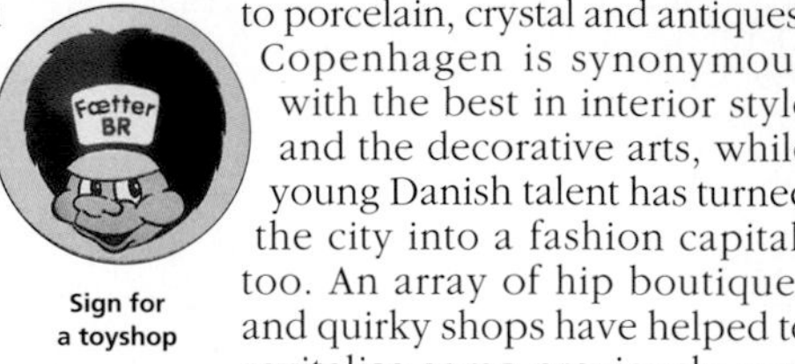

Sign for a toyshop

Magasin du Nord, one of Copenhagen's best-known department stores

WHAT TO BUY

Denmark is the home of applied design, and those looking for homewares are spoilt for choice by the vast array of ingenious, smart, unusual and extravagant items on offer. The Danes like to dress smartly too, without spending a fortune, so it is worth checking out the sales for good quality clothes and footwear at bargain prices. The best times are July and early January.

While all of the high-profile international designer labels are available, one of the pleasures of shopping in Copenhagen is discovering unusual and unique items unavailable back home.

WHERE TO SHOP

Most of the major international brands can be found along the city's two longest pedestrian streets, Strøget *(see p70)* and Købmagergade. Shops range from cheerful and inexpensive to designer and upmarket department stores (towards Kongens Nytorv). If you take detours into the side streets there is plenty of more alternative shopping on offer. On parallel Læderstræde and Kompagnistræde you will discover a variety of small independent shops; the latter is especially good for antiques. Those on tighter budgets should head west of Strøget, to Larsbjørnsstræde and Studiestræde for street fashion, secondhand shops and record stores.

On the outskirts of the old town, the Nansensgade area mixes traditional and trendy boutiques with attractive bars and cafés. There is everything here from sushi restaurants and chocolate shops to vintage clothes and accessories.

To the west of the central station, the former red light district of Vesterbro has undergone a complete transformation and is now one of Copenhagen's most vibrant areas. At its centre, Halmtorvet is a trendy café-filled square. Head to Istedgade for art and speciality shops.

Those in search of a quirky bargain should try the multi-cultural Nørrebro district, north of the city. Elmegade and Fælledvej are lined with secondhand stores, new Danish design and recycled goods. For secondhand jewellery try Ravnsborggade.

OPENING HOURS

It is not worth trying to shop in Denmark for anything other than foodstuffs before 10am. Early in the week most shops close at around 5:30pm, although many stores remain open on Fridays until 8 or 9pm. On Saturdays some shops close at 2pm, but the majority now stay open until 4 or 5pm. Department stores tend to have the longest opening hours. Most shops and shopping centres are closed on Sundays in Denmark; there are however several "trading Sundays" throughout the year.

A large shopping centre in Malmö, just across the road bridge in Sweden, has many shops open on Sunday.

HOW TO PAY

The country's currency is the Danish krone (Dkr). Some shops also accept the Swedish krone and the euro, although the rate of exchange applied in such cases may not be advantageous. A few of the smaller shops may expect payment in cash, however the vast majority of outlets accept credit cards. The prices quoted always include VAT and excise tax. Non-EU residents are entitled to a VAT refund *(see p286)*.

DEPARTMENT STORES AND SHOPPING CENTRES

Magasin du Nord was Scandinavia's first department store and is still a huge favourite. As well as clothes, cosmetics and luxury household goods it sells books, jewellery, delicious chocolate and foodstuffs. Also popular is the light and airy **Illum** on Strøget, which has several elegant floors selling high-quality goods under a glass dome, and the added advantage of a rooftop café.

Copenhagen has several shopping centres, with shops, cafés, restaurants, and cinemas under one roof. **Fisketorvet**, situated on the site of an old fish market facing the Sound, is arguably one of the best. It is also worth taking a trip out to **Fields**, the biggest shopping centre in Scandinavia with a total of 150 shops under one roof. Although a little way out of the city, it is conveniently situated at the Ørestad metro station.

DESIGN AND INTERIOR DECORATION

Denmark is justly famous for combining attractive design with functionality and quality materials. Most of its best-known brands have their own shops in the city centre. The **Bang & Olufsen** showroom has listening rooms where customers can appreciate the quality of its audio products. For a good selection of interior design under one roof, head for **Illums Bolighus**, which keeps an eye on tradition while displaying the latest trends in furnishing and lighting.

Winner of numerous awards for innovative design, **Normann Copenhagen** has converted an old cinema in Østerbro into a stunning showroom. As well as its own collection of kitchen accessories, here you can find a variety of contemporary lifestyle products and high-profile fashion brands from around the world – all in a truly unforgettable setting.

The **Louis Poulsen** showroom offers an array of designer lighting solutions set against a minimalist background, and young furniture designers display their talent for creating classics with a contemporary twist at **Hay**. Another sleek furniture store is **Paustian** in the dock area. Designed by architect Jørn Utzon, of Sydney Opera House fame, there is also a stylish restaurant.

Back in town, the interior design centre **Casa Shop** is well worth a look, as is the **Danish Design Centre (DDC)**, which hosts changing exhibitions showcasing Danish innovation. **Designer Zoo** is a working design store for eight Danish designers who create furniture, jewellery, knitwear and artistic glass. **Bolia** is a nationwide interior design store that celebrates Scandinavian traditions.

Interior of a shop selling Bodum kitchenware, a popular Danish product

Minimalist interior of leading fashion store Munthe plus Simonsen

CLOTHES AND ACCESSORIES

From high fashion to second-hand chic, Copenhagen has it all. Top international designers congregate at the Kongens Nytorv end of Strøget, while less expensive labels stretch down the street towards the town hall. Købmagergade is good for mid-price clothes whilst Kronprinsensgade, which runs off it, is known as "Copenhagen's Catwalk" for the cutting-edge clothes shops located here. Pioneering **Bruuns Bazaar** is a favourite, selling men's and women's modern designs.

The narrow streets of the Grønnegade quarter are lined with half-timbered buildings housing streetwear and classic labels from leading Danish designers. **Munthe plus Simonsen**, renowned for classy yet casual ladies-wear, is found here. Nearby on Pilestræde, **Designers Remix** have opened a large flagship store of their sexy, edgy womenswear. **Day Birger et Mikkelsen**, has also gathered all of their seven lines under one roof here: women's, men's and children's wear, lingerie, jewellery, accessories and home.

Secondhand chic lies in the "Pisserenden" area adjacent to Strøget. Check out **København K** and **Kitsch Bitch** for quality retro clothes. For vintage frocks and clever accessories, head to Nansensgade or try **Glam Vintage** in Silkegade 7. The collection of high-end 1960–70s glad rags is particularly pleasing.

JEWELLERY

Danish jewellery has a reputation for fine design and attention to detail. The city's most famous jewellery shop is silversmith **Georg Jensen**, but Julie Sandlau (stocked at **Magasin du Nord**), who creates pretty gold designs, is the name on many a celebrity's lips. For jewellery fit for Denmark's Queen, visit **Peter Hertz**. Amber washed up on Denmark's west coast makes its way into jewellery at **The Amber Specialist** and branches of **House of Amber**, which also has an amber museum. For jewellery based on Viking designs, take a look at **Museums Kopi Smykker**.

ROYAL SHOPPING

While historic royals have left their mark on Copenhagen's architecture, fans of today's very popular royal family like to follow in their footsteps to the shops. The Queen, a talented artist, book illustrator, and designer of ecclesiastical textiles and stage costumes, can often be seen shopping in the city centre while several family members frequent Copenhagen's two big department stores, **Illum** and **Magasin du Nord**.

Grand stores carrying the coveted words "Purveyors to her Majesty, the Queen of Denmark" cluster together on the Amagertorv section of Strøget – the great silversmith **Georg Jensen**, **Royal Copenhagen Porcelain**, which also boasts a charming tea room, **Holmegaard** glass and crystal, and **Illums Bolighus**, a shrine to modern design.

Crown Princess Mary is a fashion and style icon in Denmark. Among her favourite clothes designers are Julie Fagerholt at **Heart Made**, known for her subtle detailing, the sexy and sophisticated look of **By Malene Birger**, and the innovative yet classic lines of Baum und Pherdgarten, stocked at **Urban Factory**.

Should you wish to take home wine bottled on Prince Henrik's estate in France, visit **Kjaer & Sommerfeldt**.

MARKETS

Hours can be spent bargain hunting in Copenhagen's outdoor flea markets that pop up around the city between April or May and mid-October. Near Parliament in old Copenhagen, the flea market on **Gammel Strand** sells antiques, Danish design, posters, paintings and ceramics. It is particularly popular with its canalside setting and outdoor cafés. The markets on **Israels Plads** and in **Frederiksberg** tend to be cheaper, however.

In November, **Øksnehallen** hosts a deluxe indoor market at which more than 200 stands display designer clothes, lamps, furniture and homeware.

Flea market in one of Copenhagen's picturesque squares

ART AND ANTIQUES

Bredgade, in the financial district, and Ravnsborggade in Nørrebro are packed with antiques shops, bric-a-brac sellers and collectibles, especially modern Danish classics and funky retro designs. Come here for pieces by the great names in 20th-century Danish design, such as Arne Jacobsen, famed for his Egg, Ant and Swan chairs, Hans J Wegner, Kaare Klint and lighting by Poul Henningsen. For collectors of modern Danish classics, **Dansk Møbelkunst** and **Permanent Design** are essential browsing territory.

Great furniture and style from the 1950s, 1960s and 1970s can also be found at **Klassik**, while **Lysberg, Hansen & Terp** are popular for the timeless quality of their designs. Bredgade is also the home of the traditional art galleries and auction houses. Sotheby's have a house here as do the long-established Danish auction houses, such as **Bruun Rasmussen**. These offer a good potential source of finds in art, antiques, furniture and jewellery.

In vibrant Vesterbro, the side streets off Istedgade are the place to look for galleries displaying work by up-and-coming artists. The small streets in the Islands Brygge area are a hotbed of galleries specialising in experimental art. Off Strøget, Kompagnistræde is a quiet haven for collectors. Among the cluster of antiques shops there are specialists in porcelain and china, vintage watches and books, prints and comics. For the finest porcelain, silver and crystal, visit **Royal Copenhagen Antiques**.

SPECIALIST SHOPS

The array of individual and innovative little shops make strolling Copenhagen's streets a pleasure. They are also a great way to find gifts and souvenirs to take home from the city. Buy specialist teas in one of Europe's oldest teashops, **A.C. Perch's Thehandel**, which dates from 1834. Having retained its original interior, the shop and tearoom are a highlight on fashionable Kronprinsensgade. **Sømods Bolcher** is a lovely old-fashioned sweet shop where you can watch traditional treats being made in time-honoured fashion. For the finest foods, take a look at the delicious pastries at **Trianon**, the specialist breads at **Reinh van Hauen Bakery**, and explore Vaernedamsvej in Vesterbro, a great street for gourmets, with specialist cheese, wine, fish and chocolate shops, as well as cafés and grocers.

Buy a posy, or just soak up the colour and scent of **Bering Flowers**, who not only do the flowers for the Royal Theatre but royal weddings and other glitzy occasions too.

DIRECTORY

DEPARTMENT STORES AND SHOPPING CENTRES

Fields
Arne Jacobsens Allé 12.
Tel *70 20 85 05.*
www.fields.dk

Fisketorvet
Kalvebod Brygge 59.
Map 3 A5.
Tel *33 36 64 00.*

Illum
Østergade 52. **Map** 3 C1.
Tel *33 14 40 02.*

Magasin du Nord
Kogens Nytorv 13.
Map 4 D1.
Tel *33 11 44 33.*

DESIGN AND INTERIOR DECORATION

Bang & Olufsen
Kogens Nytorv 26.
Map 2 D5.
Tel *33 11 14 15.*

Bolia
Chr. IX gade 7.
Map 1 C5.
Tel *70 10 00 55.*

Casa Shop
Store Regnegade 2.
Map 1 C3.
Tel *33 32 70 41.*

Danish Design Centre
H.C. Andersens Blvd 27.
Map 3 B2.
Tel *33 69 33 69.*
www.ddc.dk

Designer Zoo
Vesterbrogade 137.
Tel *33 24 94 93.*
www.dzoo.dk

Hay
Pilestræde 29–31.
Map 3 C1.
Tel *99 42 44 00.*

Illums Bolighus
Amagertorv 10.
Map 3 C1.
Tel *33 14 19 41.*

Louis Poulsen
Gammel Strand 28.
Map 3 C1.
Tel *70 33 14 14.*

Normann Copenhagen
Østerbrogade 70.
Map 1 B1.
Tel *35 27 05 40.*

Paustian
Kalkbrænderiløbskaj 2.
Tel *39 16 65 65.*
www.paustian.dk

CLOTHES AND ACCESSORIES

Bruuns Bazaar
Kronprinsensgade 8–9.
Map 3 C1.
Tel *33 32 19 99.*

Day Birger et Mikkelsen
Pilestræde 16. **Map** 3 C1.
Tel *33 45 88 80.*

Designers Remix
Pilestræde 8D. **Map** 3 C1.
Tel *33 14 33 00.*

Glam Vintage
Silkegade 7. **Map** 3 C1.
Tel *35 38 50 41.*

Kitsch Bitch
Læderstræde 30.
Map 3 C1.
Tel *33 13 63 13.*

København K
Studiestræde 32B.
Map 3 A1.
Tel *33 33 08 89.*

Munthe plus Simonsen
Grønnegade 10.
Map 2 D5.
Tel *33 32 00 12.*

JEWELLERY

Georg Jensen
Amagertorv 4. **Map** 3 C1.
Tel *33 11 40 80.*

House of Amber
Kogens Nytorv 2.
Map 4 D1.
Tel *33 11 67 00.*

Magasin du Nord
(See Department Stores)

Museums Kopi Smykker
Grønnegade 6. **Map** 2 D5.
Tel *33 32 76 72.*

Peter Hertz
Købmagergade 34.
Map 3 C1.
Tel *33 12 22 16.*

The Amber Specialist
Frederiksberggade 28.
Map 3 B2.
Tel *33 11 88 03.*

ROYAL SHOPPING

By Malene Birger
Antonigade 10.
Map 3 C1.
Tel *35 43 22 33.*

Illum
(See Department Stores)

Illums Bolighus
(See Design and Interior Decoration)

Heart Made
Pilestræde 45.
Map 3 C1.
Tel *33 38 08 80.*

Holmegaard
Amagertorv 8.
Map 3 C1.
Tel *33 13 71 81.*

Kjaer & Sommerfeldt
Gammelmønt 4.
Map 1 C5.
Tel *33 93 34 44.*

Magasin du Nord
(See Department Stores)

Royal Copenhagen Porcelain
Amagertorv 6.
Map 3 C1.
Tel *33 13 71 81.*

Urban Factory
Ny Østergade 12.
Map 1 C5.
Tel *33 91 70 75.*

MARKETS

Frederiksberg Flea Market
Smallegade 1–3, Frederiksberg
(behind the town hall).
Apr–Oct: Sat

Gammel Strand Antique and Flea Market
Map 3 C1.
May–Sep: Fri–Sat

Israel Plads Flea Market
Map 1 A/B 5.
May–mid-Oct: Sat

Øksnehallen
Halmtorvet 11.
Tel *33 86 04 00.*
www.oeksnehallen.dk

ART AND ANTIQUES

Bruun Rasmussen
Bredgade 32.
Map 2 E5.
Tel *88 18 11 11.*

Dansk Møbelkunst
Bredgade 32.
Map 2 E5.
Tel *33 32 38 37.*

Klassik
Bredgade 3.
Map 2 D5.
Tel *33 33 90 60.*

Lysberg, Hansen & Terp
Bredgade 77.
Map 2 E4.
Tel *33 14 47 87.*

Permanent Design
St Kongensgade 32.
Map 2 D5.
Tel *21 72 01 12.*

Royal Copenhagen Antiques
Amagertorv 6.
Map 3 C1.
Tel *33 13 71 81.*

SPECIALIST SHOPS

A. C. Perch's Thehandel
Kronprinsensgade 5.
Map 3 C1.
Tel *33 15 35 62.*

Bering Flowers
Landemærket 12.
Map 1 C5.
Tel *33 15 26 11.*

Reinh van Hauen Bakery
Østergade 22.
Map 3 C1.
Tel *33 13 17 03.*

Sømods Bolcher
Nørregade 36B.
Map 1 B5.
Tel *33 12 60 46.*

Trianon
Hyskenstraede 8.
Map 3 C1.

ENTERTAINMENT IN COPENHAGEN

Copenhagen has a vibrant cultural life, from world-class opera and ballet staged at the magnificent Operaen, to jazz clubs and street performance. Nightclubs range from small café-style venues to major nightspots, where live bands and international DJs play the latest sounds, and the gay scene is one of Europe's best. Festivals come in all sizes, especially during the summer months when the city seems to breathe enjoyment. In July and August, locals make the most of the beaches, open-air swimming pools and sunbathing spots which open up along the harbour, including an urban beach on Amager island. Copenhagen is incredibly child-friendly and there is plenty to entertain young visitors, from the thrills and spills on offer at the ever-popular Tivoli amusment park to interactive fun at some of the country's top museums.

Roller-skating at Bakken

PRACTICAL INFORMATION

The first place to look for up-to-date information is the free magazine **Copenhagen This Week** (which despite its name comes out monthly) for the latest news on cultural events and club listings. It also has its own website: www.ctw.com.

BOOKING TICKETS

Tickets for theatre, opera, concerts, festivals and sport events can be booked through **Billetnet**, by phone, online, or at a post office. The **Royal Theatre/Opera Box Office** on Kongens Nytorv opens at 4pm for the sale of half-price tickets for that day's performances. Get there early to ensure yourself a ticket as queues can get long. Under-25s and over-65s are eligible for half-price tickets when booking for shows more than a week in advance.

Cinema tickets tend to be cheaper for matinee and weekday performances; these can be booked online at www.biobooking.dk.

OPERA AND CLASSICAL MUSIC

Opera fans should not miss a performance of the Royal Opera at the striking **Operaen** *(see p89)*, which also hosts regular classical music concerts. In early August, the Royal Opera presents a preview of the new season at a free open-air opera concert, held on grassy Fælledparken. Do not forget to take a picnic, as the locals do.

Tivoli Koncertsal was revamped in 2005, and those who enjoy classical music will be thrilled by concerts given here. Throughout the summer season, Danish and international conductors and soloists join the 80-strong Tivoli Symphony Orchestra for a varied programme of concerts. Be sure to check out the foyer of the Koncertsal; it has the added attraction of housing Europe's longest saltwater aquarium – home to sharks and around 1,600 fish! During the winter months, the orchestra becomes the Copenhagen Philharmonic and tours extensively.

For a less formal occasion, students from the Royal Danish Academy of Music give free Wednesday concerts during spring and autumn in various venues. See www.onsdagskoncerter.dk for details. Alternatively, classical concerts are performed upstairs every Monday at cosy **Kul Kafeen** café.

Tivoli Koncertsal, home to the Tivoli Symphony Orchestra

Ballet performance at Det Kongelige Teater

BALLET AND CONTEMPORARY DANCE

Det Kongelige Teater (The Royal Theatre) is home to the Royal Ballet, although theatre and some opera are also staged here. The season runs from August to June, finishing with a free open-air performance in the grounds of Kastellet *(see p54)*.

The main venue for contemporary dance is **Dansescenen**, a small theatre devoted to the best in Danish dance combined with guest performances from visiting international artists.

Dansk Danseteater focuses on daring experiments in choreography. It was founded in 1981 and is a leading contemporary dance company, attracting choreographers and dancers from around the world. The company presents a popular August festival Copenhagen Summerdance with free performances in the colonnaded courtyard of the

Copenhagen City Police headquarters. The **Copenhagen International Ballet Festival**, a celebration of choreography, takes place in August in Klampenborg, north of the city.

Jazz quintet playing at the Copenhagen Jazz House

JAZZ CLUBS AND LIVE MUSIC

International performers are regulars at the atmospheric **Copenhagen Jazz House**, and there is Monday Night Big Band Jazz at **Huset Magstræde**. Many city hotels and bars host their own jazz sessions – **La Fontaine** is a slightly seedy example, which has live jazz sessions every weekend. For blues fans, there is live music spanning blues, country, and folk at **Mojo Blues Bar** and the **Copenhagen Blues Festival** in late September every year.

In July, the **Copenhagen Jazz Festival** fills the streets and practically every available venue in the city. It attracts some of the world's finest jazz musicians, and most of the 800 or so performances are free.

For up-and-coming bands as well as international acts, **VEGA**, in the heart of Copenhagen's transformed Vesterbro district, is a popular, distinctly Scandinavian, venue. Housed in a 1950s trade union building it is divided into four main areas, with concert and club-night venues as well as lounge and bar with weekend DJs. For the best young indie bands, check out **Loppen** where Franz Ferdinand and Interpol played long before they hit the big time.

Last but by no means least is **Tivoli** *(see pp76–7)* where on summer nights, world-famous rock and pop acts perform on the open-air stage. Elsewhere, throughout the gardens, thousands of coloured lights illuminate the fountains. Entrance is free with general Tivoli admittance. In winter, musicals are staged when Tivoli opens for the Christmas season.

NIGHTLIFE VENUES

As Copenhagen's clubs only start getting lively after midnight, many clubbers head first to a pre-club bar, such as the trendy **Zoo Bar** or the Ideal Bar at **VEGA**. **Rust**, in the vibrant Nørrebro district, attracts top international DJs and up-and-coming bands. Indie rock and hip hop dominate the live music, while in the basement DJs play indie, punk and electro. In a former courthouse off Strøget, **The Rock** turns into a rock nightclub after a live show. **Culture Box** is a purist techno club. To hangout with the beautiful people, head to chic and exclusive **Nasa**, where house or retro soul is played.

Advertising pillar in Copenhagen

Wallmans Salonger offers something completely different – a seated dinner show where artists perform on different stages around the restaurant. Later, this former circus building turns itself into Copenhagen's biggest club.

Space age bar of intimate nightclub, Nasa

THEATRE

Although the grand old **Det Kongelige Teater** still hosts a variety of mainstream performances, most drama by the Royal and Danish Theatre is now staged in two new adjacent venues: the **Turbine Hallerne** and **Stærekassen**. As its name suggests, the former has been imaginatively converted from the city's old power station and supports the production of new Danish drama. The latest addition, **Stærekassen**, is in an Art Deco building abutting Det Kongelige Teater. With two stages, a restaurant and wonderful views out over the waterfront, this is an exciting home for Danish theatre.

In the centre, **Plex Musikteater** is a lively venue for experimental musical theatre and interactive performance art.

CINEMA

There are more than 60 cinemas in and around Copenhagen, ranging from art-house cinemas to huge multiplexes. Most films are shown in their original language version, with Danish subtitles.

To catch the latest blockbusters, the big **Cinemaxx**, which is part of the Fisketorvet shopping centre down by the harbour, screens all the major releases in its luxuriously spacious cinemas. **Metropol** is another "big screen" cinema, while, with its candlelit lounge entrance, **Empire Bio** in the Nørrebro district is a cinema with a lot of style.

To get away from the mainstream, the long established **Grand Teatret**, with its repertoire of European films, and **Cinemateket**, which is attached to the Danish Film Institute, are traditional art-house cinemas. For off-circuit and low-budget films try **Vester Vov Vov** in the Vesterbro district, which has a good bar for post-film drinks.

GAY AND LESBIAN

Copenhagen is a city with a long tradition of openness and acceptance: the city's first gay bar, **Centralhjørnet**, opened more than 80 years ago and is still going strong. Famed for its Annual Gay Pride Parade, known as "Copenhagen Pride", in August, and the long-running Gay and Lesbian Film Festival in October, the city has a stream of other events year-round, including the St Hans Midsummer Bonfire and beach party on Amager island in June, organized by the **National Gay and Lesbian Organisation (LBL)**.

The city centre gay club, bar and restaurant scene is concentrated in quite a small area, so everything is pretty much within walking distance. **Be Proud** is Copenhagen's biggest gay club, featuring a lounge area and a smoking section. As well as the occasional live event, the club offers popular music on Fridays and experimental sounds on Saturdays. **Jailhouse** is a popular concept bar and restaurant with booths kitted out as prison cells and staff dressed in police uniforms. On Friday evenings, DJs and a good atmosphere are available at the lounge-style **Oscar Bar & Café**. Young gay men favour **Masken Bar**, where the shows span live music and drag. **Mens Bar** is for the leather-clad contingent. For the really late night scene, head on to the aptly named **Never Mind Bar**, open every day until 6am.

Chaca, a bar and café on two floors, is the lesbian meeting place of choice. For up-to-date listings on women's gay parties and clubbing, see the website www.ziraf.dk.

Tables on the pavement outside the Oscar Bar and Café

BEACHES

Clean and spacious harbour swimming pools, with beaches and sports activities, are a great summer feature and only a short walk from the centre of Copenhagen. The harbour area is being revitalised with apartments, hotels and restaurants and the water really is clean enough for swimming. The pools are open from June until early September.

Havnebadet, just across the ramparts from Christianshavn at Islands Brygge, has five pools and a large grassy bathing "beach". The smaller **Copencabana** pool is by the Fisketorvet shopping centre and comes complete with sand beach and palm trees.

Further afield, the north end of **Bellevue Strand**, at Klampenborg, is a short train or bike ride from town. It's a gay-friendly place with a nudist area. **Amager Strandpark** *(see pp96–7)* on Amager island is divided into two parts: an "urban" beach with a range of fitness activities, bars, food stalls, even a Bedouin tent; and a "wild" section with wide sandy beaches and small sand dunes. A lagoon between the island and the mainland has child-friendly shallow water.

CHILDREN'S ENTERTAINMENT

No child visiting Copenhagen should miss **Tivoli** amusement park *(see pp76–7)*, which has enough rides, slides and attractions to keep even the most demanding young person happy. **Bakken** *(see p120)* in a wooded area north of the city near Klampenborg, claims to be the oldest fun park in the world and has more than 100 rides. **Zoologisk Have** *(see pp92–3)* is the city's zoo, with more than 2,000 animals, mainly outdoors. It has a mini-zoo for toddlers, pet animals to cuddle, and, in Rabbit Town, youngsters can crawl into an over-sized "warren" to experience life as a rabbit.

Miniature classic car ride in Tivoli Gardens

Several interesting museums in or near Strøget are suitable for children, including **Ripley's Believe It or Not!** *(see p73)*, **Hans Christian Andersen's Wonderful World** and **Guinness World Records Museum** *(see p69)*. There is also the **Experimentarium** *(see pp94–5)*, a science-based museum with plenty of hands-on fun; and for the star-struck, the **Tycho Brahe Planetarium** *(see p92)* has a dazzling IMAX Space Theatre. The Children's Art Museum at the **Statens Museum for Kunst** (Danish National Gallery, *see pp62–3)* exhibits original art at a child's-eye level and holds workshops.

For outdoor fun, children enjoy riding on the harbour boats that are part of the city's excellent public transportation system, going on canal cruises to see the **Little Mermaid** *(see p54)*, and watching the midday Changing of the Guard at the **Amalienborg Palace** *(see pp56–7)*, to the sounds of the the Royal Guard band on those days that the Queen is in residence.

Copenhagen is a city full of parks with public play and sports facilities. Free puppet shows take place during school holidays in **Kongens Have** (The King's Garden, *see p58*), a lovely green space with a children's playground that surrounds the fairytale Rosenborg Palace. The harbour **swimming pools** *(see Beaches)* also have slides and areas reserved for kids.

DIRECTORY

BOOKING TICKETS

Billetnet
Tel 70 15 65 65.
www.billetnet.dk

Royal Theatre/ Opera Box Office
Kongens Nytorv.
Map 4 D1.
www.kglteater.dk

OPERA AND CLASSICAL MUSIC

Kul Kafeen
Teglgårdstræde 5.
Map 3 A1.
Tel 33 32 17 77.

Operaen
Ekvipagemestervej 10.
Map 2 F5.
Tel 33 69 69 69.
www.operahus.dk

Tivoli Koncertsal
Vesterbrogade 3.
Map 3 A2.
Tel 33 15 10 12.
www.tivoli.dk

BALLET AND CONTEMPORARY DANCE

Copenhagen International Ballet Festival
www.copenhageninternationalballet.com

Dansescenen
Pasteursvej 24, 1.
Tel 33 29 10 10.
www.dansescenen.dk

Dansk Danseteater
www.danskdanseteater.dk
www.copenhagensummerdance.dk

Det Kongelige Teater
Kongens Nytorv.
Map 4 D1.
Tel 33 69 69 69.
www.kgl-teater.dk

JAZZ CLUBS AND LIVE MUSIC

Copenhagen Blues Festival
www.copenhagenbluesfestival.dk

Copenhagen Jazz Festival
www.jazzfestival.dk

Copenhagen Jazz House
Niels Hemmingsensgade 10.
Map 3 C1.
Tel 33 15 26 00.
www.jazzhouse.dk

Huset Magstræde
Rådhusstræde 13.
Map 3 B2.
Tel 33 69 32 00.
www.husetmagstræde.dk

La Fontaine
Kompagnistræde 11.
Map 3 C1.
Tel 33 11 60 98.

Loppen
Bådsmandsstræde 43, Christianshavn. **Map** 4 E2.
Tel 32 57 84 22.
www.loppen.dk

Mojo Blues Bar
Løngangstræede 21. **Map** 3 B2. *Tel 33 11 64 53.*
www.mojo.dk

Tivoli
(See Opera and Classical Music)

VEGA
Enghavevej 40.
Tel 33 25 70 11.
www.vega.dk

NIGHTLIFE VENUES

Culture Box
Kronprinsensgade 54.
Map 1 C5.
Tel 33 32 50 50.
www.culture-box.com

Nasa
Gothersgade 8F. **Map** 2 D5. *Tel 33 93 74 15.*
www.nasa.dk

Rust
Guldbergsgade 8.
Tel 35 24 52 00.
www.rust.dk

The Rock
Skindergade 45. **Map** 3 B1. *Tel 33 91 39 13.*

VEGA
(See Jazz Clubs and Live Music)

Wallmans Salonger
Cirkusbygningen, Jernbanegade 8.
Map 3 A2.
Tel 33 16 37 00.
www.wallmans.com

Zoo Bar
Kronprinsensgade 7.
Map 3 C1.
Tel 33 15 68 69.
www.zoobar.dk

THEATRE

Det Konglige Teater
(See Ballet and Contemporary Dance)

Plex Musikteater
Kronprinsensgade 7.
Map 3 C1. *Tel 33 32 38 30.*
www.plex-musikteater.dk

Staerekassen
August Bournonvilles Passage 5. **Map** 4 D1.
Tel 33 69 69 69.
www.kglteater.dk

Turbine Hallerne
Adelgade 10. **Map** 4 D1.
Tel 33 69 69 69.
www.kglteater.dk

CINEMAS

Cinemateket
Gothersgade 55.
Map 1 C5. *Tel 33 74 34 12.*
www.dfi.ck

Cinemaxx
Kalvebod Brygge 59.
Map 3 A5.
Tel 70 10 12 02.

Empire Bio
Guldbergsgade 29F.
Tel 35 36 00 36.
www.empirebio.dk

Grand Teatret
Mikkel Bryggersgade 8.
Map 3 B2. *Tel 33 15 16 11.*
www.grandteatret.dk

Metropol
Vestergade 16.
Map 3 A2.
www.biobooking.dk

Vester Vov Vov
Absalonsgade 5.
Tel 33 24 42 00.
www.vestervovvov.dk

GAY AND LESBIAN

Be Proud
Jernbanegade 9.
Map 3 A2.
www.beproud.dk

Centralhjørnet
Kattesundet 18. **Map** 3 B2.
Tel 33 11 85 49.
www.centralhjornet.dk

Chaca
Studiestræde 39.
Map 3 A1.
Tel 31 67 46 55.
www.chaca.dk

Jailhouse
Studiestræde 12.
Map 3 B1.
Tel 33 15 22 55.
www.jailhousecph.dk

Masken Bar
Studiestræde 33.
Map 3 A1.
Tel 33 91 09 37.
www.maskenbar.dk

Mens Bar
Teglgårdsstræde 3.
Map 3 A1.
Tel 33 12 73 03.
www.mensbar.dk

National Gay and Lesbian Organisation (LBL)
Nygade 7.
Map 3 B1.
Tel 33 13 19 48.
www.lbl.dk

Never Mind Bar
Nørre Voldgade 2.
Map 3 A1.
www.nevermindbar.dk

Oscar Bar & Café
Rådhuspladsen 77.
Map 3 B2.
Tel 33 12 09 99.
www.oscarbarcafe.dk

BEACHES

Bellevue Strand
Strandvejen 340, Klampenborg.

Copencabana
Kalvebod Brygge.
Map 3 A5.

Havnebadet
Islands Brygge. **Map** 3 C3.

CHILDREN'S ENTERTAINMENT

Hans Christian Andersen's Wonderful World
Radhuspladsen 57.
Tel 33 32 31 31.
www.topattractions.dk

STREET FINDER

The map references given for all of Copenhagen's sights, hotels, restaurants, bars, shops and entertainment venues included in this guide refer to the maps in this section. All major sights, famous historic buildings, museums, galleries, railway, bus, metro and suburban train stations have been marked on the map. Other features are indicated by symbols explained in the key below. The names of streets and squares contained on the map are given in Danish. The word *gade* translates as street; *plads* means square, *allé* translates as avenue and *have* means park or garden.

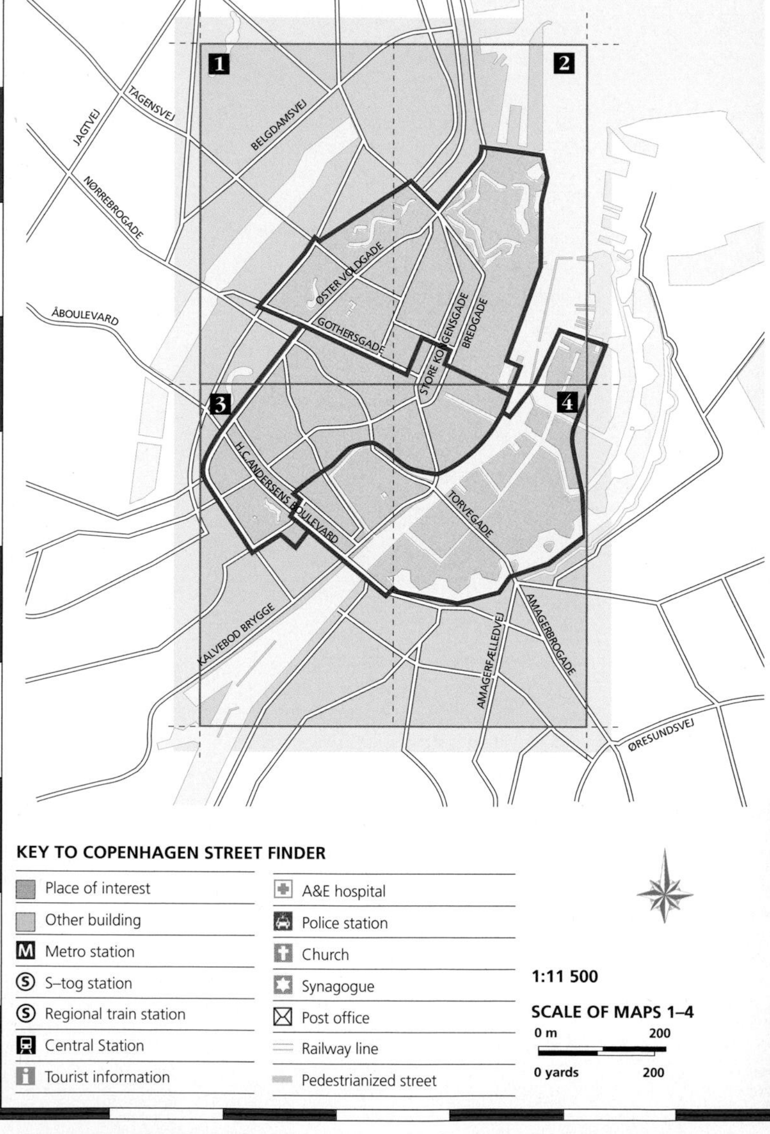

KEY TO COPENHAGEN STREET FINDER

- Place of interest
- Other building
- Metro station
- S–tog station
- Regional train station
- Central Station
- Tourist information
- A&E hospital
- Police station
- Church
- Synagogue
- Post office
- Railway line
- Pedestrianized street

1:11 500

SCALE OF MAPS 1–4

0 m 200

0 yards 200

For additional map symbols *see back flap*

Street Finder Index

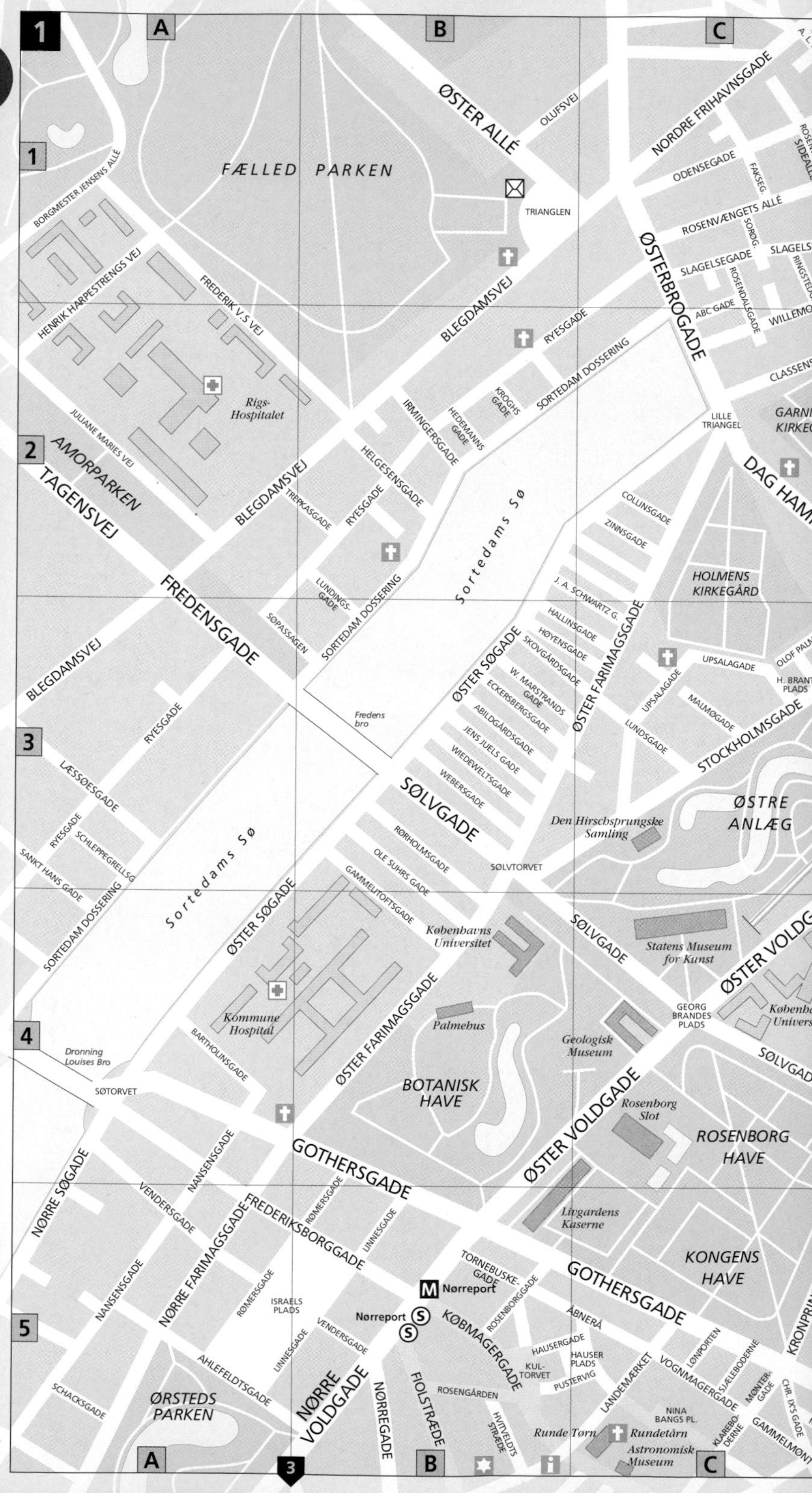
1
A
B
C
FÆLLED PARKEN
ØSTER ALLÉ
OLUFSVEJ
NORDRE FRIHAVNSGADE
ODENSEGADE
FAKSEG.
ROSENVÆNGETS ALLÉ
TRIANGLEN
ØSTERBROGADE
SORØG.
SLAGELSEGADE
ROSENDALSGADE
ABC GADE
BORGMESTER JENSENS ALLÉ
HENRIK HARPESTRENGS VEJ
FREDERIK V.S VEJ
BLEGDAMSVEJ
RYESGADE
SORTEDAM DOSSERING
Rigs-Hospitalet
IRMINGERSGADE
HEDEMANNS GADE
KROGHS GADE
LILLE TRIANGEL
2
JULIANE MARIES VEJ
AMORPARKEN
TAGENSVEJ
HELGESENSGADE
TREPKASGADE
RYESGADE
Sortedams Sø
COLLINSGADE
ZINNSGADE
HOLMENS KIRKEGÅRD
FREDENSGADE
LUNDINGS-GADE
SØPASSAGEN
SORTEDAM DOSSERING
J. A. SCHWARTZ G.
HALLINSGADE
HØYENSGADE
SKOVGÅRDSGADE
W. MARSTRANDS GADE
ECKERSBERGSGADE
ABILDGÅRDSGADE
JENS JUELS GADE
WIEDEWELTSGADE
WEBERSGADE
ØSTER SØGADE
ØSTER FARIMAGSGADE
UPSALAGADE
LUNDSGADE
MALMØGADE
STOCKHOLMSGADE
BLEGDAMSVEJ
Fredens bro
3
RYESGADE
LÆSSØESGADE
SØLVGADE
ØSTRE ANLÆG
Den Hirschsprungske Samling
RØRHOLMSGADE
OLE SUHRS GADE
GAMMELTOFTSGADE
SØLVTORVET
RYESGADE
SCHLEPPEGRELLSG
SANKT HANS GADE
Sortedams Sø
SORTEDAM DOSSERING
ØSTER SØGADE
Københavns Universitet
SØLVGADE
Statens Museum for Kunst
GEORG BRANDES PLADS
ØSTER FARIMAGSGADE
Palmehus
Kommune Hospital
BARTHOLINSGADE
Geologisk Museum
4
Dronning Louises Bro
SØTORVET
BOTANISK HAVE
ØSTER VOLDGADE
Rosenborg Slot
ROSENBORG HAVE
GOTHERSGADE
NANSENSGADE
NØRRE SØGADE
VENDERSGADE
NØRRE FARIMAGSGADE
FREDERIKSBORGGADE
RØMERSGADE
LINNESGADE
Livgardens Kaserne
KONGENS HAVE
TORNEBUSKE-GADE
GOTHERSGADE
Nørreport
NANSENSGADE
RØMERSGADE
ISRAELS PLADS
Nørreport
KØBMAGERGADE
ROSENBORGGADE
ÅBENRÅ
5
HAUSERGADE
HAUSER PLADS
KUL-TORVET
PUSTERVIG
VENDERSGADE
LINNESGADE
LANDEMÆRKET
VOGNMAGERGADE
LØNPORTEN
SJÆLEBODERNE
MØNTER-GADE
CHR. IX'S GADE
AHLEFELDTSGADE
SCHACKSGADE
ØRSTEDS PARKEN
NØRRE VOLDGADE
NØRREGADE
FIOLSTRÆDE
ROSENGÅRDEN
HVITVELDTS STRÆDE
NINA BANGS PL.
KLAREBO-DERNE
GAMMELMØNT
Runde Tårn
Rundetårn
Astronomisk Museum
A
3
B
C

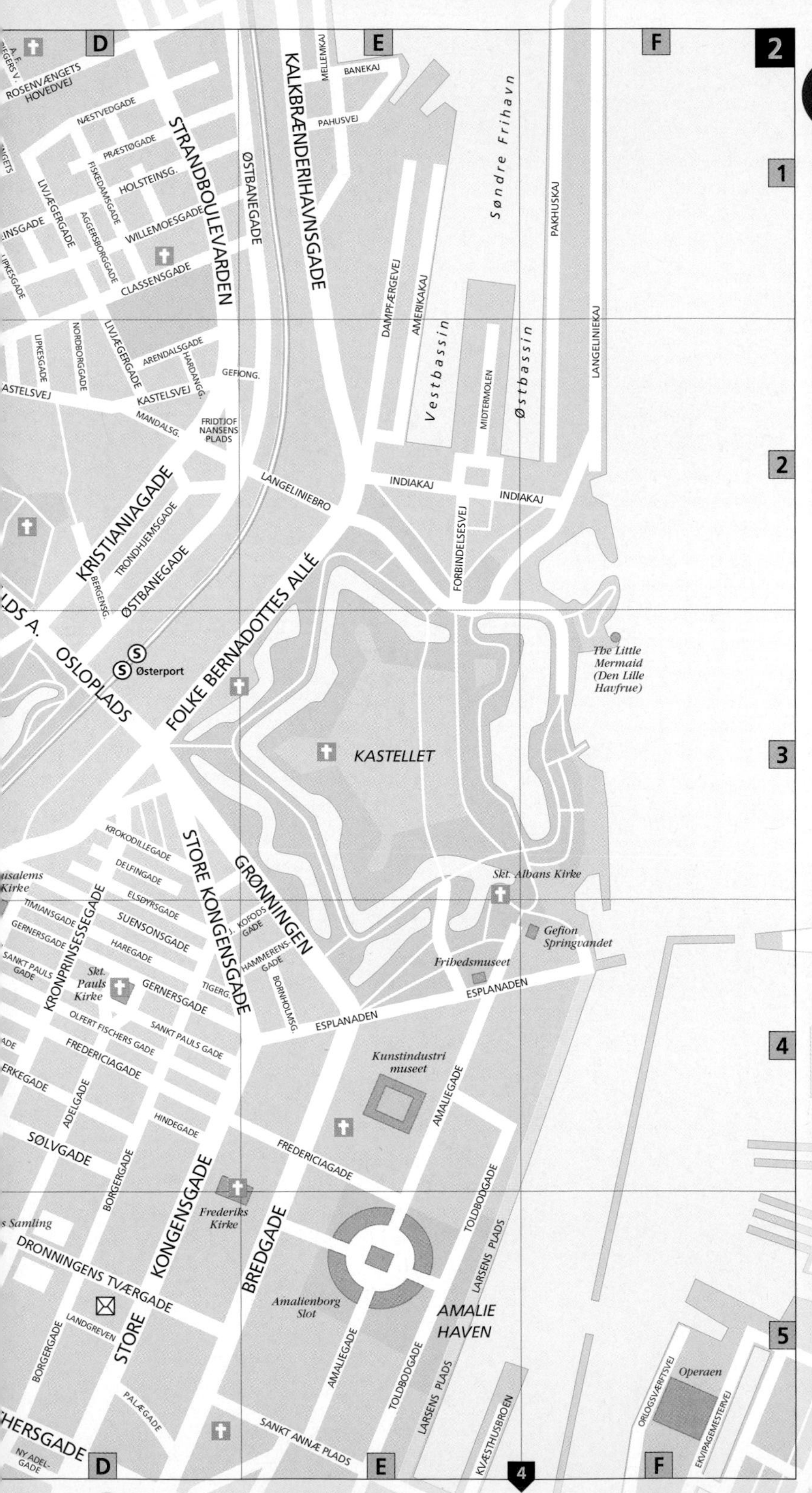
D
E
F
2
1
2
3
4
5
ROSENVÆNGETS HOVEDVEJ
NÆSTVEDGADE
PRÆSTØGADE
HOLSTEINSG.
FISKEDAMSGADE
LIVJÆGERGADE
AGGERSBORGGADE
WILLEMOESGADE
CLASSENSGADE
STRANDBOULEVARDEN
ØSTBANEGADE
KALKBRÆNDERIHAVNSGADE
MELLEMKAJ
BANEKAJ
PAHUSVEJ
Søndre Frihavn
PAKHUSKAJ
DAMPFÆRGEVEJ
AMERIKAKAJ
Vestbassin
MIDTERMOLEN
Østbassin
LANGELINIEKAJ
LIPKESGADE
NORDBORGGADE
ARENDALSGADE
HARDANGG.
GEFIONG.
KASTELSVEJ
MANDALSG.
FRIDTJOF NANSENS PLADS
LANGELINIEBRO
INDIAKAJ
INDIAKAJ
FORBINDELSESVEJ
KRISTIANIAGADE
TRONDHJEMSGADE
BERGENSG.
ØSTBANEGADE
FOLKE BERNADOTTES ALLÉ
OSLOPLADS
Østerport
The Little Mermaid (Den Lille Havfrue)
KASTELLET
KROKODILLEGADE
DELFINGADE
ELSDYRSGADE
SUENSONSGADE
HAREGADE
STORE KONGENSGADE
GRØNNINGEN
J. KOFODS GADE
HAMMERENS-GADE
BORNHOLMSG.
TIGERG.
Skt. Albans Kirke
Gefion Springvandet
Fribedsmuseet
ESPLANADEN
ESPLANADEN
TIMIANSGADE
GERNERSGADE
SANKT PAULS GADE
KRONPRINSESSEGADE
Skt. Pauls Kirke
GERNERSGADE
OLFERT FISCHERS GADE
SANKT PAULS GADE
FREDERICIAGADE
Kunstindustri museet
AMALIEGADE
ADELGADE
HINDEGADE
SØLVGADE
FREDERICIAGADE
BORGERGADE
TOLDBODGADE
Frederiks Kirke
KONGENSGADE
BREDGADE
LARSENS PLADS
DRONNINGENS TVÆRGADE
Amalienborg Slot
AMALIE HAVEN
LANDGREVEN
STORE
BORGERGADE
AMALIEGADE
TOLDBODGADE
LARSENS PLADS
Operaen
ORLOGSVÆRFTSVEJ
EKVIPAGEMESTERVEJ
PALÆGADE
SANKT ANNÆ PLADS
KVÆSTHUSBROEN
NY ADEL-GADE
4

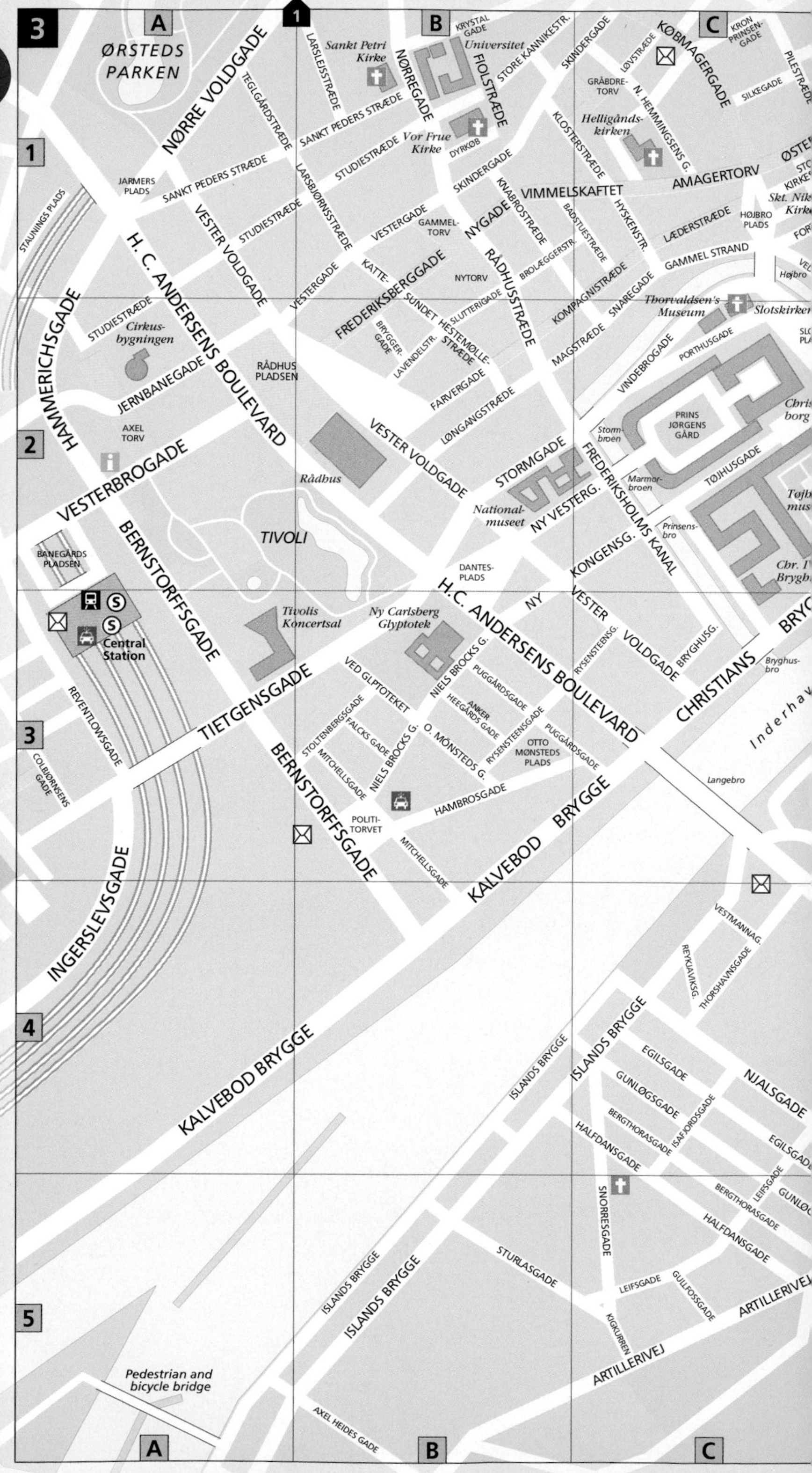
3
A
B
C
1
2
3
4
5
ØRSTEDS PARKEN
NØRRE VOLDGADE
TEGLGÅRDSTRÆDE
LARSLEJSSTRÆDE
Sankt Petri Kirke
NØRREGADE
Universitet
FIOLSTRÆDE
KRYSTAL GADE
STORE KANNIKESTR.
SKINDERGADE
LØVSTRÆDE
KØBMAGERGADE
KRON PRINSEN-GADE
PILESTRÆDE
SILKEGADE
GRÅBRØDRE-TORV
N. HEMMINGSENS G.
Helligånds-kirken
KLOSTERSTRÆDE
SANKT PEDERS STRÆDE
STUDIESTRÆDE
Vor Frue Kirke
DYRKØB
JARMERS PLADS
STAUNINGS PLADS
LARSBJØRNSSTRÆDE
SKINDERGADE
KNABROSTRÆDE
VIMMELSKAFTET
AMAGERTORV
ØSTER
Skt. Nik Kirke
HØJBRO PLADS
LÆDERSTRÆDE
HYSKENSTR.
BADSTUESTRÆDE
GAMMEL STRAND
H. C. ANDERSENS BOULEVARD
VESTER VOLDGADE
VESTERGADE
GAMMEL-TORV
NYGADE
RÅDHUSSTRÆDE
BROLÆGGERSTR.
KOMPAGNISTRÆDE
SNAREGADE
Højbro
KATTE-SUNDET
FREDERIKSBERGGADE
NYTORV
SLUTTERIGADE
HESTEMØLLE-STRÆDE
Thorvaldsen's Museum
Slotskirken
HAMMERICHSGADE
STUDIESTRÆDE
Cirkus-bygningen
JERNBANEGADE
RÅDHUS PLADSEN
BRYGGER-GADE
LAVENDELSTR.
FARVERGADE
MAGSTRÆDE
VINDEBROGADE
PORTHUSGADE
LØNGANGSTRÆDE
PRINS JØRGENS GÅRD
Stormbroen
Chris borg
AXEL TORV
VESTERBROGADE
VESTER VOLDGADE
Rådhus
STORMGADE
FREDERIKSHOLMS KANAL
TØJHUSGADE
Marmor-broen
National-museet
NY VESTERG.
Tøjh mus
TIVOLI
Prinsens-bro
BANEGÅRDS PLADSEN
BERNSTORFFSGADE
DANTES-PLADS
KONGENSG.
Chr. I Brygh
H.C. ANDERSENS BOULEVARD
NY
VESTER
VOLDGADE
Central Station
Tivolis Koncertsal
Ny Carlsberg Glyptotek
NIELS BROCKS G.
RYSENSTEENSG.
BRYGHUSG.
BRYG
Bryghus-bro
CHRISTIANS
Inderhav
VED GLPTOTEKET
PUGGÅRDSGADE
ANKER HEEGÅRDS GADE
TIETGENSGADE
REVENTLOWSGADE
STOLTENBERGSGADE
FALCKS GADE
MITCHELLSGADE
NIELS BROCKS G.
O. MÖNSTEDS G.
RYSENSTEENSGADE
OTTO MØNSTEDS PLADS
PUGGÅRDSGADE
COLBJØRNSENS GADE
BERNSTORFFSGADE
HAMBROSGADE
KALVEBOD BRYGGE
Langebro
POLITI-TORVET
MITCHELLSGADE
INGERSLEVSGADE
VESTMANNAG.
REYKJAVIKSG.
THORSHAVNSGADE
KALVEBOD BRYGGE
ISLANDS BRYGGE
ISLANDS BRYGGE
EGILSGADE
NJALSGADE
GUNLØGSGADE
BERGTHORASGADE
ISAFJORDSGADE
HALFDANSGADE
EGILSGADE
LEIFSGADE
GUNLØ
BERGTHORASGADE
SNORRESGADE
HALFDANSGADE
STURLASGADE
ISLANDS BRYGGE
ISLANDS BRYGGE
LEIFSGADE
GULLFOSSGADE
ARTILLERIVEJ
KIGKURREN
ARTILLERIVEJ
Pedestrian and bicycle bridge
AXEL HEIDES GADE

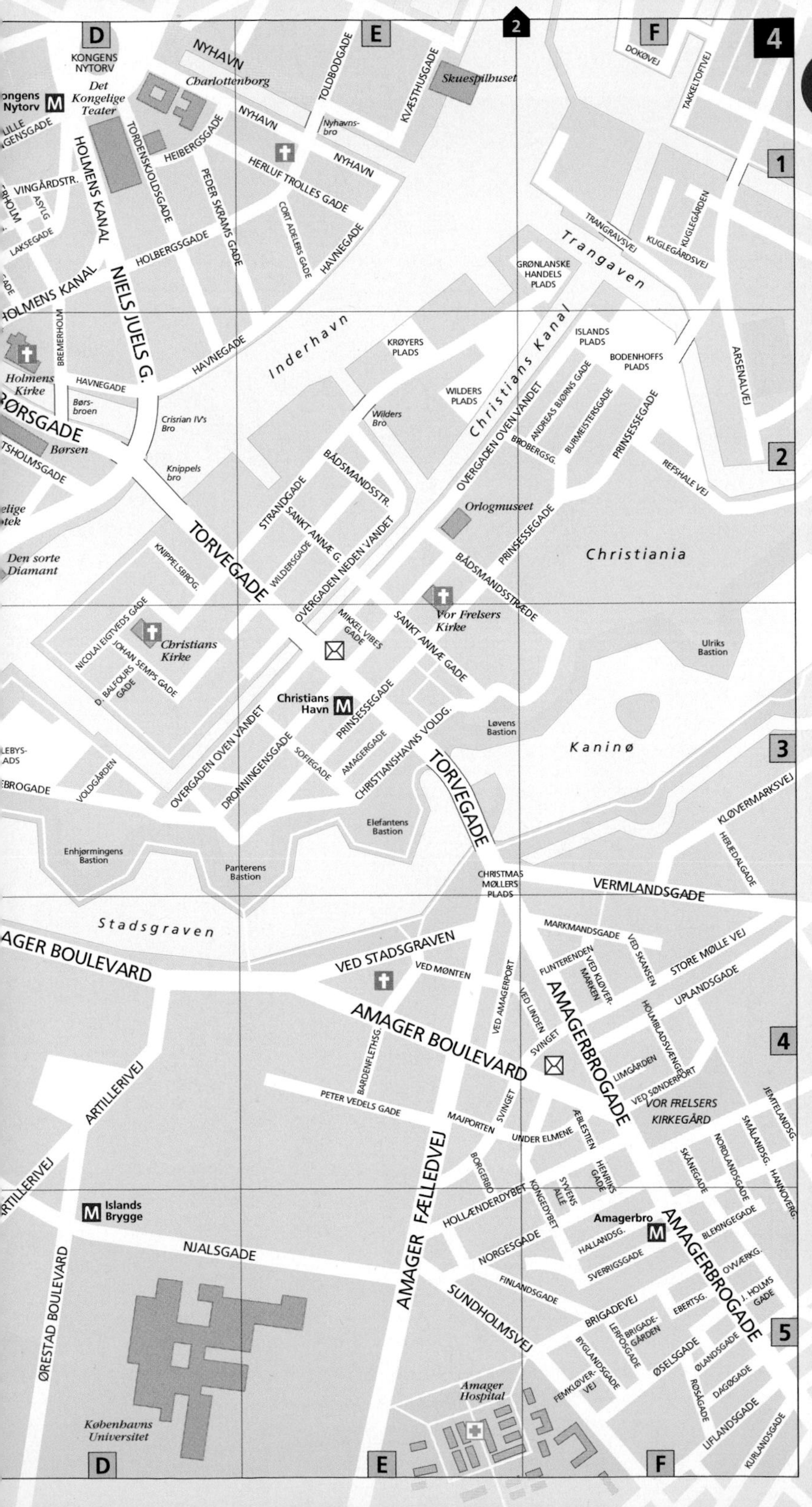

D
E
F
4
1
2
3
4
5
KONGENS NYTORV
Kongens Nytorv
Det Kongelige Teater
NYHAVN
Charlottenborg
TOLDBODGADE
KVÆSTHUSGADE
Skuespilbuset
DOKØVEJ
TAKKELTOFTVEJ
Nyhavns-bro
HEIBERGSGADE
TORDENSKJOLDSGADE
HERLUF TROLLES GADE
HOLMENS KANAL
VINGÅRDSTR.
LAKSEGADE
PEDER SKRAMS GADE
CORT ADELERS GADE
HAVNEGADE
HOLBERGSGADE
NIELS JUELS G.
TRANGRAVSVEJ
KUGLEGÅRDEN
KUGLEGÅRDSVEJ
Trangaven
GRØNLANSKE HANDELS PLADS
ISLANDS PLADS
BODENHOFFS PLADS
ARSENALVEJ
Inderhavn
KRØYERS PLADS
BREMERHOLM
Holmens Kirke
Børs-broen
BØRSGADE
Børsen
Crisrian IV's Bro
Knippels bro
Wilders Bro
WILDERS PLADS
Christians Kanal
ANDREAS BJØRNS GADE
BURMEISTERSGADE
PRINSESSEGADE
BROBERGSG.
OVERGADEN OVEN VANDET
REFSHALE VEJ
BÅDSMANDSSTR.
STRANDGADE
SANKT ANNÆ G.
Orlogmuseet
TORVEGADE
WILDERSGADE
OVERGADEN NEDEN VANDET
BÅDSMANDSSTRÆDE
Christiania
Den sorte Diamant
KNIPPELSBROG.
Vor Frelsers Kirke
NICOLAI EIGTVEDS GADE
JOHAN SEMPS GADE
D. BALFOURS GADE
Christians Kirke
MIKKEL VIBES GADE
SANKT ANNÆ GADE
Ulriks Bastion
Christians Havn
Løvens Bastion
Kaninø
VOLDGÅRDEN
DRONNINGENSGADE
SOFIEGADE
AMAGERGADE
CHRISTIANSHAVNS VOLDG.
KLØVERMARKSVEJ
HERJEDALGADE
Elefantens Bastion
Enhjørmingens Bastion
Panterens Bastion
CHRISTMAS MØLLERS PLADS
VERMLANDSGADE
Stadsgraven
AMAGER BOULEVARD
MARKMANDSGADE
VED SKANSEN
STORE MØLLE VEJ
VED STADSGRAVEN
VED MØNTEN
FLINTERENDEN
VED KLØVERMARKEN
UPLANDSGADE
VED AMAGERPORT
VED LINDEN
AMAGERBROGADE
HOLMBLADSVÆNGE
SVINGET
LIMGÅRDEN
VED SØNDERPORT
ARTILLERIVEJ
BARDENFLETHSG.
PETER VEDELS GADE
MAJPORTEN
UNDER ELMENE
ÆBLESTIEN
VOR FRELSERS KIRKEGÅRD
JEMTELANDSG.
SMÅLANDSG.
NORDLANDSGADE
SKÅNEGADE
HANNOVERG.
AMAGER FÆLLEDVEJ
BORGERBO
HOLLÆNDERDYBET
KONGEDYBET
SYVENS ALLÉ
HENRIKS GADE
Islands Brygge
Amagerbro
BLEKINGEGADE
NJALSGADE
NORGESGADE
HALLANDSG.
SVERRIGSGADE
ØRESTAD BOULEVARD
FINLANDSGADE
ØVÆRKG.
J. HOLMS GADE
SUNDHOLMSVEJ
BRIGADEVEJ
EBERTSG.
LERFOSGADE
BRIGADE-GÅRDEN
ØLANDSGADE
BYGLANDSGADE
ØSELSGADE
FEMKLØVER-VEJ
RØSÅGADE
DAGØGADE
Amager Hospital
LIFLANDSGADE
KURLANDSGADE
Københavns Universitet

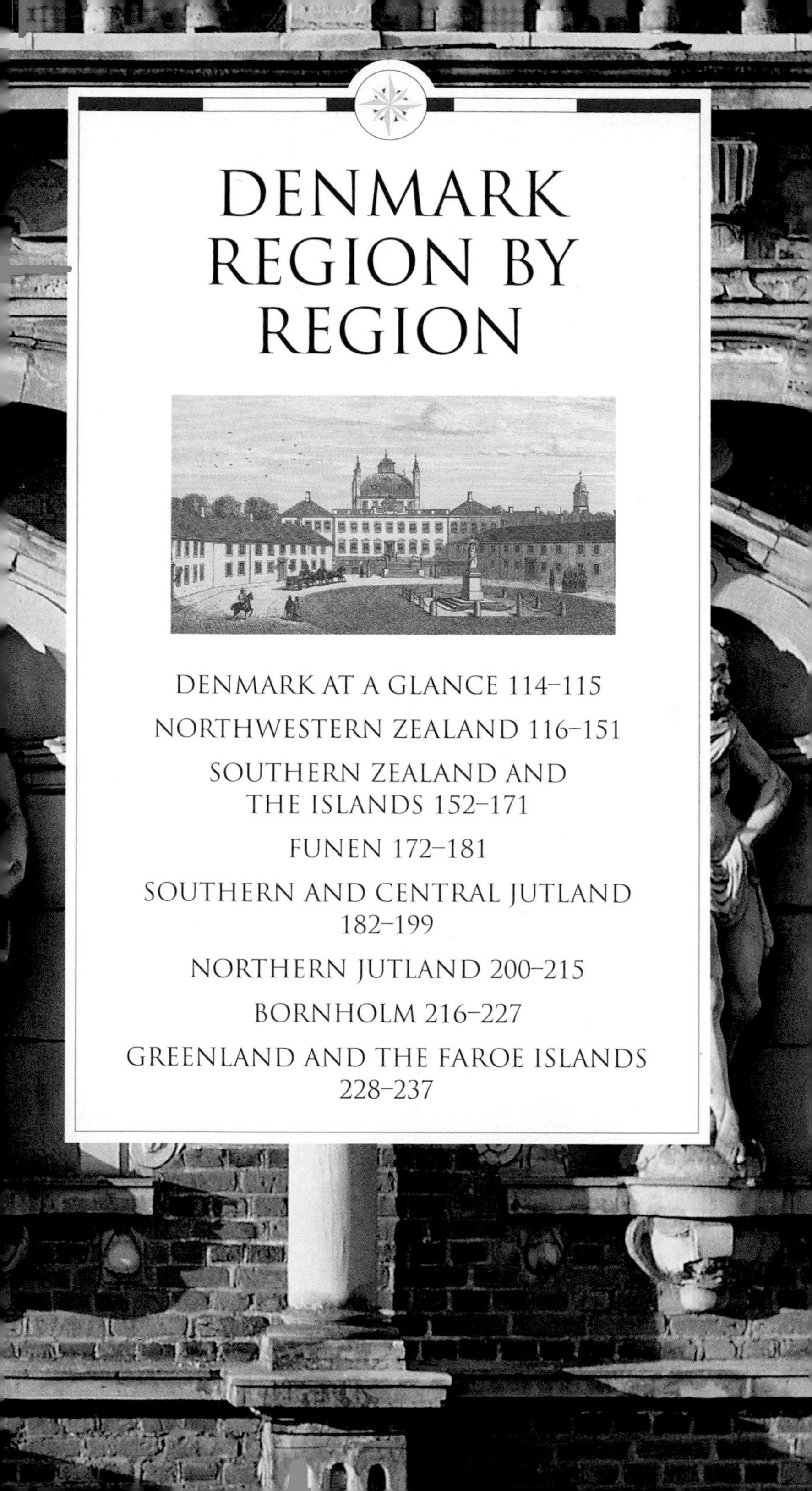

DENMARK REGION BY REGION

Denmark at a Glance

Denmark has a host of attractions for visitors. Small rural farms, rolling fields of wheat, lush woodlands and fine beaches are just some of the things that make the country especially popular with nature lovers. Those favouring outdoor activities will enjoy the many trails and cycle routes. Many of these are themed and are designed to take in some of the country's best historic churches, castles and palaces. For sightseers, there are Neolithic ruins, Viking remains and medieval villages to explore, while the various delights on offer at amusement parks such as Bakken or LEGOLAND® will not be lost on children.

NORTHERN JUTLAND
(See pp200–215)

SOUTHERN AND CENTRAL JUTLAND
(See pp182–199)

Northern Jutland *has some beautiful beaches, as well as fine buildings such as Voergård Slot. The works on display in the Skagens Museum perfectly capture the shimmering Nordic light found in this part of the country.*

Southern Jutland *is famous for towns such as Ribe, which survived flood and fire, and retains some of the best-preserved medieval architecture in Denmark. The level to which the waters of the Ribe Å River rose during a flood in 1634 are marked on a wooden column.*

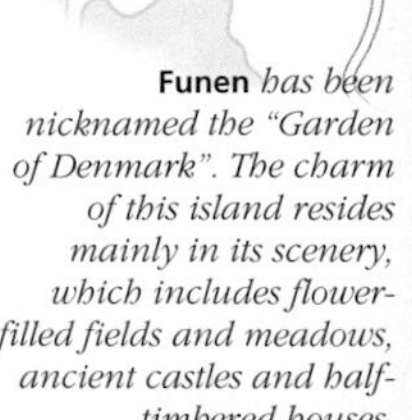

Funen *has been nicknamed the "Garden of Denmark". The charm of this island resides mainly in its scenery, which includes flower-filled fields and meadows, ancient castles and half-timbered houses.*

◁ **Neo-Classical sculpture adorning Frederiksborg Slot's façade**

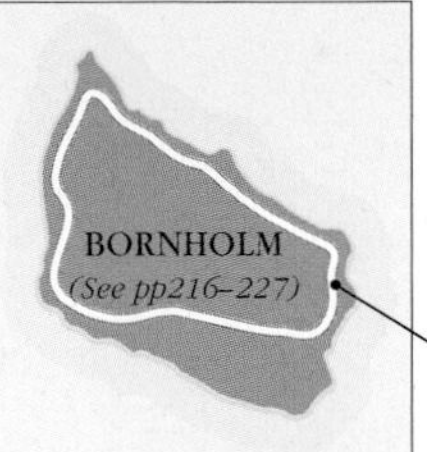

Bornholm *is sometimes described as "Scandinavia in a nutshell" because it combines many typically Scandinavian features, such as rocky shores, picturesque villages and peaceful forests.*

Northwestern Zealand *is known for its royal castles and palaces. Among these is the magnificent Kronborg Slot on the Oresund coast, which was used by William Shakespeare as the setting for* Hamlet. *The castle now contains a museum.*

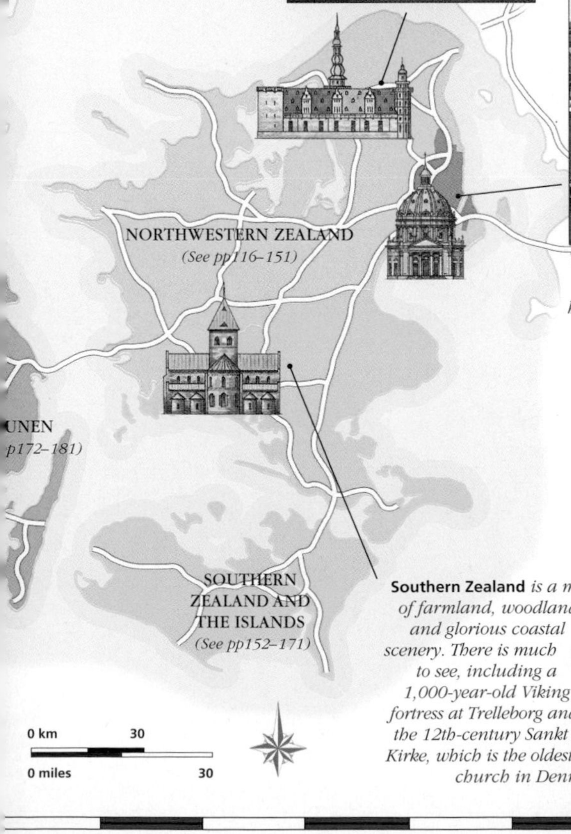

NORTHWESTERN ZEALAND
(See pp116–151)

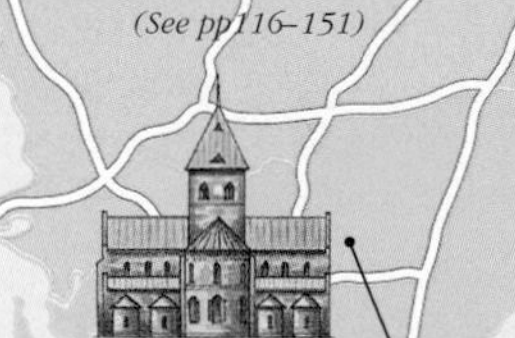

UNEN
p172–181)

SOUTHERN ZEALAND AND THE ISLANDS
(See pp152–171)

Copenhagen *is Denmark's capital and its largest city. It has many sights, both modern and old, including the magnificent Marmorkirken, which offers splendid views from its grand dome.* (See pages 46–111.)

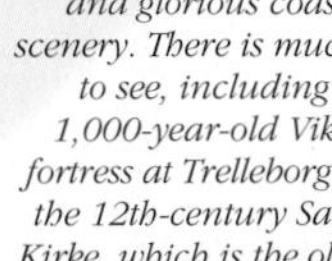

Southern Zealand *is a mix of farmland, woodland and glorious coastal scenery. There is much to see, including a 1,000-year-old Viking fortress at Trelleborg and the 12th-century Sankt Bendts Kirke, which is the oldest brick church in Denmark.*

0 km 30
0 miles 30

NORTHWESTERN ZEALAND

Zealand is the largest of the Danish islands and has an area of 7,500 sq km (2,895 sq miles). On its eastern shore lies Copenhagen (see pp46–107) *– the country's capital city as well as its cultural and commercial centre. Away from the city, there is much to enjoy, from mighty castles and historic towns to sandy beaches, rural villages and beautiful countryside.*

The island's scenery is typical of the lowland regions. Idyllic meadow scenery is broken here and there by beech forests and coastal fjords that cut deep into the land. Much of the region's wildlife can be seen around Arresø, Denmark's largest lake.

Most of the port towns were once Viking settlements. A reconstructed 10th–11th-century Viking camp can be visited in Trelleborg, while Viking ships can be seen at Roskilde's Viking Ship Museum. A visit to the Lejre Forsøgcentre, an experimental camp where Danish families volunteer to spend a week living in an Iron Age village, provides a glimpse into the past, as do the Viking plays staged at Frederikssund.

Northwestern Zealand has played an important part in the history of Denmark. Lejre was one of the first centres of Danish administration; later on this function was assumed by Roskilde, which in 1020 became a bishopric and the capital of Denmark. This lasted until 1443 when the role of the country's capital was taken over by Copenhagen. Traditionally, this area has been favoured by wealthy Danes and some of the most impressive royal castles can be found here including Kronborg, Fredensborg and Frederiksborg. In addition, there is a variety of more modest establishments worthy of a visit, such as Ermitagen, a royal hunting lodge a short way west of Klampenborg.

Hundested's popular beach

◁ **Neptune's Fountain, Frederiksborg Slot, symbolizing Denmark's power in the 17th century**

Exploring Northwestern Zealand

Most visitors to Zealand never stray beyond the limits of Copenhagen. There are, however, many other parts of the island that are well worth exploring. The list of sacral buildings includes Roskilde Domkirke (Cathedral) and Vor Frue Kirke, in Kalundborg, a 12th-century church with five spires. The region also has several areas that are conducive to carefree holidays. The northern shores, washed by Kattegat's waters, are famous for their beautiful sandy beaches, while the forests, criss-crossed with a network of trails, are perfect for cyclists and hikers.

SEE ALSO

• ***Where to Stay*** pp247–9.

• ***Where to Eat*** pp274–6.

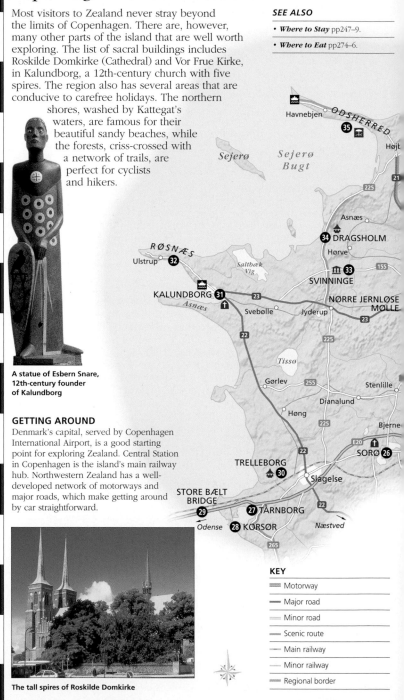

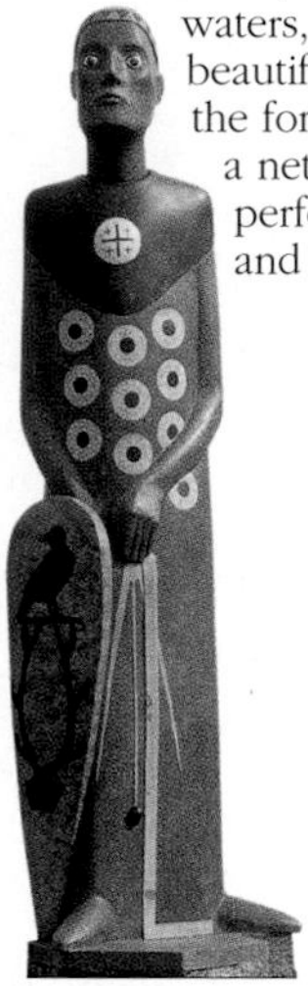

A statue of Esbern Snare, 12th-century founder of Kalundborg

GETTING AROUND

Denmark's capital, served by Copenhagen International Airport, is a good starting point for exploring Zealand. Central Station in Copenhagen is the island's main railway hub. Northwestern Zealand has a well-developed network of motorways and major roads, which make getting around by car straightforward.

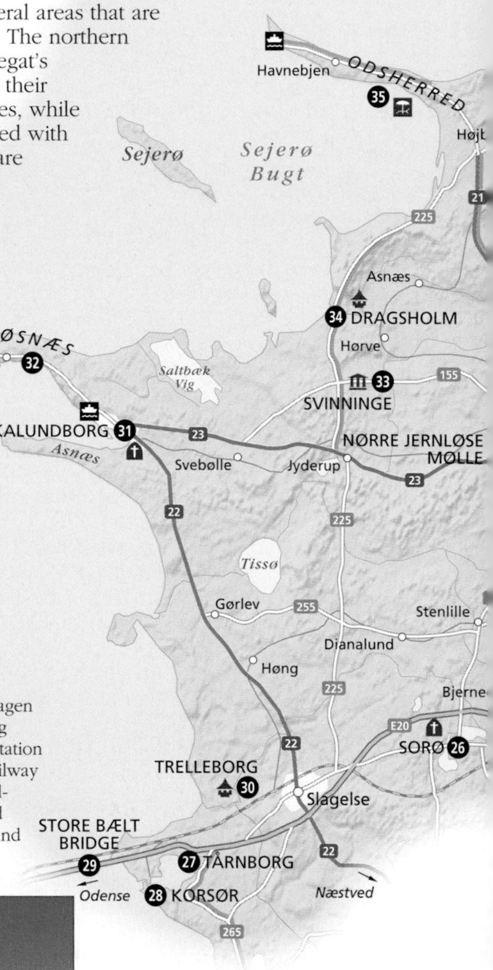

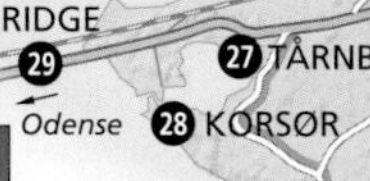

The tall spires of Roskilde Domkirke

KEY

- Motorway
- Major road
- Minor road
- Scenic route
- Main railway
- Minor railway
- Regional border

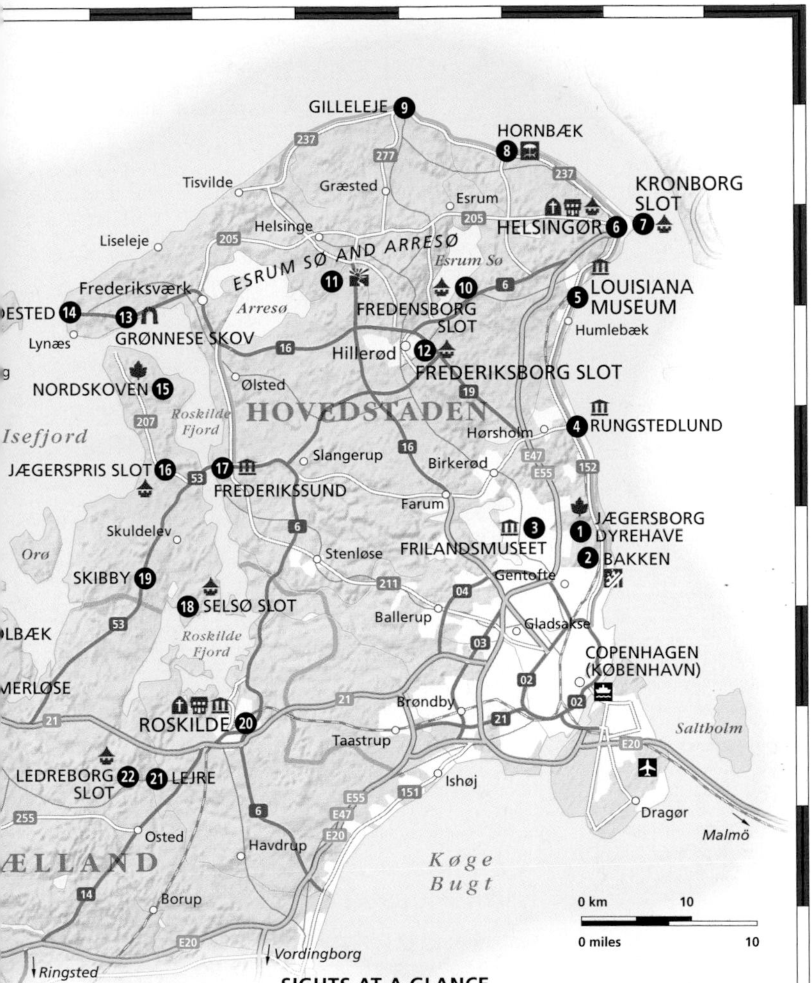

SIGHTS AT A GLANCE

Bakken 2
Dragsholm 34
Fredensborg Slot 10
Frederiksborg Slot pp132–3 12
Frederikssund 17
Frilandsmuseet 3
Gilleleje 9
Grønnese Skov 13
Helsingør pp124–5 6
Holbæk 23
Hornbæk 8
Hundested 14
Jægersborg Dyrehave 1
Jægerspris Slot 16
Kalundborg 31
Korsør 28
Kronborg Slot pp126–7 7
Ledreborg Slot 22
Lejre 21
Louisiana Museum pp122–3 5
Nordskoven 15
Nørre Jernløse Mølle 25
Roskilde pp140–43 20
Rungstedlund 4
Røsnæs 32
Selsø Slot 18
Skibby 19
Sorø 26
Store Bælt Bridge 29
Svinninge 33
Tårnborg 27
Trelleborg 30
Tveje Merløse Kirke 24

Tours

Esrum Sø and Arresø 11
Odsherred 35

Stately Dutch Renaissance entrance to Frederiksborg Slot

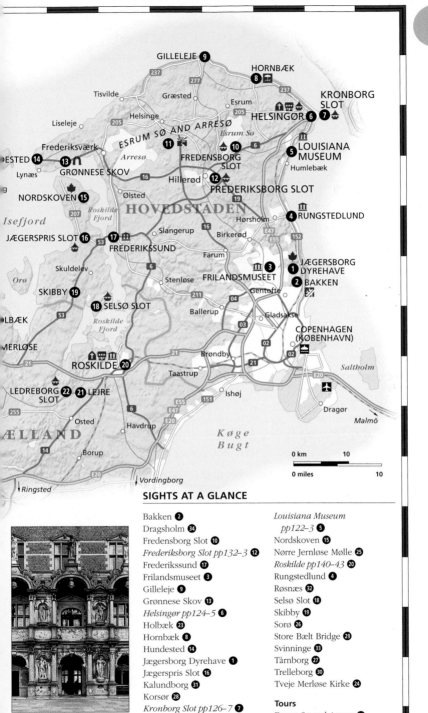

Jægersborg Dyrehave ❶

Road map F4.

The beech forests and parkland covering an area between the motorway that runs from Copenhagen towards Helsingør and the shore of the Øresund (Sound) is one of the favourite places for weekend forays out of Copenhagen. This area, which is criss-crossed with paths and cycle routes, was established as a royal hunting ground in 1669. The park still supports a herd of some 2,000 deer. A good vantage point from which to look out for them is the Ermitagen hunting lodge at the centre of the park, which was built in 1736 for Christian VI.

Among the park's other attractions are some 600-year-old oak trees, Kirsten Pils Kilde (a holy spring which was a pilgrimage destination in the 16th century) and, nearby, Bellevue (one of the area's best beaches). Horse-drawn carriages offer rides through the park and there is also a golf course and a horse racing track just to the south of Bakken.

Ermitagen hunting lodge

Bakken ❷

Road map F4. Ⓢ *Klampenborg.* ***Tel*** *39 63 73 00.* ◯ *late Mar–Aug. Opening hours vary; always consult the website before visiting.* **www**.bakken.dk

Bakken was founded in 1583 and is probably the world's oldest amusement

One of the many rides to be enjoyed at Bakken

park. Located just a short way out of Copenhagen, it is on the edge of a former royal hunting ground that is now the Jægersborg Dyrehave deer park.

The present amusement park has 100 or so rides, including roller-coasters and merry-go-rounds, as well as circus shows and a cabaret-style revue. There are 40 cafés and restaurants on site, although in keeping with Danish tradition people can bring their own supplies for a picnic. Entrance to the park is free though rides must be paid for. Profits from Bakken help to support the deer park.

Frilandsmuseet ❸

Road map F4. ***Tel*** *33 13 44 11.* ◯ *Apr–Oct: 10am–5pm Tue–Sun.* **www**.frilandsmuseet.dk

This open-air museum was founded in 1897 and contains virtually every kind of Danish country dwelling imaginable. It was originally situated near Rosenberg Slot in Copenhagen but was relocated to its present site in 1901 and is now run as part of the Nationalmuseet. Over 100 buildings are arranged into 40 groups and include many examples of rural architecture from cottages to grand manor houses, many of which are furnished and decorated in keeping with the period in which they were built. Visitors should allow a day to look round the collection, which includes fishermen's cottages, windmills, peasant huts, a post mill (still with working sails) and a smithy (kitted out with irons and a hearth). Many of the museum's staff dress in traditional costume and demonstrate such fading arts as turning clay pots and weaving cloth. The admission price also includes entry to Brede Værk, a textile mill which closed in 1956 and is now preserved as an industrial village complete with cottages, a school and the owner's country house.

A meticulously reconstructed house interior, Frilandsmuseet

Rungstedlund ❹

Road map F4. 2960 Rungsted Kyst. ***Tel*** *45 57 10 57.* **Karen Blixen Museum** ◯ *May–Sep: 10am–5pm Tue–Sun; Oct–Apr: 1–4pm Wed–Fri, 11am–4pm Sat–Sun.* **www**.karen-blixen.dk

Made famous by Karen Blixen, author of *Out of Africa,* Rungstedlund is the author's birthplace and was where she grew up and wrote most of her works under the pen name Isak Dinesen.

Karen Blixen's house was built around 1500 and was first used as an inn. In 1879 her father bought the property. It is now maintained by a foundation established by the writer, and in 1991 was converted into a museum devoted to Blixen's life and work. The rooms remain little changed from the period when she lived here, and manuscripts, photographs and personal belongings are on display. Blixen's grave is in the surrounding park.

For hotels and restaurants in this region see pp247–9 and pp274–6

Karen Blixen

Karen Blixen was born in 1885. The most colourful period in the Danish writer's life was her stay in Africa. Blixen left for Kenya at the age of 28 with her Swedish husband, Baron Bror von Blixen-Finecke, to establish a coffee plantation. While in Kenya she wrote *Seven Gothic Tales*, a collection of stories that launched her career. Safari expeditions, the raptures and miseries of her affairs, the breakdown of her marriage and the eventual failure of the plantation are all themes of her best-known work, *Out of Africa*, which established her reputation. The author returned to Rungsted in 1931 and lived here until her death in 1962. Among Blixen's other famous stories is *Babette's Feast*, which was made into a film in 1987.

Karen Blixen's House
Only part of the original house is still standing; two wings burned down when Blixen was 13 years old.

Blixen's Grave
The park behind the house contains a beech tree, with a modest gravestone underneath. This is the final resting place of Karen Blixen, who died at the age of 77.

African Room
Displayed in the room are Masai shields and spears as well as other mementos brought back from Africa.

Karen Blixen
Despite suffering from cancer Blixen wrote right up to her death. Towards the end, unable to write herself, she dictated her thoughts to her secretary.

The Film Version
The screen version of Out of Africa *stars Robert Redford and Meryl Streep. It was directed by Sydney Pollack (above) and departs markedly from the novel.*

Out of Africa
Out of Africa *was first published in 1937. It was originally written by the author in English and then translated by Blixen herself into Danish. The cover seen here is of the rare first Danish edition.*

Louisiana Museum ❺

This striking museum was established in 1958 to house a collection of modern Danish art. The museum's remit has expanded considerably since then and the collection now includes modern American and European paintings, graphic art and photography. The location and architecture are equally impressive. Light-filled galleries form a semi-circle round a 19th-century villa and open out onto a tranquil park filled with sculpture and offering stunning views of the Øresund. Among the many artists represented here are Giacometti, Henry Moore, Picasso and Warhol.

★ Big Thumb (1968)
The French artist Cesar Baldaccini was fascinated by the shape of his thumb. This bronze image is 185 cm (73 inches) high.

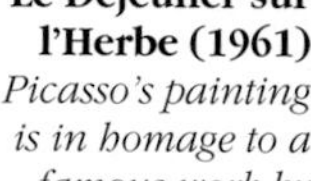

Le Déjeuner sur l'Herbe (1961)
Picasso's painting is in homage to a famous work by Edouard Manet painted nearly 100 years earlier.

Sculpture garden

Exit

GALLERY GUIDE
Single-storey galleries are connected by a corridor to the south wing and underground galleries. Works are on rotation apart from a room devoted to Giacometti. A children's wing has workshops, art materials and computers for children and their families.

★ Vénus de Meudon (1956)
This work by the French sculptor and painter Jean Arp depicts a woman's body reduced to its simplest form.

Eyes (1997)
This sculpture by Louise Bourgeois, in the interior sculpture garden, is a reminder of the sculptor's solo exhibition that took place here in 2003.

Main entrance

KEY

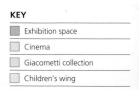

- Exhibition space
- Cinema
- Giacometti collection
- Children's wing

For hotels and restaurants in this region see pp247–9 and pp274–6

Concert hall

VISITORS' CHECKLIST

Road map F4.
Humlebæk Gl. Standvej 13.
Tel *49 19 07 19.*
11am–10pm Tue–Fri, 11am–6pm Sat, Sun & hols.
www.louisiana.dk

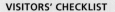

Café
Works on display in the museum's airy café include pieces by the Danish designer Arne Jacobsen.

Marilyn Monroe (1967)
Obsessed by the legendary actress's suicide in 1962, Andy Warhol set about immortalizing the film star by endlessly duplicating her image, using a silk-screen process to transfer the picture onto canvas.

Two Piece Reclining Figure No. 5 (1963–64)
In his image of the semi-reclining woman, split into two parts, Henry Moore intended to blend the female figure with the landscape.

The Graphics Wing, opened in 1991, was built underground to protect its displays from daylight.

Ground floor

★ South Wing
The south wing was added in 1982 and is half buried in the hillside. It houses the museum's permanent art collection, as well as special exhibitions.

STAR EXHIBITS

★ Big Thumb

★ South Wing

★ Vénus de Meudon

Helsingør ❻

Helsingør owes its prosperity to its location on the sound that links the North Sea with the Baltic. The town was a centre of international shipping during the 1400s, when Erik of Pomerania levied a tax on every ship passing through its local waters. In 1857 the dues were abolished, causing a temporary economic decline in the town's fortunes. This downturn was reversed in 1864 with the opening of a railway line and ferry services to Sweden. Today, most people visit Helsingør to see Kronborg Slot *(see pp118–19)*, a late-16th-century castle that was used by William Shakespeare as the setting for *Hamlet*.

Old apothecary on display in the town museum

Exploring Helsingør

When sightseeing in Helsingør it is a good idea to start with a visit to the Carmelite Monastery and the Municipal Museum, and then continue with a walk along Biergegade promenade, turning occasionally into side streets (Stengade in particular). Further south is the tourist information centre in Havnepladsen and, a little further on, the ferry terminal.

Gothic cloisters surrounding the Karmeliterklosteret's courtyard

Karmeliterklosteret Sankt Mariæ Kirke

Sankt Anna Gade 38. ***Tel*** *49 21 17 74.* *mid-May–mid-Sep: 10am–3pm daily; mid-Sep–mid-May: 10am–2pm daily.* **www**.sctmariae.dk

This Gothic building once belonged to the Carmelites and was erected in the second half of the 15th century. It is considered to be one of the best-preserved medieval monasteries anywhere in Scandinavia and was described by H.C. Andersen as "one of the most beautiful spots in Denmark". Among its many features are the chapterhouse with its barrel vault and the "Bird Room" decorated with ornithological frescoes. Christian II's mistress, Dyveke, who died in 1517, is believed to be buried in the grounds.

Helsingør Bymuseum

Sankt Anna Gade 36. ***Tel*** *49 28 18 00.* *noon–4pm daily.*

The building that currently houses the town museum was erected by friars from the neighbouring monastery, who used it as a hospital for sailors arriving at the local harbour. Some of the instruments once used by the friars for brain surgery in the hospital are on display together with other exhibits relating to the town's past including a model of Kronborg Slot as it was in 1801. Visitors to the museum can also learn about the origin of the region's name: Øresund refers to the levy demanded by Erik of Pomerania which translates as "Penny Sound" ("øre" is the Danish penny, and "sund" means "sound").

Axeltorv

Helsingør's main square has a number of restaurants and bars. On Wednesday and Saturday mornings there is a colourful local market here that sells flowers, vegetables, fresh fish, handicrafts, cheese and souvenirs.

The statue in the centre depicts Erik of Pomerania – the Polish king and nephew of Margrethe I who occupied the throne of Denmark between 1397 and 1439. Following the break-up of the Kalmar Union and his subsequent dethronement in 1439 in favour of Christoffer III of Bavaria, the ex-monarch moved to the Swedish island of Gotland. Here, he began to occupy himself with piracy and he is sometimes referred to as "the last Baltic Viking".

In his old age Erik returned to Pomerania and is buried in the Polish town of Darlowo. One legend has it that Darlowo's castle still contains hidden treasure plundered from Denmark.

Monument to Erik of Pomerania in Axeltorv

For hotels and restaurants in this region see pp247–9 and pp274–6

Stengade

Helsingør's medieval quarter includes Stengade, a pedestrianized street that is linked by various alleyways to Axeltorv. Many of the colourful half-timbered houses once belonged to merchants and ferrymen and date from the 17th and 18th centuries. Oderns Gård, at Stengade No. 66, was built in 1459.

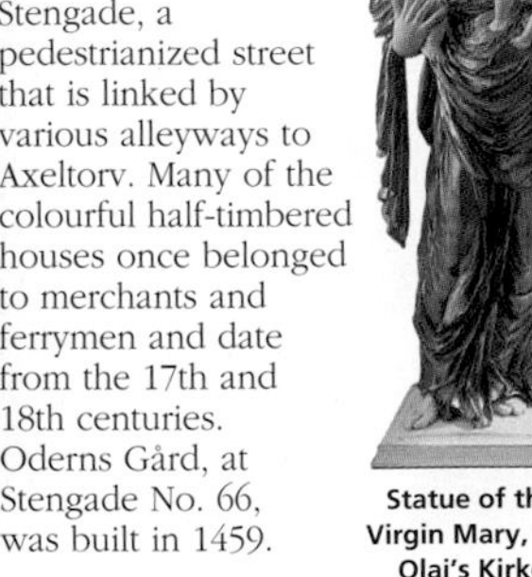
Statue of the Virgin Mary, Skt Olai's Kirke

Sankt Olai Kirke

Sankt Anna Gade 12. ***Tel*** *49 21 04 43.* *May–Jul: 10am–4pm Mon–Sat; Sep–Apr: 10am–2pm daily.*

This building was consecrated around 1200 and served for centuries as a parish church. It was elevated to the rank of cathedral in 1961. Numerous elaborate epitaphs can be seen commemorating the many rich merchants and distinguished citizens of Helsingør who are buried here. The church's present-day appearance dates from 16th-century modifications when it also acquired its current furnishings. Among its most precious possessions are a 15th-century Gothic crucifix, a Renaissance pulpit (1568) and a carved wooden altar. The church was restored in 2001.

Marienlyst Slot

Marienlyst Allé 32.
Tel *49 28 18 30.*
noon–4pm Tue–Sun.

The first palace built here dates from 1587 and was used by Frederik II. The present Neo-Classical manor house is the result of extensive remodelling work carried out between 1759 and 1763 by the French architect Nicolas-Henri Jardin, who was asked to adapt the place to the needs of the widowed queen Juliana Maria. The building now serves as a museum with a collection that includes paintings and silverware. Part of the building is also used as a hotel. The surrounding garden contains a mound known as Hamlet's Tomb from which there is a view of the sound.

VISITORS' CHECKLIST

Road map F4. *40,000.*
Havnepladsen 3.
Tel *49 21 13 33.*
www.visithelsingor.dk

Øresundakvariet

Strandpromenaden 5. ***Tel*** *49 21 37 72.* *Jun–Aug: 10am–5pm daily; Sep–May: 10am–4pm Mon–Fri, 10am–5pm Sat & Sun.*
www.oresundsakvariet.ku.dk

As well as a colourful collection of tropical fish from around the world, Helsingør's aquarium contains many species taken from the waters of the Øresund (Sound). These local varieties include Baltic jellyfish and seahorses.

Three-storey Neo-Classical Marienlyst Slot

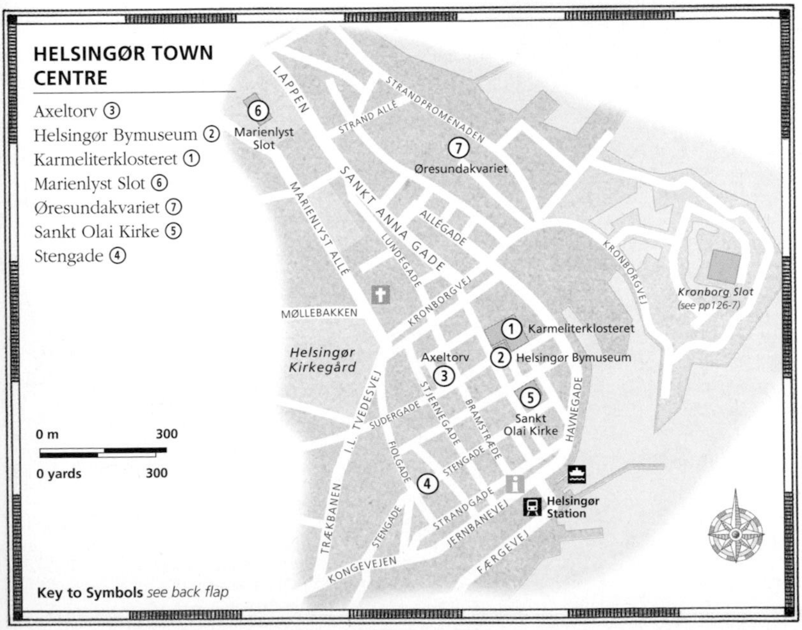

HELSINGØR TOWN CENTRE

Axeltorv ③
Helsingør Bymuseum ②
Karmeliterklosteret ①
Marienlyst Slot ⑥
Øresundakvariet ⑦
Sankt Olai Kirke ⑤
Stengade ④

0 m 300
0 yards 300

Lappen
Strandpromenaden
Strand Allé
⑥ Marienlyst Slot
⑦ Øresundakvariet
Sankt Anna Gade
Allégade
Marienlyst Allé
Lundegade
Kronborgvej
Møllebakken
Kronborg Slot *(see pp126–7)*
① Karmeliterklosteret
② Helsingør Bymuseum
Axeltorv ③
Helsingør Kirkegård
I.L. Tvedesvej
Sudergade
Stjernegade
Bramstræde
⑤ Sankt Olai Kirke
Havnegade
Folgade
Stengade
④
Strandgade
Jernbanevej
Helsingør Station
Trækbanen
Kongevejen
Færgevej

Key to Symbols *see back flap*

Kronborg Slot ❼

Hamlet's "Castle of Elsinore" was originally built by Erik of Pomerania in the early 15th century. It was remodelled by Frederik II and later by Christian IV but still retains an eerie quality that makes it perfect for the many productions of Shakespeare's play performed here. Among the most impressive rooms are the 62-m (203-ft) Great Hall, the King's Chamber, which has a ceiling painted by the Dutch artist Gerrit van Honthorst, and the "Lille Sal" containing 16th-century silk tapestries by the Flemish painter Hans Knieper. The castle was added to UNESCO's World Heritage List in 2000.

Maritime Museum
Established in 1915 the museum's collection has exhibits relating to the Danish fleet and overseas trade; also on show are the remains of the original 15th-century fortress.

Trumpeter's Tower

Viking Chief
The dungeons contain a sleeping statue of Holger Danske, a Viking chief. According to legend he will wake up should Denmark find itself in peril.

★ Great Hall
Once the longest hall in northern Europe, it was completed in 1582 and is decorated with paintings from Rosenborg Slot. The chandeliers date from the 17th century.

STAR FEATURES

- ★ Chapel
- ★ Great Hall
- ★ "Lille Sal"

HAMLET

Shakespeare probably never visited Kronborg, but it is here that he set one of his best-known plays. The prototype for the fictional Danish prince was Amlet, a Viking king whose story is recounted by the 12th-century Danish chronicler Saxo Grammaticus in his *Historia Danica* (Danish History). Shakespeare may have encounted this classic tale of murder and revenge via Francois de Belleforest's *Histoires Tragiques* (Tragic Histories), published in 1570. A festival is held in the castle each year during which *Hamlet* and other works by Shakespeare are performed.

For hotels and restaurants in this region see pp247–9 and pp274–6

King's Tower
Built during 1584-85 it was also known as the "Turner's Tower" as one of its rooms housed Frederik II's turnery containing lathes.

★ "Lille Sal"
The "small room" has seven tapestries depicting Danish kings with verses describing their various achievements.

The North Wing was completed in 1585. Its western section contained the castle offices.

The Queen's Chambers at the corner of the north wing had direct access to the chapel, via the east wing.

Royal Chambers
These rooms contain ornate ceiling decorations and marble fireplaces. At one time the walls would have been lined with gold-embossed leather.

★ Chapel
The chapel has a beautiful altar, oak benches with intricately carved ends, a royal balcony and an organ dating from the early 18th century.

The Pigeon Tower housed birds that were used for sending important royal messages.

VISITORS' CHECKLIST

Road map F4. Kronborgvej, DK 3000, Helsingør. ***Tel*** *49 21 30 78.* ***Fax*** *49 21 30 52.* *May–Sep: 10:30am–5pm daily; Jun & Oct: 11am–4pm Tue–Sun; Nov–Mar: 11am–3pm Tue–Sun.*
Maritime Museum
Same as castle.
www.kronborg.dk

Clean sandy beaches of Hornbæk

Hornbæk 8

Road map F4. *Vestre Stejlebakke 2A.* ***Tel*** *49 70 47 47.* **www**.helsbib.dk

The northern shore of Zealand is famous for its pleasant sandy beaches, clean water and the small town of Hornbæk, which has for years been a favoured resort. A large number of visitors come from Copenhagen, many of whom have built holiday homes here. In summer the resort fills with holiday-makers enjoying various outdoor pursuits, including sailing and swimming.

Former Cistercian monastery buildings

Environs

Esrum, situated southwest of Hornbæk, is famous mainly for its Cistercian monastery. Founded in 1151, it was regarded as one of the most important monasteries in Denmark during the Middle Ages. Its prominence was acknowledged even by the monarchy: in 1374 Queen Helvig, wife of Valdemar IV, was buried here. Even the fires that plagued the establishment (in 1194 and 1204) did not prevent the monastery from becoming one of the largest buildings in Scandinavia. During the Lutheran Reformation in the 16th century much of the church was demolished and the materials were used to build Kronborg Slot *(see pp126–7)*. What remained of the buildings passed into the hands of the monarch and the premises were used first as a hunting base and later as warehouses before being turned into army barracks. In the 20th century they were used as offices, as a post office and then as an orphanage. During World War II they became an air-raid shelter and a fireproof store for valuable documents brought here from the National Archives, and for the Royal Library collection.

This chequered history came to an end when a decision was reached to renovate the ancient walls and in 1997 the former monastery opened to visitors. Its main building now houses an exhibition devoted to the Cistercian order while the vaults have been transformed into a café. Also open to visitors is the herb garden, where medicinal plants are grown and used, as they once were when the monastery flourished. Some of the plants are used to produce a flavoured beverage, which is on sale in the shop.

Not far from the monastery is **Esrum Møllegard**, a 400-year old mill. The mill was first used to grind grain, and later to generate electricity. Today, it houses a centre for environmental awareness.

Gilleleje 9

Road map F4. *6,000.* *Hovedgade 6F.* ***Tel*** *48 30 01 74.* **www**.visitgribskov.dk

The northernmost town in Zealand is also one of the oldest Danish fishing ports and contains the island's largest harbour. From historical records it has been established that the local inhabitants were engaged in fishing here as early as the mid-14th century. Today, Gilleleje is an attractive town with thatched houses, a busy harbour-side fishing auction and a colourful main street that has been turned into a promenade. Rising above the fisherman's cottages is the church – Sønændenesk Kirke. During the German occupation locals used the church as a hiding place for Danish Jews who were then smuggled into neutral Sweden aboard fishing boats under cover of darkness.

Other places of interest include **Gilleleje Museum**, devoted to the town's history, and **Det Gamle Hus** an old fisherman's house, which illustrates the realities of everyday life for a mid-19th-century fishing family. A coastal trail from the town centre leads east to the Nakkehoved Østre Fyr lighthouse. Built in 1772, this is one of a very few coal-fuelled lighthouses in the world to have survived to this day. This historic building is now open to visitors.

Nakkehoved Østre Fyr, a coal-fired lighthouse near Gilleleje

For hotels and restaurants in this region see pp247–9 and pp274–6

Fishing boats in Gilleleje's harbour

Environs: Nearby Græsted, some 8 km (5 miles) south of Gilleleje, has an amusement park – **Nordsjællands Sommerpark** – which has an aqua park as well as paintball and mini golf. In summer refurbished steam and diesel trains run between Gilleleje and Græsted and also to Hornbæk.

Gilleleje Museum
Vesterbrogade 56. ***Tel*** *48 30 16 31.* *includes a visit to the lighthouse.*

Det Gamle Hus
Hovedgade 49, Gilleje.
Tel *48 30 16 31.*

Nordsjællands Sommerpark
Kirkevej 43, 3230 Græsted.
Tel *48 71 41 41.* *admission free for children up to 90 cm (3 ft) in height.* **www**.sommerpark.dk

Fredensborg Slot ⑩

Road map F4. ***Tel*** *33 40 31 87.*
Jul: 1–4:30pm daily. *every 15 min (duration about 35 min).*
Gardens *9am–5pm daily.*
www.ses.dk

Frederik IV decided to build Fredensborg Castle in order to commemorate the 1720 peace treaty concluded between Denmark and Sweden at the end of the Nordic Wars (Fredensborg means "Town of Peace"). The building was originally used as a hunting lodge. Nowadays the castle is one of the main residences of the Danish royal family and is often used to receive VIPs from all over the world. According to tradition, guests who spend the night at the palace must sign their name on a glass pane using a diamond pen.

The original design was modelled on French and Italian castles and the long list of contributors who influenced its final shape includes renowned architects such as Niels Eigtved, Lauritz de Thurah and Caspar Frederik Harsdorf. The present-day complex consists of 28 separate buildings. At its centre is the Dome Hall (Kuppelsalen), surmounted by a dome crowned with a lantern. The magnificent room is encircled by a gallery, which divides the hall into two levels. It is used for formal royal family occasions and also for entertaining special guests.

One of the most interesting rooms in the palace is Havesalon, or the Garden Room, which features a wide door leading to the castle gardens. Its ceiling is decorated with a painting by Henrik Krock depicting Denmark and Norway begging the Olympian gods for help against Sweden.

Fredensborg's gardens decorated with numerous statues

Fredenborg Slot's ornate Chinese Dining Room (Kinesisk Spisesalon) is another notable room. It is decorated in yellow and red and houses a collection of Chinese porcelain.

The palace garden was established in the 1760s, and contains a lane decorated with a sculpted group of 70 figures, created by J.G. Grund, of fishermen and farmers from Norway and the Faroe Islands. Plants sensitive to cold, including a 250-year-old myrtle shrub, are shielded from low temperatures in a greenhouse built in 1995.

Fredensborg Slot, used as a residence by the Danish royal family

A Tour Around Esrum Sø and Arresø ⓫

These beautiful lakes are the two largest in Denmark and attract a great many visitors, especially in summer. Gribskov, on the west bank of Esrum Sø, is a forested area where marked paths and bicycle trails lead through thick clusters of ancient beech and spruce trees. Arresø, to the east of Esrum Sø, is Denmark's largest lake and reaches depths of 22 m (72 ft). Ospreys and cormorants can occasionally be spotted diving for fish. As well as being perfect for anglers, bathers and enthusiastic sailors, a tour around the area takes in lush farmland, ancient church ruins, picturesque towns and historic medieval villages.

Ramløse ③
Situated on Arresø's north bank *(above)*, the town's most interesting feature is its Dutch-style windmill (1908) that can be seen working on traditional "Mill Days".

Asserbo ②
Scenic ruins surrounded by a wind-blown forest are all that remains of this former fortress, built in 1100 on the orders of Bishop Absalon.

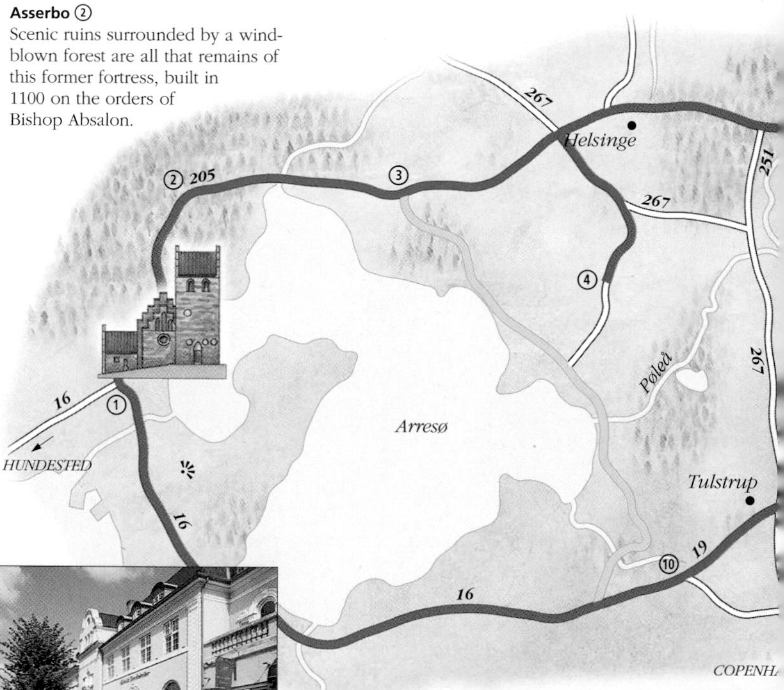

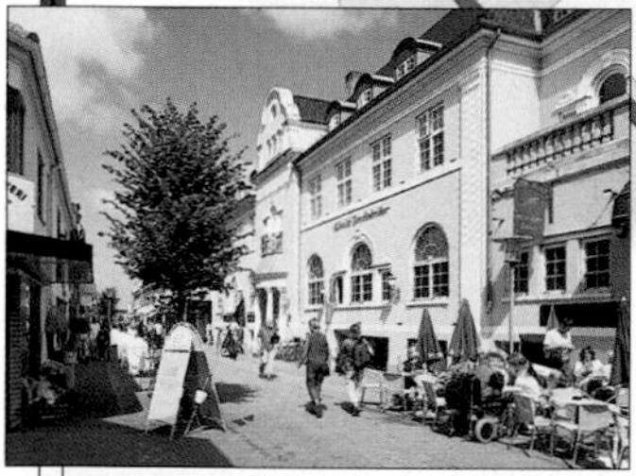

267
Helsinge
251
② 205
③
267
④
Pøleå
267
16
①
HUNDESTED
Arresø
Tulstrup
16
⑩ 19
16
COPENH

Frederiksværk ①
Frederiksværk, built alongside a canal, is Denmark's oldest industrial town. A museum in a former gunpowder factory has exhibits on the town's industrial past.

Æbelholt Kloster ⑩
This 12th-century Augustinian abbey was once a hospital. Today, as well as viewing the ruins, visitors can examine the museum's collection of surgical instruments.

Esrum ⑤
The restored buildings of this former Cistertian monastery house a museum devoted to the community that lived here, giving visitors an idea of the monk's day-to-day life.

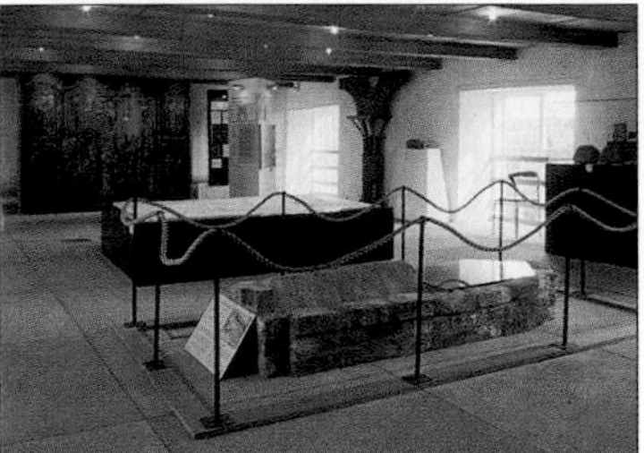

TIPS FOR DRIVERS

Length: *about 100 km (62 miles).* ***Stopping-off points:*** *There is a large choice of restaurants and accommodation in Fredensborg.*
www.visitdenmark.com
www.visitcopenhagen.com

Annisse Nord ④
Annisse Nord is a sleepy village but was strategically important for the surrounding area in medieval times; at that time numerous watchtowers were erected along the fjord.

Fredensborg Slot ⑥
The castle gardens are arranged in a Baroque style and are open to the public all year round *(see p129).*

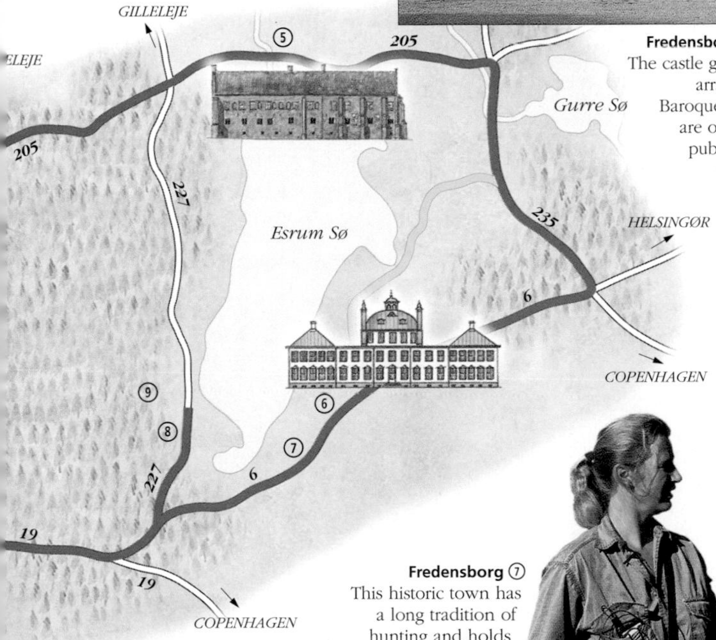

GILLELEJE
ELEJE
205
227
Gurre Sø
Esrum Sø
235
HELSINGØR
6
COPENHAGEN
19
COPENHAGEN

Fredensborg ⑦
This historic town has a long tradition of hunting and holds regular demonstrations of falconry.

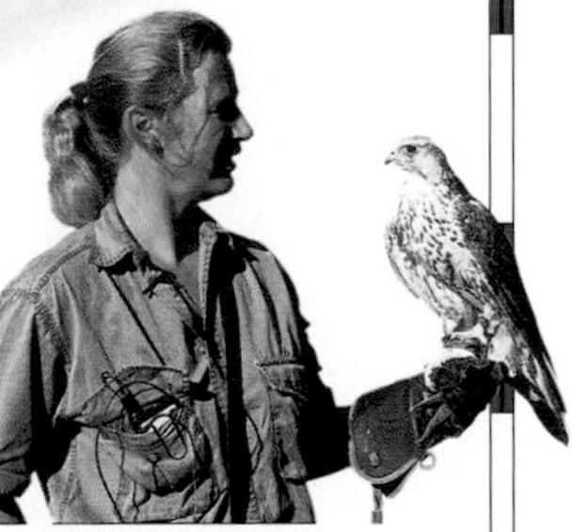

Gribskov ⑨
Growing along the undulating western shoreline of Esrum Sø, Gribskov is the second largest forest in the country.

KEY

- Suggested route
- Scenic route
- Other road
- River, lake
- Viewpoint

0 km 2
0 miles 2

Nødebo ⑧
The tiny village of Nødebo is on the banks of Esrum Sø *(left)* and surrounded by Gribskov. The pretty village church is decorated with 15th-century frescoes.

Frederiksborg Slot ⓬

The first royal residence was constructed on this site by Frederik II in 1560. A fire in 1859 destroyed most of the castle, which may well have remained a ruin were it not for Carlsberg boss J.C. Jacobsen who restored the building and helped found a national history museum. The museum now takes up 80 or so of the palace rooms. Jacobsen also donated many of his own paintings which, along with others, are arranged chronologically to chart Denmark's history. Period furnishings and some magnificent architecture help to conjure up a feel for the country's past.

★ Slotskirken
From 1671 until 1840 the castle chapel was used to crown Denmark's monarchs. Its ebony altar dates from 1606 and is the work of Jakob Mores, a German goldsmith.

★ Riddersalen
The Knights' Hall has a carved wooden ceiling. The gilded ornaments, a 19th-century black marble fireplace and intricate tapestries add to the splendour.

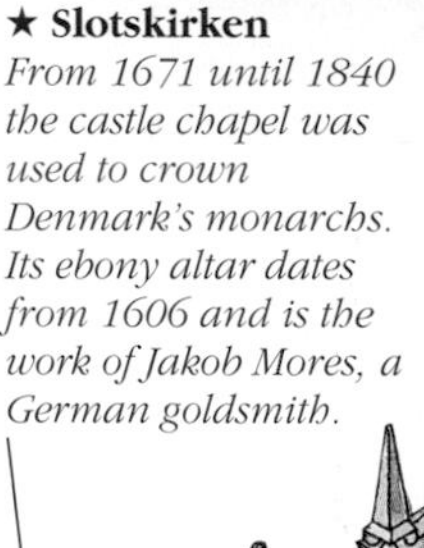

Audienssalen
The Audience Chamber was completed in 1688. Among the paintings lining the walls is a portrait of a proud-looking Christian V, depicted as a Roman emperor surrounded by his children.

Chapel Portal
The oak door, set within a sandstone portal in the shape of a triumphal arch, survived the fire of 1859 and looks as it would have done in Christian IV's day.

STAR FEATURES

★ Riddersalen

★ Slotskirken

For hotels and restaurants in this region see pp247–9 and pp274–6

VISITORS' CHECKLIST

Road map F4.
3400 Hillerød, Slotsgade 1.
Tel *48 26 04 39.*
Apr–Sep: 10am–5pm daily; Oct–Mar: 11am–3pm daily.
Baroque gardens *10am–sunset daily.*
www.frederiksborgslot.dk

Queen Sophie's Room
During the reign of Christian IV this room was used by the king's mother. When the palace became a museum, it was hung with paintings associated with Frederik III.

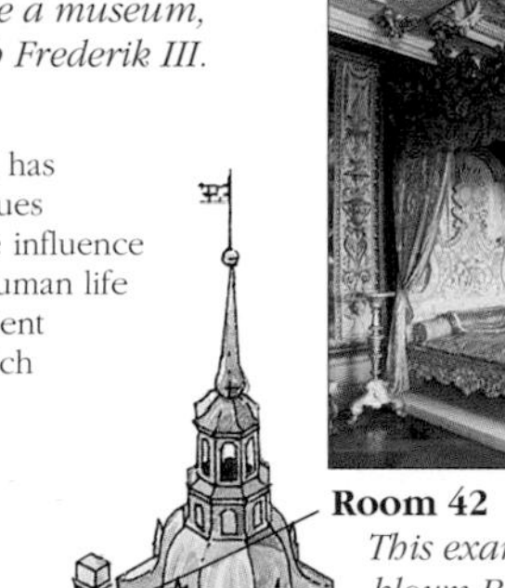

Room 42
This example of overblown Baroque is typical of the taste associated with Denmark's era of absolute monarchy (see pp38–9). The bed with silk draperies was made in France in 1724.

The Royal Wing has a gallery of statues symbolizing the influence of planets on human life and is an excellent example of Dutch Mannerism.

Gardens
The castle gardens were established in the 1720s and restored in 1996. The carefully trimmed shrubs create a symmetrical pattern typical of a Baroque garden.

Room 46
All of the items in this room, such as this ornate wall clock, are in perfect accord with the colours and Rococo excess of the overall design.

Grønnese Skov ⓭

Road map F4.

The ancient forest of Grønnese Skov is about 5 km (3 miles) east of Hundested, on the shores of Roskilde Fjord. Archaeological excavations indicate that during the Neolithic era this area was one of the more important sites of early culture in Zealand and the site now attracts thousands of visitors every year.

One of the most important relics of Denmark's Neolithic past is an extraordinary burial chamber known as a dolmen. It is one of many such tombs in Denmark and consists of a huge flat stone resting on three chunky pillars. The dolmen is referred to locally as Karlsstenen ("Karl's Stone") and is one of the biggest and best preserved of its type anywhere in Denmark. It must be reached on foot but the forest car park is only a short distance away.

Prehistoric Karlsstenen, Grønnese Skov

Hundested ⓮

Road map E4. *Jernbanegade 8.* ***Tel*** *47 93 77 88.* **www**.visithalsnaes.dk

This small town lies on a slender peninsula. Its name translates literally as "dog's place" and derives from a species of local seal commonly known as a sea dog because of its canine-like barking. The main reason to come to Hundested is to take a look around **Knud Rasmussens Hus**, which is situated on a high cliff close to Spodsbjerg lighthouse. The house was built in 1907 by the intrepid Arctic explorer, Knud Rasmussen, and now houses a museum devoted to his life and travels. Close by is a monument to him erected in 1936 made of stones brought over from Greenland.

Environs

A short way northeast is **Kikhavn**, the oldest fishing village on the Halsnæs peninsula, which dates back to the 13th century. In the 18th century there were many small farms here, some of which were partly destroyed by a storm in 1793. A handful of these have now been reconstructed to form an open-air museum. Kikhaven is also the starting point of a footpath, **Halsnæsstien**, that links the shores of Isefjord and Kattegat.

Knud Rasmussen's house, now a popular museum

Another place worth visiting is **Lynæs**, just south of Hundested. The local church, built in 1901 from huge granite blocks, serves as a navigational guide for returning fishermen. A monument standing by the church commemorates those who lost their lives at sea.

Knud Rasmussens Hus
Tel *47 93 71 61. Apr–Oct: 11am–4pm Tue–Sun.*

KNUD RASMUSSEN

Knud Rasmussen was born in 1879. Half Inuit himself, Rasmussen was fascinated by Inuit culture and language and resolved to become a polar explorer at an early age. He took part in his first scientific expedition in 1900 and soon began organizing them himself. In 1910, together with Peter Freuchen, he founded the Thule settlement in the north of Greenland. Between 1921 and 1924 Rasmussen completed a grand expedition from Greenland to the Bering Straight, covering 18,000 km (11,185 miles) by dog-sleigh. From each of his expeditions the explorer brought back many artifacts; most of these are now in the Nationalmuseet in Copenhagen *(see pp84–5)*. In the course of his seventh expedition Rasmussen fell seriously ill. He died in 1933, aged 54.

The explorer's house, full of reminders of his expeditions

Kongeegen, believed to be the oldest living oak tree in Europe

Nordskoven ⓯

Road map F4.

The peninsula that separates Roskilde Fjord from Isefjord contains one of Denmark's most beautiful beech forests. The forest has two sections, known as Fællesskoven and Studehaven. Running between them is a 15-km (9-mile) long bicycle trail with

Statue of a deer in front of Jægerspris Slot

views over Roskilde Fjord. At its highest point, called Frederikshøj, is a hunting pavilion built by Frederik VII in 1875. A number of ancient trees can be found in the forest including three famous oaks: Kongeegen, Storkeegen and Snoegen, which have inspired many artists. Kongeegen, the most ancient of the three trees, is believed to be 1,500–1,900 years old. In 1973 its last bough broke away, leaving only the vast trunk, which has a circumference of 14 m (46 ft).

Jægerspris Slot ⓰

Road map F4. *Jægerspris Slot, Slotsgården 20.* ***Tel*** *47 53 10 04.* *Apr–Oct: 11am–4pm Tue–Sun.* **Park** *all year round.*

This medieval castle, situated about 6 km (4 miles) west of Frederikssund, has been used by Danish royalty since the early 14th century and is now open to the public. The first royal building, known as Abrahamstrup, still exists although it has been swallowed by the north wing of the present complex. A life-size statue of a deer standing before the entrance to the castle is by Adelgund Vogt, a pupil of Bertel Thorvaldsen.

In the mid-19th century Frederik VII made the palace his summer residence. After his death in 1863 the monarch's widow, Countess Danner, turned part of the palace into a refuge for poor and unwanted girls. The centre became the first children's home in Denmark. A special exhibition illustrates the often austere way of life in an early 20th-century Danish orphanage.

Much of the house still retains its royal character, however, and visitors can take a look at magnificent rooms arranged by Frederik VII. There is also an exhibition of archaeological finds reflecting one of Frederik VII's abiding passions.

The gardens stretching to the rear of the castle include Zealand's largest collection of rhododendrons; standing among them are 54 obelisks with busts of famous Danish personages. The tomb of countess Danner is also in the castle gardens.

Frederikssund ⓱

Road map F4. *17,000.* *Havnegade 5A.* ***Tel*** *47 31 06 85.* *Viking Festival (mid-Jun–late Jul).* **www**.visitfrederikssund.dk

This town was founded in 1655 on the orders of Frederik III. The choice of site was not accidental, as it overlooks the narrowest part of the Roskilde Fjord and was used for many years by boats crossing to the other side.

In the town centre is the **J.F. Willumsens Museum**. Willumsen (1863–1958), a prominent Danish Symbolist painter, donated his paintings, sculptures and drawings to Frederikssund on condition that a suitable building be erected to display them. The museum also contains works by other artists that were collected by Willumsen.

Frederikssund is primarily known, however, for its reconstructed **Viking Village**. The village is open to visitors all year round but the best time to visit is during the summer Viking Festival when events are held. The most popular are the evening Viking plays that feature 200 actors and end with a grand banquet. A popular summer excursion is to take a cruise aboard the *Harald Blåtand*, a river boat named after the Viking chieftain Harald I (Bluetooth).

J.F. Willumsens Museum
Tel *47 31 07 73.*
10am–5pm daily.

Danes dressed as Vikings during Frederikssund's summer festival

Selsø Slot, built in 1578

Selsø Slot 18

Road map F4. Selsøvej 30A, 4050 Skibby. ***Tel*** *47 52 01 71.* *May–Jun: 1pm–4pm Sat & Sun; end-Jun–early Aug & mid Oct: 11am–4pm daily; Aug–Oct: 1pm–4pm Sat & Sun.* **www**.selsoe.dk

This property's history dates back to the 12th century. According to records, Bishop Absalon became interested in the site in about 1170 and by 1228 a sumptuous residence had been built here.

The present castle was built in 1578. It was reworked in 1734 and much of its original Renaissance style was replaced with Baroque details. The castle is now a museum and gives visitors an idea of what aristocratic life was like in the 1800s. The castle's stern, simple exterior hides a richer interior, including the "Grand Ballroom". With original marble panels and a decorated ceiling, it is used as a venue for classical music concerts. Wine-tasting sessions are held in the castle vaults. The castle church has an altarpiece dating from 1605.

The property owes much of its charm to its location on the banks of Selsø lake. A bird reserve established in the gardens is one of the premium places for bird-watching in Denmark. A viewing tower standing in the garden was built specifically for this purpose.

Skibby 19

Road map F4. Havnegade 5A, 3600 Frederikssund. ***Tel*** *47 31 06 85.* **www**.visitfrederikssund.dk

The main town of the peninsula between Roskilde Fjord and Isefjord, Skibby is known mainly for its early 12th-century church, which is decorated with some well-preserved frescoes. The oldest of these were found in 1855 in the Romanesque apses and date from the second half of the 12th century. Similar decorations can be found in other churches in the district, including some at nearby Dråby. In 1650 a manuscript, known as the *Skibby Chronicle*, was found buried behind the altar. The work, written in Latin, recounts the history of Denmark between 1046 and 1534.

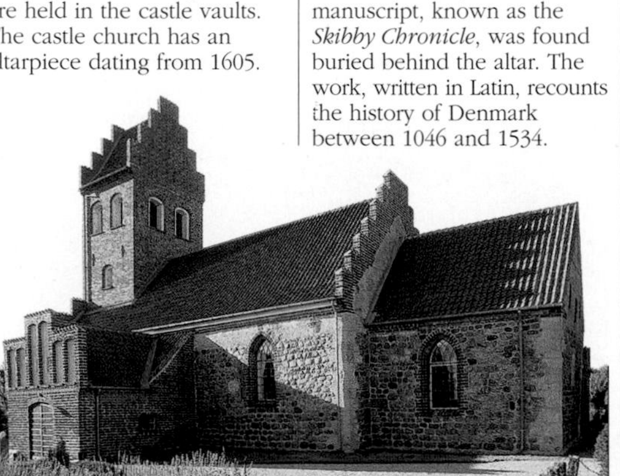

Dråby Kirke, situated near Skibby

It is uncertain why the chronicle was found here. Its style points to the authorship of Paul Helgsen, a Carmelite monk and orator. Helgsen was a native of Helsingør, however, and since the work is unfinished, its discovery has provoked debate as to the fate of its author. Skibby's other claim to fame is as the location of Scandinavia's first nudist swimming pool.

Environs

Northeast of Skibby, in the town of Skuldelev, is a **toy museum** with a collection of over 4,000 dolls. Also on display are stuffed toys, model trains, toy cars, toy soldiers and mechanical toys.

Roskilde 20

See pp140–41.

Trying out a dugout canoe at Lejre's Stone Age village

Lejre 21

Road map F4. **Open-air museum** Slangealleen 2, 4320 Lejre. ***Tel*** *46 48 08 78.* *May & Jun: 10am–4pm Tue–Fri; end Jun–mid-Aug: 10am–5pm daily; mid-Aug–end Sep: 10am–4pm Tue–Fri, 11am–5pm Sat & Sun.* **www**.sagnlandet.dk

A reconstructed village that takes visitors back to the Iron Age is the main attraction of Lejre, which is situated 8 km (5 miles) to the southwest of Roskilde. In summer Lejre Forsøgcenter is populated by volunteer Danish families who, in the

◁ Frederiksborg Slot and its surrounding gardens seen from the lake

Ledreborg Slot, surrounded by beautiful, well-kept gardens

name of research, dress in prehistoric furs and skins, use traditional tools and carry out all-but-forgotten chores such as chopping firewood and making clay pots.

The village is popular with children, especially in summer, when it is possible for them to take part in a variety of activities including archery, dying clothes and paddling a dugout canoe. The centre also has a 19th-century cottage farm that recreates the lives of Danish farmers of that period.

Research has established that Lejre was one of the earliest centres of government in Denmark. Legend has it that it was the seat of a Stone-Age king named Skjoldungs, although the building shown to the visitors, once home of the supposed sovereign, is a recreation built in the 18th century. It is quite likely, however, that the nearby grave-mound dates from the Stone Age period.

Ledreborg Slot ㉒

Road map F4. Ledreborg Alle 2, 4320 Lejre. ***Tel*** *46 48 00 38.* *Jul–mid-Aug: 11am–5pm Mon–Fri, noon–3pm Sat & Sun.* **Park** *11am–4pm daily (all year round).* **www**.ledreborg-slot.dk

Elegant on the outside and opulent on the inside, Ledreborg Slot is one of the foremost examples of Baroque architecture in northern Europe. It was built in 1739 on the orders of Count Johan Ludvig Holstein. The interior has changed little since that time and contains antique furniture, gilded mirrors, wall paintings, tapestries and massive candelabras. One of the most interesting rooms is the banqueting hall, designed by the renowned royal architect Nicolai Eigtved. In 1745 this exclusive residence acquired a chapel, which until 1899 served as a parish church.

The gardens that surround the castle are a pleasant place to explore. The neatly trimmed hedges make this place one of the most enchanting Baroque gardens in Scandinavia. There is also a maze, created from trimmed shrubs, which can be a source of much merriment.

Holbæk ㉓

Road map F4. *30,000.* *Jernbaneplads 3, 59 43 11 31.* **www**.holbaek-info.dk

An important port, Holbæk is also the main commercial town for the area. It serves as a good starting point for people wishing to visit Øro island, which lies a mere 7 km (4 miles) away. The area has several bicycle trails and Holbæk is also popular with cyclists, who set off from here.

Holbæk was granted municipal privileges in the late 13th century, making it one of the oldest of Zealand's towns. At that time it was the site of a dynamic Dominican monastery, although the oldest surviving remains are these of a Franciscan monastery, which is located next to the Neo-Gothic Sankt Nicolaj Kirke in the medieval part of the town.

Not far from this church is **Holbæk Museum**, which consists of a dozen or so period houses dating from 1660 to 1867. Their interiors include typical items and furnishings from rural and urban dwellings of the 17th and 18th centuries. There is also a reconstructed grocery shop. A café, toy shop and pottery exhibition complete the attractions. The tiny market square between the houses is a venue for numerous events staged during summer months, which often feature people dressed in period costumes.

Holbæk has some good local parks, such as Bysøparken, which has a charming fountain, and Østre Anlæg, where entire families of plump ducks can be seen waddling along the lanes and pecking about on the lawns.

Holbæk Museum
Klosterstræde 18. ***Tel*** *59 43 23 53.* *10am–4pm Tue–Fri, noon–4pm Sun.* **www**.holbmus.dk

Period interior in Holbæk Museum

Roskilde ⓴

Founded in the 10th century by the Vikings, Roskilde was Denmark's first capital. In AD 980 Harald I (Bluetooth) built Zealand's first church here, making the town an important religious centre and from the 11th century it was a bishopric. In the Middle Ages Roskilde had a population of 10,000 and was one of the largest towns in northern Europe. When Erik of Pomerania moved the capital, the town lost much of its status but it flourishes today as a market centre for the region and is popular with visitors in summer who come to see the historic Viking ships and the ancient cathedral.

Exploring Roskilde

All of the town's attractions are within easy reach. The most prestigious streets, lined with shops and cafés, are Skomagergade and Algade. The Vikingeskibsmuseet (Viking Ship Museum) is by the harbour.

Roskilde Domkirke

See pp142–3.

Fountain in front of the town hall in Stændertorvet

Stændertorvet

This small square situated by the town's main promenade has for centuries been the heart of Roskilde. In the Middle Ages it was the site of fairs. Sankt Laurence, a Romanesque church, was demolished in the mid-16th century to provide more space for the growing market. A few remaining parts of the church can be seen today including the tower, which now adorns the town hall (built in 1884) and what remains of the church foundations. The foundations are open to the public and are in the town hall's vaults. In the square is a monument depicting, among others, Roar, the legendary father of Roskilde, who established Roskilde as homage to the two pagan gods, Thor and Odyn.

Roskilde Palace

Stændertorvet 3.
***Tel** 46 31 65 65.*
9am–7pm daily (to 8pm in summer).

Built in 1733 by the Danish architect Laurits de Thurah, this yellow Baroque palace is the former seat of Roskilde's bishops. It is linked to the neighbouring cathedral by the Arch of Absalon. The palace rooms contain two museums. The Museum of Contemporary Art has a permanent collection and also organizes numerous temporary exhibitions of Danish and foreign artists. The Palace Collections has 18th- and 19th-century paintings on display as well as works of art from other periods that were collected by a number of wealthy Roskilde families such as the Bruuns and the Borchs.

Roskilde Museum

Sankt Ols Gade 18. ***Tel** 46 31 65 00.*
11am–4pm daily.
www.roskildemuseum.dk

The municipal museum in Roskilde is an excellent place for anyone interested in the town's history. Its collection – including documents, photographs, archaeological finds and works of art – explains the region's past, from the Stone Age up to the present day (which is aptly symbolized by a display devoted to the prestigious rock festival organized every year in Roskilde since 1971). The museum also includes a building in Ringstedgade, named Brødrene Luetzhøfts Købmandsgård, which is simply a shop furnished in a manner typical of a century or so ago, where potash soap and dried cod can be purchased.

Hussar's uniform, Roskilde Museum

Roskilde Kloster

Sankt Pederstræde 8.
***Tel** 46 35 02 19. Jul: 2–3:30pm; Jan–Jun & Aug–Dec: 9am–9pm.*
Jul–mid-Aug: 2pm Wed (in Danish).
www.roskildkloster.dk

In the Middle Ages Roskilde had about 20 churches and monasteries, not counting the cathedral. Their sacral functions ceased as the Reformation swept through the country in 1536.

This brick-built monastery, which stands in its own grounds, was built in 1560 and, in 1699, became Denmark's first refuge for unmarried mothers from well-to-do families. It has some fine interiors including a chapel and banqueting hall.

Brick monastery buildings of Roskilde Kloster

Gråbrødre Kirkegård

The former cemetery, where prominent and wealthy citizens of the town were buried during the Middle Ages, is now used as a park and is located near the railway station. The station was built in 1847 to serve the Copenhagen–Roskilde line and is one of the oldest train stations in Denmark.

Roskilde Jars commemorating the city's 1,000-year anniversary

Hestetorvet

The main landmark of the market square, used in medieval times for horse trading, are the three 5-m (16-ft) tall jars. These were put in place in 1998 as part of the town's millennium celebrations. Engraved on one of the jars are verses from a poem written by Henrik Nordbrandt, dedicated to Roskilde and to Margrethe I. The jar's creator, Peter Brandes, intended them to symbolize life and death.

Vikingeskibsmuseet

Vindeboder 12.
Tel *46 30 02 00.*
10am–5pm daily.
www.vikingeskibsmuseet.dk

About 1,000 years ago the boats now exhibited at the Viking Ship Museum were filled with stones and sunk in the fjord in order to block the passage of enemy ships. In 1962 five of the vessels were recovered. Although they had been underwater for so long, they are in remarkably good condition and give a good indication of Viking boat-building skills. The largest of them is a 30-m (98-ft) long warship, which could carry a crew of 70 to 80 Vikings. The best preserved is a 14-m (46-ft) long merchant ship, which sailed around the Baltic and Danish sounds. The other ships are a deep-sea trader, a longship and a ferry. The museum also has an exhibition devoted to the Vikings and a working boatyard, where replicas of old Viking ships, including those in the museum, are built using traditional methods and materials. In summer it is possible to sail on a replica ship on the Roskilde Fjord. The museum also has a pleasant café.

VISITORS' CHECKLIST

Road map F4. *50,000.*
Stændertorvet 1.
Tel *46 31 65 65.*
Roskilde Rock Festival (late Jun–early Jul).
info@destination-roskilde.dk
www.visitroskilde.com

Historic boat at Vikingeskibsmuseet

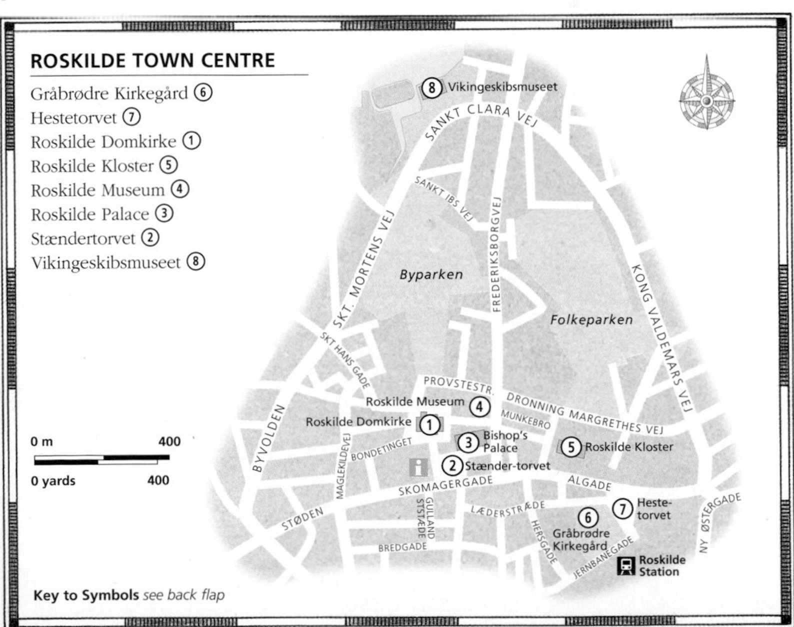

Roskilde Domkirke

The twin towers of this magnificent brick cathedral, begun in the 12th century on the orders of Bishop Absalon, are a landmark of Roskilde. The cathedral is an organic mix of styles. For centuries it was used as the burial site of Danish monarchs, 38 of whom are interred here. The remains of Harald I (Bluetooth), a 10th-century Viking king, are said to be inside one of the columns to the side of the main altar. In view of its historic value the cathedral has been declared a UNESCO World Heritage Site.

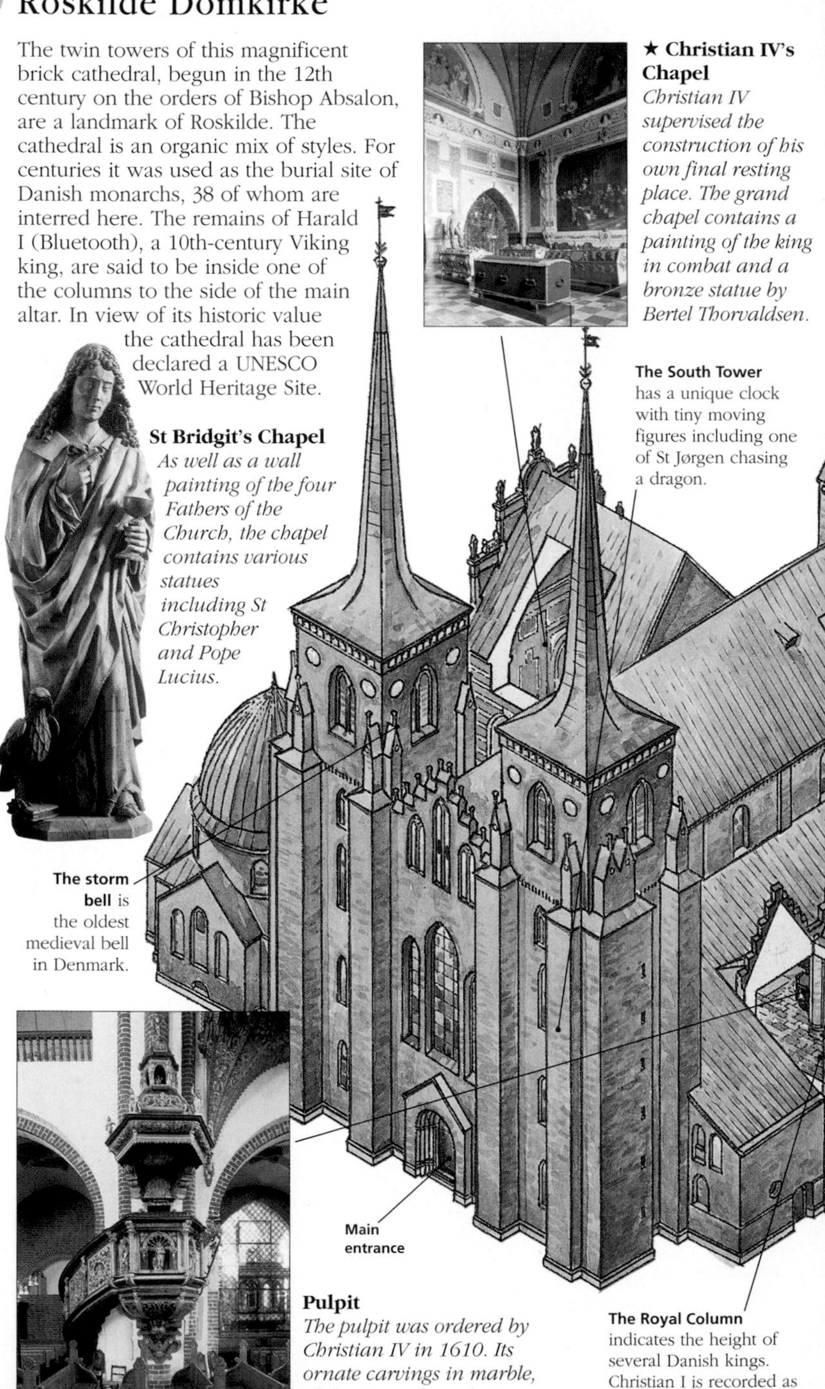

★ Christian IV's Chapel
Christian IV supervised the construction of his own final resting place. The grand chapel contains a painting of the king in combat and a bronze statue by Bertel Thorvaldsen.

The South Tower has a unique clock with tiny moving figures including one of St Jørgen chasing a dragon.

St Bridgit's Chapel
As well as a wall painting of the four Fathers of the Church, the chapel contains various statues including St Christopher and Pope Lucius.

The storm bell is the oldest medieval bell in Denmark.

Main entrance

Pulpit
The pulpit was ordered by Christian IV in 1610. Its ornate carvings in marble, alabaster and sandstone were made by Hans Brokman of Copenhagen.

The Royal Column indicates the height of several Danish kings. Christian I is recorded as 2.06 m (6 ft 9 inches), although his skeleton is 1.88 m (6 ft 2 inches).

Stalls
Set near the altar these wooden pews are beautiful examples of Gothic carving.

VISITORS' CHECKLIST

Domkirkestræde 1. ***Tel*** *46 35 16 24.* *Apr–Sep: 9am–5pm daily (from 12:30pm Sun & hols); Oct–Mar: 10am–4pm Tue–Sat, 12:30–4pm Sun & hols.* **www**.roskildedomkirke.dk

Margrethe's Spire replaced a tower destroyed by fire in 1968.

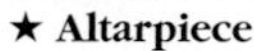

★ Altarpiece
The altar, depicting scenes from the life of Christ, was produced in Antwerp in the 1500s. It is here quite by chance, having been confiscated while on board a ship bound for Gdansk.

Chapter House contains a crucifix made from two bells that melted in the 1968 fire.

★ Sarcophagus of Margrethe I
The sarcophagus bearing an alabaster effigy of Margrethe I as a young girl is considered to be the most beautiful sculpture in the cathedral.

Interior
The cathedral has been rebuilt several times, acquiring features typical of the styles that were currently in fashion. The last major works were carried out following a fire in 1968.

STAR FEATURES

- ★ Altarpiece
- ★ Christian IV's Chapel
- ★ Sarcophagus of Margrethe I

Tveje Merløse Kirke ㉔

Road map E4. *Holbæk, Jernbaneplads 3.* ***Tel*** *59 43 11 31.*

Being a miniature version of Roskilde's original 12th-century cathedral, the church in Tveje Merløse is one of the most interesting Romanesque sacral buildings in Denmark. Its most distinctive features are the two almost identical square towers. The history of the site as a place of worship is believed to date back to the Viking era; some records suggest it was used for worship even earlier than this, in the 3rd century.

The church's interior has an altarpiece by Joakim Skovgaard. At one time the church contained some colourful 13th-century frescoes, depicting among other things, the devil and the motif of God's Majesty, which is a typical medieval theme found particularly in the region of Øresund. These were removed when the church was being restored and are now on display in Copenhagen's Nationalmuseet *(see pp84–5)*. A small cemetery is in the church grounds.

Nørre Jernløse Mølle ㉕

Road map E4.
Windmill Møllebakken 2, Regstrup. ***Tel*** *59 47 17 82. Apr–Oct: 10am–2pm 1st Sun of each month.*
www.nrjernlosemolle.dk

The small village of Nørre Jernløse, located some 25 km (16 miles) west of Roskilde, has a 12th-century church containing 16th-century frescoes. The town is best known, however, for its 19th-century windmill, which is set on an sturdy octagonal base surrounded by a distinctive gallery.

The Dutch-style windmill was built in 1893 in Nørrevold, near Copenhagen, where it was known as Sankt Peders Mølle. When financial difficulties forced its owners to sell the mill it was bought by Niels Peter Rasmussen, a miller, who dismantled it and transported it in pieces on a horse cart to Jernløse, 70 km (43 miles) away. In 1899 the windmill was bought by Ole Martin Nielsen, whose family used and maintained it for the next 60 years. Finally, in 1979 the windmill was handed over to the parish of Jernløse.

Dutch-style windmill in Nørre Jernløse

Built on a stone base, the Nørre Jernløse mill has a timber structure with a shingled roof crowned with a wooden, onion-shaped cupola. Its sails were once cloth covered and could be operated directly from the gallery. The mill, which is no longer used to grind flour, now has an information centre where visitors can learn about the mill's history and about early methods of flour production.

Well in front of the monastery in Sorø

Sorø ㉖

Road map E5. *7,000.*
Storgade 15. ***Tel*** *57 82 10 12.*
www.soroeturisme.dk

Located on the banks of the Tuel and Sorø lakes, Sorø is one of the most beautiful towns in Zealand. In 1140 Bishop Absalon, the founder of Copenhagen, began to build a monastery here. When it was complete the Klosterkirke was the largest building of its kind in Scandinavia and one of the first brick structures ever to be built in Denmark. This 70-m (230-ft) long Romanesque-Gothic church contains the remains of Bishop Absalon in a tomb at the rear of the main altar. The church also contains the sarcophagi of Christian II, Valdemar IV and Oluf III. In 1412 Queen Margrethe I was buried here, but subsequently her remains were transferred to Roskilde Domkirke *(see pp142–3)*.

A small museum is devoted to the church and to Bishop Absalon. Included in the collection is the bishop's gold sapphire ring and a 6-m (20-ft) tall crucifix, which was made by Claus Berg and brought to the church in 1527.

Sorø is perhaps best known for its Akademiet, which is set in a picturesque spot on the shores of Lake Sorø. This famous establishment, dedicated to the education of the sons of the nobility, was founded in 1623 by Christian IV in the monastery buildings left empty as a consequence of the Reformation. The Akademiet is surrounded by a park which contains a monument depicting the writer Ludwig Holberg who bequeathed his considerable fortune and library to the school after his death in 1754. The school still operates though it is no longer reserved only for the country's nobility.

Environs

Tystrup-Bavelse is a national wildlife reserve established near Sorø in the 1960s. The forests contain many prehistoric grave-mounds, including **Kellerøddysen**, Denmark's largest megalithic stone formation, which is over 120 m (394 ft) in length. The reserve's two connected freshwater lakes attract a variety of birdlife and more than 20,000 water birds winter here. **Bjernede**, near Sorø, has the only surviving round church in Zealand. Constructed of stone and brick, it is quite unlike Bornholm's round churches *(see p221)* and was built in 1160 by Sune Ebbesøn, a provincial governor to Valdemar I (The Great).

Bjernede Rundkirke – the only round church in Zealand

Tårnborg 27

Road map E5.

This ancient parish on the shores of Korsør bay, with the rising outline of a white 13th-century church, was once occupied by a castle and settlement. Tårnborg appeared as a place name for the first time in a royal land survey completed in the first half of the 13th century, though it is likely that a stronghold existed at least one hundred years prior to this and, together with Nyborg and Sprogø, controlled the passage across the Store Bælt *(see pp146–7)*. From the 13th century it was also a major centre of commerce and in the 14th century Tårnborg forged links with neighbouring estates, helping to intensify foreign trade. The castle was demolished in the 15th century following a financial crisis.

Distinct white exterior of the 13th-century church in Tårnborg

Archaeological excavations suggest that Tårnborg's original stronghold measured about 30 m (98 ft) in diameter, with an 8-m (26-ft) high tower at its centre.

Korsør 28

Road map E5. *20,000.*
Nygade 7. ***Tel*** *58 35 02 11.*
www.visitsydvestsjaelland.dk

The earliest records of this town date from 1241. The most prominent building in Korsør is a 13th-century fortress (Korsør Fæstning), which played a crucial role in the town gaining control of the Store Bælt. In 1658 the constantly enlarged fortress was captured by the Swedes, but returned to Danish control a year later. Its 25-m (82-ft) high tower now houses the **Korsør By-og Overfarts-museum** (Town and Ferry Service Museum), which has a collection that includes models of ships that once sailed across the Store Bælt.

Clusters of historic buildings, mainly from the 18th century, can be seen in the environs of Algade, Slottensgade and Gavnegade. The Rococo mansion at No. 25 Algade dates from 1761 and was built by Rasmus Langeland, a shipowner. It was originally used as an inn for sailors who were waiting for the right conditions to cross the Store Bælt. Its front is adorned with allegories of the four seasons of the year. Inside is a small art museum displaying, among other things, sculptures by Harald Isenstein who died in 1980.

Korsør By-og Overfartsmuseum
Søbatteriet 7. ***Tel*** *58 37 47 55.*
Apr–Dec: 11am–4pm Tue–Sun.

Ancient cannons outside Korsør Fæstning (Fortress)

Storebælt Bridge ㉙

Until recently the only way of travelling to Zealand was by air or ferry across the Storebælt (Great Belt). In 1998, after 12 years of construction work, the two biggest Danish islands – Zealand and Funen – were joined together. The link consists of two bridges with an artificial island in between. The journey time has now been cut to 10 minutes and the bridge is open 24 hours a day. Of the two bridges, the Østbro (Eastern) suspension bridge presents a more impressive sight. A toll charge of around 215–375 Dkr, depending on the size of your vehicle, is payable at the toll station on the Zealand side. Head to the yellow *Manuel* lanes for payment by credit card or cash.

VISITORS' CHECKLIST

Road map E5. ***Tel*** *70 15 10 15.*
www.storebaelt.dk

Bridges
The Østbro is 7 km (4.4 miles) long and carries cars (trains run in a tunnel). The Vestbro is 6.6 km (4.1 miles) long and carries cars and trains.

These pylons, at 254 m (833 ft), are the highest man-made structures in Scandinavia.

85-m (279 ft) long cables

The bridge is 48.2 m (158 ft) wide.

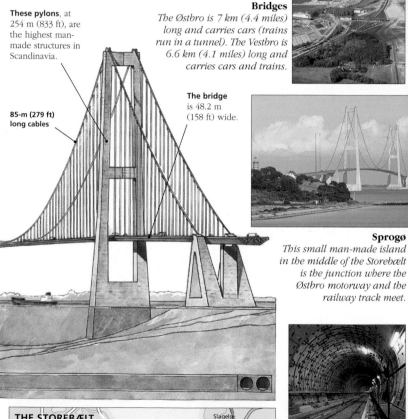

Sprogø
This small man-made island in the middle of the Storebælt is the junction where the Østbro motorway and the railway track meet.

Tunnel
An 8-km (5-mile) long rail tunnel, measuring 7.7 m (25 ft) in diameter, descends 75 m (246 ft) below the surface. It is the second largest underwater tunnel in Europe.

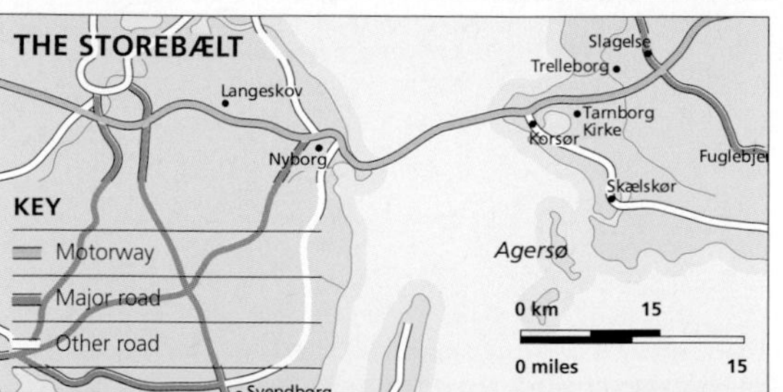

A display of Viking archery in Trelleborg

Trelleborg 30

Road map E5. 7 km (4 miles) east of Slagelse. **Tower** Trelleborg Allé 4, 4200 Slagelse. *Jun–Aug: 10am–5pm Tue–Sun; Apr–May & Sep–Oct: 10am–4pm Tue–Sun.* **www**.vikingeborg.dk

The best-preserved of Denmark's Viking fortresses was founded in the 10th century by Harald I (Bluetooth). At the height of its power it was manned by an estimated force of 1,000 warriors. Of the reconstructed buildings, the longhouse is the most impressive. It is built of rough oak beams and furnished with benches on which the Vikings slept.

Originally, there were 16 buildings in the main section of the fortress. Outside the fortress was a small cemetery, where archaeologists have counted about 150 graves.

In summer visitors can participate in fun and games. Some of the staff are dressed in Viking costume and are on hand to demonstrate such workaday jobs as grinding corn and sharpening tools. Daily workshops provide children with the opportunity to try their hand at archery and even dress up as Vikings.

A small museum exhibits finds excavated from the grounds such as jewellery and pottery. It also screens a 20-minute film about the history of Trelleborg.

Kalundborg 31

Road map E4. *20,000.* *Klosterparkvej 7.* ***Tel*** *59 51 09 15.* **Museum** Adelgade 23. ***Tel*** *59 51 21 41.* *May–Aug: 11am–5pm daily; Sep–Apr: 11am–4pm Sat & Sun.* **www**.kalmus.dk *or* **www**.kalundborg-turistbureau.dk

Kalundborg is one of Zealand's oldest towns and was populated by the Vikings as early as the 9th century. The town was also once used as a base by pirates but in 1168 a castle was built here and control of the fjord's waters was assumed by the crown.

The ruins in Volden square are all that remains of the castle. Its builder was Esbern Snare, the brother of Bishop Absalon. Snare was also the creator of the well-preserved 12th-century Vor Frue Kirke (Church of Our Lady), which has five octagonal towers and a Byzantine design based on a Greek crucifix.

Kalundborg's medieval quarter surrounds the church and includes cobbled streets and 16th-century buildings. One of these now houses the town museum. Most of the exhibits are devoted to local history and include a collection of costumes and the skeletons of two beheaded Vikings. Standing in the museum courtyard is a model of Kalundborg, providing a view of the town's 17th-century layout.

Røsnæs 32

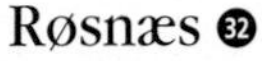

Road map D4. *Kalundborg.*

The Røsnæs peninsula, as well as the Asnæs peninsula that flanks the Kalundborg Fjord on the other side, were created by a continental glacier some 20,000 years ago. In the Middle Ages the Røsnæs peninsula, which thrusts into the Store Bælt, was covered with thick forest, making it one of the favourite areas for royal hunting trips. One hunt, in 1231, organized at the request of Valdemar the Victorious, ended in a bitter tragedy when a stray arrow killed the king's son (who was also named Valdemar).

The peninsula's tip is the westernmost point of Zealand and is marked by a lighthouse erected in 1845. The light from its lantern, mounted 25 m (82 ft) above sea level, can be seen up to 40 km (25 miles) away. A short way before the lighthouse, in the village of Ulstrup, is a Dutch-style windmill built in 1894. It was still being used in the 1950s to grind flour but is now purely a visitor attraction.

At the base of the Asnæs peninsula is Lerchenborg Slot, a Baroque castle built in 1753 by General Christian Lerche. H.C. Andersen stayed here in 1862 and some of the rooms contain items relating to the famous writer.

The unusual five-towered church in Kalundborg

Svinninge 33

Road map E4. *Hovedgaden 7.* ***Tel*** *59 21 60 09.*

The main reason people come to this town, located at the base of the Odsherred peninsula, is to visit its model electric railway, which is one of the longest in Europe. **Svinninge Modeljernbane** is housed in a building measuring 8 m by 14 m (26 ft by 46 ft) and contains over 550 model railway coaches and nearly 90 locomotives. All of the rolling stock, as well as the convincing reconstructions of many Danish stations (including Svinninge, Hilbæk, Lisebro, Hjortholm and Egaa), are built to a scale of 1:87. The creators of this extraordinary display have meticulously and painstakingly recreated entire railway routes, including the link from Holbæk to Oxneholm.

The model railway was originally a private affair and was opened to the public after it was donated to the town by its original creator. The building of this impressive display involved a great deal of work by many people including model makers, carpenters, joiners and electricians. More than 80 m (262 ft) of cable were laid in order to supply current to over 2 km (1.3 miles) of track. Even today, the display continues to grow with new sections of track and locomotives being added yearly.

Svinninge Modeljernbane
Stationen 2, 4520 Svinninge.
Tel *59 21 60 09.* *end Apr–end Oct: 10am–4pm daily.*
www.svmjk.dk

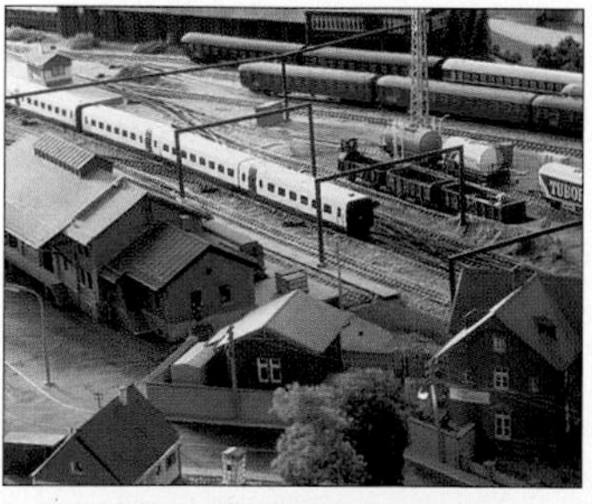

Section of the model railway in Svinninge

Dragsholm Slot, seen from the courtyard

Dragsholm 34

Road map E4. Dragsholm Allé, 4534 Hørve. ***Tel*** *59 65 33 00.* *tours only: Jun–Aug: 1:30pm Tue (in English).*
www.dragsholm-slot.dk

The castle in Dragsholm was once a fortress and later a royal residence. It is now used as a luxurious hotel and restaurant, but has lost none of its historical grandeur.

Situated on the shores of Nekselø bay, at the foot of Zealand's third highest hill – Vejrhøj (121 m/397 ft above sea level) – Dragsholm Slot is one of Denmark's oldest and biggest castles. Its origins date back to the 12th and 13th centuries, when Roskilde's bishops decided to build themselves a seat, which would also serve as a military fortress. They occupied it until 1536 at which point the bishopric was moved to Copenhagen. Dragsholm was then taken over by the king who transformed it into a palace. Following a war with Sweden in the mid-17th century the castle was converted into a prison. The dungeon's most famous inmate was Lord James von Bothwell, the husband of Mary Queen of Scots, who had sought sanctuary in Denmark after Mary's downfall. Instead he was imprisoned and languished here for five years. He eventually went mad and died in 1578. His tomb is in the castle chapel.

In the second half of the 17th century, during another war with Sweden, the castle was badly damaged. Extensive rebuilding work began in 1694 and gave the building its present distinct Baroque aspect. At that time the owners of the castle were Christian Adeler and his wife Henriette Margrete von Lente. The castle remained in the hands of the family until 1932.

Heraldic arms from Dragsholm Slot

Since 1937 the property has been owned by the Bøttger family, who run it as a hotel and restaurant. The 1-m (3-ft) thick walls, high ceilings and sumptuously decorated interiors enhance the historic aura of the place. The most interesting rooms include the magnificent Banqueting Hall (Riddersalen) and Hunting Room (Jagtværelset).

The castle and its moat are surrounded by a large expanse of parkland that contains, among other plants, a collection of rhododendrons. Like all great castles, Dragsholm is reputed to be haunted. The three ghosts that are most frequently spotted are the White Lady, the Grey Lady and, of course, Lord von Bothwell.

◁ **Sailing boats on one of Zealand's lakes**

Odsherred ㉟

Surrounded by the waters of the Kattegat, Isefjord and Serejø bay, the Odsherred peninsula is one of the most popular holiday destinations in Denmark, visited annually by sun-seekers and water sports enthusiasts. Its wide sandy beaches, the lure of the sea and the varied landscape also make this region popular with artists, some of whom have established galleries here.

Sjælland Sommerland ③
This amusement park provides a good day out for families with children. Among the many attractions are a mini train, a roller coaster and giant water slides ending in splash pools.

Havnebyen ⑤
Cutters in the harbour and the aroma from the local smokehouses make this fishing village a memorable place.

Lumsås Mølle ④
This restored mill dates from the 19th century and is open to the public. Flour ground on site can still be bought.

Højby Sø ②
The banks of this small lake are inhabited by a wide variety of birds. The lake is also popular with anglers.

Gniben ⑥
The narrow strip of land stretching westwards has wide sandy beaches and is excellent for sunbathing. Gniben, situated furthest to the west, affords magnificent views of the sea.

TIPS FOR DRIVERS

Length of route:
50 km (31 miles).
Nykøbing SJ: Algade 43.
***Tel** 59 91 08 88.*
www.visitodsherred.dk

0 km 2
0 miles 2

KEY

- Suggested route
- Scenic route
- Other road
- Viewpoint

Højby ①
The interior of the local church is decorated with frescoes depicting, among others, Sankt Jørgen.

For hotels and restaurants in this region see pp247–9 and pp274–6

SOUTHERN ZEALAND AND THE ISLANDS

The lowlands of southern Zealand are characterized by cultivated fields and beautiful lakes. Many visitors see only Vordingborg and Køge, two towns that have played a significant part in Denmark's history, but the islands of Lolland, Falster and Møn to the south are attractive holiday destinations and offer miles of sandy beaches, woodland and awe-inspiring views of coastal cliffs.

Southern Zealand (Sjælland) is an important region for the Danes. Vordingborg was the capital of the Valdemar dynasty and in the 12th century was used by Bishop Absalon as a staging post for his military expeditions to eastern Germany. The market town of Ringsted, in central Zealand, was for many years the venue of the *landsting*, a regional government assembly that formed the basis of the present-day parliament. In 1677, Køge Bay was the scene of a major naval engagement in which the Danish Admiral Niels Juel became a national hero when he dealt a crushing blow to the Swedish fleet.

The islands to the south of Zealand are more rural in character. Lolland is Denmark's third biggest island (1,243 sq km/480 sq miles) and also its flattest (at its highest point it is a mere 22 m/72 ft above sea level). The island has some pretty beaches and is popular with hikers in summer. Falster is only slightly smaller and is visited mainly for its wide beaches. Møn is the smallest of the islands and the hardest to reach. The journey is worth it, however, as Møn has rustic scenery, spectacular white cliffs, good beaches and some interesting sights including Neolithic burial places and a number of medieval churches containing some spectacular frescoes.

Ducks near the shore of Sondersø, Maribo

◁ Spectacular chalk cliffs of Møns Klint

Exploring Southern Zealand and the Islands

The largest town in southern Zealand is Næstved, which has a number of historic buildings. However, Køge, Ringsted and Vordingborg have more to offer in the way of outstanding buildings. This part of Denmark is particularly attractive to families as it has a slow pace and child-friendly attractions such as BonBon-Land, Knuthenborg Safari Park on Lolland and, on Falster, a recreated medieval village. A number of museums are also popular with children including Ålholm's Automobile Museum. Falster benefits from some of Denmark's best beaches; Lolland has a popular resort complex.

Brick-built Holsted Kirke, Næstved

GETTING AROUND

Getting from southern Zealand to Falster and Lolland presents few problems thanks to the toll-free bridges. The main arterial road – the E47 motorway – runs from Copenhagen via southern Zealand to Falster and Rødbyhavn on Lolland. Most places are easily accessible from Copenhagen by train except for Møn, which has no railway.

KEY

- Motorway
- Major road
- Minor road
- Scenic route
- Main railway
- Minor railway

SEE ALSO

- ***Where to Stay*** pp249–51.
- ***Where to Eat*** pp276–7.

For additional map symbols *see back flap*

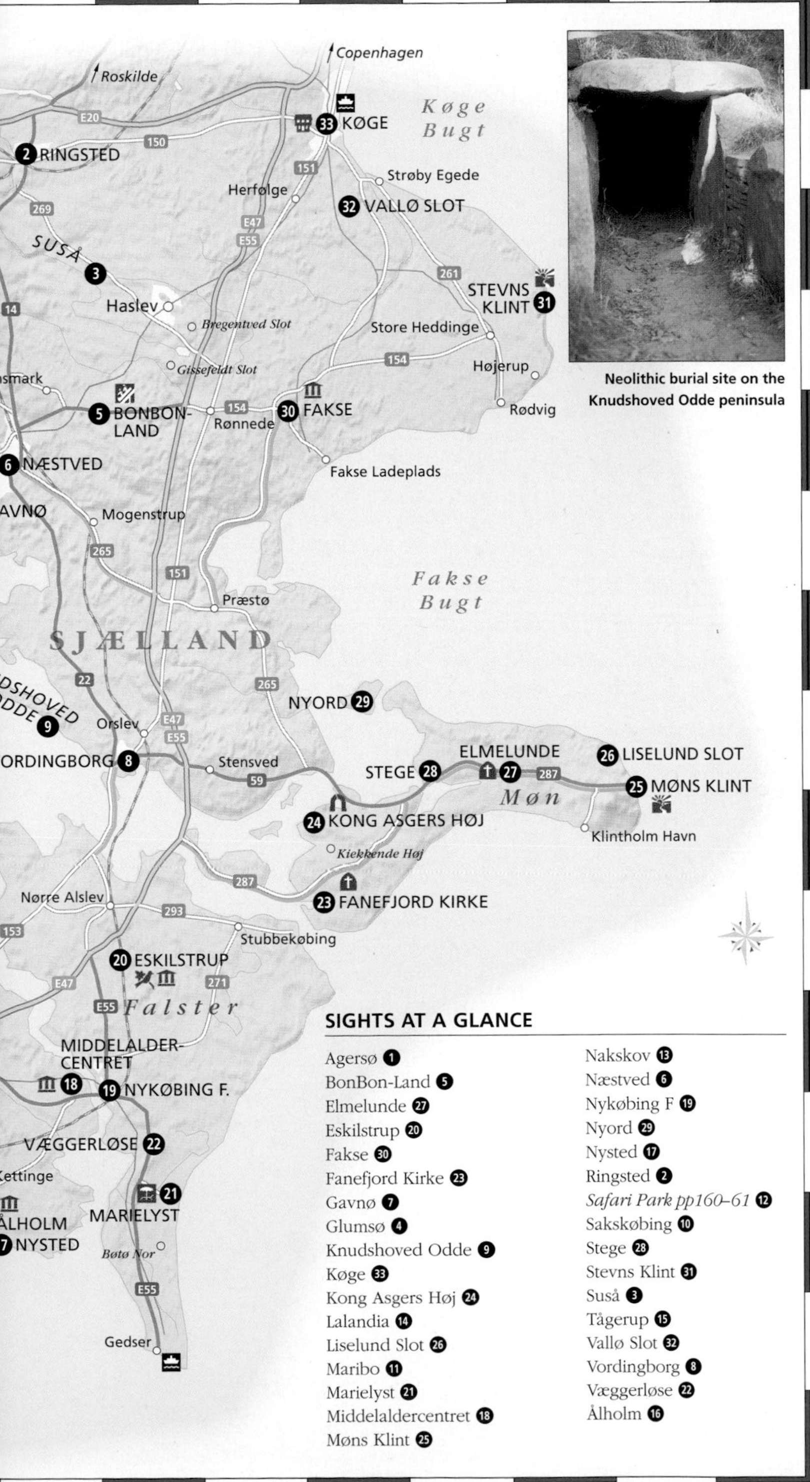

Neolithic burial site on the Knudshoved Odde peninsula

SIGHTS AT A GLANCE

Agersø 1
BonBon-Land 5
Elmelunde 27
Eskilstrup 20
Fakse 30
Fanefjord Kirke 23
Gavnø 7
Glumsø 4
Knudshoved Odde 9
Køge 33
Kong Asgers Høj 24
Lalandia 14
Liselund Slot 26
Maribo 11
Marielyst 21
Middelaldercentret 18
Møns Klint 25
Nakskov 13
Næstved 6
Nykøbing F 19
Nyord 29
Nysted 17
Ringsted 2
Safari Park pp160–61 12
Sakskøbing 10
Stege 28
Stevns Klint 31
Suså 3
Tågerup 15
Vallø Slot 32
Vordingborg 8
Væggerløse 22
Ålholm 16

Vaulted interior of Sankt Bendts Kirke, Ringsted

Agersø ❶

Road map E5. **www**.agersoe.com **Agersø Mill** ***Tel*** *58 19 81 03.* *school hols: 2–4pm Fri–Sun.* **www**.agersoe-moelle.dk

A 15-minute ferry trip from Stigsnæs, a small town 7 km (4.3 miles) southwest of Skælskør, takes visitors to the lovely island of Agersø. This strip of land is just 3 km (1.8 miles) wide and 7 km (4.3 miles) long, and it is home to a community of about 240 people.

Despite its small size, Agersø has a lot to offer, starting with the pretty harbour, which plays host to all manner of vessels, from ferries and yachts to fishing boats. There is also a comprehensive network of walking and cycling routes starting from the harbour and covering a length of 20 km (12.4 miles). The north of the island features several unspoiled beaches with good bathing.

The island's main attraction, however, is probably the Agersø Mølle, a mill built in 1892. Farmers from the surrounding areas would come here to grind their corn. Resting on a stone base, the octagonal uppermill is made of wood and covered with shingle. The mill was in use until 1959, when its owner, a baker called Erik Thomsen, gifted it to the people of Agersø. A bench was placed next to the mill in his honour.

Ringsted ❷

Road map E5. *18,000.* **www**.visitringsted.dk

Owing to its location at the crossroads of two trading routes, Ringsted was once an important market town. It was the venue for regional government assemblies – the *landsting* – which took decisions and passed laws on major national issues. The three stones standing in the market square were used hundreds of years ago by members of the *landsting*.

Ringsted gained notoriety in 1131 when Knud (Canute) Laward, duke of southern Zealand, was murdered in the neighbouring woods by his jealous cousin Magnus. He is buried in Ringsted's Sankt Bendts Kirke (St Benedict's Church) along with a number of Danish kings and queens. Sankt Bendts Kirke was erected in 1170 and is believed to be the oldest brick church in Scandinavia. Its main altarpiece dates from 1699; its baptismal font is believed to be 12th century and was for a time used as a flower pot in a local garden until it was discovered quite by chance. The magnificent frescoes were painted in about 1300 and include a series depicting Erik IV (known as Ploughpenny for his tax on ploughs).

In the 17th century it was decided to open some of the coffins. The items found in them are on display in one of the chapels. The Dagmar Cross, dating from about AD 1000, is a copy. The original cross is on display in the Nationalmuseet in Copenhagen *(see pp84–5)*. The famous cross once belonged to Queen Dagmar, the first wife of Valdemar II. Depicted on its enamelled surface is a beautiful figure of Christ with his arms outstretched. On the other side of the cross, Christ is pictured with the Virgin Mary flanked by John the Baptist, St John and St Basil.

Suså ❸

Road map E5.

At nearly 90 km (56 miles) long, Suså is one of Denmark's longest rivers. From its source near the town of Rønnede it flows through two lakes, Tystrup Sø and Bavelse Sø, to end its journey in Karrebæk Bay, near Næstved. The picturesque surroundings and slow-flowing current make the river particularly popular with canoeists. Canoe trips are usually taken over the final stretch of the river, where a canoe or a kayak can be hired for an hour or two. River traffic gets quite busy in summer, and many large family groups enjoy picnicking along the river banks.

It is easy to combine canoeing with a bit of sightseeing. Quite close to the river's source, in Rønnede, is a beautiful rhododendron park. Near Haslev are two magnificent properties. Gissefeldt Slot, completed in 1575, is one of the finest Renaissance castles in northern Europe and is surrounded by gardens

Suså – Zealand's longest river

Canoeing on the Suså past the Gunderslev Kirke in Skelby

containing about 400 species of trees and shrubs. The castle was often visited by Hans Christian Andersen – it was here that he got his idea for *The Ugly Duckling*. Bregentved Slot, on the outskirts of Haslev, was erected in the 1650s; however, the property was substantially modified in the late 1880s.

Glumsø ❹

Road map E5.

Glumsø is a good base from which to embark upon a canoeing trip along the Suså. Located about 10 km (6 miles) south of Ringsted, its other main attraction is the **Dansk Cykel & Knallert Museum** (Museum of Bicycles and Motorbikes), which has a huge collection of two- and three-wheeled transportation, from vintage cycles to trendy modern scooters. Some bikes can even be ridden by visitors.

Environs

South of Glumsø, on the banks of the Suså, is **Skelby**. The main point of interest here is Gunderslev Kirke, a 12th-century church. Its sumptuously furnished interior was paid for by the former owners of the nearby Gunderslevholm estate.

Dansk Cykel & Knallert Museum
Sorøvej 8. ***Tel*** *57 64 77 94.*
May–Sep: 11am–5pm Sat & Sun.
www.dckm.dk/cykelmuseum

BonBon-Land ❺

Road map E5. Holme-Ostrup, Gartnervej 2. ***Tel*** *55 53 07 00.* *Apr–May: 9:30am–7pm Sat, Sun & hols; Jun: 9:30am–5pm Tue–Fri, 9:30am–7pm Sat, Sun & hols; Jul–mid-Aug: 9:30am–7pm daily; mid-Aug–late Aug: 9:30am–5pm Wed–Fri, 9:30am–7pm Sat & Sun; late Aug–mid-Oct: 9:30am–5pm Sat, Sun & hols.* *children up to 90 cm (3 ft) tall are admitted free.* **www**.bonbonland.dk

This amusement park attracts large numbers of visitors in the summer. The entrance fee covers all the 100 or so attractions. In addition, children are given a free cap to take home as a souvenir. The greatest thrill is undoubtedly provided by a ride on the giant roller coaster, which races along at speeds up to 70 km/h (43 mph) and rises to a height of 22 m (72 ft) before hurtling back down again. A similar surge of adrenaline can be felt when dropping from the 35-m (115-ft) high tower. Gentler amusement can be had on the park's merry-go-rounds or mini racetracks. The queues lengthen for the water slides when the temperature rises as do those for a raft trip down some white-water rapids.

Next door to BonBon-Land, and included in its price of admission, is Fantasy World, Denmark's largest indoor attraction. This vast discovery centre is packed with a huge number of animatronic figures that are arranged in a series of colourful dioramas. One section has fairy-tale creatures inhabiting well-known scenes from the stories of Hans Christian Andersen. Elsewhere, children can see models of tigers and guitar-playing chimpanzees in a jungle setting, while a walk through an eerie forest brings visitors face to face with trolls and snickering goblins.

Fantasy World
En verden af eventyr og leg!

Fantasy World logo

As well as the rides, BonBon-Land has circus performances, magic shows, trained sea lions, a rodeo and daily concerts. It won't win any prizes for high culture, but it is a great day out for families travelling with children.

Children's attractions in BonBon-Land

Næstved 6

Road map E5. *50,000.*
Havnen 1. ***Tel*** *55 72 11 22.*
www.visitnaestved.com

Southern Zealand's largest town, Næstved has been an important centre of trade since medieval times. The 15th-century town hall in Axeltorv, the main square, is one of the oldest in Denmark. The town has two Gothic churches. The 14th-century frescoes in Sankt Peder Kirke (St Peter's Church) depict Valdemar IV and his wife Helveg kneeling in prayer. Sankt Mortens is 13th century and has a beautiful altarpiece that was completed in 1667.

Among the town's other notable buildings are Konpagnihuset, a half-timbered Guild House (1493) and Apostelhuset (Apostles' House), built in the early 16th century. Its name derives from the figures of Christ and his 12 disciples placed between the windows.

Næstved's oldest building, however, is Helligåndhuset (House of the Holy Spirit), which dates from the 14th century and was used as a hospital and almshouse. It now houses **Næstved Museum** with displays of local handicraft (pottery, silverware and glassware) and an interesting collection of medieval and contemporary woodcarvings. The Løveapoteket (Pharmacy), on Axeltorv, dates back to 1640 – a herb garden is situated in the courtyard. Munkebakken Park (a short way from Axeltorv) contains statues of seven monks which have been carved out of tree trunks.

English-style castle garden in Gavnø

Næstved Museum
Ringstedgade 4. ***Tel*** *55 77 08 11.*
10am–4pm Tue–Sun (to 2pm Sat).

Gavnø 7

Road map E5. ***Tel*** *55 70 02 00.*
mid-Apr–May: 10am–5pm daily; Jun–Sep: 10am–4pm daily; Oct–Dec: 10am–8pm Mon, Wed & Sun.
www.gavnoe.dk

Located a little way from Næstved and linked to it by road, this tiny island was used by pirates in the 13th century. In the 14th century Queen Margrethe I established a convent here.

According to legend, the convent was the scene of a tragic love affair in the 16th century between Count Henrik Hog and Ida Baggsen. The boy's father, who disapproved of the girl, sent his son away, while Ida was forced to enter the convent. When the boy returned, the lovers resumed their affair. The couple were discovered: the nuns punished the girl by burying her alive; the count narrowly escaped death and was whisked abroad.

Former Benedictine abbey in Næstved

The remains of the convent include a chapel dating from 1401. After the Reformation the convent become a privately owned manor house. The current building is 18th century and is constructed on the ruins of the convent. It owes its Rococo appearance to the Reedtz-Tholt family, who took control of the place in 1755. The pride of the house is its art collection, which includes over 2,000 paintings. It is regarded as one of the most important private collections in Scandinavia.

The grounds themselves look their best in spring when there are displays of flowers made from over half a million plants, including tulips, hyacinths and crocuses. The gardens also have a butterfly house containing specimens imported from the Far East.

Vordingborg 8

Road map F6. *20,000.*
Slotsruinen 1. ***Tel*** *55 34 11 11.*
www.visitvordingborg.dk

Vordingborg is on the strait between Zealand and Falster that leads to the Baltic, and was once Denmark's most important town. It was the royal residence of Valdemar I (The Great) who came to the throne in 1157 and built a castle here, ushering in a period of relative peace in the country's history. In 1241 Valdemar II sanctioned the Jutland Code in Vordingborg,

For hotels and restaurants in this region see pp249–51 and pp276–7

which gave Denmark its first written laws. Subsequent monarchs from the Valdemar dynasty also took a liking to the castle and enlarged it over the years. The final length of its defensive wall was 800 m (2,625 ft) and its imposing appearance was emphasized by nine mighty towers.

Most of the towers are now in ruins except for the 14th-century Gåsetårnet (Goose Tower). This 36-m (118-ft) high tower has walls that are 3.5 m (11.5 ft) thick in places. Its name dates back to 1368 when Valdemar IV placed a golden goose on top of the tower in order to express his belief that the Hanseatic League's declaration of war was no more threatening than the cackling of geese. Though it has been modified (the conical roof was added in 1871), Gåsetårnet is important as the only intact building to remain from the Valdemar era. The building opposite the tower now houses the **Danmarks Borgcenter**, which has displays on the castle's history and the three kings who lived there. Immediately behind the museum is a botanical garden.

The 14th-century Gåsetårnet in Vordingborg

Algade is Vordingborg's main street and has been pedestrianized. It leads to Vor Frue Kirke (Church of Our Lady), a 15th-century church which contains a Baroque altarpiece dating from 1642.

Tower & Danmarks Borgcenter
Jun–Sep: 10am–5pm daily; Oct–May: 10am–4pm Tue–Sun.
www.danmarksborgcenter.dk

Knudshoved Odde 9

Road map E5. *The peninsula can be reached by car, from Oreby.*

The narrow strip of the Knudshoved Odde peninsula is 20 km (12 miles) long and only 1 km (half a mile) at its widest point. The peninsula is owned by the Rosenfeldt Estate, which has managed to preserve the unique landscape. There are no towns or villages here and the only road is closed to motor traffic after about 10 km (6 miles). This inaccessibility makes it popular with people who come to sit on the seashore, gather blackberries and explore the woods (which can be reached by foot from the car park halfway along the peninsula where the trail begins). The wood's marked walking trails are not taxing and range from a short stroll to one that is just under 4 km (2 miles).

Until quite recently another local attraction was a herd of buffalo, which was imported from America by the Rosenfeldt family. The animals inhabited the top end of the peninsula, where they enjoyed a considerable degree of freedom. After a number of incidents it was finally decided that the herd caused too much damage and the buffalo have since been removed.

The peninsula is also known for its Neolithic burial mounds. One of these historic graves, which was dug about 5,500 years ago, can be seen close to the car park. Excavations have established that its ancient occupant was provided with all possible necessities for the after-life, including plenty of food and drink.

Sakskøbing 10

Road map E6. Lolland. *9,400.*
Torvegade 4. ***Tel*** *54 70 56 30 (Jun–Sep).*

One of Lolland's oldest settlements, Sakskøbing has few historic remains other than a Romanesque church (13th century). However, in view of the town's location on the E47, the main road linking Zealand to Falster and Lolland, it is a popular stopping-off point. The town's most striking feature is a water tower that resembles a smiling face.

Monument to Polish workers in Sakskøbing

A distinctive landmark in the market square is the monument erected in 1939 for the Polish men and women who worked in the local fields. The town's links with Poland date back to the end of the 19th century when many Poles came here in search of work. Many settled permanently on the island and some local Catholic churches still celebrate mass in Polish.

Shores of the Knudshoved Odde peninsula

Safari Park ⓬

Knuthenborg Safari Park provides visitors with the chance to see such exotic creatures as zebras, camels, antelopes and giraffes. The parkland itself has been in the hands of the same family since the 17th century. It was landscaped in an English style in the 19th century and the first animals were transported by ship from Kenya in 1969. Today there are about 1,000 animals. The park's botanical garden contains many rare trees and shrubs.

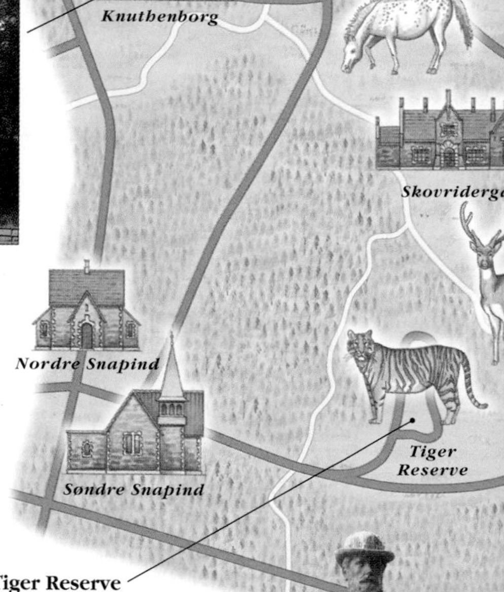

★ Knuthenborg

The house is surrounded by English-style parkland and was designed by Edward Milner. It bears clear signs of a Victorian influence. The main building is still inhabited by the Knuth family.

★ Tiger Reserve

The pride of the park are the Siberian tigers, the largest of all tigers. They enjoy bathing, which is unusual for cats. The deep marks visible on the trees have been left by the tigers' sharp claws.

Statue of the Park's Founder

Eggert Christoffer Knuth (1838–74) was a great 19th-century explorer. He brought back seeds and cuttings from his many voyages abroad. Many of these were cultivated and some are still growing in the park.

STAR SIGHTS

- ★ Knuthenborg
- ★ Tiger Reserve

Zebras
The zebras are allowed to roam freely and mingle with other animals in the park. They can run at speeds of up to 60 km/h (40 mph) when startled.

VISITORS' CHECKLIST

Road map E6. Knuthenborg, Bandholm. Lolland. ***Tel*** 54 78 80 89. *end Apr–mid-Sep: daily; mid-Sep–early Oct: Sat & Sun; for opening hours, visit the website.* **www**.knuthenborg.dk

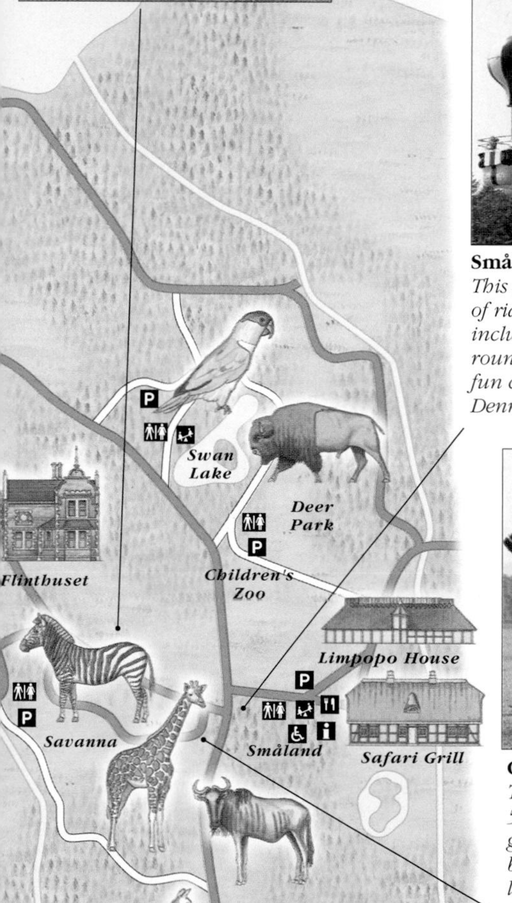

Småland
This tot-sized park contains a number of rides for "mini adventurers" including a train and a merry-go-round. Older children can also have fun climbing rope bridges in this Denmark's largest outdoor playground.

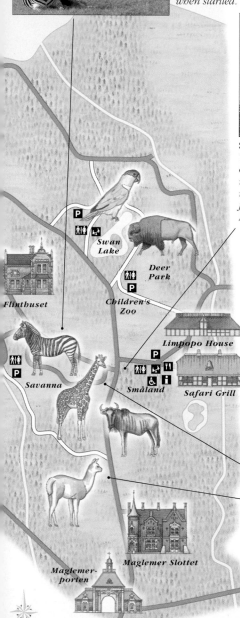

Giraffes
The giraffe can grow up to 5.5 m (18 ft) in height. The park's giraffes can sometimes be seen bending, with legs wide apart, to drink water.

Llamas
Along with donkeys, goats and camels, llamas are some of the park's more docile inhabitants and can be seen grazing near the main entrance.

Half-timbered houses in Maribo

Maribo ⓫

Road map E6. Lolland. *5,500.* *Torvet 1, Det Gamle Rådhus.* ***Tel*** *54 78 04 96.* **www**.turistlolland.dk

Situated on the northern shore of Søndersøl, a large inland lake, Maribo is Lolland's commercial centre. The town was founded in 1416 by Erik of Pomerania and soon acquired a Gothic cathedral. All that remains of an original convent and monastery complex are the cathedral's bells (that toll six times a day) and a gallery where the nuns used to pray. The convent was dissolved following the Reformation.

The cathedral is located a short way from Torvet, the town's main square, which contains a 19th-century Neo-Classical town hall and several half-timbered houses.

Maribo has two museums, with a joint admission fee. The **Lolland-Falster Stiftsmuseum** has a collection of church art and displays relating to Polish workers. The **Stortrøms Kunstmuseum** has some local history displays as well as a collection of regional art. **Frilandsmuseet**, a short way south west of Maribo, is an open-air museum where there are a number of period cottages, as well as other buildings including a windmill and a smithy.

Lolland-Falster Stiftsmuseum & Stortrøms Kunstmuseum
Tel *54 84 44 00.* *10am–4pm Tue–Sat.*

Frilandsmuseet
Tel *72 40 16 20.* *May–Oct: 10am–4pm Tue–Sun.*

Safari Park ⓬

See pp160–61.

Nakskov ⓭

Road map E6. Lolland. *16,000.* *Axeltorv 3.* ***Tel*** *54 92 21 72.*

Nakskov's origins date back to the 13th century. A reminder of its medieval past is the tower of Sankt Nikolai Kirke (Church), which rises above the old quarter. The oldest of Nakskov's houses is Dronningens Pakhus, a quayside warehouse that was built in 1590 and Den Gamle Smedie, a smithy where visitors can see a blacksmith working with 200-year-old tools. The town's greatest attraction, however, is **U-359**, a Soviet submarine built during the Cold War. Launched in 1953 the 76-m (249-ft) long submarine was able to descend to a depth of 300 m (984 ft) and carried a crew of 58. The historic vessel sailed under the Russian flag until 1989, when it was bought by the Danes. The sub's claustrophic atmosphere is intensified by the piped commands issued by the captain, which accompany the sound of alarm bells and the sonar's constant "ping".

Most of Denmark's sugar beet is grown on Lolland and **Denmark's Sugar Museum** tells the story of the crop and the Polish immigrants who arrived to work in the fields.

Russian U-359 submarine moored in Nakskov harbour

Environs

Købelevhaven, about 6 km (4 miles) north of Nakskov, is a botanical garden. Established in 1975, it has a large rhododendron collection, a Japanese garden and some rare magnolia and Asian trees.

U-359
Tel *54 95 20 16.* *Feb–Oct: 10am–4pm Mon–Fri (Jun–Aug: daily).*

Denmark's Sugar Museum
Tel *54 92 36 44.* *Nov–Apr: 1–4pm Sun; May–Oct: 1–4pm Tue–Sun.* **www**.sukkermuseet.dk

Palm trees enliven Lalandia's food and drink area

Lalandia ⓮

Road map E6. Lolland. *Rødby, Lalandiacentret 1.* ***Tel*** *54 61 06 00.* **www**.lalandia.dk

Many families come to Lalandia – Denmark's largest holiday centre – for a short break. The resort is on the southern coast of Lolland and offers numerous attractions to visitors. The local beach competes for children's attention with the aquapark where swimming pools and slides are surrounded by artificial lakes and tropical vegetation. Regardless of the outside temperature the water in the pools never falls below 28° C (82° F). For sports enthusiasts, there are tennis courts, a golf course, mini-golf, and, in the case of bad weather, a vast leisure complex that includes a gymnasium, bowling alleys, amusement arcades and indoor tennis.

Display in Polakkasernen, Tågerup

Visitors to Lalandia can stay in apartments that can sleep up to eight people. All of the apartments have their own bathrooms and kitchens. There are also numerous restaurants and bars spread around the holiday complex.

Tågerup ⓯

Road map E6. Lolland.

The main attraction of Tågerup, a small village situated a short way south of Maribo, is its Romanesque-Gothic church, which contains some fine 15th-century frescoes. At the entrance to the church is a runic stone. Many visitors are surprised to find a building displaying the Polish flag. This is **Polakkasernen**, or the Polish Barracks, and contains documents, fragments of diaries and various items left by Polish immigrants who from 1893 began arriving in Lolland in great numbers. Many Poles were on the move for political reasons as the Soviet Union had taken control of Poland. There were also economic reasons, however, and immigrants arrived from Poland between 1870 and 1920 in a bid to escape a feudal system that gave them few legal rights. Once they arrived most Poles found employment as labourers in the local sugar-beet fields.

A short way from Polakkasernen is **Lungholm**, an early 15th-century residence. Unfortunately, the house itself is not open to the public but a section of the English-style garden that surrounds it can be viewed without restrictions.

Polakkasernen
Højbygårsvej 34. ***Tel*** *54 82 23 30.*
Easter, Whitsun, Jul–Aug: 2–4pm Tue–Sun.

Lungholm
Rødbyvej 24. ***Tel*** *54 60 02 53.*
Garden *dawn until dusk.*

Ålholm ⓰

Road map E6. Lolland.

Ålholm Slot (Castle) is on the outskirts of Nysted and dates from the 12th century. It was crown property for many years and the rooms contain many royal furnishings. In 1332 Christian II was held prisoner in the dungeons here on the orders of his half-brother. The castle is now in private hands. Unfortunately it is not open to the public. Not far from the castle is the **Ålholm Automobile Museum**. This is the largest museum of its kind in northern Europe and has a collection of over 200 vehicles; the oldest of the cars on display date from the 19th century. Its exhibits also include a vintage air-plane and a model railway.

Ålholm Slot seen from the water

Ålholm Automobile Museum
Ålholm Parkvej 17. ***Tel*** *54 87 19 11.*
Jun–Aug: 10am–5pm daily; May, Sep–Oct: 10am–4pm Sat & Sun (daily mid-Oct).
www.aalholm.dk

Nysted ⓱

Road map E6. Lolland. *6,000.* *Strandvejen 18.* ***Tel*** *54 87 19 85.* **www**.nysted-turistforening.dk

This small harbour town situated on the Rødsand bay was founded in the 13th century. Nysted's main historic monuments are a large Gothic church dating from the early 14th century, and a much later 17th-century tower. There are also a number of half-timbered houses and a water tower, which now serves as a viewpoint. In Nysted it is possible to tour a local candle factory, Svane Lys, where visitors can not only see some of the factory's products, but also try their hand at making their own candles.

Environs
About 3 km (2 miles) north of Nysted is **Kettinge**, a small village which has an old Dutch windmill and a church containing some magnificent frescoes.

Woman dressed in period costume at Middelaldercentret

Middelalder-centret ⓲

Road map F6. Lolland. *Sundby, Ved Hamborgskoven 2.* ***Tel*** *54 86 19 34.* *May & Sep: 10am–4pm Tue–Sun; Jun & Aug: 10am–4pm daily; Jul: 10am–4pm daily (to 6pm Wed & Thu).* **www**.middelaldercentret.dk

Lolland's Middle Ages Centre is a recreated medieval settlement that provides an insight into what life was like in the 14th century. Crafts and games from medieval times are displayed and explained by staff wearing costumes from the period, while the local inn serves a range of "medieval" food. A replica sailing ship lies in the harbour and a huge wooden catapult is ready for firing. Jousting tournaments are a regular feature in summer, and visitors can also try their hand at archery. A marked walking trail in the nearby forest explains medieval customs and includes a site where charcoal is made. Along the walk, visitors are warned about woodland spirits and are invited to throw a ghost-repelling stick at an appropriate spot – just in case.

The centre can easily be reached from Nykøbing F by crossing the bridge that connects Lolland and Falster.

Nykøbing F ⓳

Road map F6. Falster. *25,000.* *Østergågade 7.* ***Tel*** *54 85 13 03.* **www**.tinf.dk

Falster's largest town and capital city was a busy commercial centre in medieval times and was granted municipal status in the early 13th century by Valdemar II. In order to distinguish it from two other Danish towns of the same name, this Nykøbing is followed by the letter F (standing for Falster).

Nykøbing F's main historic sight is a 15th-century brick church, which once formed part of a Franciscan monastery. Its richly decorated interior includes an eye-catching series of portraits of Queen Sophie (wife of Frederik II) together with her family, which were commissioned in 1627. Another notable sight is the half-timbered Czarens Hus (Tsar's House), which is one of the oldest buildings in town. In 1716 the Russian Tsar, Peter the Great, stopped here over night on his way to Copenhagen. Today, the building is used as a restaurant and also houses a local history museum – **Guldborgsund Museum**. Among the museum's exhibits are some reconstructed interiors including an 18th-century peasant cottage and a 19th-century burgher's house.

The most panoramic view of Nybøking F is from the early 20th-century yellow water tower. **Nykøbing F Zoo** is a little way east of the train station and has a variety of animals including deer, monkeys and goats.

Statue of a bear in Nykøbing F

Guldborgsund Museum
Langgade 2. ***Tel*** *54 85 26 71.*
11am–5pm Tue–Fri, 11am–3pm Sat, 2–4pm Sun.

Nykøbing F Zoo
Øster Alle 92. ***Tel*** *54 85 20 76.*
May–mid-Aug: 9am–5pm daily; mid-Aug–Apr: 10am–4pm daily.
www.nyk-zoo.dk

Eskilstrup ⓴

Road map F6. Falster.

This small town is situated a short distance from the E47 motorway and has two rather unusual museums.

The **Traktor-museum** is housed in a multi-storey brick building and contains over 200 tractors and engines dating from 1880 to 1960. Alongside a wide selection of vintage Fiats, Fords, Volvos and Fergusons are rare

Nykøbing F, as seen from the river

◁ **Evening horse ride along the beach**

Beautiful white beaches around Marielyst

Czechoslovakian and Romanian tractors. The oldest tractor in the museum is American and was built in 1917. There is also a steam traction engine built in England in 1889. Until 1925 it was still being used as a threshing machine. A number of small pedal-tractors are also provided for the amusement of children.

About 3 km (2 miles) from the town centre is the **Krokodille Zoo**. This is the largest collection of crocodiles in Europe and includes all but four of the 23 species of these sharp-toothed reptiles that exist worldwide. The smallest among them is the dwarf cayman, which grows up to 159 cm (62 inches) in length. At the other end of the scale, the zoo's giant Nile crocodile is called Samson and is currently the largest crocodile in Scandinavia.

As well as the many crocodiles, the zoo also contains a variety of other species including a green anaconda (the world's largest snake) and turtles. The zoo also helps towards the conservation of crocodiles by donating a percentage of the admission price to an international programme of scientific research and protection associated with crocodiles living in the wild.

Traktormuseum
Nørregade 17B. ***Tel*** *54 43 70 07.*
May–Jun, Sep: 10am–4pm Tue–Sun; Jul–Aug: 10am–5pm daily. **www**.traktormuseum.dk

Krokodille Zoo
Ovstrupvej 9. ***Tel*** *54 45 42 42.*
mid-Jun–mid-Aug: 10am–5pm daily; mid-Aug–Oct & Apr: noon–5pm Tue–Sun; Nov–Mar & May–mid Jun: noon–4pm Tue–Sun. **www**.krokodillezoo.dk

Marielyst 21

Road map F6. Falster.
Marielyst Strandpark 3. ***Tel*** *54 13 62 98.* **www**.visitlollandfalster.dk

Situated on the eastern end of the island, Marielyst gets its revenue mainly from its many summer visitors and is one of the foremost holiday resorts in the whole of Denmark. One of the main attractions is the fine white sand beach, which is a good length and easily accessible. It also benefits from clean and fairly shallow waters. The dunes running parallel to the coastline are an additional attraction and are fringed by an ancient beech forest. There are plenty of shops, restaurants and bars. Along with camp sites, guesthouses and hotels the town also has about 6,000 summer cottages.

Environs

Just south of Marielyst is the **Bøtø Nor bird sanctuary** where a variety of birds can be spotted including cranes, ospreys and plovers.

Væggerløse 22

Road map F6. Falster.

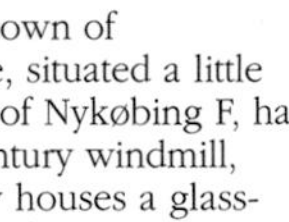

The small town of Væggerløse, situated a little way south of Nykøbing F, has an 18th-century windmill, which now houses a glass-blowing workshop, and ceiling paintings from the late Middle Ages in the church. Another nearby attraction is the **Sports Car Museum**. Road signs direct drivers to a private farmstead where one of the buildings houses a collection of motor cars. Although not as large as the car museum found at Ålholm Slot near Nysted on Lolland *(see p163)*, it is nevertheless worth visiting as it contains some interesting exhibits. Among the 65 vehicles on display are a 1917 Adler (which was once capable of reaching the giddy speed of 35 km/h/22 mph), as well as a Jaguar (which could travel as fast as 240 km/h/149 mph).

Sports Car Museum
Stovby Tværvej 11. ***Tel*** *54 17 75 89.*
10am–5pm daily.

A zoo keeper at the Krokodille Zoo picking eggs from a nest.

Frescoes in Fanefjord Kirke, painted in the mid-15th century

Fanefjord Kirke ㉓

Road map F6. Fanefjordvej, Falster. ☐ *Jun–Aug: 8am–6pm daily; Sep–May: 8am–4pm daily.* **www**.fanefjordkirke.dk

The small church of Fanefjord stands on top of an isolated hillock surrounded by green fields. It provides an excellent viewpoint and from here it is possible to look out over the Baltic, Jes and the island of Falster. The Gothic church derives its name from the Fan fjord bay, whose waters come close to the building. The fjord was in turn named after Queen Fane, wife of King Grøn Jæger.

Built about 1250, the church was at that time far too big for the needs of the 300 or so parishioners, but its builders took into account worshippers from ships anchoring in the bay as this was a busy harbour in the Middle Ages. According to records it was probably here that Bishop Absalon gathered his fleet before embarking on his raids against the Wends in eastern Germany.

Fanefjord Kirke is famous in Denmark for its frescoes. The oldest of them date from around 1350 and include an image of St Christopher carrying the infant Jesus. The later paintings date from the mid-15th century and include frescoes painted by the Elmelunde master, an artist about whom virtually nothing is known. His mark, which looks like a man with long rabbit-like ears, can be seen on one of the ribs in the northeastern vault. A collection of votive ships hangs in the church. The oldest is a frigate hanging above the entrance which commemorates a tragic shipwreck off the north coast of Møn in which three children lost their lives.

Kong Asgers Høj ㉔

Road map F6. Møn.

King Asgers mounds, located in a farmer's field near the village of Røddinge, are all that remain of Denmark's largest passage grave.

The Stone Age corridor consists of an 8-m (26-ft) long underground passage that leads to a large chamber, 10 m (33 ft) long by 2 m (6.5 ft) wide. It is dark inside, so it is wise to take a torch.

Corridor leading to the burial chamber of Kong Asgers Høj

Environs

A short way south of Kong Asgers Høj stands yet another burial mound – the **Klekkende Høj**, which has two entrances placed side by side. The chamber is 7 m (23 ft) long. The mound has been restored and is now illuminated.

At the south end of Møn is **Grønjægers Høj**, another highly unusual tomb that is thought to be about 4,000 years old. The burial site is one of the largest dolmens in Denmark and consists of 134 weighty stones arranged in an oval shape. According to one legend the site is the final resting place of Queen Fane and her husband, Grøn Jæger who ruled this part of the island in the late Stone Age.

Chalk crags of Møns Klint, rising from the waters of the Baltic

Møns Klint ㉕

Road map F6. Møn.

The white chalk cliffs soaring above the Baltic are one of Møn's main attractions. The cliffs are about 70 million years old and are formed mostly of calcareous shells. Stretching over a distance of about 7 km (4 miles), the crags reach 128 m (420 ft) in height to form a striking landscape. The highest point is near Dronningestolen (Queen's Throne). At one time these cliffs were mined for chalk but are now a legally protected zone.

The coastline can be admired from one of the

For hotels and restaurants in this region see pp249–51 and pp276–7

many viewpoints on top of the cliffs. After a cliff-top hike many people head inland to explore Klinteskoven (Klint Forest), where about 20 types of orchid can be seen flowering from May to August.

Klintholm Havn is a port south of the cliffs. In the 19th century it was a private estate and later taken over by the local authorities. Small pleasure boats leave for 2-hour cruises from here and are a good way to take in the stunning coastal scenery.

One of Stege's quieter shopping streets

Liselund Slot ㉖

Road map F6. Møn. **Palace** Langebjergvej 6. ***Tel*** *55 81 20 81.* *May–Sep: 10:30am, 11am, 1:30pm & 2pm Wed–Sun.* *free admission to the park.* **www**.liselundslot.dk

The diminutive palace of Liselund was once crown property. A subsequent owner gave the building its present name in honour of his wife. The house is set in a large park, and its whitewashed walls are reflected in the waters of a small lake. The fairytale atmosphere is enhanced by the immaculate thatch on the building's roof (locals joke that this is the world's only thatched-roof palace). Liselund Ny Slot (New Castle), a 19th-century building in the midst of the estate, is now a hotel and restaurant.

Sun dial at Liselund Slot

Elmelunde ㉗

Road map F6. Møn. **Churches in Emelunde and Keldby** *May–Sep: 8am–5pm daily; Oct–Apr: 8am–4pm daily.* **www**.keldbyelmelundekirke.dk

Along with its famous cliffs, Møn boasts a number of churches with highly original frescoes. One of them can be visited in Elmelunde; another in Keldby, a little to the west. The church in Elmelunde is one of the oldest stone churches in Denmark and was built in about 1075. The frescoes date from the 14th and 15th centuries and were whitewashed during the Reformation. Ironically this only served to preserve the paintings from fading. They were restored in the 20th century under the guidance of Copenhagen's Nationalmuseet (National Museum).

The frescoes depict scenes from the Old and New Testaments and include images of Christ and the saints as well as lively portrayals of demons and the flames of hell. Most of them are attributed to one artist, known simply as the Elmelunde Master. The paintings served to explain biblical stories to illiterate peasants and are characterized by their quirky static figures with blank faces devoid of any emotion. More frescoes can be seen in Keldby Kirke, which also has a sumptuously carved 16th-century pulpit.

Medieval fresco in Stege Kirke

Stege ㉘

Road map F6. Møn. *4,000.* *Storegade 2.* ***Tel*** *55 86 04 00.* **www**.visitvordingborg.dk

Møn's commercial centre, Stege grew up around a castle built in the 12th century and reached the height of its power during the Middle Ages, when it prospered thanks to a lucrative herring industry. A reminder of those days is Mølleporten (Mill Gate), which spans the main street of the town and once served as Stege's principal entrance. Ramparts belonging to the fortress walls are another medieval relic. **Empiregården**, Stege's museum, is a short way from Mølleporten and has local history exhibits.

Stege Kirke is in the town centre. This Romanesque church was built by Jakob Sunesen, who ruled Møn in the 13th century. Its ceiling frescoes were painted over during the Reformation and exposed again in the 19th century.

Empiregården
Storegade 75.
Tel *55 81 40 67.*
10am–4pm Tue–Sun. **www**.empiregaarden.dk

Nyord island's meadows, with marshland beyond

Nyord 29

Road map F5.

Until quite recently the only way to reach the small island of Nyord was by boat. A bridge, built in 1986, now links Nyord with Møn and has made the island more accessible and so increasingly popular with visitors. Nevertheless, both the island and the pretty hamlet of the same name have changed little since the 19th century. Nyord is particularly favoured by bird-watchers – its salt marshes attract massive flocks of birds, especially during spring and autumn, when the island is used as a stopping-off place for winged migrants. The most numerous among them include arctic terns, curlews and swans. The birds can be best viewed from an observation tower situated near the bridge.

Fakse 30

Road map F5. *Postvej 3, Fakse Ladeplads.* ***Tel*** *56 71 60 34.* **www**.visitfaxe.dk

References to Fakse can be found in late 13th-century records when it was an important area for limestone mining. Today the town is best known for its local brewery, Faxe Bryggeri, which produces over 130 million litres (28.6 million gallons) of beer each year.

The town's most historic building is the 15th-century Gothic church, which has a number of wall paintings dating from around 1500. **Geomuseum Faxe** has a collection of over 500 types of fossils including some 63 million-year-old remains of plants and animals found in the Fakse Kalkbrud quarry about 2 km (1 mile) outside the town.

Geomuseum Faxe
Torvegade 29, 4640 Fakse.
Tel *56 50 28 06. May, Jun, Aug & Sep: 2–4pm Tue–Sun; Jul: 2–4pm daily.*

Fakse's brewery, producing millions of gallons of beer a year

Stevns Klint 31

Road map F5. *Rødvig, Havnevej 21.* ***Tel*** *56 50 64 64.* **www**.visitstevns.dk

Although Denmark's most famous cliffs are found on Møn, the limestone peninsula of Stevns Klint is almost as impressive. The section between Rødvig, a small fishing port, and Gjorslev where there is a 15th-century Gothic castle is the most picturesque, especially when the sun glints against the white chalk surface.

The area was for centuries known for its limestone quarries, which supplied building material for the first castle built by Bishop Absalon in Copenhagen; this castle became the nucleus of the royal residence, which in later times was given the name of Christiansborg Slot *(see pp86–7)*. Large-scale limestone quarrying was abandoned in the 1940s.

The strip of coastal cliffs is about 15 km (9 miles) long, with the highest peaks rising to about 41 m (135 ft). The best viewpoint can be found next to the old church of Højerup (Højerup Kirke). Legend has it that this 13th-century edifice, built close to the cliff's edge, moves inland each Christmas Eve by the length of a cockerel's jump.

Another local myth recounts a story about a king of the cliffs who lives in a cave in a crag south of the church. The king of the cliffs failed, however, to save the church from the destructive forces of nature. Over the years, due to constant erosion, the sea has advanced closer and closer towards the church and in 1928 the presbytery collapsed and crashed into the water.

A short distance from the church is the small town of Højerup. Here, the **Østsjællands Museum** has a local-history collection that includes workshops, Stone-Age tools, antique toys and a collection of fire-fighting equipment from the past including pumps and fire engines. There is also an exhibition dealing with the geology of the local cliffs.

Limestone cliffs of Stevns Klint on Zealand's east coast

Environs

A few kilometres inland is **Store Heddinge**, with one of Zealand's best Romanesque churches. The 12th-century church is made from limestone excavated in the nearby quarries. Its octagonal shape probably made it easier to defend.

Østsjællands Museum
Højerup Bygade 38, 4660 Store Heddinge. ***Tel*** *56 50 28 06.*
May, Jun, Aug, Sep: 11am–5pm Tue–Sun; Jul: 11am–5pm daily.

Vallø Slot, a moated 16th-century castle

Vallø Slot 32

Road map F5. ***Tel*** *56 26 05 00.*
Castle *to visitors, but it is possible to explore the courtyard 10am–6pm daily.* **Garden** *8am–sunset daily.*

The secluded castle of Vallø is one of the most impressive Renaissance buildings in Denmark. As early as the 15th century the islet was surrounded by a moat and featured a complex of defensive buildings. The castle owes its present shape to the influence of two enterprising sisters, Mette and Birgitte Rosenkrantz, who in the 16th century owned the surrounding land. The sisters divided the estate in equal shares between themselves – the east part was managed by Birgitte, while the western section belonged to Mette.

In 1737 the castle was taken over by a trust that provided a home for unmarried daughters of noble birth during their later years. The castle is closed to visitors. The large park is open, however, as is the former stable block, which houses a museum containing a mix of agricultural implements and equestrian accessories.

Køge 33

Road map F5. *40,000.*
Vestergade 1. ***Tel*** *56 67 60 01.*
www.visitkoege.com

One of Denmark's best-preserved medieval towns, Køge was granted a municipal charter in 1288 and grew quickly thanks to its large natural harbour at the mouth of a navigable river. Køge Bay entered the annals of Danish history in 1677 when the Danish fleet, led by Admiral Niels Juel, crushed a Swedish armada heading for Copenhagen. The battle and the victorious Admiral Juel are commemorated by a 9-m (30-ft) tall obelisk standing by the harbour.

The heart of the town is its market square, which contains a monument to Frederik VI. The town hall standing in the cobbled square is the longest-serving public building of its kind in Denmark. The cobbled streets leading from the market square are lined with half-timbered houses for which Køge is famous. The most interesting street in this respect is Kirkestræde. The small house at No. 20, with only two windows, is the oldest half-timbered house in Denmark; the beam under its front door gives the year of construction as 1527.

Kirkestræde 10, now serving as a children's nursery

Another impressive historic building is Sankt Nicolai Kirke, which dates from 1324. Its tower served for many years as a lighthouse and is now used as a viewpoint.

Køge Museum is located along Nørregade and occupies two early-17th-century buildings. Its exhibits include old photographs, historic furniture, costumes and, serving as a reminder of the town's bloody past, the local executioner's sword.

Køge Museum
Nørregade 4. ***Tel*** *56 63 42 42.*
Jun–Aug: 10am–5pm Tue–Sun; Sep–May: 1–5pm Mon–Fri & Sun, 11am–3pm Sat.

THE ARISTOCRATIC LADIES OF THE CASTLE

In 1737, Vallø's owner, Queen Sophie Magdalene, donated the castle to the Royal Vallø Foundation. From then on the castle become a home for unmarried women from noble families. The famously religious queen ensured the typically cloistral character of the place and promoted a lifestyle true to Christian principles. Initially it housed 12 women, some of whom were as young as 15. The convent was run by a prioress of high birth, and the mother superior was also descended from an aristocratic family. The male staff, an administrator, doctor and servants, lived opposite the castle. Some unmarried ladies still reside in Vallø Slot.

The imposing twin towers of Vallø Slot

FUNEN

Funen (Fyn in Danish) is Denmark's second largest island and occupies an area of about 3,000 sq km (1,158 sq miles). It has some of Denmark's best scenery including wide, sandy beaches, steep cliffs and lush pasture land and orchards. A number of neighbouring islands are considered to be part of Funen including Ærø and Tåsinge, which are themselves popular destinations.

Funen is separated from Zealand by the Store Bælt (Great Belt) and from Jutland by the Lille Bælt (Little Belt). Nearly half of Funen's inhabitants live in Odense, which is the island's capital, a lively cultural centre and the birthplace of Hans Christian Andersen. Aside from Odense there are no large towns on Funen and the island is sometimes described as the "garden of Denmark" because of the large amount of produce that grows in its fertile soil.

Thanks to the fact that the island has escaped most of Denmark's wars with other nations, Funen has an exceptionally high number of well-preserved historic buildings and palaces. The best-known of these is Egeskov Slot, a Renaissance castle encircled by a moat.

The relatively small distances, gently rolling landscape and the many interesting places to visit, make Funen an ideal area for cycling trips. The south-western part of the island features a range of wooded hills. The highest of these, rising to 126 m (413 ft), are found near the town of Faaborg. Central Funen is mostly flat and only becomes slightly undulated in the northeastern region. The south has most of the island's harbours and towns, while the northern and western parts are sparsely populated.

An archipelago of southern islets includes Langeland, Ærø and Tåsinge as well as a number of tiny islands inhabited only by birds. This area is popular with Danish yachtsmen and it is possible to explore the archipelago by joining an organized cruise on board a wooden sailing ship. Some of the islands can be reached by ferry.

The imposing façade of Egeskov Slot, one of Denmark's finest castles

◁ **Cultivated fields typical of Funen's coastal region**

Exploring Funen

The university town of Odense lies at the heart of Funen. In contrast to the rest of the island, it is a busy place and Denmark's third largest city. Throughout the centuries the Danish aristocracy were keen to build their opulent residences on the island and Funen has over 120 beautifully preserved mansions, castles and palaces. The most impressive of them are Egeskov Slot and, on Tåsinge, Valdemars Slot. Funen's coastline is 11,000 km (6,800 miles) long and has some beautiful beaches. The loveliest island under Funen's administration is Ærø, a picturesque place with tiny villages and ancient farms.

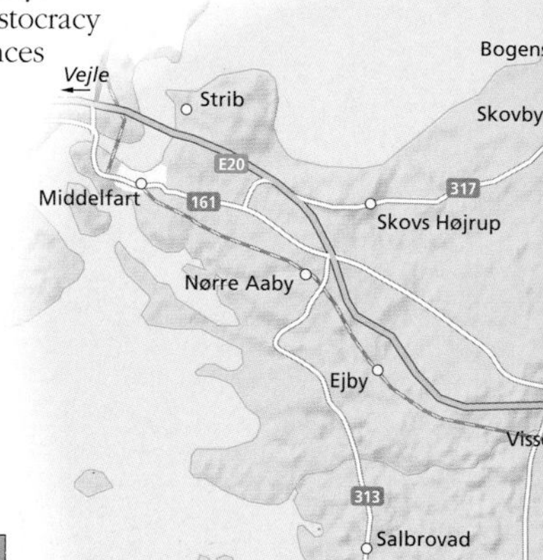

Den Gamle Gaard, a merchant's house in Faaborg

KEY

- Motorway
- Major road
- Minor road
- Scenic route
- Main railway
- Minor railway

0 km 10

0 miles 10

SIGHTS AT A GLANCE

Assens 1
Egeskov Slot 6
Faaborg 7
Hindsholm 4
Kerteminde 3
Langeland 10
Marstal 11
Nyborg 5
Odense pp178–9 2
Svendborg 8
Tåsinge 9
Ærøskøbing 12

Traditional wooden boat moored in Svendborg harbour

For additional map symbols *see back flap*

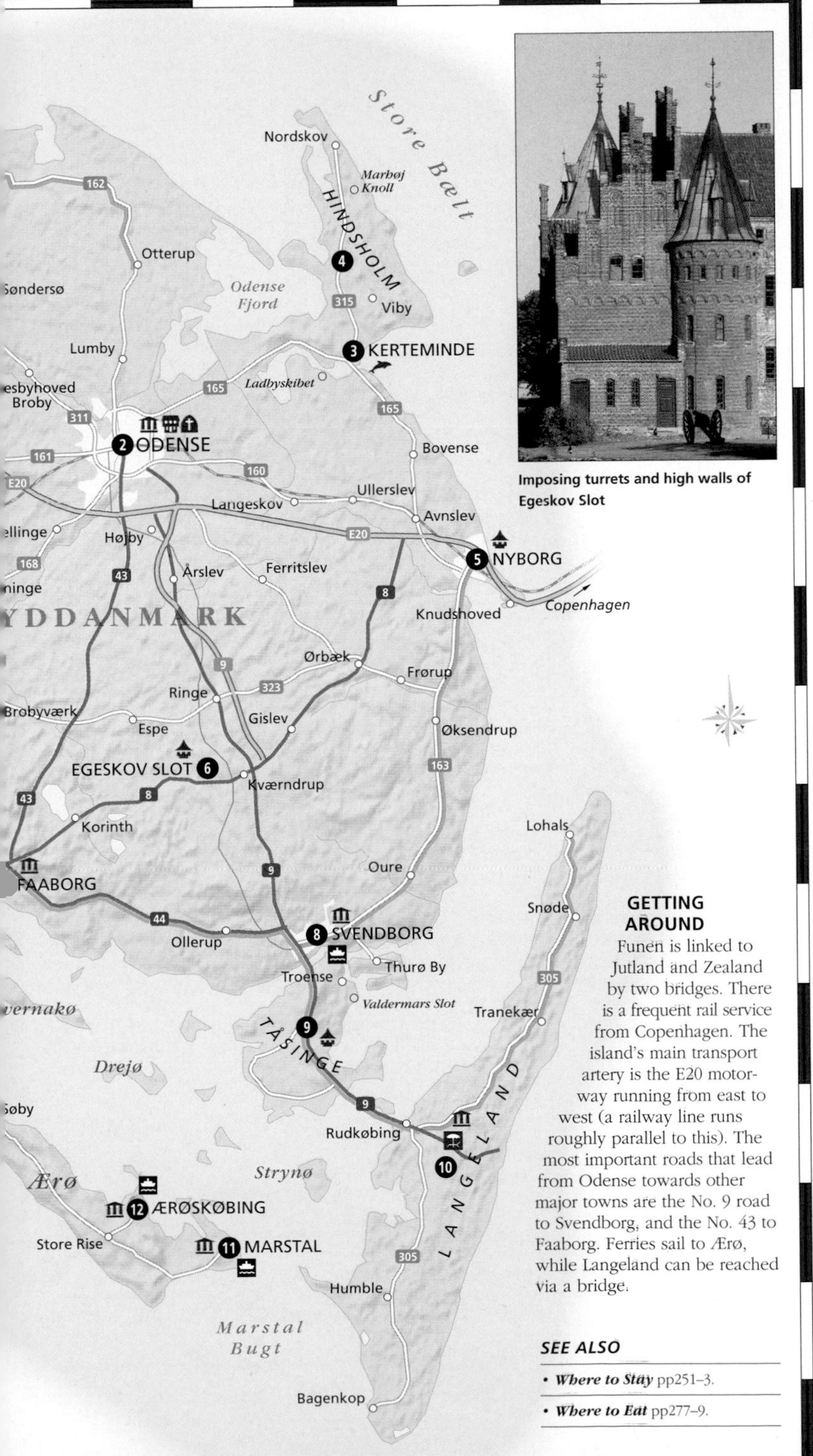

Imposing turrets and high walls of Egeskov Slot

GETTING AROUND

Funen is linked to Jutland and Zealand by two bridges. There is a frequent rail service from Copenhagen. The island's main transport artery is the E20 motorway running from east to west (a railway line runs roughly parallel to this). The most important roads that lead from Odense towards other major towns are the No. 9 road to Svendborg, and the No. 43 to Faaborg. Ferries sail to Ærø, while Langeland can be reached via a bridge.

SEE ALSO

- ***Where to Stay*** pp251–3.
- ***Where to Eat*** pp277–9.

Quiet yacht marina in Assens

Fjord&Bælt
Margrethes Plads 1.
Tel *65 32 42 00.*
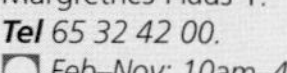
Feb–Nov: 10am–4pm Mon–Fri, 10am–5pm Sat & Sun.
Jan, Dec.
www.fjord-baelt.dk

Johannes Larsen Museum
Møllebakken 14.
Tel *65 32 11 77. Jun–Aug: 10am–5pm daily; Mar–May, Sep & Oct: 10am–4pm Tue–Sun; Nov–Feb: 11am–4pm Tue–Sun.*

Assens ❶

Road map C5. *15,000.*
Tabaksgaarden 7. ***Tel*** *64 71 20 31.* **www**.vestfyn.dk

Situated on the shores of the Store Bælt (Great Belt), Assens was for centuries a busy harbour for ferries on the route between Funen and Jutland. Following the construction of a bridge across the strait, far north of the town, it lost its importance. Assens contains numerous historic buildings including 18th- and 19th-century merchants' houses, as well as the 15th-century Vor Frue Kirke (Church of Our Lady).

The best-known citizen of Assens was Peter Willemoes (1783–1808), a war hero who, in 1801, fought against Admiral Nelson during the Napoleonic Wars and distinguished himself during Nelson's bombardment of Copenhagen. Willemoes' birthplace, **Willemoes-gården**, now houses a museum of cultural history. A monument to Willemoes has been erected near the harbour. A house by the monument was once a sailors' kitchen.

Nearby is the Ernsts Samlinger exhibition in the house of a local silversmith, Frederik Ernst, which has Denmark's largest collection of antique silver and glass.

Willemoesgården
Østergade 36. ***Tel*** *64 71 31 90.*
May–Sep, Easter & mid-Oct: 10am–4pm; mid-Oct–Apr: 10am–4pm Wed & Sat. *Mon.*

Odense ❷

See pp178–9.

Kerteminde ❸

Road map D5. *5,500.*
Hans Schacksvej 5. ***Tel*** *65 32 11 21.* **www**.visitkerteminde.dk

Much of this pretty seaside town is clustered around the 15th-century Sankt Laurentius Kirke (Church). One of the town's main attractions is **Fjord&Bælt**, a sea-life centre built in 1997. A 50-m long tunnel with large windows allows visitors to walk beneath the fjord and enjoy the underwater view. The famous Danish painter Johannes Larsen (1867–1961) once lived in Kerteminde and the **Johannes Larsen Museum** contains many of his paintings.

Environs

Four kilometres (2 miles) southwest of Kerteminde is the **Ladbyskibet**, a 22-m (72-ft) long Viking ship that dates from the 10th century and was used as the tomb of a Viking chieftain.

Statue of St Laurentius, in Kerteminde

Hindsholm ❹

Road map D5.

Rising at the far end of the Hindsholm peninsula are 25-m (82-ft) high cliffs, which provide a splendid view over the coast and the island of Samsø. A little way inland is Marhøj knoll, a 2nd-century BC underground burial chamber.

The small town of Viby, north of Assens, has a 19th-century windmill and an Early-Gothic church. According to legend, Marks Stig, a hero of Danish folklore, was buried here in 1293. Before setting off for war, Marsk Stig is said to have left his wife in the care of the king, Erik Klipping. The king took the notion of "care" somewhat too far and when the knight returned he killed the king and was outlawed. Even his funeral had to be held in secrecy.

Crops growing on the Hindsholm peninsula

Royal painting and suits of armour in the Knights' Hall, Nyborg Slot

Nyborg 5

Road map D5. *15,000.*
Torvet 9, 65 31 02 80.
www.visitnyborg.dk

The castle of **Nyborg Slot** was built in the early 13th century by Valdemar I as part of the fortifications that guarded the Store Bælt. For nearly 200 years the castle was the scene of the Danehof assemblies (an early form of Danish parliament). The castle was also the venue of the signing, in 1282, of a charter that laid down the duties of the king. Over the centuries the castle gradually fell into ruin and it was only after World War I that it was restored and turned into a museum. A number of rooms are open to the public incuding the royal chambers and the Danehof room. The castle ramparts and moat are now a park.

During July and August, on Tuesdays at about 7pm, the Tappenstreg regiment marches through the streets of Nyborg. This regiment upholds an 18th-century tradition of checking whether all the town's entertainment venues have closed on time.

Environs

In Knudshoved, about 5 km (3 miles) from Nyborg, is the **Store Bælt Centre**, devoted to the history of constructing the link between Funen and Zealand *(see p146)*.

Nyborg Slot
Slotsgade 11. ***Tel*** *65 31 02 07.* *Apr–mid-Nov: 10am–3pm Tue–Sun (Jun & Aug: to 4pm; Jul: to 5pm).*
www.museer-nyborg.dk

Egeskov Slot 6

Road map D5. Egeskov Gade 18, Kværndrup. ***Tel*** *62 27 10 16.* *May & Sep–early Oct: 10am–5pm daily; Jun–Aug: 10am–6pm daily (1 Jul–9 Aug: to 7pm).* **www**.egeskov.dk

This magnificent castle was built in the mid-16th century and is one of Denmark's best-known sights. Egeskov means "oak forest" and the castle was built in the middle of a pond on a foundation of oak trees. The interior has some grand rooms containing antique furniture and paintings, and a hall full of hunting trophies that include elephant tusks and tiger heads.

Much of the grounds were laid out in the 18th century and include a garden adorned with various fountains, as well as a herb garden. More recent additions to the layout are a bamboo maze and a vintage car museum.

Coat of arms from Egeskov Slot

Faaborg 7

Road map D5. *8,000.*
Banegårdspladsen 2A, 62 61 07 07. **www**.visitfaaborg.dk

Faaborg is a picturesque place with cobbled streets and half-timbered houses. The market square contains the town's most famous monument, produced by the Danish painter and sculptor Kai Nielsen in the early 20th century. Its main figure is Ymer, a giant who according to Nordic mythology was killed by Odin.

The view from the 15-m (49-ft) tall Klokketårnet (Clock Tower) embraces the bay. The tower is all that remains of a medieval church.

Den Gamle Gaard is a wealthy merchant's house that dates from 1725. Its rooms have been arranged to illustrate the life of a 19th-century merchant. **Faaborg Museum**, designed by Carl Petersen, has a number of works by Danish artists such as Peter Hansen and Johannes Larsen.

Den Gamle Gaard
Holkegade 1. ***Tel*** *63 61 20 00.*
Apr–May: 11am–3pm Sat & Sun; Jun–Aug: 10am–4pm daily; Sep–mid-Oct: 11am–3pm Sat & Sun; Dec: 11am–3pm daily. **www**.fkm.nu

Faaborg Museum
Grønnegade 75. ***Tel*** *62 61 06 45.*
Nov–Mar: 11am–3pm Tue–Sun; Apr–Oct: 10am–4pm daily.
www.faaborgmuseum.dk

Collection of Danish art in Faaborg Museum

Odense ❷

The city's coat of arms

One of the oldest cities in Denmark, Odense derives its name from the Nordic god Odin who was worshipped by the Vikings. In medieval times it was an important centre of trade and from the 12th century on it was a major pilgrimage destination. Since the 19th century, when a canal was built linking Odense with the sea, the city has been a major port. Odense has a rich cultural life and plenty to see including a cathedral and a museum devoted to the city's most famous son, Hans Christian Andersen.

Exploring Odense

Most attractions lie within the boundaries of the medieval district. Getting around is made easy by the Odense Eventyrpas (Adventure Pass), which entitles the holder to free travel, free admission to museums and cut-price tickets for boat cruises.

Brandts Klædefabrik

Brandts Passage 37–43.
Danmarks Mediemuseum ***Tel*** *65 20 70 10.* *10am–5pm Tue, Wed & Fri–Sun; noon–9pm Thu.* *Mon (except for weeks 7, 8 & 42).*
Museet for Fotokunst ***Tel*** *65 20 70 10.* *same as above.*
Kunsthallen Brandts ***Tel*** *65 20 70 10.* *same as above.*

For more than fifty years Brandt's textile factory was the biggest company in Odense. After its closure in 1977 it stood empty for a number of years until it was renovated and transformed into a cultural centre. Today it houses museums, a cinema, art galleries, shops, restaurants and cafés. The latest addition is the **Danmarks Medie-museum**, which has displays on the history of print production and the latest electronic media.

The **Museet for Fotokunst** exhibits works by Danish and international photographers, while the **Kunsthallen Brandts** shows contemporary art, craft, design and performance.

Childhood home of Hans Christian Andersen

H.C. Andersens Barndomshjem

Munkemøllestræde 3–5. ***Tel*** *65 51 46 01.* *Jan–May & Sep–Dec: 11am–3pm Tue–Sun; Jun–Aug: 10am–4pm daily.* **www**.museum.odense.dk

The Andersen family moved to this small house close to the cathedral when Hans was two years old. Andersen lived here until the age of 14. The museum has only a few rooms, furnished with basic period household objects, but manages to conjure up what life was like for a poor Danish family in the early 19th century.

Art gallery in Brandts Klædefabrik

Sankt Knuds Kirke

Klosterbakken 2. ***Tel*** *66 12 03 92.* *Apr–Oct: 10am–5pm daily; Nov–Mar: 10am–4pm daily.* **www**.odense-domkirke.dk

Odense cathedral is named after Canute (Knud) II, who ruled Denmark from 1080–86. The king's skeleton is on public display in a glass

16th-century cathedral altarpiece by Claus Berg

case down in the basement. The present cathedral is one of Denmark's most beautiful examples of Gothic architecture. It stands on the site of an earlier Romanesque structure, which was destroyed by fire in 1248. The cathedral's ornate gilded altar is a masterpiece of 16th-century craftmanship by Claus Berg of Lübeck. The triptych is 5 m (16 ft) high and includes nearly 300 intricately carved figures within its design.

Flakhaven

Flakhaven derives its name from an old Danish word meaning an area surrounded by meadows and gardens. For centuries the square was used as a market venue and attracted merchants and farmers from all over Funen. The main building standing in the square is the Rådhus (city hall), which has a west wing dating from the 19th century. The remainder of the building is 20th century. Guided tours are available daily in the summer and include access to the Wedding Room, the Town Council Chamber and a wall commemorating citizens who have made major contributions to the city's history. Flakhaven contains a statue of Frederik VII as well as an abstract metal sculpture made by Robert Jacobson to celebrate the 1,000-year anniversary of Odense in 1988.

Fyns Kunstmuseum

Jernbanegade 13. ***Tel*** *65 51 46 01.* *10am–4pm Tue–Sun.* **www**.museum.odense.dk

This museum has the largest collection of Danish art in Denmark outside Copenhagen. The Classicist building is adorned on the outside with a frieze depicting scenes from

For hotels and restaurants in this region see pp251–3 and pp277–9

Danish history and mythology. The interior is crammed with paintings, etchings and sculptures by Danish artists from all periods. One section contains works by local Funen artists.

H.C. Andersens Hus

Bangs Boder 29. ***Tel** 65 51 46 01.* *Jan–May & Sep–Dec: 10am–4pm Tue–Sun; Jun–Aug: 9am–6pm daily.* **www**.museum.odense.dk

Denmark's most famous writer was born in this house in 1805. It is now a museum and has undergone a substantial metamorphosis; it was greatly extended and modernized to celebrate the 200th anniversary of Andersen's birth. The exhibition includes a recreation of the author's study and numerous items belonging to Andersen including his notes and letters. There is even an old rope – apparently Andersen was terrified by the thought of a fire and carried this with him wherever he went in readiness for an emergency evacuation. Hanging on one of the walls is a world map indicating the countries in which Andersen's tales have been published in translation. A special collection includes copies of his works in 120 languages.

Close to the museum is Fyrtøjet, a children's cultural centre based on Andersen's stories.

Bust from Fyns Kunstmuseum

Carl Nielsen Museet

Claus Bergs Gade 11. ***Tel** 65 51 46 01.* *Jun–Aug: noon–4pm Fri–Sun; Sep–May: 2–5pm Mon–Wed.*

This museum, devoted to the famous Danish composer Carl Nielsen (1865–1931), was opened in 1988 to celebrate the town's millennium. The exhibits, donated by the descendents of the composer, are all associated with Nielsen, who is mainly known for his operas, symphonies and violin concertos. In addition to handwritten scores of the artist's compositions, the collection includes Nielsen's piano and works by his wife, the sculptor Anne Marie Brodersen.

VISITORS' CHECKLIST

Road map D5.
185,000.
City Hall, 66 12 75 20.
otb@odenseturist.dk
www.visitodense.com

City hall façade, crowned with an allegorical statue of Justice

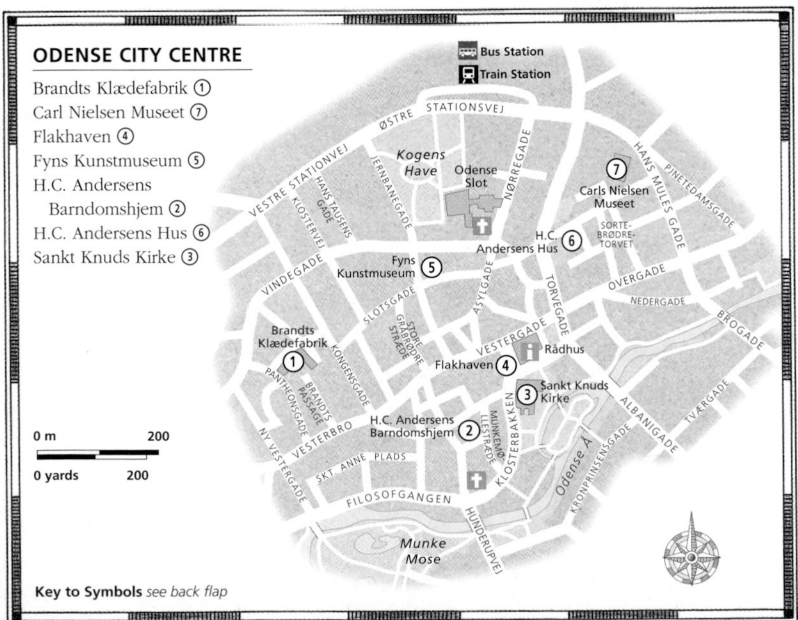

Svendborg ❽

Road map D5. *30,000.* *Centrumpladsen 4.* ***Tel*** *62 23 57 00.* *Fyn Rundt Regattas (Jul).* **www**.visitsydfyn.dk

Funen's second largest town, Svendborg is a busy port and has strong links with shipbuilding. In the 19th century its boatyards produced half of all Danish vessels.

Most of Svendborg's sights are within easy reach of Torvet, the market square. Closest to hand is the 13th-century Vor Frue Kirke, which has a carillon consisting of 27 bells. Sankt Nicolai Kirke is slightly older, though also 13th century. A short distance west of Vor Frue Kirke is **Anne Hvides Gård**, a half-timbered building dating from 1560. This is now a local history museum and exhibits locally produced ceramics and glass. Contemporary art is on display at **SAK Kunstbygningen** (SAK Art Exhibitions), which also exhibits works by the Danish sculptor Kai Nielsen (1882–1924) who was born in Svendborg. Other museums in town include a toy museum and a natural history museum. The latter is full of stuffed animals and skeletons including the bones of a whale that was washed ashore in 1955.

Anne Hvides Gård
Fruestræde 3. ***Tel*** *62 21 02 61.*
May–mid-Oct: 11am–4pm Tue–Sun.

SAK Kunstbygningen
Vestergade 27. ***Tel*** *62 22 44 70.*
11am–4pm Tue–Sat.

Kattesund, a scenic alley in Svendborg

An elegant apartment in Valdemars Slot, Tåsinge

Tåsinge ❾

Road map D6. *2,500.*

The island of Tåsinge is linked by bridge to Funen and Langeland. The major local attraction is **Valdemars Slot**, which was built by Christian IV for his favourite son Valdemar and completed in 1644. Unfortunately the prince had only a short while to enjoy the estate as he was killed in battle in 1656.

The castle's architect was Hans van Steenwinckel, who was also responsible for building Rosenborg Slot in Copenhagen *(see pp60–61)*. In 1670s the king gave the castle to Admiral Niels Juel in recognition of his successful command of the Danish fleet during the Battle of Køge Bay. The castle has remained in the hands of the Juel family ever since. A number of rooms are open to the public including the royal apartments, the reception rooms and the kitchens. In the attic there is a collection of items including trophies brought from African safaris. The domestic quarters, arranged around a lake, house a couple of small museums.

Environs

Near the castle, heading for Svendborg, is the fishing port of **Troense**. Its most attractive street, Grønnegade, is lined with half-timbered houses. The Søfartsmuseet (Marine Museum) is housed in an 18th-century school. It displays marine paintings, model ships and products brought back by merchant ships from China.

Valdemars Slot
Troense. ***Tel*** *62 22 61 06.*
Apr & Oct: 10am–5pm days vary, see website; May & Sep: 10am–5pm Tue–Sun; Jun–Aug: 10am–5pm daily.
www.valdemarsslot.dk

Statue of Hans Christian Ørsted in Rudkøbing

Langeland ❿

Road map D6.
Rudkøbing Torvet 5. ***Tel*** *62 51 35 05.*
www.langeland.dk

Langeland is positioned off the southeast coast of Funen and can be reached by bridge or from Lolland by ferry. The island has a number of good beaches and marked cycling paths. Windmills are dotted here and there, along with quaint hamlets and farms.

Rudkøbing is the capital and the island's only sizeable town. Its most famous citizen was Hans Christian Ørsted (1777–1851), a physicist who made major advances in the field of electromagnetism. The house in which the scientist was born is known as **Det Gamle Apotek** (The Old Pharmacy) and has been arranged to recreate an 18th-century pharmacist's shop. In front of it stands a statue of Ørsted. From here it is only a short distance to the market square, which contains a 19th-century town hall and a much older church with an inscription giving its year of founding as 1105. **Langelands Museum** is devoted mostly to local history and includes archaeological finds.

About 10 km (6 miles) north of Rudkøbing is **Tranekær**, whose main attraction is Tranekær Slot, a pink-coloured castle that dates from around 1200. The castle is closed to visitors but the grounds can be toured. Part of the estate now serves as a botanical garden which has a number of rare trees including some Californian sequoias. An open-air gallery exhibits sculptures and installations by artists from a number of of countries including Denmark, Germany and the USA.

Det Gamle Apotek
Brogade 15, Rudkøbing. ***Tel*** *63 51 63 00.* *by appointment only (contact Langelands Museum).*

Langelands Museum
Jens Winthersvej 12, Rudkøbing. ***Tel*** *63 51 63 00.* *for renovation until 2011.* **www.** langelandsmuseum.dk

Colourful façade of Tranekær Slot, Langeland

Picturesque 17th-century houses in Ærøskøbing

Marstal ⓫

Road map D6. Ærø. *2,200.* *Havnegade 5.* ***Tel*** *62 52 13 00.* *mid-Jun–Aug: 9am–3:30pm Mon–Sat.*

Marstal is the largest town on the island of Ærø. Its history has long been associated with the sea and in the 18th century it was a busy port with about 300 ships arriving here every year. The **Søfartmuseum** (Maritime Museum) occupies four buildings near the harbour and contains many items connected with the sea including model schooners and seafaring paintings.

The dependence of the local population on the sea is also apparent in the local church on Kirkestræde, which was built in 1738. The altarpiece in the church depicts Christ calming the rough waves, and hanging in several places within the building are votive sailing ships. Outside in the cemetery there are numerous gravestones of local sailors. The church clock was created by Jens Olsen, who also produced the World Clock in the Rådhus in Copenhagen *(see p74)*.

Exhibit from Marstal's Søfartmuseum

Søfartmuseum
Prinsensgade 1. ***Tel*** *62 53 23 31.* *Nov–Apr: 10am–4pm Mon–Fri, 11am–3pm Sat; May, Sep & Oct: 10am–4pm daily; Jun: 9am–5pm daily; Jul & Aug: 9am–6pm daily.*

Ærøskøbing ⓬

Road map D6. Ærø. *1,500.* *Vestergade 1.* ***Tel*** *62 52 13 00.*

Many of the 17th-century houses lining the cobbled streets are a reminder of a time when Ærøskøbing was a prosperous merchant town. The oldest house dates from 1645 and can be found at Søndergade 36. The town's most picturesque dwelling is Dukkehuset (Dolls' House) at Smedegade 37. Also in Smedegade is **Flaske-Peters Samling**, a museum devoted to Peter Jacobsen, who first went to sea at the age of 16. Known as "Bottle Peter", he created about 1,700 ships-in-a-bottle before he died in 1960. Also in the museum is a cross he made for his own grave. **Ærø Museum** has displays on the history of the island and its people, including a collection of 19th-century paintings.

Flaske-Peters Samling
Smedegade 22. ***Tel*** *62 52 29 50.* *early Apr–mid-Jun & mid-Aug–mid-Oct: 10am–4pm daily; mid-Jun–mid-Aug: 10am–5pm daily; mid-Oct–early Apr: 1–3pm Tue–Fri, 10am–noon Sat.*

Ærø Museum
Brogade 3–5. ***Tel*** *62 52 29 50.* *early Apr–mid-Jun: 11am–3pm daily; mid-Jun–mid-Sep: 10am–4pm daily; mid-Oct–early Apr: 10am–1pm Mon–Fri & Sun, noon–3pm Sat.*

SOUTHERN AND CENTRAL JUTLAND

As well as the scenic lowlands and undulating hills and meadows found on the eastern side of central Jutland, this region has much to recommend it. Attractions include beautifully preserved medieval towns, traditional hamlets, parks, castles and ancient Viking burial grounds. In addition, no one travelling with children should miss a trip to LEGOLAND®.

Jutland derives its name from the Jutes, a German tribe that once inhabited this peninsula. When the Vikings, who occupied the islands to the east, began to encroach on this territory, the mixing of the two tribes gave rise to the Danes as a distinct people.

After Denmark's defeat during the Schleswig Wars in 1864, Jutland was occupied by Prussia, and subsequently, as part of Schleswig, remained under German control. It was not until a plebiscite in 1920 that it once more became part of the kingdom of Denmark. After the final resolution of this Danish-German border dispute, many German families remained on the Danish side. The expatriate minority is still active in the region, and German speakers have their own newspaper.

The region has also been shaped by Dutch settlers and the lowland scenery is here and there enlivened by Dutch windmills, while some fields are bisected by canals. The Dutch influence can also be seen in many of the houses in this region, some of which are decorated with distinctive Dutch wall tiles.

The top attraction of this region is LEGOLAND®, where millions of plastic LEGO® bricks are used to create Denmark's best-known amusement park. The cities of Århus and Silkeborg, located in attractive surroundings, offer a more cultural approach.

Carved Viking figures and replica Viking ship in Vejle Fjord

◁ Farmhouses set amid the undulating fields of Jutland

Exploring Southern and Central Jutland

Jutland is the only part of Denmark that is not an island. The bottom section of the peninsula is cut across by a 69-km (43-mile) long national border with Germany and ties with this country remain close. The most popular attraction of southern and central Jutland is LEGOLAND®. Close to this theme park is the town of Jelling, which is famous for its ancient burial mounds. This region is rich in towns with long histories, of which Ribe is the oldest and best preserved. Århus is Denmark's second city and is famous for its nightlife, while Esbjerg has some good museums.

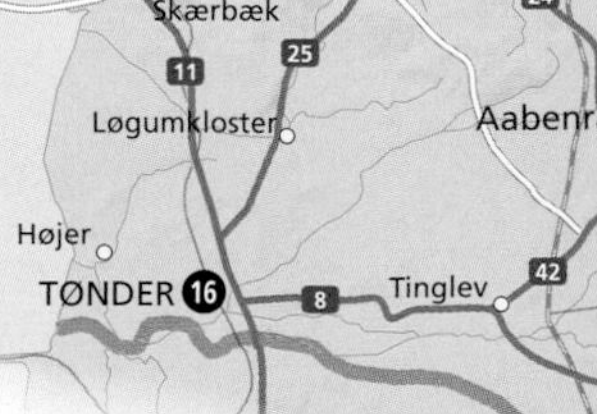

GETTING AROUND

Esbjerg's harbour handles international ferry traffic; the town's airport handles flights from the UK and Norway. The quickest route to Jutland from Copenhagen is the E20, running through Funen. This joins with the E45 that runs along the eastern coast of the peninsula, from Germany to Århus and further north. It is also possible to take a ferry from Funen to Als and from there join up with Jutland's southern section. Jutland is almost three times larger than the rest of Denmark put together and distances between towns can be significant.

SEE ALSO

- ***Where to Stay*** pp253–5.
- ***Where to Eat*** pp279–81.

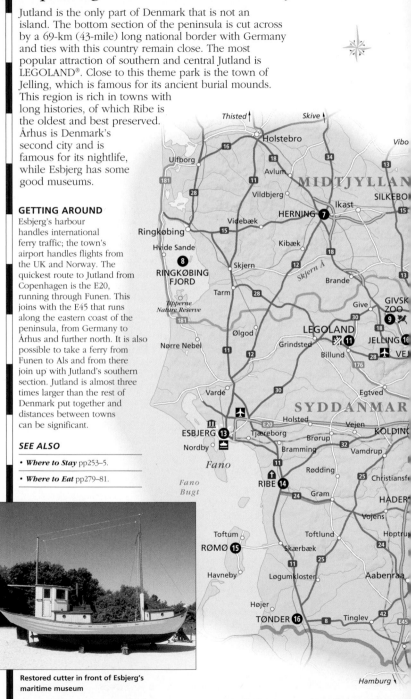

Restored cutter in front of Esbjerg's maritime museum

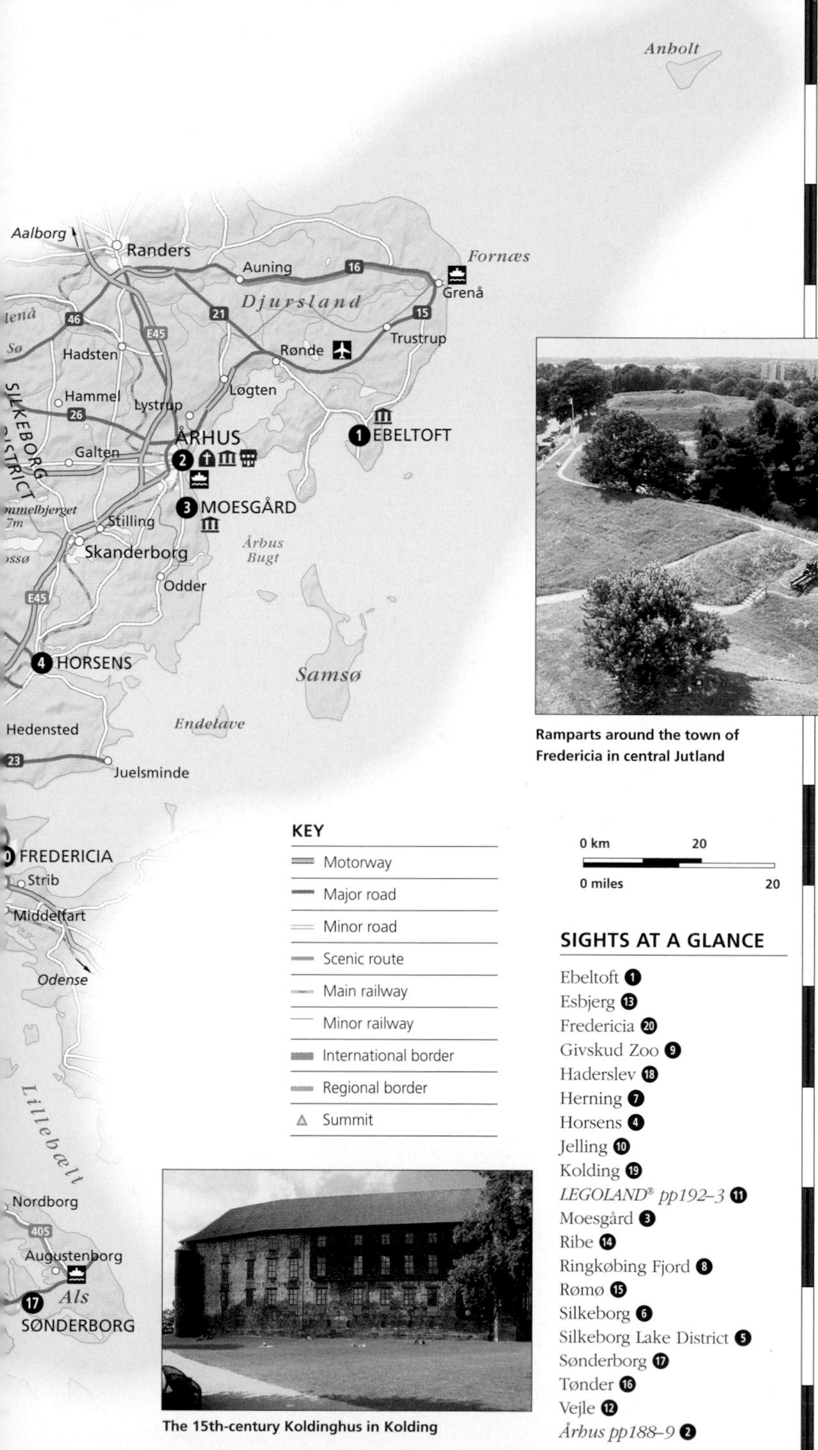

Ramparts around the town of Fredericia in central Jutland

The 15th-century Koldinghus in Kolding

KEY

- Motorway
- Major road
- Minor road
- Scenic route
- Main railway
- Minor railway
- International border
- Regional border
- △ Summit

SIGHTS AT A GLANCE

Ebeltoft ❶
Esbjerg ⓭
Fredericia ⓴
Givskud Zoo ❾
Haderslev ⓲
Herning ❼
Horsens ❹
Jelling ❿
Kolding ⓳
LEGOLAND® pp192–3 ⓫
Moesgård ❸
Ribe ⓮
Ringkøbing Fjord ❽
Rømø ⓯
Silkeborg ❻
Silkeborg Lake District ❺
Sønderborg ⓱
Tønder ⓰
Vejle ⓬
Århus pp188–9 ❷

Fregatten Jylland in Ebeltoft, now serving as a museum

Ebeltoft ❶

Road map D3. *5,000.* *S.A. Jensens Vej 3.* ***Tel*** *86 34 14 00.*

Boasting the smallest *rådhus* (town hall) in Denmark, Ebeltoft is over 700 years old. Many of the town's cobbled streets have been pedestrianized including Adelgade, which is lined with half-timbered houses. Ebeltoft Kirke dates from 1301 and contains a font that is even older as well as some 16th-century frescoes.

In the harbour is **Fregatten Jylland**, a 19th-century sailing ship that was used as a royal vessel. The displays on board give an idea of the conditions endured by the 430-strong crew, which are in stark contrast to those found in the royal apartments.

The nearby **Glasmuseet** has many glass items on display. The exhibits include works of art by a selection of international artists as well as more everyday glass items.

Bell from Fregatten Jylland

Fregatten Jylland
S.A. Jensen Vej 4. ***Tel*** *86 34 10 99.*
Jan–Mar, Nov & Dec: 11am–3pm daily; Apr–Aug: 10am–5pm daily; Sep & Oct: 11am–4pm daily; during school holidays: 10am–6pm.

Glasmuseet
Strandvejen 8. ***Tel*** *86 34 17 99.*
Jan–Mar, Nov & Dec: 10am–4pm Tue–Sun; Apr–Jun, Sep & Oct: 10am–5pm daily; Jul & Aug: 10am–6pm daily. **www**.glasmuseet.dk

Århus ❷

See pp188–9.

Moesgård ❸

Road map D4. *5 km (3 miles) south of Århus.*

The main attraction of this small town is the **Moesgård Museum**, housed in an 18th-century manor house. Its star exhibit is Graubelle Man who was discovered in 1952 in a bog by peat gatherers from Graubelle. The mummified body was found about 30 km (19 miles) from Moesgård and had been preserved thanks to a combination of acids and iron in the soil. He is believed to have been about 40 years old when he died in 80 BC. A slash across his throat indicates that he may have been murdered.

The museum also has a collection of runic stones, a reconstructed Viking church and various weapons including swords and axes. A trail leading from the museum to the beach passes by reconstructed dolmens and homesteads that represent different historic periods. Each year in late July, Moesgård becomes the venue for a lively and entertaining Viking festival.

Moesgård Museum
Moesgård Allé 20. ***Tel*** *89 42 11 00.*
Apr–Sep: 10am–5pm daily; Oct–Mar: 10am–4pm Tue–Sun.

Lichtenberg Palace, Horsens, now used as a hotel

Horsens ❹

Road map C4. *38 km (24 miles) south of Århus.* *50,000.* *Søndergade 26.* ***Tel*** *75 60 21 20.* *Medieval Festival (late Aug).* **www**.visithorsens.dk

Horsens is the birthplace of Vitus Bering (1681–1741), the explorer who discovered Alaska and the straits that separate it from Siberia (the straits were subsequently named after him). The guns from Bering's ship now stand in the town's main park. Mementos from Bering's expeditions are on display in **Horsens Museum**.

The Danish Romanesque Vor Frelsers Kirke (Our Saviour's Church) is 13th century. Nearby, Lichtenberg Palace was used by the Tsar's family after they fled Russia.

If possible, it is best to visit Horsens during its Medieval Festival, held in August, when armoured knights engage in deadly combat and robed wizards and witches cast spells on unruly children.

Horsens Museum
Sundvej 1A. ***Tel*** *76 29 23 50.*
Jul–Aug: 10am–4pm daily; Sep–Jun: 11am–4pm Tue–Sun.

Reconstructed burial chamber at Moesgård Museum

Charming harbour on one of Søhøjlandet's lakes

Silkeborg Lake District ❺

Road map C4.

The stretch between Silkeborg and Skanderborg and the area slightly to the north of it is a land of lakes and hills known as Søhøjlandet. It is here that visitors will find Jutland's largest lake – the Mossø, as well as Denmark's longest river, the Gudenå (158 km/ 98 miles). The Lake District also has some of the country's highest peaks. In summer it is a favourite destination for canoeists and cyclists, as well as hikers, all of whom make the most of the lakeland scenery.

Labyrinthia Park is one of the area's main attractions. It has many kinds of mazes and provides a fun way for the whole family to get lost. Gjern has a vintage car museum (with about 70 models, the oldest dating from the early 20th century), while Tange Sø boasts **Elmuseet**, an electricity museum situated next to the country's largest power station.

Other places worth visiting include the church in Veng which was built around 1100. It is thought to be the oldest monastery in Denmark.

Standing on the shores of Mossø are the ruins of the Øm monastery, which can be explored by visiting the attached **Monastic Museum of Denmark**. At one time this was the largest of the dozen or so local monasteries and the entire estate belonged to a Cistercian order, which included nearly 400 farms.

Silkeborg ❻

Road map C4. *45,000.* *Åhavevej 2A.* ***Tel*** *86 82 19 11.* *Jazz Festival (Jun), Country Music Festival (Aug).* **www**.silkeborg.com

Silkeborg owes much of its past prosperity to the paper factory, built in 1846, that was at one time powered by the local river.

Silkeborg's **Culture Museum** occupies a residential house built in 1767. Most visitors head straight for the remains of the Tollund Man. Only the head of the mummified Iron-Age body is genuine as the body decomposed once it was dug up.

Tollund Man

In summer a 19th-century paddle steamer travels the 15 km (9 miles) to Himmelbjerget (Sky Mountain), one of the area's most visited spots. On top of the 147-m (482-ft) high hill is a 25-m (82-ft) high tower that affords magnificent views of the lakeland scenery.

Silkeborg Museum
Hovedgårdsvej 7.
Tel *86 82 14 99.*
10am–7pm daily.

Herning ❼

Road map C4. *30,000.* *Torvet 8.* ***Tel*** *96 27 22 22.* **www**.visitherning.dk

The town of Herning was established in the late 19th century following the arrival of the railway. The **Herning Museum** tells the story of the town as well as the history and archaeology of the region. The **Herning Kunstmuseum** (Art Museum), exhibits works by artists such as Asger Jorn and Carl-Henning Pedersen. The **Danmarks Fotomuseum** has an extensive collection of cameras and interesting photographic displays including a panorama of Copenhagen.

Herning Museum
Museumgade 32. ***Tel*** *96 26 19 00.*
10am–4:30pm Tue–Fri, 11am–4:30pm Sat & Sun; Jul: 10am–4:30pm Mon.

Herning Kunstmuseum
Birk Centerpark 3. ***Tel*** *97 12 10 33.*
Nov–Apr: 10am–5pm Tue–Fri, noon–5pm Sat & Sun; May–Oct: 10am–5pm Tue–Sun (Jul: also Mon).
www.herningkunstmuseum.dk

Danmarks Fotomuseum
Museumsgade 28. ***Tel*** *97 22 53 22.*
Jan–Jun & Aug–Dec: noon–4:30pm Tue–Sun; Jul: 11am–4:30pm daily. **www**.fotomuseum.dk

One of Herning's tranquil streets

Århus ❷

Denmark's second largest city dates back to Viking times, when a small settlement was established here. It was originally named Aros, meaning "at the mouth of the river", and due to its location on Jutland's eastern coast it became a major seaport. After the Reformation Århus grew into an important trading centre. Many merchants' houses were built as a result, and the 19th century saw the development of the harbour. The founding of a university in 1928 led to an expansion of culture and today Århus has some fine museums, as well as lively cafés and bars.

Town panorama from the Rådhus tower

Exploring Århus

Most of the town's attractions are concentrated within a small area; the only site located some distance away is Den Gamle By. Sightseeing is made easier by the Århus Pass, which gives free admission to museums, a guided tour of the Rådhus (city hall) and free use of public transport.

Musikhuset

Thomas Jensens Allé 2. ***Tel*** *89 40 40 40.* *10am–9pm daily.*
www.musikhusetaarhus.dk

The city's concert hall opened in 1982 and is one of Denmark's foremost cultural centres. The glass-fronted building is home to several prestigious music and theatre organizations, including a symphony orchestra, the Filuren Children's Theatre and the Danish Institute of Electroacoustic Music. The building is worth visiting if only to see its vast glazed hall planted with palm trees. The centre has its own café, which often has concerts, and a restaurant, the Richter, named after Johan Richter, the main architect of the building.

Rådhus

Rådhuspladsen. ***Tel*** *89 40 20 00.*

The modern city hall was designed by Arne Jacobsen and Erik Møller and completed in 1947. The building is a prime example of Danish Modernism. It is clad on the outside with dark Norwegian marble and topped with a rectangular clock tower, which affords a good view of the city. The interior has a lighter feel. The large council chamber and Civic Room are worth seeking out.

The Rådhus with its strikingly Modernist clock tower

ARoS Kunstmuseum

Aros Allé 2. ***Tel*** *87 30 66 00.* *10am–5pm Tue, Thu–Sun, 10am–10pm Wed.* **www**.aros.dk

Hard to miss, the rust-coloured cubic block that is the ARoS art museum is as ambitious as it is big: the collection includes works from the Danish Golden Age and Modernist eras to rival those in Copenhagen. It also shows the latest light, video and installation art. There is an interactive Junior Museum, shop and a chic restaurant on the top-floor.

Vikingemuseet

Sankt Clemens Torv. ***Tel*** *89 42 11 00.* *10am–4pm Mon–Wed, Fri, 10am–5:30pm Thu.*
www.vikingemuseet.dk

Situated in the basement of the Nordea Bank next to the cathedral is a museum devoted to the Viking era. The prime exhibit is a section of archaeological excavation that was conducted in Clemens Torv. Fragments of the original Viking ramparts, discovered in 1964, are on display along with items dating from 900 to 1400 including a skeleton, a reconstructed house, woodworking tools and pottery. Similar discoveries at nearby Store Torv have confirmed the importance of Århus as a major centre of Viking culture.

Domkirke

Store Torv. ***Tel*** *86 20 54 00.*
May–Sep: 9:30am–4pm Mon–Fri; Oct–Dec: 10am–3pm Mon–Sat.
www.aarhus-domkirke.dk

Århus's main place of worship is at the heart of the city's oldest district. The cathedral was built in 1201 but destroyed by fire in the 14th century. It was rebuilt in the late 15th century in a Gothic style, and is easily Denmark's longest cathedral with a nave that spans nearly 100 m (328 ft). Until the end of the 16th century most of the cathedral walls were covered with frescoes. During the Reformation these were whitewashed over, but many have since been restored. The five-panel altarpiece dates from 1479 and is the work of Bernt Notke of Lübeck. The Baroque pipe organ dates from 1730.

For hotels and restaurants in this region see pp253–5 and pp279–81

Kvindemuseet

Domkirkeplads 5. ***Tel*** *86 18 64 70.* *Sep–May: 10am–4pm Tue–Fri, 10am–8pm Wed, 11am–4pm Sat & Sun; Jun–Aug: 10am–5pm daily.* **www**.kvindemuseet.dk

The Women's Museum has made a name for itself with its imaginative temporary exhibitions relating to women's issues – past and present. Since 1982 the museum has been collecting objects, photographs and documents illustrating the many changes that have taken place over the centuries in the lives of women in Danish society.

Figure from Bernt Notke's altarpiece

Vor Frue Kirke

Frue Kirkeplads. ***Tel*** *86 12 12 43.* *May–Aug: 10am–4pm Mon–Fri; Sep–Apr: 10am–2pm Mon–Fri, 10am–noon Sat.* **www**.aarhusvorfrue.dk

The oldest section of this church is the 11th-century Romanesque stone crypt. Its vault rests on a dozen or so stone arches. Built above it is the main structure of the church, whose star adornment is a 16th-century wooden altarpiece carved by Claus Berg.

The 11th-century crypt of Vor Frue Kirke

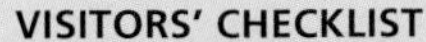

VISITORS' CHECKLIST

Road map D4. *255,000.* *Banegårdspladsen 20, 8000 Århus C.* ***Tel*** *87 31 50 10.* *Århus International Jazz Festival (2nd half of Jul), Århus Festuge/Cultural Week (1st week Sep).* info@visitaarhus.com **www**.visitaarhus.com

Den Gamle By

Viborgvej 2. ***Tel*** *86 12 31 88.* *Jan: 11am–3pm daily; Feb–Mar: 10am–4pm daily; Apr–Jun & early Sep–mid-Nov: 10am–5pm daily; Jul–early Sep: 9am–6pm daily, mid-Nov–late Dec: 9am–7pm daily; late Dec–early Jan: 10am–5pm daily.* **www**.dengamleby.dk

This open-air museum consists of 75 or so Danish buildings including shops, workshops, a mayor's house, a post office and a school as well as a theatre and a windmill. Covering the period from the Middle Ages to the 1900s, the overall effect is to recreate a typical Danish mercantile town and the way of life of its inhabitants.

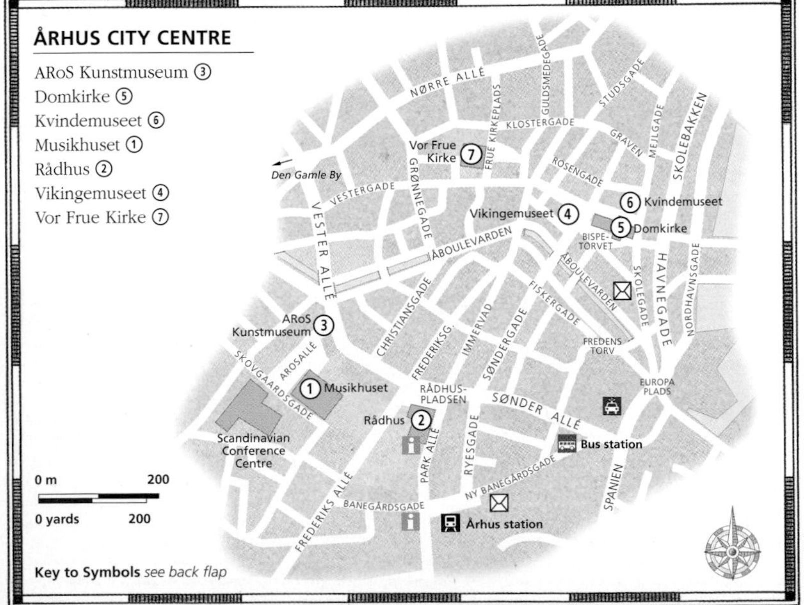

Harbour with Ringkøbing Fjord in the background

Ringkøbing Fjord ❽

Road map B4. ℹ *Ringkøbing, Nørregade 2.* ***Tel*** *70 22 70 01.* **www**.visitvest.dk

A thin strip of land some 35 km (22 miles) long separates Ringkøbing Fjord from the North Sea. This sandy spit is about 1 km (half a mile) wide and has a large number of summer cottages tucked amongst the dunes. The only water access between the sea and Ringkøbing Fjord is through a channel and lock in the town of Hvide Sande. Ringkøbing Fjord is popular with windsurfers and the calm waters of the bay are suitable for novices; the North Sea on the other side of the spit offers more challenging conditions.

On the bay's northern shore is **Ringkøbing**, which is the largest town in this region. Ringkøbing was once a sea-port but over the centuries the entrance from the bay to the sea shifted southwards and the town became an inland harbour. Standing in Torvet, the town's main square, are some of the most historic buildings including Hotel Ringkøbing, a timbered building that dates from 1600. The local museum exhibits various objects that are associated with 20th-century explorations of Greenland.

The locality includes many attractions. **Fiskeriets Hus** (House of Fisheries) at Hvide Sande contains an aquarium with fish and shellfish from the North Sea and fjord waters as well as displays on the area's fishing industry. A paved footpath, suitable for wheelchair users, leads from the museum to **Troldbjerg**, Hvide Sande's main viewpoint. The mast at the top was once used by sailors to warn them about water levels. Another good view is from the 60-m (197-ft) high lighthouse on the Nøre Lyngvig dune, 5 km (3 miles) north of Hvide Sande.

A different kind of scenery can be found on the southern shores of Ringkøbing Fjord, where the marshes form **Tipperne Nature Reserve**, one of Denmark's most important sites for waterfowl. Access has been restricted to a few hours on Sunday mornings so as not to disturb the migrating birds. The reserve contains an observation tower and a small museum. Skjern-Egvad Museum on the eastern shores of the fjord can arrange visits.

Givskud Zoo ❾

Road map C4. **Løveparken Givskud Zoo** ***Tel*** *75 73 02 22.* ◯ *late Apr–late Jun & early Aug–late Aug: 10am–5pm daily (to 6pm Sat, Sun & hols); late Jun–early Aug: 10am–8pm daily; Sep–mid-Oct: 10am–4pm daily (to 5pm Sat, Sun & hols).* ♿ **www**.givskudzoo.dk

A short way north of Jelling is Givskud Zoo (sometimes referred to as Løveparken), home to the largest pride of lions in Scandinavia. When the park was established in 1969 the pride had 29 members; today it has over 40. In addition to the lions, Givskud has about 1,000 other animals representing 120 species. Givskud is part-zoo, part-safari park and many of the animals are left to wander freely within their allocated areas. Car drivers can travel along marked routes. Visitors on foot can enjoy a safari by bus. For obvious reasons, no one should step out of the car or bus while on safari.

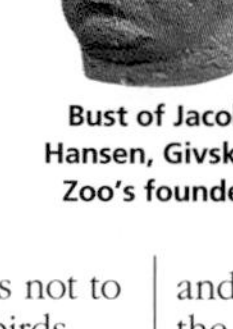

Bust of Jacob Hansen, Givskud Zoo's founder

The lions are the most popular sight but there is no denying the appeal of the giraffes, zebras, buffalos, ostriches and other species that inhabit the park. One of the zoo's other attractions is the gorilla enclosure; the family of apes was brought over from Copenhagen's zoo in 2001.

Fenced-off areas provide children with the opportunity to stroke some of the park's

Small herd of zebra wandering freely in Givskud Zoo

For hotels and restaurants in this region see pp253–5 and pp279–81

Ancient burial mounds in Jelling

more domesticated animals or have fun feeding the camels.

Givskud Zoo is not only a family attraction but also a major scientific establishment. A third of the species at the park are endangered. One of Givskud's programmes resulted in deer and antelope reared at the park being re-introduced into the wilds of Pakistan in the late 1980s.

Jelling ⑩

Road map C4. 2,500.
Gormsgade 23. ***Tel*** *75 87 23 50.*
Viking Fair (Aug).
www.visitvejle.com

For the Danes Jelling is a special place: this unassuming village served as the royal seat of Gorm the Old, a 10th-century Viking who conquered Jutland and then Funen and Zealand to create a new state. The dynasty he established has ruled Denmark continuously to this day.

Although no trace is left of the old royal castle, **Jelling Kirke** and the two burial mounds beyond it have revealed much of Denmark's ancient history. The church was built in about 1100, but it is now known that the site was occupied far earlier than this by at least three wooden churches. The first of these was, according to legend, built by Gorm's son, Harald I (Bluetooth) who came to the throne in 950 and adopted Christianity a short time afterwards. For a long time it was believed that the two knolls outside the church contained the remains of Denmark's first ruler but when they were excavated in the 19th century nothing was found. In the late 1970s, however, archaeologists began a series of digs beneath Jelling Kirke and found the remains of the three earlier wooden churches, along with Viking jewellery and human bones. Forensic examinations, conducted at Copenhagen's Nationalmuseet, concluded that the bones were indeed those of Gorm and in the year 2000, in the presence of the current royal family, the remains were reburied under the floor of Jelling's church. It is likely that Gorm was moved by his son Harald I as an act of piety so that his remains might reside in a Christian shrine. Close to the church are two runic stones. The larger one, known as the "Danes' baptism certificate", was erected in 983 by Harald I, in memory of his parents – Gorm and Thyra. Still visible on the stone is a picture of Christ – the oldest representation of Christ in Scandinavia. The stone's inscription proclaims that "Harald king ordered this monument to be erected to Gorm his father and Thyra his mother for the glory of Denmark". This inscription is considered to be the first written record in which the word "Denmark" appears. In 1994 the entire complex was declared a UNESCO World Heritage Site.

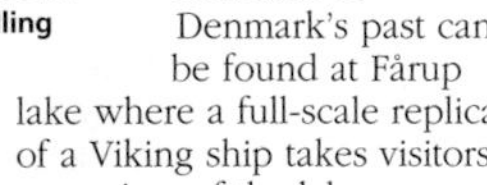

Runic stone in Jelling

Kongernes Jelling, an exhibition centre opposite the church is devoted to the history of the Vikings and the establishment of the Danish monarchy.

The atmosphere of Jelling can best be enjoyed during the annual Viking Fair. This weekend-long event is popular with many Danes, some of whom take it as an opportunity to dress up as Vikings and parade through the streets of the town. Another reminder of Denmark's past can be found at Fårup lake where a full-scale replica of a Viking ship takes visitors on cruises of the lake.

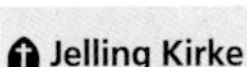

Jelling Kirke
8am–5pm Fri & Sat, noon–5pm Sun.

Kongernes Jelling
Gormsgade 23.
Tel *75 87 23 50.* *Jun–Aug: 10am–5pm Tue–Sun; Sep–May: noon–4pm Tue–Sun.*
www.kongernesjelling.dk

Runic writing including the oldest record of the name "Denmark"

LEGOLAND® ⓫

LEGO® bricks, known and loved by children throughout the world, were invented in the 1930s by Ole Kirk Christiansen. This popular amusement park was opened in 1968. Its attractions include amazingly detailed miniature versions of cities as well as famous landmarks constructed entirely from plastic LEGO® bricks. In addition there are thrilling rides, miniature trains and water chutes.

A LEGO® figure greets visitors

Imagination Zone
Hands-on fun is the main theme of this area. Among the activities are an interactive musical fountain and the chance to build a robot.

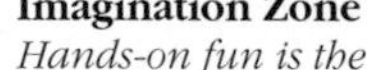

DUPLO® Land is for the youngest children.

★ Miniland
Over 20 million LEGO® bricks were used to construct famous buildings, airports, trains and even African animals.

Entrance

LEGO® Train
Miniland can be explored aboard a train or viewed from a revolving platform that gradually ascends to the top of a tower.

Round the World Voyage
The famous LEGO® structures include the Statue of Liberty and can be seen while cruising in a miniature boat.

For hotels and restaurants in this region see pp253–5 and pp279–81

★ X-treme Racers
This popular 400-m (1,312-ft) roller coaster negotiates bends at 60 km/h (37 mph) and provides thrill seekers with a hair-raising experience.

VISITORS' CHECKLIST

Road map C4. ***Tel*** *75 33 13 33.* *opening days and times vary, but usually: early Apr–Aug: from 10am daily; Sep, Oct: from 10am Fri–Tue; Nov: from 10am Sat & Sun. Always consult the website before visiting. Please note that rides close 1 to 2 hours before the park.* **www**.legoland.dk

Jungle Rally
Visitors who are too young to try Adventure Land's more breathtaking attractions can race around in these small electric cars.

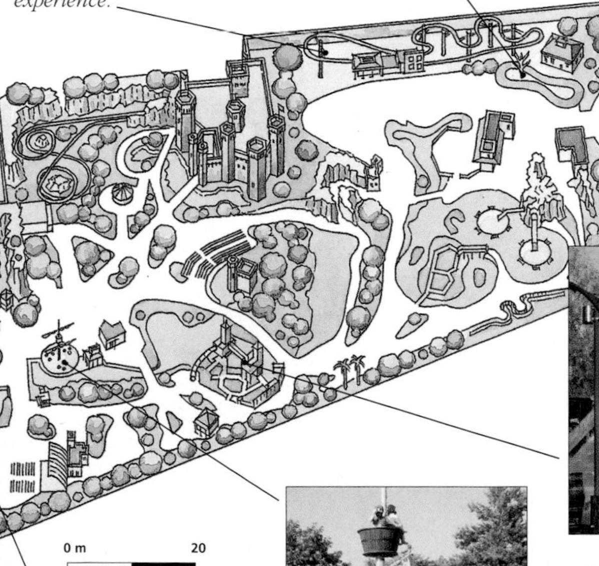

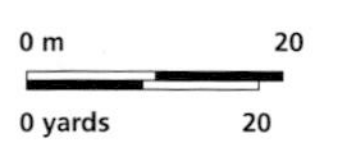

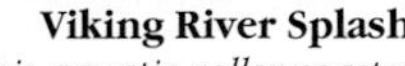

Viking River Splash
This aquatic roller coaster ride sends rafts splashing down wild water rapids and waterfalls and through a world of dragons and Vikings.

Merry-go-rounds
Many rides in LEGOLAND®, such as the merry-go-rounds in Pirateland, are aimed at younger children.

Pirate Splash Battle
Board a pirate ship and take position behind the water cannon in this playful recreation of a sea battle.

STAR SIGHTS

★ Miniland

★ X-treme Racers

Vindmølle, a Vejle landmark with a flour milling museum

Vejle ⓬

Road map B4. 55.
Banegårdspladsen 6. ***Tel*** *75 81 19 25.* **www**.visitvejle.com

The harbour town of Vejle makes a good base for visiting LEGOLAND® *(see pp192–3)* and the burial mounds at Jelling *(see p191)*. Aside from these nearby attractions, its main point of interest is Sankt Nicolai Kirke, a Gothic church dating from the 13th century. Inside the church, resting in a glass-lidded coffin, is the mummified body of a woman. The body was discovered in 1835 in a nearby peat bog and nick-named Queen Gunhilde, the legendary queen of the Vikings. However, recent forensic examinations have revealed that the woman lived during the Iron Age around 450 BC. Another curiosity of the church, though they can't be seen, are the 23 skulls hidden in its walls, which belonged to 23 robbers executed in 1630.

Rådhustorvet, Vejle's main square, contains the town hall. It stands on the site of a Dominican monastery and its medieval bell can be heard ringing each day from the tower. The **Vejle Museum** is spread over a number of locations in town and beyond. The main venue is a short way northwest of Rådhustorvet housed in Den Smidtske Gard, an early 19th-century burgher's residence. The exhibition covers 800 years of Vejle's history. On the edge of town, Vejle Vindmølle is also part of the museum. Built in 1890 and operational until 1960, the windmill houses an exhibition devoted to flour milling.

While in Vejle it is also possible to visit the Ecolarium, a centre that aims to raise awareness of environmental issues and the potential of alternative energy.

Vejle Museum
Den Smidtske Gard. Søndergarde 14. ***Tel*** *76 43 12 01.*
Jun–late Aug: 11am–5pm Tue–Fri, 10am–2pm Sat.
www.vejlemuseum.dk

Esbjerg ⓭

Road map B5. *85,000.*
Skolegade 33. ***Tel*** *75 12 55 99.*
Rock Festival (mid-Jun); Esbjerg Festival Week (mid-Aug), Chamber Music (Aug). **www**.visitesbjerg.com

When Prussia invaded the southern part of Jutland in 1864 Denmark lost the regions of Schleswig and Holstein. As a result, the former fishing village of Esbjerg began to develop into a harbour from which Jutland's farmers and producers could export goods. Today it is Denmark's largest commercial port and a centre for North Sea oil operations.

Seals, a favourite sight at Esbjerg's aquarium

Because of its 19th-century origins, Esbjerg lacks a medieval district. Nevertheless, it has several places worth visiting. For years the town's main symbol was its **Vandtårnet** (Water Tower), which was erected in 1897. Today, it serves as an observation platform, from which there is a panoramic view of the town. Close to the tower is the Musikhuset (Concert Hall) designed by Jørn Utzon and built in 1997.

Esbjerg Museum presents an historical portrait of the town and also has a large collection of amber. The **Fiskeri-og Søfartsmuseet** (The Fisheries and Maritime Museum), 4 km (2 miles) northwest of Esbjerg's centre, contains a large aquarium and various marine-related displays. Most of the sea life in the aquarium comes from the North Sea. Its most popular inhabitants are the seals. This vast museum complex also features a collection of navigation instruments and model vessels, a number of fishing boats placed outside the building and a reconstructed coastal lifeboat station. Outside the museum grounds, on the seashore, are four 9-m (30-ft) tall snow-white stylised figures of seated men, which are

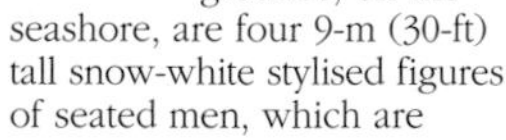

Exhibition room in Esbjerg's Fiskeri-og Søfartsmuseet

entitled *Man Meets the Sea* and were created by Svend Wiig Hansen to mark the city's centennial in 1995. The maritime theme continues in Esbjerg harbour where the 20th-century **Horns Rev Lightship** is moored.

Vandtårnet
Havnegade 22. ***Tel*** *76 16 39 39.* *Jun–mid-Sep: 10am–4pm daily.*

Esbjerg Museum
Torvegade 45. ***Tel*** *76 16 39 39.* *10am–4pm.* *Sep–May: Mon.*

Fiskeri-og Søfartsmuseet
Saltvandsakvariet Tarphagevej 2–6. ***Tel*** *76 12 20 00.* *Sep–Jun: 10am–5pm daily; Jul–Aug: 10am–6pm daily.*

Horns Rev Lightship
Tel *21 62 11 04.* *May–Aug: 10:30am–4pm daily.*

Ribe ⓮

Road map B5. *18,000.* *Torvet 3, 75 42 15 00.* **www**.visitribe.com

Scandinavia's oldest town is also one of the best preserved and contains many fine buildings including a medieval cathedral and a 16th-century schoolhouse. The medieval centre is beautifully preserved and features a maze of cobbled streets lined with crooked, half-timbered houses.

Ribe was once a seaport. With the passage of time the mouth of the river that flows through it became silted up, and now the town is quite a way from the seashore.

In 856 it was visited by the missionary Ansgar, known locally as the Apostle of Scandinavia. He built a small wooden church in Ribe, intending it to be a base for clergymen arriving here from Germany.

The night watchman in Ribe

In the 10th century Ribe became a bishopric, and in the mid-12th century acquired an impressive cathedral, which still stands today. **Ribe Domkirke** is built of a soft porous rock called tufa that was quarried near Cologne. The most prominent entrance, used by the bishops, is on the south side of the church. This entrance features a 13th-century "Cat's Head" doorway that got its name from the knocker made in the shape of a lion's head. Another feature of the portal is the pediment portraying Jesus and Mary – positioned at their feet are the images of Valdemar II and his wife Dagmar who died in childbirth in 1212. To this day at noon and 3pm the cathedral bells chime the tune of a folk song dedicated to the queen. The most notable features of the church's interior are the 16th-century frescoes and the modern mosaics created by Carl-Henning Pedersen. The left wing of the transept contains a marble floor slab from the tomb of Christoffer I, who died in 1259 and is laid in the adjacent sarcophagus. It is thought to be the oldest royal tombstone in Scandinavia. Stunning views can be obtained from the top of the 14th-century tower.

Nave of Ribe Domkirke

Det Gamle Rådhus, opposite the cathedral's southeast corner, was built in 1496. The town hall's museum has a small collection of medieval objects including torture instruments and executioners' swords. From here it is not far to the river, where the Stormflodssøjlen (Flood Column) indicates the floods that have submerged the town. Moored along the jetty is a replica of the *Johanne Dan*, a windjammer dating from 1867.

Ribe has two Viking museums. Standing opposite the railway station on Odyna square is **Ribes Vikinger** where the market town atmosphere of late 8th-century Ribe is recreated. The **Vikingecenter**, 3 km (2 miles) south of the town centre, is an open-air museum that offers a portrait of Ribe during the Viking era.

Ribe Domkirke
Albert Skeelsgade 11. ***Tel*** *75 42 06 19.* *Nov–Mar: 11am–3pm daily; Apr & Oct: 11am–4pm daily; May & mid-Aug–Sep: 10am–5pm daily; Jul–mid-Aug: 10am–5:30pm.*

Det Gamle Rådhus
Von Støckens Plads. ***Tel*** *76 88 11 22.* *Jun–Aug 1–3pm daily.*

Ribes Vikinger
Odin Plads 1. ***Tel*** *76 88 11 22.* *Jul–Aug: 10am–6pm (until 9pm Wed) daily; Sep–Oct & Apr–Jun: 10am–4pm daily; Nov–Mar: 10am–4pm Tue–Sun.*

Ribe Vikingecenter
Lustrupvej 4. ***Tel*** *75 41 16 11.* *May–Jun, Sep: 10am–3:30pm, Jul–Aug: 11am–5pm.*

Half-timbered houses, adding to the charm of Ribe

Palisade by Rømø dyke

Rømø 15

Road map B5. *850.* *Tvismark, Havnebyvej 30.* ***Tel*** *74 75 51 30.* **www**.romo.dk

The largest Danish island in the North Sea, Rømø was a prosperous whaling base in the 18th century. Its western shores are fringed with wide stretches of beach. The island is connected to Jutland by a causeway that passes through marshland rich in birdlife.

In the village of **Toftum** is Komandørgaard (Captain's House), which dates from 1748. The house, which now serves as a museum, has a thatched roof and some original interior decor, including wall coverings consisting of 4,000 Dutch tiles. Close by is an 18th-century school. A short distance further north, in the hamlet of **Juvre**, is a whale jawbone fence constructed in 1772. In **Kirkeby**, next to the walls that surround the Late-Gothic church, are whalers' gravestones that were brought back from Greenland. The histories of captains and their families have been carved by local artists.

The main point of interest at the south end of the island is **Havneby**, which has an amusement park and a mechanical dolls' museum. A ferry goes from here to the tranquil island of Sylt, just to the southwest.

Tønder 16

Road map B5. *8,200.* *Torvet 1.* ***Tel*** *74 72 12 20.* *Tønder Festival (Aug).* **www**.visittonder.dk

In the Middle Ages Tønder was a major fishing port. During subsequent centuries it became the centre of a lace-making industry, which is now commemorated by a lace-makers' festival held every three years. Examples of fine lace and the sophisticated tools used in its production are on display in the **Tønder Museum**. During the 17th and 18th centuries Tønder also produced ceramics that were used as wall tiles, some of which can be seen in the museum. The Tønder Museum is part of the **Museum of Southern Jutland** which shows a collection of modern art.

Font in Haderslev Domkirke

Tønder's town centre is a pleasant place to explore and the narrow streets contain many houses with decorative doorways and picturesque gables and window shutters. The best-known house is Det Gamle Apotek (The Old Pharmacy), at Østergade 1, which has a Baroque doorway dating from 1671. The market square contains a 16th-century Rådhus (town hall). Also in the square is the 16th-century Kristkirken, which has some fine paintings and carvings.

Tønder Museum & Museum of Southern Jutland
Kongevejen 51. ***Tel*** *74 72 89 89.*
Jun–Aug: 10am–5pm daily; Sep–May: 10am–5pm Tue–Sun.
www.sonkunst.dk

Doorway of a house in Østergade, Tønder

Sønderborg 17

Road map C5. Als. *30,000.* *Rådhustorvet 7.* ***Tel*** *74 42 35 55.* **www**.visitsonderborg.com

Sønderborg, meaning "South Castle", is on the island of Als. It owes its name to a castle fortress built by Valdemar I in 1170. Over the centuries the castle served a variety of purposes. Christian II was held prisoner here for 17 years in the early 16th century. Later on it was used in turns as a warehouse, a hospital, a prison and as a military barracks.

The town's turbulent history is brought to life at the **Historiecenter Dybbøl Banke** which is situated near Sønderborg, close to the village of Dybbøl. In the spring of 1864 this area was the scene of a fierce and protracted battle between Danish and Prussian forces. Dybbøl Mølle, a windmill that was damaged during the fighting, is now regarded as a national symbol. As a result of Denmark's defeat

For hotels and restaurants in this region see pp253–5 and pp279–81

Søndenborg was destroyed and southern Jutland was incorporated into Prussia and later into Germany (the territory was returned in 1920).

Historiecenter Dybbøl Banke
Dybbøl Banke 16. ***Tel*** *74 48 90 00.* *early Apr–mid-Oct: 10am–5pm daily.*

Haderslev ⓲

Road map C5. *25,000.*
Honnørkajen 1, 74 52 55 50.
www.haderslev-turist.dk

The present-day capital of southern Jutland is situated between a narrow fjord and a lake that was formed by the construction of a dam. In the 13th century Haderslev was a market town and its historic centre contains many period buildings.

During the Reformation Haderslev was a major centre of Protestantism and in 1526 it became the site of the first Protestant theological college. The town's main place of worship is Haderslev Domkirke. This cathedral was built in the 13th century but during its long history has been remodelled many times. It boasts a magnificent altarpiece featuring a 14th-century crucifix and alabaster statues of the apostles.

The most enchanting of the town's buildings are to be found on Torvet, a square flanked by half-timbered houses. From here it is easy to find the **Haderslev Museum**, which has exhibits on the archaeological history of the area, a local-history collection and its own mini open-air museum.

Interior of the 13th-century cathedral in Haderslev

Courtyard at Koldinghus castle

Haderslev Museum
Dalgade 7. ***Tel*** *74 52 75 66.* *Jun–Aug: 10am–4pm Tue–Sun; Sep–May: 1–4pm Tue–Sun.*

Kolding ⓳

Road map C5. *59,000.*
Akseltorv 8.
Tel *76 33 21 00.*
www.visitkolding.dk

Kolding is close to the bridge that links Jutland to Funen. The town's most important historic building is Koldinghus – a mighty castle that has a distinctive square tower with a flat roof (called the Heroes' Tower). The first fortress on this site was built in 1268 but the oldest surviving walls date from about 1440. More of the castle's history can be learned at the **Museet på Koldinghus**. Kolding's main square is Akseltorv, which contains the beautiful Renaissance Borchs Gård dating from 1595. The **Kunstmuseet Trapholt** on the town's eastern outskirts has a collection of Danish modern art.

Museet på Koldinghus
Adelgade 1. ***Tel*** *76 33 81 00* *10am–5pm daily.*
www.koldinghus.dk

Kunstmuseet Trapholt
Æblehaven 23. ***Tel*** *76 30 05 30.* *10am–5pm daily (to 8pm Wed).*

Fredericia ⓴

Road map C5. *36,000.*
Vendersgade 30D. ***Tel*** *72 11 35 11.*
www.visitfredericia.dk

Frederik III decided to build Fredericia on this strategic section of the Lille Bælt (Little Belt) in 1650. In 1657 the fortress town was captured by the Swedes who slaughtered the entire garrison stationed here. In 1849, during the Schleswig conflict, it was the scene of a battle fought by the Danes against the advancing Prussian army. Special ceremonies are held in Fredericia on the anniversary of that event; a daily reminder of it is the Landsoldaten monument by the Prince's Gate. The Danes killed in the battle were buried in a communal grave in the local cemetery. The town ramparts remain from the original fortress. The best section is by Danmarksgade, where the grassy embankments reach 15 m (49 ft) in height. The nearby water tower dates from 1909 and provides the best view of the surrounding area. **Fredericia Museum** has displays relating to the town's military and civilian history. Madsby Park, a short way outside the old town, contains a miniature version of Fredericia.

Coat of arms on gate in Fredericia

Fredericia Museum
Jernbanegade 10. ***Tel*** *72 10 69 80.* *mid-Jun–mid-Aug: noon–4pm; mid-Aug–Dec & Feb–mid-Jun: noon–4pm.* *Mon.*

Man Meets the Sea, **sculpture outside Esbjerg ▷**

NORTHERN JUTLAND

Visitors to northern Jutland can enjoy beautiful scenery and peace. Remote from Denmark's main tourist attractions, this part of Jutland is sparsely populated. Aalborg is the area's only large city and for the most part the diverse landscape is made up of farmland and fields, heathland and dunes. There are a number of places to visit including a Viking burial ground at Lindholm Høje.

The least populated and the wildest part of this region is its northern end where numerous coves make up the Limfjord straits. This part of the country provides excellent nesting grounds for a variety of birds. On the northwestern side, facing Skagerrak, the scenery is dominated by dunes, which display the clear effects of frequent sea breezes that shift the sand by up to 10 m (33 ft) each year.

Many visitors embark on trips to Grenen, Denmark's northernmost point, which is washed over by the waters of the Baltic and the North Sea. This area is sometimes referred to as the "Land of Light" and enjoys more hours of sunshine than anywhere else in Denmark. The extraordinary light has long been appreciated by artists, who came here in search of inspiration in the 19th century. Many settled around Skagen which became a magnet for prominent painters and writers who formed the Skagen School.

Another distinct feature of northern Jutland's landscape are its heathlands. As recently as the mid-19th century they covered one third of this region; now they can be seen only here and there. Northern Jutland also boasts Rold Skov, Denmark's largest forest, which forms part of Rebild Bakker, the country's only national park.

The most important of the area's historic sights are the Lindholm Høje prehistoric cemetery and the 1,000-year-old Viking fortress at Fyrkat, which has a replica Viking farmstead.

Some of Denmark's best beaches can also be found in northern Jutland and there are many holiday cottages and camp sites in the area.

Renaissance palace in Voergård

◁ **Lindholm Høje – the largest Viking burial ground in Scandinavia**

Exploring Northern Jutland

Aalborg makes a good base for exploring this part of the country, while smaller towns such as Thisted, Løgstør, Mariager or Skagen can also serve as good jumping-off points. When heading north, it is best to travel by car, since many of the most attractive areas are some distance from each other, and there may be problems with finding suitable public transport. Even when travelling by car it pays to allow plenty of time as many roads are fairly minor and pass through villages. The advantage of travelling on these minor routes is that the scenery is varied and offers a portrait of Denmark quite different from any seen from motorways.

Viking enthusiast sharpening a blade in the village of Fyrkat

View of the cathedral from the shore of the lake in Viborg

SIGHTS AT A GLANCE

Frederikshavn 4
Fyrkat 17
Fårup 1
Gammel Estrup 19
Grenen 3
Hirtshals 2
Hjerl Hedes Frilandsmuseum 11
Holstebro 10
Kongenshus Mindepark 12
Limfjorden pp210–11 9
Lindholm Høje 7
Mariager 16
Mønsted 13
Randers 18
Rebild Bakker 15
Sæby 5
Viborg 14
Voergård Slot 6
Aalborg pp208–9 8

For additional map symbols *see back flap*

GRENEN
3
Skagen
40
Ålbæk Bugt
HIRTSHALS 2
597
Ålbæk
55
Hjørring
Sindal
35
4 FREDERIKSHAVN
Tårs
585
Løkken
553
Vrå
Ør Vrå
E39
5 SÆBY
Læsø
FÅRUP 1
543
585
541
Brønderslev
180
6 VOERGÅRD SLOT
Pandrup
E45
Hjallerup
Aabybro
Asaa
55
11
Vodskov
Brovst
7 LINDHOLM HØJE
AALBORG 8
583
Nibe
595
Hals
Svenstrup
NORDJYLLAND
Aalborg Bugt
187
Støvring
E45
541
Skørping
Aars
REBILD BAKKER 15
13
507
180
29
Hadsund
541
Aalestrup
Hobro
16 MARIAGER
FYRKAT 17
13
507
180
547
16
GAMMEL ESTRUP
RANDERS 18
19
VIBORG
503
Auning
Langå
Grenå
525
46
E45
21
Bjerringbro
Gudenå
Rosenholm Slot
26
Hornslet
Århus
Århus

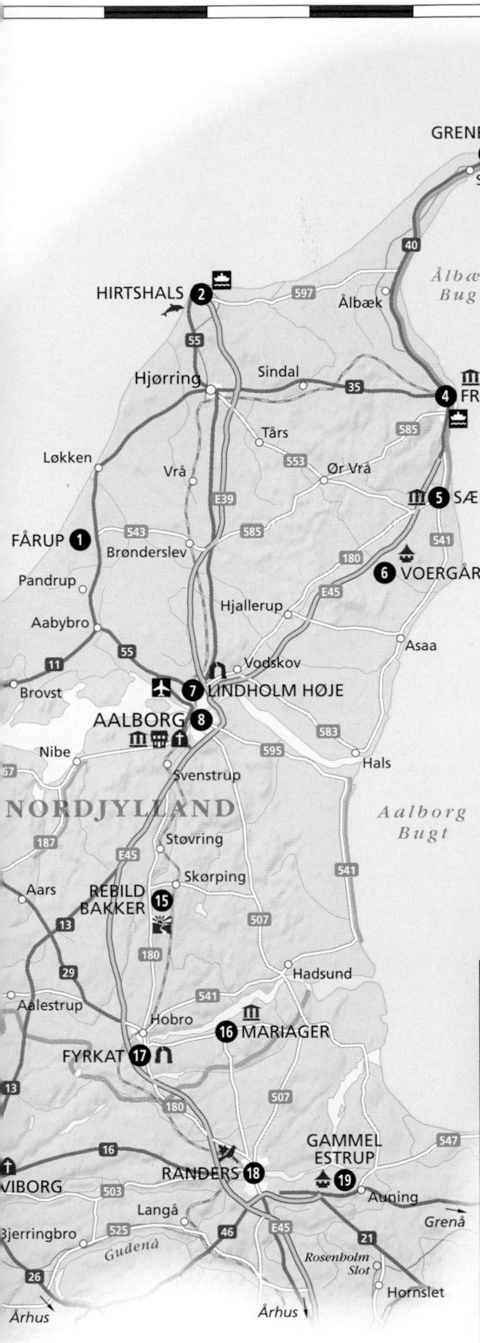

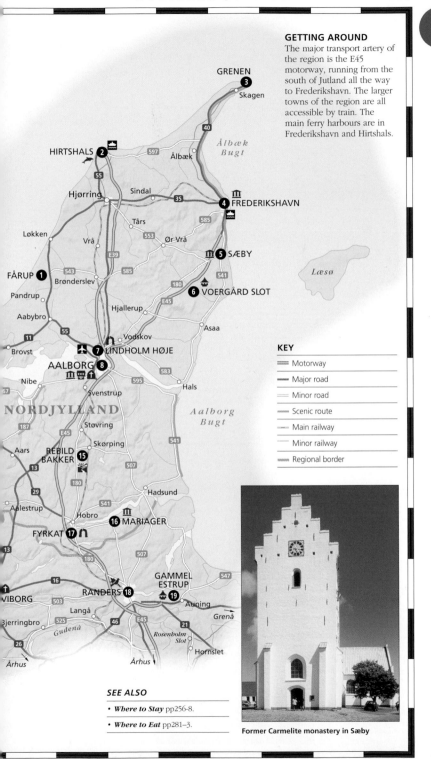

GETTING AROUND

The major transport artery of the region is the E45 motorway, running from the south of Jutland all the way to Frederikshavn. The larger towns of the region are all accessible by train. The main ferry harbours are in Frederikshavn and Hirtshals.

KEY

- Motorway
- Major road
- Minor road
- Scenic route
- Main railway
- Minor railway
- Regional border

Former Carmelite monastery in Sæby

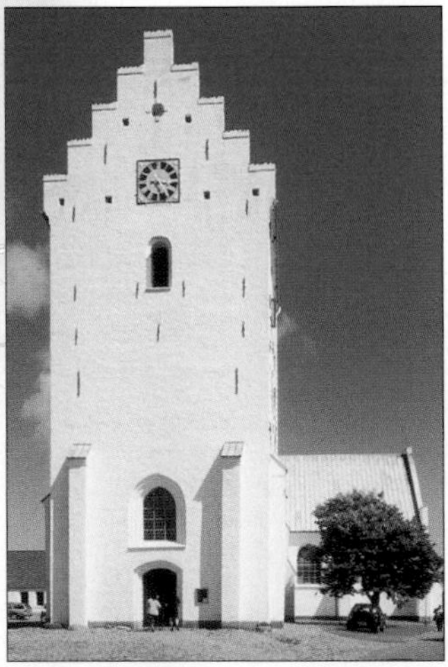

SEE ALSO

- ***Where to Stay*** pp256-8.
- ***Where to Eat*** pp281–3.

Fårup Sommerland, a vast amusement park

Fårup ❶

Road map C2. Pirupvejen 147. ***Tel*** *98 88 16 00.* *May & early Sep: from 10am Sat & Sun; early Jun–late Aug: from 10am daily. Always consult the website before visiting.* **www**.faarupsommerland.dk

Fårup Sommerland is an amusement park set amid forests and heathlands, between Saltum and Blokhus. The park's history is linked with the Krageland family of merchants, who ran a wholesale business in Aalborg. When in the early 1970s the chain stores went into decline, the Kragelands switched their energy to creating a place that would combine relaxation with amusement. In June 1975 Fårup opened its doors for the first time. Among the thrills and spills on offer are water chutes, white-water rafting and roller-coasters. In addition, there are gentler attractions for younger visitors.

Hirtshals ❷

Road map C1. *15,000.* *Nørregade 40.* ***Tel*** *98 94 22 20.* **www**.hirtshals-tourist.dk

Towards the end of the 19th century Hirtshals was no more than a small fishing hamlet; now it is one of Jutland's major ports. Regular ferry links with the Norwegian towns of Kristiansand, Oslo and Moss make this small town an important bridge with Denmark's Scandinavian neighbours on the other side of Kattegat. The town has a thriving fishing harbour and every day, at 7am, it becomes the venue for auctioning the night's catch.

The greatest attraction is the **Nordsøen Oceanarium**, a sea-life centre that is situated about 1 km (half a mile) east of the town centre. Since it opened in 1984, the oceanarium has attracted thousands of visitors every year. Its vast tank contains 4.5 million litres (990,000 gallons) of water, making it one of Europe's biggest aquariums. The aquarium includes an amphitheatre that looks onto a huge glass pane that is 8 m (26 ft) high and 45 cm (18 in) thick. The fish include schools of herring and mackerel as well as sharks. A diver enters the tank every day at 1pm to feed the fish.

As well as the aquarium, the Nordsøen Oceanarium has numerous displays that explain about the issues surrounding fishing in the North Sea and the ecology of the region. Outside is a seal pool, which has regular feed times at 11am and 3pm.

Aquarium at Nordsøen Oceanarium, Hirtshals

Hirtshals also offers a network of walking and cycling trails, including one leading to a 57-m (187-ft) tall lighthouse and also to Husmoderstrand – a clean beach with many safe places for children to play and swim.

Hirtshals Museum is in a former fishermen's cottage that dates from 1880. This has an exhibition of everyday objects illustrating the lifestyle of the local population in the early 20th century.

Nordsøen Oceanarium
Willemoesvej. ***Tel*** *98 94 41 88.*
Jan–Mar & Nov: 9am–4pm daily (to 5pm Sat, Sun & hols); Apr–Jun, Sep & Oct: 9am–5pm daily; Jul & Aug: 9am–6pm daily.
www.nordsoenoceanarium.dk

Grenen, where the Baltic meets with the North Sea

Grenen ❸

Road map D1. *Vestre Strandvej 10, Skagen.* ***Tel*** *98 44 13 77.* **www**.skagen-tourist.dk

Grenen is the northernmost point of Denmark. Standing by the car park, from which a 2-km (1-mile) trail leads to the point, is the Skagen Odde Naturcenter. Designed by the Danish architect Jørn Utzon, the centre aims to enable visitors to appreciate the natural environment of this region through a series of imaginative displays utilizing sand, water, wind and light.

The environs of Grenen consist of vast sand dunes, here and there overgrown with heather. This wild landscape captivated the Danish writer Holger Drachmann (1846–1908) to such an extent that he made it his wish to be buried in the sands of Grenen. His grave can be found on one of the nearby dunes.

For hotels and restaurants in this region see pp256–8 and pp281–3

Skagen Artists

The former fishing port of Skagen is now a fashionable resort, full of brightly painted yellow houses and a good number of local restaurants and shops. The town's character is accurately represented by its coat of arms, which features a painter's palette in the shape of a flounder. In the late 19th century many artists flocked here in order to "paint the light" and formed what is now known as the Skagen School. Its members included the writer Holger Drachmann, and painters Anna and Michael Ancher, Peder Severin Krøyer, Lautitz Tuxen, Carl Locher, Christian Krogh and Oskar Bjørck. The Skagens Museum exhibits many of their works and it is also possible to visit the former home of Michael and Anna Ancher.

The extraordinary light, *produced by the reflection of the sun's rays in the waters surrounding Skagen and the dunes, was the inspiration for the 19th-century artists arriving here from all over Denmark, as well as from Sweden and Norway.*

The Skagens Museum *houses a huge collection of works. Most of the paintings are of local scenes and all of the Skagen School of artists are well represented.*

The fishing harbour *is crowded with cutters as Skagen is still one of the major centres of fishing in northern Denmark, although much of the town's income now derives from tourism.*

Brøndums Hotel *was founded by Erik Brøndums in 1859. Hans Christian Andersen once stayed here and the hotel was also popular with artists, who often met in the bar at night. The Skagens Museum is in the grounds.*

The Skagen artists' work *is often characterized by vibrant seascapes and naturalistic portraits. The painting above, by P.S. Krøyer, depicts Anna Ancher and the artist's wife, Marie.*

Michael Ancher *lived for four years in Brøndums Hotel. Ancher married Anna Brøndum, step-sister of the hotel's owner, who was herself a talented artist. This 1886 portrait of Ancher is by P.S. Krøyer.*

Frederikshavn ❹

Road map D1. 30,000. Skandiatorv 1. ***Tel*** *98 42 32 66.* *Tordenskiold Festival.* **www**.frederikshavn-tourist.dk

The main international ferry port of Jutland has a number of historical sights. The Krudttårnet (Gunpowder Tower) is all that remains of a 17th-century citadel that once guarded the port. Today the tower houses a small military museum. Frederikshavn Kirke dates from the 19th century and contains a painting by Michael Ancher, one of the best-known of the Skagen School *(see p205)*. The **Bangsbo-Museet** is about 3 km (2 miles) south of the centre. This 18th-century manor house has an eclectic collection that includes objects relating to the town's history and the Danish Resistance during World War II. There is also a display of artifacts made from human hair. Perhaps the best exhibit is a reconstructed 12th-century Viking merchant ship.

Bangsbo-Museet
Dronning Margrethes Vej 6. ***Tel*** *98 42 31 11.* *10am–5pm Tue–Sun.* **www**.bangsbo.com

Sæby ❺

Road map D1. *18,000.* *Krystalgade 3.* ***Tel*** *98 46 12 44.* **www**.visitsaeby.dk *or* **www**.saeby-tourist.dk

The town skyline is dominated by the tower of Vor Frue Kirke (Church of Our Lady), which once formed part of a 15th-century Carmelite monastery. The church is richly decorated with frescoes. Its beautiful Late-Gothic altarpiece dates from around 1520. Next to the church is the grave of Peter Jakob Larssøn, a 19th-century buccaneer who went on to become Sæby's mayor.

Sæby has a compact centre with half-timbered houses and an attractive harbour. In summer a trumpeter heralds the end of each day, which is followed by the ceremonial lowering of a flag. **Sæby Museum**, housed in the 17th-century Ørums Consul's House, contains a 1920s schoolroom and a violinmaker's workshop.

Environs

A short distance north of town is **Sæbygård**, a beautifully preserved 16th-century manor house set in a small beech forest.

Sæby Museum
Algade 1–3. ***Tel*** *98 46 10 77.* *Jun–Aug: 10am–4pm Tue–Sun; Sep–May: 10am–4pm Tue–Fri.*

Opulent dining room in Voesgård Slot

Voergård Slot ❻

Road map D2. Voergård 6, Dronningelund. ***Tel*** *98 86 71 08.* *Easter: 11am–4pm; May–mid-Jun: 1–4pm Sat, 11am–4pm Sun & hols; mid-Jun–Aug: 10am–5pm daily; Sep–early Oct: 1–4pm Sat, 11am–4pm Sun; autumn hols: 1–4pm.* **www**.voergaardslot.dk

This Renaissance castle is one of Denmark's most stylish buildings. Its splendid portal was intended originally for the royal castle of Fredensborg. Initially the estate was part of a religious complex, but following the Reformation it passed into private hands. The parts open to visitors include the main wing, which has a large collection of paintings and antiques. The collection includes works by Raphael, Goya, Rubens and Fragonard. Also on display are many fine pieces of furniture and porcelain (including a dinner set made for Napoleon I).

Lindholm Høje ❼

Road map C2. **Cemetery** *until dusk.* **Museum** *Vendilavej 11.* ***Tel*** *99 31 74 40.* *Apr–Oct: 10am–5pm daily; Nov–Mar: 11am–4pm Tue–Sun.* **www**.nordjyllandshistoriske museum.dk

Denmark's largest Iron Age and Viking cemetery has survived so well due to a thick layer of sand that blew over it, burying it for many centuries. The 4-m (13 ft) thick sand deposit kept the site hidden until 1952, when archaeologists happened upon

Half-timbered house in one of Sæby's picturesque streets

it and unearthed nearly 700 graves of various shapes. The oldest ones are triangular; others are circular. Some have even been made to resemble ships. Other finds discovered in the vicinity, including traces of houses and hearths, indicate that between the 7th and 11th centuries this was a trading settlement. Lindholm Høje comes to life each year during the last week of June, when a Viking festival is held here. Throughout the rest of the year it is possible to learn about the lives of its former inhabitants by visiting the small museum by the car park.

Village house in Hjerl Hedes Frilandsmuseum

Aalborg ❽

See pp208–9.

Limfjorden ❾

See pp210–11.

Holstebro ❿

Road map B3. *31,000.* *Den Røde Plads 14.* ***Tel*** *97 42 57 00.* **www**.visitholstebro.dk

The earliest records of Holstebro can be found in 13th-century documents. The town was often plagued by fire, however, and has few historic sights. Continuing a centuries-old tradition the town bells chime every day at 10pm reminding citizens to put out fires for the night.

In front of the mid-19th-century Rådhus (town hall) in the centre of town is a sculpture by Alberto Giacometti. The nearby Neo-Gothic church is 20th century and contains the remains of a 16th-century altar.

The **Holstebro Kunstmuseum** has a sizeable collection of paintings (including works by Picasso and Matisse) as well as sculpture and ceramics, which are mainly by contemporary Danish artists.

Façade of the Holstebro Kunstmuseum

Holstebro Kunstmuseum
Museumsvej 2. ***Tel*** *97 42 45 18.*
Jul–Aug: 11am–5pm Tue–Sun; Sep–Jun: noon–4pm Tue–Fri, 11am–5pm Sat–Sun.

Hjerl Hedes Frilandsmuseum ⓫

Road map B3. Hjerl Hedevej 14. ***Tel*** *97 44 80 60.* *Apr & Oct: 11am–4pm, days vary; May–Sep: 10am–5pm daily (late Jun–mid-Aug: to 6pm); late Nov–mid-Dec: 10am–5pm Sat & Sun.* **www**.hjerlhede.dk

A short distance northeast of Holstebro is an open-air museum that re-creates the development of a Danish village from 1500 to 1900. The collection of buildings includes an inn, a school, a smithy and a dairy. In summer, men and women wear period clothes and demonstrate traditional skills such as weaving and bread-making. Young children can dress in Stone Age costumes, while older ones can try their hand at spear fishing.

Kongenshus Mindepark heathland reserve

Kongenshus Mindepark ⓬

Road map C3. Venstre Skivevej 142, Viborg. ***Tel*** *87 28 10 13.* *all year round.* **www**.kongenshus.dk

A small section of Demark's uncultivated heathland, of which just 800 sq km (309 sq miles) remains, can be explored at Kongenhus Mindepark. For many years early pioneers attempted to cultivate this windswept and inhospitable area. In the 18th century an army officer from Mecklenburg leased the land from Frederik V, intending it for cultivation. Assisted by the king's generosity he built a house, which he named Kongenshus (King's House). However, the German officer abandoned the project after 12 years and returned to his homeland. The house is now a visitor centre.

Aalborg 8

North Jutland's capital city is situated on the south bank of the Limfordjen. It was founded by the Vikings in the 10th century and rapidly acquired a strategic significance as a hub of trade and transport. It prospered in the 17th century thanks to a thriving herring industry and many of its finest buildings date from this time. Aalborg remains a commercial centre and is the seat of the regional government and a university town. The local industry includes the country's leading producer of Danish schnapps, *akvavit*.

Satyr sticking out its tongue toward city hall

Panoramic view of Aalborg, capital of northern Jutland

Coat of arms from Jens Bangs Stenhus

Exploring Aalborg

Aalborg consists of two parts separated from each other by Limfjord. Most of the historic buildings are clustered around the compact medieval quarter. Jomfru Ane Gade has restaurants and bars and is the centre of the city's nightlife.

Vor Frue Kirke

Niels Ebbesens Gade. *9am–2pm Mon–Fri, 9am–noon Sat.*
www.vorfrue.dk

The Church of Our Lady dates back to the 12th century. In the 16th and 17th centuries it was the main place of Christian worship in Aalborg. It has been remodelled many times, however, and all that remains of the original building is the Gothic portal decorated with stone reliefs depicting Christ and a number of biblical scenes. The wooden crucifix seen over the presbytery entrance is 15th century. In the vicinity of the church are some cobbled streets lined with half-timbered merchants' houses. Many have been turned into shops.

Aalborghus Slot

Slotspladsen. *8am–9pm daily.* **Dungeons** *May–Sep: 8am–3pm Mon–Fri.* **Underground passages** *8am–9pm daily.*

This modestly-sized castle was built on the orders of Christian III and completed in 1555. It is surrounded by deep moats. The building was never used as a royal residence, however; instead it was the office of the king's functionaries. The dank castle dungeons and underground passages leading off them make for an eerie walk.

Jens Bangs Stenhus

Østerågade 9. *to the public.*

A Dutch Renaissance-style house, this five-storey edifice, decorated with gargoyles and floral ornaments, was built in 1624 for Jens Bang, a wealthy merchant. Its façade facing the Rådhus (city hall) includes a stone figure of a satyr sticking its tongue out – this was intended to symbolize the owner's attitude towards the city's councillors who refused to admit him into their ranks. The cellars house a wine bar that has changed little over the years.

Rådhuset

Gammel Torv 2. *to the public.*

The yellow-painted Baroque city hall was completed in 1762 and stands on the site of a demolished Gothic town hall. The motto written above the main door translates as "Wisdom and Determination" and was used by Frederik V, who was on the throne when the city hall was built.

Soldiers preparing for a parade, Aalborghus Slot

Budolfi Domkirke

Algade 40. ***Tel*** *98 12 46 70.* *Jun–Aug: 9am–4pm Mon–Fri, 9am–2pm Sat; Sep–May: 9am–3pm Mon–Fri, 9am–noon Sat.*

The Gothic cathedral's white plastered front was built around 1400, although some of its elements originate from an earlier church. Among the notable interior features are portraits of wealthy merchants, a gilded Baroque altarpiece and 16th-century frescoes. The church's patron, St Budolfi, is the patron saint of sailors whose cult was propagated by English missionaries.

Delightfully simple interior of Budolfi Domkirke

Historiske Museum

Algade 48. ***Tel*** *99 31 74 00.* *10am–5pm Tue–Sun.* **www.**nordjyllandshistoriskemuseum.dk

Just west of the cathedral is the local history museum. Its varied collection includes archaeological finds from Lindholm Høje *(see pp206–7)* and rare glassware and ancient coins. The museum's star exhibits include a reconstructed drawing room from an early 17th-century merchant's house. Most interesting of all, perhaps, is the skeleton of a 40-year-old female discovered in a peat bog who died around AD 400.

Helligåndsklostret

Kloster Jordet 10, C.W. Obels Plads. *late Jun–mid-Aug: 2pm Mon–Fri.* *(phone 99 30 60 90).*

This convent was founded in 1431 and is one of the best preserved buildings of its type in Scandinavia. The only original part is the west wing; the north and the east wings are 16th century. Guided tours allow visitors to look at the frescoes in the hospital chapel, step into the refectory with its starry vault and listen to the story of a nun who was buried alive for having a relationship with a monk.

VISITORS' CHECKLIST

Road map D2. *216,000.* *Østerågade 8.* ***Tel*** *99 30 60 90.* *Aalborg Carnival (May).* info@visitaalborg.com **www.**visitaalborg.com

Helligåndsklostret

Kunsten Museum of Modern Art Aalborg

Kong Christians Allé 50. ***Tel*** *99 82 41 00.* *10am–5pm Tue–Sun.* **www.**nordjyllandskunstmuseum.dk

Designed by Alvar Aalto in conjunction with Danish architect Jean-Jacques Baruël, this striking museum has a great collection of Danish and European modern art.

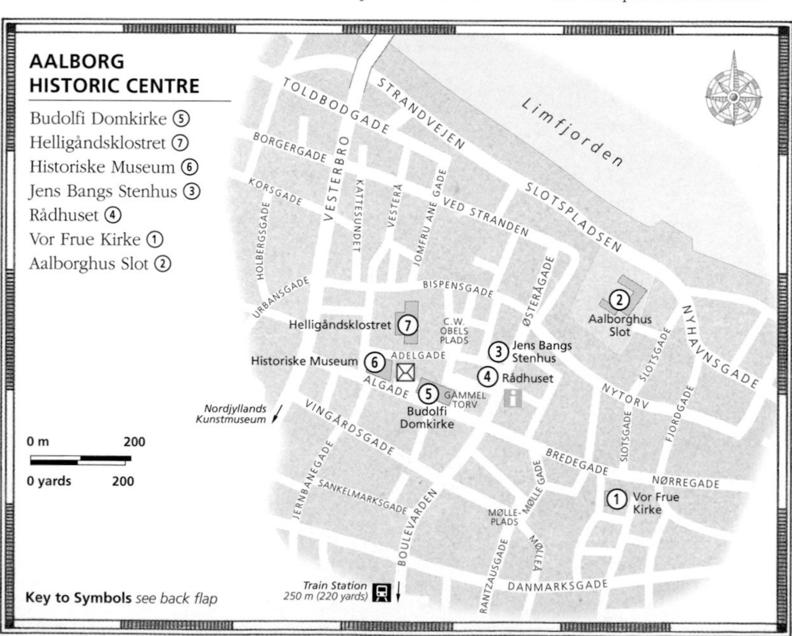

Limfjorden ❾

Limfjorden is Denmark's largest body of inland water. Although narrow inlets connect it to both the Kattegat and the North Sea, Limfjorden resembles an inland lake. It has some good beaches and is popular as a holiday destination in summer. Just how significant this area was at one time can be deduced from the many surviving churches and castles. In the middle is the island of Mors, whose aerial shape resembles Jutland. According to legend, when God created Jutland he first built a model. It was so good that he decided to place it at the centre of Limfjorden.

★ Jesperhus Park
This park is planted with half a million flowers. Some are planted to form figures of animals found in the park zoo, such as a crocodile.

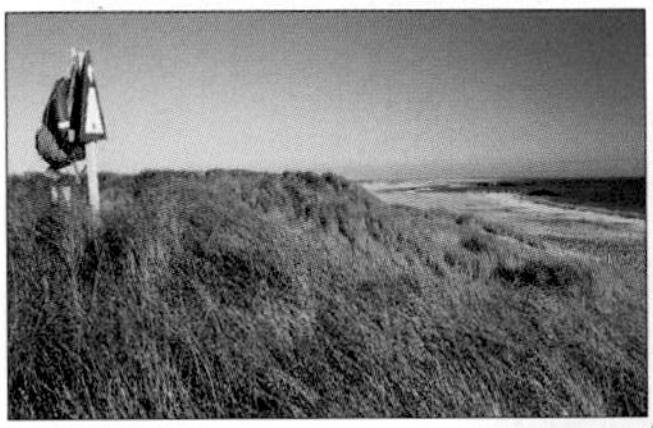

Spit
A narrow 10-km (6-mile) spit leads from Thyborøn to Harboøre. The west side is flanked by the fjord, the eastern side by the North Sea.

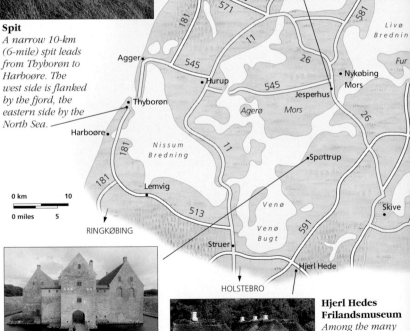

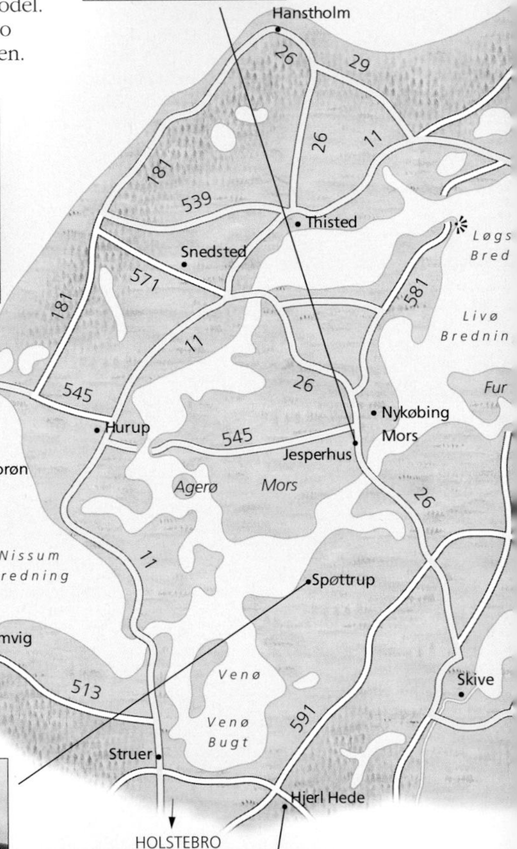

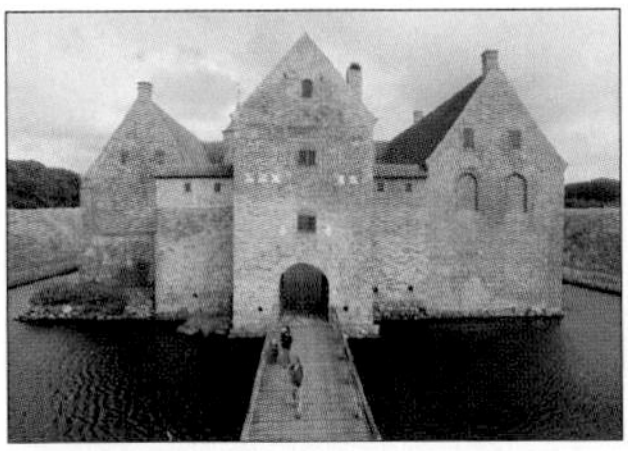

Hanstholm
Thisted
Snedsted
Løgs Bred
Livø Bredning
Fur
Agger
Hurup
Nykøbing Mors
Jesperhus
Thyborøn
Agerø
Mors
Harboøre
Nissum Bredning
Spøttrup
Lemvig
Venø
Venø Bugt
Skive
Struer
Hjerl Hede
RINGKØBING
HOLSTEBRO
0 km 10
0 miles 5

★ Spøttrup Borg
Protected against attack by a moat and high ramparts, this medieval castle has changed little since it was built in 1500.

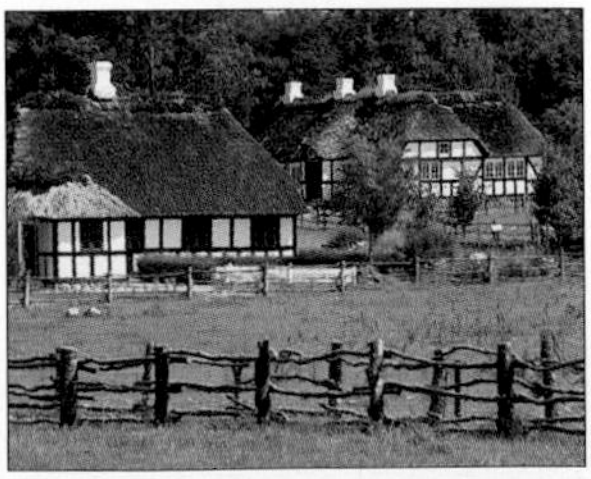

Hjerl Hedes Frilandsmuseum
Among the many historic buildings at this open-air museum are an inn, a smithy, a dairy, a school, a vicarage and a grocer's shop.

Fjerritslev
Situated between the fjord and the North Sea, Fjerritslev is surrounded by beautiful scenery. The town brewery has been preserved as a museum.

VISITORS' CHECKLIST

Road map C2.
Aalborg *Østerågade 8.* ***Tel*** *99 31 75 00.*
Nykøbing Mors *Havnen 4.* ***Tel*** *97 72 04 88.*
www.visitnordjylland.dk
www.visitaalborg.dk
www.visitskive.dk

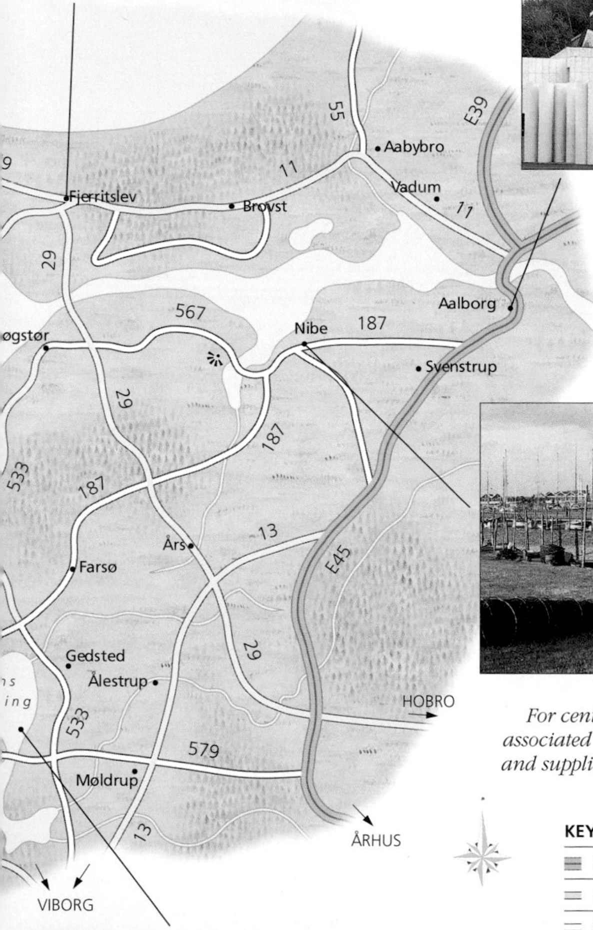

Aalborg
Northern Jutland's capital city has many interesting sights, including the superb Kunsten Museum of Modern Art (see p209).

Nibe
For centuries this small town was associated with the herring industry and supplied fish for the royal table.

KEY

- Motorway
- Major road
- Other road
- River
- Viewpoint

Lovns Bredning
This section of Limfjorden, which has some enchanting coves, is a protected area because of the rich diversity of birdlife found here.

STAR SIGHTS

★ Jesperhus Park

★ Spøttrup Borg

Mønsted's limestone mine

Mønsted ⓭

Road map C3. Mønsted Kalkgruber, Kalkværksvej 8. ***Tel*** *86 64 60 11.* *Apr–Oct: 10am–5pm daily.* **www**.monsted-kalkgruber.dk

As far back as the 10th century the area around Mønsted was famous as a centre of limestone mining. The mine, which was still in operation in the 20th century, is now an unusual local attraction. Although only 2 km (1 mile) of the entire 60 km (37 miles) of its tunnels are open, a walk through the underground maze is an unforgettable experience. Visitors can wander at their own pace through the galleries, but they must wear safety helmets. In view of the mine's steady humidity and temperature, which stays at 8° C (46° C), some of the caves situated 35 m (115 ft) below the surface are used for ripening cheese.

Viborg ⓮

Road map C3. *30,000.* *Nytorv 9.* ***Tel*** *86 60 02 38.* **www**.visitviborg.dk

Viborg is scenically located on the shores of two lakes. Its history dates back to the 8th century and it became one of Denmark's bishoprics in 1060. The 12th-century cathedral was used for coronation ceremonies by the Danish monarchy until the 17th century. The present twin-towered Domkirke (cathedral) was completed in 1876. This huge granite building has some valuable relics as well as a crypt dating from 1130, which is all that remains of the original cathedral. Other features include a gilded altarpiece and a vast 15th-century candelabra. The cathedral's frescoes form an illustrated Bible and were created by the Danish artist Joakim Skovgaard (1901–06). Other works by the artist can be seen in the **Skovgaard Museet** which is next to the cathedral. The **Viborg Stiftsmuseum** (District Museum) contains a variety of exhibits relating to the town's history including some items that date from the Viking era.

Figures from Viborg Domkirke

Viborg Domkirke
Domkirkepladsen, Sankt Mogensgade 4. ***Tel*** *87 25 52 50.* *Jan–Mar: 11am–3pm Mon–Fri, noon–3pm Sun; Apr–Sep: 11am–4pm Tue–Sat, noon–4pm Sun; Oct–Dec: 11am–3pm Tue–Sat, noon–3pm Sun.*

Skovgaard Museet
Domkirkstræde 4. ***Tel*** *86 62 39 75.* *Jun–Aug: 10am–5pm Tue–Sun; Sep–May: 11am–4pm Tue–Sun.*

Viborg Stiftsmuseum
Hjultorvet 4. ***Tel*** *87 87 38 38.* *mid-Jun–Aug: 11am–5pm Tue–Sun; Sep–mid-Jun: 1–4pm Tue–Fri, 11am–5pm Sat & Sun.*

Rebild Bakker ⓯

Map C3. *Rebild-Skørping Turistbureau, Kultur Stationen.* ***Tel*** *99 88 90 00.* **www**.visitrebild.dk

Rold Skov is the largest forest in Denmark. In 1912, after fund-raising among the Danish expatriate community in the USA, a section of it was purchased and turned into this national park. Covering 77 sq km (30 sq miles), an array of wildlife lives in the park, including foxes, deer, squirrels, wild boar, martens, badgers and numerous birds. The park contains a small museum and the **Lincoln Log Cabin**, which has photographs and other items relating to Danish emigration to America.

Lincoln Log Cabin
Tel *98 39 14 40.* *Jun: 11am–4:30pm daily; Jul–Sep: 11:30am–5pm daily.* **www**.rebild.org

Interior of the Lincoln Log Cabin, Rebild Bakker

Mariager ⓰

Road map D3. *2,500.* *Torvet 1B, 98 54 13 77.* **www**.visitmariager.dk

In the Middle Ages Mariager was a major centre of pilgrimages, owing to the nunnery that was established here in 1410. Today, it is a quiet fjord town, with cobbled streets and picturesque houses engulfed in roses. The main reminder of the convent is the church standing on a wooded hill. Though it is much smaller

◁ **Lighthouse in Oddesund Nord, Limfjorden**

Banks of Limfjorden, near Mariager

than the original 14th-century building it is possible to imagine what the convent would have been like from a scale model in **Mariager Museum**, which is housed in an 18th-century merchant's house.

At **Danmarks Saltcenter** visitors can learn about methods of salt production, make their own crystals and take a bath in Denmark's version of the Dead Sea, which has pools filled with warm water so salty that it's quite impossible to dive beneath the surface.

Small bag of salt from Danmarks Saltcenter

Mariager Museum
Kirkegade 4A. ***Tel*** *98 54 12 87.*
mid-May–mid-Sep: 1–5pm daily.

Danmarks Saltcenter
Ny Havnevej 6. ***Tel*** *98 54 18 16.*
10am–4pm daily (to 5pm Sat, Sun & hols).

Fyrkat 17

Road map C3. Fyrkatvej 37B. ***Tel*** *98 51 19 27. Apr: 10am–4pm Sat & Sun; May & 10–18 Oct: 10am–4pm daily; Jun–Aug: 10am–5pm daily; Sep: 10am–3pm daily.* **www**.sydhimmerlandsmuseum.dk **www**.fyrkat.dk

In 1950 the remains of a Viking settlement dating from around AD 980 were discovered in fields 3 km (2 miles) from the town of Hobro. A modern visitor centre has since been built around the site.

The entire settlement was surrounded by ramparts 120 m (394 ft) in diameter. The entry gates to the fortress, aligned strictly with the points of the compass, were linked with each other by two intersecting streets. An ancient cemetery containing 30 graves was discovered outside the main camp. One of the graves contained a skeleton of a woman buried together with her jewellery. A Viking-style farmstead north of the settlement recreates many aspects of Viking life.

Randers 18

Road map D3. *60,000.* *Rådhustorvet 4.* ***Tel*** *86 42 44 77.* **www**.visitranders.com

Jutland's fourth largest city was already a major market town in the Middle Ages. Its most important historic sight is the 15th-century Sankt Morten's Kirke. Hanging inside is a model of a ship dating from 1632. The three-storey Paaskesønnernes Gård nearby is late 15th century and one of the city's oldest houses. The most popular attraction is **Randers Regnskov**, an unusual tropical zoo that houses 200 animal species and 450 species of plants in a tropical rain forest environment. Here, regardless of the time of the year, the temperature remains at a constant 25° C (77° F), accompanied by very high humidity. Among the many animals kept at the zoo are crocodiles, gibbons, colourful butterflies, tapirs and snakes.

Randers Regnskov
Tørvebryggen 11.
Tel *87 10 99 99. 10am–4pm Mon–Fri, 10am–5pm Sat & Sun.*
www.regnskoven.dk

Gammel Estrup 19

Road map C3. Randersvej 2. ***Tel*** *86 84 30 01. Jan–Mar & Nov–Dec: 10am–3pm Tue–Sun; Apr–Jun, mid-Aug–Oct: 10am–5pm; Jul–mid-Aug: 10am–6pm.* **www**.gammelestrup.dk

One of the region's major attractions is the Gammel Estrup estate, near the village of Auning on the Djursland peninsula. The estate's 15th-century manor house is surrounded by a moat and provides an insight into Denmark's rural life. The house is now a museum and its interiors, complete with period furniture, paintings and tapestries, include reception rooms, bedrooms, a chapel and an alchemist's cellar. Some of the gardens and outbuildings form the Dansk Landbrugs-museum, which focuses on the estate's agricultural past and includes farm machinery and tools.

Environs

Rosenholm Slot, near Hornslet, is a 16th-century castle built on a small island in the middle of a lake. Boasting a large tapestry collection, the castle is said to be haunted by the ghost of an insane former owner.

Façade of Gammel Estrup's manor house

BORNHOLM

Far out in the Baltic, the idyllic island of Bornholm has an atmosphere all of its own. For years it remained relatively unknown to outsiders but the beauty of the island's sprawling beaches, its rugged coastal cliffs and distinctive architecture have made it a popular holiday destination. Tourism remains a low-key affair, however, and the villages and towns have changed little over the years.

Bornholmers are proud of their ancestry and have their own flag and, among the older generation, a distinctive dialect that is as unique to the island as the *rundkirke* (round churches) that are found here.

The discovery of ancient burial mounds and engravings suggest that the island was inhabited by 3000 BC. At one time Bornholm was an important centre for trade, and coins have been unearthed from as far afield as Rome and the Near East. The name "Bornholm" appeared for the first time in AD 890 at a time when the island was inhabited by the Vikings.

From the mid-12th century much of Bornholm became the property of the Archbishop of the city of Lund, which at that time belonged to Denmark. For a period in the 17th century it was controlled by Sweden but the islanders' strong allegiance to Denmark resulted in a rapid withdrawal of Swedish forces. Following the surrender of Germany in May 1945 Bornholm was occupied by the Soviets until the Danish army established a permanent garrison.

Today, Bornholm has a thriving fishing industry and no visitor should leave without sampling its smoked herring, known as *bornholmers*.

A wide variety of natural habitats is found here ranging from secluded forests and pasture land to rugged cliffs and long, sandy beaches. Another of the island's assets is its climate, with mild winters and Denmark's highest percentage of sunny days. The local flora features many species typical of the Mediterranean, including orchids, figs, grapes and mulberry trees.

Svaneke's yacht marina

◁ Entrance to Natur Bornholm in åkirkeby, one of Bornholm's few modern landmarks

Exploring Bornholm

Bornholm has some good cycle paths and exploring by bicycle is both convenient and enjoyable. The northern shore is marked by steep cliffs while sandy beaches are the main feature of the south and southeast coasts. Bornholm is known for its round churches and for the atmospheric ruins at Hammershus Slot. Rønne, the island's main town, has some well-preserved quarters, as do many of the smaller harbour ports. Children will enjoy a visit to Joboland Park, which includes an aquapark and a small zoo, and Østerlars' history centre where they can see what life was like in a medieval village.

Modern power-generating windmills north of Hasle

One of Bornholm's fortified 12th-century round churches

SIGHTS AT A GLANCE

Allinge 2
Gudhjem 12
Hammershus Slot 1
Hasle 4
Joboland 10
Nyker 5
Nylars 7
Olsker 3
Rønne 6
Svaneke 9
Aakirkeby 8
Østerlars Kirke 11

SEE ALSO

- ***Where to Stay*** pp258–60.
- ***Where to Eat*** pp283–4.

For additional map symbols *see back flap*

The scenic coast of Bornholm

GETTING THERE

Bornholm's airport is 5 km (3 miles) southeast of Rønne. A flight from Copenhagen takes half an hour. Many visitors arrive by ferry. The journey from Køge takes six to seven hours (overnight ferries are an option). As an alternative, visitors can take a three-hour train to Ystad in Sweden, and pick up a ferry from there to Rønne. Buses are also available from Copenhagen to Ystad and cost a little less.

One of Rønne's many colourful half-timbered houses

Picturesque ruins of Hammershus Slot

Hammershus Slot ❶

Castle ◯ *all year round.*
Hammershus Exhibition
Langebjergvej 26, Allinge. ◯ *mid-Apr–mid-Oct: 10am–4pm daily; Jun–Aug: 10am–5pm daily.*

The atmospheric ruins of Hammershus Slot are the largest in northern Europe and stand on a 70-m (230-ft) high cliff. The castle was built in the 13th century on the orders of the Archbishop of Lund. Legend has it that Hammershus was originally to be built at a different site, but the walls erected during the day vanished each night. A change of location was thought necessary and horses were let loose; the spot where they finally stopped was chosen as the new site.

The entrance to the castle leads over a stone bridge that was once a draw-bridge. The ruins also include what remains of a brewery, a cistern, a granary and a bakery.

The impressive square tower, Manteltårnet, was used in the Middle Ages for storing the country's tax records and later served as the quarters of the castle commander and also as a prison. In 1660 Leonora Christina, daughter of Christian IV, and her husband were imprisoned in the tower, accused of collaboration with the Swedes. Technological improvements in artillery eventually diminished the castle's defensive capabilities as its walls became vulnerable to attack from powerful cannons. It was abandoned in 1743 and much of the castle was used as building material for local homes. An exhibition includes a model of Hammerhus Slot as it was at the peak of its might.

Allinge ❷

2,000. *Kirkegade 4.* ***Tel*** *56 48 64 48.* **www**.bbc.dk

Allinge and nearby Sandvig, 2 km (1 mile) to the northwest, are treated as one town though the two have slightly different characters. Allinge has the majority of commercial facilities while Sandvig is quieter, with walking trails and neatly-tended gardens. Allinge's church is mostly 19th century, although the church itself grew out of a chapel erected five centuries earlier. Inside is a painting that once adorned the chapel in Hammershus Slot as well as tombstones of the castle's past commanders. On the outskirts of Allinge there is a well-kept cemetery for Russian soldiers, with a granite obelisk proudly displaying the Soviet star at the top. This is a reminder of the Red Army, who occupied Bornholm from the end of World War II until March 1946.

Granite obelisk at Allinge Cemetery

On the outskirts of Allinge is Madsebakke Helleristininger – the biggest and the most precious set of rock paintings to be found in the whole of Denmark. These simple enigmatic Bronze Age drawings, depicting ships, boats and the outlines of feet, are thought to be 4,000 years old. Another local curiosity is the Moseløkken quarry, where between May and September visitors can learn all about the excavation of granite on Bornholm and even have a go at splitting a piece themselves.

12th-century three-storey round church in Olsker

Olsker ❸

1,700.

The village of Olsker, south of Allinge, has one of the best known of Bornholm's distinctive round churches. Historians once believed they were of pagan origin. This hypothesis has now been discarded and the current theory is that they were intended for defensive purposes, as well as being used for storage. This three-storey granite building is the slenderest of Bornholm's four round churches and has nine windows. It was erected in the mid-12th century in honour of St Olaf, a Norwegian king who died in 1031, and who is revered in Denmark. The hill on which the church stands affords a beautiful view of the surrounding countryside.

For hotels and restaurants in this region see pp258–60 and pp283–4

Round Churches

Bornholm's four sparkling-white *rundkirke* (round churches) are each dedicated to a different saint. They were built between 1150 and 1200 at a time when pirate attacks were a constant threat to the island and have 2-m (7-ft) thick granite walls. Apart from the one at Nyker, all are three-storey buildings. The bottom level was used mainly for worship. The first floor served as a supply warehouse and also stored the church's valuables and donations received from the faithful. In times of danger the first floor also provided shelter for women and children, while the third, top level was used for surveillance and was an ideal place from which to shoot and throw stones at the advancing enemy.

Østerlars rundkirke *has a central pillar 6 m (20 ft) in diameter. It is adorned with a 14th-century frieze depicting scenes from the life of Christ.*

The churches *are decorated with paintings dating from the 13th and 14th centuries. The most popular themes are biblical.*

The conical roofs are not an original feature. When they were first built the church roofs were flat.

ØSTERLARS RUNDKIRKE
Sankt Laurentius Kirke was built around 1150 and is the oldest round church on the island. It has a whitewashed interior that features a number of Gothic wall paintings *(see p226)*.

Apses

Main door, for men only

The ground level was used for worship. Women came in through a separate entrance.

Many elements of furnishing *are not as old as the churches themselves. A notable feature of Olsker's church is its richly ornamented 16th-century pulpit.*

Top floors *were accessed by a stairway leading through narrow passages knocked out of the thick walls.*

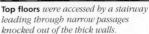

Hasle 4

1,800. Havnegade 1. **Tel** 56 96 44 81. **www**.hasle.dk

One of Bornholm's oldest towns, Hasle is mentioned in records as early as 1149. The herring industry has long been the town's main source of revenue although many locals were once also employed in excavating brown coal until the mine closed in 1946. The town is popular with visitors, many of whom come to sample the herring from local smoke-houses, which can be found thanks to their conspicuous chimneys. Many of these houses also function as museums, where visitors can watch the smoking process. The Silderogerierne Museum is probably the best of these and contains an exhibition illustrating the history of Hasle as well as the surrounding area.

In the centre of town stands an interesting 15th-century church with a lovely two-winged altarpiece made in Lübeck in 1520. According to one local story the altar was a gift from a sailor who miraculously escaped from a sinking ship.

A monument in the town square commemorates Peder Olsen, Jens Kofød and Porl Anker who became the local heroes of an uprising against the Swedes that erupted in Bornholm in 1658.

On the outskirts of the town, on the road leading towards Rønne, is a huge runic stone – the largest one on the island.

Nykirke's pillar with scenes from the Stations of the Cross

Nyker 5

2,000.

The smallest of Bornholm's historic round churches *(see p221)* is in Nyker. It is only two storeys high and lacks external buttresses. In keeping with its name (Nykirke or New Church) it is also the most recently built of the churches. A Latin inscription found on the Late-Gothic chalice kept in the church proclaims that the church is dedicated to All Saints. Other items to look out for include the frescoes that decorate the main pillar of the church, which depict the Stations of the Cross, and a stone laid in the portico with a Resurrection scene that dates from 1648. Another interesting object is an 18th-century tablet carved with the names of the local inhabitants who died during two plagues that devastated the area in 1618 and 1654.

Rønne 6

15,000. Nordre Kystvej 3. **Tel** 56 95 95 00. Wed, Sat. **www**.bornholm.info

One third of Bornholm's population live in Rønne. The town has grown up around a natural harbour and two of the first buildings that can be seen when approaching from the sea are the 19th-century lighthouse and Sankt Nicolai Kirke.

Rønne has two main squares – Store Torv and Lille Torv (Big Market and Little Market). Store Torv was originally used for military parades but is now the venue for a twice-weekly market.

The Tinghus at Store Torv 1 dates from 1834 and was once used as the town hall, court-house and jail. A number of picturesque cobbled streets lead off from Store Torv and many of the early 19th-century houses are still standing, despite a series of bombing raids carried out by the Soviets in May 1945. One of Rønne's most unusual buildings is in Vimmelskaftet – its width allows for one window only. Standing at the corner of Østergade and Theaterstræde is the restored Rønne Theatre, one of the oldest theatres in Denmark, dating from 1823. **Bornholm Museum** has a good local-history section that includes archaeological finds, a small collection of paintings and a selection of 6th-century golden tablets known as *goldgubber*. Over 2,000 of these tablets engraved with small figures have been found on the island.

Distinctive white chimneys of a smokehouse in Hasle

For hotels and restaurants in this region see pp258–60 and pp283–4

Harbourside smithy in Rønne

The **Forsvarsmuseet** (Military Museum) is housed in a citadel south of the town centre that was built around 1650. The defensive tower houses a large collection of weapons, ammunition, uniforms and one of the oldest cannons in Denmark.

Bornholm Museum
Sankt Mortensgade 29. ***Tel*** *56 95 07 35.* *Jan–mid-May & mid-Oct–Dec: 1–4pm Mon–Sat; mid-May–Jun & Sep–mid-Oct: 10am–5pm Mon–Sat; Jul & Aug: 10am–5pm daily.*

Forsvarsmuseet
Arsenalvej 8. ***Tel*** *56 95 65 83.* *mid-May–mid-Sep & school hols: 10am–4pm Tue–Sat.*

Nylars 7

Situated some 7 km (4 miles) east of Rønne, Nylars Rundkirke is one of Bornholm's four well-preserved round churches *(see p221)*. It was built in 1150 and is dedicated to St Nicholas, the patron saint of sailors. To climb the stairs to the upper levels it is necessary to squeeze through narrow passages knocked through thick walls. For invaders trying to reach the upper floor this presented a big obstacle. The frescoes that adorn the distinctive pillar that rises through all three levels of the building depict biblical scenes including Adam and Eve's expulsion from the Garden of Eden.

Aakirkeby 8

1,600. *Hans Rømersvej 1.* ***Tel*** *56 97 45 20.*

During the Middle Ages this was the most important town on the island and the seat of Bornholm's church and the lay authorities. As a result, the 12th-century Aekirke is Bornholm's largest church. The Romanesque building contains a number of treasures including a 13th-century baptismal font and an early 17th-century pulpit. Climbing to the top of the church's high bell tower affords great views of the town. Aakirkeby's latest attraction is **NaturBornholm**, a state-of-the-art natural history museum situated on the southern outskirts of town. A trip to the museum takes visitors back 2,000 years and provides an entertaining and informative way to learn about the flora and fauna of the island. Behind this centre is a gigantic natural fault in the bedrock created some 400 million years ago, which marks the geological boundary between the continental plates of Europe and Scandinavia.

Denmark's national emblem, Åkirke

NaturBornholm
Grønningen 30. ***Tel*** *56 94 04 00.* *Apr–Oct: 10am–5pm.*

Svaneke 9

1,200. *Havnebryggen 2.* ***Tel*** *56 49 70 79.* *Sat.*

In the 1970s this appealing town won the European Gold Medal preservation award and Svaneke continues to maintain its unspoilt historic character. A short distance south of the town centre is Svaneke Kirke. A majestic swan adorns the spire of this 14th-century church (Svaneke translates as "Swan Corner"), and the image of a swan is also included in the town emblem.

In the local glass factory, Pernille Bulow, visitors can watch as skilled workers produce glassware. As well as being known as one of the most photogenic towns on Bornholm, Svaneke is also famous for its windmills. These can be seen standing by each of the town's exit roads. The best preserved is the Årsdale Mølle (1877) on the road leading to Nexø. The mill is open to visitors and also sells its own flour.

Horse-drawn tram in Svaneke, a popular way to see the town

Joboland ⑩

3 km (2 miles) from Svaneke, Højevejen 4. ***Tel*** *56 49 60 76.* *early May–Jun: 11am–5pm Thu–Tue; Jul–early Aug: 10am–6:30pm daily; early Aug–late Aug: 11am–5pm daily.* **www**.joboland.dk

This amusement park has enough entertainment to last an entire day. Its greatest attraction is the aquapark with pools of water kept at a constant 25° C (77° F). The aquapark contains five water slides and a 125-m (410-ft) long Wild River, which adventurous visitors can ride on a rubber tyre. It is also possible to sail a boat, whizz down a "death slide" and walk across a rope bridge. During high season the park lays on additional shows and games for children, including treasure hunts. As well as the amusements, Joboland also has its own small zoo with a variety of animals including peacocks, goats, monkeys and exotic birds.

Climbing frames at Joboland amusement park

Østerlars Kirke, the largest of the island's round churches

Østerlars Kirke ⑪

Gudhjemvej 28. ***Tel*** *56 49 82 64.* *mid-May–mid-Oct: 9am–5pm Mon–Sat (Jul: 1–5pm Sun).*

The largest of Bornholm's round churches *(see p221)* is Østerlars Kirke, which is scenically located in the middle of wheat fields. The church dates from 1150 and is dedicated to Sankt Laurentius (St Laurence). The sturdy buttresses and conical roof are later additions. Inside, the central pillar is decorated with 14th-century frescoes. A rune stone at the entrance dates from 1070 and bears the inscription: "Edmund and his brother erected this stone to the memory of their father Sigmund. May Christ, St Michael and St Mary help his soul."

A short way from the church is Middelalder-center, a recreated village where staff in medieval dress work in the smithy, grind corn and tend sheep. There are daily demonstrations of medieval skills such as making clay pots and archery.

Middelaldercenter
Stangevej 1. ***Tel*** *56 49 83 19.* *May–Sep: 10am–4pm Mon–Fri (Jul–mid-Aug: to 5pm); selected days in Apr & wk 42: 11am–4pm.* **www**. bornholmsmiddelaldercenter.dk

Gudhjem ⑫

900. *Åbogade 9.* ***Tel*** *56 48 52 10.*

The village of Gudhjem ("God's Home") is built on a steep hill overlooking the sea. The picturesque harbour, cobbled streets and brightly painted half-timbered houses with red-tiled roofs make it a popular spot with visitors in summer.

The village has long been associated with the fishing industry and in 1893 Gudhjem acquired the first proper smokehouse in Bornholm. The famous "Sun over Gudhjem", a herring smoked in its skin and served with egg yolk, is well worth trying.

In the centre of the village is a late 19th-century church. Close by are the remains of a much older chapel dating from the 13th century. The **Oluf Høst Museet** has a large selection of paintings by the Bornholm artist Oluf Høst who died in 1966. The collection is housed in the artist's home, which he built in 1929. An old railway station houses the **Gudhjem Museum**, which has displays on local history.

Oluf Høst Museet
Løkkegade 35. ***Tel*** *56 48 50 38.* *early May–end Sep: 11am–5pm daily.* *early May–mid-Jun: Mon.*

Gudhjem Museum
Stationsvej 1. ***Tel*** *56 48 54 62.* *10am–5pm Mon–Sat, 2–5pm Sun.*

Half-timbered houses in Gudhejm

◁ Sankt Nicolai Kirke towering over Rønne's harbour

Cycling on Bornholm

The best way to explore Bornholm is by bicycle and cycle groups are a common sight. The island has 235 km (146 miles) of well signposted cycling routes, many of which connect to the main towns. The routes provide an ideal way to enjoy Bornholm's meadows, fields and forests. Most are far away from busy roads. Rønne, Allinge, and Gudhjem are good places to start. An English language brochure entitled *Bicycle Routes on Bornholm* is available at tourist information centres. Be aware that cycling on Bornholm requires a reasonable level of fitness as there are numerous hills.

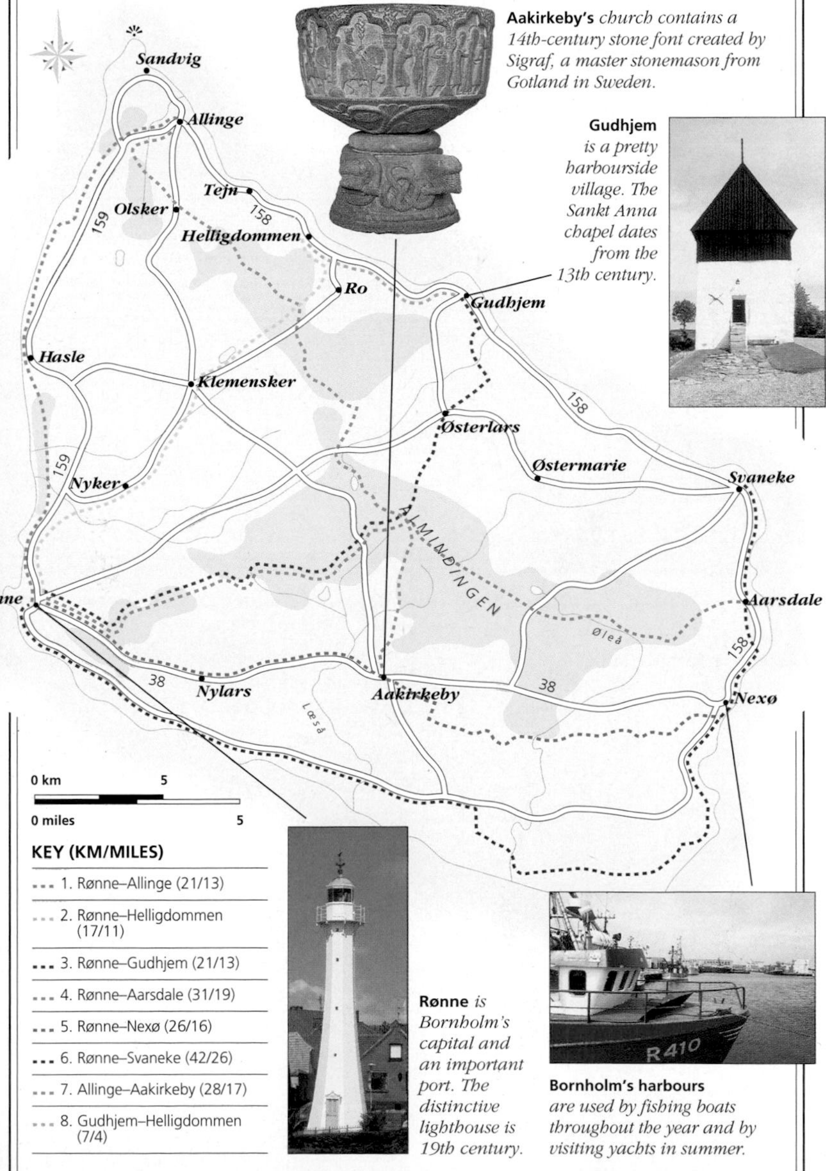

Aakirkeby's *church contains a 14th-century stone font created by Sigraf, a master stonemason from Gotland in Sweden.*

Gudhjem *is a pretty harbourside village. The Sankt Anna chapel dates from the 13th century.*

KEY (KM/MILES)

1. Rønne–Allinge (21/13)
2. Rønne–Helligdommen (17/11)
3. Rønne–Gudhjem (21/13)
4. Rønne–Aarsdale (31/19)
5. Rønne–Nexø (26/16)
6. Rønne–Svaneke (42/26)
7. Allinge–Aakirkeby (28/17)
8. Gudhjem–Helligdommen (7/4)

Rønne *is Bornholm's capital and an important port. The distinctive lighthouse is 19th century.*

Bornholm's harbours *are used by fishing boats throughout the year and by visiting yachts in summer.*

AVIAQ ITTUK
STINA

GREENLAND AND THE FAROE ISLANDS

These two far-flung territories of Denmark offer spectacular adventure and some of the world's most stunning scenery. Greenland's vast frozen glaciers and wondrous northern lights, and the remote settlements and varied birdlife on the Faroe Islands, are ideal for visitors attracted by solitude and natural beauty.

Denmark's two distant island territories enjoy a particular status. Greenland was granted home rule in 1979; the Faroe Islands in 1948. Both have their own government but due to the fact that Denmark retains responsibility for matters such as defence, both are represented in the Danish parliament.

Native Greenlanders share a common heritage with the Inuit of Alaska and northern Canada. Denmark's links with the island began in the 10th century when Viking settlers arrived here and began trading with the Greenlanders. The island was named by Erik the Red, a Viking chief who reached the southern end of Greenland around AD 985.

Early settlers on the Faroe Islands were from Norway. When Norway came under Danish rule in the 14th century the islands also became part of Denmark. Denmark ceded Norway to Sweden in 1814 under the Treaty of Kiel but the Faroes continued under the Danish crown until demands for independence led to eventual home rule. The local name for the Faroes is Føroyar, which translates as "sheep island". The Faroes are aptly named and there are currently almost twice as many sheep as people.

Both Greenland and the Faroe Islands are perfect for nature lovers. A boat tour through parts of Greenland, for instance, takes visitors through crystal-clear waters teeming with marine life including seals and whales. Dog-sled tours across frozen lakes are possible during the winter. The Faroe Islands are a paradise for hikers and ramblers and have a huge variety of birdlife.

Typical Faroe Islands scenery with rocky islets jutting out into the sea

◁ Distinctive houses in Qaqortoq's harbour, Greenland

Exploring Greenland

Greenland is the world's largest island (assuming Australia is a continent) and has a total area of 2,175,600 sq km (840,000 sq miles) and 40,000 km (25,000 miles) of coast. About 85 per cent of the land mass is covered by a huge ice-sheet that is up to 3 km (2 miles) thick. Despite its great size, the island has a population of just 55,000, the majority of whom are descended from a mixture of Inuits and European immigrants. For much of the year Greenland is a vast frozen wilderness. During spring and summer, however, the southern coastal regions thaw and the temperature can rise to as much as 21° C (70° F). Most of the towns and villages have both Inuit and Danish names.

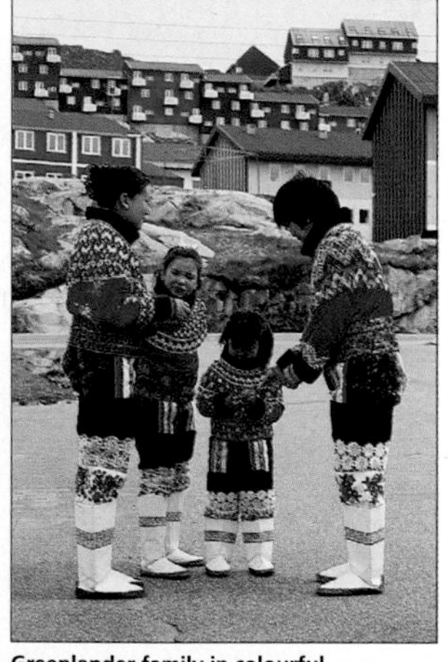

Greenlander family in colourful Inuit costumes

Midnight sun during summer months

For additional map symbols *see back flap*

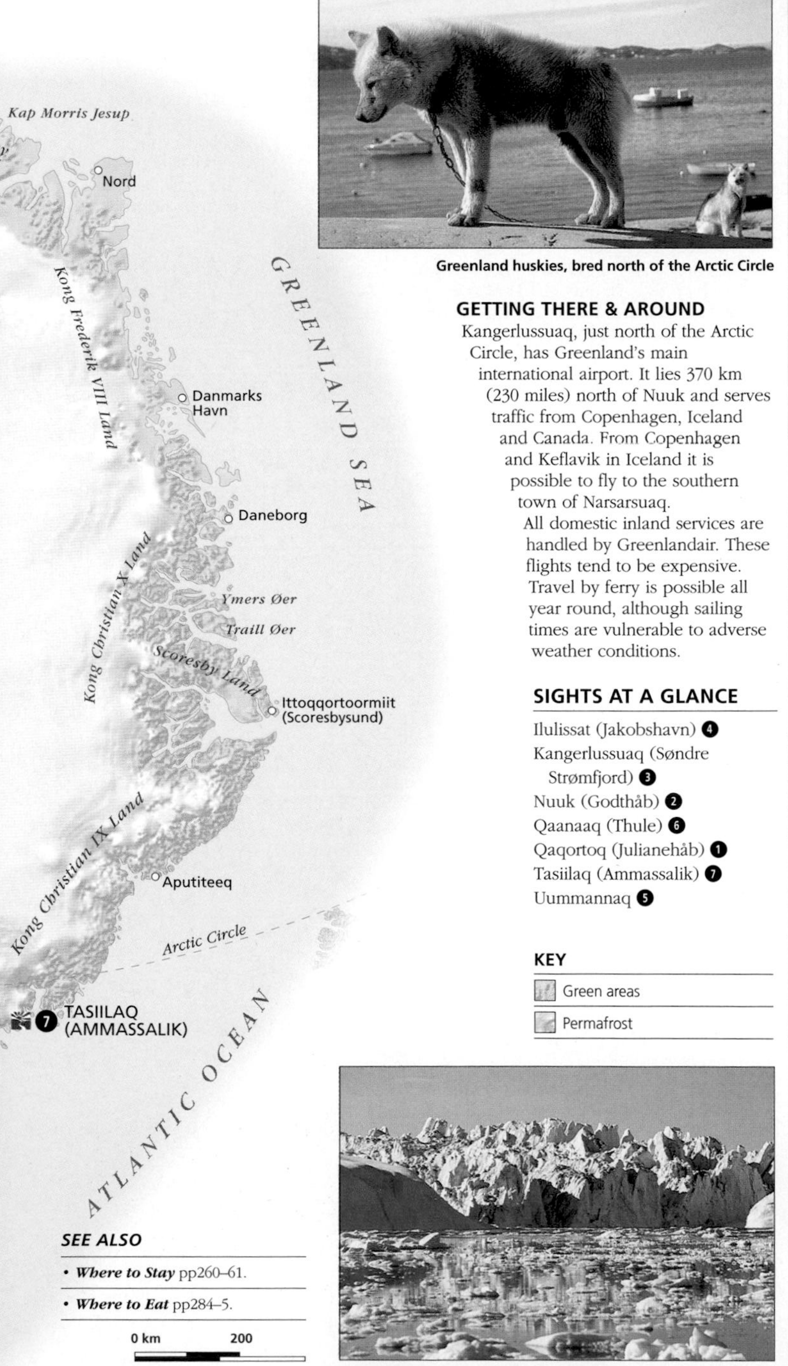

Greenland huskies, bred north of the Arctic Circle

GETTING THERE & AROUND

Kangerlussuaq, just north of the Arctic Circle, has Greenland's main international airport. It lies 370 km (230 miles) north of Nuuk and serves traffic from Copenhagen, Iceland and Canada. From Copenhagen and Keflavik in Iceland it is possible to fly to the southern town of Narsarsuaq.

All domestic inland services are handled by Greenlandair. These flights tend to be expensive. Travel by ferry is possible all year round, although sailing times are vulnerable to adverse weather conditions.

SIGHTS AT A GLANCE

Ilulissat (Jakobshavn) 4
Kangerlussuaq (Søndre Strømfjord) 3
Nuuk (Godthåb) 2
Qaanaaq (Thule) 6
Qaqortoq (Julianehåb) 1
Tasiilaq (Ammassalik) 7
Uummannaq 5

KEY

Green areas
Permafrost

SEE ALSO

- ***Where to Stay*** pp260–61.
- ***Where to Eat*** pp284–5.

Glacier near the small town of Ilulissat

The 19th-century church of St Saviour in Nuuk

Qaqortoq (Julianehåb) ❶

3,600. (+299) 64 24 44.
www.qaq.gl

The town of Qaqortoq was established in 1775. Traces of earlier, 10th-century Viking settlers can be seen in nearby Hvalsey where the remains of a local settlement and church are the best-preserved Nordic ruins in Greenland.

Other local attractions include the hot springs in Uunartoq and the research station in Upernaviarsuk which grows the only apple trees in Greenland.

Qaqortoq participates in Greenland's Stone and Man programme, an open-air sculpture project that uses natural rock formations as base material for a variety of abstract shapes and figures.

Nuuk (Godthåb) ❷

14,000. *Hans Egedesvej 29, P.O. Box 199.* ***Tel*** *(+299) 32 27 00.*
www.nuuk-tourism.gl

Greenland's capital was founded in 1728 by Hans Egede, a Danish missionary who established a year-round trading post here. Nuuk is the largest and oldest town on the island and the seat of Greenland's government. Egede's monument is on a hill, close to the cathedral.

More information about the history of Nuuk can be found at the **National Museum**, which has a collection of Inuit costumes as well as other Greenland artifacts.

According to some traditions Santa Claus lives in Nuuk and even has his own box number (2412 Nuuk Post Office). Next to the post office is a huge letterbox for Santa's letters.

The best time to visit is summer – in June humpback whales can be seen in the bay.

National Museum
Hans Egedesvej 8. ***Tel*** *(+299) 32 26 11.* *1–4pm Tue–Sun (Jun–Sep: from 10am).* **www**.natmus.gl

Kangerlussuaq (Søndre Strømfjord) ❸

600. *Kangerlussuaq Tourism, P.O. Box 49.* ***Tel*** *(+299) 84 16 48.*
www.kangtour.gl

Situated near the fjord of the same name, Kangerlussuaq was until 1992 home to Blue West 8, a US base. A museum, located in the former HQ building, contains memorabilia from the base's history including a replica of the commander's hut.

This area is an excellent venue for hiking, biking, camping and fishing and is inhabited by large herds of reindeer as well as musk ox, arctic foxes and polar hares. A popular day-trip destination

Gently sloping green coastline near Kangerlussuaq

For hotels and restaurants in this region see pp260–6 and pp284–5

is to Russells Glacier, an ice cap some 25 km (16 miles) away. Rising about 10 km (6 miles) from Kangerlussuaq is Sugarloaf Mountain, which has a wonderful view of the inland ice from its peak.

Ilulissat (Jakobshavn) ❹

*4,600. Kussangajaannguaq 20B. **Tel** (+299) 94 33 37.* **www**.northgreenland.com

The town of Ilulissat looks out over Disko Bay, which is full of floating icebergs. It has been calculated that almost 10 per cent of the icebergs floating on Greenland's waters come from the nearby 40-km (25-mile) long glacial fjord, where the ice can be up to 1,100 m (3,600 ft) thick. The glacier can be reached by boat from Ilulissat.

The most famous inhabitant of Ilulissat was the polar explorer Knud Rasmussen. His former house contains objects associated with Inuit art and the everyday life of Greenlanders.

Other museums include the Museum of Hunting and Fishing and the so-called Cold Museum (it has no heating), which has a selection of tools and machinery from a former trading settlement.

Uummannaq ❺

*2,600. Trollep Aqqutaa B 1342. **Tel** (+299) 95 15 18.* **www**.icecaphotels.gl

Despite its location 600 km (373 miles) north of the Arctic Circle, this place enjoys more days of summer sunshine than anywhere else in Greenland. Such favourable conditions have for a long time been a magnet for hunters and whalers. The charm of this town, situated on a small island, is due in part to its colourful houses set on a rocky shore against the backdrop of the 1,175-m (3,855-ft) high Hjertetjeldet ("Heart Shaped") mountain. The old stone cottages with turf roofs date from 1925. The nearby museum, housed in a late 19th-century hospital, contains hunting implements, kayaks and a display devoted to German scientist Alfred Wegener's expedition across the inland ice in 1930 on propeller-driven sledges.

Children dressed in traditional Inuit costumes

Nearby is the Inuit village of Qilaqitsoq, where some mummified bodies were discovered in a cave in 1972. The mummies can be seen in Nuuk's National Museum.

In winter it is possible to take a dog-sled trip across the frozen fjord.

Qaanaaq (Thule) ❻

*800. P.O. Box 75. **Tel** (+299) 97 14 73.* **www**.turistqaanaaq.gl

Greenland's northernmost town was built in the 1950s. Its inhabitants follow a traditional way of life hunting for seals, walruses and polar bears. Visitors can participate in hunts, which involve sleeping in igloos and travelling by sled. Hunts such as these are an important means of survival in this area and not for the squeamish.

About 500 km (311 miles) from Qaanaaq is the North and East Greenland National Park, covering an area of 1,000,000 sq km (386,000 sq miles). The park is mostly covered by an inland ice cap and contains musk ox, polar bears and, in summer, walruses. Permission to enter must be obtained from the Dansk Polarcenter in Copenhagen *(www.dpc.dk).*

Tasiilaq (Ammassalik) ❼

*1,700. P.O. Box 120, Skaven Ujuaap Aqqutaa B 48. **Tel** (+299) 98 22 43 or 98 15 43.* **www**.eastgreenland.com

Situated on the shores of a fjord, surrounded by high mountains, Tasiilaq is one of eastern Greenland's larger towns. The first Europeans arrived here about 100 years ago, and tourism is becoming increasingly important. From here, visitors can go whale watching, visit the nearby "Valley of Flowers" (in summer this is a splendid opportunity to enjoy the Arctic flora) or climb the mound that towers over the town (it was raised in 1944 to celebrate the 50th anniversary of Tasiilaq), from which there are some stunning views.

The town's other points of interest include a modern church decorated with Greenland artifacts. The oldest of Tasiilaq's houses dates from 1894 and was built by a Danish missionary.

Uummannaq, built on the rocks of a small island

Exploring the Faroe Islands

This cluster of 18 islands, sandwiched between the Atlantic and the Norwegian Sea, is home to about 48,000 people, almost half of whom live in the capital Tórshavn on Streymoy. The Faroes have a total area of 1,399 sq km (540 sq miles) and are 450 km (280 miles) from the Shetland Islands and 1,500 km (900 miles) from Copenhagen. Many of the islands are interlinked by a network of tunnels and causeways. The Faroes are perfect for ramblers, and marked trails cover many routes. This is rough terrain and the right equipment, including maps and a compass, should always be carried. The island's seafaring past is evident in the busy harbours, while the town museums have displays on island customs and folklore. Sea cruises are an ideal way to explore the Faroes.

Garden gate made from a ship's wheel

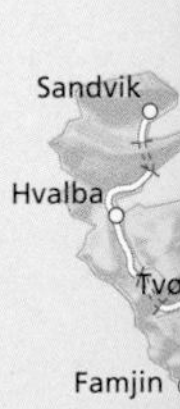

Rugged cliffs on the tiny island of Koltur

KEY

Minor road

Tunnel

For additional map symbols *see back flap*

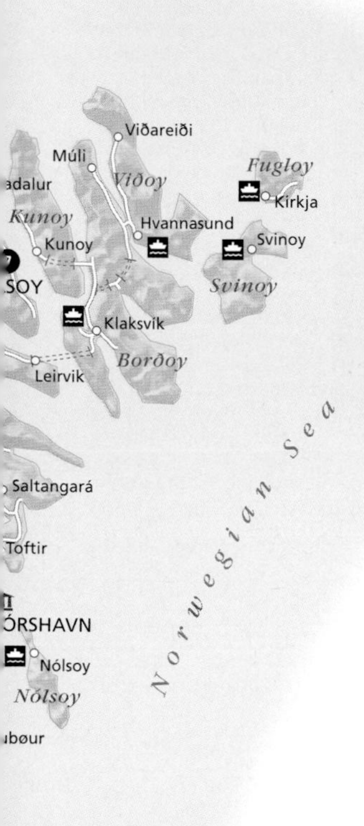

Steel sheep sculpture on the outskirts of Tórshavn

GETTING THERE & AROUND

The Faroe Islands Smyril Lane ferry service operates regularly between Tórshavn, the island's capital, and Hanstholm in northern Jutland. In summer there are additional services from Bergen in Norway, Lerwick on the Shetlands and Seyðisfjörður in Iceland. Atlantic Airlines, Stirling and Air Iceland serve routes from Copenhagen in Denmark. Atlantic Airlines also flies from Oslo in Norway. From April to September twice-weekly routes operate from London and Aberdeen. The Faroe Islands' international airport is near the town of Sørvágur, on the island of Vágar, about 70 km (43 miles) from Tórshavn. A bus connects the airport with Tórshavn. Most of the towns and villages are connected by road, while local ferries cater for the more outlying settlements.

SEE ALSO

- ***Where to Stay*** p261.
- ***Where to Eat*** p285.

0 km 10

0 miles 10

SIGHTS AT A GLANCE

Eysturoy 6
Kalsoy 7
Mykines 4
Streymoy 2
Sud-uroy 5
Tórshavn 1
Vágar 3

Fishing boats in Klaksvik's harbour

Brightly coloured houses lining Tórshavn harbour

Tórshavn ❶

19,000.

Niels Finsens Gøta 13, Tórshavn. **Tel** (+298) 31 57 88.

The Faroe Islands' capital is a lively and picturesque place with a well preserved old centre, although much of the town is fairly modern. Tórshavn was granted municipal status in 1909, but its history stretches back much further.

In the 11th century Tórshavn became a venue for annual Viking gatherings known as the Althings, an early form of the Faroese parliament. The meetings were held in summer and were used to settle quarrels and to trade. A permanent settlement developed around the annual event, and eventually became Tórshavn.

Some of the Faroes' earliest inhabitants were Irish friars, and Tórshavn's oldest building is the 15th-century Munkastovan, or Monks' House, which is one of the few buildings to survive a fire in 1673.

The ruins of Skansin Fort, which was built in 1580 to defend the village from pirates, can still be seen to this day. The fort acquired its present shape in 1780 and was used by British troops during World War II. Today, it provides a good viewpoint for surveying the town's busy harbour, which is crammed with fishing boats, ferries and pleasure craft.

Føroya Fornminnissavn (Historical Museum) has a wide-ranging collection tracing the Faroes' seafaring history, including boats and fishing equipment, as well as religious artifacts and items dating back to the Viking era.

Føroya Fornminnissavn
Brekkutún 6, Hoyvík. **Tel** (+298) 31 07 00. *mid-May–mid-Sep: 10am–5pm daily (from 2pm Sat & Sun); mid-Sep–mid-May: 2–5pm Sun.* **www**.natmus.fo

FAROE ISLANDS WEBSITES

www.faroeislands.com

www.visit-faroeislands.com

Streymoy ❷

22,000. Vaglið, P.O. Box 379, Tórshavn. **Tel** (+298) 30 24 25.

The largest of the Faroe Islands has a varied terrain and is criss-crossed by ancient paths that were used to travel between settlements.

Saksun is a small village on the shores of an inlet that leads into Pollur lake – a fine spot to fish for trout and salmon.

The **Dúvugaröar Museum**, located in an old turf-roofed farmhouse, has exhibits on island life from medieval times to the 1800s.

Traces of a group of 8th-century Irish friars have been found in the village of Kirkjubøur, at the south end of Streymoy. Written records show that Kirkjubøur was a busy place in medieval times. A reminder of those days is the 12th-century church of St Olaf, the archipelago's oldest historic site.

Southwest from Tórshavn are the Vestmannabjørg (Bird Cliffs) where hundreds of sea birds inhabit the 640-m (2,100-ft) high cliff face.

Dúvugaröar Museum
FO436, Saksun. **Tel** (+298) 42 23 03. *mid-Jun–mid-Aug: 2–5pm Fri–Wed (or on request).*

Vágar ❸

2,800. At the airport. **Tel** (+298) 35 33 00.

The Faroe Islands' modern airport is on Vágar and was originally used as a landing strip by the RAF. This mountainous island has some of the region's most stunning sights including the 313-m (1,027-ft) tall needle rock called "Trollukonufingur" ("Troll Woman's Finger"). Lake Sorvagsvatn is a little way from Midvagur, Vágar's largest town, and is a great place for fishing. Sandavagur, a nearby village, is the birthplace of Venceslaus Ulricus Hammershaimb (b. 1819), creator of the Faroese alphabet.

House hugging the cliff on Streymoy

For hotels and restaurants in this region see p261 and p285

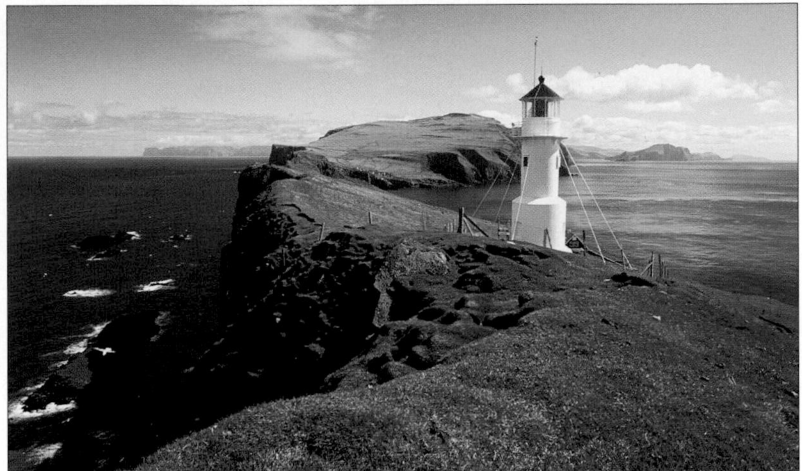

Lighthouse standing on the cliffs of Mykines

Mykines ❹

20.

On this tiny island of only 10 sq km (4 sq miles), the inhabitants are vastly outnumbered by the birds, including thousands of puffins. All the islanders live in the same village, which is a pretty place with colourful houses topped by turf roofs. This is one of the hardest islands to reach but the trip is worth it, especially for keen hikers. Mykineshólmur, a tiny islet, is a good spot from which to view gannets, as well as large colonies of puffins. It is connected to the island by a footbridge that has been built 24-m (79-ft) above the sea.

Suðuroy ❺

5,000. Kunningarstovan á Tvøroyri, Tvørávegur 37, Tvøroyri. ***Tel*** *(+298) 37 24 80.* **www**.visitsuduroy.fo

The largest town on Suðuroy, the Faroes' southernmost island, is Tvøroyri, which has a population of 1,800. The little village of Famjin, on the west coast, is more historically important, however, as its church contains the original Faroe Islands' flag. The red-and-blue cross on a white background was designed by two students and accepted as the national ensign in 1940. A short hike above the village is Kirkjuvatn ("Church Lake"), one of the Faroes' largest lakes.

The village of Sandvik, at the northern end of the island, has an isolated and expansive beach. In AD 1000 Sigmund Bresterson, an early Norwegian settler and hero of the Faroe Sagas, was murdered here while preaching Christianity. On the way from Sanvik to Hvalba are two stones that, according to legend, were brought here by Bresterson. Passing between them is believed to be unlucky and can spell misfortune or even death.

Goat on one of the islands' rural smallholdings

Eysturoy ❻

10,000. Kunningarstovan í Runavík, Heiðavegur, P.O. Box 200, Saltangará. ***Tel*** *(+298) 41 70 60.* @ kunningarstovan@runavik.fo

The second largest island of the archipelago is connected to Streymoy by a road bridge, which is often jokingly described by locals as the only bridge across the Atlantic.

Eysturoy has a number of unique features. At 882 m (2,894 ft), Slættaratindur is the Faroes' highest point. The summit can easily be reached by climbing the mountain's eastern ridge – the views from the peak are breathtaking.

Close to Fuglafjørdur are the Varmakelda hot springs. Their water remains at a constant 18° C (64.4° F) and is believed to have medicinal properties.

Further north is the village of Oynadarfjordur. Just beyond its shore are the Rinkusteinar, or rocking stones, two huge blocks that constantly rock, moved by the motion of the sea.

At nearby Gjøgv there is a 200-m (656-ft) long gorge that with time has eroded to become a sea-filled bay.

Kalsoy ❼

140.

Nicknamed the "flute" because of its elongated shape, this rugged island is ideal for hikes. Many walkers head towards Kap Kallur, at the island's northern tip, where the lighthouse makes an excellent point from which to view the cliffs. Puffins are a frequent sight. The sea stacks at Eysturoy's northern tip can be seen on a clear day.

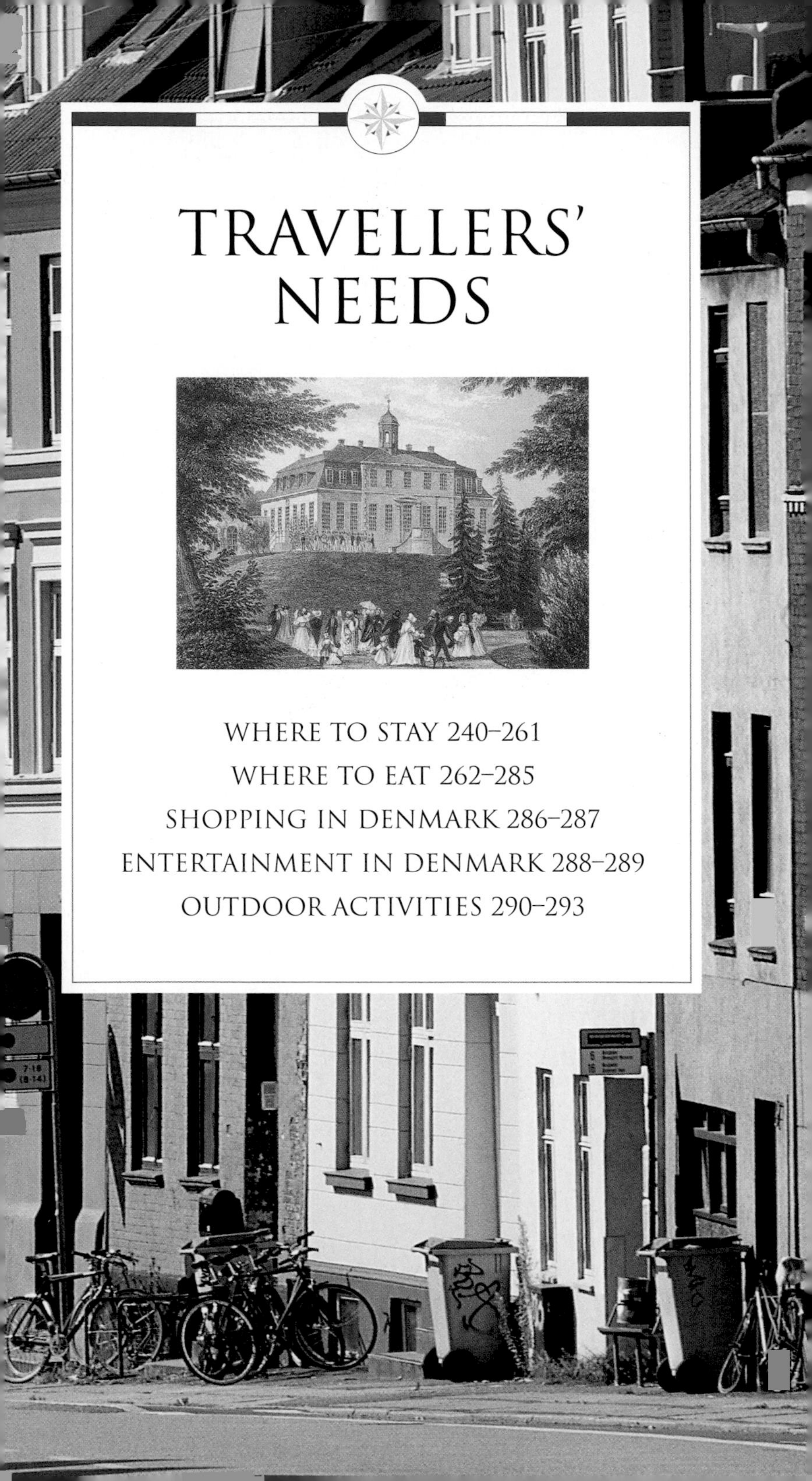

TRAVELLERS' NEEDS

WHERE TO STAY

Holiday accommodation in Denmark is of a high standard and provides visitors with plenty of options. The choice ranges from luxury hotels and apartments to roadside inns, budget hotels, family hostels, private homes and camp sites. Information is readily available from tourist offices and on the Internet. Some of Denmark's hotels can be expensive, however. For those on a tight budget, staying on a camp site or in one of the country's well-run hostels provides a cheaper alternative. Those seeking something a little different might choose to stay in an historic castle or on one of the farms taking part in Denmark's agritourism scheme. Visitors to Greenland can even choose to stay in an igloo. Whatever your preference, Danish accommodation has a reputation for professionalism and a warm welcome is generally assured.

Copenhagen hotel porter

Main entrance to a hotel in Sandvig, Bornholm

CHOOSING A HOTEL

Travellers in Denmark have a wide choice of hotel accommodation. Information is readily available and details of hotels found in brochures and on websites is generally both up to date and accurate. Many of Denmark's hotels are 3-star establishments, and are aimed at holiday-makers as well as business travellers. The majority of three-star hotels offer rooms with a private bathroom, telephone and TV. Be clear when booking a room if a bath is specifically required, as some hotels have showers rather than baths in rooms. Visitors may be able to use their laptops as rooms often have Internet access but it is wise to enquire. The cheaper hotels tend to be rather plain but even these are generally clean and well run. An all-you-can-eat breakfast, consisting of pastries, bread, cereal, coffee/tea and fruit, is often included in the price of a room.

When planning a journey to Denmark by car, take into account the cost of parking in town centres. It is worth finding out in advance whether the hotel has its own car park or off-street parking.

Hotels on Greenland and the Faroe Islands are not plentiful. Those that do exist can be fairly costly.

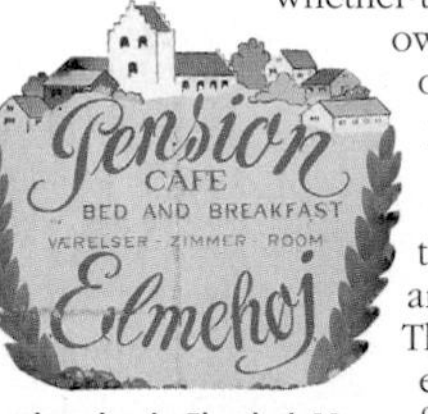

Pension sign in Elmehøj, Møn

HOW TO BOOK

During peak season, hotels are often booked up in Denmark so it pays to reserve a room in advance. Hotel accommodation can be booked via the Internet at www.danishotels.dk or www.visitdenmark.dk. Many individual hotels in Denmark also have their own websites. Alternatively, bookings can be made by telephone, fax or e-mail. It may also be worth contacting a travel agent, as they often have details about special offers or schemes. Local tourist offices can also provide accommodation lists in their towns.

HOTEL PRICES

Hotel prices in Denmark can be rather high. There are many hotels at the lower end of the scale, however, which charge about 600 to 700 Dkr per night; the most expensive ones may quote up to 10,000 Dkr for a luxury suite. The majority of room prices fall into the 900–1,400 Dkr bracket. During summer and at weekends when business visitors are scarce, many hotels offer discounted rates. Another way to save money is by purchasing "Inn Cheques" from one of the tourist offices or online at www.krohotel.dk. More than 70 hotels belong to this scheme, which allows rooms to be booked in advance at a reduced price.

ADDITIONAL COSTS

Some hotels and hostels belonging to the Green Key association add 35 Dkr "ecological tax" to the price of an overnight stay. This

◁ Colourful houses lining a street in Århus, central Jutland

A guest room in the Admiral Hotel, Copenhagen *(see p244)*

scheme, which began in 1994, ensures that the hotel has fulfilled certain ecological criteria such as using low-energy light bulbs, low-water consumption toilets and environmentally friendly cleaning products.

CHAIN HOTELS

The majority of hotels in Denmark belong to large hotel chains including First & Clarion, Hilton, Radisson and Scandic. Some chains, such as Best Western, have their own schemes whereby visitors can get discounts at weekends or during the holiday period. It is best to book in advance for these, though deals can sometimes be struck on the spot.

HISTORIC HOUSES

A small number of Denmark's manor houses and palaces offer accommodation. These historic buildings are run by **Danske Slotte & Herregaarde** (The Danish Association of Castles and Manor Houses), which can provide a brochure of the 60 or so historic houses available for overnight stays. The venues are undeniably romantic, although they can be rather expensive.

INNS

Outside larger towns, it is possible to stop for a night in an inn, known as *kro* in Denmark. The variety on offer ranges from modern roadside inns to meticulously restored period houses. Some country inns have retained much of their 18th or 19th-century rusticity; others are downright luxurious. Many *kro* offer a family atmosphere, and it is not unusual for inns to be used for family gatherings and big occasions.

Camp site on Hindsholm peninsula, Funen

CAMP SITES

Denmark has over 550 camp sites. Of these, as many as 100 are open all year round. All are rated by the **Dansk Camping Union** using a system of stars from one to five. Prices depend on the number of stars, which reflect not only comfort and a site's attractiveness but also specific facilities, such as whether the site has a playground and the distance to the nearest grocery store. The cost generally includes a charge for pitching a tent or parking a caravan, plus a charge for each occupant. One-star sites will have little more than fresh drinking water and toilets. Three-star sights and above will have a TV room, on-site shop and a café or restaurant. Whatever the rating, it is rare to find a Danish camp site that is not well run. Roughly 400 of Denmark's camp sites feature chalet accommodation or cabins that can sleep four to six. Many cabins have cooking facilities but visitors usually have to supply their own linen and towels. Most cabins do not have private washing or toilet facilities.

A comprehensive database at *www.camping.dk* allows a search according to location and facilities. Tourist offices can provide a leaflet listing all the sites and the basic rules of camping in Denmark.

Anyone wishing to camp in Denmark will need a Visitor's Pass. These annual permits are readily available and can be bought on the spot at any of the official camp sites.

Pitching a tent in areas not designated as camp sites is not encouraged and anyone caught camping in a field or on the beach without permission may be fined.

Distinctive architecture of the Royal Holstebro, Jutland *(see p256)*

Historic hotel room in Liselund Slot, Møn

HOSTELS

All of Denmark's 180 or so hostels or *vandrehjem* are incorporated into the **Danhostel** association, which registers its hostels in five categories marked (as in the case of hotels and camp sites) by stars. Along with communal dormitories, most hostels have private "family" rooms, which usually sleep four to six and must be booked well in advance. Blankets and pillows are usually provided, but it is generally the case that visitors supply their own bed linen and towels. In all hostels it is possible to buy breakfast; many also offer dinner, charging half-price for children up to the age of 12. Most hostels have kitchen facilities, where guests can prepare their own meals, although plates and cutlery are rarely provided.

The prices of family rooms can vary, but the maximum price of a bed in a communal dormitory is fixed each year for the entire country. Prices for an overnight stay vary between high and low seasons. From September until May a place in a provincial hostel must be booked at least three days in advance. During peak season all hostels should be booked as early as possible and couples wishing to rent a private room during this period may be asked to pay for all the beds in the room.

In order to stay at a hostel it is necessary to have a Youth Hostel Association (YHA) card. Holders of YHA cards pay the normal full price. Non-members can buy temporary membership for each night spent in the hostel, which may make sense if staying only one or two nights. For visits that exceed five days it is worthwhile buying a full membership.

Danhostel's website has telephone numbers and website addresses for all of its hostels, where additional information can be found.

BED & BREAKFASTS

Denmark's bed and breakfasts offer good quality and value, and usually charge about 150 Dkr per person per night. Many can be booked from local tourist offices. Alternatively, a list is available from **Dansk Bed & Breakfast**. Some Danish B&Bs quote a price that only includes accommodation. Breakfast may be at extra cost or may not be available at all.

DISABLED TRAVELLERS

Many hotels can accommodate disabled guests. The majority of multi-storey hotels have lifts. VisitDenmark, the tourist board *(see p297)*, has a leaflet entitled *Access in Denmark – a travel guide*, which has information on disabled access to hotels.

TRAVELLING WITH CHILDREN

Taking children on holiday to Denmark is not a problem. Many hotels and hostels, particularly establishments aimed at holiday-makers, offer family rooms for three to four people. Hotels belonging to the Scandic group are also ready to receive young guests; many of these have playrooms. Hotel restaurants not only provide high chairs for babies and toddlers, but also offer special menus that will satisfy all but the most picky children.

Sign advertising one of Denmark's bed & breakfasts

COTTAGES AND HOLIDAY CENTRES

Cottages are available to rent for longer stays in a summer resort. Some summer cottages are let out by their owners, and are only available for the period when they are not using the house themselves. Others are run purely as commercial ventures. Both must be booked well

Entrance to one of Denmark's converted manor houses

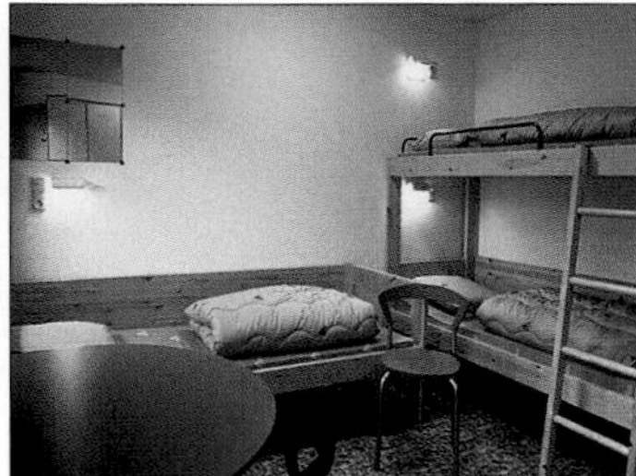
Youth Hostel dormitory

in advance. Many companies are able to handle bookings nationwide.

Holiday centres, which have purpose-built accommodation, children's playgrounds, swimming pools and other family-friendly amenities, have lots of space for children to play. Prices vary widely.

FARM HOLIDAYS

Spending time on a farm is becoming an increasingly popular activity in Denmark. There are now more than 100 Danish farms where a stay is possible, and most are far away from busy resorts. Such rural retreats provide a chance to relax in pastoral surroundings and, in some cases, to muck in with the chores. An association called **Landsforeningen for Landboturisme** can book stays on farms and assist in selecting a farm for visitors depending on the facilities and location required.

A holiday of this sort can be arranged in several ways. It is possible to choose B&B or full-board accommodation. Cottages, a simple apartment with a kitchen, or a room can be rented. Alternatively, visitors can pitch a tent or park a caravan on farm land. Some farms offer theme holidays that may include angling, cookery courses or environmental studies.

Another possibility is to travel from farm to farm by bicycle or car. When travelling along well-marked routes this can provide an attractive alternative to camp sites and hostels. Regardless of what type of vacation is on offer, visitors can be sure of a clean room and warm rural atmosphere. Prices start from 200 Dkr per adult (for bed and breakfast).

DIRECTORY

INFORMATION ON ACCOMMODATION & RESERVATIONS

www.hotel.dk
www.visitdenmark.com

INFORMATION ON ACCOMMODATION & RESERVATIONS IN COPENHAGEN

Copenhagen Right Now Information and Booking Service
Vesterbrogade 4A.
Tel *70 22 24 42.*
Fax *70 22 24 52.*
@ touristinfo@woco.dk
www.visitcopenhagen.com

HISTORIC HOUSES

Danske Slotte & Herregaarde
Frederiksberggade 2, 1. th, 1459 Copenhagen K.
Tel *86 60 38 44.*
Fax *86 60 38 31.*
@ danskeslotteogherregaarde@mail.dk
www.slotte-herregaarde.dk

INNS

Danske Kroer & Hoteller
Vejlevej 16, 8700 Horsens.
Tel *75 64 87 00.*
Fax *75 64 87 20.*
@ info@krohotel.dk
www.krohotel.dk

CAMP SITES

Campingrådet
Mosedalvej 15, DK-2500 Valby.
Tel *39 27 88 44.*
Fax *39 27 80 44.*
@ info@campingraadet.dk
www.campingraadet.dk

Dansk Camping Union
Korsdalsvej 135
2605 Brøndby.
Tel *33 21 06 00.*
@ info@dcu.dk
www.dcu.dk

DK-CAMP 2002
Industrivej 5, Bredballe, 7120 Vejle Ø.
Tel *75 71 29 62.*
Fax *75 71 29 66.*
@ info@dk-camp.dk
www.dk-camp.dk

FDM Camping
Firskovvej 32.
2800 Kgs. Lyngby.
Tel *45 27 07 07.*
@ camping@fdm.dk
www.fdmcamping.dk

HOSTELS

Danhostel Danmarks Vandrehjem
Vesterbrogade 39, 1620 Copenhagen V.
Tel *33 31 36 12.*
@ ldv@danhostel.dk
www.danhostel.dk

B&BS

Dansk B&B
Sankt Peders Stræde 41, 1453 Copenhagen K.
Tel *39 61 04 05.*
@ bed@bbdk.dk
www.bedandbreakfast.dk

COTTAGES AND HOLIDAY CENTRES

Danland & DanCenter
Lyngbyvej 20, 2100 Copenhagen Ø.
Tel *33 63 02 00.*
Fax *70 13 70 71.*
@ info@danland.dk
www.danland.dk

Dansk Folkeferie
Hedegaardsvej 88, 2300 Copenhagen.
@ danmark@danskfolkeferie.dk
www.folkeferie.dk

Dansommer
Voldbjergvej 16, 8240 Risskov.
Tel *86 17 61 22.*
Fax *86 17 68 55.*
@ dansommer@dansommer.dk
www.dansommer.dk

Novasol
Rygårds Alle 104, 2900 Hellerup.
Tel *70 42 44 24.*
@ novasol@novasol.dk
www.novasol.co.uk

Sol & Strand
Ilsigvej 21, Hune, 9492 Blokhus.
Tel *99 44 44 44.*
Fax *99 44 44 45.*
@ info@sologstrand.dk
www.sologstrand.com

FARM HOLIDAYS

Landsforeningen for Landboturisme
Lerbakken 7, 8410 Ronde.
Tel *86 37 39 00.*
Fax *86 37 35 50.*
www.bondegaardsferie.dk

Choosing a Hotel

The hotels in this guide have been selected across a wide price range for facilities, good value, and location. All rooms have an ensuite bathroom and TV unless otherwise stated. The hotels are listed by area. For Copenhagen map references, *see pp106–111*. For regional map references, *see inside back cover.*

PRICE CATEGORIES
Price categories are for a standard double room with bath or shower per night in high season including breakfast, tax and service.
Ⓚ Under 600 Dkr
ⓀⓀ 600–1,000 Dkr
ⓀⓀⓀ 1,000–1,500 Dkr
ⓀⓀⓀⓀ 1,500–2,000 Dkr
ⓀⓀⓀⓀⓀ Over 2,000 Dkr

COPENHAGEN

NORTH COPENHAGEN Christian IV ⓀⓀⓀ

Dronningens Tværgade 45, 1302 **Tel** *33 32 10 44* **Fax** *33 32 07 06* **Rooms** *42* **Map** *4 D3*

A central, unassuming hotel that is situated away from the hustle and bustle of the city centre yet still well placed for Nyhavn. The rooms all have a refined, Scandinavian look and feel. They serve excellent continental breakfasts, hire out cycles and offer free wi-fi in the rooms. **www.hotelchristianiv.dk**

NORTH COPENHAGEN Comfort Hotel Esplanaden ⓀⓀⓀ

Bredgade 78, 1260 **Tel** *33 48 10 00* **Fax** *33 48 10 66* **Rooms** *117* **Map** *2 D5*

An ornate, period building with lavish decor leading to somewhat smallish rooms that feel a bit worn at times. Though the Esplanaden is a bit of a hike from the city centre, it is set in quiet green surroundings, the staff are very friendly and efficient and the breakfasts are large. **www.choicehotels.dk**

NORTH COPENHAGEN Copenhagen Admiral ⓀⓀⓀ

Toldbodgade 24–8, 1253 **Tel** *33 74 14 14* **Fax** *33 74 14 16* **Rooms** *366* **Map** *2 E4*

This 1780's-era warehouse has been turned into a modern hotel that is swimming in nautical and maritime detail. No two rooms are alike, but they do all boast mod cons and portal-style windows, and many look out to the sea. Despite the inviting atmosphere, it sees few tourists and exists mostly as a business hotel. **www.admiralhotel.dk**

NORTH COPENHAGEN Scandic Front ⓀⓀⓀ

Sankt Annae Plads 21, 1022 **Tel** *33 13 34 00* **Fax** *33 11 77 07* **Rooms** *132* **Map** *2 D5*

Scandic Front is riding high as Copenhagen's hotel of the moment. All the rooms are lavish in their comforts, with deep beige and brown accents, Barcelona chairs, and flat-screen TVs, as well as tiled bathrooms with vanity mirrors. Breakfast is included, and guests can enjoy free coffee throughout the day. **www.scandichotels.com**

NORTH COPENHAGEN Clarion Hotel Neptun ⓀⓀⓀⓀ

Sankt Annae Plads 14–20, 1250 **Tel** *33 96 20 00* **Fax** *33 96 20 66* **Rooms** *133* **Map** *2 D5*

This is a top-notch hotel attractively located near to the royal palace and close to the bars and restaurants of Nyhavn. Many of the rooms look onto a quiet internal courtyard, and while the bathrooms are a little small they are clean and there is never any want for hot water. **www.choicehotels.dk**

NORTH COPENHAGEN Phoenix ⓀⓀⓀⓀ

Bredgade 37, 1260 **Tel** *33 95 95 00* **Fax** *33 33 98 33* **Rooms** *213* **Map** *2 D5*

The Phoenix is housed in an 18th-century building close to Amalienborg Slot and Nyhavn. The lavish, elegant rooms proffer silk bedspreads, original art on the walls, Louis XIV furniture and gold fixtures in the large marble bathrooms. The staff are very welcoming. Breakfast is included at weekends. **www.phoenixcopenhagen.com**

NORTH COPENHAGEN Adina Apartment Hotel Copenhagen ⓀⓀⓀⓀⓀ

Amerika Plads 7, 2100 **Tel** *39 69 10 00* **Fax** *88 19 36 99* **Rooms** *128* **Map** *4 F3*

Adina Apartment Hotel is a four-star establishment just minutes away from the Little Mermaid monument. With its modern design and vibrant colour scheme, it offers the perfect home-away-from-home experience for both business and leisure guests. Facilities include an indoor pool, Jacuzzi, sauna and gym. **www.adina.eu**

CENTRAL COPENHAGEN Bed and Breakfast Bonvie Ⓚ

Frederiksberggade 25 C, 2, 1459 **Tel** *33 93 63 73* **Fax** *33 93 63 73* **Rooms** *4* **Map** *3 B1*

This family-style guesthouse, set along Strøget, is one of Copenhagen's most central budget hotels. Rooms are decorated in an eclectic homely style but can suffer from street noise. There is only one bathroom. Guests can sit in the small courtyard and there is a washing machine available for their use. **www.bbbonvie.dk**

CENTRAL COPENHAGEN Carstens Guest House Ⓚ

Christians Brygge 28, 1559 **Tel** *33 14 91 07* **Rooms** *5* **Map** *3 C3*

Chipper, gay-friendly bed and breakfast that has woodsy rooms set in two separate apartment buildings. The staff will cook a full breakfast for you, if you book in advance. The rooftop terrace is good for evening drinks. There are also shared, dormitory-style rooms in the loft, a Finnish sauna and laundry facilities. **www.carstensguesthouse.dk**

Key to Symbols *see back cover flap*

CENTRAL COPENHAGEN Danhostel Copenhagen City Kr

H.C. Andersens Boulevard 50, 1553 ***Tel*** *33 18 83 32* ***Fax*** *33 29 80 59* ***Rooms*** *192* ***Map*** *3 A1*

Do not be deceived by the anonymous high-rise exterior: the interior furnishings and sleekly-styled rooms would put most mid-level hotels to shame. Many of the rooms have superb views over the city. Facilities include an internet café, comfortable TV lounge, laundry and large kitchen. **www.danhostel.dk/copenhagencity**

CENTRAL COPENHAGEN Alexandra KrKr

H.C. Andersens Boulevard 8, 1553 ***Tel*** *33 74 44 44* ***Fax*** *33 74 44 88* ***Rooms*** *61* ***Map*** *3 A1*

Housed in what were once fashionable city apartments, the decor of this chic hotel is stylish and upmarket, with plenty of attention to detail. The walls are hung with original artworks and much of the furniture is classic Danish design, including pieces by Arne Jacobsen. **www.hotel-alexandra.dk**

CENTRAL COPENHAGEN Hotel Fox KrKr

Jarmers Plads 3, 1551 ***Tel*** *33 95 77 55* ***Fax*** *33 14 30 33* ***Rooms*** *61* ***Map*** *3 A1*

Easily one of the most unusual hotels in the city, the Fox was fashioned by a group of graphic designers, street artists and illustrators. Their off-the-wall creations range from the ultra-minimalist (floor-to-ceiling white formica) to the fantastical (walls covered in outlandish murals). Friendly reception and a great restaurant to boot. **www.hotelfox.dk**

CENTRAL COPENHAGEN Hotel Selandia KrKr

Helgolandsgade 12, 1653 ***Tel*** *33 3146 10* ***Fax*** *33 31 46 09* ***Rooms*** *84* ***Map*** *3 A3*

Just minutes from the train station and a short walk from Halmtorvet, where you can find a number of classy cafés and inexpensive ethnic restaurants, the Selandia features bright, renovated rooms, many with shared baths. Excellent value, and prices drop by 20 per cent in the winter. **www.hotel-selandia.dk**

CENTRAL COPENHAGEN Jørgensen KrKr

Rømersgade 11, 1362 ***Tel*** *33 13 81 86* ***Fax*** *33 15 51 05* ***Rooms*** *37* ***Map*** *1 A5*

Denmark's first gay-friendly hotel. Just minutes from Nørreport station, this is an excellent place from which to explore the city. The rooms are simply furnished, and the staff are very friendly. There are also a number of inexpensive, cramped dormitory-style rooms. Laundry available next door. **www.hoteljoergensen.dk**

CENTRAL COPENHAGEN Sømandshjemmet "Bethel" KrKr

Nyhavn 22, 1051 ***Tel*** *33 13 03 70* ***Fax*** *33 15 85 70* ***Rooms*** *30* ***Map*** *4 D1*

This neo-Gothic building was once a popular stopping-off point for merchants on their way out to the high seas. The decor is traditional Scandinavian and the rooms, though at times a bit on the small side, are well equipped. Several of the larger corner rooms have excellent views to the harbour. **www.hotel-bethel.dk**

CENTRAL COPENHAGEN Ascot KrKrKr

Studiestræde 61, 1554 ***Tel*** *33 12 60 00* ***Fax*** *33 14 60 40* ***Rooms*** *120* ***Map*** *3 A1*

The wall reliefs of men and women bathing are a reminder that this building was once a public baths. The bathrooms, rather appropriately, are prodigious and luxurious. Though the hotel was renovated a few years back, it does manage to maintain an old-world atmosphere. **www.ascothotel.dk**

CENTRAL COPENHAGEN DGI-byens Hotel KrKrKr

Tietgensgade 65, 1704 ***Tel*** *33 29 8050* ***Fax*** *33 29 80 59* ***Rooms*** *104* ***Map*** *3 A3*

Situated within a massive sporting complex just south of Halmtorvet, DGI-byens' rooms are homages to chic Scandinavian design, featuring bleached oak flooring and leather sofas. Guests get free access to the massive pool and discounted spa treatments. Parking is available for a fee. **www.dgi-byen.dk/hotel**

CENTRAL COPENHAGEN Ibsens KrKrKr

Vendersgade 23, 1363 ***Tel*** *33 13 19 13* ***Fax*** *33 13 19 16* ***Rooms*** *118* ***Map*** *1 A4*

Set within a classic French-style apartment building, this modern boutique hotel has individually styled rooms, ranging from modern Scandinavian to classical English, though all are modestly decorated. The hotel is hidden away in a narrow café-lined street close to Nansensgade – great for a night out. **www.ibsenshotel.dk**

CENTRAL COPENHAGEN Kong Frederik KrKrKr

25 Vester Voldgade, 1552 ***Tel*** *33 12 59 02* ***Fax*** *33 37 06 30* ***Rooms*** *110* ***Map*** *3 A1*

There has been a hotel on this site for more than 700 years. Today, the English-style Frederik offers inviting rooms with fabric wallpaper, deep woods, plush carpeting and comfortable love seats. The lobby has a great sitting room. Splendidly located, close to Tivoli Gardens and Copenhagen's pedestrian street, Strøget. **www.hotelkf.dk**

CENTRAL COPENHAGEN Marriott KrKrKr

Kalvebod Brygge 5, 1560 ***Tel*** *88 33 99 00* ***Fax*** *88 33 99 99* ***Rooms*** *395* ***Map*** *3 A4*

This 11-storey, high-class chain hotel offers superb views of the city and harbour. The rooms, while plush enough, are in classic international Marriott style which can, at times, veer towards the uninspiring. However, if you want to be guaranteed a safe and welcoming stay, this is your place. **www.copenhagenmarriott.dk**

CENTRAL COPENHAGEN Opera KrKrKr

Tordenskjoldsgade 15, 1055 ***Tel*** *33 47 83 00* ***Fax*** *33 47 83 01* ***Rooms*** *91* ***Map*** *4 D1*

The location of the Opera, next to the Royal Theatre, accounts for the large number of Danish and international actors who have stayed here over the years. The rooms, though sometimes on the small side, are decorated in impeccable, elegant English style. At weekends there is a sizeable discount on the standard rate. **www.hotelopera.dk**

CENTRAL COPENHAGEN Copenhagen Strand ⓀⓀⓀⓀ

Havnegade 37, 1058 ***Tel*** *33 48 99 00* ***Fax*** *33 48 99 01* ***Rooms*** *174* ***Map*** *4 D2*

Set in an original harbourside warehouse, with a vague maritime atmosphere throughout the hotel lobby. The Strand's rooms are uninspiring but comfortable. However, many of them look right across the water to Christianshavn. **www.copenhagenstrand.dk**

CENTRAL COPENHAGEN Grand Hotel Copenhagen ⓀⓀⓀⓀ

Vesterbrogade 9, 1620 ***Tel*** *33 27 69 00* ***Fax*** *33 27 69 01* ***Rooms*** *161* ***Map*** *3 A2*

The bright, smallish rooms here bring a touch of modern style to this classic Copenhagen hotel, which dates from 1890. The more upmarket rooms have leather reading chairs, mahogany writing desks, large windows and all mod cons. Wi-Fi access is available throughout. Breakfast is included at the weekend. **www.grandhotel.dk**

CENTRAL COPENHAGEN Radisson Blu Royal Hotel ⓀⓀⓀⓀ

Hammerichsgade 1, 1611 ***Tel*** *38 15 65 00* ***Fax*** *33 42 63 00* ***Rooms*** *260* ***Map*** *3 A1*

This is *the* designer hotel. The entire place, inside and out, was designed in 1960 by Arne Jacobsen, including Swan and Egg chairs, a spiral staircase and anodized doorknobs. The comfortable rooms have internet access, a sophisticated decor and all modern amenities. **www.radissonblu.com/royalhotel-copenhagen**

CENTRAL COPENHAGEN The Square ⓀⓀⓀⓀ

Rådhuspladsen 14, 1550 ***Tel*** *33 38 12 00* ***Fax*** *33 38 12 01* ***Rooms*** *267* ***Map*** *3 A2*

The entire place epitomises all there is to love about Denmark: sleek design, efficient service, friendly reception but with high prices to match. The superbly designed rooms are to die for, with some of the most comfortable beds in the entire city, and some of them with very fetching views. Breakfast available. **www.thesquare.dk**

CENTRAL COPENHAGEN First Hotel Skt Petri ⓀⓀⓀⓀⓀ

Krystalgade 22, 1172 ***Tel*** *33 45 91 00* ***Fax*** *33 45 91 10* ***Rooms*** *268* ***Map*** *3 B1*

Super-chic colourful establishment offering rooms which are impeccably designed by top Danish architects. The rooms on the upper floor have great views over to the nearby Latin Quarter, at a supplement. There is a trendy café, cocktail bar and parking (for a fee). **www.hotelsktpetri.com**

CENTRAL COPENHAGEN Hotel D'Angleterre ⓀⓀⓀⓀⓀ

Kongens Nytorv 34, 1022 ***Tel*** *33 12 00 95* ***Fax*** *33 12 11 18* ***Rooms*** *123* ***Map*** *4 D1*

One of the most respected hotels in Copenhagen, the D'Angleterre has been in business for more than 250 years and remains the choice for visiting dignitaries. The rooms are very large, classic in decor, and filled with every amenity you could want. The queen's official residence is just around the corner. **www.dangleterre.com**

SOUTH COPENHAGEN Danmark ⓀⓀ

Vester Voldgade 89, 1552 ***Tel*** *33 11 48 06* ***Fax*** *33 14 36 30* ***Rooms*** *88* ***Map*** *3 A1*

A stone's throw from Rådhuspladsen and the shopping neighbourhood of Strøget, this is an ideal location for a short break in the capital. The building is late 18th century and the rooms are on the small side though all have good beds and some boast small French balconies. Weekends are quite a bit cheaper. **www.hotel-danmark.dk**

SOUTH COPENHAGEN Radisson Blu Scandinavia ⓀⓀⓀ

Amager Boulevard 70, 2300 ***Tel*** *33 96 50 00* ***Fax*** *33 96 55 00* ***Rooms*** *540* ***Map*** *3 C3*

The largest hotel in Denmark also holds the country's only casino. Most of the rooms have views of Copenhagen. The fitness centre features a huge indoor pool and squash courts, and there are four separate restaurants – Danish, Italian, Japanese and Thai – on the ground floor. Free parking. **www.radissonblu.com/scandinaviahotel-copenhagen**

FURTHER AFIELD Danhostel Ishøj Strand Ⓚ

Ishøj Strandvej 13, 2635 ***Tel*** *43 53 50 15* ***Fax*** *43 53 50 45* ***Rooms*** *40*

This huge hostel lies south of Copenhagen, but the S-Bane E line train takes you within a kilometre of it. It is ideal for families, offering jungle gyms, table tennis, miniature golf and bike rental, as well as being close to a sandy beach for swimming, sunbathing and windsurfing. The dormitory beds are cheaper. **www.ishojhostel.dk**

FURTHER AFIELD Løven Ⓚ

Vesterbrogade 30, 1620 ***Tel*** *33 79 67 20* ***Fax*** *33 79 67 30* ***Rooms*** *67*

The Løven, located on the lively Vestbrogade, gets lots of return guests. The bright rooms are simply furnished and without televisions. Some of them have hardwood floors. A few have private facilities, while others share. You can use a guest kitchen for preparing meals. Definitely one of the better bargains in this area. **www.loevenhotel.dk**

FURTHER AFIELD Sleep-In Green Ⓚ

Ravnsborggade 18, 2200 ***Tel*** *35 37 77 77* ***Rooms*** *66 beds*

Environmentally-conscious dormitory-style hostel that is perfect for those wishing to keep tabs on their carbon footprint. All the furniture and beds are made from recycled materials, solar panels light the rooms and the breakfasts are organic. Welcoming vibe at one of the cheapest places in Copenhagen. **www.sleep-in-green.dk**

FURTHER AFIELD Sleep-In Heaven Ⓚ

Struenseegade 7, 2200 ***Tel*** *35 35 46 48* ***Rooms*** *76 beds*

The small beds at this basement hostel might not offer a heavenly night's sleep but they do attract a variety of students, boho types and backpackers. As it gets crowded, especially in summer, be prepared to wake up early to get a hot shower. Free internet access, a bar, no curfew, breakfast and bed linen extra. **www.sleepinheaven.com**

Key to Price Guide *see p244* **Key to Symbols** *see back cover flap*

FURTHER AFIELD Ansgar ⓚⓚ

Colbjørnsensgade 29, 1652 ***Tel*** *33 21 21 96* ***Fax*** *33 21 61 91* ***Rooms*** *81*

Set immediately opposite the train station, this tourist-class hotel has rooms with fairly predictable Ikea-style furnishings, but all are bright and have TV, phone and Wi-Fi internet access. The bathrooms are small. Free indoor parking is available to guests. **www.ansgar-hotel.dk**

FURTHER AFIELD Bertrams Hotel Guldsmeden ⓚⓚ

Vesterbrogade 107, 1620 ***Tel*** *33 25 04 05* ***Fax*** *33 25 04 02* ***Rooms*** *47*

The lofty, elegant rooms of this gable-roofed boutique hotel are furnished in French-colonial style and feature lavish trimmings such as Oriental carpets, canopied beds and sumptuous linens. The Bertrams is a good choice for this part of town, especially if you look at the great price tag. **www.bertramshotel.dk**

FURTHER AFIELD City Hotel Nebo ⓚⓚ

Istedgade 6–8, 1650 ***Tel*** *33 21 12 17* ***Fax*** *33 23 47 74* ***Rooms*** *84*

Located right next to the train station, this ecumenical hotel is an affordable option for this part of town. There are three different price levels of room, though all have their own private shower and toilet. The cheapest rooms are great for budget travellers who wish to avoid staying in a youth hostel. **www.nebo.dk**

FURTHER AFIELD Radisson Blu Falconer Hotel ⓚⓚ

Falkoner Alle 9, 2000 ***Tel*** *38 15 80 01* ***Fax*** *38 15 80 02* ***Rooms*** *166*

Though usually favoured by businessmen and conferences, this high-class hotel makes a nice stop if you are looking to stay further from the city. A bright and airy lobby leads to clean, if slightly dated rooms. Service can be unreliable. The fitness centre has massage rooms and a sauna. **www.radissonblu.com/falconerhotel-copenhagen**

FURTHER AFIELD Sct Thomas ⓚⓚ

Frederiksberg Allé 7, 1621 ***Tel*** *33 21 64 64* ***Fax*** *33 25 64 60* ***Rooms*** *50*

A renovation several years ago turned the small, tranquil Sct Thomas into a well-run modern hotel offering excellent value for money. The rooms are modestly decorated (with the exception of flat-screen TVs) and those with shared facilities are somewhat cheaper. The 250S bus from the airport stops right outside. **www.hotelsctthomas.dk**

FURTHER AFIELD Avenue ⓚⓚⓚ

Åboulevard 29, 1960 ***Tel*** *35 37 31 11* ***Fax*** *35 37 31 33* ***Rooms*** *68*

Originally built in 1898, the Avenue has been getting glowing reviews from guests since its renovation in 2005. It now melds the best of Danish interior design with a cosy ambience. The bright rooms are very stylish, and there is an excellent breakfast buffet. A short walk from the city centre. **www.avenuehotel.dk**

FURTHER AFIELD Skovshoved Hotel ⓚⓚⓚ

Strandvejen 267, 2920 ***Tel*** *39 64 00 28* ***Fax*** *39 64 06 72* ***Rooms*** *22*

A short drive outside the city, in leafy Charlottenlund village, this hotel has been around since 1660, but a design overhaul has earned it a coveted spot on the "hip hotels" circuit. The rooms are very modern and have views over the Øresund; there is even a private bathing jetty, not to mention a superb restaurant. **www.skovshovedhotel.dk**

FURTHER AFIELD Tiffany ⓚⓚⓚ

Halmtorret 1, 1700 ***Tel*** *33 21 80 50* ***Fax*** *33 21 87 50* ***Rooms*** *29*

The Tiffany is on a little square in Vesterbro just half a block from the train station. The spacious rooms have every amenity imaginable, including microwaves, dining tables for four and fetching tiled bathrooms. The service is remarkably friendly. Breakfast costs extra. **www.hoteltiffany.dk**

FURTHER AFIELD Hotel Kong Arthur ⓚⓚⓚⓚ

Nørre Søgade 11, 1370 ***Tel*** *33 11 12 12* ***Fax*** *33 32 61 30* ***Rooms*** *117*

This former orphanage is on a small lake just by Rosenborg Slot. The smallish rooms have classic, turn-of-the-century Scandinavian decor with a good number of antique furnishings. Breakfast is taken in a sunroom that looks onto a quaint courtyard. There are several restaurants, free parking and frequent special discounts. **www.kongarthur.dk**

NORTHWESTERN ZEALAND

BIRKERØD Hotel Birkerød ⓚⓚ

Birkerød Kongevej 102–104, 3460 ***Tel*** *45 81 44 30* ***Fax*** *45 82 30 29* ***Rooms*** *29* ***Map*** *F4*

A good-value hotel convenient for Copenhagen as well as Northwestern Zealand, the Birkerød is bright with uninspired rooms. The reception, however, is very friendly and the whole place is set in lovely grounds just minutes from a forest and rolling hills. Facilities include tennis courts. **www.hotelbirkerod.dk**

ESKEBJERG Myrehøj Bed and Breakfast ⓚ

Vilhelmshøjvej 1, 4593 ***Tel*** *59 29 00 26* ***Fax*** *59 29 00 28* ***Rooms*** *13* ***Map*** *E4*

Set in a farmhouse built in 1686, the grounds of this modest B&B feature an orchard, flower gardens and a large outdoor terrace. The lovely rooms are done up in a variety of styles and many feel quite dainty, with light colours and simple cast iron or shaven-wood furniture. The beach is a fair walk away. **www.myrehoj.dk**

FREDENSBORG Fredensborg Store Kro ⓀⓀⓀⓀ

Slotsgade 6, 3480 ***Tel*** *48 40 01 11* ***Fax*** *48 48 45 61* ***Rooms*** *48* ***Map*** *F4*

Store Kro is located in a quiet scenic area, close to Esrum Lake and next to Fredensborg Castle, Queen Margrethe II's summer residence. The hotel was built by King Frederick IV in the 18th century and has a long royal history. Each room is individually decorated with taste and elegance. **www.storekro.dk**

FREDERIKSSUND Villa Bakkely Ⓚ

Roskildevej 109, 3600 ***Tel*** *30 63 45 10* ***Rooms*** *7* ***Map*** *F4*

A small bed and breakfast with seven distinctive rooms, all of which have large double beds and flatscreen TVs. None have en-suite facilities, but there is a cosy breakfast café, terrace, and a beautiful old garden. A good option if you want to get a bit outside of Frederikssund, which tends to be busy in high season. **www.villabakkely.dk**

FREDERIKSSUND Rådhuskroen ⓀⓀ

Østergade 1, 3600 ***Tel*** *47 31 54 55* ***Rooms*** *9* ***Map*** *F4*

While the elongated white building might look a bit bland from the outside, step in to find a number of warm, friendly bedrooms with bright floral quilts, wall-to-wall carpeting, and folk art on the walls. The restaurant is a popular place where locals come to get their fill of traditional Danish cuisine. **www.hotel-raadhuskroen.dk**

GILLELEJE Gilleleje Badehotel ⓀⓀ

Hulsøvej 15, 3250 ***Tel*** *48 30 13 47* ***Fax*** *48 36 04 69* ***Rooms*** *27* ***Map*** *F4*

This splendid beach hotel was built in 1895 for wealthy, weekending Copenhageners. It has since been given a bright maritime makeover which succeeds in being contemporary. The best part: downstairs you will find a sauna, steam room and jacuzzi – perfect after a dip in the sea. **www.gillelejebadehotel.dk**

HELSINGØR Danhostel Helsingør Vandrerhjem Ⓚ

Ndr Strandvej 24, 3000 ***Tel*** *49 21 16 40* ***Fax*** *49 21 13 99* ***Rooms*** *38* ***Map*** *F4*

A few steps away from a small beach, this youth hostel occupies some of the best real estate in the country. It consists primarily of double and triple rooms, though there are a few very spacious dormitory-style rooms as well. Reception is professionally run and their is wireless internet access throughout. **www.helsingorhostel.dk**

HELSINGØR Hamlet ⓀⓀ

Bramstrade 5, 3000 ***Tel*** *49 21 05 91* ***Fax*** *49 49 26 01* ***Rooms*** *36* ***Map*** *F4*

The building itself is one of the town's oldest and is centrally located. The Hamlet is also very close to the train station. Some of the rooms have been renovated in rich, deep colours; others still have very cramped bathrooms which are worth shying away from. **www.hotelhamlet.dk**

HELSINGØR Marienlyst ⓀⓀⓀⓀ

Nordre Strandvej 2, 3000 ***Tel*** *49 21 40 00* ***Fax*** *49 21 49 00* ***Rooms*** *222* ***Map*** *F4*

This massive establishment was Denmark's first official seaside resort. Situated right on the shores of the Kattegat, there are views straight to the Sound or to Kronborg Castle. The rooms are beautifully furnished. In summer you can find excellent discounts if you want to stay for more than just a night or two. Onsite casino. **www.marienlyst.dk**

HOLBÆK Holbæk Vandrerhjem ⓀⓀ

Ahlgade 1B, 4300 ***Tel*** *59 44 29 19* ***Fax*** *59 43 94 85* ***Rooms*** *26* ***Map*** *F4*

An outstanding hostel option that never ever feels like a hostel, with Oriental rugs, Alpine-style rooms and the friendliest of staff. This place makes other Danish hostels green with envy. The ground-floor restaurant also happens to be one of the best places to eat in town. **www.holbaekvandrerhjem.dk**

HORNBÆK Ewaldsgården Ⓚ

Johannes Ewaldsvej 5, 3100 ***Tel*** *49 70 00 82* ***Fax*** *49 70 00 82* ***Rooms*** *12* ***Map*** *F4*

This 150-year-old guesthouse is set around a cobblestone courtyard. The rooms are bright and spacious, with large comfortable beds, and there is such a perfectly rustic ambience throughout the hallways and living rooms that it almost feels as though you are in an old ethnographic museum. **www.ewaldsgaarden.dk**

HORNBÆK Hotel Bretagne ⓀⓀⓀ

Sauntevej 18, 3100 ***Tel*** *49 70 16 66* ***Fax*** *49 25 65 04* ***Rooms*** *26* ***Map*** *F4*

This one-time hospital has outstanding views over the Hornbæk lake, the Kattegat and the surrounding forest. Today the Bretagne boasts pastel-coloured rooms with wireless internet and cooking facilities, though there is also a hotel restaurant. **www.hotelbretagne.dk**

HORNBÆK Havreholm Slot ⓀⓀⓀⓀ

Klosterrisvej 4, 3100 ***Tel*** *49 75 86 00* ***Fax*** *49 75 80 23* ***Rooms*** *26* ***Map*** *F4*

Situated amongst sprawling lawns bordered by woodlands and looking onto a pristine lake, this bright modern-meets-classic hotel has spacious well-equipped rooms. There are numerous sports activities available, including golf, tennis, and swimming in the pool or lake. There is also an excellent terrace restaurant. **www.havreholm.dk**

HUNDESTED Hundested Kro ⓀⓀⓀ

Nørregade 10, 3390 ***Tel*** *47 93 75 38* ***Fax*** *47 93 78 61* ***Rooms*** *58* ***Map*** *F4*

Most of the rooms at this much-loved inn are very elegant, though be sure to ask for one with views to the Isjefjorden. Facilities include a gym, pool and sauna, and it is just a short distance from the beach. The inn restaurant is well known for serving excellent food and there is also a lively bar. **www.hundested-kro.dk**

Key to Price Guide *see p244* **Key to Symbols** *see back cover flap*

HØRVE Dragsholm Slot ⓚⓚⓚⓚ

Dragholm Allé, 4534 **Tel** *59 65 33 00* **Fax** *59 65 30 33* **Rooms** *36* **Map** *E4*

Finding more luxury and class than is offered by this establishment would be tough. Set in a 13th-century castle built to defend the town, the rooms here are unique, with a distinctive antique feel to them. The Dragsholm is popular for weddings, so check ahead of time to be sure you are not next door to some newlyweds. **www.dragsholm-slot.dk**

KORSØR Svenstrupgård Feriecenter ⓚ

Svenstrup Strandvej 3, 4220 **Tel** *22 18 58 38* **Fax** *58 38 15 09* **Rooms** *35* **Map** *E5*

Located in the middle of the forest on the water's edge, the rooms in this rustic holiday centre are spacious and feel new, while featuring exposed beams and vaulted brick ceilings. There are also cheaper dormitory rooms, a common sitting room and communal kitchen that guests can use. Ideal for outdoor enthusiasts. **www.svenstrupgaard.dk**

NYKØBING S Anneberg Vandrerhjem ⓚ

Egebjergvej 162, 4500 **Tel** *59 66 55 44* **Fax** *59 66 55 45* **Rooms** *13* **Map** *E4*

This gorgeous youth hostel is set within a 17th-century estate that from the outside looks like it should be lived in by royalty. The rooms are clean and tasteful, though undeniably hostel-like, and the grounds lead to a private beach. Families are welcomed. **www.annebergvandrerhjem.dk**

ROSKILDE Roskilde Vandrerhjem ⓚ

Vindeboder 7, 4000 **Tel** *46 35 21 84* **Rooms** *40* **Map** *F4*

Situated in the harbour next to the Viking Ship Museum, the Vandrerhjem is a 15-minute walk from the centre of town. This spectacular youth hostel feels more like a minimalist design hotel with a maritime ambience than a regular hostel. It is clean and very well run. There are good offers for families. **www.rova.dk**

ROSKILDE Scandic Hotel Roskilde ⓚⓚ

Søndre Ringvej 33, 4000 **Tel** *46 32 46 32* **Fax** *46 32 02 32* **Rooms** *98* **Map** *F4*

Situated near the park, this prestigious hotel has many facilities including a sauna and solarium. The rooms are comfortable and furnished in a traditional style, though they can feel quite bland at times. Located outside of town on the ring road, the Scandic is best if you have a vehicle. **www.scandic-hotels.com/roskilde**

ROSKILDE Prindsen ⓚⓚⓚ

Algade 13, 4000 **Tel** *46 30 91 00* **Fax** *46 30 91 50* **Rooms** *76* **Map** *F4*

A very attractive and smartly furnished hotel, whose guests have included Hans Christian Andersen and members of the Danish royal family. The rooms are comfortable and warmly furnished, though for a really memorable stay it is worth going for one of the more expensive classically-furnished suites. **www.prindsen.dk**

SORØ Hotel Postgården ⓚⓚ

Storgade 25, 4180 **Tel** *57 83 22 22* **Fax** *57 83 22 91* **Rooms** *18* **Map** *E5*

The Danish writer Ludvig Holberg composed a number of his stories here. Centrally located right on the main street in Sorø, the rooms at this classy hotel are elegant and smart and the reception friendly and helpful. There is also a great pan-Asian restaurant just next door. **www.hotelpostgaarden.dk**

TISVILDELEJE Kildegaard ⓚⓚ

Hovedgaden 52, 3220 **Tel** *48 70 71 53* **Fax** *48 70 72 19* **Rooms** *27* **Map** *F4*

This tiny family guesthouse has quaint little rooms which have hardly changed since the place was established in over a hundred years ago. Some of the original furnishings are still present. The leafy garden out back is a great place to spend a quiet sunny afternoon and there is a bathing beach nearby. **www.kildegaard-tisvildeleje.dk**

TISVILDELEJE Strand Hotel ⓚⓚ

Hovedgade 75, 3220 **Tel** *48 70 71 19* **Rooms** *27* **Map** *F4*

This gorgeous *fin-de-siècle* building was originally the town's general store. Today it is a modern hotel with a sparky colourful interior created by local designers; all rooms are individually decorated. The Strand has, however, retained a number of older features such as exposed beams and traditional wicker chairs. **www.strand-hotel.dk**

SOUTHERN ZEALAND AND THE ISLANDS

KØGE Centralhotellet ⓚⓚ

Vestergade 3, 4600 **Tel** *56 65 06 96* **Fax** *56 66 02 07* **Rooms** *12* **Map** *F5*

The rooms at this small comfortable hotel, situated right next to the tourist office, are basic. The perfectly acceptable doubles are fairly priced, for such a great location right in the middle of town and the cheery reception is run by helpful locals who have plenty of recommendations. **www.centralhotellet.dk**

KØGE Hvide Hus ⓚⓚⓚ

Strandvejen 111, 4600 **Tel** *56 65 36 90* **Fax** *56 66 33 14* **Rooms** *126* **Map** *F5*

Popular with business conferences and weekend golfers, Hvide Hus offers basic rooms with design features such as minimalist lighting and boutique textiles. This, combined with expansive grounds inhabited by wandering flamingoes and the fact that the beach is nearby, make this a real find. **www.hotelhvidehus.dk**

MARIBO Hotel Maribo Søpark ⓚⓚ

Vestergade 29, 4930 **Tel** *54 78 10 11* **Fax** *54 78 05 22* **Rooms** *110* **Map** *E6*

This superb hotel enjoys an exceptionally lovely location. Its spacious rooms are elegantly furnished, and many have balconies looking onto the beautiful Maribo Sø lake. A wellness centre and spa was added in 2006. The Søpark also has a fantastic restaurant and an outdoor swimming pool. **www.maribo-soepark.dk**

MARIELYST Hotel Nørrevang ⓚⓚ

Marielyst Strandvej 32, 4873 **Tel** *54 13 62 62* **Fax** *54 13 62 72* **Rooms** *66* **Map** *F6*

Set in a 19th-century landscape in the centre of town, this is by far the nicest place to stay in Marielyst. It is close to the beach but an indoor/outdoor swimming pool is great for cooling off during the day. A number of the rooms are set within chalet-style duplex buildings with lofted beds. Attracts a fair share of large groups. **www.norrevang.dk**

MØN Bakkagården B&B ⓚ

Busenevej 64, 4791 **Tel** *55 81 93 01* **Fax** *55 81 94 01* **Rooms** *12* **Map** *F6*

Set in a large farmhouse on sprawling lawns towards the eastern half of Møn (a 20-minute walk from the stunning chalk cliffs of Møns Klint), this B&B offers pleasant and sparsely-decorated rooms. Breakfast is taken in a large sunroom or in a covered gazebo out on the lawn, from which you can see the Baltic. **www.bakkegaarden64.dk**

MØN Møns Klint Youth Hostel ⓚ

Langebjergvej 1, 4791 **Tel** *55 81 20 30* **Fax** *55 81 28 18* **Rooms** *29* **Map** *F6*

This efficiently run hostel is set on the quiet Hunosøen lake, where guests can go fishing. Rooms are large and have a rustic feel to them, and it is not uncommon to have an entire room to yourself. The hostel is just 15 minutes by foot to the chalk cliffs of Møns Klint. Horse-riding is available next door. **www.danhostel.dk/moen**

MØN Liselund ny Slot ⓚⓚ

Langebjergvej 6, 4791 **Tel** *55 81 20 81* **Fax** *55 81 21 91* **Rooms** *17* **Map** *F6*

This tiny thatched castle is a unexpected gem. Each room is named after one of H.C. Andersen's fairy tales and retains original wall panelling and ceiling frescoes, plus old wooden planks for floors and private baths. For a particularly memorable stay there is the tower honeymoon suite with panoramic views. **www.liselundslot.dk**

NAKSKOV Hotel Harmonien ⓚⓚ

Nybrogade 2, 4900 **Tel** *54 95 91 90* **Fax** *54 95 91 30* **Rooms** *33* **Map** *E6*

Situated close to the sights of central Nakskov, the spacious, minimalist rooms and suites are elegantly decorated in whites, blues and light greys, with dark wooden furniture and large bathrooms. Probably Nakskov's best hotel option. **www.hotel-harmonien.dk**

NÆSTVED Hotel Kirstine ⓚⓚ

Købmagergade 20, 4700 **Tel** *55 77 47 00* **Fax** *55 72 11 53* **Rooms** *31* **Map** *E5*

Long ago, Næstved's mayors lived within the walls of this 250-year-old brick and timber building. The top-class hotel that now occupies the premises makes good use of this history, with classical rooms with antique furnishings. The Kirstine also offers several budget rooms which they do not advertise. **www.hotelkirstine.dk**

NÆSTVED Hotel Vinhuset ⓚⓚ

Skt Peders Kirkeplads 4, 4700 **Tel** *55 72 08 07* **Fax** *55 72 03 35* **Rooms** *57* **Map** *E5*

A thorough renovation in 2006 has brought this classic 1778 building up to modern standards while retaining its antique charm. The rooms are now individually decorated in rich colours and with a few feature canopy beds. Cellar restaurant and modern wine-and-tapas bar on site. **www.hotelvinhuset.dk**

PRÆSTØ Kirsebærkroen ⓚ

Kirsebærvej 1, 4720 **Tel** *55 99 39 55* **Rooms** *7* **Map** *F5*

Run by a friendly elderly Danish couple, this one-time farmstead features nicely decorated rooms, each with minibar and TV, all set in quiet grounds just a few minutes' walk from a beach on Præstø fjord. Each room has an adjoining patio with table and chairs – ideal for relaxing in the picturesque surroundings. **www.kirsebaerkroen.dk**

RINGSTED Scandic Hotel Ringsted ⓚⓚ

Nørretorv 57, 4100 **Tel** *57 61 93 00* **Fax** *57 67 02 07* **Rooms** *75* **Map** *E5*

A four-storey hotel south of the town centre with comfortable, simply decorated rooms. This chain is popular with business travellers. High standards throughout with generous breakfast buffet, however for dinner it is recommended to head into town. You can even borrow the hotel's bicycles. **www.scandic-hotels.dk/ringsted**

RINGSTED Sørup Herregård ⓚⓚⓚ

Sørupvej 26, 4100 **Tel** *57 64 30 02* **Fax** *57 64 31 73* **Rooms** *102* **Map** *E5*

Set in an old manor house, this hotel overlooks a small lake and even has its own landing stage. The rooms are particularly well furnished, with dark hardwood floors, fine linens, all mod cons and great views of the hillside. There is also an indoor pool, sauna and terrace restaurant. **www.sorup.dk**

RØDVIG STEVNS Rødvig Kro og Badehotel ⓚⓚ

Østersøvej 8, 4673 **Tel** *56 50 60 98* **Rooms** *16* **Map** *F5*

An old, atmospheric family-run inn with particularly fetching views out to the Baltic and to the Stevns Klint cliffs. The tidy rooms come in a variety of sizes, but all are impeccably decorated with modern furnishings and comfortable beds. The hotel restaurant is worth trying, and in summer guests can eat outside. **www.roedvigkro.dk**

Key to Price Guide *see p244* **Key to Symbols** *see back cover flap*

SAKSKØBING Våbensted Ⓚ
Kårup Møllevej 6, 4990 ***Tel*** *54 70 63 63* ***Rooms*** *15* ***Map*** *E6*

This pleasant hotel, with its inviting rustic ambiance, is a good place to stay in an otherwise uneventful part of Lolland. The rooms are elegantly simple and the staff are uncharacteristically animated. The on-site restaurant serves excellent Thai food and is one of the best in this region. Breakfast available. **www.hotel-vaabensted.dk**

SØLLESTED (LOLLAND) Gammelgaard Bed and Breakfast ⓀⓀ
Ryde Kirkevej 1, 4920 ***Tel*** *40 50 82 88* ***Fax*** *54 94 10 26* ***Rooms*** *6* ***Map*** *E6*

Surrounded by a double moat and set within a castle, this luxurious bed and breakfast is an interesting place to stay. The lavish rooms feature lots of original furnishings, including marble tiled floors in the bathrooms and the opulent sitting room sports wall tapestries and crystal chandeliers. **www.gammelgaardgods.dk**

VORDINGBORG Hotel Kong Valdemar ⓀⓀ
Slotstorvet, 4760 ***Tel*** *55 34 30 95* ***Rooms*** *60* ***Map*** *F6*

Located opposite the ruins of Vordingborg castle, the Valdemar may lack style but it certainly makes up for it in the friendliness of its reception. By far the most central hotel in Vordingborg and there is a decent restaurant and internet access. **www.hotelkongvaldemar.dk**

FUNEN

ASSENS Marcussens ⓀⓀⓀ
Strandgade 22, 5610 ***Tel*** *64 71 10 89* ***Fax*** *64 71 41 75* ***Rooms*** *33* ***Map*** *C5*

Located in the old merchant's town of Assens, this is an ideal place to soak up the small-town atmosphere that Funen is known for. The hotel is set just off a pedestrianised street and though most of the rooms feel somewhat dated, many do boast views of the water. There is also a pleasant terrace for meals. **www.marcussens.dk**

FAABORG Fåborg Vandrerhjem Ⓚ
Grønnegade 71–2, 5600 ***Tel*** *62 61 12 03* ***Fax*** *62 61 35 08* ***Rooms*** *18* ***Map*** *D5*

A superb youth hostel that feels as if you have stepped into an old museum, with creaky floors, uneven window panes, and subdued matte colours that call to mind homesteads of the early 19th century. It could not be more central too, placed equidistant from the ferry terminal, train station and town square. **www.danhostel.dk/faaborg**

FAABORG Hotel Fåborg ⓀⓀ
Torvet 13–15, 5600 ***Tel*** *62 61 02 45* ***Rooms*** *21* ***Map*** *D5*

Originally built in 1916, this gorgeous Gothic-style brick renovation of an old warehouse sits right on Fåborg's central square. All the rooms, soft and somewhat dainty in their colouring and furniture, have private facilities. The Mediterranean-style restaurant downstairs is one of the best spots to eat in town. **www.hotelfaaborg.dk**

FAABORG Hvedholm Slot ⓀⓀⓀ
Hvedholm Alle 1, 5600 ***Tel*** *63 60 10 20* ***Fax*** *63 60 10 29* ***Rooms*** *42* ***Map*** *D5*

Hvedholm is one of Denmark's largest castles and has been in the same family since 1570. The rooms have chandeliers, canopy beds, and plenty of regal ambience. The excellent restaurant, with a wine cellar beneath it, specialises in game and fish dishes. **www.slotshotel.dk**

KERTEMINDE Danhostel Kerteminde Ⓚ
Skovvej 46, 5300 ***Tel*** *65 32 39 29* ***Rooms*** *30* ***Map*** *D5*

A good budget option set in a wooded area and only a few minutes' walk from the town beach. The bucolic, cabin-like rooms hardly feel like a youth hostel, though the many visiting youth groups will be enough of a reminder. About a ten minute walk the town centre. **www.dkhostel.dk**

KERTEMINDE Tornøes Hotel ⓀⓀ
Strandgade 2, 5300 ***Tel*** *65 32 16 05* ***Fax*** *65 32 48 40* ***Rooms*** *30* ***Map*** *D5*

This brick building, originally built in 1643, is set right on the harbourside. The bright rooms have been renovated to a high standard and the best ones feature canopy beds and views out to Kerteminde fjord. The hotel succeeds in retaining a very old-world feel and there is a good restaurant. **www.tornoeshotel.dk**

MARSTAL Hotel Marstal ⓀⓀ
Dronningestræde 1A, 5960 ***Tel*** *62 53 13 52* ***Rooms*** *18* ***Map*** *D6*

Located in an old harbour town at the easternmost point of the island of Ærø, this classic hotel has a number of plain but clean and comfortable rooms offering sea views and private access to an enclosed garden. The hotel restaurant is the best in town, serving fine seafood in an English pub setting. **www.hotelmarstal.dk**

MIDDELFART Toldboden Bed & Breakfast Ⓚ
Brogade 1, 5500 ***Tel*** *64 41 47 37* ***Rooms*** *3* ***Map*** *C5*

This small bed-and-breakfast is just across from the harbour in the old quarter of Middelfart. The three colourful rooms all have sea views, as does the spacious balcony. There are two clean bathrooms shared between the rooms, and a large kitchen is also available for guests. **www.toldboden-bb.dk**

MIDDELFART Hindsgavl Slot ⓀⓀⓀ

Hindsgavl Allé 7, 5500 ***Tel*** *64 41 88 00* ***Rooms*** *70* ***Map*** *C5*

Occupying a medieval castle, this partially modernised hotel enjoys a magnificent lakeside location. The rooms feature quilted beds, window sashes, small crystal chandeliers and elegant trimmings. Verdant grounds and a gourmet restaurant add to its attractions, making it a choice stay for this part of Funen. **www.hindsgavl.dk**

MUNKEBO Munkebo Kro ⓀⓀⓀ

Fjordvej 56, 5330 ***Tel*** *65 97 40 30* ***Fax*** *65 97 55 64* ***Rooms*** *22* ***Map*** *D5*

This one-time country inn has been converted into a semi-luxurious hotel. The rooms are airy, modern, and attractively lit, featuring hardwood furnishings and bright bathrooms. There is also a gourmet restaurant, which is country-renowned for its authentic Danish cuisine. **www.munkebokro.dk**

NYBORG Hotel Hesselet ⓀⓀⓀⓀ

Christianslundsvej 119, 5800 ***Tel*** *65 31 30 29* ***Fax*** *65 31 29 58* ***Rooms*** *43* ***Map*** *D5*

Located north of the city on the edge of a beech forest, the stylish, spacious, and individually-decorated rooms of this grand old hotel are typified by wooden furniture and luxurious bathrooms with granite floors and double washbasins. There is also an indoor pool, sauna, two tennis courts and free cycle hire for guests. **www.hesselet.dk**

ODENSE Det Lille Hotel Ⓚ

Dronningensgade 5, 5000 ***Tel*** *66 12 28 21* ***Fax*** *66 12 28 21* ***Rooms*** *12* ***Map*** *D5*

Located in the centre of Odense, this little hotel housed in a pretty building from the 1800s offers single, double and family-sized rooms. The affordable price includes breakfast and coffee, and cake is also served in the evening by the friendly owners. Parking is available. **www.lillehotel.dk**

ODENSE Domir Ⓚ

Hans Tausensgade 19, 5000 ***Tel*** *66 12 14 27* ***Fax*** *66 12 13 14* ***Rooms*** *38* ***Map*** *D5*

Quiet and independently-run, the Domir is simply and elegantly decorated with friendly low-key service. Here you will find very comfortable beds, TV and a phone in every room, although a few of the rooms are on the small side ask to take a look first. The owners also run the smaller, less expensive Ydes next door. **www.domir.dk**

ODENSE Motel Ansgarhus Ⓚ

Kirkegårds Allé 19, 5000 ***Tel*** *66 12 88 00* ***Fax*** *66 12 88 65* ***Rooms*** *16* ***Map*** *D5*

Just ten minutes southeast of the city centre, this quaint family-run hotel is in a very desirable location next to the Å river. The rooms are small but cheery and there is wireless internet access throughout. Nearby you can take a river boat all the way down to the Fynske Landsby open-air museum. **www.ansgarhus.dk**

ODENSE Odense City Hostel Ⓚ

Østre Stationsvej 31, 5000 ***Tel*** *63 11 04 25* ***Rooms*** *39* ***Map*** *D5*

Situated in the same complex as the train station, this spacious and bright hostel is the most central and inexpensive place in town. The reception is very friendly and hands out brochures on activities in and around town. Wireless internet access included. **www.cityhostel.dk**

ODENSE Pjentehus Ⓚ

Pjentedamsgade 14, 5000 ***Tel*** *66 12 15 55* ***Fax*** *66 17 82 09* ***Rooms*** *4* ***Map*** *D5*

Set in the heart of old Odense, the Pjentehus' rooms are tidy and feature TV and radio although little else in the way of amenities, though some of them have pleasant floral decorations. The bathrooms are shared. Breakfast is served in the old-fashioned kitchen downstairs. **www.pjentehus.dk**

ODENSE City Hotel Odense ⓀⓀ

Hans Mules Gade 5, 5000 ***Tel*** *66 12 12 58* ***Fax*** *66 12 93 64* ***Rooms*** *43* ***Map*** *D5*

This centrally located establishment, close to the train station, is popular with businessmen. The rooms are comfortable enough, with all mod cons, though quite bland in their decor; an alternative might be one of the hotel's five apartment-style rooms. Great roof terrace for breakfast. **www.city-hotel-odense.dk**

ODENSE Hotel Ansgar ⓀⓀ

Østre Stationsvej 32, 5000 ***Tel*** *66 11 96 93* ***Fax*** *66 11 96 75* ***Rooms*** *74* ***Map*** *D5*

The rooms here boast plenty of classical charm thanks to their Italian-style chairs and window sashes. Catering to business and leisure travellers alike, the Ansgar also features a bar and restaurant, which offers a very good lunchtime buffet. **www.millinghotels.dk**

ODENSE Radisson Blu H.C. Andersen ⓀⓀ

Claus Bergs Gade 7, 5000 ***Tel*** *66 14 78 00* ***Fax*** *66 14 78 90* ***Rooms*** *145* ***Map*** *D5*

In a cobblestone district, minutes from the Andersen museums, this plush hotel has been around for a while and at times shows its age. The business-like rooms are perfectly adequate, though, especially if you are planning on spending time at the museums or going to hear the city's orchestra. **www.radissonblu.com/hotel-odense**

ODENSE Clarion Collection Hotel Plaza ⓀⓀⓀ

Østre Stationsvej 24, 5000 ***Tel*** *66 11 77 45* ***Fax*** *66 14 41 45* ***Rooms*** *68* ***Map*** *D5*

The Plaza is located on the edge of the Kongs Haven park in an old building that, from certain angles, resembles a castle. The rooms here are rather endearing, with classical furniture and a vague air of glamour. Copious breakfasts, large common areas, Wi-Fi internet and friendly staff. **www.millinghotels.dk**

Key to Price Guide *see p244* **Key to Symbols** *see back cover flap*

RUDKØBING Rudkøbing Skudehavn ⓚⓚ

Havnegade 21, 5900 ***Tel*** *62 51 46 00* ***Fax*** *62 51 49 40* ***Rooms*** *32* ***Map*** *D6*

Down at Langeland's largest marina, a ten minute walk from the centre of Rudkøbing, this Swedish-style hotel has spacious chalet-style rooms and a large indoor pool. Each room has its own bathroom. Nearby you will find an excellent selection of restaurants and shops. **www.rudkobingskudehavn.dk**

SVENDBORG Ærø Hotel ⓚ

Brogade 1, 5700 ***Tel*** *62 21 07 60* ***Fax*** *63 20 30 51* ***Rooms*** *33* ***Map*** *D5*

Svendborg's oldest hotel, dating from 1870, is placed in a charismatic old building just across from the ferry harbour, meaning that you get whiffs of the sea whenever you open your window. The modern rooms are very well equipped and have an old-world, somewhat sumptuous feel to them. **www.hotel-aeroe.dk**

ÆRØSKØBING Pension Vestergade 44 ⓚⓚ

Vestergade 44, 5970 ***Tel*** *62 52 22 98* ***Rooms*** *10* ***Map*** *D6*

This British-run guesthouse is set along one of Ærøskøbing's many atmospheric cobblestone streets and has lots of charm and some very comfortable, quite exquisite rooms. There is a pretty garden out back for taking meals, including afternoon English tea, in the fresh island air. **www.vestergade44.com**

SOUTHERN AND CENTRAL JUTLAND

BILLUND Hotel Propellen ⓚⓚⓚ

Nordmarksvej 3, 7190 ***Tel*** *75 33 81 33* ***Fax*** *75 35 33 62* ***Rooms*** *94* ***Map*** *C4*

This cosy three-storey hotel is a no-frills establishment with efficient friendly service. The rooms are cheery and comfortable and there are plenty of activities available such as table tennis and swimming. For children the hotel has its own playroom and outdoor playground. **www.propellen.dk**

BILLUND Legoland ⓚⓚⓚⓚ

Aastvej 10, 7190 ***Tel*** *75 33 12 44* ***Fax*** *75 35 38 10* ***Rooms*** *176* ***Map*** *C4*

Set up mainly for visitors to LEGOLAND®, this hotel is connected to the park by an overhead walkway and the price for the first night includes two days admission to the attraction. Some of the rooms provide a view of the entire park and all of them have wireless internet access. **www.hotellegoland.dk**

EBELTOFT Ebeltoft Park ⓚⓚ

Vibæk Strandvej 4, 8400 ***Tel*** *86 34 32 22* ***Fax*** *86 34 49 41* ***Rooms*** *74* ***Map*** *D3*

Close to a white-sand beach, this hotel provides an ideal stay in a comfortable environment. A heated indoor swimming pool is available as an alternative to the sea in inclement weather. The nearby ferry terminal provides links with Zealand. Wireless internet access is available. **www.ebeltoftparkhotel.dk**

EBELTOFT Hotel Ebeltoft Strand ⓚⓚ

Nordre Strandvej 3, 8400 ***Tel*** *86 34 33 00* ***Fax*** *86 34 46 36* ***Rooms*** *110* ***Map*** *D3*

This modern beachfront hotel is surrounded by stunning scenery. Each of the brightly coloured rooms has a view over the enchanting Ebeltoft Vig cove. Facilities include a heated indoor swimming pool and sauna. This is a popular area for surfers. Internet access available. **www.ebeltoftstrand.dk**

ESBJERG Scandic Olympic Esbjerg ⓚⓚⓚ

Strandbygade 3, 6700 ***Tel*** *75 18 11 88* ***Fax*** *75 18 11 08* ***Rooms*** *90* ***Map*** *B5*

Centrally located in the heart of the city, this modern hotel offers clean, well-maintained accommodation. The comfortable rooms are decorated in cool hues of white and blue with modern wooden furnishings. All the rooms have free wireless internet. **www.scandichotels.com**

FANØ Sønderho Kro ⓚⓚⓚ

Kropladsen 11, 6720 ***Tel*** *75 16 40 09* ***Fax*** *75 16 43 85* ***Rooms*** *14* ***Map*** *B5*

Nestled behind the sand dunes in the heart of Sønderho, this 18th-century thatched inn has a pleasant atmosphere and four-poster beds. The rooms are individually furnished and enjoy views over the marshland and the sea. The French-Danish restaurant, one of the best on the island, attracts gourmets from afar. **www.sonderhokro.dk**

FREDERICIA Kronprinds Frederik ⓚⓚⓚ

Vestre Ringvej 96, 7000 ***Tel*** *75 91 00 00* ***Fax*** *75 91 19 99* ***Rooms*** *78* ***Map*** *C5*

This comfortable hotel is located in the scenic, recreational area of Madsby Enge. This expansive hilly area is a lively centre for many leisure activities and is not far from Fredericia and the local beach. Next to the Kronprinds Frederik is the large Subtropical Waterland tourist attraction. **www.hkf.dk**

FREDERICIA Kryb-i-ly-Kro ⓚⓚⓚ

Kolding Landevej 160, 7000 ***Tel*** *75 56 25 55* ***Fax*** *75 56 45 14* ***Rooms*** *77* ***Map*** *C5*

Built in 1610, this cosy manor house has plenty of character. Its name means "take shelter". Situated in peaceful surroundings, this popular and highly regarded establishment is within an hour's drive of Givskud Safari Park and LEGOLAND®. The facilities include an indoor swimming pool and billiard room. **www.krybily.dk**

GRENÅ Grenå Strand Kr Kr

Havneplads 1, 8500 ***Tel*** *86 32 68 14* ***Fax*** *86 32 07 92* ***Rooms*** *12* ***Map*** *D3*

This delightful seaside hotel is in a conspicuous early-20th-century yellow building. Next to it is a sailing jetty and a pleasant beach. The Strand's rooms are individually designed in a typically Danish style. Local attractions include Denmark's Kattegat Centre (shark centre). **www.grenaastrand.dk**

HERNING Østergaards Hotel Kr Kr Kr

Silkeborgvej 94, 7400 ***Tel*** *97 12 45 55* ***Fax*** *97 12 01 52* ***Rooms*** *84* ***Map*** *C4*

Located in Central Jylland in quiet and peaceful surroundings, this modern hotel offers tastefully decorated rooms with contemporary furnishings. The peace is only broken when the football stadium next door is being used. There is an outdoor swimming pool. **www.oestergaardshotel.dk**

HORSENS Scandic Bygholm Park Kr Kr

Schüttesvej 6, 8700 ***Tel*** *75 62 23 33* ***Fax*** *75 61 31 05* ***Rooms*** *142* ***Map*** *C4*

Located in the beautiful Bygholm Park, this modernized manor house dates back to 1775. The hotel overlooks Bygholm Lake and visitor attractions in the area include the Museum of Art. All the rooms feature wireless internet access. **www.scandic-hotels.com**

HORSENS Best Western Hotel Danica Kr Kr Kr

Ove Jensens Allé 28, 8700 ***Tel*** *75 61 60 22* ***Fax*** *75 61 66 63* ***Rooms*** *39* ***Map*** *C4*

This modern and comfortable hotel is situated in the town centre close to the town hall. The rooms are tastefully decorated and equipped with all modern amenities. The hotel restaurant is well worth a visit as it has received widespread recognition for its gourmet menu. Internet access is available. **www.hoteldanica.dk**

KOLDING Comwell Kolding Kr Kr

Skovbrynet 1, 6000 ***Tel*** *76 34 11 00* ***Fax*** *76 34 12 00* ***Rooms*** *180* ***Map*** *C5*

The Comwell Kolding is a modern hotel equidistant from the town centre and Koldinghus Castle. It lies adjacent to a small lake and is decorated in contemporary Danish style. All the rooms are bright and cheerful. Facilities include internet access and an indoor swimming pool. **www.comwell.com**

KOLDING Saxildhus Hotel Kr Kr

Jernbanegade 39, Banegårdspladsen, 6000 ***Tel*** *75 52 12 00* ***Fax*** *75 53 53 10* ***Rooms*** *87* ***Map*** *C5*

Situated in the centre of Kolding, opposite the train station, this international establishment exudes an air of nostalgia and history. Renovated in 2002, the beautifully decorated rooms have been refurbished respecting the original character of the building. The rooms facing the main street can be slightly noisy. **www.saxildhus.dk**

RIBE Weis Stue Kr Kr

Torvet 2, 6760 ***Tel*** *75 42 07 00* ***Fax*** *75 41 17 95* ***Rooms*** *8* ***Map*** *B5*

An atmospheric inn-style hotel situated in the heart of Ribe not far from the town's famous 12th-century cathedral. The hotel building is half-timbered and dates back to the year 1600. The rooms are small and cosy with shared bathroom facilities. **www.weis-stue.dk**

RIBE Dagmar Kr Kr Kr

Torvet 1, 6760 ***Tel*** *75 42 00 33* ***Fax*** *75 42 36 52* ***Rooms*** *50* ***Map*** *B5*

Denmark's oldest hotel, built in 1581, the Dagmar is in a charming half-timbered building which has been gently restored over the years. Low ceilings, windows with deep sills and sloping floors take you back in time. The individually decorated rooms are stylish with canopy beds. Internet access in the lobby. **www.hoteldagmar.dk**

RINGKØBING Fjordgården Kr

Vesterkær 28, 6950 ***Tel*** *97 32 14 00* ***Fax*** *97 32 47 60* ***Rooms*** *98* ***Map*** *B4*

A modern hotel located a short walk from the town centre, where each evening Ringkøbing's night-watchman sings in the streets. The rooms are a good size with pleasant sea and country views. Free wireless internet access and indoor swimming pool available. **www.hotelfjordgaarden.dk**

RØMØ Havneby Kro Kr Kr

Skansen 3, 6792 ***Tel*** *74 75 75 35* ***Rooms*** *9* ***Map*** *B5*

This charming inn is situated close to the harbour, and the rooms offer views over the Wadden Sea. However, if you want to swim, the beach is only a short bike or car ride away. For those without a car, there are buses to the mainland. An ideal place to escape to. **www.havneby-kro.dk**

SABRO Hotel Nilles Kro Kr Kr

Hadstenvej 209, 8471 ***Tel*** *86 94 88 99* ***Fax*** *86 94 80 89* ***Rooms*** *25* ***Map*** *D3*

Built in 1954, this charming little hotel is surrounded by magnificent countryside. Considered one of the most beautiful inns in this part of Jutland, the Nilles Kro has a five-star restaurant that is well known for its delectable cuisine. Close to Moesgård Museum, Tivoli Friheden, golf courses and beaches. **www.nilleskro.dk**

SILKEBORG Radisson Blu Kr Kr Kr

Papirfabrikken 12, 8600 ***Tel*** *88 82 22 22* ***Fax*** *88 82 22 23* ***Rooms*** *88* ***Map*** *C4*

Silkeborg's old paper mill was thoroughly refurbished and remodelled a few years back into this hotel. Located in the centre of town, near the harbour and the Aqua Aquarium, it overlooks the Remstrup River. The interior is bright and modern and all the expected facilities are available. **www.radissonsas.com**

SILKEBORG Dania ⓀⓀⓀⓀ

Torvet 5, 8600 ***Tel*** *86 82 01 11* ***Fax*** *86 80 20 04* ***Rooms*** *49* ***Map*** *C4*

Located in the town square and built in 1848, the Dania provides panoramic views of the lake. The rooms are uncluttered with modern decor and many of them have been named after personalities who have stayed at the hotel: Hans Christian Andersen stayed for several years! **www.hoteldania.dk**

SKANDERBORG Skanderborghus ⓀⓀⓀ

Dyrehaven 3, 8660 ***Tel*** *86 52 09 55* ***Fax*** *86 52 18 01* ***Rooms*** *46* ***Map*** *C4*

Situated in the centre of Skanderborg Dyrehave, this lakeside hotel is surrounded by some breathtaking natural scenery, visible from all the hotel's rooms. The interiors are bright and airy. It is possible to charter a boat, the "Dagmar", that passes just outside the hotel from May to September. **www.hotelskanderborghus.dk**

SØNDERBORG Scandic Hotel ⓀⓀ

Ellegårdvej 27, 6400 ***Tel*** *74 42 26 00* ***Fax*** *74 42 76 00* ***Rooms*** *102* ***Map*** *C6*

This modern hotel is conveniently situated 3 km (2 miles) from the centre of town. The hotel is designed with high ceilings and bright airy rooms. It is close to attractions such as Sønderborg castle and the Sommerland Syd amusement park. It offers a playroom for children and free wireless internet access. **www.scandichotels.dk**

SØNDERBORG Comwell Sønderborg ⓀⓀⓀ

Rosengade 2, 6400 ***Tel*** *74 42 19 00* ***Rooms*** *95* ***Map*** *C6*

This splendid hotel is not far from the picturesque town centre of Sonderborg, just across from the castle and very close to the beach. The rooms are bright and comfortable and the staff are renowned for their personable professional service. The facilites include internet access and an indoor swimming pool. **www.comwell.dk**

TØNDER Schackenborg Slotskro ⓀⓀⓀ

Slotsgaden 42, Møgeltønder, 6270 ***Tel*** *74 73 83 83* ***Fax*** *74 73 83 11* ***Rooms*** *25* ***Map*** *B6*

An elegant hotel with an enchanting atmosphere, the Slotskro stands close to the ducal palace of Schackenborg where Prince Joachim has lived since 1995. Many of the hotel rooms were decorated under the supervision of his former wife, the Countess of Frederiksborg, Alexandra Manley. Wireless internet is available. **www.slotskro.dk**

VEJLE Park ⓀⓀ

Orla Lehmannsgade 5, 7100 ***Tel*** *75 82 24 66* ***Fax*** *75 72 05 39* ***Rooms*** *32* ***Map*** *C4*

Vejle's oldest hotel proudly occupies a corner plot right in the town centre. This small and friendly establishment has comfortable and bright rooms with a relaxed atmosphere. It is well maintained and the staff have gained a reputation for their excellent and personal service. Wireless internet is available. **www.park-hotel.dk**

VEJLE Hotel Australia ⓀⓀⓀ

Dæmningen 6, 7100 ***Tel*** *76 40 60 00* ***Fax*** *76 40 60 01* ***Rooms*** *102* ***Map*** *C4*

Located in the heart of Vejle with panoramic views of the harbour and the town, this modern high-rise is the tallest building in the area. The rooms are spacious and clean. The service is efficient and the hotel is conveniently placed close to all the shops and restaurants. **www.hotelvejle.dk**

ÅRHUS Cab Inn Århus Ⓚ

Kannikegade 14, 8000 ***Tel*** *86 75 70 00* ***Fax*** *86 75 71 00* ***Rooms*** *192* ***Map*** *D4*

Opened in 2001 and conveniently located right in the heart of Århus, the Cab Inn has been designed with the budget-conscious traveller in mind. The petite rooms are modelled on ship cabins and the hotel's facilities are all shared. There is a café located on the premises. **www.cabinn.dk**

ÅRHUS Guldsmeden ⓀⓀ

Guldsmedgade 40, 8000 ***Tel*** *86 13 45 50* ***Fax*** *86 13 76 76* ***Rooms*** *27* ***Map*** *D4*

This small hotel is discreetly positioned amongst the winding lanes close to the canal. It offers a warm and homely atmosphere. The rooms vary in size but are all simply decorated with references from around the world and rustic furniture. All the art is by Knud Weinert. Free wireless internet available. **www.hotelguldsmeden.dk**

ÅRHUS Best Western Hotel Ritz ⓀⓀⓀ

Banegårdspladsen 12, 8000 ***Tel*** *86 13 44 44* ***Fax*** *86 13 45 87* ***Rooms*** *67* ***Map*** *D4*

Built in 1932 near to the town's Musikhuset (concert hall), theatres and restaurants, Best Western's Ritz has been redecorated and carefully refurbished in keeping with the original architecture. The hotel restaurant is one of the best in town. Access to the internet is available in the lobby. **www.hotelritz.dk**

ÅRHUS Helnan Marselis Hotel ⓀⓀⓀ

Strandvejen 25, 8000 ***Tel*** *86 14 44 11* ***Fax*** *86 14 44 20* ***Rooms*** *100* ***Map*** *D4*

Designed by the famous architects Friis & Molkte in 1967, this hotel has been cleverly designed to offer a view of Århus Bay from every room. Some distance from the town centre, the Marselis is next to the beach with several golf courses nearby. The interiors display the simple lines of Scandinavian design. **www.marselis.dk**

ÅRHUS Hotel Royal ⓀⓀⓀⓀ

Store Torv 4, 8000 ***Tel*** *86 12 00 11* ***Fax*** *86 76 04 04* ***Rooms*** *69* ***Map*** *D4*

Situated in the heart of Århus, this famous hotel is next to the cathedral in the Latin Quarter. Built in 1838, it has been sensitively restored. The walls are decorated with fascinating art pieces. Past guests have included such names as Madonna, Sting and David Beckham. A casino is on site. **www.hotelroyal.dk**

NORTHERN JUTLAND

DRONNINGLUND Dronninglund

(Kr)(Kr)

Slotsgade 78, 9330 ***Tel*** *98 84 15 33* ***Fax*** *98 84 40 50* ***Rooms*** *72* ***Map*** *D2*

Located amid the picturesque countryside of Ostvendsyssel, close to Dronninglund Castle, this simple provincial hotel offers comfortable, bright surroundings and a family-friendly atmosphere. White sandy beaches are a short car or bike ride away. The hotel also has its own indoor swimming pool. **www.dronninglundhotel.dk**

FARSØ Himmerland Golf & Country Club

(Kr)(Kr)

Centervej 1, Gatten, 9640 ***Tel*** *96 49 61 00* ***Fax*** *98 66 14 56* ***Rooms*** *60* ***Map*** *C2*

A golfer's paradise: this hotel has two international golf courses as well as a three-par course on site. Surrounded by a lovely wooded area and overlooking a lake, it has modern rooms, all with internet access. For the non-golfer there are bowling facilities, indoor/outdoor swimming pools and a wellness centre. **www.himmerlandgolf.dk**

FARUP Purhus Kro

(Kr)(Kr)

Præstevejen 6, 8990 ***Tel*** *86 45 28 55* ***Fax*** *86 45 22 08* ***Rooms*** *21* ***Map*** *C3*

A cosy and family-friendly hotel built in 1752, the Purhus Kro has modern and comfortable rooms. There is a lake and lovely gardens in the grounds as well as a playground for children. Disabled facilities are available and there is free internet access in all rooms. **www.purhus-kro.dk**

FREDERIKSHAVN Lisboa

(Kr)(Kr)

Søndergade 248, 9900 ***Tel*** *98 42 21 33* ***Fax*** *98 43 80 11* ***Rooms*** *32* ***Map*** *D1*

This comfortable family hotel was built in 1958 and offers all the facilities you might expect. It is situated between beautiful woodlands and sandy beaches, on the outskirts of Frederikshavn, and has its own playground for children. A good stopping off point for those on their way to Norway or Sweden. **www.lisboa.dk**

FREDERIKSHAVN Turisthotellet

(Kr)(Kr)

Margrethevej 5–7, 9900 ***Tel*** *98 42 90 55* ***Fax*** *98 42 90 91* ***Rooms*** *18* ***Map*** *D1*

Simple and cosily furnished, this hotel is close to Frederikshavn's famous Palm Beach and local golf courses. Some of the rooms have access to a garden. All of them have wireless internet. The restaurant is only available for breakfast. **www.turisthotellet.dk**

FREDERIKSHAVN Radisson Blu Jutlandia

(Kr)(Kr)(Kr)

Havnepladsen 1, 9900 ***Tel*** *98 42 42 00* ***Fax*** *98 42 38 72* ***Rooms*** *95* ***Map*** *D1*

An elegant hotel, centrally located and overlooking the harbour, the Jutlandia is occasionally used by the Danish royal family. The rooms feature simple modern decor and the service is impeccable. The Jutlandia is close to both shops and ferries. Internet available in the lobby. Superb restaurant. **www.hotel-jutlandia.dk**

FREDERIKSHAVN Scandic Stena Line Hotel Frederikshavn

(Kr)(Kr)(Kr)

Tordenskjoldsgade 14, 9900 ***Tel*** *98 43 32 33* ***Fax*** *98 43 33 11* ***Rooms*** *213* ***Map*** *D1*

Conveniently situated in the middle of town, this well-equipped hotel offers comfortable rooms all with wireless internet access. Downstairs there is a large heated swimming pool. The hotel is close to local attractions such as Bangsbro Museum and the Frederikshavn Kirke (church). **www.scandic-hotels.com**

HANSTHOLM Hotel Hanstholm

(Kr)(Kr)

Chr. Hansensvej 2, 7730 ***Tel*** *97 96 10 44* ***Fax*** *97 96 25 84* ***Rooms*** *76* ***Map*** *B2*

Surrounded by sand, water, as well as lovely woods, the Hanstholm is in a small paradise all of its own. The rooms are bright and simply decorated, most of them with a balcony or terrace attached. It is ideal for families and has its own playground and indoor swimming pool. **www.hotelhanstholm.dk**

HIRTSHALS Skaga

(Kr)(Kr)

Willemoesvej 1, 9850 ***Tel*** *98 94 55 00* ***Fax*** *98 94 55 55* ***Rooms*** *108* ***Map*** *C1*

The Skaga is situated along the E39 motorway, close to the Color Lines ferry terminal (for ships to Norway). Mainly for the business traveller, facilities include a conference centre, indoor pool, solarium, sauna, bar and nightclub. Families are well-placed for the North Sea Centre, bowling alley, woodland and excellent beaches. **www.skagahotel.dk**

HOLSTEBRO Best Western Hotel Schaumburg

(Kr)(Kr)(Kr)

Nørregade 26, 7500 ***Tel*** *97 42 31 11* ***Fax*** *97 42 72 82* ***Rooms*** *57* ***Map*** *B3*

Now thoroughly modernised, the Schaumburg has a copy of Copenhagen's Little Mermaid statue in the front hall. It offers all the facilities you would expect from Best Western, and some of the rooms have views of the town's old city hall. The price includes free admission to the nearby Holstebro Badeland waterpark. **www.hotel-schaumburg.dk**

HOLSTEBRO Royal Holstebro

(Kr)(Kr)(Kr)

Den Røde Plads 10, 7500 ***Tel*** *97 40 23 33* ***Rooms*** *40* ***Map*** *B3*

Located in the heart of the town, this business hotel is topped by a striking glass pyramid. The well-equipped rooms have wireless internet and overlook the Musikteater (concert hall). For golf enthusiasts, the beautiful Holstebro Golfklub course is nearby. A complimentary breakfast is available in the hotel's Cafe Royal. **www.hotel-royal.dk**

Key to Price Guide *see p244* **Key to Symbols** *see back cover flap*

NYKØBING Pakhuset Hotel & Restaurant ®®

Havnen 1, 7900 **Tel** *97 72 33 00* **Fax** *97 72 52 33* **Rooms** *18* **Map** *B2*

This pleasant hotel is located in an old warehouse on the harbour front and combines original 19th-century features with modern Danish design. In summer, the harbour is abuzz with activity and the hotel is a popular place to stay, so do reserve in good time. American Express is not accepted. **www.phr.dk**

RANDERS Scandic Hotel Kongens Ege ®®

Gl. Hadsundvej 2, 8900 **Tel** *86 43 03 00* **Fax** *86 43 22 73* **Rooms** *130* **Map** *D3*

High on a hilltop overlooking the town, the Kongens Ege offers modern comfortable rooms with stunning views of the city centre, Randers Fjord and the surrounding park. It is only a five minute drive from the city centre. All rooms have free wireless internet access. **www.scandic-hotels.com/KongensEge**

RANDERS Randers ®®®

Torvegade 11, 8900 **Tel** *86 42 34 22* **Fax** *86 40 15 86* **Rooms** *79* **Map** *D3*

With the reputation of being one of the town's best (and oldest) hotels, the Randers has spacious and stylish rooms with all the amenities you would expect. It is close to the railway station and within short walking distance of a fitness centre. **www.hotel-randers.dk**

SKAGEN Color Hotel Skagen ®®®

Gl. Landevej 39, 9990 **Tel** *98 44 22 33* **Fax** *98 44 21 34* **Rooms** *152* **Map** *D1*

This pleasant, rather formal hotel is located in quiet surroundings between old Skagen and the maritime centre. The rooms are spacious with large windows which make the most of Skagen's famous natural light. On site amenities include an outdoor swimming pool. Close to Den Tilsandede Kirke (The Sand-buried Church). **www.skagenhotel.dk**

SKAGEN Plesner ®®®®

Holstvej 8, 9990 **Tel** *98 44 68 44* **Fax** *98 44 36 86* **Rooms** *16* **Map** *D1*

With unpolished wooden floor boards, muted decor, and the famously comfortable Hästens beds in all rooms, the Plesner makes for a real haven of luxurious peace in this remote outpost of the country. Close to the beach and the countryside, yet plumb in the centre of town. Fabulous light and airy restaurant, too. **www.hotelplesner.dk**

SKAGEN Ruths Hotel ®®®®

Hans Ruths Vej 1, 9990 **Tel** *98 44 11 24* **Fax** *98 45 08 75* **Rooms** *26* **Map** *D1*

This atmospheric establishment is in the old part of Skagen and close to the beach. Built in the late 19th century, it has been completely renovated and the rooms are spacious and light, all with internet access. There is an indoor pool. The hotel's gourmet restaurant, run by head chef Michel Michaud, is worth visiting. **www.ruths-hotel.dk**

SKIVE Best Western Hotel Gl. Skivehus ®®

Søndre Boulevard 1, 7800 **Tel** *97 52 11 44* **Fax** *97 52 81 68* **Rooms** *56* **Map** *C3*

Located in the heart of Skive, this modern family-run hotel is in a grand former manor house overlooking the river. The rooms are clean, simple and uncluttered. Close to the park, beach and golf courses. The hotel restaurant is recommended. **www.skivehus.dk**

SKØRPING Comwell Rebild Bakker ®®

Rebildvej 36, 9520 **Tel** *98 39 12 22* **Fax** *98 39 24 55* **Rooms** *151* **Map** *C2*

This modern low-rise hotel and conference centre is nestled in between the hills and unspoiled nature at the edge of the Rebild Bakker National Park. All the rooms are well equipped and have stunning views of the countryside. Local attractions include the limestone caves at Thingbæk and a golf course. **www.comwell.dk**

SÆBY Stiholt ®

Trafikcenter Sæby Syd 1, 9300 **Tel** *96 89 66 69* **Fax** *96 89 66 67* **Rooms** *10* **Map** *D1*

Although situated next to a petrol station, this modest and inexpensive hotel is an excellent stopping-off place for travellers on their way to Skagen. All the rooms are light and airy and there is a tourist office within the hotel. It is also only a short drive to the beach. **www.tcss.dk**

SÆBY Hotel Viking ®®

Frederikshavnsvej 70-72, 9300 **Tel** *98 46 17 00* **Fax** *98 46 24 93* **Rooms** *84* **Map** *D1*

A comfortable family-friendly hotel, located in the heart of the town and a short stroll from a sandy beach. The rooms are bright with all the usual modern amenities. The Viking also has a courtyard garden, with a playground for children, and is known for its good food and wellness centre. Nearby is the "Old Water Mill". **www.hotelviking.dk**

VIBORG Best Western Palads ®®®

Sct. Mathiasgade 5, 8800 **Tel** *86 62 37 00* **Fax** *86 62 40 46* **Rooms** *100* **Map** *C3*

Centrally located and in one of the town's most beautiful buildings, this grand hotel combines tradition with comfort. Hotel guests have free access to Viborg Vandland, an indoor water complex with fitness facilities, as well as an internet café. **www.hotelpalads.dk**

AALBORG Helnan Phønix Hotel ®®

Vesterbro 77, 9000 **Tel** *98 12 00 11* **Fax** *98 10 10 20* **Rooms** *210* **Map** *D2*

A major feature of the town, this historic hotel was built in 1783 as a palace to Brigadier William Von Halling and converted into a hotel just over 100 years later. Located in the heart of Aalborg, the hotel provides classic hospitality in an elegant setting. **www.helnan.dk**

AALBORG Hotel Aalborg Sømandshjem Kr Kr

Østerbro 27, 9000 ***Tel*** *98 12 19 00* ***Fax*** *98 11 76 97* ***Rooms*** *54* ***Map*** *D2*

This is a family-friendly economy hotel located just opposite the amusement park "Karolinelund," and only a five minute walk to the main shopping streets. The rooms are comfortable and simply decorated, and the hotel restaurant serves good Danish food at moderate prices. Parking available. **www.hotel-aalborg.com**

AALBORG Hotel Hvide Hus Kr Kr

Vesterbro 2, 9000 ***Tel*** *98 13 84 00* ***Fax*** *98 13 51 22* ***Rooms*** *198* ***Map*** *D2*

This 16-floor hotel sits surrounded by the lovely Kilde Park, in the city centre. The rooms are bright with balconies and large windows, and the staff are efficient and friendly. Modern, sleek design is throughout and facilities include top-notch business facilities and panoramic restaurant. Breakfast included. **www.hotelhvidehus.dk**

AALBORG Park Hotel Aalborg Kr Kr

John F Kennedys Plads 41, 9000 ***Tel*** *98 12 31 33* ***Fax*** *98 13 31 66* ***Rooms*** *81* ***Map*** *D2*

Reportedly one of the oldest hotels in the city, all of the Park's rooms are tastefully decorated in a romantic style. Over the years the hotel has been gently restored and modernized so that today it is a cosy, well equipped establishment with a distinguished atmosphere and focus on personal service. **www.park-hotel-aalborg.dk**

AALBORG Hotel Scandic Kr Kr Kr

Hadsundvej 200, 9220 ***Tel*** *98 15 45 00* ***Fax*** *98 15 55 88* ***Rooms*** *101* ***Map*** *D2*

In a rather unpromising block some 5 km (3 miles) away from the centre of Aalborg, the rooms of the Scandic are light, inviting, and feature wireless internet access. There are well-organised facilities including a children's playroom. **www.scandic-hotels.dk**

AALBORG Radisson Blu Limfjord Kr Kr Kr

Ved Stranden 14, 9000 ***Tel*** *98 16 43 33* ***Fax*** *98 16 17 47* ***Rooms*** *188* ***Map*** *D2*

Located in the heart of Aalborg, the rooms are comfortably furnished and most of them offer fabulous views over the city and Limfjord. The hotel is just opposite the famous café, Jomfru Anne Gade. Casino Aalborg is located at the hotel. Wireless internet access is available. **www.radissonblu.com/hotel-aalborg**

AALBORG Scheelsminde Hotel & Gastronomi Kr Kr Kr

Scheelsmindevej 35, 9100 ***Tel*** *98 18 32 33* ***Fax*** *98 18 33 34* ***Rooms*** *96* ***Map*** *D2*

Built in 1808, this was once one of the most beautiful manor houses in Denmark. Converted into a hotel and then extensively restored, the rooms feature under-floor heating in the bathrooms. It is worth checking out the restaurant with its exceptional wine cellar. There is also an indoor swimming pool, sauna and spa. **www.scheelsminde.dk**

BORNHOLM

ALLINGE Danchels Hus Kr

Havnegade 38, 3770 ***Tel*** *56 48 22 18* ***Fax*** *56 48 22 18* ***Rooms*** *4*

The individual rooms at this small Swedish-run guesthouse have stylish furniture and chintzy-decorations: room No.2 is particularly atmospheric. There is also an apartment available by the week. Set in its own grounds, you can take a pleasant stroll from the door of your room right down to the water. **www.danchelshus.dk**

ALLINGE Strandhotel Abildgaard Kr

Tejnvej 100, 3770 ***Tel*** *56 48 09 55* ***Fax*** *56 48 08 35* ***Rooms*** *83*

This modern complex is popular with group tours. The rooms are sizable, though somewhat bland, and they all have small kitchens and coffee-makers, as well as TV and phone. There is a good-sized pool, but you are also only minutes from a gorgeous beach on Bornholm's northern shore. **www.hotel-abildgaard.dk**

ALLINGE Byskrivergården Hotel Garni Kr Kr

Løsebækgade 3, 3770 ***Tel*** *56 48 08 86* ***Fax*** *56 48 18 86* ***Rooms*** *20*

Set in a converted 18th-century farmhouse on the Baltic, this is one of the most cherished overnight spots on this part of the island. The cosy rooms are in the converted stables. The dining room/lounge looks out from the top floor to the water – a perfect place to enjoy the complimentary breakfasts. Small beach nearby. **www.byskrivergaarden.dk**

ALLINGE Friheden Kr Kr

Tejnvej 80, 3770 ***Tel*** *56 48 04 25* ***Fax*** *56 48 16 65* ***Rooms*** *44*

Set in the tiny coastal hamlet of Sandkås, this upmarket hotel features a wellness and health centre with spa treatments, a sauna and heated pool. A dozen of the rooms have views right out to the water, and some have small terraces to catch the morning sun. Bicycles for hire and complimentary breakfast. **www.hotelfriheden.dk**

ALLINGE Hotel Romantik Kr Kr

Strandvejen 68, 3770 ***Tel*** *56 48 03 44* ***Fax*** *56 48 06 44* ***Rooms*** *50*

In the 19th century this was Bornholm' best-known hotel and it is still popular today. Many of the neat rooms have sea views from their small-ish windows. All have telephone and satellite TV. The Romantik also offers some larger apartment-style rooms with jacuzzis. Complimentary breakfast. **www.hotel-romantik.dk**

Key to Price Guide *see p244* **Key to Symbols** *see back cover flap*

CHRISTIANSØ Christiansø Gæstgiveri Ⓚ

Christiansø, 3760 ***Tel*** *56 46 20 15* ***Fax*** *56 46 20 86* ***Rooms*** *6*

Set on the idyllic tiny island of Christansø, with one boat a day to Bornholm, the rooms in this 18th-century ex-garrison all have bathrooms, large beds, creaky floorboards, and views to the harbour. The owner is an affable irreverent Dane who ensures only scrumptious meals are served in the restaurant. **www.christiansoekro.dk**

DUEODDE Dueodde Vandrehjem Ⓚ

Skrokkegårdsvejen 17, 3730 ***Tel*** *56 48 81 19* ***Fax*** *56 48 81 12* ***Rooms*** *36*

Dueodde Vandrehjem is located in a beautiful forest area right by the beach. In high season, four- to eight-person bedrooms are available, but camping is also possible. The hostel features an indoor swimming pool and spa area, and plenty of activities like table tennis and ball games. Open May–Sep. **www.dueodde.dk**

DUEODDE Dueodde Badehotel ⓀⓀⓀ

Sirenevej 2, 3730 ***Tel*** *56 48 86 49* ***Fax*** *56 48 89 59* ***Rooms*** *52*

This modern, two-storey beach hotel has sleek rooms with brushed oak flooring and balconies that look onto a garden. There are also several larger apartment-style suites. The facilities include a sauna and tennis courts. They generally rent by the week, but it is possible to get one- or two-night stays too. **www.dueodde-badehotel.dk**

GUDHJEM Gadegård Ⓚ

Gudhjemvej 52, 3760 ***Tel*** *56 48 52 85* ***Rooms*** *1*

Several kilometres south of Gudhjem, the Hansens, a gregarious couple, rent out a section of their enchanting farmhouse to summer boarders. The two-floor apartment is done out in an elegant, countrified style. They rent the room most often for week-long stays, though shorter stays are possible. **www.pfunch.dk**

GUDHJEM Gudhjem Vandrerhjem Ⓚ

Løkkegade 7, 3760 ***Tel*** *56 48 50 35* ***Fax*** *56 48 56 35* ***Rooms*** *37*

This harbourside hostel is in a weathered old building that was once the town's general store. The rooms have exposed wood beam ceilings and half-timbered walls, and there are common toilets and kitchen facilities. Cycle hire also available. **www.danhostel-gudhjem.dk**

GUDHJEM Jantzen's Hotel ⓀⓀ

Brøddegade 33, 3760 ***Tel*** *56 48 50 17* ***Rooms*** *16*

Founded in the 1870's, this hotel is one of the oldest on Bornholm. Many of the rooms have small, cast iron balconies that look out to the water. In summer you can enjoy a sumptuous breakfast buffet outside in the attractive back courtyard. The perfect romantic hide-away. **www.jantzenshotel.dk**

GUDHJEM Melsted Badehotel ⓀⓀⓀ

Melstedvej 27, 3760 ***Tel*** *56 48 51 00* ***Fax*** *56 48 55 84* ***Rooms*** *18*

This hotel consists of several small buildings set on a sprawling lawn a stone's throw from the Baltic. The dainty rooms are all done in bright whites with very comfortable Swedish beds. TVs and phones are nowhere to be seen ensuring blissful peace. **www.melsted-badehotel.dk**

NEXØ Strand Hotel Balka Søbad Ⓚ

Vestre Strandvej 25, 3730 ***Tel*** *56 49 22 25* ***Fax*** *56 49 49 48* ***Rooms*** *106*

One of the few hotels on Bornholm with its own bathing beach (and a pool to boot), the modern rooms here come with balconies and feature extra fold-out beds, making them great for families. The Balka Søbad is also placed right by several walking and cycling paths that lead to Nexø. Cycle hire is available. **www.hotel-balkasoebad.dk**

NEXØ Hotel Balka Strand ⓀⓀ

Boulevarden 9A, 3730 ***Tel*** *56 49 49 49* ***Fax*** *56 49 49 48* ***Rooms*** *95*

A large, four-star hotel with modern interiors and a good restaurant, the Balka Strand is very family friendly. It is only a short walk from a nature reserve and beautiful bathing beaches (though the hotel has its own outdoor pool and sauna). **www.hotelbalkastrand.dk**

RØNNE BB-Hotel Rønne Ⓚ

Store Torv 17, 1, 3700 ***Tel*** *70 22 55 30* ***Rooms*** *21*

This bed and breakfast offers fairly priced rooms right on the main square in Rønne, close to restaurants, shops and public transport to the entire island of Bornholm. The rooms are small but well designed, and the kitchen offers free access to coffee and tea 24 hours a day. Parking is available, and there is a golf course nearby. **www.bbhotels.dk**

RØNNE Danhostel Rønne Ⓚ

Arsenalvej 12, 3700 ***Tel*** *56 95 13 40* ***Fax*** *56 95 01 32* ***Rooms*** *29*

Danhostel Rønne is within walking distance of the ferry and only a stone's throw away from the beach and the forest. It is furnished in a homely style and offers different activities – both indoors and outdoors – like table tennis and mini golf. Note that they accept only the Danish credit card Dankort. **www.danhostel-roenne.dk**

RØNNE Hotel Skovly Ⓚ

Nyker Strandvej 40, 3700 ***Tel*** *56 95 07 84* ***Fax*** *56 95 48 23* ***Rooms*** *31*

Lying next to a babbling brook and within a protected forest several kilometres north of Rønne, this is one of the town's hidden gems. Each of the rustic, apartment-style rooms has its own terrace. There is a beach nearby where you can swim and fish. Breakfast is included. **www.hotel-skovly.dk**

RØNNE Griffen

Ndr Kystvej 34, 3700 ***Tel*** *56 90 44 45* ***Fax*** *56 90 44 43* ***Rooms*** *142*

This lovely modern hotel is on the Baltic shoreline and offers large rooms with sofas, desks, and balconies. Half of the rooms have a view to the sea; the other half look onto a cobblestone street of old Rønne. All have wireless internet. The Griffen also has a restaurant, an indoor pool and spa, and a small private beach. **www.hotelgriffen.dk**

RØNNE Radisson Blu Fredensborg

Strandvejen 116, 3700 ***Tel*** *56 90 44 44* ***Fax*** *56 90 44 43* ***Rooms*** *72*

From the outside, this modern establishment does not promise much, but inside everything is business class. Rooms are meticulously decorated in modern Scandinavian style; all have wireless internet and small balconies or terraces with views out to the Baltic. There is also a private beach. Complimentary breakfast. **www.ronne.radissonsas.com**

SANDVIG Hotel Hammersø

Hammershusvej 86, 3770 ***Tel*** *56 48 03 64* ***Fax*** *56 48 10 90* ***Rooms*** *40*

Located on the edge of the tranquil Hammersø (Denmark's only mountain lake), this business-style hotel has a heated outdoor swimming pool and a sunny terrace with table tennis tables. Several of the rooms have small balconies with pretty views. **www.hotel-hammersoe.dk**

SANDVIG Hotel Pepita

Langebjergvej 1, 3770 ***Tel*** *56 48 04 51* ***Fax*** *56 48 18 51* ***Rooms*** *36*

A yellow, half-timbered farmhouse dating from the 16th century houses the Pepita, one of Sandvig's more modern hotels. Some of the rooms overlook the terrace, others the sea, and there is a very popular *á la carte* restaurant on-site as well. **www.pepita.dk**

SVANEKE Hotel Østersøen

Havnebryggen 5, 3740 ***Tel*** *56 49 60 20* ***Fax*** *56 49 72 79* ***Rooms*** *22*

Open year-round, the individual apartment-style accommodation here opens onto a gorgeous courtyard with a heated pool. Rooms are full of character with exposed beams. Between June and August the apartments can only be rented on a weekly basis. **www.oestersoen.dk**

SVANEKE Siemsens Gård

Havnebryggen 9, 3740 ***Tel*** *56 49 61 49* ***Fax*** *56 49 61 03* ***Rooms*** *49*

The Siemsens Gård has Ikea-styled rooms set within an old merchant's house dating from the 17th century. Most of the rooms have cooking facilities, views to the sea (or, alternatively, to a garden), and private access to the terrace and lawns. The hotel's restaurant is a great place to try out the local *smørrebrød*. **www.siemsens.dk**

ÅKIRKEBY Danhostel Boderne

Bodernevej 28, 3720 ***Tel*** *56 97 49 50* ***Fax*** *56 97 49 48* ***Rooms*** *20*

A short drive from Åkirkeby, this family-friendly hostel is set in a large rural farmhouse lying among the conifers on Bornholm's southern coast. Most rooms are en-suite. The hostel offers bicycles for hire, internet access, a television room and childrens' playground. Close to some sandy beaches. **www.rosengaarden.dk**

GREENLAND

ILULISSAT Hotel Icefiord

Box 458, 3952 Ilulissat ***Tel*** *94 44 80* ***Fax*** *94 40 95* ***Rooms*** *31*

Delightful rooms abound at this wonderful hotel in an old wooden building. Several rooms, including two deluxe suites, have stunning sea views, and there is a lounge with a fireplace and a terrace from which you can watch the icebergs in Disko Bay. Price includes transport to the airport. Wireless internet in the rooms. **www.hotelicefiord.gl**

KANGERLUSSUAQ Hotel Igloo Village

3910 Kangerlussuaq ***Tel*** *84 11 80* ***Fax*** *84 12 84* ***Rooms*** *5*

Everything in this five-roomed hotel, basically a large igloo, is made entirely out of ice! Ice tunnels lead to individual igloos, where double beds with extra-warm sleeping bags are covered with reindeer skins. In winter, this unusual establishment also has an on-site ice bar where the menu and the glasses themselves are made out of ice.

KANGERLUSSUAQ Hotel Kangerlussuaq

P.O. Box 1006, 3910 Kangerlussuaq ***Tel*** *84 11 80* ***Fax*** *84 12 84* ***Rooms*** *70*

Conveniently located at the town's airport, this modern facility is a great base for exploring the region, though it tends to fill up with business groups and tours. Attached to the hotel is a smaller annex with cheaper rooms available (shared bathrooms). The nearby fitness centre has a pool and sauna. **www.airporthotels.gl**

NUUK Bed and Breakfast

Hans Egedesvej 29, 3900 Nuuk ***Tel*** *32 27 00* ***Fax*** *32 27 10* ***Rooms*** *3*

Not one location but many are available through the Nuuk tourist office which organizes stays (and meals) with local families at very affordable prices. While comfort may vary, you are nearly always guaranteed a memorable time, since as everyone knows, the best way to get to know Greenland is from its people. **www.nuuk-tourism.gl**

Key to Price Guide *see p244* **Key to Symbols** *see back cover flap*

NUUK Sømandshjemmet ⓀⓀⓀ

Marinevej 3, 3900 Nuuk ***Tel*** *32 10 29* ***Fax*** *32 21 04* ***Rooms*** *41*

Made up of several red wooden buildings at the foot of an Alpine mountain, the Sømandshjemmet offers modern, bright, very clean rooms with TV and phone. Be sure to ask for a room with a view, as they can be spectacular. The cafeteria-restaurant produces a good range of warming stews and desserts. **www.soemandshjem.gl**

NUUK Hotel Hans Egede ⓀⓀⓀⓀ

Aqqusinersuaq 1–5, 3900 Nuuk ***Tel*** *32 42 22* ***Fax*** *32 44 87* ***Rooms*** *140*

This luxurious four-star establishment is right in the centre of Nuuk. The rooms are modern and somewhat soulless, but the service is superb. The hotel's gourmet restaurant and bar are on the top floor, and both offer unequalled views to the harbour and icebergs further out. Popular with large conference groups. **www.hhe.gl**

QAANAAQ Hotel Qaanaaq ⓀⓀ

Box 88, 3971 Qaanaaq ***Tel*** *97 12 34* ***Rooms*** *5*

A tiny, red wooden building with a handful of small rooms, the Qaanaaq is the only hotel in town. It does away with "unnecessary" facilities such as television, instead offering a cheery sitting room with local art on the walls, a washing machine and a quaint restaurant. Internet access is available. **www.turistqaanaaq.gl/hotel.htm**

UUMMANNAQ Hotel Uummannaq ⓀⓀⓀ

Trollep Aqqutaa B, 3961 Uummannaq ***Tel*** *95 15 18* ***Fax*** *95 12 62* ***Rooms*** *40*

This modern hotel, attractively situated with panoramic views across the ice fjord, has comfortable rooms with all mod cons, including TV and phone. The hotel's restaurant looks out onto the world's only year-round ice golf course. There are also cheaper dormitory-style beds in the annex. **www.icecaphotels.gl**

THE FAROE ISLANDS

MYKINES Kristianshus Ⓚ

Mykines, 388 ***Tel*** *31 29 85* ***Fax*** *32 19 85* ***Rooms*** *12*

A colourful and quaint guesthouse run by a jovial local woman who also runs many nature expeditions out to the surrounding areas. The dozen rooms are furnished in a homely fashion, with basic amenities. There is also a small cafeteria: try the tasty fried puffin if it is available. **www.mykines.dk**

STREYMOY, VESTMANNA B&B Krákureiðrð Ⓚ

Niðari vegur 34, 350 ***Tel*** *42 47 47* ***Rooms*** *6*

This quaint old guesthouse consists of six small, simply furnished rooms presided over by a friendly local couple. The toilets are shared between the rooms and use of the kitchen is free, though there is also a well-liked restaurant nearby. Internet connection is available. **sf.egilsness@kallnet.fo**

SUDUROY, TVØROYRI Gistingarhúsið undir Heygnum Ⓚ

Tvøroyri, 800 ***Tel*** *37 20 46* ***Fax*** *37 24 46* ***Rooms*** *9*

An excellent modern guesthouse set at the tip of the bay, with tables and chairs placed out front for taking in the sun (when it is shining). The rooms are clean and bright, and the comfortable common room has satellite TV and stereo. This hotel tends to get quite busy with groups of travellers, so book well in advance. **www.guest-house.dk**

TÓRSHAVN Bláýpi Guesthouse Ⓚ

Dr. Jakobsensgøta 14–16, 100 ***Tel*** *50 06 00* ***Fax*** *31 94 51* ***Rooms*** *19*

This guesthouse is close to the centre of town. The pristine rooms have views onto the street, and there are three dormitory-style rooms available for those travelling on a budget. There is a small kitchen available to guests, though breakfast is included in the price during the summer. Internet access is available. **www.bladypi.fo**

TÓRSHAVN Hotel Streym ⓀⓀ

Yviri vi ð Strond 19, 100 ***Tel*** *35 55 00* ***Fax*** *35 55 01* ***Rooms*** *14*

This small place has bright rooms with comfortable beds, heated floors, satellite TV and internet access; the double rooms also have views out to the sea. The lobby is decidedly modernist, with funky seating and polished matte wood floors. Friendly reception and complimentary breakfast. **www.hotelstreym.com**

TÓRSHAVN Hotel Føroyar ⓀⓀⓀ

Oyggjarvegur 45, 100 ***Tel*** *31 75 00* ***Fax*** *31 75 01* ***Rooms*** *108*

Set a bit above the town, the rooms and excellent restaurant in this hotel have panoramic views over the colourful rooftops of Tórshavn. Great facilities and room service. The hotel also organises horse riding excursions in the countryside. **www.hotelforoyar.com**

TÓRSHAVN Hotel Tórshavn ⓀⓀⓀ

Tórsgøta 4, 100 ***Tel*** *35 00 00* ***Fax*** *35 00 01* ***Rooms*** *43*

With rooms decked out in warm colours, this establishment is appealing, with flatscreen TVs and wireless internet access in all rooms. Oddly, or thoughtfully, it also has a number of "women's rooms", which boast extra facilities such as bathrobes, hair dryer and footspa. Good weekend rate. **www.hoteltorshavn.fo**

WHERE TO EAT

Visitors to Denmark can be assured of a good meal wherever they go. The choice ranges from city restaurants serving a fusion of Danish and French cuisine, to country inns catering for the lunchtime market with generous servings of *smørrebrød*. In small villages visitors can get a meal in a *kro* (inn), which often also provides overnight accommodation. Cafés are popular in Denmark. As well as pastries and coffee, they often serve main meals and also beer and wine. Many cafés in Copenhagen open late into the night. At the bottom end of the spectrum are the street stalls selling *pølser*, a sausage or hot dog wrapped in a bun and served with onions and sauces. Spicier takeaway alternatives include Greek or Middle Eastern kebabs, which are in plentiful supply in larger towns.

Restaurant sign, Randers

The elegant interior of Era Ora in Copenhagen *(see p272)*

WHEN TO EAT

Danish breakfast tends to be a fairly modest affair. It is usually eaten at home and apart from hotel restaurants there are few places that serve morning meals. As an alternative, many bakeries serve delicious bread, pastries and coffee and provide a table at which to sit.

Frokost (lunch) is the main meal of the day and is consumed between noon and 2pm. It can take various forms, from a light meal to a large banquet of open sandwiches and salads. At lunchtime many restaurants also serve hot main courses such as meatballs, but the helpings are smaller and prices lower than the same meal at dinnertime. *Aftensmad* (dinner) is from 6pm onwards and can be expensive. It is not unusual for prices to rise between lunch and dinner at the same establishment. At weekends many restaurants serve a brunch between 11am and 3pm. Late night snacks are generally limited to hot dogs or kebabs from a stall.

OPENING HOURS

Bakeries open early; in some places it is enough to knock at the bakery door for the baker to open up and sell a loaf even before the shop is open. Fast-food restaurants that serve breakfast open at around 8 or 9am. Restaurants that cater for the lunchtime trade generally open around 10 or 11am. Pubs remain closed until early afternoon, except for the village *kros* (inns), which open earlier, especially during the holiday season. Most restaurants finish serving by 10pm, and restaurants that are not licensed to remain open all night close at 1am. Cafés tend to stay open all day and often late into the night.

MENU

Many restaurants have menus written in English. In addition to the full menu, some offer a specially priced *dagens ret*, or "dish of the day", which is often written up on a board. Some restaurants serve good value fixed-price three-course lunches.

Glass-fronted counter displaying cakes at La Glace *(see p269)*

Visitors at tables in front of a herring smokehouse in Svaneke

CHILDREN

Most restaurants in Denmark offer high chairs and special "child-friendly" menus and activity packs. The best time to take children to a restaurant is late afternoon, when they are far less busy. This time of day is less stressful and generally means that no one need wait long to be served.

Café terraces lining one of Nykøbing F's little streets

PRICES AND TIPS

Prices in restaurants vary enormously. Many cheaper Danish establishments offer set-price all-you-can-eat buffets at lunchtime, as do some of the Thai and Indonesian restaurants. Some hostels also serve good value lunch and evening meals for about 60 Dkr. A three-course meal in a restaurant will cost about 150–200 Dkr not including alcohol. At an upmarket restaurant, diners should be prepared to pay in excess of 800 Dkr.

Soft drinks, beer and *akvavit* (a kind of schnapps) cost about the same in most places. Prices for wines and liqueurs vary and tend to be steep in some of the upmarket restaurants.

Although a service charge and tax are included in the price, it is customary to tip in Danish restaurants (this can be as little as 5 per cent). In less prestigious places it is unusual to leave a tip, unless the service has been particularly good. Even then, simply rounding up the bill is sufficient. Leaving no tip is not considered bad manners in Denmark. Tipping is not practised in fast-food restaurants.

Most restaurants accept credit cards and display the appropriate signs at their entrance. It is unusual for there to be a minimum limit set for credit card payments.

RESERVATIONS

Guests are generally required to book well in advance at the most popular restaurants. Even in quieter restaurants it is advisable to make a booking at the weekend, especially for Sunday brunch, which is often a busy time.

If it is too late to book then the best option is to go somewhere where there are clusters of restaurants. For small groups, there will normally be at least one restaurant that will have a table available after a short wait.

DRESS CODE

The Danes are, for the most part, a relaxed people and do not attach too much importance to etiquette concerning their appearance. Nevertheless, it is customary to smarten up when visiting a restaurant. Dress requirements rise in step with the price of the menu; some upmarket restaurants expect diners to wear evening attire or at least a shirt and tie.

VEGETARIANS

The diet in Denmark is based on meat and fish. However most restaurants have at least a few vegetarian dishes on their menus, as well as green salads. Restaurants that serve only vegetarian food are rare.

DISABLED GUESTS

As elsewhere in Europe, restaurants providing facilities for disabled people cannot be taken for granted. However, many restaurants in Denmark are accessible for disabled people, but it is advisable to check when making a reservation.

A Danish-language database, researched by Danish wheelchair users, lists all the restaurants (as well as attractions and cultural institutions) that are accessible to wheelchairs in Denmark. Local tourist offices can often help with this.

Aalborg's Mortens Kro ***(see p283)*****, with its floor-to-ceiling windows**

The Flavours of Denmark

Denmark's cuisine, like that of other Scandinavian countries, has always been rich in meat and fish dishes. Specialities from the sea include smoked salmon, pickled herring, eel and haddock. Cod is served baked, steamed, fried or dried *(klipfisk)*. The *kolde bord*, a lunchtime buffet, is a good way to try out various local dishes, with a selection of *smørrebrød*, cold cuts and hearty pork dishes. Most Danes have a sweet tooth and *wienerbrød* (Danish pastries) are eaten at any time of day. Berries appear in many desserts, and Danish ice cream is among the best in the world.

Danish pastries

Punnets of ripe strawberries, freshly harvested on Samsø Island

SMØRREBRØD

The classic *smørrebrød* (open sandwich) is as popular as ever with the Danes. Preparation is easy enough: buttered slices of *rugbrød* (unleavened rye bread) are topped with any number of sliced meats, fish or cheeses, such as prawns, smoked eel, ham, lamb and beef. They are then garnished with dill, cucumber, tomato or lemon, a remoulade (mayonnaise-based sauce), caviar, or even a raw egg yolk served in its shell. Among national favourites are *Sol over Gudhjem* and *Bornholmer*, both variations on smoked herring fillets topped with an egg yolk, raw onion, chives and radishes. *Marineredsild* (vinegar-cured herring with onions and capers) and *Stjerneskud* ("shooting star", fried fish fillet with prawns, lemon and dill are also popular). Meat varieties include *dyrlægens natmad*, a towering creation laden with liver pâté, salt beef, flavoured lard, onion rings and dill; *smørrebrødsmad*, rare roast beef with fried onions and grated horseradish; and *rullepølsemad,* slices of pork belly seasoned with herbs, horseradish and watercress.

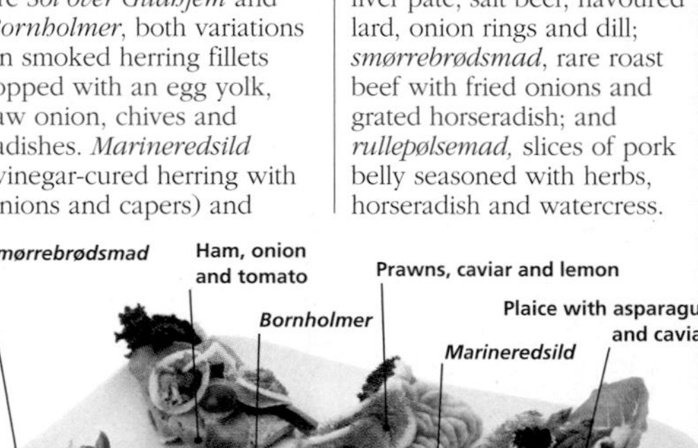

Selection of typical Danish *smørrebrød*

DANISH DISHES AND SPECIALITIES

To this day, Danish cuisine retains a flavour of pre-industrial times, when the diet centred around rye bread, salted pork and herring – basically whatever could be grown and harvested in a short summer or pulled from the sea and preserved. Typical are dishes such as *øllebrød* (barley porridge), *æbleflæsk* (slices of pork with apples fried in the fat), *finker* (haggis), *stuvet oksekød* (beef stew), *rullepølse* (mutton rolls) and *grønlandkål* (thick kale stew). Many dishes are served with new potatoes, root vegetables and cabbage. Cucumber salad, pickled beetroot, and peas and carrots in white sauce also appear. Desserts include Apple Charlotte with whipped cream, breadcrumbs and almonds, and *rødgrød med fløde*, a jellied fruit juice served with thick cream.

Dill

Frikadeller *meatballs made of pork and veal are fried in olive oil and served with boiled new potatoes.*

Herrings hanging in a Bornholm smokery

FISH & SEAFOOD

With its several hundred Baltic islands, Denmark abounds with seafood. Herring is the most caught, cooked and consumed fish in the country. It is eaten fresh or preserved by salting, drying and smoking, and is served with sauces including curry, garlic, mustard and, most popularly, tomato. Salmon also features prominently, smoked, roasted, poached or cured in a salt-sugar-dill mixture, as does jellied eel, roe, mackerel and plaice. Fish fillets are often fried in butter and served with new potatoes and a buttery parsley sauce, washed down with lager or *akvavit* (Danish schnapps). Seafood is best enjoyed in the distinctive *røgeri* (smokehouses) found in harbours all over the country.

MEAT

Pork is the most common meat; there are twice as many pigs as people in Denmark, and Danish bacon is famous throughout the world. Traditional preparations include *stegt flæsk med persillesovs,* fried slices of pork with parsley sauce, served with potatoes; and *medisterpølse*, a thick and spicy pork sausage.

Sausages are widely popular, no more so than the ubiquitous *pølse*, an inexpensive hotdog that is sold in kiosks everywhere and flavoured with any number of toppings. Though it is hardly *haute cuisine*, it is still a must for any visitor.

Beef, veal and lamb appear widely on menus, often in stews or minced to make rissoles and *frikadeller* (meatballs). Game birds such as duck are often smoked.

Romsnegl **(literally "rum snail") pastries in a baker's window**

DANISH PASTRIES

The "Danish" was introduced to Denmark in the 1870s, when striking Copenhagen bread-makers were replaced by Viennese immigrant bakers, with their repertoire of sweet breads, cakes and puff pastries. Pastries are still prepared by hand today. They come in all shapes and sizes, and are filled with raisins, fruit compotes, custards and *remonce* (a very rich butter), then topped with nuts and sweet icing. Some of the best examples are marzipan horn, a crispy swirl of flaky pastry rolled up with *remonce*, *spandauer*, a flat twist of dough filled with vanilla custard, and the almond-filled *hanekam*. Moist and light, all are perfect with a coffee or shot of Gammel Dansk *(see p267)*.

Flæskesteg *is a joint of roasted pork with crackling. It is usually served with cabbage and gravy.*

Rødbeder, *a popular side dish, consists of sliced, pickled beetroot (beets) with horseradish sauce and dill.*

Risalamande *is a rice pudding with almonds. It is served cold, topped with a rich, fruity cherry sauce.*

What to Drink in Denmark

As far as drinks are concerned the Danes have two passions – coffee and beer. They are also very attached to their liqueurs, which come in a variety of flavours and appear under the common name of *akvavit*. The beer market is dominated by a handful of companies, of which Carlsberg is the best known, but there are also many microbreweries. Danish beer comes in a variety of strengths and colours, from fairly tame draught Pilsner through to stout with an alcohol content of about 10 per cent. Wine was not always so popular but is readily available in supermarkets and restaurants. Non-alcoholic drinks include mineral water and numerous soft drinks.

Drinkers enjoying the sun outside one of Denmark's extremely popular bars

Faxe Royal lager

LAGER

Lager is the most popular Danish beverage. Most Danish beers are of the Pilsner type with an alcohol content of about 4.5 per cent. They include brands such as Carlsberg, Grøn Tuborg, Faxe and Star. Before Christmas and Easter the shops sell Julebryg and Påskebryg in standard and strong varieties. These beers are slightly sweet and make perfect additions to *akvavit*. Bars and restaurants serve both draught beer *(fadøl)* and bottled beers. Sometimes draught beer is ordered in a jug. Beer is most often sold in bottles rather than cans. Carlsberg and Tuborg beers are also sold in plastic bottles.

Beer is consumed throughout the day. It is not uncommon, and perfectly respectable, for Danes to drink beer in the park at lunchtime. Drunkenness is rare and drink-driving is not tolerated.

Logo of the Carlsberg brewery

Carlsberg Pilsner

Tuborg lager

Faxe Classic

BROWN ALE

There are about 150 varieties of beer produced in Denmark and among these are many fine brown ales. They generally have more flavour and are often stronger than Pilsner beers, with an alcoholic content of about 8 per cent or above. Some cafés and bars specialize in these dark beers, which tend to be slightly sweeter and less fizzy than lager. Among the popular brown ales are Carlsberg's Elephant and Sort Guld from the Tuborg brewery. The darkest beers are stouts and porters; these often have a higher percentage of alcohol.

Carlsberg stout

Carlsberg Elephant

WINE

The Danish climate does not allow for the cultivation of grapes, although a few enthusiasts are trying to introduce the hardier varieties to southern Scandinavia. So far their efforts have not yielded any commercially viable vintages, and Danes, who are increasingly swapping a tankard of beer for a glass of wine, have to settle for imported wines. White wine is referred to as *hvidvin*, red wine is *rødvin* and sparkling wine is *mousserende-vin*. Hot mulled wine, or *gløgg*, is served with almonds and raisins in the run–up to Christmas.

Gløgg – mulled wine

An aromatic herbal tea

A cup of black coffee

HOT DRINKS

The Danes are coffee connoisseurs and coffee is the most popular drink in the country. Roasted beans are freshly ground on café premises and brewed in special jugs. Strong Italian espressos are also available, as are cappuccinos and increasingly popular lattes. Caffeine-free coffee can also be found (ask for a *koffeinfri*). For children there are delicious hot chocolates served with whipped cream. Tea is not as popular in Denmark as coffee and consists of no more than a tea bag placed in a cup. Caffeine-free herbal teas are available in some cafés.

LIQUEURS

The traditional Christmas feast is often accompanied in Denmark by chilled *akvavit*. This schnapps-like beverage comes in a variety of herbal flavours and often bears the name *akvavit* on the label. It is usually drunk in a single shot and is followed by a glass of beer. As well as schnapps, the Danes drink other strong alcoholic herb infusions. The most popular of these is Gammel Dansk, which is traditionally drunk early in the morning. Danes used to regard a small glass of this bitter herbal preparation as a preventative medicine. Another local drink is Peter Heering, a sweet liqueur made from cherries, which is sipped after meals.

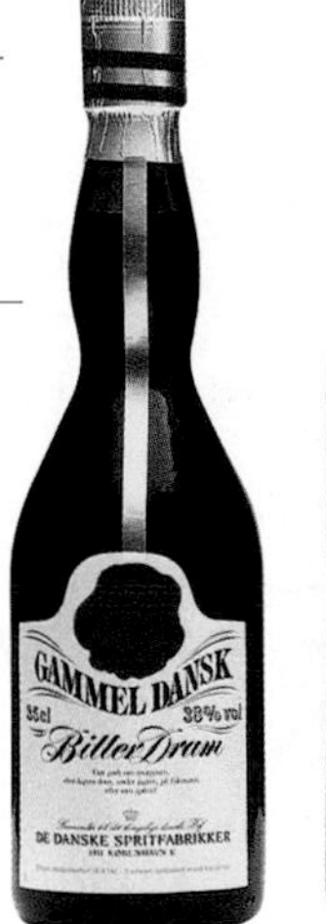

Herb-flavoured Gammel Dansk

Akvavit – Danish schnapps

Sparkling mineral water

Fizzy soft drink

SOFT DRINKS

When ordering a meal it is customary to ask for a bottle or jug of water. Danish tap water is perfectly safe – ask for *postevand* to be brought to your table. Still bottled water is *minaralvand;* the sparkling variety bears the proud name of *danskvand* (Danish carbonated water). All restaurants, bars and pubs also serve low-alcohol beer, known as *let øl*. Soft drinks such as Coca-Cola go by the name of *sodavand*, while orange juice is *appelsinjuice*. Drinking chocolate is popular both hot *(varm chokolade)* and cold *(chokolademælk)*.

Bottle of chocolate milk

Choosing a Restaurant

The restaurants listed here have been selected across a wide price range for their fine food, good value and interesting location. They are listed alphabetically according to area, beginning with Copenhagen. For Copenhagen map references *see pp106–111*, for regional map references *see inside back cover*.

PRICE CATEGORIES:
The following price categories are for a three-course meal for one without alcohol or tip, but including tax:
Ⓚ Under 150 Dkr
ⓀⓀ 150–200 Dkr
ⓀⓀⓀ 200–300 Dkr
ⓀⓀⓀⓀ 300–350 Dkr
ⓀⓀⓀⓀⓀ Over 350 Dkr

COPENHAGEN

NORTH COPENHAGEN The Coffee Factory Ⓚ

Gothersgade 21, 1123 ***Tel*** *33 14 15 82* ***Map*** *1 A4*

A complete experience for coffee lovers, this has to be one the most outstanding places to drink coffee in Copenhagen. There are also brownies, croissants, and chocolate-chip cookies. And if you are not into coffee, there are smoothies or chai, served with milk and honey. Free wireless internet access too.

NORTH COPENHAGEN Biscaya Tapas Bar ⓀⓀ

Jernbanegade 4, 1608 ***Tel*** *33 32 44 77* ***Map*** *3 A2*

One of Copenhagen's better tapas bars, this authentic Spanish restaurant (including Spanish pop music) is spread over two floors. Dozens of tapas dishes are on offer as well as other, more filling Iberian fare, as well as a good list of Spanish wines and *sangria*. Close to several cinemas so ideal as a pre- or post-film meeting place.

NORTH COPENHAGEN Café Petersborg ⓀⓀ

Bredgade 76, 1260 ***Tel*** *33 12 50 16* ***Map*** *2 D5*

Housed in what used to be the Russian consulate, this charming old place dates back to the early 18th century. Among the Danish dishes served here are *biksemad* (a meat and potato hash), smoked salmon, and curried *sild* (herring). There is also a varied selection of *smørrebrød* dishes.

NORTH COPENHAGEN Eastern Corner ⓀⓀ

Sølvgade 85A, 1307 ***Tel*** *33 11 58 35* ***Map*** *1 B3*

You will get a very friendly reception at this large, much-loved Thai restaurant whose affordable prices make it a big hit with Danish families, though it would make a great spot for a date, too. Favourite dishes include chicken and coconut milk soup, grilled whole fish *á la thailandaise*, and pork filet with basil, chilli and garlic.

NORTH COPENHAGEN Ida Davidsen ⓀⓀ

Store Kongensgade 70, 1264 ***Tel*** *33 91 36 55* ***Map*** *2 D3*

With nearly 250 *smørrebrød* sandwiches on offer, this family-run lunchtime-only cellar restaurant is a great place to try out this Nordic speciality. Best are the smoked duck, lobster, liver pâté, and the many variations on herring. The staff are well-informed about everything they serve and the walls are covered in photographs of famous Danes.

NORTH COPENHAGEN O's American Breakfast & Barbeque ⓀⓀ

Gothersgade 15, 1123 ***Tel*** *33 12 96 12* ***Map*** *1 A4*

Here the "early morning brunch" begins at 3am, making this a good place for those leaving the city's clubs or bars. This American-style restaurant, with Cajun and Caribbean flavours, is best known for its filling pancakes, doused in maple syrup. There are also barbecued meats, including great burgers and inexpensive grilled chicken or ribs.

NORTH COPENHAGEN Sult ⓀⓀⓀ

Vognmagergade 8B, 1120 ***Tel*** *33 74 34 17* ***Map*** *1 C5*

Somewhat confusingly named after Knut Hamsun's famed novel, Sult (Hunger), the fusion menu here includes scrumptious dishes with influences from all over the world, including Spain, France, Italy and North Africa. Set inside the Danish Film Institute's cultural centre, Sult is ideal both for a quick snack or a longer, more filling meal.

NORTH COPENHAGEN Umami ⓀⓀⓀ

Store Kongensgade 59, 1264 ***Tel*** *33 38 75 00* ***Map*** *2 D3*

Heralded as Copenhagen's best Japanese restaurant, but with a French twist, Umami's menu includes rabbit loin stuffed with shiitake mushrooms. The decor is decidedly minimalist, with brushed wood floors and massive portraits on the walls. On weekends the local hip crowd are attracted to the DJ sets of smooth low-key music.

NORTH COPENHAGEN Restaurationen ⓀⓀⓀⓀⓀ

Møntergade 19, 1116 ***Tel*** *33 14 94 95* ***Map*** *1 C5*

Placed a few blocks from Norreport station at Gothersgade, this is a fine dining establishment where you can eat gourmet Danish cuisine in rooms lined with classical paintings. The only thing served is a constantly changing five-course menu, but the food certainly justifies the price.

Key to Symbols *see back cover flap*

CENTRAL COPENHAGEN Den Grønne Kælder ⓚ

Pilestræde 48, 1112 ***Tel*** *33 93 01 40* **Map** *3 C1*

Much loved by Copenhagen's growing number of vegetarians, the "Green Cellar" is one of the few city restaurants that serves vegetarian, vegan, and dairy-free meals. Friendly staff, welcoming ambience, huge portions, and inexpensive meals make this an excellent choice. It also offers take-away meals during the day.

CENTRAL COPENHAGEN Huset Med Det Grønne Træ ⓚ

Gammeltorv 20, 1457 ***Tel*** *33 12 87 86* **Map** *3 B1*

This well-liked lunch restaurant is popular with lawyers and businessmen. It is an excellent place to try typical Danish meals, such as *smørrebrød* sandwiches, local cheeses, *frikadeller* (Danish meatballs), as well as any of a dozen varieties of Danish schnapps. Well worth a stop if you are in the area.

CENTRAL COPENHAGEN Kanal Cafèen ⓚ

Frederiksholms Kanal 18, 1220 ***Tel*** *33 11 57 70* **Map** *4 F2*

This simple restaurant opposite the Frederiksholms Kanal is best known for its wealth of *smørrebrød* dishes. The boiled, pickled herring is a well-regarded house speciality. The decor is maritime in theme, though it also sports signed photographs of its more famous diners.

CENTRAL COPENHAGEN La Galette ⓚ

Larsbjørnsstræde 9, 1454 ***Tel*** *33 32 37 90* **Map** *3 B1*

This Breton-style restaurant serves only *galettes* (savoury pancakes) topped or filled with any number of items including smoked salmon, ham, eggs, tomatoes, goat's cheese, or walnuts. There are also a number of sweet pancakes too. La Galette is small so you may want to book ahead.

CENTRAL COPENHAGEN La Glace ⓚ

Skoubogade 3, 1158 ***Tel*** *33 14 46 46* **Map** *3 B1*

Situated in a small maze of streets just south of the university, this is Copenhagen's oldest *konditori* (cake shop) and serves great cakes and pastries along with coffee and hot chocolate. Locals come here for a take-away or to enjoy a quick bite over the morning paper. An institution that should not be missed during your stay in the capital.

CENTRAL COPENHAGEN Slotskælderen ⓚ

Fortunstræde 4, 1065 ***Tel*** *33 11 15 37* **Map** *3 C1*

Excellent, well-known lunch-only spot right by the Strøget that specializes is *smørrebrød*. Select what you want from behind the glass counters and they bring it to your table. Slotskælderen also serve good *frikadeller* (meatballs) and *sild* (herring). Poplar with the parliamentarians who hold sessions nearby.

CENTRAL COPENHAGEN Atlas Bar ⓚⓚ

Larsbjørnsstr. 18, 1454 ***Tel*** *33 15 03 52* **Map** *3 B1*

This cosy and unpretentious basement bar serves, in its own words, "food from the hot countries". Antique maps adorn the walls, alluding to the changing menu of dishes from all over the world; though the focus is on Asia and India. The Atlas is also known for its freshly pressed juices. Very busy, especially in the evenings. Excellent service.

CENTRAL COPENHAGEN Cafe Flottenheimer ⓚⓚ

Skindergade 20, 1159 ***Tel*** *35 38 32 12* **Map** *3 C1*

Flottenheimer is located just a stone's throw away from popular Grabrødre Torv. Striking a balance between old and new Scandinavian design, it is a cosy little café with a well-assorted menu. In addition, it offers wireless internet access and a selection of papers and magazines. From Thursday to Saturday, it is also possible to enjoy cocktails.

CENTRAL COPENHAGEN Flow ⓚⓚ

Gyldenløvesgade 10, 1369 ***Tel*** *33 14 43 43* **Map** *3 A1*

A few minutes walk from the train station, Flow is a vegetarian buffet restaurant that has been nominated one of Copenhagen's best places for dinner. The ample buffet includes fennel, organic carrots, and feta. Alcohol free, the drinks list includes lassi, chai, various teas and fruit juices.

CENTRAL COPENHAGEN Nyhavns Færgekro ⓚⓚ

Nyhavn 5, 1051 ***Tel*** *33 15 15 88* **Map** *4 D1*

A Danish restaurant in a building that once served as the last stop for immigrants on their way to the New World. The fetching interior features a spiral staircase from an old tram and marble floors from the old Dagmar theatre. The popular lunch buffet includes a host of herring dishes alongside Danish favourites including smoked salmon.

CENTRAL COPENHAGEN Restaurant Cap Horn ⓚⓚ

Nyhavn 21 3tv, 1051 ***Tel*** *33 12 85 04* **Map** *4 D1*

Weathered walls, original wood floors, and an open fireplace are the setting for the Cap Horn's classic Danish menu, which focuses on regularly changing seafood and organic dishes. The organic theme extends to the beer, wine, and coffee. Service is fast and courteous and they occasionally have live jazz sessions.

CENTRAL COPENHAGEN The Living Room ⓚⓚ

Larsbjørnstrædet 17, 1454 ***Tel*** *33 32 66 10* **Map** *3 A1*

Come to The Living Room for a range of natural and organic foods and drinks, including soups, sandwiches, muffins, smoothies, milkshakes and juices. The place has a grungey, funky look, and diners can relax downstairs by the fireplace or head upstairs for views of the Latin Quarter.

CENTRAL COPENHAGEN Wagamama ⓀⓀ

Tietgensgade 20, 1704 ***Tel*** *33 75 06 58* **Map** *3 A3*

Well-known to Londoners, this pan-Asian noodle bar opened in 2006 and now ranks as one of the most popular casual dining spots in the city. With seating for 250, the Wagamama team offer inexpensive soups, dim sum, noodles, rice dishes and curries. Guests can also enter directly into the Tivoli park from the restaurant.

CENTRAL COPENHAGEN Café Bjørg's ⓀⓀⓀ

Vestervoldgade 19, 1552 ***Tel*** *33 14 53 20* **Map** *3 A1*

A very social café-restaurant decorated in the style of an American diner. They serve good-sized brunches and lunches during the day and hot meals at night, including excellent club sandwiches accompanied by *jalapeños*, olives, and red pesto. There are also tasty curries, ample salads and wireless internet access.

CENTRAL COPENHAGEN Café Dan Turèll ⓀⓀⓀ

Store Regnegade 3–5, 1110 ***Tel*** *33 14 10 47* **Map** *1 C5*

This comfy place is named after renowned Danish author Dan Turéll and decorated with the covers from his many books. Locals come here for morning coffee and pastries, but there are also sandwiches, soups and burgers. In summer the outside terrace gets busy in the evenings and on weekends. Wireless internet access available.

CENTRAL COPENHAGEN Det Lille Apotek ⓀⓀⓀ

Store Kannikestrade 15, 1169 ***Tel*** *33 12 56 06* **Map** *3 B1*

The interior of Det Lille Apotek is decorated in deep, dark woods and gilded lamps. The menu features classic Danish dishes including roast pork, prawn cocktail with tournedos, and a wide variety of pickled *sild* (herring). Their speciality is *apotekaregrytan*, a tasty stew of pork tenderloin in a paprika cream sauce with mushrooms and pineapple.

CENTRAL COPENHAGEN Domhuskælderen ⓀⓀⓀ

Nytorv 5, 1450 ***Tel*** *33 14 84 55* **Map** *3 B1*

The clientele here is traditionally local businessmen and families, but a number of tourists find their way here as well. The smartly-prepared Danish dishes include veal, steak and a host of seafood dishes such as lobster and many types of herring. In the summer you can eat right on Nytorv.

CENTRAL COPENHAGEN Dubrovnik ⓀⓀⓀ

Studiestrade 32, 1455 ***Tel*** *33 13 05 64* **Map** *3 A1*

A convivial atmosphere is to be enjoyed here where the waiters walk around in Croatian costumes. The menu features a colourful and eclectic selection of Balkan cuisine, including rich grilled meat and fish dishes, such as thick soups, tripe and whitefish. All in all, a unique dining experience for downtown Copenhagen.

CENTRAL COPENHAGEN Glyptoteket ⓀⓀⓀ

Ny Carlsberg Glyptotek, Dantes Plads, 1556 ***Tel*** *33 41 81 28* **Map** *3 B3*

This tranquil, atrium café-restaurant is set within the Glyptoteket Museum winter garden. It is a great place to stop for a coffee or quick snack. Here you will find probably the best cookies and cakes in Copenhagen. Beware, however, of the crowds on Sunday, when the museum opens its doors for free.

CENTRAL COPENHAGEN Indian Taj ⓀⓀⓀ

Jernbanegade 5, 1608 ***Tel*** *33 13 10 10* **Map** *3 A2*

Copenhagen's first Indian restaurant is centrally located just a block away from the train station and serves unforgettable classic Indian cuisine. Here you will find a wide range of dishes, including a large number of vegetarian options, as well as favourites such as spicy jingha soup with king prawn and saffron.

CENTRAL COPENHAGEN Madklubben ⓀⓀⓀ

St Kongensgade 66, 1262 ***Tel*** *33 32 32 34* **Map** *2 D5*

This Nordic bistro in the centre of Copenhagen serves traditional Scandinavian dishes with a modern touch. The relaxed and trendy surroundings, friendly service and simple, affordable menu attract a wide variety of diners. Groups of more than nine people have access to a fixed-price menu.

CENTRAL COPENHAGEN Magstræde 16, Spiseri & Enotek ⓀⓀⓀ

Magstræde 16, 1204 ***Tel*** *33 16 12 92* **Map** *3 B2*

This restaurant is housed in a building dating back to 1733 and features a rustic and relaxed interior. On the menu is Italian food with a Nordic twist, which translates into a selection of quick snacks, the best pizza in town (according to the *Copenhagen Post*) and three-course meals accompanied by a great range of Italian wines.

CENTRAL COPENHAGEN Peder Oxe ⓀⓀⓀ

Gråbrødretorv 11, 1154 ***Tel*** *33 11 00 77* **Map** *3 C1*

Press a button at your table and the waiters will appear at this Asian-influenced 70s-style restaurant. The Peder Oxe serves good lunch dishes – the organic beefburgers are a big hit – but they are best known for their salad bar buffet, which includes such exotic vegetables as escarole endives and poupier. Great wine list too.

CENTRAL COPENHAGEN Alberto K ⓀⓀⓀⓀ

Hammerischsgade 1, 1611 ***Tel*** *33 42 61 61* **Map** *3 A1*

Situated at the top floor of the Radisson Blu Royal Hotel, with superb views across the city, every detail (including the cutlery) of the Alberto K was designed by Arne Jacobsen, so there is a lot to feast your eyes upon here. The Italian-inspired menu includes lumpfish roe, king crab *tortellini*, and thyme-spiced lamb. Outstanding Italian wine list.

Key to Price Guide *see p268* **Key to Symbols** *see back cover flap*

CENTRAL COPENHAGEN Thorvaldsens

Gammel Strand 34, 1202 ***Tel*** *33 32 04 00* — ***Map*** *3 C1*

Located in the oldest part of Copenhagen, formerly the site of the fish market, Thorvaldsens offers splendid views of the old port and Christiansborg Palace. The interior is elegant and classic, with a cosy lounge on the ground floor. At weekends, the place transforms into a funky cocktail bar called Nouvel, with DJs and urban vibes.

CENTRAL COPENHAGEN 1.th

Herluf Trollesgade 9, 1052 ***Tel*** *33 93 57 70* — ***Map*** *4 E1*

A very romantic (and absurdly expensive) gourmet Danish fusion restaurant set in a converted apartment. You will be treated like royalty here. The menu is dominated by seafood dishes, and you are bombarded with many small tasters (such as elegantly prepared shellfish, mushrooms and berries) before the main dishes arrive.

CENTRAL COPENHAGEN Divan 2

Tivoli, Vesterbrogade 3, 1620 ***Tel*** *33 75 07 50* — ***Map*** *3 B2*

This Oriental-style garden restaurant opened in 1843 and to this day the fabrics that once adorned the restaurant's walls can be seen in the Tivoli Museum. Divan 2 offers top-notch Danish (and some French) cuisine in a pristine, chandeliered dining room. The exceptional international wine list is particularly strong on French vintages.

CENTRAL COPENHAGEN Krogs Fiskerestaurant

Gammel Strand 38, 1202 ***Tel*** *33 15 89 15* — ***Map*** *3 C1*

The French-Scandinavian gourmet seafood served at this white-tablecloth establishment is regularly heralded in the Danish press. Their "surprise menu" is a collection of small, superbly-prepared courses guaranteed to satisfy your appetite. Comparatively inexpensive lunches are also served on the street in summer.

CENTRAL COPENHAGEN Noma

Strandgade 93, 1401 ***Tel*** *32 96 32 97* — ***Map*** *4 D2*

One of the city's several Michelin-starred restaurants, the Noma draws upon Greenland, Iceland, and the Faroe Islands for its inspiration. Though there are only a handful of dishes on the menu, they are all prepared with immaculate attention to detail. A meal to remember.

CENTRAL COPENHAGEN Prémisse

Dronningens Tværgade 2, 1302 ***Tel*** *33 11 11 45* — ***Map*** *4 D3*

Set under the vaulted ceilings of the Molktes Palæ, this adventurous restaurant is right in the centre of royal Frederiksstaden. The refined menu includes suckling pig, Ayurvedic-prepared Dover sole, creamy jasmine bouillon, sea scallops, and a caviar dish that is to die for.

SOUTH COPENHAGEN Lagkagehuset

Torvegade 45, 1400 ***Tel*** *32 57 36 07* — ***Map*** *4 D2*

Out by the Christianshavn canal, this gem of a bakery is one of the best in the city. Locals in the know come here to stock up on muffins, breads, and, of course, Danish pastries. Light lunches of well-prepared sandwiches and salads are also served. Great coffee.

SOUTH COPENHAGEN Morgenstedet

Bådsmandsstræde 43, 1407 — ***Map*** *4 F2*

Set in the self-governing, alternative society of Christiania, this bright and unpretentious rustic community restaurant serves an exclusively organic menu, with items such as tofu, vegetable curries, hoummus, and great salads. The tables are laid out with small pots of fresh rosemary, pickled ginger, and chilli to use as a garnish.

SOUTH COPENHAGEN Nemoland

Fabriksområde 52, 1440 ***Tel*** *32 95 89 31* — ***Map*** *4 E2*

This is one of Christiania's best-known café-bistros and has an appropriately laid-back hippie atmosphere. The food is simple and hearty, and most people eat outside in the small courtyard when the weather is good. A great place to come to after a walk around this wonderful part of Copenhagen.

SOUTH COPENHAGEN Café Wilder

Wildersgade 56, 1408 ***Tel*** *32 54 71 83* — ***Map*** *4 E3*

A relaxed, corner café on a quiet street in Christianshavn. The seasonal, French-inspired menu here changes quite often, but it always includes great meat and fish dishes. Wilders is a good choice for a late-night meal, and if you need to save your money then try the *dagens rett* ("selection of the day"). Vegetarian meals are booked in advance.

SOUTH COPENHAGEN La Novo

Torvegade 49–51, 1400 ***Tel*** *32 57 75 10* — ***Map*** *4 D2*

Classic Italian fare served in an Italian setting. The interior of dark wood, terracotta, and wine bottles sets the ambiance, where you will find a wide range of tasty pizza and pasta dishes. Their *tiramisu* dessert is the best in the city. Tends to get lively later on, with lots of drinking and, occasionally, some dancing in the dining room.

SOUTH COPENHAGEN Oven Vande Café

Overgaden Oven Vandet 44, 1415 ***Tel*** *32 95 96 02* — ***Map*** *4 D3*

An inviting café serving big brunches and good fish dishes at tables in front of large bay windows, perfect for watching the world (as well as well-dressed Danes) go by along the Christianshavn canal. The meals are mostly Danish, but the chef has added a French-touch more recently, something that is currently very popular in Denmark.

SOUTH COPENHAGEN Ravelinen ⓀⓀⓀ

Torvegade 79, 1400 ***Tel*** *32 96 20 45* ***Map*** *4 D2*

This garden restaurant on a tiny island, accessible via a small bridge, proudly serves traditional Danish cuisine, with a focus on *smørrebrød*. Their dishes include several types of herring, Danish potatoes, apple pie with whipped cream, and the much beloved *gammel ost* cheese, all of which should be accompanied by an *akvavit* (Danish schnapps).

SOUTH COPENHAGEN Spiseloppen ⓀⓀⓀ

Bådsmandsstræde 43, 1407 ***Tel*** *32 57 95 58* ***Map*** *4 E2*

This gourmet restaurant attracts a well-heeled, but casually-dressed crowd to its candle-lit tables in a large warehouse. A range of international, organically-prepared meals – from Lebanese to Italian – are on the menu and as this is Christiania expect your neighbours to smoke something aromatic after their meal.

SOUTH COPENHAGEN Bastionen og Løven ⓀⓀⓀⓀ

Christianshavns Voldgade 50, 1424 ***Tel*** *32 95 09 40* ***Map*** *4 D3*

One of the defining spots of Christianshavn, this one-time mill is a very popular place given its lush outdoor garden and views to the Frelserkirken tower. The food is typically Danish, and includes filet of wild boar with red wine sauce, blue mussels steamed in white wine, and oven-baked flounder doused in saffron butter.

SOUTH COPENHAGEN Era Ora ⓀⓀⓀⓀⓀ

Overgaden Neden Vandet 33B, 1414 ***Tel*** *32 54 06 93* ***Map*** *4 E2*

Regularly nominated as the best Italian restaurant in Denmark, Era Ora has had its Michelin star for well over a decade for its sophisticated Tuscan-inspired menu. Here you do not order, instead the chef simply presents you with what he has cooked. It's worth the wait. Extensive wine cellar.

SOUTH COPENHAGEN Kanalen ⓀⓀⓀⓀⓀ

Wilders Plads 2, 1403 ***Tel*** *32 95 13 30* ***Map*** *2 F4*

This quaint café serves great candlelit meals along one of Christianshavn's most idyllic canals. The food is seasonally-inspired Danish cuisine such as roasted gurnard fish and lamb with asparagus. French items such as oysters and an inventive goat's cheese *creme brulée* also show up. Choose from the modern dining room or the terrace umbrellas.

SOUTH COPENHAGEN Søren K ⓀⓀⓀⓀⓀ

Søren Kierkegaards Plads 1, 1221 ***Tel*** *33 47 49 49*

Located in the "Black Diamond" *(see p93)*, businessmen and fashionistas alike come to this minimalist restaurant for its fabulous views and great cuisine. There are lots of fish dishes and the six-course "tasting" menu is reasonably priced. If it is sunny out then take a table next to the water. Great wine list.

FURTHER AFIELD Café Det Gule Hus Ⓚ

Istedgade 48, 1650 ***Tel*** *33 25 90 71*

This hip café serves *smørrebrød*-type lunches, with toppings that include local cheese, Danish ham, smoked bacon, fresh melon, garden tomato, spicy sausage, and marmelade. Some of their other popular menu items include pancakes and smoothies. Often remains packed throughout the day.

FURTHER AFIELD Castro Ⓚ

Nørrebrogade 209, 2200 ***Tel*** *35 85 35 85*

Pictures of Fidel Castro adorn the walls of this enormous Cuban-themed café-bistro. In addition to salads, burgers, and other hot dishes, they serve a range of fabulous coffees (Hiatian, Colombian, and Kenyan brews) that are unrivalled in the city. Salsa and Afro-Cuban music accompanies everything.

FURTHER AFIELD Den Persiske Stue Ⓚ

Nørrebrogade 102, 2200 ***Tel*** *35 35 35 72*

Small, simple, and cosy ethnic restaurant offering affordable Persian and Turkish food. Beside the usual kebabs, yoghurt dips, and some tasty vegetarian main courses, the house speciality is the traditional Persian dish *koresht khemer*, delicatedly-prepared lamb with peas, potatoes, and saffron rice.

FURTHER AFIELD Den Sorte Gryde Ⓚ

Nørrebrogade 46, 2200 ***Tel*** *35 35 25 64*

The meaty burgers served at "The Black Cauldron" are legendary in Copenhagen. Cooked by a friendly Kurdish owner, the *buggi* burger is a handmade concoction of beef plus a number of toppings, such as cheese, bacon, egg, and even caviar. Primarily a take-away place, the Cauldron can be found at four other locations in the city.

FURTHER AFIELD Front Page Ⓚ

Sortedam Dossering 21, 2200 ***Tel*** *35 37 38 29*

Right by one of Copenhagen's lakes, the tasty Danish and continental meals served here are light and elegantly prepared. The seasonal menu changes monthly and the weekend brunch draws a diverse crowd. Ask for one of the small tables looking out onto the lake.

FURTHER AFIELD Golden Bamboo Ⓚ

Vesterbrogade 41, 1620 ***Tel*** *33 21 71 58*

Opened in 1973, the interior of Copenhagen's first Chinese restaurant can feel a bit dated at times, but do not let that keep you from ordering off their delicious pan-Asian menu. Recommendations include the king prawns with sweet and sour sauce, curry chicken with vegetables, and beef with mushrooms and bamboo shoots.

Key to Price Guide *see p268* **Key to Symbols** *see back cover flap*

FURTHER AFIELD Kate's Joint

Blågårdsgade 12, 2200 ***Tel*** *35 37 44 96*

A simple, much-loved budget restaurant serving Asian and Caribbean fusion cuisine, much of which is geared towards vegetarians. The feel of the place is vaguely bohemian and there is always interesting world music being played. Be sure to try the mango lassi.

FURTHER AFIELD Pussy Galore's Flying Circus

Sankt Hans Torv 30, 2200 ***Tel*** *35 24 53 00*

Salads, burgers, and interesting renditions of Danish classics are served at this cosmopolitan but casual restaurant. They prepare brunch, lunch, and dinner as well as café-style snacks and well-priced drinks at a cocktail bar. When the weather's fine, be sure to get a spot out on the square.

FURTHER AFIELD Riccos Kaffebar

Istegade 119, 1650 ***Tel*** *31 21 04 40*

This cosy streetside café serves good snacks, as well as great hot chocolate, coffee and tea. Both the modest but colourful interior and the selection of music played lend a bohemian air to the place. There are a few tables out front for when the weather is fine. There is another branch at Studiestræde 24.

FURTHER AFIELD Sticks 'n' Sushi

Gammel Kongvej 120, 1850 ***Tel*** *33 29 00 10*

Although this particular restaurant opened in 2007, its sister establishments have been around the city for some time. The whole chain is child friendly, and serve sushi, sashimi, and all the trimmings, including lots of great spicy dip sauces, as well as other traditional Japanese (non-raw) fish and meat dishes.

FURTHER AFIELD Ankara

Vesterbrogade 35, 1620 ***Tel*** *33 31 92 33*

A large, dimly lit, buffet-style Turkish restaurant with reasonably priced Middle Eastern dishes – hoummous, falafel, mousakka – in addition to an inexpensive buffet of warm and cold items. Views from the top floor windows look out onto the lively Vesterbrogade. There is a sister branch on the same street at number 96.

FURTHER AFIELD Den Franske Café

Sortedam Dossering 101, 2100 ***Tel*** *35 42 48 45*

Set right in the atmospheric Trianglen near a "lake" (really an old reservoir) at the heart of Østerbro, this typically Danish café has a relaxed feel and offers great views over the water. There are a number of well-priced lunch dishes and good coffee.

FURTHER AFIELD Floras Kaffebar

Blågårdsgade 27, 2200 ***Tel*** *35 39 00 18*

Fairly standard café fare, including soups, cakes, and coffees either in the sleek but casual interior or else outside when the sun is shining. During the evenings Floras turns into a popular place for drinks serving some of the cheapest beer in the neighbourhood.

FURTHER AFIELD Hackenbusch

Vesterbrogade 124, 1620 ***Tel*** *33 21 7474*

An irreverent café with wacky waiters, this is the most exciting place along Vesterbrogade. It is regularly patronised by local boho-types, students, and other people with time on their hands. A recommendation if you like burgers: the scrumptious *frøburgeren* comes highly recommended.

FURTHER AFIELD Hansens Gamle Familiehave

Pile Allé 10–12, 2000 ***Tel*** *36 30 92 57*

This garden restaurant draws both locals as well as the fashionable media crowd with its lovely, out-of-the-way setting. It serves mostly traditional Danish dishes, including several house specialities such as smoked salmon with a sweet dill and mustard sauce or filet of veal with paprika. A great choice for getting away from the hustle and bustle.

FURTHER AFIELD Himalaya

Blågårdsplads 10 ***Tel*** *35 36 85 05*

A rare opportunity to taste Tibetan (and Nepalese) food in Denmark, the Himalaya is presided over by the affable Tibetan chef/owner who knows his *thenthuk* from his *tukpa*. A house speciality is *momo*, a steamed dumpling filled with vegetables, chicken or beef, and served with a mouth-scalding chilli sauce.

FURTHER AFIELD Kaffesalonen

Peblinge Dossering 6, 2200 ***Tel*** *35 35 12 19*

This classic and colourful café with a maritime flavour has been around since 1933. It occupies an enviable location right on the small Peblinge lake and serves cakes, pastries, and drinks both inside and out. Opens early, so you can get your breakfast coffee and croissant from 8am.

FURTHER AFIELD Lê Lê Nhà Hàng

Vesterbrogade 40, 1620 ***Tel*** *33 22 71 35*

Outstanding Vietnamese food is served here for lunch. Instead of having a traditional single-plate meal, it is worth putting together a number of tasty noodles, soups, curries, ravioli, and spring rolls to sample all the great tastes that come out of the kitchen. Do not miss one of their great Thai milkshakes.

FURTHER AFIELD Thai Esan 1

Lille Istedgade 7, 1700 ***Tel*** *33 24 98 54*

This Thai restaurant has large windows, atmospheric lighting, and spicy meals to enliven your day. Their Tom Yom shrimp soup is worth trying, and although the food is inexpensive the chefs do not skimp on quality ingredients. There are many other Thai restaurants in the vicinity, most run by the same family.

FURTHER AFIELD Formel B

Vesterbrogade 182, 1800 ***Tel*** *33 25 10 66*

This boutique restaurant was recommended as a "rising star" by Michelin in 2006. Delectable Danish-French dishes are served here by two talented young cooks. The divine dining room attracts its fair share of businessmen looking to impress and wealthy jetsetters. Reservation essential.

NORTHWESTERN ZEALAND

FREDENSBORG Restaurant Skipperhuset

Skipperallé 6, 3480 ***Tel*** *48 48 17 17* **Map** *F4*

The long Skipperallé leads past the castle down towards the sea, where this one-time boathouse serves great Danish meals in a charming ambiance right at the water's edge. Chicken and delicately-prepared fish dishes are some menu favourites, though it would be hard to go wrong with anything they serve here.

FREDERIKSSUND Regnbuen

Ny Østergade 5C, 3600 ***Tel*** *47 38 58 10* **Map** *F4*

This cosy little restaurant offers a rather large menu of international dishes, including Danish, Italian, Turkish and Greek. There are nearly two dozen different pizzas, and as many types of steak, including *tournedos*, gorgonzola and T-bone. The lobster tail or French onion soup starters are both worth trying.

FREDERIKSSUND Toldboden

Færgevej 1, 3600 ***Tel*** *47 36 17 77* **Map** *F4*

Situated in an old tax collector's home, Toldboden offers meals with strong roots in traditional Danish cooking complemented with touches of modern European cuisine. The finely-prepared dishes are extremely tasty, as are the wines picked to go with them. Pricy, but the waterside location is idyllic.

GILLELEJE Røgeriet

Havnen 1, 3250 ***Tel*** *48 39 22 31* **Map** *F4*

This smokehouse, with its location right on the harbour, is one of the most atmospheric of Gilleleje's eating spots. Ideal for those on a budget, Røgeriet sells seasoned filets of mackerel, halibut, herring, eel and salmon from the counter which can then be eaten on the picnic tables out front.

GILLELEJE Gilleleje Havn

Havnevej 14, 3250 ***Tel*** *48 30 30 39* **Map** *F4*

Impeccably turned-out restaurant in an old merchants' inn on the harbour. Arrive early to get one of the booths at the front, each with individual French doors, that look out to the harbour. The lunch menu features many simple herring, salmon and other fish dishes; while for dinner the offerings are pricier and more sophisticated.

HELSINGØR Cafeteria San Remo

Stengade 53, 3000 ***Tel*** *49 21 00 55* **Map** *F4*

An inexpensive restaurant that features friendly service and no-frills Danish fare served from a counter. The dishes include fish and chips, scampi, *smørrebrød*, burgers and the *dagens ret* (day's selection). Moreover, the menu has photos of everything so you know exactly what you are getting. Ideal for a quick snack.

HELSINGØR Pakhus Pizza

Stengade 26, 3000 ***Tel*** *49 21 10 50* **Map** *F4*

This country-style *trattoria* serves excellent pastas and pizzas, drawing families from as far away as Copenhagen for its low-key atmosphere, friendly staff and central location. Situated on a pedestrianised street in downtown Helsingør, Pakhus Pizza offers an easy-going meal out.

HELSINGØR Rådmand Davids Hus

Strandgade 70, 3000 ***Tel*** *49 26 10 43* **Map** *F4*

One of the oldest addresses in town, this café-style restaurant has a few delectable bite-sized dishes on the menu but the real attraction is the interior: meticulously restored stonework and evocative furnishings. There is even a view into the cellar, whose passageways reportedly run all the way up to Kronborg castle.

HELSINGØR Madame Sprunck

Stengade 48, 3000 ***Tel*** *49 26 48 49* **Map** *F4*

A café-restaurant in an atmospheric old building with a menu of Danish and international dishes. The five-course "tasting menu" gives a great sample of what the superb chef is capable of cooking. A very large wine list, including some exceptional (and pricey) vintages, complements all the dishes served here.

HILLERØD Spisesteder Leonora Kr Kr

Frederiksborg Slot, 3400 ***Tel*** *48 26 75 16* ***Map*** *F4*

A lunch-only restaurant, with a large terrace garden, delightfully placed near the Frederiksborg Slot. The menu is extensive, but to order something typically Danish try *det store kolde bord* (a *smorgasbord*-like selection of fish, meat, vegetables and cheese dishes): a filling sampler of the best the country has to offer.

HILLERØD Encore Café & Brasserie Kr Kr Kr

Torvet 11, 3400 ***Tel*** *48 22 14 88* ***Map*** *F4*

A brasserie-style restaurant in a rounded atrium building right on the main square, near to the picturesque Fredensborg Slot. The brunch is large and could last you nearly all day, while the lunch menu features chicken sandwiches, wraps and salads. Tasty beers dominate the drinks list.

HOLBÆK Bryghuset No.5 V Kr Kr Kr Kr

Nygade 5, 4300 ***Tel*** *59 44 25 11* ***Map*** *E4*

This micro-brewery with café-restaurant attached has a good value *á la carte* menu. As well as snacks, it offers larger plates such as beef carpaccio, salmon roulade and beer-battered steamed mussels. The mini grill is placed on the table allowing guests to cook their own meat. Live music in the evenings.

HORNBÆK Restaurant Hansens Café Kr Kr Kr

Havnevej 19, 3100 ***Tel*** *49 70 04 79* ***Map*** *F4*

Just inside Hornbæk's oldest house, this inn-style restaurant has a changing menu that features a variety of typical Danish dishes. There are two terraces, for eating outdoors, and on Sundays the brunch menu attracts many locals to the place creating quite an atmosphere.

HORNBÆK Søstrene Olsen Kr Kr Kr

Øresundsvej 10, 3100 ***Tel*** *49 70 05 50* ***Map*** *F4*

Set within a thatched, late-19th-century summer cottage next to the town beach, this traditional Danish restaurant looks towards France for flashes of inspiration. The menu changes every two weeks, but you can always find a selection of fine seafood dishes on offer.

HUNDESTED Lynæs Kro Kr Kr

Frederiksværkvej 6, 3390 ***Tel*** *47 98 01 81* ***Map*** *E4*

An old Danish inn serving a range of Danish favourites as well as a selection of international dishes including an especially tasty mulligatawny soup. The children's menu reverts to such standbys as fish and chips and nuggets. The interior is filled with antique furniture, adding to the bygone atmosphere of the place.

HØRSHOLM Mikkelgaard Kr Kr Kr Kr

Rungsted Strandvej 302, 2970 ***Tel*** *45 76 63 13* ***Map*** *F4*

The walls of this French restaurant are lined with wine bottles, adding to the homely feel of the bright interior. There are a few *á la carte* dishes, but most diners are confident enough in the skills of the chefs to choose one of the fixed-price meals.

KALUNDBORG Café Bogart V Kr

Kordilgade 17, 4400 ***Tel*** *59 51 00 57* ***Map*** *E4*

Café Bogart owes its popularity to its good food and its convenient location right on a pedestrian area in the centre of town. It serves baguettes, sandwiches, salads and baked potatoes topped with any assortment of fillings including bacon, shrimp, tuna and garlic butter. A great place for watching the world go by.

KORSØR Havfruen V Kr Kr

Algade 24, 4220 ***Tel*** *58 37 61 65* ***Map*** *E5*

Placed at the end of Korsør's central pedestrian walkway, this bright and comfy restaurant has a great atmosphere, with a modern wooded interior that has a touch of the maritime about it. Dishes include burgers, steaks, salads and sandwiches (though there are more formal dishes as well), all served by friendly staff.

NYKØBING Madkunsten V Kr Kr Kr Kr

Algade 44, 4500 ***Tel*** *59 93 17 27* ***Map*** *F6*

The food at this little hole in the wall will make your mouth water (its name means "The Art of Food"). For lunch they serve inventive dishes, often incorporating seafood, though there are good burgers, omelettes and snack-sized meals. Dinner is a bit more formal, accompanied by a surprisingly extensive wine list.

ROSKILDE Snekken V Kr Kr Kr

Vindeboder 16, 4000 ***Tel*** *46 35 98 16* ***Map*** *F4*

Large, bright and airy, this café enjoys views over the marina at the edge of Roskilde Fjord. Come the evening, Snekken is transformed into a chic restaurant when the metal-and-glass architecture perfectly complements the contemporary menu. The spectacular all-you-can-eat sushi buffet is worth a try.

ROSKILDE Store Bors T Kr Kr Kr Kr

Havnevej 43, 4000 ***Tel*** *46 32 50 45* ***Map*** *F4*

Fresh and local sums up the approach of this upmarket restaurant, with views onto the harbour. The menu features fresh fish and shellfish straight out of the water in front, whilst many of the other ingredients are locally sourced or produced, including cheeses, smoked salmon, vegetables and beer.

RUNGSTED KYST Nokken

Rungsted Havn 44, 2960 **Tel** *45 57 13 14* **Map** *F4*

A stylish and bright harbourside restaurant that serves Scando-Mediterranean cuisine with such specialities as fresh seafood and classic French meat dishes. The large bay windows allow views out to Rungsted harbour. At night, it becomes one of the most popular bars on the coast. The terrace overlooking the harbour is especially pleasing.

RØRVIG Rørvig Fisk og Røgeri

Toldbodvej 81, 4581 **Tel** *59 91 81 33* **Map** *E4*

A simple, family-run smokehouse-cum-restaurant right at the ferry terminal, where boats leave to cross the fjord to Hundested. Do not expect anything more than fish and shellfish: herring, salmon, mackerel, pike, perch and shrimp, all caught from the fjord that morning. Fresher (and tastier) fish would be hard to find.

SORØ Hotel Postgården

Storgade 25, 4180 **Tel** *57 83 22 22* **Map** *E5*

The warm and cosy atmosphere at this *à la carte*, candlelit restaurant make it a popular place. The menu is traditional Danish, with a few surprises from further afield. The interior features a fireplace and light music. Recommendations include the fish soup and the venison medallions.

SORØ Støvlet Katrine's Hus

Slagelsevej 63, 4180 **Tel** *57 83 50 80* **Map** *E5*

Located in a picturesque, half-timbered country house, this inn has plenty of character. The interior is as traditional as the menu, which features plenty of herring, fillets of fish and a half-dozen steak dishes prepared according to century-old recipes. A short walk from the town centre, but far the most atmospheric place to eat in Sorø.

TISVILDELEJE Tisvildeleje Caféen

Hovedgaden 55, 3220 **Tel** *48 70 88 86* **Map** *F4*

This indoor/outdoor informal restaurant, with checkered tablecloths and a family atmosphere, could easily pass for a barbecue joint on Cape Cod. They put on a popular unlimited grilled buffet of steaks and fish, but there is also an inexpensive *à la carte* lunch menu. Perfect after a day at the beach.

SOUTHERN ZEALAND AND THE ISLANDS

FAKSE Skovfogedstedet

Ny Strandskov 4, 4640 **Tel** *56 71 02 27* **Map** *F5*

A very simple spot that is perfectly placed on a small plot of land between the forest and the Fakse bay (and with views to both). They only serve a few simple Danish dishes, but they tend to be well prepared and elegantly presented. Try the breast of duck with berries and raspberry vinaigrette.

KØGE Slagter Stig & Co

Carlsensvej 8, 4600 **Tel** *56 65 48 09* **Map** *F5*

With a host of burgers, fish filets, *charcuterie* and cheese plates, this brasserie-style restaurant is a good local option for picking up a quick tasty Danish meal. Unusually there is no menu: you just point at what you want from the counter and they prepare it before your eyes.

KØGE Milas Pizzabar

Nørregade 35, 4600 **Tel** *56 65 61 60* **Map** *F5*

A simple pizza restaurant that serves delicious pizzas with a variety of toppings. Milas tends to fill up with families at dinner time, so you are well advised to arrive early or to come for lunch instead, when things are a little quieter.

MARIBO Bangs Have

Bangshavevej 23, 4930 **Tel** *54 78 19 11* **Map** *E6*

By far the most atmospheric spot to eat in Maribo, this large pavillion restaurant is right on the town's lake and pulls in diners from all over Lolland. They serve traditional Danish plates such as fried fillet of mullet and fillet of lamb with summer vegetables sautéed in butter.

MARIELYST Larsens Plads

Marielyst Strandvej 57, 4873 **Tel** *54 13 21 70* **Map** *F6*

This large indoor-outdoor establishment has room for 700 and has long been the most popular place to eat – and drink – in Mareilyst. They have a number of themed rooms, all of which are usually teeming with Danish families. Their large all-you-can-eat buffet offers a dozen types of meat, a huge salad bar and any number of side dishes.

MØN Liselund Slot

Langebjergvej 6, 4791 **Tel** *55 81 20 81* **Map** *F6*

Set within an alluring 19th-century manor house, this upscale restaurant serves lunch in a café-style room and dinner in more formal surrounds. The menu features delicious Baltic fish and lamb. With its appealing old-world atmosphere, this is a must-stop while on the island.

Key to Price Guide *see p268* **Key to Symbols** *see back cover flap*

NAKSKOV Lido ⓀⓀ

Sondergade 8–10, 4900 ***Tel*** *54 92 23 13* **Map** *E6*

The Danish menu at this long-standing restaurant features a number of fairly-priced dishes, such as fish fillet, schnitzel, many different burgers, and a number of tasty *smørrebrød* dishes. Many of the starters are also competitively priced, including the prawn cocktail, so it is worth giving them a try.

NÆSTVED Café Oliver ⓀⓀⓀ

Jarnbanegade 2, 4700 ***Tel*** *55 77 88 81* **Map** *E5*

A bright, airy brasserie-style restaurant right at the centre of Næstved. Their lunch offerings include sandwiches, bruschetta, burgers and nachos. With only three dishes, dinner is somewhat less varied. Ideal for a quick bite before heading out to explore the town.

NÆSTVED Rådhuskroen ⓀⓀⓀ

Skomagerrækken 8, 4700 ***Tel*** *55 72 01 56* **Map** *E5*

The name means "Town Hall Inn", yet once inside it seems more like an English gentlemen's club with a decor of deep dark woods, tanned leather seats and shelves of antique tomes. The menu comprises a collection of Danish and French dishes such as pepper and garlic steaks and *weinerschnitzel* with mashed potatoes, peas and gravy.

RINGSTED Café Aspendos ⓀⓀ

Møllegade 11, 4100 ***Tel*** *57 67 05 08* **Map** *E5*

A relaxed corner café which is also a popular hangout for local teenagers. The menu is what you would expect from such a place – salads, burgers, sandwiches and the like, but it is also just a great place to come and have a coffee or a beer as you watch the world go by.

RINGSTED Rådhuskroen ⓀⓀⓀ

Sct. Bendtsgade 8, 4100 ***Tel*** *57 61 68 97* **Map** *E5*

This local Danish inn is about as traditional as you are going to find in this part of Denmark, and it is very popular with the locals. It specialises in beef and steak dishes – English, French, garden, pepper and Bearnaise – though there are a few unexpected (but equally good) items such as blini and *escargot*.

STEGE Slagter Stig & Co. Stoeberiet ⓀⓀ

Storegade 59, 4780 ***Tel*** *70 33 70 22* **Map** *F6*

This nationwide chain combines an eclectically decorated, cosy brasserie with a well-stocked delicatessen shop. On the menu is Danish food with worldwide inspiration. Help yourself at the side-dish buffet and the draught beer bar, then choose your own cut of meat and leave it up to the expert staff to grill it and serve it to your liking.

VORDINGBORG Babette ⓀⓀⓀⓀⓀ

Kildemarksvej 5, 4760 ***Tel*** *55 34 30 30* **Map** *E5*

One of the best restaurants in Denmark. Named after the 1987 Danish film *Babette's Feast* this Michelin-starred establishment has a changing menu featuring Danish and French delicacies such as local asparagus with fjord prawns and Italian sardines *au gratin*. A worthwhile treat if you are in this part of the country.

FUNEN

KERTEMINDE Rudolf Mathis ⓀⓀⓀⓀⓀ

Dosseringen 13, 5300 ***Tel*** *65 32 32 33* **Map** *D5*

This well-regarded fish restaurant sits right on the waterfront in Kerteminde. Inside find cosy rooms elegantly decorated. Here the three-, four- and five-course meals are excellent samplings of Danish gastronomy. The "daily catch" at lunchtime is a reliable option.

MIDDELFART Hindsgavl Slot ⓀⓀⓀⓀⓀ

Hindsgavl Allé 7, 5500 ***Tel*** *64 41 88 00* **Map** *C5*

Set within a fetching old manor estate, this upmarket restaurant offers a few fixed-priced menus, all of which are quite delicious: gratinated lobster tail with sautéed spinach, buttered asparagus delicately wrapped in bacon, and pan-fried mullet with peas. All in all, a great place to splash out.

MILLINGE Falsled Kro ⓀⓀⓀⓀⓀ

Assensvet 513, 5642 ***Tel*** *62 68 11 11* **Map** *D5*

This charming old inn offers gourmet French cuisine created with locally sourced ingredients and home-grown produce. The menu changes according to the seasons, and one of the highlights is the home-smoked salmon served with horseradish sauce and pickled cucumber. Advance booking recommended.

MUNKEBO Restaurant Anden ⓀⓀⓀⓀⓀ

Fjordvej 56, 5330 ***Tel*** *65 97 40 30* **Map** *D5*

A charming Danish inn, the Munkebo Kro has a nationwide reputation for its food, even hosting the Danish royal family on occasion. The menu is dominated by fish dishes, though the seasonal menus can bring surprises to your table. There is also an enormous wine list. Booking is advisable.

NYBORG Teglværksskoven Ⓚ Ⓚ Ⓚ

Strandalleen 92, 5800 ***Tel*** *65 31 41 40* ***Map*** *D5*

An indoor/outdoor establishment that does a good trade in a range of herring dishes, though there are lots of other items on the menu including Funen *æggekage* (omelette), steamed fish filet, and shellfish salad. Be sure to get a table on the covered terrace, which has a wonderful view out to sea.

ODENSE Badstuen Ⓚ

Østre Stationsvej 26, 5000 ***Tel*** *66 13 48 66* ***Map*** *D5*

Located very near to the train station at the north end of town, Odense's central cultural and youth centre also happens to be a great place to stop for a coffee, cookie or inexpensive dish of the day. Badstuen puts on regular concerts, dance performances and festivals.

ODENSE Café Biografen Ⓚ

Brandts Passage 39–41, 5000 ***Tel*** *66 13 16 16* ***Map*** *D5*

For a long time now Biografen has been one of the most popular places in Odense for lingering lazily over a tasty meal. The menu includes a good brunch or a dinner of *chile con carne*, burgers, or a selection of *tapas*. Afterwards, head further inside to catch one of the art house films at the restaurant's cinema.

ODENSE Djengis Khan Ⓚ

Overgade 24–25, 5000 ***Tel*** *66 12 88 38* ***Map*** *D5*

Exotically decorated, Djengis Khan's speciality is Mongolian barbecue, a massive offering where you select from dozens of meat and vegetable ingredients to be topped with any number of exotic sauces. There is also a large salad bar, and the wine list includes French, Spanish and Californian vintages.

ODENSE Druen & Bønnen Ⓚ

Vestergade 15, 5000 ***Tel*** *66 11 18 13* ***Map*** *D5*

This friendly, airy restaurant serves a combination of simply-prepared Danish and Mediterranean *tapas*-like dishes: think *charcuterie* platters and freshly made sandwiches with fresh olives and *tzatziki*. There are chess tables and board games in the back room, making it a great place to spend the day.

ODENSE Café Cuckoo's Nest Ⓚ Ⓚ

Vestergade 73, 5000 ***Tel*** *65 91 57 87* ***Map*** *D5*

Cosy intimate tables, deep sofas, and several different rooms for dining and hanging out make this chic café-style restaurant popular among students and young professionals. They serve lots of *tacos*, pastas, salads, *nachos* and steaks. The weekend brunches are especially enjoyable, when a jazz group usually plays outside.

ODENSE Marco Polo Ⓚ Ⓚ

Jernbanegade 14, 5000 ***Tel*** *66 14 27 60* ***Map*** *D5*

The emphasis here is decidedly Italian, with plenty of chicken and pork dishes in addition to many different types of pasta. The food is cooked in an open kitchen, so you can see just how your meals are being prepared. Several specially-priced two-course meals make this a good lunch- and dinner-time bargain.

ODENSE Bryggeriet Flakhaven Ⓚ Ⓚ Ⓚ

Flakhaven 2, 5000 ***Tel*** *66 12 02 99* ***Map*** *D5*

A multi-level restaurant on the town square that doubles as a micro-brewery, with all the beer-making paraphernalia and plumbing running throughout the eating areas. The food includes spare ribs, pepper steak, scampi and catches of the day from the nearby shores. Be sure to try their homemade brews.

ODENSE Den Gamle Kro Ⓚ Ⓚ Ⓚ

Overgade 23, 5000 ***Tel*** *66 12 14 33* ***Map*** *D5*

Set in a wonderful old building dating from 1683, this atmospheric restaurant is decorated with memorabilia from the past. Some of the more unexpected Danish dishes on the menu include fried mullet with shellfish ragout, and strawberries soaked in champagne. There are several dining rooms to choose from and a great wine cellar.

ODENSE Under Lindetræet Ⓚ Ⓚ Ⓚ Ⓚ Ⓚ

Ramsherred 2, 5000 ***Tel*** *66 12 92 86* ***Map*** *D5*

Just minutes from the H.C. Andersen museum, this formal restaurant is housed in an original half-timbered building dating from 1771. The dishes tend to be pricey but come excellently prepared and include king crab, beef stroganoff and Funen asparagus. The best place in Odense for a romantic meal.

RUDKØBING Pichardt's Ⓚ Ⓚ Ⓚ Ⓚ

Bystræde 2, 5900 ***Tel*** *62 53 33 53* ***Map*** *D6*

Langeland's newest restaurant, the friendly Pichardt's features gastronomic food at reasonable prices. The menu includes such things as pâté of Danish lamb, cream of asparagus soup, and oven-baked quail. The dessert menu is equally fine, and the chef/owner is happy to share his knowledge about the food.

SVENDBORG Jettes Diner Ⓚ

Kullinggade 1, 5700 ***Tel*** *62 22 17 48* ***Map*** *D5*

Just next to the ferry terminal, this burger bar is popular among families on their way to visit the islands off Svendborg's coast. It serves up sandwiches, steaks, salads, snacks and, most famously, outstanding burgers – Danes come from all over Funen to have one. The weekend brunch is popular with locals.

Key to Price Guide *see p268* **Key to Symbols** *see back cover flap*

SVENDBORG Oranje ⓚⓚⓚ

Jessens Mole, 5700 ***Tel*** *62 22 82 92* ***Map*** *D5*

The speciality at this bright wood-panelled restaurant is most definitely seafood, with unique dishes such as "fish symphony", though they also do good *tournedos* and fillet of wild boar (served with fresh vegetables and homemade cream sauce). If the weather is nice, eat outside on the covered terrace.

ÆRØSKØBING Mumm ⓚⓚⓚ

Søndergade 12, 5970 ***Tel*** *62 52 12 12* ***Map*** *D6*

Although the building dates back several centuries and the decor is mostly traditional, a few touches, such as umbrellas out back, add somewhat of a modern feel to Mumm. The menu includes both American and Scandinavian standards – steak, salads and seafood. Recommended are the snails, shrimp and sole.

SOUTHERN AND CENTRAL JUTLAND

EBELTOFT Molskroen ⓚⓚⓚⓚⓚ

Hovedgaden 16, 8400 ***Tel*** *86 36 22 00* ***Map*** *D3*

The chef at Molskroen has a reputation for conjuring up a range of French fare with imaginative Danish twists. In 2006, this exceptional restaurant was honoured with the "best restaurant" prize according to the Danske Spise Guide (Danish Restaurant Guide). Wheelchair access is available in some areas.

ESBJERG Café Bøgen ⓚⓚ

Torvet v, Hotel Britannia, 6700 ***Tel*** *75 13 01 11* ***Map*** *B5*

French- and Italian-inspired dishes are prepared by Café Bøgen's chef, whose aim it is to offer inexpensive food of high quality in a casual but exciting setting. There is a nice view onto the restaurant's garden, the staff are very friendly, and in the summer there are tables outside.

ESBJERG Jensens Bøfhus ⓚⓚ

Kongensgade 9, 6700 ***Tel*** *75 18 18 70* ***Map*** *B5*

Located in the centre of Esbjerg, this family restaurant (part of a nationwide chain) has its own courtyard, which is a pleasant place to enjoy the grilled meats in the summer. The menu consists mainly of meat dishes, served in generous portions, and there is a large salad bar to choose from too. To finish off, do not miss the ice cream bar.

ESBJERG Pakhuset ⓚⓚⓚⓚⓚ

Dokvej 3, 6700 ***Tel*** *75 12 74 55* ***Map*** *B5*

Built in 1902, this former red-brick auction hall now functions as an art gallery and restaurant and has plenty of atmosphere. Situated in the harbour area, the food is delicate and well prepared. A "tasting menu" is available, which consists of five mini-portions of the most popular main dishes.

FREDERICIA Simon's ⓚⓚⓚ

Torvegade 2, 7000 ***Tel*** *75 91 49 11* ***Map*** *C5*

Located in Axeltorv, right in the centre of town, this cosy café-cum-restaurant provides a relaxed atmosphere in which to enjoy your coffee, snack or full meal. The chef's concoctions draw heavily upon Italian and French cuisines. There is a good wine list too.

GRENÅ Det Gyldne Krus ⓚⓚⓚⓚⓚ

Lillegade 18, 8500 ***Tel*** *86 32 47 22* ***Map*** *D3*

Popular with the locals and located in the middle of town, this restaurant attracts a mixed crowd; young and old meet up to enjoy the live local and international music, which is often played in the evening. The menu features some excellent meat dishes. Outdoors, there is also a lovely patio.

HADERSLEV Dannevang ⓚⓚⓚ

Kelstrupvej 73, 6100 ***Tel*** *74 58 29 75* ***Map*** *C5*

The operative words for this pleasant hotel-restaurant are "cosy and comfortable" or, as the Danes would say, "*hygge*". Here they serve a mix of Danish and international cuisine from a small menu; however, the meals are prepared from the freshest of seasonal ingredients. Lively service and good wine list.

HERNING Herreford Beefstouw ⓚⓚⓚⓚⓚ

Lundvej 16, 7400 ***Tel*** *97 12 35 44* ***Map*** *C4*

Now part of a leading chain of restaurants, this is the perfect place for all meat-lovers who dream of high quality, juicy steaks and spare ribs – and for vegetarians there is a salad bar. The paintings on the walls are by the former owner, Aage Damgaard. Wheelchair access needs to be arranged in advance. Closes at 9:30pm.

HORSENS Lille Hejmdal ⓚⓚⓚ

Rædersgade 8–10, 8700 ***Tel*** *75 61 02 00* ***Map*** *C4*

A family restaurant that originally opened its doors as a café back in 1888. Lille Hejmdal is the town's oldest and largest restaurant, with a huge *á la carte* menu that includes Danish open sandwiches, organic chocolate fondue and a fantastic selection of other delicacies, also organic.

KOLDING Den Blå Café ⓀⓀ

Slotsgade 4, 6000 ***Tel*** *75 50 65 12* ***Map*** *C5*

Offering a cosy intimate atmosphere, Den Blå is Kolding's oldest café. The menu is decidedly French, and for a mouth-watering experience try the barbeque marinated chicken served with roasted potatoes and salad. Live music every Thursday from 11pm. Outdoor seating available in the summer.

KOLDING Den Gyldne Hane ⓀⓀ

Christian IV's Vej 23, 6000 ***Tel*** *75 52 97 20* ***Map*** *C5*

Located only a few minutes from the centre of town in a timber-framed house, this restaurant provides excellent Danish and French cuisine in a lovely setting. The menu is being constantly tweaked, but at the same time "tried and tested" Danish staples are always served. Outside serving is available.

KOLDING Herreford Beefstouw ⓀⓀⓀⓀⓀ

Helligkorsgade 20, 6000 ***Tel*** *75 52 00 87* ***Map*** *C5*

One of a reliable chain of meat restaurants known for stylish interiors serving juicy steaks and ribs in rich sauces. In Kolding, the building dates back to the 17th century and a massive olive mill stands in the middle of the restaurant. Gaining a good reputation for itself locally.

RIBE Kammerslusen ⓀⓀ

Bjerrumvej 30, 6760 ***Tel*** *75 42 07 96* ***Map*** *B5*

Located 15 km (9.5 miles) east of Ribe, this popular hotel restaurant has four 19th-century dining rooms and space to seat 300 guests. The menu is international in flavour, and includes some good beef and fish dishes. It is also possible to order lunch boxes to take away.

RIBE Sælhunden ⓀⓀⓀ

Skibbroen 13, 6760 ***Tel*** *75 42 09 46* ***Map*** *B5*

As the name, which means "seal tavern", might suggest, this restaurant is know for its selection of reasonably priced fish dishes. Situated next to a river, the menu also includes non-fish dishes such as *Wienerschnitzel* served in a butter sauce. A terrace is open in the summer.

RY Motel Julsø ⓀⓀⓀⓀ

Julsøvej 14–16, 8680 ***Tel*** *86 89 80 40* ***Map*** *C4*

Housed in a former hotel in the heart of the Danish lake district, Motel Julsø is known for its experimental gourmet cuisine: for example, cake served with green peppers. The menu is international, with an Italian twist, and always contains culinary surprises. Highly recommended.

SILKEBORG Angus Steak House Ⓚ

Christian d.8 Vej 7, 8600 ***Tel*** *86 82 28 54* ***Map*** *C4*

Located in the heart of town, this family-friendly steakhouse serves a variety of grilled meat dishes as well as fish. The decor is bright and cheery, and the desserts, such as pancakes with ice cream and fresh fruit, are definitely worth saving space for. There is also a good selection of wines.

SILKEBORG Zorba ⓀⓀⓀ

Nygade 19, 8600 ***Tel*** *86 81 21 55* ***Map*** *C4*

Chef Andreas Fergadis returns each year to his native Greece to collect new recipes and sample wines, which he then brings back to Zorba. With its modern interior and freshly-prepared meals, this spacious establishment has gained a good reputation for its food, not to mention its excellent coffee, and has an open fireplace for use in the winter.

SILKEBORG Piaf ⓀⓀⓀⓀ

Nygade 31, 8600 ***Tel*** *86 81 12 55* ***Map*** *C4*

Named because of the owner's resemblance to the French cabaret singer Edith Piaf, this popular restaurant strives to be a little different with paintings and posters on the walls and a mishmash of furniture and potted plants in the dining room. The menu includes outstanding fish, smoked in the restaurants own smoking oven.

TØNDER Torvets ⓀⓀⓀ

Storegade 1, 6270 ***Tel*** *74 72 43 73* ***Map*** *B6*

Situated in a former bank on the market square, this restaurant offers a wide selection of dishes in its restaurant and bistro. The restaurant is more upmarket and consequently more expensive, while the bistro offers a range of *smørrebrød*, pickled herring and pasta dishes. A large salad bar is available.

TØNDER Schackenborg Slotskro ⓀⓀⓀⓀⓀ

Slotsgade 42, 6270 ***Tel*** *74 73 83 83* ***Map*** *B6*

Prince Joachim, who lives in the nearby Schackenborg Slot, has designated this restaurant as his official royal inn. The hotel's gourmet restaurant is highly regarded and serves a mix of French and Danish cuisine. The salmon soufflé is particularly good. Reservations are recommended.

VEJLE Merlot ⓀⓀⓀⓀⓀ

Skyttehusgade 42, 7100 ***Tel*** *75 83 88 44* ***Map*** *B4*

This small intimate restaurant, situated in a historic building, serves a selection of French food and wines. Particularly fine are the *foie gras* and the delicious desserts. For wine lovers, the Merlot also has its own wine shop. In summer, outdoor tables are available.

Key to Price Guide *see p268* **Key to Symbols** *see back cover flap*

ÅBENRA Royal

*Nørretorv 1, 6200 **Tel** 74 62 03 30* — ***Map** C6*

Located in the town's oldest hotel, the Royal serves sumptuous roast beef, grilled meats and hamburgers all at reasonable prices. They are renowned for their quick and efficient service, and it is wise to book in advance as it is popular with locals and tourists alike.

ÅBENRA Knapp

*Stennevej 79, Stollig, 6200 **Tel** 74 62 00 92* — ***Map** C6*

A smart hotel-restaurant situated in a former water mill that offers an extensive menu, formal but friendly atmosphere, and excellent service which makes you instantly feel expected. Its small size, only 35 places, adds an air of intimacy. Good for a romantic meal.

ÅRHUS Italia

*Åboulevarden 9, 8000 **Tel** 86 19 80 22* — ***Map** D4*

The classic Italian cuisine on offer here includes pasta, grilled meat, and fish. The pizzas, cooked in a wood-fired oven, are especially good. Not only that but there is an excellent Italian buffet, the prices are low, and the setting truly romantic. Italian all the way.

ÅRHUS Jacob's BarBQ

*Vestergade 3, 8000 **Tel** 87 32 24 20* — ***Map** D4*

The restaurant is situated in an attractive 18th-century merchant's house. The menu consists mainly of grilled meats and a selection of fish dishes. Once you have finished your meal, you can move on to the bar where there is live piano music from Tuesday until Saturday.

ÅRHUS Olive

*Kaløgade 2, 8000 **Tel** 86 12 95 61* — ***Map** D4*

Drawing inspiration from southern European cuisines, the menu in this cosy restaurant is small but varied. Reasonably priced and with the chance to bring your own bottle of wine, Olive is a popular place to eat and can get crowded and somewhat noisy at the weekends. The desserts are simply divine.

ÅRHUS Dauphine

*Frederiksgade 43, 8000 **Tel** 86 19 39 22* — ***Map** D4*

Rapidly gaining a reputation for its experimental cuisine using the finest ingredients, the Dauphine offers a constantly changing French-based menu in a pleasant, relaxed and smoke-free atmosphere. The food is accompanied by an extensive wine list.

ÅRHUS Navigator

*Marselisborg Havnevej 46D, 8000 **Tel** 86 20 20 58* — ***Map** D4*

A lively restaurant, decked out in cobalt blue and creamy white, serving well-cooked Danish-French staples in tune with the seasons. When the weather permits, there is an outdoor grill and salad bar. Dinner and dance evenings are on every Saturday. It is necessary to book in advance.

ÅRHUS L'Estragon

*Klostergade 6, 8000 **Tel** 86 12 40 66* — ***Map** D4*

Located in the heart of the city's Latin quarter, this intimate restaurant concentrates on producing high-quality French food using the best of local ingredients. The atmosphere is cosy, with only 22 guests, and on Sundays the menu extends to classic as well as experimental dishes.

NORTHERN JUTLAND

FREDERIKSHAVN Nikolines Cafeteria

*Nordvej 4, 9900 **Tel** 98 47 90 16* — ***Map** D1*

Fast service and a wide selection of filling food are offered by this classic Danish café-restaurant. The menu is simple and unfussy, and there are many dishes that will appeal to children. Every Sunday they serve a traditional Danish meal of pork and red cabbage with potatoes and sauce.

FREDERIKSHAVN Møllehuset

*Skovalléen 45, 9900 **Tel** 98 43 44 00* — ***Map** D1*

Ideal for coffee, lunch or an evening meal, the cosy Møllehuset offers a mainly Danish *á la carte* menu with a good selection of dishes, all of which are made from fresh ingredients. Their chicken with sauce, vegetables and roasted potatoes is recommended.

HJØRRING Messen

*Nordre Klitvej 21, 9800 **Tel** 98 96 81 85* — ***Map** D1*

A cosy restaurant with a varied menu, Messen offers reasonably-priced dishes and welcomes families. On Saturdays there is a carvery buffet, with salad and potatoes to accompany the meat, as well as a special children's buffet too. For family entertainment after, the bowling centre is just across the road. Does not accept American Express.

HJØRRING Jensens Bøfhus Ⓚ Ⓚ

Sankt Olai Plads 1, 9800 ***Tel*** *98 90 35 55* ***Map*** *D1*

One of the Bøfhus chain, known for using only top-quality meat, this reliable, centrally located restaurant serves tasty grilled meat and stews as well as a variety of tempting desserts. The atmosphere is cosy and relaxed, the salad bar extensive, and there is a good children's menu.

HOBRO Fyrkat Møllegaard Ⓚ Ⓚ

Fyrkatvej 45, 9500 ***Tel*** *98 52 10 65* ***Map*** *C3*

Located just outside Hobro in a peaceful setting overlooking the Vikingecenter Fyrkat (Viking Fortress), this is a friendly restaurant with a menu inspired by classic Italian cuisine, but which serves German dishes as well. In summer there are tables outside. Enjoy a tour of the fortress after a fine meal.

RANDERS Niels Ebbesens Spisehus Ⓚ Ⓚ Ⓚ

Storegade 13, 8900 ***Tel*** *86 43 32 26* ***Map*** *D3*

The ghost of Niels Ebbersen is said to roam in this house. However, do not let that put you off the restaurant's seasonal menu of modern Danish dishes, based on excellent, often local, ingredients. Outdoor serving is available in the summer.

RANDERS Fru Larsen Ⓚ Ⓚ Ⓚ Ⓚ Ⓚ

Østergade 1, 8870 Langå ***Tel*** *86 46 83 88* ***Map*** *D3*

This is a small, romantic hotel-restaurant where the guests are made to feel whole-heartedly welcome. Fru Larsen's is known for its exceptional quality and attention to detail: from growing their own vegetables and herbs for the table to the exquisite French cuisine that they serve. The service is friendly and the menu is changed every 3–4 weeks.

SALTUM Fårup Skovhus Ⓚ

Saltum Strandvej 63, 9493 ***Tel*** *98 88 11 45* ***Map*** *C1*

Charming and reasonably priced, this restaurant has gained a good reputation over the years for its traditional kitchen. Worth trying are their omelettes or the *frikadeller* with rye bread and red cabbage. The varied menu provides something for all tastes. Live music and seasonal decorations are all part of the atmosphere.

SKAGEN Jakobs Café & Bar Ⓚ Ⓚ

Havnevej 4, 9990 ***Tel*** *98 44 16 90* ***Map*** *D1*

A popular Skagen café-bar, this lively establishment has good food and often hosts live music at the weekend. The varied menu is mainly Danish in character. For something fresh, try the catch-of-the-day fish, served with vegetables and potatoes.

SKAGEN McCurdies Ⓚ Ⓚ

Sct Laurirtiivej 56B, 9990 ***Tel*** *98 44 39 00* ***Map*** *D1*

With the Stars and Stripes on the wall, McCurdies American-influenced menu includes hot wings, barbecue spare ribs, burgers and salads, but also an excellent Mexican buffet. The decor is bright and cosy, and children are welcomed. Take-away available. Internet hotspot.

VIBORG Mønsted Kro Ⓚ Ⓚ

Viborgvej 43, Mønsted, 8800 ***Tel*** *86 64 50 17* ***Map*** *C3*

Serving traditional Danish food, Mønsted Kro is located in a historic building in a quiet setting. The menu includes excellent soups, for lunch, and scrumptious desserts, including home-made ice cream. The restaurant can cater for large groups and parties.

VIBORG Bones Ⓚ Ⓚ Ⓚ

Preislers Plads 5, 8800 ***Tel*** *86 60 36 66* ***Map*** *C3*

American-style salads and steaks are the main feature of the menu at this reasonably priced chain restaurant. You can design your own burger, with all the trimmings, and choose from the extensive salad bar, and later from their equally tempting ice cream bar. Children's menu and playroom are provided.

AALBORG Duus Vinkælder Ⓚ

Østerågade 9, 9000 ***Tel*** *98 12 50 56* ***Map*** *D2*

Located in the cellar of the famous Jens Bang's Stenhus, this is a convivial restaurant and bar which serving light lunches only. They are known for their delicious *frikadeller*, and in summer serve a wide variety of Danish *smørrebrød*. This place is full of character and makes a good stopping-off point while sightseeing.

AALBORG Layalina Ⓚ

Ved Stranden 7–9, 9000 ***Tel*** *98 11 60 56* ***Map*** *D2*

A Lebanese restaurant serving a variety of spicy Middle Eastern meat dishes in a warm and friendly atmosphere. The vegetarian plate, which is filled with roasted vegetables and Mediterranean delicacies, is particularly recommended, as are the succulent kebabs.

AALBORG Provence Ⓚ

Ved Stranden 11, 9000 ***Tel*** *98 13 51 33* ***Map*** *D2*

Inspired by French tradition, the interior design, music and gastronomy of Provence all reflects this. The bread is imported from the world famous bakery Poilâne in Paris, while the classic menu includes soufflés, fish and meats. Several times a year the restaurant stages exhibitions with works by Danish and international artists.

Key to Price Guide *see p268* **Key to Symbols** *see back cover flap*

AALBORG Il Mulino ⓚⓚⓚ

Ved Stranden 14–16, 9000 ***Tel*** *98 12 39 99* ***Map*** *D2*

Set in an 18th-century warehouse, this gourmet Italian restaurant has a traditional menu that includes a varied selection of pasta dishes, grilled meats and pizza. All the pasta is home-made and freshly rolled each day. The Casino Aalborg shares the same address.

AALBORG Restaurant Brigaderen ⓚⓚⓚ

Vesterbro 77, 9000 ***Tel*** *98 12 00 11* ***Map*** *D2*

Bright and spacious, with cream-coloured walls and gold furnishings, Brigaderen offers Danish and international dishes on an *à la carte* menu. It is located in the Helnan Phønix Hotel, Aalborg's oldest hotel, and is known for its cosy atmosphere, excellent service and outstanding wine list. Closed on Sundays.

AALBORG Restaurant Papegøjehaven ⓚⓚⓚ

Europa Plads 2, 9000 ***Tel*** *98 12 54 99* ***Map*** *D2*

Located in the Aalborg Culture & Congress Centre, with views of the Kilde Park, this family-run restaurant is known for its delicious home-made meals served in a charming setting and friendly atmosphere. There are a variety of local dishes on offer. The lunch buffet is a good bet too, served everyday except Sunday.

AALBORG Mortens Kro ⓚⓚⓚⓚ

Mølleå 4–6, 9000 ***Tel*** *98 12 48 60* ***Map*** *D2*

Morten Nielsen, owner and head chef, is something of a celebrity cook in Denmark. The wide-ranging menu reflects his attention to detail: your meal might include filets of red snapper with an apricot-flavoured curry sauce. Every weekend the restaurant plays host to local and international DJs.

BORNHOLM

ALLINGE Algarve ⓚⓚⓚ

Havnegade 9, 3770 ***Tel*** *56 48 11 08*

A modest inn-style restaurant with a relaxed atmosphere and good selection of beautifully prepared Danish and French favourites. The restaurant is right on the harbour in Allinge, which means it can get quite busy at night, though reservations are not a necessity.

ALLINGE Cafe Sommer ⓚⓚⓚ

Havnegade 19, 3770 ***Tel*** *56 48 48 49*

With its chic modern interior, Cafe Sommer is particularly well known for its fish dishes. Though the portions are rather small, all the food is well cooked and served with a smile. Ask for the scrumptious *bruschetta* appetizer, with island mushrooms, berries, rosemary and parmesan. Food is served on a terrace during the summer.

CHRISTIANSØ Christiansø Gæstgiveri ⓚⓚⓚ

Christiansø 10, 3760 ***Tel*** *56 46 20 15*

Lunches here are crowded with day trippers coming over to Christiansø for a few hours, but if you are staying the night then you will be treated to a wonderful evening meal. The dishes are traditional Danish prepared with an island flare. The baked cod and the salt-fried herring seasoned with island-grown sloe schnapps are especially tasty.

GUDHJEM Gudhjem Røgeri ⓚ

Ejner Mikkelsensvej 9, 3760 ***Tel*** *56 48 57 08*

The best place in Bornholm to try Sol Over Gudhjem, a *smørrebrød* sandwich with herring, onion and egg that is surprisingly tasty. If it is fish you are after, then there are nearly a dozen varieties, depending on the day's catch. The best option is to buy inside and then picnic on the harbourside.

GUDHJEM Pandekagehuset ⓚ

Brøddegade 15, 3760 ***Tel*** *56 48 55 17*

A great place for a quick bite, this roadside *crêperie* serves great savoury and sweet pancakes. The fillings include everything from mushrooms and local cheese to peaches, chocolate and almonds. There is diner-style seating inside, or you can sit outside at one the cast-iron tables and watch the world go by.

GUDHJEM Bokulhus ⓚⓚⓚⓚ

Bokulvej 4, 3760 ***Tel*** *56 48 52 97*

Situated in a large estate on top of a hill, Bokulhus serves a great mix of traditional Danish cuisine and local island specialities. It is worth trying one of their sampler plates, which give a taste of local herring, shrimp and Bornholm cheeses; alternatively, there are tuna and cod main courses. The dining room looks out onto a beautiful garden.

HASLE Silderøgeriet ⓚ

Fælledvej 53, 3790 ***Tel*** *56 96 44 11*

Characterized by the island's traditional four-chimney design, this smokehouse is a characterful place where you can sample the catch of the day. Inexpensive fish, such as mackerel, herring and salmon, are served as pre-prepared fillets ready to eat inside or to take with you down to the harbour.

HASLE Le Port ®®®®

Vang 81, 3790 ***Tel*** *56 96 92 01*

A traditional restaurant offering excellent food in a spectacular location overlooking the sea, perfect for a romantic sunset dinner. During the summer, diners can sit out on the terrace and choose one of several French dishes that are Le Port's speciality. The lunch menu, which is served until 4pm, is a cheaper option.

NEXØ Dueodde Badehotel ®®®

Sirenevej 2, 3730 ***Tel*** *56 48 86 49*

Set within one of the best beach hotels on the island, this café-restaurant offers a hearty salad buffet and light sandwich-based meals during the day. On summer evenings, fresh fish and meats are cooked on a mesquite-fired barbecue on the beach – well worth staying around for.

RØNNE Casa Mia ®®

Antoniestræde 3, 3700 ***Tel*** *56 95 95 73*

Run by a born-and-bred Italian who has since settled on Bornholm, the rustic-style decor of Casa Mia recalls a Tuscan countryside inn, with lots of authentic decorations on the walls. The pizza and pasta dishes here are excellently prepared and well priced too.

RØNNE Fyrtøjet ®®

Store Torvegade 22, 3700 ***Tel*** *56 95 30 12*

Stylish and well-run, this restaurant serves international staples, such as *coq au vin*, as well as many local Bornholm specialities including grilled Baltic salmon. The atmosphere is very bright and airy, and there is an abundant salad bar. Great weekend brunch.

RØNNE Di 5 Stâuerna ®®®®

Strandvejen 116, 3700 ***Tel*** *56 90 44 44*

Spread across five separate rooms inside the Radisson SAS hotel, this popular restaurant is known for its award-winning chefs and superb Danish-French cuisine. All the dishes on the menu are top-notch and there is also a very impressive wine cellar.

SVANEKE Pakhuset ®®

Brænderigænget 3, 3740 ***Tel*** *56 49 65 85*

Just off Svaneke's market square, Pakhuset is known for its steaks, of which they serve over a dozen different kinds, including Bearnaise, chilli, onion and blue cheese. For dessert, the choice includes a divine chocolate mousse and a plate offering a selection of Bornholm cheeses. Especially popular with families just back from the beach.

SVANEKE Bryghuset ®®®

Torvet 5, Havnebryggen 12, 3740 ***Tel*** *56 49 73 21*

Right on the central square in Svaneke, where there is always lots of lively goings-on, the Bryghuset's typically Danish menu includes marinated and grilled spare ribs, which can be washed down with beer from the restaurant's own brewery, braised lamb, and breast of chicken with a creamy pepper sauce.

ÅKIRKEBY Restaurant Kadeau ®®®®®

Baunevej 18, Vestre Sømark, Pedersker, 3720 ***Tel*** *56 97 82 50*

Open only from 1 May until the end of September, this restaurant offers Nordic-inspired food prepared with local produce. Kadeau is located right on the coast, and diners can enjoy splendid ocean views while sampling dishes such as seasonal fish with hollandaise sauce and dill, or Piggy-Wiggy (pork loin and brisket).

GREENLAND

ILULISSAT Ulo ®®®

Hotel Arctic, Postcode 1501, 3952 ***Tel*** *94 41 53*

The restaurant attached to the Hotel Arctic has superb views of icebergs afloat in the bay. The menu includes international dishes as well as Greenlandic shrimps and other good fish platters. In the summer, weekend parties are held out on the deck.

KANGERLUSSUAQ Roklubben ®®®

3910 ***Tel*** *84 19 96 or 86 16 40*

Just south of Kangerlussuaq on the shores of the idyllic Lake Tasersuatsiaq, the enviably located "Rowing Club" serves local dishes, including fried reindeer fillet and marinated musk ox. After a meal, you can walk or cycle around the lake to see reindeer and musk oxen grazing. A great spot to catch the Northern Lights. Hourly buses from town.

NUUK Charoen Porn ®®

Aqqusinersuaq 5, 3900 ***Tel*** *32 57 59*

Alongside some excellent Thai dishes and several types of sushi, expect to find a few unique dishes here, including whale meat and crocodile satay. Their renowned "Greenlandic coffee" consists of coffee, sugar and three different spirits topped with whipped cream. The decor is "pan-Asian" which makes a nice change from Danish-Greenlandic.

Key to Price Guide *see p268* **Key to Symbols** *see back cover flap*

NUUK Isikkivik

Narsaviaq 26 1sal, 3905 **Tel** *34 85 06*

Set in Nuussuaq, just outside of central Nuuk by the marina, this restaurant has simple, well-cooked meals that include burgers and pizzas, though you can also get a decent fixed-price meal. The tables have pleasant views across the harbour.

NUUK Nipisa

Hans Egedesvej 29, 1. sal, 3900 **Tel** *32 12 10*

Nuuk's premiere dining spot manages at the same time to feel wonderfully low-key. The menu features lamb, reindeer, musk ox and fish. All the dishes are elegantly prepared and served, and some even border on works of art. The traditional lunch dishes are more affordable. Reservations a must.

QAANAAQ Hotel Qaanaaq

Box 88, 3971 **Tel** *97 12 34*

Friendly, family-style restaurant located within Qaanaaq's only hotel. The walls are decked with paintings by local artists. The Greenlandic food here features basic lunch and dinner dishes, but perhaps more importantly it is the only place to eat in town.

UUMMANNAQ Hotel Uummannaq

Trollep Aqqutaa B, 3961 **Tel** *95 15 18*

A hotel restaurant with some spectacular views of the sea. This is really the only place in town to have a decent, sit down meal. On the menu are tasty Arctic char, caribou and lamb dishes, as well as a few international standards including pasta and burgers.

THE FAROE ISLANDS

KLAKSVIK Hereford

Klaksvíksvegur 45, 700 **Tel** *45 64 34*

An atmospheric old steakhouse with lots of rustic charm. The menu is full of scrumptious steak dishes and burgers, but there are also a couple of surprises such as *escargot*. The restaurant is in the same building as a popular café, great for morning coffees or a glass of island beer during the day.

RUNAVIK (EYSTUROY) Hotel Runavik

Runavík, 620 **Tel** *44 74 20*

Situated in the centre of Runavik near to both the harbour and shops, this well-respected hotel restaurant serves *smyrjibreyð* (open sandwiches), as well as many chicken and fish dishes with fries. Breakfast, lunch and dinner are available, and take-away too.

SUDUROY Hotel Øravik

Øravik 827 **Tel** *37 13 02*

Situated in a remote, creek-side town along Suduroy's eastern coast, the Øravik occupies a rickety old building near to the town's harbour. This hotel-restaurant serves good pizzas and salads, but hold out if you can for a unique Faroese speciality: a tasty mélange of dried lamb, dried fish and whale blubber.

TÓRSHAVN Kliché

Vágsbotnur, 100 **Tel** *32 24 04*

This restaurant on the second floor on the corner of Vágsbotn combines Faroese culture with Mediterranean flavours. Kliché is renowned for its steaks, which are served in a variety of ways, including *à la katalana*, with pears, jam, salad and spicy chips. Please note that there are no vegetarian options on the menu.

TÓRSHAVN Rio Bravo

Tórsgøta 11, 100 **Tel** *31 97 67*

This traditional steakhouse has a sophisticated interior made up of old, English-style furnishings. In addition to many varieties of steak, the specialities on the menu include lobster tail soup, asparagus with Hollandaise sause, and lamb cutlet with black olives and fennel.

TÓRSHAVN Marco Polo

Sverrisgøta 12, P.O. Box 1140, 110 **Tel** *47 15 05*

This casual diner in the centre of town is the ideal place for an evening with friends. The menu includes dishes such as grilled fillet of salmon with a green herb sauce, and fillet of venison served with Waldorf salad and fig confit. Marco Polo is also renowned for its griddled steaks. Reservations recommended.

TÓRSHAVN Gourmet

Gr. Kambans Gøta 13, 100 **Tel** *32 25 25*

This upmarket restaurant serves a changing fish-oriented menu. Other items include marinated beef, Bouillabaisse fish soup and rolled lamb with basil and tomato. To follow, you can select any one of several delectable chocolate desserts. One of the country's top restaurants.

SHOPPING IN DENMARK

Most major towns in Denmark have large, shopping centres and department stores such as the country-wide chain Magasin du Nord. Prices can be high, however, especially in the more exclusive shops such as those found along Strøget in Copenhagen. Many bargains on clothes can be found, especially during the post-seasonal sales. Flea markets are widespread in Denmark. Much of what is on sale is tat, but persistence and a keen eye can sometimes uncover real treasures. The many independently run shops selling beautiful household goods satisfy the Danes' love of good design. Jewellery made from Danish amber is also popular and relatively cheap. Danish herb-flavoured *akvavit* (a kind of schnapps) comes in a variety of flavours and colours and makes a good present.

Bearded Viking toy

Busy Saturday market in Svaneke, popular with Danes and visitors

OPENING HOURS

In Denmark shopping days and opening hours are highly regulated due to union demands for reasonable working hours. The regulated hours are, for the most part, rigorously adhered to, although during the Christmas season and around busy tourist centres longer openings are usual. Most shops open at 9 or 9:30am and remain open until 5:30pm Monday to Thursday. On Fridays many shops are open until 7 or 8pm. On Saturdays most shops close at about 2pm; some larger shops and department stores remain open until 4pm. Most shops are closed on Sundays.

Some smaller, independent shops keep longer opening hours. Stores attached to petrol stations and kiosks found in town centres remain open 24 hours but offer a limited choice of goods.

In the run-up to Christmas and other festivals many shops and department stores in the capital and in larger towns extend their opening hours and often trade on Sundays.

MARKETS

Produce markets are becoming increasingly rare in Denmark and only occasionally will visitors stumble upon a fruit and vegetable market. On the other hand the Danes relish their flea markets, which are held periodically in many towns. Genuine antiques are mixed up with piles of bric à brac and a morning spent at a flea market offers a trip down memory lane for many Danes and also provides a good opportunity to munch on a hot sausage from one of the many snack bars.

Pre-Christmas fairs are also common. Seasonal fairs sell a variety of festive decorations including baubles, handmade wooden items, candles and colourful elves and gnomes fashioned from balls of bright wool.

Sign in Ærøskøbing

VAT

The rate of VAT (locally known as MOMS) is 25 per cent in Denmark. Some goods, such as alcohol, tobacco and petrochemical products, carry an additional excise. Visitors from outside the EU can claim a tax refund of between 13 and 19 per

12th-century cellars being used for wine storage

Hvide Hus – a handicraft shop in Gudhjem on Bornholm

cent of the total price of an item on purchases over 300 Dkr. Shops operating this scheme carry a Tax Free logo. When making a purchase ask for a Global Refund certificate. The shopkeeper may ask to see a passport. On leaving the country the certificate must be stamped by a customs officer, who will need to see that the product is intact in its original packaging. The stamped certificate may be used when reclaiming VAT in allocated banks or border agencies. For more information visit *www.globalrefund.com*.

SEASONAL REDUCTIONS

Reductions on many items can be obtained by shopping during the sales, which are known locally as "Tilbud" or "Udsalg". In Denmark, the traditional months for sales are January and July, although many stores shift their dates by one or two weeks either way. Sales are also held to mark the anniversary of a shop's opening or even the founding of a chain. One-off sales held at the start of the school year or before Easter are also common. As with most promotions, it pays to be cautious, however, as reductions can often be quite insignificant or apply only to a limited number of goods.

METHODS OF PAYMENT

Cash is the easiest form of payment but for larger sums it is safer to use credit cards, which are widely accepted throughout the country. Cards can be used in many shops, restaurants, hotels and museums. This method of payment does not carry any surcharge.

CONTEMPORARY DESIGN

Denmark is famous for its cutting edge design of ceramics, contemporary furniture and home accessories. Copenhagen has a wealth of independent outlets, but many brands are available throughout the country. The price of such merchandise can be high, especially for items by major designers, but smaller, less expensive items are available such as glasses by Bodum, silver Christmas tree decorations by Georg Jensen and "Olefant" bottle openers designed exclusively for the Carlsberg brewery.

FOOD PRODUCTS

Many types of cheese are produced in Denmark so there is no excuse for sticking to a simple Danish blue. Those who like sharp-tasting cheeses should go for "Gamle Ole". This strongly flavoured cheese goes particularly well with Danish rye bread, a dense loaf made with seeds and grains.

For those with a sweet tooth, chocolates and sweets are also well worth seeking out. Often these are handmade, beautifully presented and far superior to the mass-produced variety. Handmade boiled sweets are also good quality.

One of the Danes' favourite foodstuffs is pickled herring, which is served on its own and often on bread as *smørrebrød*. Many different recipes are used when marinating the fish to produce a wide range of tastes. Smoked fish, especially from Bornholm, is also popular.

The southern region of Jutland is famous for its meat products, which include salamis of various flavours and seasonings, all of which are delicious.

Assorted coffee-related gadgets such as grinders and percolators are often on sale in coffee shops, which sell a bewildering range of roasted beans from around the world.

ALCOHOLIC DRINKS

While in Denmark it is worth sampling *akvavit* (a form of schnapps). Many regions, and even individual restaurants, have their own special recipes for these flavoursome drinks, which are then sold as *husets snaps*. Visitors can, for instance, savour an Aalborg Porse flavoured with Jutland herbs. As well as *akvavit*, Denmark produces some excellent beers *(see p266)*. Some of the lesser known brands and dark beers are worth trying, and make a welcome alternative to the ubiquitous light Pilsners.

An antique shop in Copenhagen

ENTERTAINMENT IN DENMARK

Denmark is a vibrant country with a wide range of culture and entertainment on offer. Clubs and bars promote all kinds of music from mainstream pop and jazz to the latest in alternative sounds, while venues such as Det Kongelige Teater (The Royal Theatre) put on world-class theatre and ballet. Summer time is the season for a number of high-profile festivals such as Roskilde's rock festival in June. Local festivals include re-creations of Denmark's Viking past. Cinemas can be found in most towns and often screen English language films with Danish subtitles. Sport, too, is popular and Danish soccer clubs are among the best in the world. Children are sure to enjoy a visit to one of the country's amusement parks, including LEGOLAND®. For entertainment in Copenhagen see pages 102–105.

Viking Festival

Pierrot, Harlequin and Columbine at Tivoli

THEATRE, MUSIC, DANCE AND CINEMA

Visits to the cinema or theatre are some of the most popular pastimes in Denmark. Cultural life blossoms not only in Copenhagen but throughout the country, and university towns, such as Århus and Odense, have much to offer.

Århus is probably the biggest cultural centre after Copenhagen and has the **Musikhuset Århus**, a modern venue that stages musical and dance performances, and is home to Den Jyske Opera (The Jutland Opera). Aalborg in northern Jutland has four cinemas, several theatres and a resident symphony orchestra, which often gives concerts in the Aalborg Kongres and Kultur Center.

Along with three cinemas, Funen's capital, Odense, has several theatres including **Mimeteatret**, which, as the name suggests, is devoted to mime. The **Amfiscene** is a major venue that provides a platform for various kinds of live performance, including jazz and rock, and contemporary dance, while the **Odense Koncerthus** has a regular programme of classical music, which includes performances of music by Carl Nielsen (1865–1931), a native of Odense.

AMUSEMENT PARKS

Denmark's amusement parks provide entertainment for children and adults alike. The parks are open mainly in summer, although some of them start their season earlier. One of the most famous is **LEGOLAND**® in central Jutland *(see pp192–3)*, which includes LEGO® sculptures along with high-octane rides. As with many of Denmark's amusement parks, the admission price to LEGOLAND® includes free use of all the attractions. Less high-profile amusement parks are dotted throughout the country and include fairgrounds, water parks and science centres. **BonBon-Land** in southern Zealand *(see p157)*, for instance, is packed with rides and amusements as is **Fårup Sommerland** in northern Jutland *(see p204)*.

In addition to its traditional zoos, Denmark has numerous safari parks and aquariums where visitors can see wild animals and aquatic creatures. Two of the best known are **Knuthenborg Safari Park** *(see pp160–61)* and Esbjerg's **Fiskeri-og Søfartsmuseet** aquarium *(see p194)*.

Miniature buildings in LEGOLAND®

Royal Theatre performance in Copenhagen *(see p69)*

NIGHTLIFE

The best clubs, apart from Copenhagen, are in university towns, such as Århus, Aalborg and Odense, where they cater for the exacting demands of the student population. Among the most popular places in Århus are **Train**, **VoxHall** and **Musikcaféen**, which play a mixture of rock and techno depending on the night. In Aalborg **Skråen** and **The Irish House** have a lively feel. Two of the best clubs in Odense are **Rytmeposten** and **Jazzhus Dexter**. The latter has live jazz at the weekend.

Performances in Danish music venues range from local bands to major acts from abroad. Many concerts are free although prices can be fairly steep for the biggest international names. Nightclubs are also popular and can be found even in some of the smaller towns. Clubwise, nothing really gets going until about 11pm in Denmark. Pubs and clubs usually stay open until 1am on weekdays. At weekends many of them don't close their doors until dawn.

SPECTATOR SPORTS

Football (soccer) is a passion in Denmark and the Danish national side is one of the top teams in the world and achieved its greatest success when it defeated Germany in the final of Euro '92. Watching football is a popular pastime and many games are attended by entire families. Three of the best-known clubs are **Brøndby IF**, **FC København** and **Aalborg BK**. International matches are played at Parken, Denmark's national stadium and home ground of FC København.

Handball is another popular sport and has quite a high profile following the gold-medal success of the women's team at the 2000 Olympics. Other common sports include ice hockey, badminton, dirt-bike racing and cycling. Gymnastics clubs are also popular, and shows and competitions are frequently advertised in smaller towns.

Feeding the seals at the Fiskeri-og Søfartsmuseet, southern Jutland

DIRECTORY

THEATRE, MUSIC, DANCE & CINEMA

Amfiscenen
Brandts Passage 26, 5000 Odense C. *Tel 66 13 78 97.*
www.amfiscenen.dk

Granhøj Dans
Klosterport 6, 8000 Århus C. *Tel 86 19 26 22.*
www.granhoj.dk

Mimeteatret
Vestergade 95B, Odense C. *Tel 66 17 86 61.*
www.mimeteatret.dk

Musikhuset Århus
Thomas Jensens Allé, 8000 Århus C.
Tel 89 40 40 40.
www.musikhuset aarhus.dk

Odense Koncerthus
Claus Bergs Gade 9, Odense C.
Tel 62 12 00 52.

Odense Teater
Jernbanegade 21, 5100 Odense C.
Tel 62 12 00 52.
www.odenseteater.dk

Teatret Katakomben
Søstedvej 1, 5792 Årslev.
Tel 66 13 25 10.
www.katakomben.dk

Århus Teater
Teatergaden, 8000 Århus C.
Tel 70 21 30 21.
www.aahusteater.dk

NIGHTLIFE

The Irish House
Østerågade 25, 9000 Aalborg.

Jazzhus Dexter
Vindegade 65, 5000 Odense C.

Musikcaféen
Mejlgade 53, 8000 Århus C.

Rytmeposten
Ostre Stationsvej 35, 5000 Odense C.

Skråen
Strandvejen 19, 9000 Aalborg.

Train
Toldbodgade 6, 8000 Århus C.

VoxHall
Vester Allé 15, 8000 Århus C.

SPECTATOR SPORTS

Brøndby IF
Brøndby Stadion 30, 2605 Brøndby.
Tel 43 63 08 10.
www.brondby.com

FC København
Parken, Øster Allé 50, 2110 Copenhagen.
Tel 35 43 74 00.
www.fck.dk

Aalborg BK
Hornevej 2, 9220 Aalborg Øst.
Tel 96 35 59 00.
www.aabsport.dk

OUTDOOR ACTIVITIES

The Danes are keen on sport and fitness and many adults and most children participate in one sport or another. The country's gentle terrain and the many miles of well maintained cycle routes have helped to make cycling an integral part of Danish culture – it is not unusual for entire Danish families to embark on cycling holidays. Golfers are also well catered for and Denmark has over 100 courses, many of which can be found close to hotels and camp sites. With its many fjords, protected waters and tiny islands to explore, Denmark is a good place for sailors. The country is also ideal for water sports such as windsurfing and canoeing. The same sheltered fjords are perfect for novice windsurfers and there are many companies near Danish holiday resorts that can arrange lessons. Horse riding is another popular activity.

A successful catch

HORSE RIDING

Equestrian pursuits are popular in Denmark and the country has a large number of riding stables. Some Danes have their own horses and keep them in community-style stables, where members are expected to make contributions both in cash and labour for the upkeep of the horses and ponies. Those who are unable to keep their own horses make use of the numerous riding clubs that offer riding lessons and provide horses for individual unsupervised rides. Prices vary widely though most clubs will expect a fee for the use of a horse and also for membership. A small number of clubs will accept riders paying an hourly rate. A good way for beginners to learn about riding and looking after horses is to sign up for a farm holiday *(see p243)*, some of which include riding lessons and accompanied treks through the countryside.

Horse riding – a popular pastime in Denmark

Horse and driver on a carriage racetrack

For something a little different, it is possible to travel the country by wagon. Four to six people can usually be carried in the wagons, which are hired complete with horses from companies such as **Prærievognsferie Og Hesteudlejning** on Funen. Training is provided on the first day and the wagon is equipped with everything that travellers might need while on the road. A map is provided marking the route to the camp site, where there is pasture for horses and often a welcoming bonfire. Prairie wagon holidays can be great fun, particularly for children.

WATER SPORTS

The many Danish lakes and some 7,300 km (4,536 miles) of coastline make Denmark a perfect location for water sports enthusiasts. Equipment for windsurfing, water skiing and sea kayaking can be readily hired in waterside resorts, as can jet skis and other related gear.

Visitors intending to take up some form of water sport should check in advance whether the region they plan to visit allows for such pursuits as certain water sports, such as water skiing, are prohibited in some ecologically sensitive areas.

FISHING

Denmark is an ideal destination for anglers. Its many streams and lakes are well maintained and have healthy stocks of fish including plentiful supplies of pike and trout both for coarse and fly-fishing. The long coastline is also good for saltwater fishing and anglers can realistically hope to catch sea trout, plaice, mackerel and cod.

Windsurfers making the most of Denmark's coastal waters

Anglers between the age of 18 and 67 must carry an appropriate licence. These are sold at post offices, tourist information offices and shops that sell angling equipment. Licences are issued for one day, one week or annually and cost 30, 90 and 125 Dkr respectively. Fishing in lakes and streams requires the permission of the owner, which very often is the local angling club. Tourist offices will have details of angling holidays and some camp sites are especially geared for anglers with rooms set aside for gutting and cleaning fish.

Anyone fishing in Denmark will be expected to know the regulations concerning the size and types of species that may be caught. Some clubs may impose restrictions concerning the number or the total weight of the catch.

Those keen on deep-sea fishing can join the crew of a fishing vessel and head out to offshore fishing grounds where high-tech gadgetry, such as echo sounders, increases the likelihood of hauling in a big fish.

Anyone interested in a fishing holiday in Denmark should contact **Danmarks Sportsfiskerforbund** (The Danish Fishing Council).

MOTORCYCLE TOURS

Touring around Denmark by motorcycle is a pleasant way to get to know the country. Traffic is reasonably light and many Danes are themselves keen motorcyclists, and so visitors on motorbikes are unlikely to be treated with suspicion.

As a result of the popularity of riding motorbikes in Denmark there are many motorcycle rallies, known as *motorcykeltraft*, which are organized countrywide. The size of events varies from small weekly meetings to large rallies that feature live music and competitions for the most impressive bikes. Major events can last days and attract locals as well as foreign enthusiasts.

Denmark has a network of scenic roads known as the Marguerite Route, which takes in some of the most beautiful parts of the country. The route consists mostly of secondary and minor roads and is marked on road signs by a white daisy on a brown background *(see p308)*. Maps mark the route with green dots or a green line.

Bikers and bikes at an annual motorcycle rally

Anyone travelling in Denmark on a motorcycle should take into account the wind, which at times can be very strong and make riding difficult and sometimes even hazardous. When crossing bridges, particularly over some of the long straits, the wind can be especially strong and take the form of sudden and unexpected gusts. When strong winds prevail, motorcyclists may be banned from using these bridges.

Motorcyclists in Denmark must adhere to the highway code. Riders and passengers are required by law to wear helmets and carry the necessary documentation.

Cyclists on one of the country's many cycling routes

CYCLING

Riding a bike is a hugely popular activity in Denmark and the lowland areas especially are excellent regions for a cycling holiday, as is the island of Bornholm *(see p227)*. The whole country is criss-crossed with an extensive network of cycling routes. It is easy to plan a journey and routes take in most of the big towns and cities as well as more rural parts of the country.

Organized cycle races are common in Denmark. Many cover short distances and are open to amateurs. Races for elite riders include the Grand Prix Aalborg and the prestigious CSC Classic, where teams compete to earn points for use on the world ranking list. Races such as the CSC Classic are for serious competitors only.

Playing the green at a golf club near Gilleleje, northwestern Zealand

CYCLING TOURS

Cycling is an excellent way to tour Denmark, and enthusiasts are very well catered for. Specialist bicycle shops are found throughout the country. Alongside traditional touring bikes, they sell the very latest in cycling equipment. Dedicated cycling maps make planning a cycling tour fairly straightforward. Maps are widely available and cover virtually every part of the country. The maps include not only cycle routes but all the major sights along the way such as museums and castles. In addition, they indicate which roads have cycle paths and on which roads it is forbidden or too dangerous to ride. Cycling maps are useful in a number of other ways. They often include details of camp sites and hostels, for instance, as well as grocery stores. Maps can be ordered from **Dansk Cyklist Forbund** (The Danish Cycling Federation) as well as from bookshops or tourist offices.

The Dansk Cyklist Forbund can also provide details of packaged cycling tours. Tours can be expensive but they have the advantage of providing suitable cycles and organizing the accommodation along the route. Tour operators often arrange for luggage to be carried, so that riders need not be weighed down by tents and other items.

There are numerous places in Denmark where visitors can hire a bicycle although many bikes will only be suitable for short distances. One company that hires good quality touring bikes is **Københavns Cykler** in Copenhagen.

Tandem bicycle, popular in Denmark

Finding someone to fix a bike is easy. Most cycling maps include details of cycle workshops where minor repairs such as mending a punctured tyre or fixing a spoke can be carried out quickly and cheaply.

GOLF

Denmark has more than 100 golf courses. The majority of them will honour the membership card of your own club, and most clubs admit novices as well as experienced players. Green fees vary but are fairly reasonable, averaging around 350 Dkr per day. Buying a package golfing holiday that also includes accommodation can work out cheaper. Golf clubs generally hire and sell golfing equipment and also run improvement courses for all levels. The **Dansk Golf Union** can provide information about the country's golf courses.

SAILING

The waters around Denmark are dotted with islands, many of which have harbours in which to moor a boat. The coastline is highly diversified and there is plenty of scope for sailing at all levels of ability. Storms and gales are uncommon in bodies of water such as the sea between Zealand and Lolland as well as many of the fjords and these calm, forgiving conditions are perfect for less experienced sailors and novices.

A sailing boat can be hired in Denmark for about 4,500 Dkr per week, while larger motor-cruisers cost about 17,000 Dkr per week.

All craft intended for charter must carry a seaworthiness certificate issued by the State Inspectorate of Shipping. When chartering a boat, it is important to ask to see this certificate before sailing.

Sailing boats, a common sight on Danish waters

Coastal dunes, an ideal area for walks

BOAT CRUISES

For visitors with little or no experience of sailing, boat cruises are the best option. Boat cruises are popular in Denmark and depart regularly from Nyhavn in Copenhagen, bound for the islands situated in the Øresund (Sound). It is even possible to book a cruise on a reconstructed Viking ship. Stationed in Roskilde harbour are several small ships that are faithful copies of 10th-century wooden Viking boats and these embark on regular cruises. Cruises of the lakes and rivers are another option. One popular jaunt is to jump aboard one of the small ships that depart from Ry harbour on a cruise along the Gudena river. Another alternative is to take a trip back in time on the *Hjejlen*, a paddle steamer that travels daily from Silkeborg to Himmelbjerget.

WALKING

Walking trails in Denmark are clearly signposted, with information boards giving the names of the destination points, the length of the route and – when applicable – the route number. These numbers correspond to those on local tourist maps. In Denmark the public have access to the coast even if the land is privately owned. Many signed walks follow the shoreline and are especially beautiful. The country's forests are also good for walking. Some marked trails lead across private land. When this is the case it is important to stick to the trail, otherwise walkers risk being arrested (although this is highly unlikely). Many routes are through nature reserves and are marked with the sign of a daisy. Tourist offices and libraries often have brochures listing some of Denmark's best walks.

Denmark's hostels and inns are used to catering for the needs of walkers, as are the country's camp sites. **Dansk Vandrelaug** (The Danish Ramblers Association) can provide a list of camp sites in Denmark that are open only to walkers and cyclists.

SWIMMING

Denmark has many beautiful beaches. Most are ideal for swimming although the temperature can be on the chilly side. Even in summer, the water temperature rarely rises above 17° C (63° F). As an alternative, virtually all cities and major towns have swimming baths, which are well maintained.

Children, of course, are more likely to enjoy a visit to one of the water parks, such as **Fårup Sommerland** *(see p204)* and **Joboland** *(see p226)*, which have splash pools and waterslides.

DIRECTORY

VisitDenmark
www.visitdenmark.com

SPORTING ORGANIZATIONS

Dansk Idræt Forbund
Idrættens Hus, Brøndby Stadion 20, 2605 Brøndby.
Tel 43 26 26 26.
www.dif.dk

HORSE RIDING

Dansk Ride Forbund
Idrættens Hus, Brøndby Stadion 20, 2605 Brøndby.
Tel 43 26 28 28.
www.rideforbund.dk

Prærievognsferie Og Hesteudlejning
Holmdrup Huse 3 - 5881 Skårup, Funen.
Tel 62 23 18 25.

WATER SPORTS

Danish Sailboard Association
Idrættens Hus, Brøndby Stadion 20, 2605 Brøndby.
Tel 43 26 21 82.
www.sejlsport.dk

FISHING

Danmarks Sports-fiskerforbund
Skyltevej 4, Vingsted, 7082 Bredsten.
Tel 75 82 06 99.
www.sportsfiskeren.dk

CYCLING

Bornholm Velcomstcenter (Visitors Centre)
Nordre Kystvej 3, 3700 Rønne.
Tel 56 95 95 00.
www.bornholminfo.dk

Dansk Cyklist Forbund
Rømersgade 5, 1362 Copenhagen K.
Tel 33 32 31 21.
www.dcf.dk

Københavns Cykler
Reventlowsgade 11, 1651 Copenhagen V.
Tel 33 33 86 13.
www.copenhagen-bikes.dk

GOLF

Dansk Golf Union
Idrættens Hus, Brøndby Stadion 20, 2605 Brøndby.
Tel 43 26 27 00.
www.dgu.org

WALKING

Dansk Vandrelaug
Kultorvet 7, DK-1175 Copenhagen K.
Tel 33 12 11 65.
www.dvl.dk

SURVIVAL GUIDE

PRACTICAL INFORMATION

Large numbers of holidaymakers arrive in Denmark each year, drawn by the wide range of attractions and accommodation on offer. The peak season is relatively short, however, as the winter months are cold and the daylight hours short. The country has a good tourism infrastructure with a network of efficient tourist offices. Information is easy to obtain, especially on the Internet, and planning a trip should be a straightforward undertaking as most hotels and attractions have dedicated web sites, many of which have English versions. Denmark's hotels and inns are welcoming and clean, as are the many good-value camp sites and hostels. The major museums and galleries have world-class collections, and usually have English language displays and guidebooks to help visitors get the most from the exhibits.

Tourist information sign

WHEN TO VISIT

The best time to visit Denmark is during the mild months between mid-April and mid-October, or in December, when most of the country's towns and villages sparkle with festive Christmas decorations.

For cycling holidays it is best to plan for the period between mid-June and late August. The Danes take their holidays mainly during the school vacations – from the third week in June to the end of the first week in August – and the peak holiday season is during the first three weeks of July, which are generally warm and dry. During this time the camp sites, beaches and resorts tend to be full. Children go back to school in mid-August in Denmark and this can be a good time to visit as the days are still warm, while the attractions and beaches are less busy.

TOURIST INFORMATION

Most towns and resorts throughout Denmark have well-run tourist information centres. The qualified staff can provide visitors with maps and comprehensive details concerning the area including local attractions, festivals and events. Staff will also be pleased to give you free pamphlets containing a wealth of information about topics such as cycling routes, walking trails, fishing and disabled access to hotels and attractions. The personnel usually speak English and German. In smaller towns and villages, where there are no special tourist centres, visitors can usually get local information from their hotel. Visitors can also learn a great deal from the official website of VisitDenmark, the new name for the Danish Tourist Board.

Sign for historical site

CUSTOMS REGULATIONS

Duty-free goods were abolished in the EU in 1999. Nevertheless, Denmark continues to impose a limit on what can be brought into the country. Visitors arriving from EU countries are allowed to bring 800 cigarettes (or 200 cigars) and 10 litres of spirits or 90 litres of table wine; persons from outside the EU can bring 200 cigarettes (or 50 cigars) and 1 litre of spirits or 4 litres of table wine. Food articles that are not vacuum-packed by the manufacturer cannot be brought into Denmark. Articles imported in commercial quantities and presents of a value exceeding 1,350 Dkr are subject to customs duty. When bringing a large amount of cash (equivalent to over 40,000 Dkr) visitors must carry a certificate confirming the legality of its source.

There is no limit within reason on how much alcohol or tobacco EU citizens can take out of the country. US citizens are allowed to take home $400 worth of goods before duty must be paid.

Visitors enjoying a guided tour in Copenhagen

◁ Beach huts in Tisvildeleje, northwestern Zealand

Tourist information office in Copenhagen

VISA REGULATIONS

Citizens of the EU do not need a visa to enter Denmark; other visitors should check if their country has reciprocal agreements on waiving visa requirements. Visitors not obliged to have a visa are allowed to stay in Denmark for up to 90 days.

EMBASSIES

Visitors to Denmark should contact their embassy in an emergency if all other avenues of assistance have been exhausted. Emergencies might include the loss of a passport or a motoring accident. Embassies will expect you to have your own travel insurance, however, and are not likely to help if you been jailed or fined for committing a crime. Most embassies are in Copenhagen.

ADMISSION PRICES

The cost of admission to museums and historic attractions is not expensive in Denmark. In larger cities, such as Copenhagen, Odense and Århus, visitors can purchase special weekly passes that combine reduced or free admission costs to museums, galleries and other attractions with unlimited use of public transport.

Copenhagen Card, entitling visitors to cut-price tickets

OPENING HOURS

Office hours in Denmark are normally from 9am to 5pm. Once a week (usually on Thursday), the hours are from 9am until 6pm.

Shops open at about 9am, and remain open until 5:30pm. On Friday they close at 7 or 8pm; on Saturday at about 2 or 3pm. Most shops are closed on Sunday.

People interested in visiting churches should check their opening hours because Danish churches are only open on certain days and only between certain hours. Churches are closed to sightseers during services.

MUSEUMS AND HISTORIC SIGHTS

Many tourist attractions make seasonal changes to their opening days and hours, reducing or extending them, as required. Some attractions and hotels close altogether during the darkest winter months.

Sightseeing is easiest in the period from April until the end of September, and also in the run-up to Christmas and the New Year. Tourist information centres provide current lists of museums, historic sights and attractions, including their opening hours.

PUBLIC TOILETS

Public toilets are generally free. In Copenhagen there are also automatic toilets which charge a small fee. Many public toilets are adapted for disabled users and also have baby-changing facilities. In larger railway stations, along with toilet facilities, there are often showers and sockets for electric shavers.

DIRECTORY

VisitDenmark
Islands Brygge 43,
2300 Copenhagen S.
Tel *32 88 99 00.*
www.visitdenmark.com

Copenhagen Right Now & Booking Service
Vesterbrogade 4A,
1620 Copenhagen V.
Tel *70 22 24 42.*
www.visitcopenhagen.com

Bornholms Booking Center
Postgade 2, Tejn, 3770 Allinge.
Tel *56 48 00 01.*
www.bbc.dk

Køge Tourist Office
Vestergade 1, 4600 Køge.
Tel *56 67 60 01.*
www.koegeturist.dk

Odense Tourist Office
Vestergade 2, 5000 Odense C.
Tel *63 75 75 39.*
www.visitodense.com

Roskilde Tourist Office
Stændertorvet 1,
4000 Roskilde.
Tel *46 31 65 65.*
www.visitroskilde.com

Aalborg Tourist Office
Østerågade 8, 9000 Aalborg.
Tel *99 31 75 00.*
www.visitaalborg.com

UK Embassy
Kastelvej 36–40,
2100 Copenhagen.
Tel *35 44 52 00.*
www.britishembassy.dk

US Embassy
Dag Hammarskjøld Allé 24,
2100 Copenhagen 2.
Tel *33 41 71 00.*
www.denmarkusembassy.gov

Personal Security and Health

Police sign

Denmark is a safe country with a low level of crime. Even in the larger cities there is little likelihood of visitors encountering problems. In the event of a crime or accident, the Danish police and emergency services work very efficiently. In case of any unpleasant incident it is worth asking passers-by or witnesses to the event for their help. As a rule, Danes will not refuse such a request. The chances of falling victim to crime can be further minimized by keeping credit cards, mobile phones and money hidden away and by not carrying excessive amounts of cash.

EMERGENCIES

In case of a road accident, a life-threatening situation, fire, attack or any other predicament that requires immediate intervention by the emergency services, visitors should telephone 112. This toll-free line is staffed by qualified operators who are able to speak foreign languages including English; they will decide which service should be sent to the scene of the incident.

Emergency telephones installed along the hard shoulders of motorways can be used to report a breakdown or accident. When in need, special telephones found on S-tog railway stations and on the metro lines enable people to contact railway duty officers.

An accident or mugging should be reported to the police. The victim and any witnesses to the incident are entitled to give evidence in their native language.

Consulates and embassies can help to contact a visitor's family in the event of an incident, and may also be able to provide financial help or advance the money for a ticket home.

Navy blue police van

POLICE

During the summer season the police are dressed in blue shirts and black trousers; in winter they also wear black jackets. Road police generally wear all-in-one leather suits and ride large white motorcycles. Ordinary police patrol cars are white with the word-"POLITI" in blue lettering. Cars driven by the criminal division are dark blue. Criminal division police usually wear civilian clothes and will show their ID cards when required.

In Copenhagen visitors may encounter traffic wardens, sporting dark green jackets. Traffic wardens are not a part of the police force but are entitled to check if someone has a valid parking ticket and can impose a fine for illegal parking.

Most Danish policemen and policewomen will have at least a working knowledge of the English language. In most cases they will be able to provide some assistance, such as getting in touch with a breakdown service.

Danish policeman

Sign outside a Copenhagen police station

AVOIDING THEFT

Summer and the run-up to Christmas are the times when thieves are most likely to be operating, especially in busy places. Valuables should be deposited with the hotel reception or kept in the safe in your room; money and documents should be carried under clothing rather than in handbags or trouser pockets. Make sure all valuable items are out of sight if parking a car.

PERSONAL BELONGINGS AND LOST PROPERTY

Any theft of money, travel documents, credit cards, as well as any theft from a car or hotel room should be reported immediately at the police station, where an officer will issue a note confirming that the crime has been reported. This note may well be required when filling out an insurance claim or visiting an embassy or consulate.

If documents or personal belongings have been lost you should enquire at the lost property office closest to the area in which the belongings went missing. Any items left behind on a railway train, S-tog or metro should be reported to the duty personnel at the station and, if lost on a bus, to the passenger service office of the appropriate bus company. Lost or stolen credit cards should be reported as soon as possible to the card issuer.

Red-and-white ambulance

MEDICAL ASSISTANCE

Anyone with a medical emergency is entitled to free treatment in hospitals and doctor's surgeries in Denmark, providing that the person has not arrived in the country specifically for that treatment and is unfit to return home. Visitors from the EU are covered by Danish national health insurance but will need to present a European Health Insurance Card (EHIC). Non-EU citizens must have travel insurance.

For all visitors, travel insurance is advisable, however, as it can make it easier to get treatment and should cover the cost of an ambulance (which the patient is responsible for) or an emergency flight home.

Addresses of doctors and hospitals can be obtained from hotel receptions or a camp site manager, and can also be found in a telephone directory. Most Danish doctors speak English.

PHARMACIES

Pharmacies display the word "Apotek" and a green logo in which the letter "A" is combined with the head of a snake. Pharmacies are usually open from 9:30am until 5:30pm on weekdays, and until 2pm on Saturdays. In larger towns there will be a small number of pharmacies open 24 hours a day. The addresses of 24-hour pharmacies can be found displayed on the doors or windows of any pharmacy. Controlled drugs require a doctor's prescription.

Danish pharmacy logo

HEALTH

Travellers to Denmark do not require any special vaccinations. Visitors to the country should pack pain-killers, as well as antidiarrhoeal and travel sickness remedies. Anyone requiring constant medication should take an adequate supply with them as medicines can be very expensive in Denmark.

It is perfectly safe to drink the tap water in Denmark and stomach upsets are uncommon; any stomach problems that do occur are likely to be mild. In many shops and offices visitors should be able to get a free drink of water from one of the water dispensers.

Modern window of a pharmacy in Copenhagen

DIRECTORY

Emergency telephone line – police, ambulance, fire brigade
Tel *112 (toll free).*

HOSPITALS

Amager Hospital, Copenhagen
Italiensvej 1, 2300 Copenhagen S.
Tel *32 34 32 34.*

Odense Universitets Hospital
Sønder Blvd 29, 5000 Odense C.
Tel *66 11 33 33.*

Roskilde Amtssygehuset
Køgevej 7–13, 4000 Roskilde.
Tel *46 32 32 00.*

24-HOUR PHARMACIES

Aalborg Budolfi Apotek
Algade 60, 9000 Aalborg.
Tel *98 12 06 77.*

Copenhagen Steno Apotek
Vesterbrogade 6C, 1620 Copenhagen V. **Tel** *33 14 82 66.*

Copenhagen Sønderbro Apotek
Amagerbrogade 158, 2300 Copenhagen S. **Tel** *32 58 01 40.*

Odense Apoteket Ørnen
Vestergade 80, 5000 Odense C.
Tel *66 12 29 70.*

Roskilde Dom Apotek
Algade 52, 4000 Roskilde.
Tel *46 32 32 77.*

LOST PROPERTY

Buses
Tel *36 13 14 15 (Zealand only).*

S-tog
Tel *70 13 14 15.*
Items left on a train should be reported at the railway station.

Banks and Local Currency

Visitors arriving in Denmark are obliged to have adequate means to pay for their food and accommodation for the duration of their stay. Immigration authorities are usually satisfied with a verbal assurance regarding a visitor's credit card limit. It is also worth having some Danish currency, although most places in Denmark accept credit cards as the Danes do not usually carry much cash. Most Danish banks have ATMs (cash machines) from which Danish kroner can easily be withdrawn by using a credit or debit card.

BANK OPENING HOURS

Banks in Denmark are usually open from 10am until 4pm, Monday to Wednesday and Fridays. On Thursdays banks remain open later, until 6pm. They are closed on Saturdays, Sundays and public holidays including, among others, Maunday Thursday, Good Friday, Christmas Day, Ascension Day and New Year's Day.

One of Denmark's many bureaux de change

EXCHANGING MONEY

Foreign currency can be exchanged in a wide variety of places in Denmark. Exchange booths are open most of the day at Copenhagen Airport. Hotels can also exchange money but offer the least favourable rates of exchange. Banks and special automatic money-exchange machines, available in some places, offer a slightly better rate, but also charge commission. The best deals can be obtained at branches of Forex, Exchange or any other similar bureau de change, which do not charge a commission. In addition, their opening hours are usually more flexible than those of the banks. Exchange rates are usually displayed by the door.

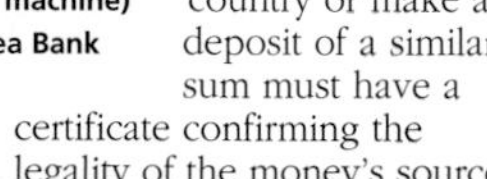

ATM (cash machine) of Nordea Bank

Anyone who wishes to bring more than 40,000 Dkr into the country or make a deposit of a similar sum must have a certificate confirming the legality of the money's source.

A branch of Danske Bank

CREDIT CARDS

There should be no problem with using credit cards such as Visa, Eurocard or MasterCard. American Express and Diners Club may be less readily accepted in Denmark. In many shops and restaurants staff will use a reader to enter a card's data and ask the customer to sign a receipt or key in the card's pin number.

Some shops may refuse to accept a card as payment for low-cost items.

DIRECTORY

BANKS

Danske Bank
Højbro Plads 5,
1200 Copenhagen K.
Map 3 C1.
Tel *45 12 45 50.*
www.danskebank.dk

Jyske Bank
Vesterbrogade 9,
1780 Copenhagen V.
Map 3 A2.
Tel *89 89 00 10.*
www.jyskebank.dk

Nordea
Kongensnytorv 28,
1050 Copenhagen K.
Map 4 D1.
Tel *33 12 11 11.*
www.nordea.dk

Sydbank A/S
Kongens Nytorv 30,
1050 Copenhagen K.
Map 4 D1.
Tel *33 69 78 00.*
www.sydbank.dk

BUREAUX DE CHANGE

Copenhagen
Forex, Nørre Voldgade 90.
Map 1 B5. ***Tel*** *33 32 81 00.*
Hovedbanegården. **Map** 3 A3.
Tel *33 11 22 20.*

Odense
Banegardscentret.
Østre Stationsvej 27.
Tel *66 11 66 18.*

Århus
Ryesgade 28.
Tel *86 80 03 40.*

CURRENCY

Denmark is one of the few EU countries to reject joining the European monetary union, keeping the krone instead. The Danish krone (or crown) is divided into 100 øre. The plural of krone is kroner. Coins come in denominations of 50 øre, and 1, 2, 5, 10 and 20 kroner. Notes come in denominations of 50, 100, 200, 500 and 1,000 kroner. In many places, especially large towns and tourist resorts, prices are often quoted in both kroner and euros.

The Danish krone is written as DKK in most international money markets but is written as Dkr in northern Europe and as kr in Denmark.

New note designs are slowly being introduced until 2011. All Danish notes issued after 1945 will still be valid.

Banknotes
Danish banknotes differ from each other in terms of size and colour. The lowest denomination banknote in circulation is the violet-blue 50-krone note. The largest denomination is the reddish-brown 1,000-krone note.

50 kroner

100 kroner

200 kroner

500 kroner

1,000 kroner

20 kroner

10 kroner

5 kroner

2 kroner

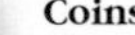

1 krone

50 øre

Coins
The 10 and most of the 20 Dkr coins are golden in colour with the queen's image on the reverse. The 5, 2 and 1 Dkr coins are nickel with a hole in the centre. The 50 øre coin is copper-coloured.

Communications

Danish postal services' logo

Danish postal services are highly efficient. Letters and postcards take between two and four days to reach their destinations within Europe, and between one and two days within Denmark. Telephoning abroad from Denmark is straightforward, although there are fewer public telephones than there once were due to the popularity of mobile phones. Nevertheless, visitors should be able to find a public telephone at a post office, railway station, camp site reception or hotel lobby. Before using the telephone in your hotel room it is best to check the price as hotels sometimes charge a premium rate for calls.

Entrance to a post office building in Copenhagen

USING THE TELEPHONE

Public telephone boxes have become an endangered species in Denmark, due to the prevalence of mobile phones. However, those public phones that do remain are well maintained. There are three types of phone booth: coin only, card only and phones that except both. Card phones can also accept credit cards. Phone cards can be purchased in about 1,500 outlets including post offices and many shops. Calling from a payphone is more expensive than using a private phone, but is cheaper than phoning from a hotel room. The minimum charge for a call from a public phone is 5 Dkr.

Public payphones in Denmark have clear instructions on how to make a call and usually have the dialling codes for many countries listed.

Logo for Denmark's main phone. company

MOBILE TELEPHONES

Most subscription networks can provide the facilities for making international calls. You should check before departure whether your phone will work in Denmark on your current package. It is sometimes possible to get an upgrade for the duration of your holiday. When using a prepaid mobile phone in Denmark you should likewise check whether your package covers international roaming. The price of outgoing calls from Denmark will be higher than calls made at home and incoming calls will also be charged at an international rate. Receiving texts from abroad is free, but sending them is usually subject to a substantial charge.

DIALLING CODES

- Calling Denmark from abroad: 0045.
- From Denmark to the UK: 0044.
- From Denmark to the US/Canada: 001.
- Services: (customer) 80 80 80 80, (wake-up call) 80 20 00 49.

USING A CARD PHONE

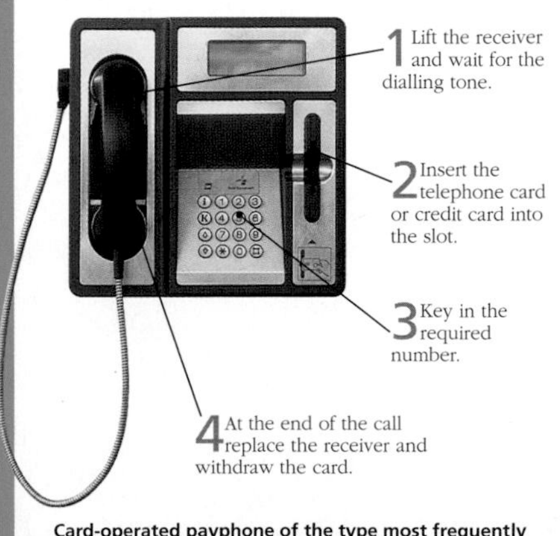

1 Lift the receiver and wait for the dialling tone.
2 Insert the telephone card or credit card into the slot.
3 Key in the required number.
4 At the end of the call replace the receiver and withdraw the card.

Card-operated payphone of the type most frequently encountered in hotels and restaurants

USING A COIN-OPERATED PHONE

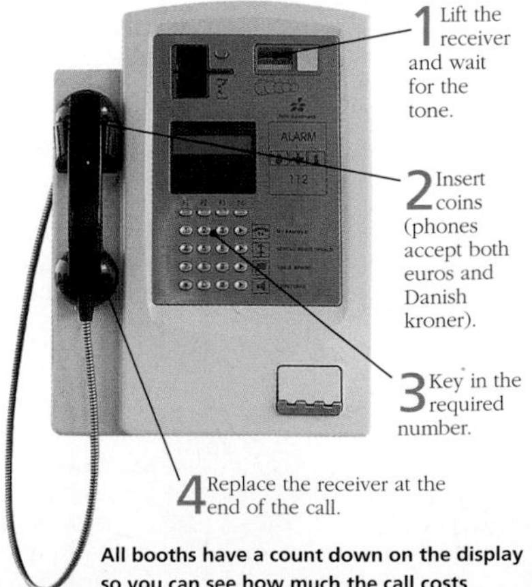

1 Lift the receiver and wait for the tone.
2 Insert coins (phones accept both euros and Danish kroner).
3 Key in the required number.
4 Replace the receiver at the end of the call.
ALARM
112

All booths have a count down on the display so you can see how much the call costs

POSTAL SERVICES

Danish post offices are indicated by the word POST written in white letters on a red background. Most post offices are open Monday to Friday, from 10am to 5pm, until 6pm on Thursdays, and on Saturday from 10am until noon. From some post offices you can make telephone calls, post parcels or registered letters and purchase stamps and envelopes. Poste restante mail can be collected from all of Denmark's post offices.

SENDING A LETTER

Stamps can be purchased at post offices and in many souvenir shops. A small number of stamp-vending machines can also be found. A letter sent to a European country requires a "Europa" tariff postage stamp. Danish postboxes are painted red and feature the crown and trumpet insignia of the national postal service. They display information on the next collection time. Post offices have separate boxes for cheaper local mail (so-called B-post) and for fast delivery A-post or Prioritare mail, including international mail. International mail sent from Copenhagen should leave the country within 24 hours.

An address in Denmark should include the name of the addressee, street, house number, town and postcode. It is very important to include the post code as many Danish towns, as well as streets within Copenhagen, have the same name.

Easy to recognise Danish letterbox

Colourful examples of Danish postage stamps

Addresses for an apartment may sometimes include the floor and staircase as well as the number of a flat within the building itself. For example the address may be written as Bjergvej 20, 3.tv (3 stands for 3rd floor and tv stands for "til venstre", meaning "to the left").

INTERNET AND EMAIL

More than half of Denmark's population has access to the internet. The internet is not regarded a luxury in Denmark, and it is easy to check for personal email in many places, including internet cafés. In most of the more upmarket hotels each room has an internet link, while other hotels have dedicated spaces or special business rooms where visitors can plug in their laptops or use the hotel's computers. Most hotels in Denmark's holiday resorts can provide internet access at reception. Many youth hostels and camp sites also have computers with broadband links to the internet.

Copenhagen has quite a number of internet cafés, as do many of the other large towns. These are ideal places to surf the net, send an email or even download and print some documents. The cost is not prohibitive, although printing can add up, and the connection speeds tend to be fast. Staff at internet cafés are usually knowledgeable and generally willing to help.

MEDIA

Most of the major foreign papers including US and UK dailies such as *The Times, Guardian* and the *Wall Street Journal* are on sale in Copenhagen and other large towns and can be picked up at train-station kiosks and from some of the larger newsagents. Magazines such as *Time* and the *Economist* are also readily available. Denmark's own press consists of about 50 daily newspapers. Of these, *Politiken* and *Jyllandsposten* have the largest circulation. The weekly *Copenhagen Post* has Danish news and a short listings section in English.

Denmark has three public-service television channels, DR1, DR2 and TV2. These screen news and current affairs along with light entertainment such as music and game shows. Other channels, such as Kanal 4 and Kanal 5, are more commercial in character, with soaps and comedy. TV3 is aimed at families while TV3+ is the main sport channel. Many US and British shows appear on TV with Danish subtitles. English-language news is often available on cable and satellite. News in English is broadcast Mon–Fri at 10:30am, 5:10pm and 10pm by Radio Denmark International (1062 Mhz).

***Politiken* and *Copenhagen Post*, two of Denmark's newspapers**

TRAVEL INFORMATION

Flights to Denmark from most parts of northern Europe are fast and frequent. Planes land at Copenhagen from over 100 destinations worldwide and the airport receives over 20 million passengers every year. Fewer people arrive by train and ferry, although ferries are popular with visitors from elsewhere in Scandinavia. Ease of travel has been vastly improved with the construction of the Store Bælt (Great Belt) bridge, linking Zealand and Funen, and the fixed-link Øresund bridge between Zealand and Sweden. Getting to the smaller Danish islands requires taking a ferry. Travelling on the mainland and around the major islands is fairly easy, thanks to a network of well-maintained motorways and railway lines, and the country's efficient coach service.

SAS aircraft

AIR TRAVEL

Most visitors to Denmark arrive at Copenhagen Airport (Kastrup), which is 2 km (7 miles) southeast of the city centre. **Scandinavian Airlines** (SAS) connects Copenhagen with most European capitals including Dublin and also has non-stop flights from New York and Chicago. From Australasia the best connections are via Bangkok. Billund airport (for LEGOLAND®) has flights from many European cities including Amsterdam, Frankfurt and London. **Ryanair** has daily low-cost flights from London Stansted to Århus and Esbjerg, and also to Malmø in Sweden with a special connecting coach to Copenhagen. Other airlines serving Copenhagen include **Aer Lingus**, **bmi** (British Midland), **British Airways**, **easyJet** (from London Stansted and Newcastle) and **Cimber Sterling**.

TARIFFS

Ticket prices charged by SAS are comparable with most airlines. However, intense competition means that airlines vary their prices continuously and it is difficult to be precise about tariffs. There are nevertheless certain set rules. Business class travel will always cost more than economy. The cheapest ticket will always be linked to some conditions, such as having to purchase it by a certain date and a limited period of validity. People who can afford to spend more on their tickets have more freedom to decide when to travel and to amend flight details if necessary. Visitors who book at short notice will inevitably pay higher prices.

A number of concessions are available from some airlines. SAS offer discounts to pensioners over 65 and also to children and students. To get the best deal visitors should contact their local travel agent or browse the Internet for last-minute deals. Following the liberalization of the aviation market, many cheap, no-frills flights are now available within Europe.

Terminal
Terminal 3
Ankomsthal
Arrival hall
Told VAT - Tax free
Customs VAT - Tax free
Valuta veksling
Exchange
Postkontor
Post office
Garderobe
Left luggage

Information board at Copenhagen Airport

DOMESTIC FLIGHTS

Air travel within Denmark is relatively inexpensive, provided that you book your tickets a couple of weeks before your departure date. The major inland carriers are SAS and Cimber Sterling. SAS flies from Copenhagen to Århus and Aalborg. Cimber Sterling flies from Copenhagen to Bornholm. The routes particularly worth recommending include Copenhagen to Aalborg (a six-hour journey by car) and Copenhagen to Bornholm.

General view of Copenhagen Airport

Modern entrance to Copenhagen Airport

AIRPORTS

The country's main airport is Copenhagen Airport (formerly known as Kastrup). It has three terminals: two for international flights, and one for internal flights. The airport is situated on Amager Island, a short way from the city centre. Like many of the country's airports, it has helpful staff and excellent information services. The airport's facilities include shops and restaurants, cash machines (ATMs) and lockers. Rooms can be rented at the Transfer Hotel, located within the transit hall, for a minimum of four hours and a maximum stay of 16 hours. Cars can be hired at terminals 1 and 3.

A fast and economical train service runs every 10 minutes from the airport's Terminal 3 to Central Station in Copenhagen. Trains run throughout the day and most of the night (between 03:57am and 00:29am) and take 12 minutes. The metro and buses also make the journey and drop passengers off at Rådhuspladsen. The price of a bus ticket is much the same as the train, however, and the journey time is nearly three times as long. The taxi rank by the exit of Terminal 3 is a good option for visitors with a lot of heavy luggage.

Billund international airport is served by buses running from Århus, Vejle, Horsens and LEGOLAND® as well as by long-distance buses from Kolding and Esbjerg. Car rental companies at Billund include international names Avis, Europecar and Hertz.

Århus airport is 40 km (25 miles) northeast of the city centre. Buses link the airport to the city and drop passengers off at Århus's railway station. The journey time is about 45 minutes.

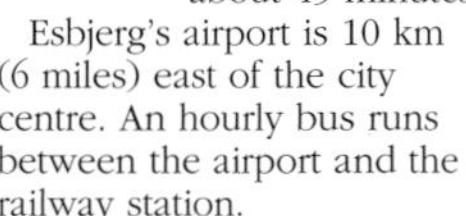

Logo of Scandinavian Airlines

Esbjerg's airport is 10 km (6 miles) east of the city centre. An hourly bus runs between the airport and the railway station.

An express bus links Aalborg's airport with the city centre. Parking around the airport is free, although drivers must pay if they wish to leave their car at the attended car park.

Check in at Copenhagen Airport

DIRECTORY

SAS

Denmark **Tel** *70 10 20 00.*
Ireland **Tel** *01 844 5440.*
UK **Tel** *0871 521 2772.*
USA/Canada
Tel *1800 221 2350 (toll free).*
www.sas.dk

OTHER AIRLINES

Aer Lingus
Tel *0818 365 000 (Ireland).*
www.aerlingus.com

bmi (British Midland)
Tel *0870 607 0555 (UK).*
www.flybmi.com

British Airways
Tel *0844 493 0787 (UK).*
www.britishairways.com

Cimber Sterling
Tel *70 10 12 18 (DK).*
www.cimber.dk

easyJet
Tel *0871 244 2366 (UK).*
www.easyjet.com

Ryanair
Tel *0871 246 0000 (UK).*
www.ryanair.com

DANISH AIRPORTS

Københavns Lufthavn (Copenhagen Airport)
Lufthavnsboulevarden 6,
2770 Kastrup.
Tel *32 31 32 31.*
www.cph.dk

Billund Lufthavn
Postboks 10, 7190 Billund.
Tel *76 50 50 50.*
www.bll.dk

Karup Lufthavn
N.O. Hansens Vej 4,
7470 Karup J.
Tel *97 10 06 10.*
www.karup-airport.dk

Aalborg Lufthavn
Lufthavnsvej 100,
9400 Nørresundby.
Tel *98 17 11 44.*
www.aal.dk

Århus Lufthavn
Stabrandvej 24, 8560 Kolind.
Tel *87 75 70 00.*
www.aar.dk

Travelling by Train and Ferry

Danish trains are not particularly cheap but are reliable, fast and extremely comfortable. The Danish railway system is currently undergoing a programme of modernization on many lines, which should make journey times even faster in the future. Holders of an InterRail or similar pass are entitled to unlimited use of the extensive railway network throughout the country. A network of ferry links provides a convenient way to travel to some of Denmark's many islands as well as between Denmark and countries such as Germany, Sweden and Norway.

19th-century railway station building in Roskilde

DOMESTIC TRAINS

The Danish state railway or **DSB** has an extensive network that covers both local and long-distance lines and, with an InterRail or similar pass, provides an extremely cheap and efficient way of seeing the country. Danish trains are modern and safe. The long-distance trains, such as those that run between Copenhagen and Aalborg, are stylish and sophisticated. Intercity trains have comfortable air-conditioned carriages. They are open-plan, with seating arranged in pairs facing each other. Above each seat is a reading light and, often, individual music jacks for headphones and power supply sockets for laptops. Information displayed above each seat indicates whether a seat has been reserved and to which station. Intercity trains also contain payphones, baby-changing facilities, space for oversize luggage and even children's play areas. In some parts of the train dogs are not allowed; in others, known as rest sections, silence must be maintained and the use of mobile phones is prohibited. On some of the busiest routes DSB operate "business class" trains which, along with all the creature comforts of intercity trains, feature luxuries such as free drinks and snacks.

Local trains, many of which have double-decker carriages, are generally slower and have fewer facilities but are perfectly adequate for shorter distances.

Details of the network and main train schedules are available in a booklet from all DSB stations.

TICKET AND TRAVEL CARD DISPENSER FOR LOCAL TRAINS

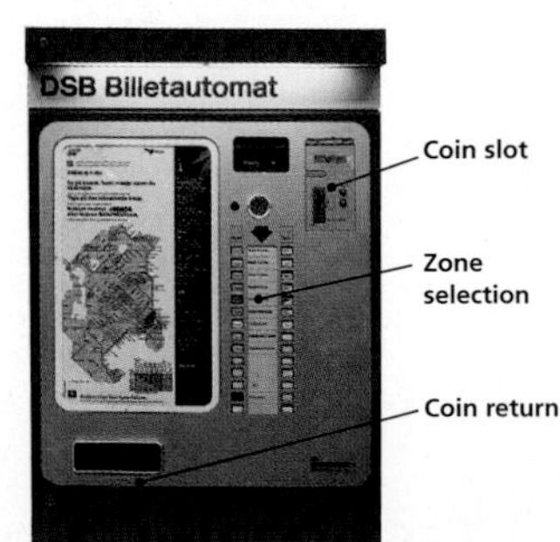

INTERNATIONAL RAIL SERVICES

DSB is responsible for most of Denmark's internal railway system and some of the international routes. Train services operate to Denmark from most parts of northern Europe including Germany, Sweden and Norway. The most common route to Jutland is through Germany, while many people travel to Zealand by train from Sweden across the Øresund Bridge. Travel from the UK is generally via the Netherlands. Once in the country, Copenhagen's Central Station is the main point of arrival for international rail services and allows passengers to disembark in the centre of the capital.

The *Thomas Cook European Timetable*, available from Thomas Cook travel agents, gives a complete listing of train schedules in Europe.

Express train waiting at a platform in Copenhagen

TRAIN TICKETS

Tickets can be bought at stations or reserved by calling the DSB reservation line or logging onto the DSB website, which has an English language version.

Anyone wishing to travel extensively by train should consider one of the special passes. InterRail tickets are available to residents of European countries. Visitors from outside Europe can purchase a Eurail Pass. Both passes are available in a flexible range of options and give substantial discounts on travel in Europe.

Many other rail concessions are available within Denmark and you should always ask about discounts for off-peak travel, family tickets and discounted return fares. Children aged between 10 and 15 travel for half price; children under 12, when with someone with a ticket, travel for free. Further information can be obtained from DSB ticket offices.

A hydrofoil in Nexø, Bornholm

RAILWAY STATIONS

Danish railway stations are clean and well maintained. Facilities include heated waiting rooms and snack bars. Copenhagen's Central Station is a major hub and has a small shopping centre with a variety of shops, and a supermarket, post office and police station.

DOMESTIC FERRIES

Denmark's territory covers a large number of populated islands. These islands are linked by an extensive domestic ferry service making ferry services an important element in the country's transport infrastructure. Some routes are very short, taking a matter of minutes. The longest route, from Køge to Bornholm, takes nearly seven hours.

Ferries in Denmark, especially the long-distance ones, are clean and comfortable with cafés, bars and passenger lounges.

INTERNATIONAL FERRIES

Most ferries are run by **DFDS Seaways**. The other major ferry company is **Stena Line**, which operates mainly between Denmark, Norway and Sweden.

The opening of the bridges spanning the Øresund (Sound) and the Store Bælt has to a degree reduced the demand for ferry travel between Denmark and Sweden, as well as between Zealand and Funen. Nevertheless, the Danes and visitors to the country continue to use many of the ferry services.

FERRY TICKETS

Tickets for ferry services within Denmark as well as services between Denmark and other countries can usually be reserved using Internet websites. Fares can vary widely depending on the season or the time of day. Substantial discounts are often available for students and young people who have an international rail pass.

For many local routes it is not necessary to book a ticket and passengers need only arrive shortly before departure. Longer routes generally require a ticket to be purchased well in advance. Reservations should also be made in advance when travelling at busy times or if you are planning to bring a vehicle.

International ferry docking in Copenhagen

DIRECTORY

TRAVEL INFORMATION

DSB Train Tickets Reservation and Information
Tel 70 13 14 15.
www.dsb.dk

Train and Coach Service Information
www.rejseplanen.dk

DOMESTIC FERRY SERVICES

DFDS Seaways (Denmark)
Dampfærgevej 30, 2100 Copenhagen Ø.
Tel *33 42 30 00.*
www.dfdsseaways.dk

Scandlines
Dampfærgevej 10, 2100 Copenhagen Ø.
Tel *33 15 15 15.*
www.scandlines.dk

Smyril Line
Yviri við Strond 1, 110 Tórshavn, Faroe Islands.
Tel *(+298) 34 59 00.*
www.smyril-line.com

INTERNATIONAL FERRY SERVICES

Color Line
Norgeskajen 2, 9850 Hirtshals.
Tel *99 56 20 00.*
www.colorline.com

DFDS Seaways (UK)
Scananavia House, Refinery Road, Harwich, Essex, CO12 4QG.
Tel *+44 871 522 9955.*
www.dfdsseaways.co.uk

Fjordline
Nordsøterminalen Trailerkajen 1, 9850 Hirtshals.
Tel *97 96 30 00.*
www.fjordline.dk

Stena Line
Trafikhavnen, 9900 Frederikshavn.
Tel *96 20 02 00.*
www.stenaline.dk

Travelling by Car

Sign indicating scenic route

Notwithstanding Denmark's excellent public transport, a car can still be a convenient method of travel for visitors, particularly when travelling in groups of three or four. Using a car can reduce travel costs significantly and is good for visiting out-of-the-way places. Danish motorways are toll-free, the major roads are well signposted and of a good standard, and travelling over one of the new bridges, such as the Store Bælt Bridge between Zealand and Funen, can be a truly breathtaking experience on a clear day. Particularly scenic roads are signposted by a marguerite on a brown background.

ARRIVING BY CAR

Anyone driving to Denmark must travel via Germany as this is the country's only land border. Following the implementation of the Schengen Treaty in 2001, immigration checkpoints between EU countries have been abolished. There are still customs checkpoints at sea and land borders with Germany and drivers may expect customs but generally you will not be required to stop and produce a passport. The main route into Denmark is the E45 which forms part of a European network and runs through Jutland, ending up at Frederikshavn.

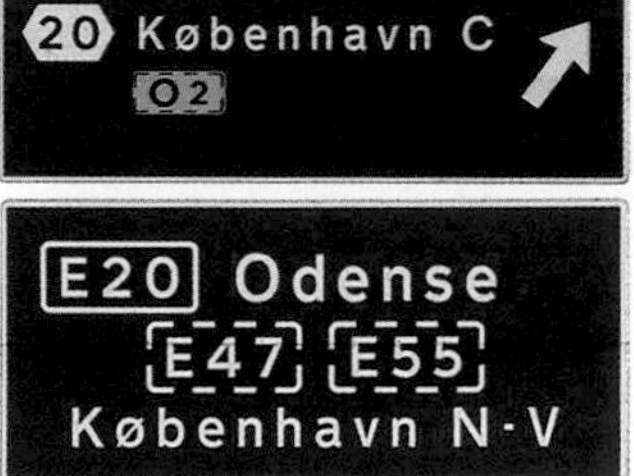

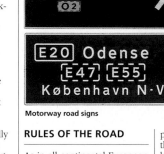

Motorway road signs

RULES OF THE ROAD

As in all continental European countries, the Danes drive on the right. Cars from the UK will need to have their headlights adjusted. Both cars and motorcycles must have dipped headlights on during the day and seat belts must be worn at all times. Children under three must be in a child seat. When turning to the right, drivers must give way to cyclists on the inside. A warning triangle must be kept in the car in case of a breakdown.

The speed limit is usually 50 km/h (30 mph) in town, 80 km/h (50 mph) on most roads and up to 130 km/h (80 mph) on the motorways. Hefty fines may be charged on the spot for breaking the speed limit as well as for other motoring offences such as not wearing a seat belt or talking on a mobile phone while driving. Being caught driving under the influence of alcohol will incur even stiffer penalties and possibly imprisonment.

Self-service Fuel Pump at a Petrol Station
Many stations in Denmark are equipped with special self-service fuel pumps. These are easy to use and accept both cash and credit cards.

Hertz
Biludlejning

Hertz Car Hire logo

PARKING

Tickets for parking are obtained from kerbside machines. Known as *billet-automat*, these accept most coins.

In many smaller towns, parking is free and is regulated by a parking disk available from all garages. The plastic disk has an hour hand that you leave on your dash board. Different zones are marked with a blue sign with the letter "P". Also on the sign is the time limit for parking. Signs marked as *1 time* mean you can stay for an hour; *2 timer* is two hours and so on. When parking within these time zones set the hour hand to indicate the time when you parked the car so that the wardens can check whether the limit has been exceeded.

In larger towns parking is often free between 6pm and 8am, after 2pm on Saturdays and all day Sundays. The Danish for no parking is *parkering forbudt*. For parking in towns, see page 303.

BREAKDOWNS

In the event of a breakdown drivers should telephone the emergency number given by their hire company or breakdown organization. Phones on motorways are placed at 2-km (1-mile) intervals. For other emergencies dial 112 and ask for the relevant service.

CAR HIRE

Representatives of most major car hire firms can be found at airports, upmarket hotels and in city centres. Car hire tends to be expensive in Denmark; booking beforehand through an international firm can work out much cheaper. Three of the major firms in Denmark are **Avis**, **Europcar** and **Hertz**.

ROADS, MOTORWAYS AND BRIDGES

Motorway signs in Denmark are colour coded and easy to understand. Exits are indicated by blue signs while green signs indicate cities that can be reached along the motorway.

There are five trans-European motorways in Denmark. The E20 runs west to east from Esbjerg though Kolding and Odense, across the Store Bælt and onto Køge and Copenhagen; the E29 links Hirtshals to Nørresundby; the E45 crosses the German border and links Kolding, Århus, Aalborg and Frederikshavn; the E47 links Helsingør, Copenhagen, Køge, Maribo and Rødbyhavn. The E55 runs between Helsingør, Copenhagen, Køge, Nykøbing F and Gedser.

Danish motorway sign

Caravans – a common sight on Denmark's roads

Part of the E20 consists of bridges over the Storebælt and Øresund (Sound). A toll is charged to cross and is collected at entry or exit points. The toll stations are equipped with card machines or are manned by staff at busier times. The yellow *Manuel* lanes are for payment by credit card or cash.

The Store Bælt bridge toll charges are between 200 and 350 Dkr, depending upon the size and height of your vehicle. The toll charges for the Øresund Bridge are similar in price.

ROAD MANNERS

Danes are generally careful drivers and tend to observe the country's speed limits, both on motorways and local roads and when driving in town. On motorways cars often cruise along the middle lane, leaving the left one for faster traffic and the right one for slower vehicles. It is compulsory to indicate when changing lane.

WHAT TO TAKE

Anyone driving in Denmark must have all the relevant documents including insurance and an international driver's licence. Check that you have breakdown cover with a company that has reciprocal arrangements with Denmark. **FDM**, the Danish motoring organization, can provide further information.

It is not compulsory to carry a first-aid kit, but it is good to have one in the car, as well as a car fire extinguisher, a torch and a towrope.

Motorway entrance

DIRECTORY

INFORMATION

FDM
Firskovvej 32, 2800 Lyngby
Tel *45 27 07 07.*
www.fdm.dk

TOLL CHARGES

Øresund Bridge
Tel *70 23 90 60.*
www.oresundbron.com

Store Bælt Bridge
Tel *70 15 10 15.*
www.storebaelt.dk

CAR HIRE

AVIS
Avis Biludlejning,
Sluseholmen 3,
2450 Copenhagen SV.
Tel *33 26 80 00*
www.avis.dk

Europcar
Gl Kongevej 13, Copenhagen.
Tel *70 11 66 99.*
www.europcar.dk

Hertz
Vester Farimagsgade 1,
1606 Copenhagen V.
Tel *33 17 90 00.*
www.hertzdk.dk

Getting Around Danish Towns

A cycle lane's markings

Most Danish towns and cities can easily be explored on foot. Cycling is widespread and all Danish towns, including the capital, have good cycle lane networks. On normal roads, drivers treat cyclists as they would any other legitimate road users. All this makes cycling an enjoyable way to explore a town. Public transport in most cities is efficient, safe and reasonably priced. Taxis are another good way to get around and are especially convenient for anyone that is carrying heavy luggage or large amounts of shopping.

Pedestrian crossing lights at a busy city intersection

ON FOOT

All of Denmark's towns and cities are compact and most have pedestrianized areas. In addition, many sights tend to be closely grouped together and signposting is good, making getting around on foot a pleasurable experience.

Nevertheless, pedestrians should observe the traffic regulations. Care should be exercised when crossing the road, although Danish drivers are very attentive towards pedestrians and would never enter a crossing when there are people on it; nor would they force their right of way in any other situation.

Pedestrians who step onto the cycle lanes that run along beside the pavements are strongly frowned upon, however, especially during the busy rush hour. Danish cities such as Copenhagen, Århus and Odense often have walking tours, which offer an alternative way to explore the city.

BICYCLES

Most Danes own and use bicycles – it has been estimated that Danes cycle, on average, over 600 km (373 miles) a year. Danish cities make many allowances for cyclists including numerous cycle paths and advantageous laws regarding right of way.

Copenhagen is especially cycle-friendly and even runs a scheme known as Bycykler, which allows anyone to borrow a bike for free. The scheme, which runs during summer, is aimed at reducing congestion in the city centre and provides over 2,000 bikes for anyone who wishes to use one. The bicycles have solid wheels and punctureless tyres and, to deter theft, are unsuitable for travelling long distances. They are available from 125 stands throughout the city. Many of the stands are located close to the main attractions and can also be found at some of the larger S-tog stations. A 20 Dkr coin must be deposited in the Bycykler stand to release a bike. This deposit is returned once the bike is placed back in a stand.

Bikes and accessories such as helmets and child seats can be hired in many of Denmark's towns and cities from companies including **København Cykler** in Copenhagen, **City Cykler** in Odense or **Morten Mengel Cykelværksted** in Århus.

Although cycling can be a fun way to get around, there are a number of factors that should be taken into account. No bike should be left unlocked and expensive bikes should be avoided as they are highly desirable to thieves. In larger towns it is advisable to attach the bicycle to a cycle rack. On the busy streets of Copenhagen cyclists new to the city should exercise special care, as many of the city's native cyclists whizz around at an alarming pace and expect others to do the same.

When using cycle lanes cyclists must observe general traffic regulations, such as not jumping red lights. Bicycles must be equipped with lights after dark and have reflectors fitted at the back and front. Cyclists stopped under influence of alcohol may not only incur a hefty fine but also lose their driver's licence. Everybody, especially children, should wear safety helmets when riding a bicycle.

Outside of peak hours, bicycles can be taken onto trains. Carrying a bicycle on

Bicycles, a popular form of transport in Danish towns and cities

City bus – tickets can be bought on board or in advance

the train or metro in the city requires a special bicycle ticket. The fee is minimal, however, and multiple-journey cards for transporting a bicycle are also available.

DRIVING IN TOWN

In accordance with their environmental concerns, the Danish government does its best to discourage people from using their car, and driving in the larger towns and cities is to be avoided if at all possible. Major cities are often congested and parking and fuel are very expensive, as is the cost of hiring a car. Pedestrians and cyclists take precedence on city roads and car drivers are obliged to give way when turning right to cyclists coming up on the inside and, even if there is a green light, to pedestrians crossing the road.

PARKING IN TOWN

A fee is charged for on-street parking in Denmark's city centres between 8am and 6pm Monday to Friday and from 8am–2pm on Saturdays. At all times it can be difficult to find a parking space, especially in the centre of towns and cities. It can also be expensive to park a car. Some Danish cities have parking zones, with zones closest to the centre costing the most. Non payment of parking charges or exceeding the permitted time limit incurs high fines. See page 300 for more on parking in Denmark.

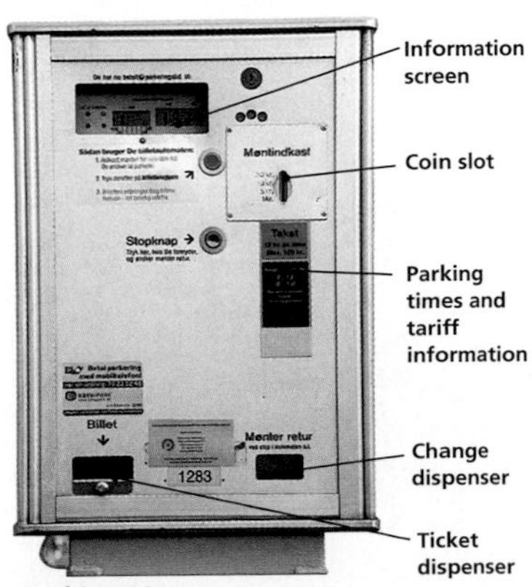

Parking Meter
Parking meters are found within all pay-zones. The driver has to estimate the parking time and pay the price. The meter then prints out a time-coded ticket.

PUBLIC TRANSPORT

Most cities in Denmark have well-run, modern systems of public transport, and anyone planning to stay in the larger towns will have little need of a car. Many Danish cities, including Copenhagen, Odense and Århus, have their own travel cards, which entitle the user to unlimited use of local transport for a set period.

Maps and timetables are available from tourist offices in the major cities that list the main bus and rail routes as well as the main sights close to the stops. Central bus stations in towns and cities are usually situated next to the main train station or by the ferry terminal.

Books of tickets *(klippekort)* are readily available in the major cities, such as Århus, Copenhagen and Odense, which are valid on buses and local trains. Weekly or monthly passes such as the Århus Pass and Odense Eventrypas allow unlimited travel on public transport and include discounted or free admission to city attractions. Reduced-fare travel cards for children are available up to the age of 16 and are valid for the same periods and zones as adult travel cards.

For more detailed information on public transport in Copenhagen see pages 312–13.

TAXIS

In Denmark there is little problem with finding a taxi, although they can be rather expensive. Taxi ranks can be found in front of all railway stations, airports and ferry terminals, as well as in town centres and major shopping centres. Taxis can be booked by phone. Those with a lit sign saying *fri* can be flagged down in the street. Fares start at 24–30 Dkr and are then charged by the kilometre. A higher rate is levied at night and when booked by phone. Most taxis in Denmark accept credit cards, and there is no need to offer a tip.

TAXI
4 vogne

Sign for a taxi rank

DIRECTORY

BICYCLE HIRE

City Cykler
Odense. ***Tel*** *66 12 97 93.*
www.citycykler.dk

København Cykler
Copenhagen. ***Tel*** *33 33 86 13.*
www.rentabike.dk

Morten Mengel Cykelværksted
Århus. ***Tel*** *86 19 29 27.*
www.mmcykler.dk

TAXIS

Århus Taxa
Århus. ***Tel*** *89 48 48 48.*

Dantaxi
Nationwide. ***Tel*** *70 33 83 38.*

Odense Taxa
Odense. ***Tel*** *66 15 44 15.*

Public Transport in Copenhagen

Logo of the S-tog train

Copenhagen is an easy city to explore thanks to its up-to-date system of public transport. The metro and the network of buses and trains run throughout the week and are cheap and efficient. Waterbuses make the most of Copenhagen's canals and provide an excellent means of getting around. The city's transport system has an integrated fare structure, which means that you can use *klippekort* (clip cards) and travel passes on the metro, buses and S-tog. Copenhagen is one of the safest cities in Europe and there should be no problem travelling alone, even at night.

BUSES

One of the easiest and most pleasant ways to get around in Copenhagen is by bus. Copenhagen's efficient HT bus network, run by **HUR**, has a common fare structure with the city's S-tog and metro trains. Bus stops are marked by posts carrying a yellow signboard with the letters BUS. Buses run according to a schedule displayed at the stop. When asked to stop at a specific stop the driver will announce its approach. Otherwise the driver is entitled to drive past the stop if no one is waiting. Tickets can be purchased at the time of boarding providing you have the correct change. Travel cards should be clipped by inserting them into the yellow time clock next to the driver. Disembarking takes place via the central or back doors.

Buses, like trains, begin operating at about 5am (6am on Sundays). Unlike trains, however, a number of buses run throughout the night and operate on special routes, according to a night timetable.

METRO

The newest form of transport in Copenhagen is the **Metro**, which links the airport to the city centre and Vanløse. The metro system, which has been designed to complement the S-tog rail network, is constantly being extended, and by 2018 there should be a route circling the entire city.

The bright, modern trains were produced in Italy and are fully in accord with the Danes' love of elegant design. Each train can hold up to 300 passengers, with seating for 96. Even at peak times they do not feel crowded, and a journey through Copenhagen in a light and spacious metro carriage is an enjoyable experience in itself.

Metro trains are fully automated and consist of single driverless carriages. The doors open automatically in line with the platform doors, making it impossible for anyone to fall onto the track. Call points by each of the carriage doors can be used in an emergency or by passengers in wheelchairs.

Travel cards must be punched into the yellow time clocks on the platform before boarding.

Metro stations are marked with the red letter "M" and can easily be spotted above ground by the 5-m (16-ft) high illuminated information posts outside them.

Metro station in Copenhagen

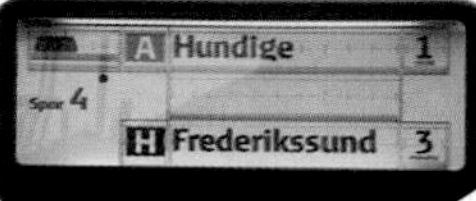

Board on platform showing S-tog departure information

S-TOG

Copenhagen's rail system is known as **S-tog** and is run by DSB (Danish State Railways). This fast and convenient service consists of 10 lines that all pass through Central Station and run to the distant outskirts of the city. The DSB's website has a journey planner, allowing you to work out the best route around Copenhagen.

Tickets can be bought at the station. Travel cards must be punched into one of the yellow time clocks on the platform by inserting it with the magnetic strip facing downwards.

All trains are marked with a red hexagon bearing a white letter "S". Those marked with an "x" are express trains with limited stops. Much of the system is adapted for disabled passengers, with lifts from street level to the platforms. Outside peak hours, passengers are allowed to carry bicycles on the train. Trains begin operating from about 5am and run till about half past midnight.

Modern S-tog at the platform

TICKETS AND TRAVEL PASSES

Copenhagen's public transport system has a common fare structure, which means that tickets are valid on trains, buses and the metro, and transferring from one mode of transport to another is possible on the same ticket. You can purchase tickets from ticket offices, vending machines at stations and bus drivers.

The metropolitan area is split into seven zones. Coloured zone maps can be found at information desks and are also on display at bus and train stations. The cheapest ticket *(billet)* allows you to travel within two zones. A *klippekort* is valid for 10 journeys within two zones. For travel between three or more zones you will need to buy the appropriate ticket or clip the appropriate number of tickets on your *klippekort*. Clipping stamps your travel card with the date and time and the zone from which you are departing. Cards stamped for journeys within the same zone or between two or three zones are valid for one hour. Four-, five- and six-zone tickets are valid for an hour and a half. Tickets and stamped 10-trip cards for all zones are valid for two hours. Travelling without a valid ticket carries a high penalty.

Between 1am and 5am fares double. If you are using a *klippekort*, you will need to clip an extra ticket. Special tickets are available which allow for unrestricted travel over a 24-hour period. Tourist passes, such as the Copenhagen Card, allow unlimited travel on public transport, as well as discounted admission to many of the city's attractions.

Two children up to the age of 12 travel free when accompanied by an adult carrying an appropriate ticket. Four children up to the age of 12 can travel on one ticket, or one clip of an adult *klippekort*. Children below the age of 16 pay a child's fare when travelling alone and may take another child up to the age of 12 at no extra cost.

WATERBUSES

Canal boats are a popular form of transport in the city and are a particularly good way to avoid any traffic congestion. A trip aboard a waterbus is also a good way to see Copenhagen as the city's canals lead past many of the major historic sights and attractions. One of the most popular tourist routes is the trip from Nyhavn, along Holmenskanal. Along the route the boat stops at the statue of the Little Mermaid, Amalienborg Slot, Christianshavn, Vor Frelsers Kirke, the Nationalmuseet, Christiansborg Slot, Holmens Kirke and back to Nyhavn.

Some trips on the canal are run privately by companies such as **DFDS** and are accompanied by a guide, who provides information about the sights. These are particularly appealing to families with small children as they keep the kids amused and avoid tired legs.

Cards can be purchased which allow unlimited travel on the yellow harbour bus network for a limited period. Holders of the Copenhagen Card and the weekly travel cards are also entitled to use the yellow harbour bus (guided tours must be paid for). Alternatively, it is possible to pay on the boat for a short ride from one stop to another. On some routes waterbuses run only at weekends; others operate only on weekdays.

Waterbus departure point

DIRECTORY

COPENHAGEN TRANSPORT INFORMATION (HUR)

Information Centre
Gammel Køge Landevej 3,
2500 Valby.
Tel *36 13 14 15.*

TRAINS

S-tog
Tel *70 13 14 15.*
www.dsb.dk

Metro
Tel *70 15 16 15.*
www.m.dk

WATERBUSES

DFDS Canal Tours
Tel *32 96 30 00.*
www.canaltours.dk

General Index

Page numbers in **bold** type refer to main entries. The Danish letters å (aa), æ and ø fall at the end of the alphabet *(see p325)*.

N

R

S

T

U

V

W

Y

Z

A (AA)

Æ

Ø

Acknowledgments

HACHETTE LIVRE POLSKA would like to thank the following people whose contribution and assistance have made the preparation of the book possible:

Additional Text
Sue Dobson, Roger Norum, Marek Pernal, Jakub Sito, Barbara Sudnik-Wójcikowska, Jennifer Wattam Klit.

Additional Illustrations
Dorota Jarymowicz, Paweł Pasternak.

Additional Photographs
Oldrich Karasek, Ian O'Leary, Laura Pilgaard Rasmussen, Jakub Sito, Jon Spaul, Barbara Sudnik-Wójcikowska, Monika Witkowska, Andrzej Zygmuntowicz and Ireneusz Winnicki, Juliusz Żebrowski.

DORLING KINDERSLEY would like to thank the following people whose contribution and assistance have made the preparation of the book possible:

Publisher
Douglas Amrine.

Publishing Managers
Anna Streiffert, Vicki Ingle.

Managing Art Director
Kate Poole.

Senior Editor
Kathryn Lane.

Editorial Assistance
Sam Fletcher, Anna Freiberger.

Additional Picture Research
Rachel Barber, Ellen Root.

Cartography
Vinod Harish, Vincent Kurien, Azeem Siddiqui, Casper Morris.

DTP Designers
Uma Bhattacharya, Mohammad Hassan, Jasneet Kaur, Alistair Richardson.

Factcheckers
Britt Lightbody, Katrine Anker Møller.

Proofreader
Stewart J. Wild.

Indexer
Helen Peters.

Jacket Design
Tessa Bindloss.

Additional Design and Editorial
Conrad van Dyk, Mariana Evmolpidou, Laura Jones, Priya Kukadia, Delphine Lawrance, Catherine Palmi, Laura Pilgaard Rasmussen, Pollyanna Poulter, Simon Ryder, Sands Publishing Solutions, Dora Whitaker.

Special Assistance and Permissions
The Publishers also wish to thank all persons and institutions for their permission to reproduce photographs of their property, for allowing us to photograph inside the buildings and to use photographs from their archives:

Amager Youth Hostel; Amalienborg, Copenhagen (S. Haslund-Christensen, Lord Chamberlain and Colonel Jens Greve, Palace Steward); Amber Museum, Copenhagen; Aquarium, Charlottenlund; Arbejdermuseet, Copenhagen (Peter Ludvigsen); Bornholm Tourist Information Centre (Pernille Larsen); Carlsberg Brewery; Ceramics Museum, Rønne; Christiansborg, Copenhagen; Copenhagen Airports A/S (Bente Schmidt – Event- and visitor department); Copenhagen Town Hall (Allan Johansen); Corbis (Łukasz Wyrzykowski); Danish Tourist Board Photo Database (Christian Moritz – Area Sales Manager); Dansk Moebelkunst (Dorte Slot) (Bredgade 32, Copenhagen K) www.dmk.dk; Davids Samling, Copenhagen; Danish Chamber of Tourism & SAS Group PR (Agnieszka Blandzi, Director); Egeskov Castle; Experimentarium, Copenhagen; H. Ch. Andersen Museum, Odense; Holmegaard Glass Factory; Jagna Noren – a guide to Bornholm; Jesper T. Møller and other employees of the National Museum in Copenhagen; Karen Blixen Museum; Knud Rasmussens Haus; Kronborg castle; Legoland, Billund; Lene Henrichsen – assistant to the director of the Louisiana museum; Louisiana – Museum for Modern Kunst (Susanne Hartz); The Museum of Holbæk and Environs, Holbæk; Det Nationalhistoriske Museum på Frederiksborg, Hillerød; Nationalmuseet, Copenhagen (Heidi Lykke Petersen); The Nobel Foundation (Annika Ekdahl); Ny Carlsberg Glyptotek in Copenhagen (Jan Stubbe Østergaard); Palaces and Properties Agency, Denmark (Peder Lind Pedersen); Pritzker Prize (Keith Walker) for making available the photographs of the interiors of Jørn Utzon's house; Ribe VikingeCenter (Bjarne Clement – manager); Rosenborg Castle – The Royal Danish Collection (Peter Kristiansen – curator); Roskilde Cathedral; The Royal Library, Copenhagen (Karsten Bundgaard – photographer); Royal Porcelain Factory, Copenhagen; Skagens Museum (Mette Bøgh Jensen – curator); Scandinavian Airlines SAS (Wanda Brociek i Małgorzata Grążka); Statens Historiska Museum, Stockholm; Statens Museum for Kunst: (Eva Maria Gertung & Marianne Saederup); Stine Møller Jensen (Press coordinator, Copenhagen Metro); Bo Streiffert; Tivoli, Copenhagen – Stine Lolk; Tobaksmuseet, Copenhagen (W.Ø. Larsens); Tycho Brahe Planetarium, Copenhagen; Tønder Tourist Office (Lis Langelund-Larsen – tourist officer); Voergård Slot; Aalborg Symfoniorkester (Jan Bo Rasmussen); Østerlars Kirke, Bornholm (Ernst A Grunwald).

Picture Credits
t = top; tc = top centre; tr = top right; tl = top left; cla = centre left above; ca = centre above; cra = centre right above; cl = centre left; c = centre; cr = centre right; clb = centre left below; cb = centre below; crb = centre right below; bl = bottom left; b = bottom; br = bottom right.

4CORNERS IMAGES: SIME / Gräfenhain Günter 10cl.

AALBORG OPERA: 31t. ALAMY IMAGES: Phil Degginger 8–9; Bernie Epstein 76cb; FAN travelstock / Sabine

Lubenow 11c; Ionotec / Thierry Lauzun 218clb; Leslie Garland Picture Library 10crb; LOOK Die Bildagentur der Fotografen GmbH / Holger Leue 10tc; OJPHOTOS 157tl; Robert Harding Picture Library Ltd / Adina Tovy 11tl; Robert Harding World Imagery 235b; Pep Roig 264cl; Frantisek Staud 237t; vario images GmbH & Co.KG / Stephan Gabriel 265tl; Ken Welsh 264c. Artothek: 205bl.

Bang & Olufsen Products: 24cla. BonBon-Land A/S: 157c. The Bridgeman Art Library: Nordiska Museet, Stockholm *Bella and Hanna Nathansson* (1783–1853) Christoffer-Wilhelm Eckersberg 42tr; Thorvaldsens Museum, Copenhagen *Shepherd Boy* (1817) Bertel Thorvaldsen 42bl.

Corbis: © Archivo Iconografico, S. A. 38–39c, 41br; © Bettmann 37bl, 38tc, 43 bl, 44cr, 121 crb; © Werner Forman 34b, 36bl; © Hulton–Deutsch Collection 45t; © Robbie Jack 122b; © Wolfgang Kaehler 236t, 236b; © Douglas Kirkland 121bl; © Bob Krist 135b, 182, 200, 205tl, 205cr; © Stefan Lindblom 28tclb, 45br; © Massimo Listri 27b, 50; © Wally McNamee 45c; Royalty Free 297tl; © Adam Woolfitt 54br, 172.

Dansk Moebelkunst; 24clb, 25cla. Niels Jakob Darger; 89b.Davids Samling: 58cra.

Fredensborg; 129tr, 131ca. Frederiksborg: Hans Petersen 39t, 40c, 41t, 41crb; Larsen, Lennart 38cla, 40t; Ole Haupt 36t.

Hemispheres Images: Jean du Boisberranger 11br. Horsens Kommune: Hartmann-Schmidt Fotografi 29br.

Jakub Sito: 22t, 23tc, 23ca, 27tr, 27cl.

Oldrich Karasek: 48t, 48b, 49b, 57b, 228, 230t, 233t, 290t.

Legoland: 193bl, Anders Brohus 193cr. Louisiana – Museum for Moderne Kunst: *Dead Drunk Danes* (1960) Asger Jorn © DACS, London 2008 26b; *Big Thumb* (1968) Cesar Baldaccini © ADAGP, Paris and DACS, London 2008 122tr; *Breakfast on the Grass* (1961) Pablo Picasso © Succession Picasso/DACS, London 2008 122cra; *Venus de Meudon* (1956) Jean Arp © DACS, London 2008 122clb; *Eyes* (1997) Louise Bourgeois © DACS, London/VAGA, New York 2008 122b; *Marilyn Monroe* (1967) Andy Warhol © Licensed by the Andy Warhol Foundation for the Visual Arts, Inc/ARS, New York and DACS, London 2008 123cra; Henry Moore, *Two Piece Reclining Figure No.5* (1963–4) © by kind permission of the Henry Moore Foundation 123clb.

MEPL: 9c, 34clb, 36cr, 37t, 37bra, 38bl, 42bl, 43t, 44t, 44bla, 44brb, 47c, 113c, 239c, 295c. Munthe plus Simonsen: 99tr.

Nationalmuseet: 33bl, 84t, 84cra, 84clb, 84b, 85cla. naturepl.com: Michael Hutchinson 19tr. Nimb Hotel and Restaurant: 64, 77bl.

B. V. Petersen; 20cl, 20clb, 20cra, 20c, 21cla, 21clb, 21cra, 21ca, 21crb. POLFOTO: Hansen Claus 167br.

Restaurant Era Ora: 262cl; Ribe Vikinge Center: 28b; Rosenborg Castle: 60b, 61ca, 61b. Royal Library: (Karsten Bundgaard) 121br

Safari Park: (Finn Brasen) 160t, 160b, 161cra, 161crb. Skagens Museum P. S. Krøyer, Michael Ancher (1886) phot. Esben Thorning 205br. Skuespilhuset - Royal Danish Playhouse: JensMarkus Lindhe 71bl; Anna and Janusz Starościk: 5t. Statens Museum for Kunst (Copenhagen): SMK Foto 26tra, 26tlb, 32, 42cl, 42br, 42–43c, 62cla, 62clb, 63cra, 63cr; *Seated Woman* (1934) Henri Laurens © ADAGP, Paris and DACS, London 2008 63bc; *Portrait of Mrs Matisse* (1905) Henry Matisse © Succession H Matisse/DACS, London 2008 63crb; *Last supper* (1909) Emil Nolde 63tl. Barbara Sudnik-Wójcikowska; 20bla, 21cl.

Tivoli: Henrik Stenberg 76cla, 77t. Tønder Tourist Office: 30t.

Jørn Utzon: 24–25c.

VisitDenmark: 59b, 83c; Aalborg Tourist- og Kongressbureau 211ca; Bent Næsly 29c, 117, 205cl; Bob Krist 288c; Cees van Roeden 2–3, 34cra, 100t, 174b, 183b, 210bla, 291cr; Danmarks Turistråd 125cl, 216; Dorte Krogh 287b, 308tr; Henrik Steberg 164–165; Ireneusz Cyranek 90; Jan Kofoed Winther 96b; Jette Jørs 102cr; John Sommer 38cl, 58clb, 201d, 292c, 309t; Jørgen Schytte 266t; Juliusz Żebrowski 229b, 234t, 234b, 235t; Klaus Bentzen 136–137, 278–279; Peter Søllner 33t; Strüwing 25br; Ted Fahn 46–47, 112–113; Thomas Nykrog 238–239; ukendt 1, 289t; VisitAalborg 263br; Wedigo Ferchland 212–213; WoCo 6b.

Monika Witkowska: 230b, 231t, 231b, 232t, 232b. Wonderful Copenhagen: 297bl.

Jacket
Front - Alamy Images: nagelestock.com main image; DK Images: Dorota & Mariusz Jarymowicz clb. Back - Alamy Images: Frantisek Staud clb; DK Images: Demetrio Carrasco cla; Dorota & Mariusz Jarymowicz tl; Hemispheres Images: Fred Derwal bl. Spine - Alamy Images: nagelestock.com t; DK Images: Dorota & Mariusz Jarymowicz b.

All other images Dorling Kindersley.
For further information see www.dkimages.com

Phrasebook

In an Emergency

Can you call an ambulance? **Kan du tilkalde en ambulance?** kann do till-kalleh ehn ahm-boo-lang-seh?
Can you call the police? **Kan du tilkalde politiet?** kann do till-kalleh po-ly-tee'd?
Can you call the fire brigade? **Kan du tilkalde brand-væsenet?** kann do till-kalleh brahn-vaiys-ned?
Is there a telephone here? **Er der en telefon i nærheden?** e-ah dah ehn tele-fohn ee neya-hethen?
Where is the nearest hospital? **Hvor er det nærmeste hospital?** voa e-ah deh neh-meste hoh-spee-tahl

Useful Phrases

Sorry **Undskyld** ons-gull
Goodnight **Godnat** goh-nad
Goodbye **Farvel** fah-vell
Good evening **Godaften** goh-ahf-tehn
Good morning **Godmorgen** goh-moh'n
Good morning (after about 9am) **Goddag** goh-dah
Yes **Ja** yah
No **Nej** nye
Please **Værsgo/ Velbekomme** vehs-goh/ vell-beh-commeh
Thank you **Tak** tahgg
How are you? **Hvordan har du det?/ Hvordan går det?** voh-dann hah do deh?/voh-dan go deh?
Pleased to have met you **Det var rart at møde dig** deh vah rahd add meutheh die
See you! **Vi ses!** vee sehs!
I understand **Jeg forstår** yay fuh-stoah
I don't understand **Jeg forstår ikke** yay fuh-stoah egge
Does anyone speak English? **Er der nogen, der kan tale engelsk?** e-ah dah noh-enn dah kann tah-leh eng-ellsgg?
on the left **til venstre** till vehn-streh
on the right **til højre** till hoy-reh
open **åben** oh-ben
closed **lukket** luh-geth
warm **varm** vahm
cold **kold** koll
big **stor** stoah
little **lille** lee-leh

Making a Telephone Call

I would like to call... **Jeg vil gerne ringe til...** yay vill geh-neh ring-eh till...
I will telephone again **Jeg ringer en gang til** yay ring-ah ehn gahng till

In a Hotel

Do you have double rooms? **Findes her dobbelt-værelser?** feh-ness he-ah dob-belld vah-hel-sah?
With bathroom **Med bade-værelse** meth bah-the-vah-hel-sah
With washbasin **Med hånd-vask** meth hohn-vasgg
key **nøgle** noy-leh
I have a reservation **Jeg har en reservation** yay hah ehn res-sah-vah-shohn

Sightseeing

cathedral **domkirke** dom-kia-keh
church **kirke** kia-keh
museum **museum** muh-seh-uhm
railway station **banegård** bah-neh-goh
airport **lufthavn** luhft-havn
train **tog** toh
ferry terminal **færgehavn** fah-veh-havn
a public toilet **et offentligt toilet** ehd off-end-ligd toa-led

Shopping

I wish to buy... **Jeg vil gerne købe...** yay vill geh-neh kyh-beh...
Do you have...? **Findes der...?** feh-ness de-ah...?
How much does it cost? **Hvad koster det?** vath koh-stah deh
expensive **dyr** dyh-ah
cheap **billig** billy
size **størrelse** stoh-ell-seh
general store **købmand** keuhb-mann
greengrocer **grønthandler** grund-handla
supermarket **supermarked** suh-pah-mah-keth
market **marked** mah-keth

Eating Out

Do you have a table for... people? **Har I et bord til... personer?** hah ee ed boah till... peh-soh-nah?
I wish to order... **Jeg vil gerne bestille...** yay vill geh-neh beh-stilleh...
I'm a vegetarian **Jeg er vegetar** yay eh-ah veh-gehta
children's menu **børnemenu** byeh-neh-meh-nye
starter **forret** foh-red
main course **hovedret** hoh-veth-red
dessert **dessert** deh-seh'd
wine list **vinkort** veen-cod
May I have the bill? **Må jeg bede om regningen?** moh yay beh-theh uhm rahy-ning-ehn

Menu Decoder

brød **bread** bruth
danskvand **mineral water** dansg vann
fisk **fish** fesgg
fløde **cream** flu-theh
grøntsager **vegetables** grunn-saha
is **ice cream** ees
kaffe **coffee** kah-feh
kartofler **potatoes** kah-toff-lah
kød **meat** kuth
kylling **chicken** killing
laks **salmon** lahggs
lam **lamb** lahm
leverpostej **liver paté** leh-vah-poh-stie
mælk **milk** mailgg
oksekød **beef** ogg-seh-kuth
ost **cheese** ossd
pølse **sausage** pill-seh
rejer **shrimps** rah-yah
røget fisk **smoked fish** roy-heth fesgg
saftevand **squash** sah-fteh-vann
salat **salad** sah-lad
salt **salt** sald
sild **herring** sil
skaldyr **shellfish** sgall-dya
skinke **ham** sgeng-geh
smør **butter** smuah
sodavand **fizzy drink** sodah-vann
svinekød **pork** svee-neh-kuth
te **tea** teh
torsk **cod** tohsgg
vand **water** vann
wienerbrød **Danish pastry** vee-nah-bryd
æg **egg** egg
øl **beer** uhl

Numbers

0 **nul** noll
1 **en** ehn
2 **to** toh
3 **tre** tray
4 **fire** fee-ah
5 **fem** femm
6 **seks** seggs
7 **syv** siu
8 **otte** oh-deh
9 **ni** nee
10 **ti** tee
20 **tyve** tyh-veh
30 **tredive** traith-veh
40 **fyrre** fyr-reh
50 **halvtreds** hahl-traiths
60 **tres** traiths
70 **halvfjerds** hahl-fyads
80 **firs** fee-ahs
90 **halvfems** hahl-femms
100 **hundrede** hoon-dreh-the
200 **tohundrede** toh-hoon-dreh-the
1,000 **tusind** tooh-sin-deh
2,000 **totusinde** toh-tooh-sin-deh

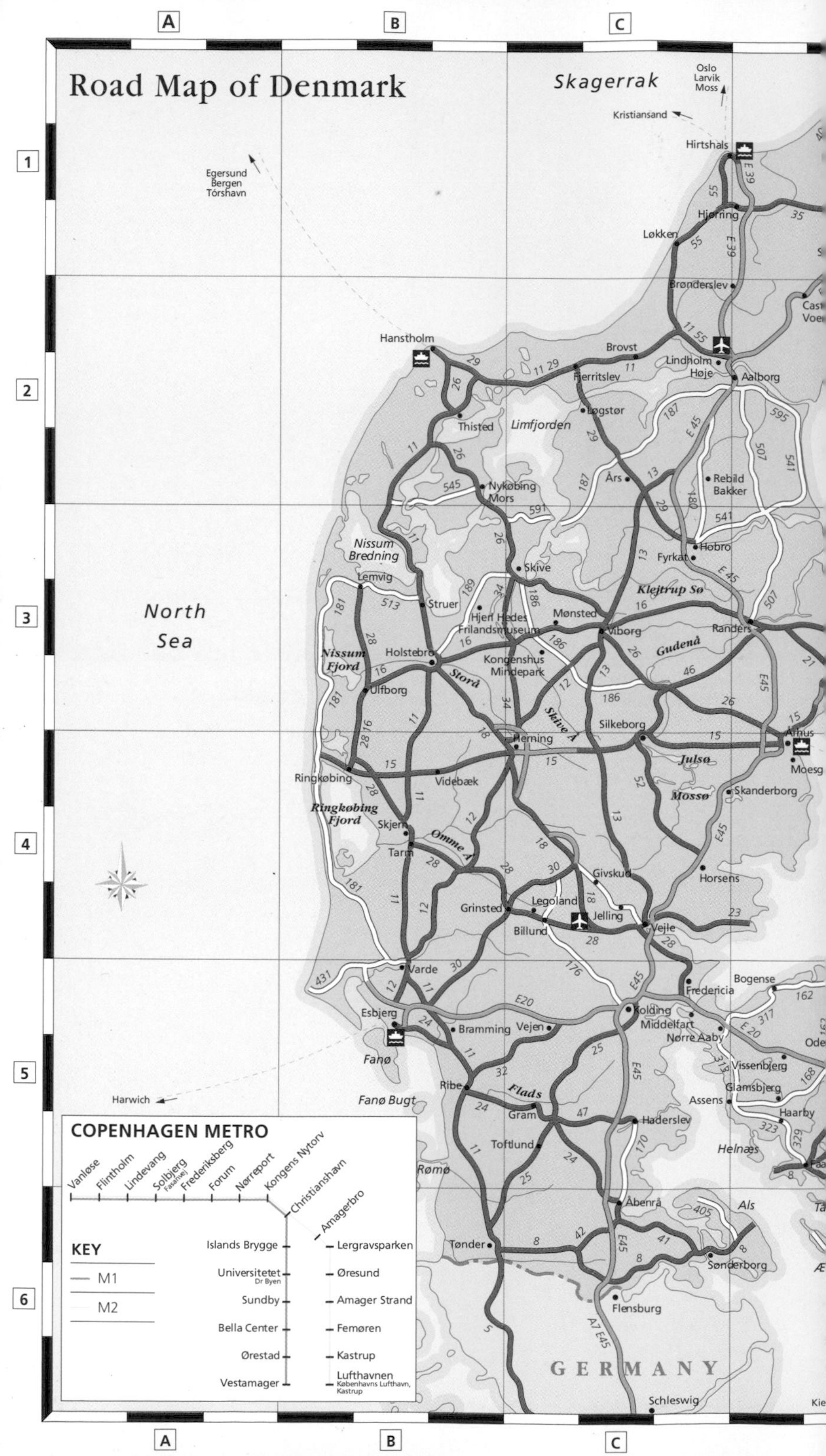

Road Map of Denmark
A
B
C
1
2
3
4
5
6
Skagerrak
Oslo
Larvik
Moss
Kristiansand
Hirtshals
Egersund
Bergen
Tórshavn
Hjørring
Løkken
Brønderslev
Hanstholm
Brovst
Lindholm Høje
Aalborg
Fjerritslev
Løgstør
Thisted
Limfjorden
Nykøbing Mors
Års
Rebild Bakker
Hobro
Fyrkat
Nissum Bredning
Skive
Lemvig
Struer
Hjerl Hedes Frilandsmuseum
Mønsted
Klejtrup Sø
Viborg
Randers
North Sea
Holstebro
Nissum Fjord
Kongenshus Mindepark
Storå
Gudenå
Ulfborg
Skive Å
Silkeborg
Herning
Århus
Moesg
Julsø
Ringkøbing
Videbæk
Skanderborg
Mossø
Ringkøbing Fjord
Skjern
Tarm
Omme Å
Horsens
Givskud
Legoland
Grinsted
Jelling
Billund
Vejle
Varde
Fredericia
Bogense
Esbjerg
Bramming
Vejen
Kolding
Middelfart
Nørre Aaby
Fanø
Vissenbjerg
Glamsbjerg
Ribe
Assens
Harwich
Fanø Bugt
Flads
Gram
Haderslev
Haarby
Toftlund
Helnæs
Rømø
Åbenrå
Als
Tønder
Sønderborg
Flensburg
GERMANY
Schleswig
COPENHAGEN METRO
Vanløse
Flintholm
Lindevang
Solbjerg (Fasanvej)
Frederiksberg
Forum
Nørreport
Kongens Nytorv
Christianshavn
Amagerbro
Islands Brygge
Universitetet (Dr Byen)
Sundby
Bella Center
Ørestad
Vestamager
Lergravsparken
Øresund
Amager Strand
Femøren
Kastrup
Lufthavnen (Københavns Lufthavn, Kastrup)
KEY
M1
M2